Library of
Davidson College

A HISTORY OF EAST CENTRAL EUROPE

Volume IV

EDITORS

Peter F. Sugar
Donald W. Treadgold

A HISTORY OF EAST CENTRAL EUROPE

VOLUMES IN THE SERIES

I. *Historical Atlas of Central Europe*
   BY PAUL ROBERT MAGOCSI

II. *The Early Middle Ages in East Central Europe**
   BY CHARLES R. BOWLUS

III. *East Central Europe in the Middle Ages, 1000–1500*
   BY JEAN W. SEDLAR

IV. *The Polish-Lithuanian State, 1386–1795*
   BY DANIEL STONE

V. *Southeastern Europe under Ottoman Rule, 1354–1804*
   BY PETER F. SUGAR

VI. *The Peoples of the Eastern Habsburg Lands, 1526–1918*
   BY ROBERT S. KANN AND ZDENĚK V. DAVID

VII. *The Lands of Partitioned Poland, 1795–1918*
   BY PIOTR S. WANDYCZ

VIII. *The Establishment of the Balkan National States, 1804–1920*
   BY CHARLES AND BARBARA JELAVICH

IX. *East Central Europe between the Two World Wars*
   BY JOSEPH ROTHSCHILD

X. *East Central Europe since 1939**
   BY IVO BANAC

* Forthcoming

The Polish-Lithuanian State, 1386–1795

DANIEL STONE

UNIVERSITY OF WASHINGTON PRESS
Seattle and London

In Memory of

Mary Charal Stone, 1910–1980

Adolph Stone, 1908–1998

Copyright © 2001 by the University of Washington Press
Printed in the United States of America

All rights reserved. No part of this publication may be reproduced or transmitted in any form or by any means, electronic or mechanical, including photocopy, recording, or any information storage or retrieval system, without permission in writing from the publisher.

Library of Congress Cataloging-in-Publication Data

Stone, Daniel, 1942–
   The Polish-Lithuanian state : 1386–1795 / Daniel Stone.
     p. cm.— (History of East Central Europe ; v. 4)
   Includes bibliographical references and index.
   ISBN 0-295-98093-1 (alk. paper)
    1. Poland—History—To 1795. I. Title. II. Series.

DJK4.S93 vol. 4 [DK4188]
943 s—dc21 [943.8'02]   00-051179

The paper used in this publication is acid-free and recycled from 10 percent post-consumer and at least 50 percent pre-consumer waste. It meets the minimum requirements of American National Standard for Information Sciences—Permanence of Paper for Printed Library Materials, ANSI Z39.48-1984.♾♲

The maps on pages xiii-xvii are adapted from Paul Robert Magocsi, *Historical Atlas of East Central Europe* (Seattle: University of Washington Press and Toronto: University of Toronto Press, 1993), by permission of the author.

CONTENTS

Foreword vii
Preface ix
Maps xiii–xvii

PART ONE: THE JAGIELLONIAN PERIOD, 1386–1572

1. Jogaila/Jagiełło   3
2. Jagiełło's Successors: Władysław III, Kazimierz IV, Jan Olbracht, and Aleksander   21
3. Zygmunt I the Old   36
4. Zygmunt II August   51
5. Economics and Society in the Jagiellonian Period   67
6. Artistic Culture and Education in the Jagiellonian Period   94
7. First Interlude: Henri Valois and Stefan Batory   116

PART TWO: THE VASA PERIOD

8. Zygmunt III Vasa (Waza)   131
9. Władysław IV   149
10. Jan Kazimierz   159
11. Noble Democracy as a Political System   177
12. Economics and Society in the Vasa Period   190
13. Culture in the Vasa Period   211
14. Second Interlude: Michał Wiśniowiecki and Jan III Sobieski   233

PART THREE: THE EIGHTEENTH CENTURY

15. August II   245
16. August III   259
17. Stanisław August Poniatowski   268
18. Economics and Society in the Eighteenth Century   289
19. Culture in the Eighteenth Century   309

Epilogue   336
Bibliographical Essay   339
Index   357

FOREWORD

The systematic study of the history of East Central Europe outside the region itself began only in the last generation or two. For the most part historians in the region have preferred to write about the past of only their own countries. Hitherto no comprehensive history of the area as a whole has appeared in any language.

This series was conceived as a means of providing the scholar who does not specialize in East Central European history and the student who is considering such specialization with an introduction to the subject and a survey of knowledge deriving from previous publications. In some cases it has been necessary to carry out new research simply to be able to survey certain topics and periods. Common objectives and the procedures appropriate to attain them have been discussed by the authors of the individual volumes and by the coeditors. It is hoped that a certain commensurability will be the result, so that the ten volumes will constitute a unit and not merely an assemblage of writings. However, matters of interpretation and point of view have remained entirely the responsibility of the individual authors.

No volume deals with a single country. The aim has been to identify geographical or political units that were significant during the period in question, rather than to interpret the past in accordance with latter-day sentiments or aspirations.

The limits of "East Central Europe," for the purposes of this series, are the eastern linguistic frontier of German- and Italian-speaking peoples on the west, and the political borders of Russia/the former USSR on the east. Those limits are not precise, even within the period covered by any given volume of the series. The appropriateness of including the Finns, Estonians, Latvians, Lithuanians, Belorussians, and Ukrainians was considered, and it was decided not to attempt to cover them systematically, though they appear repeatedly in these books. Treated in depth are the Poles, Czechs, Slovaks, Hungarians, Romanians, Yugoslav peoples, Albanians, Bulgarians, and Greeks.

There has been an effort to apportion attention equitably among regions and periods. The first volume is an historical atlas. Three volumes deal with the area north of the Danube-Sava line, three with the area south of it, and three with both areas. Three treat premodern history, six modern times. Each volume is supplied with a bibliographical essay of its own, but we all have attempted to keep the scholarly apparatus at a minimum in order to make the text of the volumes more readable and accessible to the broader audience sought.

The whole undertaking has been longer in the making than originally planned. Several of the original list of projected authors died before they could finish their volumes and have been replaced. Volumes of the series are being published as the manuscripts are received. We hope that the usefulness of the series justifies the long agony of its conception and birth, that it will increase knowledge of and interest in the rich past and the many-sided present of East Central Europe among those everywhere who read English, and that it will serve to stimulate further study and research on the numerous aspects of this area's history that still await scholarly investigators.

PETER F. SUGAR
DONALD W. TREADGOLD

Publisher's Note

The publisher deeply regrets that neither Professor Sugar (d. 1999) nor Professor Treadgold (d. 1994) was able to see the completion of the series, A History of East Central Europe. We are committed to the publication of the remaining volumes as planned by the editors.

PREFACE

The rise and fall of the Polish-Lithuanian state offers one of the great dramatic spectacles of European history. This rise and fall did not equal Rome's in chronological and geographical grandeur, but it covered a substantial period of 409 years and encompassed a major geographic region. Even if the story lacks a Brutus or a Caesar, figures such as Jogaila, Zygmunt August, Bohdan Khmelnytsky, and Stanisław August Poniatowski were complex and significant personages who deserve to be as well known in the West as they are in their home countries. At its peak, the Polish-Lithuanian state covered much of the contemporary lands of Poland, Lithuania, Belarus, Ukraine, Russia, Lithuania, Latvia, Estonia, and Romania. It was linked dynastically at various times to the predecessors of the modern states of Austria, the Czech Republic, France, Hungary, Slovakia, Sweden, and parts of Germany. As a result, historians of many East Central European countries have found a rich field for description and analysis in the fall of the Polish-Lithuanian state.

Until recent decades, most historians approached the subject to uncover its importance to their own nation and ignored or criticized the other players in the drama. This attitude is easily understood, since East Central European nations struggled throughout the nineteenth and twentieth centuries to achieve the secure independence that western European nations could generally take for granted, not to mention the well-protected countries of North America. Nineteenth-century Polish historians created a morality play linking the past and present. "Pessimists" or "Realists" understood the selfishness of the Polish nobility to be the cause of the fall, and supported monarchical institutions that would maintain a strong state. In contrast, "Optimists" or "Romantics" blamed foreign powers and rallied as many citizens as possible to support an expanded Polish democracy. The stark alternatives of these schools faded after Poland gained its independence in 1918, but many of the old polemical debates remain touchy to this day. Both groups generally boasted of Polish tolerance toward minority nationalities and religions, but criticized them harshly when they sought to improve their position in society. Ukrainian, Lithuanian, and Russian historians have traditionally seen the Polish-Lithuanian state as an oppressor. For them, its fall represents justice long overdue, finally permitting the Ukrainian and Lithuanian nations (or their Russian would-be protectors) to take their proper place in the world. Jewish historians have also recognized the importance of the Polish-Lithuanian state in creating modern Jewish institutions and identity, but they often criticize it for anti-Jewish attitudes and acts. German historians confront the historical legacy of the Polish-Lithuanian state as part of their history, particularly in Prussia. Historians from the English-speaking countries often identify with the national tradition of one or another country in the region.

Communist domination of the region since World War II has both deformed and informed historical studies. At its worst, simplistic Marxism produced propagandistic attacks on the enemies of the system and their forebears; at its best, Marxism stimulated the study of economic and social history. Historians who found themselves forced into the Marxist straitjacket succeeded in loosening the strings until they wrote from a position virtually indistinguishable from late nineteenth-century liberalism. As a result, most Polish historical writing since 1956 and some writing in other Communist countries retain their position in the historical literature in the post-Communist age. East European historiography has lagged in adopting the most recent international trends of historical writing such as gender studies, but it is catching up quickly.

In the past few decades, historians have moved away from national history toward regional studies or have placed their national studies in a broad context. The editors and initiators of this series played a significant role in the process. *Polin: A Journal of Polish-Jewish Scholarship* has shown that cooperation between formerly rival national groups is possible and productive, and similarly *Harvard Ukrainian Studies* regularly includes contributions by non-Ukrainian historians. Historians from East European nations have taken part in the effort to understand the interrelated nature of their various societies, a trend that stems, in part, from their common subjugation by the Soviet Union as well as from the greater national security that Soviet domination afforded. Contemporary Polish historiography has produced many objective studies of the non-Polish inhabitants of the Polish-Lithuanian state. The distinguished Polish historian and director of Cracow (Jagiellonian) University's Jewish Studies Program, Józef Andrzej Gierowski, recently reminded us that "the history of the first Republic cannot be seen entirely in the categories of Polish national history; it was rather the common history of all the nationalities which comprised the Polish-Lithuanian state."

The present volume tries to present a regional history with a broad focus. The development of the Polish state and nation is an obvious part of the task but so is the development of other nations such as the Lithuanians, Ukrainians, Prussians, and Jews. Indeed, the whole concept of "nation" is of dubious value for most of the period covered in this book, since religious, regional, estate/class, family, and personal factors generally decided an individual's or a group's course of action.

The aim of this volume, as with the series as a whole, is to provide information useful to readers who are not specialists in East European history. To assist such readers, geographical names generally appear in their year 2000 form. Readers can find alternative place names in the index of this volume and in the *Historical Atlas* that forms part of this series. Hence, for example, Vilnius (not Wilno) and Lviv (not Lwów or Lvov). I have kept some place names in the form that is most familiar to English readers: Cracow (not Kraków), Vasa (not Waza), and Königsberg (not Kaliningrad).

Personal names of historical figures are given in the original language because anglicization creates even more contradictions and infelicities than unfamiliar forms. For example, King John Casimir sounds better in English than King Jan Kazimierz, but his predecessor's name Władysław, has no English equivalent, and using the old-fashioned Ladislaus does not help. Despite its presence in older histories of Poland, the old-fashioned and Germanic "Sigismund" is less familiar to English speakers than the Polish "Zygmunt" (which resembles the familiar name, Sigmund), and, on this side of the Atlantic at least, "Augustus" seems less plausible than "August." Slavic names such as Michał, Mikhail, Antoni, and Józef pose no barrier and provide a taste of the original cultures. English and other equivalents are given on first reference in the text and in the index.

Insofar as possible for an age of mixed identities, names are connected to the modern nationality that seems most appropriate. Hence, I use the anglicized Ukrainian form Bohdan Khmelnytsky instead of the Polish form Bogdan Chmielnicki. Again, the Latin alphabet versions of Kostiantyn Ostrozsky and Adam Kysil in their Ukrainian form seem more appropriate than the Polish versions, Konstantin Ostrogski and Adam Kysiel, because these are men who championed the Ruthenian cause within the Commonwealth. The Lithuanian name Vytautas is an easy choice over the Polish equivalent Witold, but I use Grand Duke Jogaila in the Lithuanian context and King Jagiełło in the Polish context, relying on the reader to remember that they are the same person. In contrast, I have kept the Polish form Radziwiłł instead of the Lithuanian form Radvilas, because the family seems more Polish than Lithuanian by the seventeenth century and because English-language readers are already familiar with the Polish form. The author can only beg the readers' tolerance for these decisions; I have found no fully adequate solution.

Against tradition, I identify the Polish legislature as a "parliament" instead of a "diet" in order to avoid the impression that the institution's antiquated nature doomed it to inevitable failure. Illogically, I have left the traditional term "dietine" to describe the local assemblies in Poland-Lithuania. The terms "local assembly" and "county assembly" used by some contemporary historians seem too obscure, even though they are accurate. I also describe the noble assembly of Ducal Prussia as "Estates" in order to differentiate it from the Polish gatherings.

I would like to thank the late Professor Peter F. Sugar and the late Professor Donald W. Treadgold for inviting me to write this volume, taking a place alongside some of my undergraduate and graduate instructors who wrote earlier volumes in the series. I am particularly grateful for Professor Sugar's patient and thoughtful editorial supervision. I wish to thank the International Research and Exchanges Board (IREX) for two grants that helped me do research on this topic and for others in the past; I could not have pursued my path of scholarship over the last three decades without this support. I would also like to thank the University of Winnipeg Research and Travel Committee, Dean John Hofley, and the library staff at the University of Winnipeg. Several individuals have assisted my work greatly; they bear no responsibility for the errors of fact and interpretation contained in this volume, of course. Dr. Jerzy Kowecki of the Polish Academy of Sciences (Warsaw) has provided invaluable aid for many years in staying abreast with Polish scholarly literature. Without him, I could not have completed this project. Professors Donald Bailey, Richard I. Frost, Karin Friedrich, Janusz Duzinkiewicz, Gershon Hundert, and Paul W. Knoll read portions of this book in manuscript form and corrected many embarrassing errors. Karin Friedrich kindly provided an advance copy of her forthcoming book. Robert Paul Magocsi generously gave permission for me to adapt maps from his *Historical Atlas of East Central Europe,* and Weldon Hiebert of the University of Winnipeg gave me the benefit of his professional expertise in making the adaptations. This is a good place to thank the late Professor Andrzej Zahorski of Warsaw University, who took a twenty-one-year-old exchange student under his wing in 1963 and inspired him to spend his academic career studying Polish history.

I am grateful to my wife and friend, Kay, for all the usual reasons and some special ones.

D.S.

January 2001

Poland-Lithuania in the 13th and 14th Centuries

Poland-Lithuania, c. 1480

Poland-Lithuania, c. 1570

Poland-Lithuania in the 16th and 17th Centuries

The Partitions of Poland

PART ONE

The Jagiellonian Period, 1386–1572

CHAPTER 1

Jogaila (Jagiełło)

The marriage of Grand Duke Jogaila to "King" Jadwiga in 1386 linked the Kingdom of Poland and the Grand Duchy of Lithuania in a personal union that developed into a dynastic union in the fifteenth century and finally, in 1569, became a full union of the two states that held no matter who the sovereign was. This large united state played an important role in the history of East Central Europe until the end of the eighteenth century. Within Jogaila's reign, the combined strength of Poland and Lithuania defeated the Teutonic Knights and paved the way for Poland-Lithuania's eventual conquest of the Baltic coast as well as for a limited intervention in the Hussite Wars of the Czech Kingdom.

THE GRAND DUKE AND THE LITHUANIAN STATE

Grand Duke Jogaila (c. 1351–1434) was born to Grand Duke Algirdas and his second wife, Juliana. Mindaugas (c. 1200–1263) founded the Lithuanian state in the mid-thirteenth century, and Gediminas (c. 1275–1341) consolidated it, making it a regional power by absorbing most of Belarus and Ukraine through marriage alliances with the local Orthodox princes and through conquest; his son, Liubartas, took Volhynia. Algirdas (c. 1296–1377) reorganized the Grand Duchy, moving the capital a short distance from Trakai in ethnically Lithuanian territory to Vilnius on the Belarussian border. Algirdas cooperated with his brother Kestutis (c. 1297–1382) to extend Lithuanian rule to Kiev after beating the Tatars in battle in 1362. Lithuania also expanded northeast to the borders of the Moscow and Tver principalities in Russia. Enjoying good relations with the free cities of Pskov and Novgorod, the dukes began to think of Lithuania as the successor to Kievan Rus. Lithuania faced major challenges from the Muscovite Russian state in the east and the Golden Horde (Mongols) to the south, but its principal enemy was the Teutonic Knights in the west, who attacked Lithuania ceaselessly in order to conquer Samogitia (Żmudź/Žemaitia), the coastal region that sepa-

3

rated the Teutonic Knights from the Livonian Knights of modern Latvia and Estonia. Lithuania enjoyed generally good relations with Poland, despite some competition for control of Galicia and Volhynia as well as some localized border warfare. When Jogaila succeeded his father, Algirdas, as grand duke in 1377, he had to share power with his uncle Kestutis and later with Kestutis's son, Vytautas (Witold, c. 1350–1430), whose political program differed sharply from Jogaila's.

Jogaila presided over a duchy composed of two different nationalities and two political systems: Lithuania proper and the Ruthenian territories of former Kievan Rus. Lithuania proper spoke Lithuanian, an Indo-European language of the Baltic family, and worshipped nature spirits. The Lithuanian nobility was a warrior caste subject to the duke, who rewarded nobles with the use of landed estates governed by princely law; only a handful of former tribal leaders owned their estates outright. Lithuanian dukes rewarded state officials with estates in economically better developed Belarus, where they ran the danger of assimilating and losing their Lithuanian identity. Gediminas's descendants dominated the powerful Lithuanian state, but rivalries among them weakened it. Grand Duke Jogaila held extensive political, economic, and judicial power, subject only to informal control from his relatives and other Lithuanian war leaders who met in council to make important decisions.

More than a century of statehood created Lithuanian political, administrative, and judicial traditions that are as yet little known, although the bureaucrats were sufficiently sophisticated to correspond with the West in Latin, with the Teutonic Order in German, and with the princes of Rus in chancery Ruthenian, a medieval East Slavic language. The Lithuanian state was open to new influences early in the fourteenth century, as evidenced by political flirtations with the papacy over acquiring the title "king" through conversion, by the presence of Roman Catholic and Greek Orthodox Churches in Vilnius, and by invitations to immigrants to settle in exchange for tax relief. Intermarriage linked the Lithuanian ducal house with other royal families, as when Gediminas's daughter Aldona married Crown Prince Kazimierz (Casimir), later King Kazimierz III the Great of Poland, in 1325.

Jogaila also presided over vast Ruthenian territories—the lands of modern Ukraine, Belarus, and western Russia—which the Lithuanian state had acquired in the fourteenth century. It secured Polotsk in 1307, Minsk in 1340, Smolensk in 1356, and Kiev in 1363. Many descendants of the house of Rurik, the founder of Kievan Rus ("Ruthenia" in medieval Latin), recognized Lithuanian sovereignty voluntarily in exchange for protection against the Mongols; and the Grand Duchy adopted their traditions, legal standards, and administrative practices, including the use of chancery Ruthenian in state documents. Ruthenians practiced Orthodox Christianity, and Lithuanian dukes boasted that they were restoring unity to Rus rather than subduing it. Four of Gediminas's eight sons converted to Orthodoxy.

Grand dukes pursued centralizing policies over their vast realm, controlling crown domains and ruling directly over noble and commoner inhabitants. They collected regular taxes, but needed council approval for additional military taxes. Regalian rights to coinage, salt, alcohol, and other resources brought in revenue. Royal stewards ran the military, judicial, and economic affairs of their districts, and noble estates supplied the grand duke with soldiers. The central offices of marshal, chancellor, and treasurer developed in the fifteenth and sixteenth centuries, however. Over time, Lithuanian grand dukes took effective control over nominally autonomous Ruthenian duchies from their Slavic dukes.

The King and the Polish State

Duke Mieszko's conversion to Roman Catholicism provides the symbolic date for establishing the Polish state in 966. Poland expanded and became a kingdom in 1025, but it fragmented politically in the thirteenth century. King Władysław Łokietek reunited much of the Polish Kingdom in 1320, and his son Kazimierz III the Great (1310–70) reorganized the state, bringing it prosperity and military strength at the price of surrendering Silesia to Bohemia (the Czech Kingdom) and the Baltic coast to the Teutonic Knights. The renewed Polish Kingdom pressed southeast into western Ukrainian lands and Moldavia. Kazimierz died without heirs and left the throne to his cousin, King Louis of Hungary, who was succeeded by his daughter, Jadwiga, in 1382. Raised in Hungary, Jadwiga came to Poland to be crowned "king" in 1384.

Recent dynastic changes gave many Polish nobles the sense that the state existed independently of the monarch, and they felt that they shared responsibility for running it. Having gained extensive privileges in return for their political support, Polish nobles came to regard kings as executive officers subject to supervision by the political nation composed of state officials meeting in groups such as the royal council and the *sejm*, which later became the Polish parliament. At his coronation in 1386, Jogaila swore to uphold his subjects' existing rights and privileges, as did his successors. Polish nobles enjoyed the legal right to resist if the king violated his oath, but Polish kings still held extensive powers as heads of state who directed civil and military affairs. They freely appointed royal governors to provinces and lands subject only to the limitation that local appointees must be acceptable to the region and must live there. Officials enjoyed life tenure. The king was the source of justice and the highest judge, although lower courts, while royal in name, really represented local nobles. The king commanded the army, either in person or through his appointees, and he directed foreign policy, though custom demanded that he consult with high officials on international treaties and gain their approval.

The strength of royal authority depended on the crown's financial resources, which were substantial throughout the Jagiellonian dynasty (1386–1572). Kazimierz III's reforms had made the extensive royal domains highly profitable, even after his successors distributed estates lavishly to political supporters. Prefects administered some estates under treasury supervision; other estates were leased to nobles or clerics or lent to nobles in exchange for additional military service. Internal and external customs duties contributed to the royal treasury, as did the royal monopoly on subsoil wealth, particularly salt near Cracow. Manipulation of currency values at the royal mint also produced revenue. Taxation brought in less income than the king's direct revenues. Nobles paid a small annual tax on arable landholdings, while cities paid real-estate and road taxes, especially in wartime. Special needs led to levying special taxes.

The king made decisions with the help of a council composed of the highest dignitaries of the state: ministers (chancellor, vice-chancellor, marshal, and treasurer); palatines, or provincial governors; castellans, or governors of major castles; and Catholic bishops. The king rarely used his right to invite other advisers. The royal council lacked statutory or formal constitutional power, but custom granted it a major role in political decision-making. An inner council composed of about ten of the highest dignitaries headed by the archbishop of Gniezno (the primate of the Polish Church) met regularly with the king to advise him on political matters. Membership depended more on the king's favor than on the precise office filled.

The army consisted mainly of noble volunteers and their retainers. When summoned, most nobles served personally and brought three mounted archers, although poor nobles served alone and on foot, if necessary. Military service was generally limited to wars of defense within Poland's borders, and the monarch was obliged to ransom nobles if they were captured while taking part in a foreign war. Noble clerics owed military service for their landed estates but their secular relatives generally campaigned in their stead. The army was organized in "flags," either by region or by clan (*herb*). The king maintained a small detachment of elite shock troops at his own expense and provided a network of castles throughout the realm for defense. Peasants helped defend their own regions, and burghers defended city walls.

THE POLISH LANDS

Poland consisted of two provinces, Great Poland in the west (chief cities, Poznań and Gniezno) and Little Poland in the south (chief city, Cracow), which were subdivided in counties (*województwa*) and lands (*ziemie*). The two forms were equal, and both eventually gained parliamentary representation, although the former were larger and were governed by palatines (*wojewodowie*). Each county contained several regions (*kasztelanie*) headed by a castellan and subdivided into districts (*powiaty*). These subdivisions existed until the Third Partition in 1795 with only minor border adjustments. In each county, the royal palatine stood at the head of the dietine and presided over the royal court as the king's representative; lands also held dietines. The palatine also supervised cities and Jews in the king's name. The local function of the castellan declined in the fifteenth century as previous duties passed to central bodies, but castellans continued to attend the royal council (later, the senate). The prefect (*starosta*), or regional governor, still fulfilled important local responsibilities in the fourteenth and fifteenth centuries, exercising many royal prerogatives such as summoning the noble levy (*levée en masse/pospolite ruszenie*) for defense.

Mazovia, one of the largest independent Polish states in the period of feudal divisions (c. 1227–1320), remained closely linked with the Polish crown, although Mazovia guarded its independence jealously and maneuvered for support among its neighbors: Poland, Lithuania, and the Teutonic Knights. Mazovian Duke Siemowit III had recognized the personal suzerainty of his cousin Kazimierz the Great, but not the suzerainty of the Polish state. Siemowit IV enjoyed substantial support from western Poland when he competed with Jogaila to marry Jadwiga and assume the Polish crown. After losing out, Siemowit IV recognized Jagiełło's suzerainty. Mazovia profited from the end to Lithuanian incursions brought about by the Polish-Lithuanian union and from Polish-Lithuanian intervention against the Teutonic Knights. It drew closer to Poland, recognizing common historical and ethnic links, but Mazovian dukes maintained their independence and Polish-Mazovian relations underwent more than one crisis. Extensive trade kept Mazovia friendly to the Teutonic Knights.

Although formally part of the Bohemian Kingdom after 1339, Silesia remained linked to Poland by the ecclesiastical jurisdiction of the archbishop of Gniezno, and Polish officials considered it part of the Polish Kingdom. The region, originally a single duchy, had been subdivided in the twelfth and thirteenth centuries into twenty smaller duchies, each ruled by a collateral line of the Piast family. Nevertheless, ethnic Germans increasingly dominated the nobility and, to a somewhat lesser extent, the urban patriciate. Similarly, the duchy of western Pomerania retained its Slavic dukes, who owed allegiance to the elector of Brandenburg in Berlin, while the Pomeranian population became largely German.

The Dynastic Union of Jadwiga and Jogaila

The Piast dynasty, which had ruled Poland since about 900 A.D., virtually ended with the death of Kazimierz III (the Great) in 1370. He was succeeded by his nephew, Louis the Great of Hungary, who died in 1382 after a largely absentee reign. Great nobles from Little Poland dominated Poland's regency council and arranged for Louis's second daughter, twelve-year-old Jadwiga, who grew up in Hungary, to succeed instead of rival claimants. Jadwiga was crowned "king," or legal ruler in her own right, but her future husband was expected to exercise power. The Polish regency council overruled her family's plans for Jadwiga to marry Wilhelm Habsburg of Austria. Several factors dictated that decision. First, Poland and Hungary were rivals for control of southeastern lands, particularly Galicia (Red Russia) and Moldavia; severing the dynastic connection with Hungary would prevent a joint ruler from subordinating Polish interests to Hungary's. Second, Poland and Lithuania had undergone increasing strife over the borders, particularly in the Ukrainian lands of Galicia and Volhynia, which might be eased through a closer relationship. Third, and most important, Poland and Lithuania faced a common enemy in the Teutonic Knights of Prussia.

The Little Polish nobles who "advised" Jadwiga met Grand Duke Jogaila at Kriavas/Krewo (now Krevo, Belarus), southeast of Vilnius, and concluded an agreement on August 14, 1385. The grand duke agreed to convert to Roman Catholicism along with all his subjects, to cede lands captured from Poland, and to unite the Grand Duchy with Poland in exchange for marrying Jadwiga and assuming the Polish crown. The exact intent of this union has been hotly debated by historians, but it seems likely that Jogaila and the Poles both intended to unite the realms fully. However, Jogaila's influential first cousin Vytautas (Witold) successfully kept the two states distinct within his lifetime, and indeed until 1791 (significant differences continued until 1795).

Polish fears that Jogaila (who reigned with the Polish name Władysław II Jagiełło, Władysław being his baptismal name) would try to govern the Kingdom of Poland in an authoritarian manner proved groundless; some medieval chroniclers dogmatically ascribed Jogaila's good behavior to his conversion. As ruler, he followed Polish political traditions and accepted direction from Polish lords so fully that even the critically inclined mid-fifteenth-century chronicler Jan Długosz acknowledged that the king was "sincere and honest, [and without] double-dealing." Jogaila gained much of his popularity by distributing landed estates to noble supporters, usually as leaseholds with little or no payment. Short and slightly built, Jogaila was physically strong and showed great endurance on campaigns and hunts. He dressed unassumingly in a robe covered by a sheepskin coat instead of royal sable and wore a plain velvet gown on state occasions. His habits were good. He drank no alcohol and ate lightly except at occasional banquets. Hunting was his favorite activity and he also liked music, especially by Ruthenian fiddlers.

Jagiełło (Jogaila) as King of Poland

Władysław Jagiełło (Jogaila) came to Poland a stranger and followed the policies recommended to him by the royal advisers who arranged for his accession to the Polish throne, mostly great lords from Little Poland, and Queen Jadwiga. After gaining confirmation as king of Poland in his own right when Jadwiga died in 1399, Jagiełło built his own core of advisers slowly, starting with a chancellery of several secretaries that increased to a dozen after 1417 because the number of documents handled by the chancellery approximately doubled in Jagiełło's long reign. Jagiełło gradually freed himself from control of the Little Poland magnates by promoting well-educated clerics from the lesser nobility or burgher class who owed their rise solely to him, but the magnates remained influential and sometimes followed their own policies, particularly in Lithuania.

Royal policy constantly aimed at establishing royal power within the state and ensuring the succession of Jagiełło's heirs to the Polish throne. Much of his power came from personal supervision and decision-making during lengthy annual inspection tours on which he and his ministers met with local officials. While traveling, Jagiełło and his large entourage stayed mostly on his own far-flung estates, spending the winter months hunting in Lithuania. He spent little time in Cracow, the Polish capital, a practice that slowed urbanization and inhibited political centralization. His journeys also laid the groundwork for the parliament (*sejm*). With members of his inner council, the king met local officials in groups to discuss problems or settle legal disputes, and local nobles or city officials also came to petition him on personal matters and voiced their opinion on policy questions that were raised. These gatherings became known as dietines (*sejmiki*), and custom dictated that they approve all new taxes and legislation. Throughout the fourteenth and fifteenth centuries, Polish kings generally preferred meeting provincial gatherings to convening national ones. The practice led to the decline of "confederations," or leagues of nobles (sometimes cities) that had gathered in the past for specific purposes such as military defense or protection of noble interests. Confederations were revived during the interregnum of 1573, and nobles used them extensively in the seventeenth and eighteenth centuries.

In practice, much authority rested in the hands of the royal chancellery, which regarded itself as responsible to the realm and not solely to the king. Bishops invariably filled high office such as chancellor and vice-chancellor (whose authority was equal). About one-third of higher officials had studied at a university, mostly in Cracow. In contrast, the Lithuanian chancellery consisted mainly of secular nobles who worked under the grand duke's direct supervision.

Lesser nobles succeeded in securing their position in the state. Taking advantage of Jagiełło's need for troops to pursue war against the Teutonic Knights, they forced him to issue the Czerwińsk Privilege in 1422 (confirmed by the 1423 parliament at Warta) granting nobles a court trial before their property could be confiscated and also preventing individuals from serving as both prefect and local judge. Succession problems allowed the lesser nobles to gain further concessions. Jagiełło had no male heir until his fourth marriage in 1422 to a young Lithuanian noble woman, Zofia Holsztyńska, and some courtiers accused the queen of infidelity because they doubted Jagiełło's ability to sire children at his advanced age. To secure popular support for the dynasty, he agreed at the Jedlnia (1430) and Cracow (1433) parliaments to guarantee court trials for nobles accused of crimes.

Lithuania in the Polish-Lithuanian Union

Union with Poland forced the Grand Duchy of Lithuania to make major adjustments that affected the structure of the Grand Duchy and the nature of Lithuanian government. Lithuanian-Polish relations remained difficult for centuries, and Lithuanian-Ruthenian relations required redefinition.

Grand Duke Jogaila (Jagiełło) probably expected the Union of Kriavas (Krewo) to unify the two realms under his control, while Polish nobles expected it to give them unlimited access to the Grand Duchy, but Duke Vytautas led Lithuanian resisters who maintained Lithuanian legal distinctiveness, reserving offices and landed estates for Lithuanians. Just as Vytautas's father had contested Jogaila's father's rule, Vytautas vied with Jagiełło, now king of Poland, for his position as grand duke of Lithuania. He revolted in 1389 against Jagiełło's brother and deputy in Lithuania, Skirgaila, allying himself with the Teutonic Knights after early military reversals. A destructive civil war ensued that devastated Lithuania and left Samogitia under the Teutonic Order's control.

Jagiełło and Vytautas ended their differences with the Astravas (Ostrowo) Agreement of 1392 that recognized Vytautas as grand duke in Lithuania and recognized Jagiełło, who lived in Cracow, as supreme duke. Vytautas repudiated his alliance with the Teutonic Order, and Skirgaila relinquished the duchy of Trakai to become prince of Kiev. This left Vytautas free to direct Lithuania's internal affairs and pursue the traditional Lithuanian drive to expand in Ruthenian lands as far as Novgorod and Smolensk until he lost the important battle of the river Vorskla, near the Don River, against the Tatars in 1399 despite three years of preparation and the assistance of Polish, Muscovite, and Teutonic Order troops. Vytautas suffered such heavy losses in that battle that he could no longer pursue an eastern empire. His weakened position made him abandon dreams of breaking the union with Poland and becoming king in his own right, but he retained control over Lithuania. A 1401 agreement largely restated the Astravas

Agreement of 1392. It also made provisions for the future. Jogaila would inherit Lithuania if Vytautas died first, and Vytautas was to be consulted on the election of a Polish king if Jagiełło died first. Lithuanian boyars confirmed the arrangement at Vilnius, as did Polish nobles at Radom. The new agreement gave Vytautas the freedom to launch a campaign against his former allies, the Teutonic Order. He reclaimed Samogitia in 1401 after encouraging a popular uprising against the Order, handed it over to them again in 1404, and retook it again in 1409 in conjunction with another popular uprising. The border was finally set in 1422, giving Lithuania the province of Samogitia with the port of Palanga (Połąga) but leaving the city of Klaipėda (Kłajpeda, Memel) to the Order.

After the victorious campaign of 1410 by Lithuania and Poland against the Teutonic Knights, the Union of Horodło (1413) cemented the two realms more closely. This act changed the personal union of the two states under Jagiełło into a permanent dynastic union between Poland and Lithuania, united in the person of the grand duke, who would also be king of Poland. Future grand dukes would inherit their position while the Polish crown remained electoral. However, Polish nobles were required to choose a member of the Lithuanian ruling family, and they also pledged to consult Vytautas and the Lithuanian boyars when they elected the next Polish king. Joint meetings of the Lithuanian and Polish officials were discussed but did not take place until the sixteenth century.

Lithuanian separatism persisted nonetheless. Vytautas accepted Emperor Sigismund's offer of a royal crown in 1429, apparently with Jagiełło's agreement, but Polish forces intercepted the crown in transit and the coronation was canceled. When Vytautas died in 1430, a struggle for succession broke out. As supreme duke, Jogaila (Jagiełło) named his brother Švitrigaila (Świdrygiełło, c. 1370–1452) as grand duke but ran into serious opposition from Poles, who wanted to name Vytautas's successor themselves. When Švitrigaila sought additional support by allying himself with the Teutonic Knights, Poland seized Podolia, which Jogaila had awarded to Lithuania in 1411, and Volhynia. Švitrigaila sought to bolster his position by promising Ruthenian nobles a greater role within the Lithuanian state, arousing serious resistance from some Lithuanian nobles. Jogaila then attempted to replace Švitrigaila on the ducal throne with a more tractable relative, Vytautas's brother Žygimantas (Zygmunt Kiejstutowicz). Civil war between supporters of the two claimants and foreign intervention took almost a decade to resolve.

ETHNIC IDENTITIES IN THE GRAND DUCHY OF LITHUANIA

Despite the danger of a Polish takeover, union with Poland strengthened the Lithuanian element in the Grand Duchy and protected it against absorption into the much larger and better educated Ruthenian nobility. Bolstered by the relationship with Poland, the grand dukes of Lithuania issued legal privileges in 1387 and 1413 that restricted high state offices to ethnic Lithuanian nobles. The custom of treating Poles as foreigners, ineligible for such positions, became written law in 1447 and continued until 1795, with the exception (enacted in 1566) of nobles who served in the Lithuanian army. Polish nobles could apply for naturalization after marriage or military service in Lithuania. Native-born Ruthenians counted as citizens, but Ruthenian nobles in the Grand Duchy did not gain political rights until 1434. Separate legal privileges defined Tatars and Jews as free persons without political rights.

Lithuanian identity was stressed in Ruthenian, Polish, German, and Latin language chronicles such as the *Genealogy of Lithuanian Princes* (c. 1398) and *Eulogy of Vytautas* (c. 1428). The grand duke's council used the Lithuanian language in its discussions and even in international negotiations, although secretaries recorded discussions in Ruthenian or Polish; only judicial oaths have survived in written Lithuanian. Lithuanian must have been spoken extensively at court, since more than four hundred words entered Ruthenian and Polish chancellery language after 1400. However, because the Grand Duchy lacked educated officials, Vytautas used former members of the Teutonic Order as chancellery officials at first and then recruited Poles.

The Orthodox Ruthenian component of Lithuania played an important but secondary role in the affairs of the Grand Duchy as their demographic, economic, and cultural weight made itself felt. Population figures are inexact and subject to wide disagreement. Lithuanian historians tend to think that Ruthenians (persons speaking East Slavic languages and professing the Orthodox religion) outnumbered Lithuanians approximately 2:1, while Russian and Ukrainian historians think that a relationship of 3:1 or even 4:1 is more accurate. The difference is significant because a higher percentage of Ruthenians implies a greater role in running the Lithuanian state. Ruthenian Orthodox nobles clung to their traditional identities and privileges granted by the Kievan Rus state without distinction on a national or ethnic basis among the inhabitants of modern Ukraine, Belarus, and Russia. Originally seen as second-class citizens by the dominant Lithuanian dynasty, Orthodox nobles gradually achieved equal status.

The grand dukes gained control of their Ruthenian territories by replacing hereditary princes with their appointees (some of whom were Ruthenian in origin), but they also adopted many state traditions from Kievan Rus and the Galician-Volhynian principalities, including the form of consultation between the grand duke and his boyar council. Orthodox magnates formed part of the ducal council, although Orthodox clerics did not. Lithuania adopted the Ruthenian law code, and Orthodox clerics provided the educated bureaucracy that held the state together. State officials used the chancery Ruthenian language (distinct from Moscow usage) for state documents. Ruthenian military expertise was also utilized, particularly in constructing fortifications and attacking them.

The Lithuanian dukes needed help from Orthodox nobles in order to govern. An aristocracy developed from descendants of the Lithuanian ducal house (Gedyminovichi) and the royal house of Kievan Rus (Rurikovichi) as well as some lesser princes, all of whom received equality with Polish nobles by the Unions of Krewo and Horodło. Lithuanian grand dukes rewarded Lithuanian and Ruthenian supporters with land grants in the west (Volhynia) and northeast which were, however, subject to central control. Volhynia was a particular center of Ruthenian noble families such as the Chartoryskis, Vishnevetsys, and Zbarazhskys. The Mstislavl and Zaslavsky families dominated eastern Belarus and enjoyed extensive economic rights, particularly after the 1430s. Local nobles remained on the land and jealously protected their traditional rights, resenting appointment of Lithuanians to local offices, and they supported local Orthodox churches with grants of land and money. Many lesser nobles enjoyed secure tenure on their estates, while others held land in exchange for service to the state, as in Muscovite Russia, although they could travel freely. Traditional noble privileges confirmed by charter in the Grand Duchy included: secure ownership of estates, military service in one's district, and local trials.

Reliance on the Orthodox element in the Grand Duchy led Lithuanian grand dukes to maintain a strong Orthodox Church under their political control even though Roman Catholicism was the state religion. Throughout the fourteenth century, Orthodox metropolitans in Ruthenian lands struggled to claim successor status to the metropolitanate of Kiev and deny the claims of the metropolitan who had moved to Vladimir and then to Moscow. Grand Duke Vytautas set up a "Metropolitanate of Kiev and All Rus" in 1415 as a religious instrument of Lithuanian state power that failed to gain the recognition of the patriarch of Constantinople and faded from the scene after 1421. There was a brief revival in the 1430s. Vytautas supported a literary revival in Smolensk, and founded cathedral schools in Vilnius (1397) and Trakai (1409). Orthodox clerics rewarded him with a panegyric, the *Chronicle of the Grand Duchy of Lithuania,* written in 1420–40, which portrayed Vytautas as the successor to the princes of Rus. Despite his occasional use of the title "grand prince" (*vieliki kniaz*), borrowed from Kievan Rus, Vytautas did not plan to create a large Ruthenian state. He intended to subordinate Ruthenian lands to Lithuania.

Lithuanian campaigns in Ukrainian lands brought frequent contact with Tatars and led to the establishment of a small Tatar community in the Grand Duchy that lasted into the twentieth century. Lithuanian grand dukes settled captured Tatar and Mongol warriors on their lands as early as the 1320s, and offered them lands and self-governing rights that attracted refugees from the internecine warfare within the declining Mongol state. Vytautas organized the Tatars into regiments (hordes or flags) and used them frequently in battles such as the great battle of Grunwald (1410). In 1400, more than one thousand Tatars lived on lands granted by grand dukes in exchange for military service.

THE TEUTONIC ORDER STATE

The coordination provided by their union allowed the Polish and Lithuanian states to withstand pressure from the Teutonic Knights. The Teutonic Knights originated near Acre in Palestine in 1191 as the crusading "Order of the Hospital of the Blessed Virgin Mary of the German House of Jerusalem." Reconstituted in 1198 as a military religious order, it derived its rules from the Templars and Hospitalers. The pope authorized the Teutonic Order to convert pagans, and it took control of the Chełmno region in 1228 by agreement with Duke Konrad of Mazovia, who wanted protection against border raids by pagan tribes of Prussians, a Baltic people related to the Lithuanians. The Order enthusiastically realized the provisions of Emperor Friedrich II's Golden Bull of 1226 that authorized them to keep other lands by building a strong regional state after conquering and subjugating the Prussian tribes. The Teutonic Order then captured the major port city of Gdańsk (Danzig) with its surrounding region in the course of multiparty warfare in 1309 and established a new capital at nearby Malbork (Marienburg), where it built an impregnable castle-fortress. By the fifteenth century, colonization and assimilation had changed the primary meaning of the term "Prussian" from an ethnic to a territorial identification.

The grand master of the Teutonic Order, chosen by thirteen electors including eight knights-brothers, served as commander in chief and presided over annual "general chapters" at which representatives from different provinces of the Order made statutes, elected senior officers, received postulants, and resolved economic issues. A council of the grand master composed of five senior officers and the commanders of Gdańsk and Toruń (Thorn) administered day-to-day affairs. Prussian bishops and learned jurists joined the council in the fifteenth century. Grand masters tried to maintain their independence by choosing advisers and subordinates from the Germanies, where the Order also owned large estates, rather than from Prussia. Authority was essentially secular and military, but the knights-brothers accepted religious regulations as well. Most knights were younger sons of poor noble families in western and central Germany, and they reserved the top jobs in the Order for themselves, excluding even Prussian-born subjects of German ethnicity. Councils of brothers and half-brothers exercised local authority from regional palaces and forts. Prussian residents did not gain admittance as brothers until the early fourteenth century. Prussian burghers provided most of the personnel for the commercial bureau of the highly centralized state structure, which controlled outlying regions by correspondence delivered by an efficient system of relay runners and post riders. The central treasury of the Order in Malbork supervised the separate treasuries of the grand master and the regional masters. Monastic brethren proved to be ideal administrative personnel, working without material reward or family. They made frequent inspections and produced precise inventories of offices. The confessional, informing, and harsh punishment provided control over less idealistic workers. The Order also ran twenty-four alms houses and good medical facilities for brothers.

Excluded from playing a leading role in the Teutonic Order, the Prussian gentry became highly integrated with the urban patriciate. Nobles often came from urban families and held small estates. They generally resented the Teutonic Order's practice of recruiting new brothers from the Germanies rather than from Prussia; celibate brother-knights did not intermarry with local families, of course. As professional soldiers supplanted local gentry in the fifteenth century, local opportunities for advancement declined further. Dissatisfied nobles formed the Lizard Union in 1397 to prevent exploitation by the Order. That society was headed by four "elders," and its members pledged to observe absolute obedience and secrecy. A public arm of the society gained permission to set up a church brotherhood in Toruń in 1408. The Order suspected that members aimed to join Poland.

The commercialized Order state was well organized for war under the command of the grand master. Mercenaries and volunteer foreign knights constituted a powerful heavy cavalry that no eastern European country could challenge before 1400. They adopted the latest in western European technology, modifying heavy plate armor with chain mail so that their knights could fight Lithuanian light cavalry more effectively. Infantry supplemented these formations. The Order stationed professional troops in regional fortresses and added local militia when necessary. Nobles served as heavy or light cavalry depending on their wealth. Free peasants also served. Cities provided heavy cavalry, supplies, and infantry. The Order introduced artillery in the 1370s, although it did not become a significant force until the fifteenth century.

Polish-Lithuanian Struggles with the Teutonic Knights

The expansionist Teutonic Order state collided with Poland and Lithuania. Pagan Lithuania was most threatened, for the Order state sought to conquer the Baltic coast and may have considered moving inland as well. The danger became greater after the Prussian-based Knights merged with the Riga-based Livonian Knights in 1237 and tried to link the two states by taking Lithuania's coastal region and converting the pagan inhabitants to Christianity. Disputes with Poland centered on control of areas that had once belonged to the Polish crown, especially the valuable port of Gdańsk at the mouth of the Vistula River and its surrounding region. Similarly, both Poland and the Teutonic Order claimed the territories of New March and Dobrzyń that separated Great Poland from Pomerania. The Teutonic Order tried to bolster its territorial claims before European public opinion by refusing to recognize Jagiełło's conversion to Christianity and the conversion of Lithuania that threatened to end the Order's reason for existence. Grand Master Konrad Zollner von Rottenstein rejected Jagiełło's invitation to act as godfather at his christening and declined to attend his wedding. The grand master challenged the sincerity of Jagiełło's conversion at the papal court, supported by Sigismund of Luxemburg, the Hungarian king who was fighting against Poland for control of Moldavia and Galicia.

In 1410, warfare finally decided who would control the Baltic coast. The more numerous but more lightly armed Polish-Lithuanian force brought the war into Prussian territory. King Jagiełło commanded a Polish army of 20,000 mounted nobles, 15,000 armed commoners, and 2,000 professional cavalry, mostly hired from Bohemia. The Lithuanian army, commanded by Vytautas but under Jagiełło's overall command, consisted of about 11,000 light cavalry drawn from both the Lithuanian and the Ruthenian areas of the Grand Duchy; Tatars also fought under the Lithuanian flag. The army of the Teutonic Knights numbered 16,000 cavalry supported by 5,000 infantry. German, Slavic, and Prussian subjects of the Order fought in both the cavalry and the infantry. A heavily armed group of 500 Knights of the Cross, supplemented with a modest number of foreign guests drawn from as far away as Burgundy, provided a powerful, professional shock force that had won many battles for the Order in previous decades.

The decisive battle took place at the Prussian village of Grunwald on July 15, 1410, starting about noon and lasting until dusk. The lightly armed Lithuanian force attacked first and was driven back after heavy fighting. Several hours of fierce combat ensued as both commanders sent in reserve units. Grand Master Ulrich von Junginen resolved to break the deadlock by leading his elite troops in a flanking maneuver that unintentionally uncovered Jagiełło's command post; a single knight attacked the king and might have killed him except for the intervention of the king's secretary, Zbigniew Oleśnicki, a noble who later became the bishop of Cracow and one of the most powerful personages of the realm. Polish and Lithuanian troops exploited the division of the Order's forces and overwhelmed the Knights' elite troops, sparing no one for ransom. Grand Master von Junginen and Grand Marshal Friedrich von Wallenrode died, among other key personnel. The victorious Polish-Lithuanian army then stormed the Knights' fortified camp and slaughtered its defenders. Most of the surviving Teutonic Knights of high rank were captured and eventually ransomed. Contemporary figures of dubious reliability reported that several thousand soldiers died on either side.

The Polish-Lithuanian army emerged completely victorious on the battlefield but failed to win the campaign decisively. Key to the Prussian realm was the heavily fortified capital of the Teutonic Knights, Malbork, which Jagiełło might have captured if he had attacked immediately. But he took ten days to move his victorious army, by which time a new grand master, Heinrich von Plauen, had made preparations. Jagiełło lacked the artillery and infantry needed to storm the castle. During the ensuing siege, major Prussian cities such as Gdańsk, Toruń, and Elbląg (Elbing) acknowledged Polish sovereignty in exchange for generous economic privileges. However, the Order had powerful allies in Vaclav IV of Bohemia and Sigismund of Hungary, who supported the Order diplomatically and allowed it to raise troops; Sigismund also sent troops into Little Poland as a brief armed demonstration. In addition, the Livonian Knights attacked Prussia from the east to wrest it from Poland. More important, the majority of Polish and Lithuanian noble levies insisted on returning home, forcing Jagiełło to withdraw the Polish-Lithuanian army in mid-August. Poland-Lithuania and the Teutonic Order signed a peace agreement on February 1, 1411. The Peace of Toruń granted the Teutonic Knights most of their possessions, including Prussia. However, the Order surrendered the Dobrzyń and Samogitia regions, and paid substantial reparations for the return of prisoners and castles taken in the fighting. The settlement accurately reflected the overall military and economic balance of the two sides.

Decline of the Teutonic Order State

The Teutonic Order never recovered from its unsuccessful 1409–11 war against Poland, and its aggressive efforts to rebuild alienated its Prussian subjects, leading ultimately to revolt and unification with Poland. Destructive hostilities between the Teutonic Order and the Polish Kingdom continued for another fifty-five years on a smaller scale. Polish forces ravaged the region again in 1414, 1422, and 1431–33. To spite Sigismund for supporting the Order (Sigismund also claimed the Czech throne and was crowned Holy Roman emperor in 1433), Jagiełło hired Czech Hussite mercenaries in 1433 who despoiled Prussia with a ferocity learned in their war-torn homeland. By 1419, 20 percent of Order land lay abandoned. In areas such as southern Pomerelia, more than 50 percent of landholdings were abandoned, and in the Schwetz (Świecie) region, 80 percent. Crops failed and plague broke out. There was a shortage of human and draft labor. The Prussian mark declined by 80 percent in the fifteenth century, most sharply after the 1410 war as the Order debased the currency to meet expenses. Institutional decline accompanied economic decline, and reform efforts failed. The number of monastic brothers fell after 1410 from seven hundred to four hundred as members sought private property instead of a religious life. Warmia peasants resisted tax increases in 1440–42, and two hundred Pomeranian villages refused to pay tithes in the 1450s. Six village priests were killed in 1452.

Agricultural depression kept German bailiwicks from sending the embattled Order money, supplies, and troops for the wars that dragged through the 1420s and 1430s, and its efforts to collect more money in Prussia made it increasingly unpopular. The Order continued to favor German knights over Prussian knights for appointments, and it arbitrarily interfered with sales of private property, claiming lands where ownership was not fully documented and expropriating the inheritance of orphaned daughters because they could not serve in the army. Estates created in this manner were settled with rent-paying peasants, who were subjected to such extreme demands that they could not even afford the time to attend church, and monks complained that pagan customs were reviving in the countryside. Needless to say, peasants had trouble cultivating their own fields to feed themselves and pay their rent. The need to rebuild forced the Order to colonize abandoned villages with Polish peasants.

Changing trade patterns weakened the Order's hold over the Prussian economy and led it into conflict with Prussian merchants. The Hanseatic League declined while trade grew with English and Dutch customers, whose increasing demands for timber and grain could not be satisfied without greater participation by Prussian merchants and even Polish merchants, who settled in Prussian cities. The transit trade also brought Polish and Prussian merchants together. The Order's efforts to regain its commercial dominance led it into deepening conflicts with local merchants. The Order regulated Baltic trade more stringently, reserving low Hanse duties for its own use and imposing new regulations, licenses, taxes, and fees. The unpopular cargo tax was even applied to ships that put into Gdańsk to find shelter during storms. City officials resented the Order's practice of settling nonguild artisans on its suburban properties to compete with Prussian city guilds. The Order's first general taxation in 1411 provoked a rising in Gdańsk that was harshly suppressed. Three city councillors were executed.

The Order attempted to respond constructively to growing discontent by creating the Prussian Estates, where representatives could voice their grievances, but the gap proved too large to bridge. Representatives of the six largest Prussian cities (Braunsberg, Chelmno, Elbląg, Gdańsk, Königsberg, and Toruń) started meeting with the grand master in the 1370s to discuss commerce, mutual relations, and external relations. The addition of noble representatives made the Prussian Estates more formal but stimulated a sense of common interest within the nobility, which asserted a growing sense of historical commonality by claiming to be the primary settlers and Christianizers of Prussia rather than the Teutonic Order. The Estates were not satisfied by the creation in 1412 of a council composed of thirty-two knights and fifteen city representatives, and they refused to attack Polish lands in 1413 as merchants developed closer links with Poland. In 1422, the Estates demanded that the Order release them from their oath of service if the Order launched an aggressive war, and in 1433 it forced the grand master to sign a truce with Poland ending a destructive war. Both cities and nobles gave clear signals that they would refuse to support future wars with Poland. The Estates found procedural excuses to avoid paying war taxes while acknowledging their obligation to pay. A head-on collision between the Estates and the Order was imminent.

The Order's international position weakened, as well. Representatives of the Teutonic Knights, especially Jan Wallenrode, archbishop of Riga, made strong presentations at the Council of Constance (1414–18) to ask for help against Polish attacks claiming once again that Poland-Lithuania was not a true Christian nation. Paweł Włodkowic (Paulus Vladimiri), rector of the Jagiellonian University, defended Poland's Christianity at the council, showing that both sides had used pagan allies in the recent war, and he also demonstrated Poland's Christian sincerity by bringing sixty newly converted Samogitians to the conference. This argument impressed the council more than Wlodkowic's theoretical proposition that pagans had a right to remain pagan if they chose. More telling yet was Vytautas's creation of an Orthodox Metropolitanate of Galicia and Kiev in 1415, which kindled hopes of reconciliation or even union between the Catholic and Orthodox Churches. The Council of Constance condemned a satirical pamphlet attacking Jagiełło but refused to imprison its author, a Dominican priest. Polish representatives took part in the general work of the council as full members of the European community for the first time.

Poland-Lithuania and the Hussite Wars

One of the major issues confronting the Council of Constance was the influence of Jan Hus, reformist Czech preacher and rector of Prague's Charles University, who was declared a heretic and burned at the stake in 1415. Polish cleric-diplomats helped establish their legitimacy by condemning Hus, but Polish state policy remained hesitant and ambiguous. Factors leading to Polish support for Hussitism include the resentment of papal and imperial assistance for the Teutonic Knights, the dislike of papal centralization (particularly strong among Orthodox nobles in Galicia and Lithuania), and the hope of acquiring the Bohemian crown. Factors acting against Polish support for Hussitism included Jagiełło's need as a recent convert to avoid the appearance of heretical sympathies and his concern that his realm might fall prey to civil war between Hus's sympathizers and opponents. As a result, the king reluctantly declined an invitation from the Bohemian estates in 1418 to become king; he took three years to think it over. Nevertheless, Jagiełło refused to participate in military expeditions against the

Hussites and made no effort to stop Polish enthusiasts and mercenary soldiers from joining the Hussite armies in their fight against Holy Roman emperor Sigismund of Luxemburg. Jagiełło even hired Czech Hussite mercenaries for his 1433 campaign against the Teutonic Order. Acting independently, Vytautas sent his nephew Zygmunt Korybut to Prague as his representative in 1422 and again in 1423 with an eye to assuming the throne himself, but papal and imperial pressure forced Vytautas to withdraw.

CHAPTER 2

Jagiełło's Successors: Władysław III, Kazimierz IV, Jan Olbracht, and Aleksander

Władysław II Jagiełło's long reign established the Jagiellonian dynasty firmly on the Polish and Lithuanian thrones, but the transition to his successors was not entirely smooth, owing to the youth of the sons he fathered late in life. Jagiełło placed his oldest son, Władysław, on the Polish, Czech, and Hungarian thrones, a development that increased the dynasty's prestige but did little for Poland and Lithuania. Władysław was succeeded by Kazimierz IV Jagiellończyk (Casimir IV the Jagiellonian), who reigned for half a century and established economic prosperity, good administration, cultural enrichment, and military strength. However, he secured his position by granting further privileges to the nobility. Although he continued a process that led ultimately to the collapse of the Polish-Lithuanian state, Kazimierz cannot be held responsible for the excessive growth of noble power, because the consequences of his actions were not obvious until a century later, and the worst consequences emerged only after two hundred years. The short reigns of two sons provided a bridge to the next generation.

THE REIGN OF WŁADYSŁAW III

The short reign of Władysław III was filled with conflicts that had been brewing at the end of his father's long reign. Opposition to the dominant faction rallied behind Władysław's younger brother, Kazimierz, over the issue of dynastic expansion.

When Jagiełło died in 1434, a regency council headed by Bishop Zbigniew Oleśnicki of Cracow (1389–1455), Jagiełło's principal adviser and perhaps the real power behind the throne in his last years, ran the Polish state for Władysław III (1425–44). Oleśnicki followed a policy of expanding the Jagiellonian dynasty to the south, extending Polish influence in Lithuania, and asserting Catholic hostility against Hussitism; he distributed landed estates lavishly to the Little Poland magnates who supported him. Anti-Oleśnicki forces drawn primarily from Great Poland but headed by a Little Poland magnate, Spytek of Melsztyn, unsuccessfully challenged Oleśnicki's dominance and voiced opposition to the growing wealth and political influence of the Catholic Church in Poland, expressing some sympathy with Czech Hussitism. Their influence waned, however, after a Polish army unsuccessfully invaded Silesia in 1438 in order to place young Prince Kazimierz on the Bohemian throne at the invitation of Bohemian Hussites. Spytek rebelled the following year to prevent Władysław from assuming the throne as he approached the age of majority, but Spytek died in battle against pro-Oleśnicki forces and the rebellion petered out. Despite his failure, Spytek and Polish Hussitism left some traces in Kazimierz IV's policy of asserting control over the Catholic Church and relying on the lesser nobility to check the strength of the great Polish lords.

The regency council's aggressive policies in Lithuania prolonged the civil war that had broken out after Vytautas died in 1430. Jagiełło's death in 1434 ended the personal union between the two realms, and it was not clear what would take its place. Polish military intervention assured Żygimantas's victory in his struggle with nativist Prince Švitrigaila in 1435, but Żygimantas did not enjoy the fruits of victory for long; he was assassinated in 1440. Švitrigaila ruled Volhynia with the support of the Ruthenian nobles, abandoning his wider aspirations. Lithuanian magnates turned instead to Władysław's younger brother, Kazimierz, and made him grand duke in order to maintain their independence from Poland.

Oleśnicki was more successful in his dealings with Hungary, at least in the short run. After the death of Albert Habsburg, nephew of Sigismund of Luxemburg, Oleśnicki arranged for Władysław's election to the Hungarian throne in 1440 in exchange for promises of Polish military assistance against Turkish encroachment. A second election organized by Hungarian magnates favored Albert's posthumously born son. An inconclusive two-year civil war was resolved by Pope Eugene IV in favor of Władysław in exchange for his agreement to lead a crusade against the Turks. Eighteen-year-old Władysław won a great victory over the Turks in 1442 with the help of the experienced Hungarian general, János (John) Hunyadi. The Turks and Hungarians signed a ten-year peace that protected Hungary against attack and assured it some influence in the Balkans. However, Władysław promptly violated the agreement at the urging of the papal legate, Julian Cesarini, who insisted that an oath taken to Muslims was not binding. The ensuing campaign led to a crushing defeat at the battle of Varna, in present-day Bulgaria, on November 10, 1444. Władysław III died, but Hunyadi escaped with part of the army.

Kazimierz IV and Polish-Lithuanian Relations

Kazimierz IV (1427–92) was the third son of King Władysław II Jagiełło. The Polish court attempted to place Kazimierz on the Czech throne at age eleven, and he became grand duke of Lithuania in 1440 as well as king of Poland after his brother's death. Jagiełło's second son, also named Kazimierz, had died in infancy. The fifteenth-century historian Maciej of Miechów described Kazimierz IV as similar to his father, Władysław II Jagiełło—taller but with the same long face. Like his father, he loved to hunt, showed great endurance in harsh weather, and avoided alcohol. He lived to age sixty-five, long for the period but not long for the Jagiellonian dynasty. Kazimierz loved banquets and enjoyed numerous love affairs although he nonetheless had thirteen children with his wife, Elizabeth Habsburg (known in Poland as Elizabeth the Hungarian), of whom eleven survived. Kazimierz provided a good education for his sons, four of whom became crowned heads: Władysław in Bohemia and Hungary, Jan Olbracht (John Albert) in Poland, Aleksander in Lithuania and then Poland, and Zygmunt in Poland-Lithuania. Another son, Fryderyk, became a cardinal of the Catholic Church, and two of Kazimierz's children who died in infancy were canonized.

Kazimierz IV's education was supervised by Bishop Oleśnicki, who may have neglected his duties in this respect since no examples of Kazimierz's writing have survived, even his signature. When Grand Duke Žygimantas died in 1440, a delegation of Lithuanian nobles headed by Jonas Gostautas (John/Jan Gasztołd) brought Kazimierz to Lithuania, promising his reluctant Polish advisers that Kazimierz would act as King Władysław III's viceroy. Instead, Gostautas immediately arranged Kazimierz's election as grand duke, and, under Gostautas's direction, young Kazimierz followed his father's policy of maintaining a strong Lithuania with close links to Poland. On the one hand, he strongly opposed and defeated Polish efforts to annex Lithuania as a whole or pick off provinces adjacent to Little Poland such as Volhynia. On the other, he opposed those Lithuanians who wished to break the union with Poland and restore full independence, such as his uncle Švitrigaila. Under Kazimierz, Gostautas and Kazimierz's mother's influential family, the Holszańskis, monopolized higher offices, often appointing themselves to several at the same time. Jonas Gostautas, for example, held the important posts of chancellor of Lithuania and palatine of Vilnius in addition to acting as Kazimierz's guardian. Kazimierz placed his allies in regional capitals such as Kiev and Smolensk, and confirmed Samogitia's traditional autonomy. The Lithuanian leadership established a separate Catholic archbishopric in Vilnius to keep Church operations under its own control while acknowledging the formal primacy of the Gniezno archbishopric in western Poland. An early form of national consciousness manifested itself strongly within ethnic Lithuania, especially in Samogitia, but Ruthenian nobles also worked to keep the Grand Duchy legally distinct from the Polish Kingdom to ensure their rights.

Kazimierz IV succeeded his brother on the Polish throne at age seventeen without abandoning his support for Lithuania. Under Gostautas's supervision, Kazimierz bargained hard to maintain Lithuanian prerogatives when he received the delegation that came to invite him to rule Poland. The two sides finally reached an agreement at Brześć (Brest-Litovsk) in 1446 to maintain two separate countries united only in the person of their common sovereign and to divide the disputed border provinces, Podolia and Volhynia. Faced with strong opposition from Polish nobles, Kazimierz and his Lithuanian advisers yielded more territory, and Kazimierz finally took the Polish throne on June 25, 1447. In compensation, Kazimierz granted Lithuanian nobles far-reaching rights and privileges including a monopoly on officeholding, courts run by nobles, full ownership of their landed estates, and greater control over their peasants. Polish and Lithuanian nobles held joint meetings in 1448, 1451, and 1453 to discuss the terms of the union and finally agreed in 1453–54 without finding any new solution to difficulties. Lithuania was not entirely satisfied and expressed its displeasure by remaining neutral during the long war between Poland and the Teutonic Order (1454–66), thereby missing the opportunity to conquer ethnic Lithuanian territory around Klaipėda in eastern Prussia (Lithuania Minor). Kazimierz resided in Cracow after 1447 but ruled over Lithuania personally, unlike his father, and visited it regularly.

Throughout his reign as grand duke, Kazimierz regularized the Lithuanian state by building a stronger administration in which a council of lords shared his power, although it received official status only under Kazimierz's son and successor, Grand Duke Aleksander. Some fifteen to twenty Lithuanian Catholic families monopolized the highest territorial, ministerial, and clerical positions and another sixty to seventy families filled territorial governorships. The role of Orthodox nobles grew. They served in the ducal council and filled high offices in their own districts, but they never achieved equality with Lithuanian Catholics in numbers or rank. Federated principalities such as Kiev were subordinated to central appointments, although most local privileges remained intact. Kazimierz regularized the offices of chancellor and treasurer, which had previously existed sporadically and which had lacked clear definition. Local particularism manifested itself strongly within ethnic Lithuania, especially in Samogitia. In 1468, Kazimierz issued a law code in chancery Ruthenian on limited issues; a full law code appeared a half-century later. In 1478, he promised to leave the Lithuanian ducal throne to one of his sons and the Polish royal throne to another.

The strength of Lithuanian identity was reflected in the theory of Roman origins that developed after 1450, probably among Lithuanian students in Cracow. The fifteenth-century Polish historian Jan Długosz reported that Lithuanians were descended from followers of the Roman consul Pompey, who left Rome rather than live under Julius Caesar's tyranny. Pompey and his followers allegedly emigrated to distant Lithuania, where they were called "Litali" (Italians), a name which corrupted in time to "Lituani" as the Latin language supposedly evolved into Lithuanian. This fanciful theory elevated the status of Lithuania, and some boyars wanted to make Latin the common speech of Lithuania, "returning" to the pure language of their ancestors.

THE DECLINE OF THE RUTHENIAN NOBILITY AND LOSS OF WESTERN RUSSIA

While the Ruthenian nobility retained its position in Lithuania, it declined in the Kingdom of Poland, and many Ruthenians polonized or emigrated to Volhynia and the Ukrainian lands. Some Ruthenian nobles lost their lands when Kazimierz III the Great of Poland took Galicia (Red Russia) by stages in 1340–70, even though he granted full recognition as Polish nobles to Orthodox boyars with secure titles to their estates. Kazimierz and his successors confiscated vacated estates and granted them to Poles or immigrant nobles. Sometimes the royal judiciary declared land vacant if the Orthodox occupant lacked adequate documentation of ownership; some Orthodox magnate families lost their leaseholds on royal estates in this fashion. The Orthodox nobility also lost out in the competition for important state offices to Polish newcomers. The eastern section of Galicia polonized more slowly than the western section, and some Ruthenian aristocrats maintained their position into the fifteenth century, as evidenced by Cyrillic seals on official documents. The Catholic Church accepted mixed marriages, probably hoping to expand its influence in this manner. Ruthenian magnate families virtually disappeared from Galicia by the sixteenth century, although lesser noble families maintained their status longer even though they tended to be poorly educated and lacked opportunities for advancement. On occasions such as agitation over the Union of Brest in 1596 and the Cossack Uprising of 1648, Ruthenian consciousness reemerged as a force in Galicia.

Ruthenian interests also suffered because Kazimierz IV failed to pursue Lithuanian expansion in the Ruthenian east and left the field open for Muscovite Russia. The independent principalities of Novgorod and Pskov were trading republics ruled by noble and commercial oligarchs who invited princes from Lithuania, Moscow, and other neighboring states to act as war leaders without allowing them to dominate domestic politics. When invited, Ruthenian princes from the Grand Duchy of Lithuania fulfilled their duties as rulers in Pskov and

Novgorod without helping the Lithuanian state, but at least their presence prevented Moscow from taking over. They enjoyed little support from Kazimierz IV, who saw their strength as an obstacle to his consolidation of Lithuania. He exiled strong rulers such as Prince Aleksander Vasilievich Chartoryski (Czartoryski). Kazimierz failed to block Tsar Ivan III's absorption of Pskov in 1464 and he failed to support his cousin Prince Mykhailo Olelkevych, the newly elected prince of Novgorod, against Muscovite opposition in 1470. When Prince Mykhailo left Novgorod the following year in hopes of succeeding his recently deceased brother on the Kievan ducal throne, he found that Kazimierz had abolished the principality and appointed a Lithuanian governor. Tsar Ivan III added greatly to Muscovite Russia's power and prestige by conquering Novgorod in 1471 before a new government could establish itself, and Kazimierz failed to intervene to help the pro-Lithuanian faction. Ivan now called himself "Tsar of All the Russias" and laid claim to Ruthenian parts of the Grand Duchy of Lithuania. These and other tensions led two Lithuanian magnates, Fedor Bielski and Ivan Holszański, to conspire to kill Kazimierz IV in 1480 and place Prince Mykhailo on the throne, probably without his knowledge. The plot was uncovered and the leaders executed. Bielski managed to flee to Moscow.

Two decades later, Prince Mikhail Lvovich Glinskii tried again to separate Lithuania from Poland. Glinskii, born into an Orthodox noble family of Mongol origin, studied in Germany, Italy, and Spain, converted to Roman Catholicism for a time, and served in the Saxon army before returning to Lithuania. His abilities impressed Lithuanian Grand Duke Aleksander, who promoted him to high rank and gave him rich estates. Rumors that Glinskii aimed to make himself grand duke of a restored Kievan Rus convinced Aleksander's successor, Zygmunt I, to remove Glinskii from the ducal council and strip him of his offices. Glinskii led an unsuccessful revolt in 1508 against Zygmunt with support from Vasilii III of Moscow. He fled to Moscow in 1510, demanding to be made viceroy of areas that he conquered from Lithuania. When Vasilii refused, Glinskii reopened relations with Polish King Zygmunt I and Vasilii retaliated by throwing him into prison until 1526, when the tsar married Glinskii's niece, Elena, who gave birth to Ivan IV (the Terrible) in 1530. Prince Mikhail Glinskii regained his influence at the Russian court until Ivan IV turned eighteen.

Parliament and the Centralization of the Polish State

Like "new monarchs" further west, Kazimierz secured the independence of his realm against papal and imperial claims. Kazimierz IV demanded the right to control all benefices in Poland and Lithuania and appoint bishops rather than leave the choice to the local church chapter, which had previously appointed bishops, or to the pope. No decision was ever made in principle and each case was fought out separately, but in general King Kazimierz gained control over these valuable appointments. The most celebrated case came in 1460, when the king banished the papal candidate for bishop of Cracow, Jacob of Sienna, along with some of his Polish supporters, and took control of Church lands. Pius II retaliated by excommunicating Jacob's rivals, but in time the pope removed his ban and let the king appoint his own bishops. The papacy took revenge by supporting the Teutonic Order in disputes with the Polish-Lithuanian state and by encouraging Matthias Corvinus (son of János Hunyadi) in his contest against the Jagiellonian Prince Władysław for the Czech crown. Imperial claims were easy to shake off, since they had diminished over the centuries.

Modernization of fiscal and military organizations provided another element of centralization. Jan Ostroróg, castellan of Poznań, gave these tendencies a strong voice in his tract, "On the Organization of the State" (c. 1475). Ostroróg called for greater independence from the papacy in symbolic and practical relations; the king should address the pope as an equal and should not swear obedience to him. Ostroróg opposed sending Church taxes to Rome and wanted the Church to pay taxes to the Polish state on its extensive landholdings; he favored taxing Polish nobles as well. Ostroróg advocated establishing a uniform court system to replace the regional courts left by the period of feudal divisions and the different urban law codes observed in different cities. He wanted strong, constitutional royal power and hoped for some improvement in burgher and peasant status, although he was an opponent of guilds.

Ostroróg and other advocates of a centralized state cooperated with King Kazimierz IV in increasing the power of parliament, particularly the lower house (*sejm*). Having grown up in Poland and Lithuania under the tutelage of powerful magnates, Kazimierz IV devoted much of his political attention to developing his own independent support among lesser nobles, whom he rewarded by giving them important state offices. Kazimierz IV also cultivated support from Great Poland as an alternative to the great nobles from Little Poland who had dominated his youth. This political decision led him to adopt the traditional interest of Great Poland in closer links with Prussia based on proximity and trade, despite the risk of conflict with the Teutonic Order. King Kazimierz also garnered support from Polish cities, though they were still too weak to contribute much in the way of money or troops.

Kazimierz allowed the lesser nobility to gain strength to counterbalance the role of the great nobles. Traditionally, great nobles and state officials influenced decision-making through their participation in the royal council, while the lesser nobility only shouted approval of these decisions after they were made. Changing political procedures, Kazimierz encouraged local noble assemblies (dietines/ *sejmiki*) to elect delegates to meet at the same time as the large royal council of government officials and bishops, and he accorded those assemblies more power. In 1454, knights from Great Poland met King Kazimierz IV at their military encampment near Cerekwica and demanded concessions before they fought against the Teutonic Order. The king promised that he would not call a noble levy without the agreement of noble assemblies or impose new taxes. A serious defeat at Chojnice shortly thereafter forced Kazimierz to summon a levy from Little Poland and offer the nobles similar concessions. In addition, Kazimierz promised not to lease royal estates to magnates without proper payment and to limit the economic freedoms of burghers and peasants. He soon put these provisions together in the general privilege issued at Nieszawa that limited royal power significantly. The king may not have been unhappy about this, because the lesser nobility provided him with significant political support.

The practice of holding bicameral parliamentary sessions developed gradually throughout the reign of Kazimierz IV. At first, leading cities such as Gdańsk, Cracow, and Poznań also sent delegates, but the nobles refused to let them speak and they stopped coming. Jan Olbracht, Kazimierz IV's son, officially sanctioned the bicameral legislature in 1493. In 1496, he granted dietines the right to control prices of artisanal manufactures (*taksy wojewodzińskie*) and prohibit burghers from buying landed estates (except the clergy). The latter provision was largely ignored until the seventeenth century. In return, the nobles agreed to new taxation to launch his ambitious, but ill-fated, military expedition to Moldavia.

Overall, Kazimierz's reign had a modernizing tendency, but the king failed to provide solid institutions that would strengthen royal power permanently. While controlling important secular and clerical appointments, Kazimierz made no effort to develop a systematic bureaucracy. He never sought regular new taxes and continually fell into debt to pay for military ventures. Kazimierz helped cities develop their trade as much as possible, but he taxed them heavily and failed to see their potential for significant political support as did western European "new monarchs." The reason is probably that the cities were not rich and strong enough and he probably shared medieval prejudices against burghers, as illustrated by his reaction to a Cracow mob that killed one of his military commanders for beating up a Cracow armorer who failed to complete work on time. Kazimierz overrode Cracow's judicial autonomy to execute several city councillors who objected to the noble's high-handed assault.

Prussian Dissatisfaction and Polish Expansion to the Baltic Coast

Kazimierz's interest in Great Poland led to the Polish conquest of the Baltic coast after Prussians revolted against the Teutonic Order, hoping to abolish the Order's irksome restrictions on economic and political freedoms. As conflict increased between the Order and the Prussian Estates, an association of cities and nobles formed the Prussian Union in 1440 along the lines of the Lizard Union of 1397 to protest Order practices in taxation, coinage, land sales, and milling monopolies. Grand Master Konrad von Erlichshausen tried to resolve the problems politically through a mixture of concessions and subtle moves to play the nobles and cities off against each other, while Bishop Franz of Warmia more directly denounced the Prussian Union as immoral and illegal. After Erlichshausen died in 1449, his successor, Grand Master Heinrich Reuss von Plauen, tried desperately to get agreement on the form of his oath of office, but the Estates insisted on discussing its grievances and forcing confirmation of all privileges and liberties. The pope and emperor supported the Order, which seemed to be preparing an armed coup against the Estates. In 1453, Emperor Friedrich III ordered the Prussian Union's dissolution and threatened to execute three hundred of its members.

The Thirteen Years' War and Union with Prussia

The Prussian Union revolted on February 4, 1454, quickly conquering most of Prussia, and asked Kazimierz IV to admit it to the Polish-Lithuanian state. Poland declared war on the Order on March 6, 1454, and incorporated Prussia, making it an autonomous part of the Polish Kingdom (not Lithuania), with its own parliament, legal system, and mint. The Prussian nobility gained equal status with the Polish nobility, urban privileges were confirmed, and lower Polish taxes replaced much higher Order taxes. Prussian nobles gained a monopoly of Prussian state offices. Gdańsk took over several nearby villages that had belonged to the Teutonic Order, along with their revenues. In exchange, King Kazimierz IV only asked for 2,000 florins annually and accommodations for three days per year in a newly constructed court with stables for two hundred horses.

Despite the Prussian Union's initial successes against the Teutonic Order, the war proved long and difficult. Polish armies failed to drive the Teutonic Order out of its fortified strongholds, so the Order had time to recruit mercenaries to recapture much of Prussia with diplomatic but not military support from Emperor Friedrich III and Pope Nicholas V. The port cities of Gdańsk and Toruń hired their own mercenaries to defend themselves. When the Order ran out of money to pay their wages, its mercenaries offered their fortresses to Poland, notably Malbork in 1457. Kazimierz had no trouble convincing the Polish parliament to levy enough taxes to let him buy castles from the disaffected mercenaries and hire his own troops, even though the intervention of the elector of Brandenburg propped up the Order for several more years. Finally, a complete Polish victory over the Order's army and river fleet at Gniew on September 15,

1463, reopened the Vistula to Polish commerce. Gdańsk prevented German reinforcements from coming to the Order's aid, allowing Polish troops to achieve additional gains in 1465 and 1466. However, Brandenburg's support permitted the Order to hold a line of forts in eastern Prussia.

The war ended when Poland-Lithuania and the Teutonic Order reached their financial limit and signed a compromise peace agreement in Toruń on October 19, 1466. The Peace of Toruń awarded Poland western Pomerania, which became known as Royal Prussia and was governed according to the 1454 decree on incorporation; it included Gdańsk, Elblag, Toruń, the Chełm lands, and the bishopric of Warmia. The Teutonic Order kept eastern Prussia with its capital at Königsberg as a feudal dependency of Poland, which obliged it to provide armed assistance in wartime. Lithuania had not participated in the war and made no gains at the Order's expense. Mazovia supported the Order at some times and Poland at others; it also made no gains. The Slavic princes of western Pomerania made some small gains, and the elector of Brandenburg retained New March, an important trade link between his lands and Prussia that he had purchased from the Order in 1455.

Continuing Tensions Between Ducal Prussia and Poland

The Teutonic Order accepted defeat reluctantly and sought to minimize its new feudal dependence on Poland. Despite provisions in the Peace of Toruń, Polish subjects were never admitted into the Order and the grand master rarely attended the Polish royal council (senate). Part of the difficulties that Poland faced in dealing with the Teutonic Order came from the latter's continuing support from the Holy Roman Empire and the papacy, as indicated by the dispute over appointment of the bishop of Warmia, an important position due to the bishopric's size and wealth and the bishop's position as president of the Prussian diet. King Kazimierz IV wanted to appoint Polish churchmen to bind Prussia closer to Poland, while the Warmia lay leadership wished to emphasize Prussian autonomy by appointing a regional figure. Kazimierz prevailed in 1478 by threatening military intervention, but a dispute over Kazimierz's appointment of his son Fryderyk as bishop of Warmia dragged on until Kazimierz's death. Kazimierz's son and successor Jan Olbracht confirmed the appointment of a Prussian churchman, Lucas Watzenrode, while Zygmunt I worked out a compromise early in the sixteenth century that allowed him to appoint Poles to the important bishopric.

The long war pushed the Teutonic Order into decline, leaving the last grand masters Friedrich of Saxony and Albert of Brandenburg, to act as feudal territorial princes presiding over the impoverished region of eastern Prussia. Lacking cash, the Teutonic Order granted large landed estates with judicial rights over the peasants to its mercenary leaders and local nobles. Other mercenary officers used war booty to buy landed estates or, if unpaid, seized properties. This new "Junker" class of nobles dominated eastern Prussia until the twentieth century. The 1453–66 war caused massive devastation that kept many districts deserted until 1500. Lübeck merchants traveling from Gdańsk to Toruń in 1464 found that "there was not a living being, dog or cat for ten miles." Forty-five percent of villages near Königsberg were devastated. However, landowners prospered when they could farm, because their produce, grown mostly with hired labor, sold easily in nearby cities for domestic use and export. To prevent peasants from taking advantage of the new situation, a 1494 ordinance required the return of runaway peasants and gave masters the right to punish runaways harshly. A 1503 ordinance required servants to take another job two weeks after leaving a previous job or face arrest.

THE JAGIELLONIAN DYNASTY IN BOHEMIA AND HUNGARY

With Prussia secured, King Kazimierz turned his attention to the south to find thrones for his large family. Bohemia continued to be attractive. The Hussite Wars had ended with the election of the Bohemian noble George (Jiří) of Poděbrady as king. Poland's favorable links with the Hussite Kingdom gave Kazimierz the chance to place his son Władysław on the throne after George's death in 1471, but the Hungarian king, Matthias Corvinus, also claimed the Bohemian throne and won election by Moravian and Silesian nobles. The papacy supported Corvinus's candidacy because he seemed more likely to suppress Hussitism and because Hungary formed a crucial defense line against Turkish expansion; Emperor Friedrich III Habsburg supported the Jagiellonians in Bohemia in order to weaken Corvinus and take the Hungarian throne for himself. A war broke out between Władysław, supported by his father, Kazimierz IV, and Corvinus that devastated the Czech lands and encroached on parts of southern Poland. The Czech lands remained divided until Corvinus's death in 1490, when Władysław became king of all the Czech lands (Bohemia, Moravia, and Silesia). King Kazimierz also tried to put his third son, Jan Olbracht, on the Hungarian throne but found himself unexpectedly checked by his older son, Władysław, who gained the support of great lords. A two-year war ensued in Hungary between the two Jagiellonian brothers, which Władysław's supporters won; he gave Jan Olbracht the duchy of Głogów in Silesia in 1491 as compensation for relinquishing his claim to Hungary.

JAN OLBRACHT

Jan Olbracht (1459–1501), third son of Kazimierz IV, was known for impulsiveness and boldness, qualities that stood him well in battle but poorly in politics. Jan Olbracht received a careful education under the direction of Jan Długosz, the court historian, with a humanistic leavening from Philippo Buonaccorsi. He also gained a political education by traveling around Poland-Lithuania with his father. With his elder surviving brother Władysław serving as king of Bohemia after 1471, Jan Olbracht became the heir apparent to the Polish throne. In 1486 he undertook his first independent role as his father's representative in the Ukrainian provinces and distinguished himself in battle against the Tatars. His attempt to become king of Hungary failed.

Jan Olbracht was chosen king of Poland when Kazimierz IV died on June 7, 1492, while his younger brother Aleksander was chosen grand duke of Lithuania, thereby breaking the union between the two countries once again. To gain the Polish throne, Jan Olbracht had to outmaneuver several rivals including his brother Władysław and the duke of Mazovia. In power, Jan Olbracht continued his father's policy of building a centralized, parliamentary state based on noble privileges. He showed no greater interest in developing burgher economic strength or political support than his father had. His real interest was international expansion to the southeast, although he paid some attention to rounding out Polish possessions by incorporating the duchies of Płock in Mazovia and Oświęcim (Auschwitz) in Silesia.

Jan Olbracht's Moldavian Failure

The Jagiellonian expansion into Bohemia and Hungary played out against the background of Turkish expansion into the Balkans. The Ottomans had leapfrogged the Straits and taken most of the Balkans before capturing Constantinople in 1453, renaming it Istanbul. King Kazimierz tried to avoid war with the Turks, but he came into conflict with them as he tried to secure Poland-Lithuania's economic interests in trade along the Danube and Dniester Rivers by protecting the princes of Moldavia (Romania), who controlled the mouth of the Danube. In 1475 the Turks conquered Kaffa (Feodosiya) in Crimea from the Genoans (Italians) and the Tatars became vassals of the sultan; in addition, the Turks forced Stepan the Great, prince of Moldavia, to acknowledge their suzerainty after defeating him in battle. In 1484 the Turks took Kiliia and Bilhorod (Akkerman) in Moldova at the mouth of the Prut. Kazimierz negotiated an armistice with the Turks when the papal court turned down his request for war subsidies.

More aggressively, Jan Olbracht aimed to expand to the southeast by conquering Moldavia, but he met disaster. The aim was to reopen Black Sea trading routes that had been closed to Poland by Turkish conquest. The Turkish Empire required that Polish goods, particularly grain, be sold in Turkey below market price. Jan Olbracht probably planned to install his younger brother Zygmunt (later king of Poland-Lithuania) on the Moldavian throne. He tried to mount a powerful coalition with the Hungarian king (brother Władysław),

Lithuanian grand duke (brother Aleksander), and Moldavian prince Stepan, but the coalition quickly unraveled. Hungary held equally valid claims to Moldavian overlordship and quickly pulled out of the coalition, warning the Poles not to interfere. Ivan III of Russia used a recent treaty with Lithuania to force Aleksander to withdraw, and Aleksander complied, sending Jan Olbracht only a few troops. Sensing Stepan's hand behind these diplomatic defeats, Jan Olbracht redirected his troops toward the Moldavian capital, Suceava, to punish him. Poorly armed and disciplined Polish noble levies failed to capture the city. Jan Olbracht negotiated their exit from Moldavia, but Turkish and Tatar troops summoned by Stepan harassed the Polish withdrawal, and Moldavian forces attacked the Poles in the Bucovinian forests on October 26, 1497, causing substantial losses, greater disorder, and loss of prestige. Negotiations ensued and, in 1499, Olbracht recognized Stepan of Moldavia as an equal rather than as a feudal dependent.

The remaining years of Jan Olbracht's kingship passed more quietly as the king suffered from battle wounds, psychological scars from his defeat, and syphilis. He died on June 17, 1501.

ALEKSANDER

Jan Olbracht's younger brother Aleksander (1461–1506) succeeded to the Polish throne after serving as grand duke of Lithuania for nine years. Aleksander had been destined from birth for the Lithuanian throne, as indicated by his name, which had been Vytautas's baptismal name. As grand duke, Aleksander had little opportunity to regain control of the Lithuanian magnates who had dominated the Grand Duchy during his father's long reign. As the price of his ascendence to the ducal throne, Aleksander agreed to recognize the previous ducal council instead of reconstituting it with his own supporters, and he granted it the formal right to be consulted on all governmental appointments. Aleksander also strengthened the nobility's freedom to dispose of its estates and reduced its obligations to the state. He turned to Orthodox nobles such as Konstiantyn Ostrozky to build his own faction without much success, and his attempt to unify his subjects by promoting the union of the Catholic and Orthodox Churches aroused scant interest. He used his marriage to Helena, daughter of Russian Tsar Ivan III and Sophia Paleologus, niece of the last Byzantine emperor, to strengthen his claim to rule Ruthenian lands. The wedding took place in 1494 after a border war in which Russia prevailed; Helena was used as a pledge of peace. Despite political differences, the marriage was a loving one in which Helena supported her husband against her father. She remained Orthodox in religion and gave up her right to be crowned queen of Poland in 1501. Conflicts with Russia continued.

A Lithuanian parliament (*seim*) met several times to approve the choice of

Aleksander as grand duke and ratify decisions by the ducal council. The parliament consisted of provincial officeholders selected by the duke and was dominated by some fifteen to twenty families. Decisions were made informally by a small inner cabinet of territorial officials and ministers which controlled the formal Ducal council composed of thirty-five bishops, territorial officers, ministers, and lesser officeholders.

Aleksander had greater success in exercising royal power in Poland. At first, he seemed to give way to the magnates who supported his election by issuing the Mielnik privilege of 1501, which conceded what had been a primary aim of Little Poland magnates since 1385: a closer constitutional union dominated by Poland. It declared that the Polish and Lithuanian states made "a single body, indivisible and identical" and that the Polish and Lithuanian nations would merge into "a single nation, a single people, a single brotherhood, with common assemblies" that would have "a single head, king, and sovereign." Kings were to be elected by all Polish nobles together with bishops, palatines, and castellans from Lithuania. Election to the throne of the Grand Duchy would now be linked to election in Poland, making the Lithuanian throne electoral instead of inherited. The senate, or royal council, became more independent of the crown. Senators came under judicial supervision of a senate council, and they gained the right to refuse obedience if the king violated their privileges.

Grand Duke Aleksander soon regained power by arranging for both the Lithuanian and Polish nobles to reject the Mielnik privilege. In Poland, lesser nobles refused to pay taxes and ignored court decrees in protest against senate domination. The senators tried to buy their support by issuing favorable social legislation, but King Aleksander appointed a leader of the lesser nobility, Jan Łaski from Great Poland, as chancellor and had him lead the lesser nobility at the 1504 Piotrków parliamentary meeting in rejecting the senate's demands. Parliament insisted that high state offices be distributed more widely and not concentrated in the hands of a few families; specifically, parliament barred anyone from holding certain high bishoprics or provincial governorships and the office of chancellor or vice-chancellor at the same time. The battle over these so-called *incompatibilites* lasted for a century, with limited results. More successful was the parliament's campaign to distribute leases on royal domains more widely and to ensure that proper payments be made on them. Similarly, in 1505 the Lithuanian parliament met at Brześć under the leadership of Aleksander's lieutenants, Mikhail Glinskii and the Radziwiłłs, and refused to confirm the Mielnik privilege. Aleksander removed the accord's leading proponents from his ducal council.

Now in control, Aleksander rewarded his supporters at the next session of parliament held in Radom by issuing the law "Nothing New" (*Nihil novi*) in

1505, which promised to enact "nothing new by us and our successors without the common agreement of the council and the representatives of the lands." This compromise arrangement recognized the upper chamber of service magnates and the lower chamber of deputies as equally important. As chancellor, Łaski helped establish the superiority of the Polish Church over Rome with regard to appointments of bishops and tried to prevent Rome and the Empire from supporting the Teutonic Order. King Aleksander later rewarded him with promotion to archbishop of Gniezno. Łaski also researched and printed a collection of previously issued statutes and privileges to guide parliament and the courts in making decisions; the statutes were not edited, and contradictions were not reconciled. Like his older brothers, Jan Olbracht and Cardinal Fryderyk, Aleksander died in 1506 of syphilis after designating his younger brother Zygmunt as his successor in Lithuania and virtually dictating his election to the Polish throne. Aleksander was buried in the Vilnius Cathedral, unlike other kings, who were buried in the Wawel Castle in Cracow. It is not clear whether this represented his fondness for his Lithuanian capital or the dislike with which the Polish magnates held him.

CHAPTER 3

Zygmunt I the Old

The long reign of Zygmunt I, from 1506 to 1548, saw Poland-Lithuania reach unparalleled heights of international power and influence thanks to its thriving economy. While lacking charismatic qualities and dramatic policies, Zygmunt provided effective government with the help of a newly appointed senatorial elite and carefully chosen administrative personnel. He exercised his royal prerogatives and maintained domestic peace by evading increasingly assertive parliamentary representatives rather than suppressing them and by granting religious toleration in practice, although not in theory.

ZYGMUNT I

Zygmunt I succeeded to the Lithuanian throne at his brother's death in 1506 and quickly won election to the Polish throne; he was crowned in January 1507. Born in 1467, the fifth son of Kazimierz IV (eighth of thirteen children), Zygmunt came to the throne at age forty with little background in Polish affairs. The new king had acquired a good education under Jan Długosz's tutelage. He spent several years (1498–1501) in Buda at the court of his brother Władysław, king of Hungary and Bohemia, where he encountered Italian humanism and came to appreciate Renaissance architecture. Buda was a meeting place for international diplomacy and Zygmunt became familiar with Turkish, Venetian, Habsburg, and French affairs. King Władysław made Zygmunt ruler of the Głogów principality (1498) and the duchy of Opawa (1501), naming him viceroy of Silesia and Lusatia in 1504. Living near Poland, Zygmunt developed close ties with Polish magnates such as Rafał Leszczyński and Krzysztof (Christopher) Szydłowiecki, whom he appointed as ministers when he became king of Poland-Lithuania. Zygmunt's main accomplishment as viceroy was to unify Silesian currency in 1505.

Zygmunt was unmarried when he ascended the Polish-Lithuanian throne,

Zygmunt I the Old

although he had a recognized liaison with Catherine von Telnetz, a noblewoman from Moravia with whom he had three children. Before contracting a state marriage as king, Zygmunt married her off to Crown Treasurer Andrzej (Andrew) Kościelecki, but he still acknowledged his children openly; he gave his son the name "Jan of the Lithuanian Princes," and appointed him bishop of Vilnius (later bishop of Poznań) while he arranged good marriages for his daughters. As king, Zygmunt married Barbara Zápolya (daughter of the national king of Hungary) in 1512 in order to get Hungarian support against the Teutonic Order and its Habsburg friends. The queen died in 1515 after giving birth to two children, Anna, who died in infancy, and Jadwiga, who married the elector of Brandenburg. Zygmunt then cemented relations with the Habsburgs by marrying a thirty-five-year-old Italian princess, Bona Sforza, who had become a Habsburg ward after her family lost its principality. Bona was a powerful and controversial personality whom Polish and Lithuanian nobles disliked, especially when compared with her domestic, apolitical predecessor.

The Growth of Royal Authority

Zygmunt I (the Old) proved an effective king of Poland-Lithuania who controlled policy by installing his own supporters in high secular and clerical posts. Papal law confirmed the king's right to appoint bishops in 1512–13. Zygmunt leaned toward aristocratic government, as prevailed at the Czech and Hungarian courts, and relied more on the Polish senatorial aristocracy than his father or brothers had. As a result, reforms demanded by the lesser nobles began to take an antiroyalist complexion, and the nobility became a strong independent force in Polish affairs instead of remaining the prop for royal authority that it had become under Kazimierz IV. Zygmunt scrupulously obeyed most reform laws, although he sometimes ignored important ones that limited his authority. For example, he violated the law against multiple officeholding with some of his appointments and he ignored tradition by electing his son and heir, Zygmunt II August, to the Polish-Lithuanian throne in 1530. The father became known as Zygmunt the Old at that point.

Zygmunt developed new sources of royal power in keeping with the European "age of new monarchies." His senatorial elite were his own appointees; the older families either cooperated or lost political influence at court. Much impressed by humanistic scholarship, he selected well-educated young nobles and occasionally burghers as royal secretaries in his personal chancellery, promoting them later to clerical and secular senatorial posts. More than half the bishops gained preferment by this route, and fewer than one-quarter came from old senatorial families. About two-thirds of the new senators studied either in Cracow or abroad. Many earned doctorates in law. Some of the most famous were Jan Dantyszek,

Marcin (Martin) Kromer, and Jan Łaski, who was particularly renowned for his extensive correspondence with Erasmus; many were noted poets and historians. Three-quarters were clergy, although some had taken the lowest orders. On average, Zygmunt appointed secretaries in their late thirties who served for about a dozen years before moving on to state office.

The secretaries provided a firm basis for the royalist system of government that prevailed throughout the sixteenth century. They carried on the king's domestic and foreign correspondence, traveled around Poland-Lithuania to represent the king at dietines and other important political meetings, and served as ambassadors abroad. This kind of day-to-day management enabled Zygmunt I and his son, Zygmunt II August, to issue laws, act as supreme judge, command the army, set foreign policy, and direct the administration. Even though both kings shared power with parliament to some extent, that body could do no more than veto legislation and approve new taxes; regular taxation needed no confirmation.

Royal independence was primarily contingent on the king's financial independence, and Zygmunt devoted considerable attention to finances. Expert advice from Chancellor Jan Łaski and Cracow banker Jan Boner helped him put them in such good order that the Polish-Lithuanian state collected taxes efficiently, tapped new sources of revenue, and reclaimed uneconomic leases on the royal estates. Zygmunt had to withstand challenges from parliament to retain his control over the revenues.

Expanded revenues allowed modernization of the Polish and Lithuanian armies and won Poland-Lithuania its dominant position in East Central Europe for the next century. The most important branch of service remained the cavalry, which now included both heavy units needed to break through infantry and light units needed to fight the highly maneuverable forces of Poland's eastern neighbors. The Polish and Lithuanian armies adopted modern techniques, too. Infantry and artillery provided effective fire power. Adoption of the Czech Hussite innovation of tabors, or armed wagon trains, supplied effective field fortifications for the eastern campaigns. Crown Great Hetman Jan Tarnowski (Polish commander in chief) and Lithuanian Great Hetman Konstiantyn Ostrozsky (Lithuanian commander in chief) achieved notable success in combining the different branches of service in battle. They were well read in sixteenth-century military theory as well as the military classics of ancient Rome uncovered by Renaissance humanists.

Royal reform also touched on legal issues. Poland-Lithuania, like other countries, was moving from customary law toward codified law. Chancellor Łaski issued his collection (not codification) of laws in 1506. Although court procedures were codified in 1523–24, parliament rejected the full codification of Polish law prepared by Mikołaj (Nicholas) Taszycki in 1534 because it defined parliament's political role in narrow terms; it approved only a so-called Correction, consisting of 929 articles describing court procedures, criminal law, and constitutional law. Books on Polish law published by Jakub Przyłuski and others achieved general acceptance and quasi-legal standing as law codes. Particularistic law systems were codified at the same time, such as Armenian law in 1519 and Church law in 1527; the Prussian Estates rejected proposed codes for Royal Prussia in 1523 but accepted a codification in 1598. Lithuania issued a law code in 1529, revised it in 1566, and modified it again in 1588. Mazovian law was codified in 1540 and revised in 1577.

Each city retained its own legal system based on German law in the Magdeburg or Chełmno variant, but there was a broad similarity in practice. Translation of Charles V's 1532 criminal law code from German into Polish by Bartłomiej (Bartholomew) Groicki and other legal experts introduced the formal use of torture as an investigative tool. City courts adapted it by including elements of Polish traditional practice, particularly recognizing extenuating circumstances to avoid condemning criminals to death in some cases.

Queen Bona Sforza

Queen Bona Sforza (1494–1557) was a political figure of the first rank even though her Italian birth and her sex made Polish nobles suspicious of her political initiatives. She came to Poland with a large private fortune and received generous land grants from the king. The queen provided model economic management on her properties, introducing administrative reforms that made her Lithuanian estates far more productive than before and using her profits to buy new estates, particularly in Mazovia. She also introduced Italian crops into cultivation such as parsley, lettuce, and cauliflower. The law treated Queen Bona Sforza's estates as tax-exempt royal properties, but, unlike King Zygmunt, she made no contributions to state expenditures. Instead, she used her funds to build her own political faction and became the first magnate of the realm. Sometimes she supported the king's policies and sometimes she combated them. Although the royal couple's goals were largely compatible, the queen's policies were unclear and seemed mostly aimed at developing personal influence or dynastic strength with greater vigor than her consensus-minded husband.

Queen Bona engineered the election of their son, Zygmunt II August, to the Lithuanian and Polish thrones in 1529, when he was nine, and he was crowned in Cracow in 1530. This election during his father's lifetime violated tradition and evoked a storm of protest that Zygmunt calmed by promising that future Jagiellonians would never repeat the practice. The episode left lingering traces of antiroyal feeling among many nobles. Queen Bona sought to come to terms with the movement for effective government that was developing in the parliamentary lower chamber, but the deputies rebuffed her overtures because she was a monarch and a monarchist. In foreign policy, she hoped to pursue Polish power in the Baltic and Silesia based on alliance with France, mostly to develop a dynastic power base not subject to constitutional restrictions. Her cultural influence was considerable.

"Execution of the Laws"

Assured of legislative equality since 1505, the chamber of deputies developed an assertive parliamentary reform movement that served as a counterpart to Zygmunt's policy of strengthening royal government. Loosely based on the concept that old laws provided the best government, and modern governments need only carry them out, "Executionists" came mostly from the stratum of rich nobles who chose to pursue a political career rather than enter the Church or compete for appointment as royal secretary. Growing prosperity enabled them to acquire good educations at Polish and foreign universities, hold local offices, and serve as parliamentary deputies. Executionists felt that as experienced officials they had a right to participate constructively in governmental affairs, not just veto unpopular legislation. And they expected to enjoy the financial rewards of government service, just like Zygmunt I's coterie of handpicked appointees. Andrzej Frycz Modrzewski was the main ideologist and theoretician.

The Executionist program emphasized strengthening the central power of the state, improving administration, and eliminating the differences in legal status afforded to different geographical regions for historical reasons. One key element was treasury reform. The Jagiellonian practice of distributing royal estates to magnate supporters had two negative features in their opinion: the state was deprived of income, and the Executionists gained none of the benefits. The lower chamber first demanded the redistribution of royal estates at the 1520 parliament held in Bydgoszcz. A second key issue was the independence of the lower house of parliament itself. The chamber of deputies asserted its equality by barring senators from its debates and requiring the election of deputies by dietines instead of allowing local senators to nominate them as in the past. Zygmunt I acceded because he needed new taxes to pursue war against Prussia, but he failed to honor his promises. Deputies made no gains until the 1530s when, provoked by the premature election of Zygmunt II August as co-ruler and heir, nobles from Great Poland asked Zygmunt I to review all laws, privileges, and decrees and abolish those that might be incompatible with older laws. The issue came to a head in the Cracow parliamentary meeting of 1536–37 when Executionist nobles demanded confirmation of the principle of elective kingship. They insisted that all nobles be invited to take part in future royal elections and expressly condemned the election of an heir apparent during the predecessor's lifetime.

The Executionist movement also aimed to strengthen the state in its relations with foreign bodies such as the Church in Rome and to strengthen the position of the nobility in relation to the lower classes. The Church came in for strong criticism, reflecting both national traditions and the inroads of the Protestant Reformation in Poland. Clerical estate holders would be required to perform military service, some clerical estates would be subject to state taxes for military service, appeal to Rome would be abolished in Church law, clerical courts would no longer have jurisdiction over laypersons, and high Church positions would be reserved exclusively for nobles. The Executionists also wanted full incorporation into the Kingdom of Poland of Royal Prussia and the Silesian principalities (Oświęcim and Zator) as well as full union with Lithuania. They aimed to bolster their economic position by demanding complete freedom from tariffs for nobles and limiting the rights of cities and peasants. The unenforced 1496 law prohibiting burghers and peasants from owning land was reaffirmed. Some guilds were closed and Jewish competition was encouraged.

Zygmunt I reluctantly accepted these demands in order to gain noble support for a planned military expedition against Moldavia, but the leaders doubted his sincerity and refused to cooperate until he acted. Gathering near Lviv for the expedition in 1537, a noble levy refused to obey orders and presented thirty-six demands. The armed nobles made their point with threatening demonstrations even if royalists contemptuously called the action a "chicken war," since foraging in the countryside for food provided the major activity for troops. In the end, Zygmunt I had to accept the nobles as partners in state affairs and grant Executionist demands, reluctantly and partially. The last decade of Zygmunt I's reign passed in inconclusive tension between the resistant king and assertive nobles. The parliaments of 1538–39 forced Zygmunt to affirm his obligation to respect the rights of the lower house and admit that the election of his son was contrary to traditional law. Polish nobles gained official exclusivity in parliament despite Zygmunt's halfhearted efforts to seat several incorporated cities. Parliament asserted that estates purchased by Queen Bona Sforza belonged to the state, not to her and her heirs, but could not force her to hand them over. Several Executionist leaders who criticized her vehemently were convicted of lèse-majesté, although they escaped punishment. Parliament also failed to gain control of the royal mint in order to prevent the king from financing his political operations by debasing the currency. The clergy withstood demands to pay regular taxes.

The Protestant Reformation and Its Political Implications

The Protestant Reformation began during the reign of Zygmunt I and proved attractive to many Polish-Lithuanian citizens. There were few pressing issues, since Polish monarchs already had the right to appoint bishops without papal interference and keep Church taxes at home. But papal support for the Teutonic Knights and opposition to Czech Hussites had alienated many Poles and Lithuanians. And the Church's wealth remained a tempting target, even though it owned much less arable land in Poland-Lithuania (10–12 percent) than it did in western European countries such as England (40 percent). Still, Church holdings were substantial. The possessions of the archbishopric of Gniezno (292 villages and 13 cities) and the bishopric of Cracow (225 villages and 11 cities) put their appointees among the wealthiest nobles in Poland, with eight to ten times the possessions of most great secular lords; other bishops and monastic orders also owned large estates. Many educated Poles and Lithuanians wanted to see the Bible translated into their own language, and some of the clergymen wanted to marry.

The Polish-Lithuanian state and Church leaders condemned the Reformation from the start and tried to stop it from taking hold. In 1520, Zygmunt I barred Luther's publications from entering Poland. Additional edicts in 1522–25 threatened to burn heretics at the stake and created a censorial commission with the power to search houses for forbidden literature. The 1523 synod excommunicated heretics and approved confiscation of their property. It also created a censorship bureau to supervise publications. In 1527 the synod called on bishops to watch over their parishes more closely, and some commoners suffered as a result. Among them was the wealthy seventy-nine-year-old burgher Katarzyna Malcherowa Waiglowa (Weigel), who died at the stake in 1539 for allegedly converting to Judaism; she may have been an early Anti-Trinitarian. Royal emissaries who went to Lithuania in 1539–40 to root out an alleged Judaizing cult could find no evidence and satisfied themselves by harassing Jews. Edicts in 1535–40 banned travel to Wittenberg and study in Protestant universities. The edicts were moderated somewhat by the 1543 parliament.

Despite this strong legislation, Zygmunt was not personally committed to maintaining Catholicism at all costs and he refrained from severe measures that might upset the unity of his realm. He made little effort to enforce his own anti-Protestant edicts, since he looked to a general council to reform the Church. Laws that prohibited visiting heretical countries and importing heretical literature were rarely enforced against nobles, and reform-minded clergy ignored anti-Protestant edicts with impunity. As early as 1521, Zygmunt protected a Protestant convert against charges of heresy by telling the complaining bishop that denouncing Luther in public would complicate foreign relations. Neither King Zygmunt nor his advisers, several of whom were bishops, challenged Albrecht Hohenzollern's conversion to Lutheranism and his secularizing Ducal Prussia in 1525 or the rapid spread of Lutheranism there. In fact, they helped Duke

Albrecht withstand pressure from the aggressively Catholic Habsburg emperor, Charles V, in order to keep him within the Polish-Lithuanian political orbit. The capital of Ducal Prussia, Königsberg, became a center for Polish-language Protestant publications. Zygmunt took no action against Orthodox Christians or Armenians, and Jews enjoyed his protection against ritual murder charges and anti-Jewish riots. Ethnic Germans in Prussia, Pomerania, Silesia, and parts of Great Poland received Protestantism readily, and many ethnic Poles and Lithuanians accepted the new faith as well.

Nobles turned to other forms of Protestantism as they came to associate Lutheranism with German burghers. Calvinism appealed to nobles because its democratic form of organization and local control resembled Polish political practice. Just as they assailed secular magnates in parliament, nobles now attacked Roman Catholic bishops in Protestant synods and abolished tax payments to centralized authority. Other forms of Protestantism also gained adherents. Anabaptism split off from Calvinism and spread. Powerful nobles in Great Poland such as Jakub Ostroróg and Rafał Leszczyński helped the Czech Brethren settle there after their expulsion from Bohemia, and they themselves converted.

THE INCORPORATION OF MAZOVIA

Mazovia entered the Polish state in 1526 when the last Piast princes of the Mazovian line died out. Until then Mazovia had enjoyed the unusual status of an independent duchy within the Polish crown, with a supreme duke and autonomous lesser duchies ruled by collateral lines. Mazovia lacked a formal parliament. After the mid-fifteenth century, regular noble gatherings discussed the full spectrum of political, legal, and economic issues; 134 such gatherings occurred in 1455–1526. The Warsaw district held the most, fifty-seven, while some districts held very few. An administrative council of ministers and territorial officers also met, like the Polish ducal council. Polish kings exercised sovereignty over Mazovia by confirming all new dukes in office. This right opened the door for the Polish crown to take over individual lands when their holders died: Rawa in 1462; Sochaczew in 1476; and Płock in 1495. Zygmunt took over the rest of Mazovia in 1526 when Dukes Stanisław and Janusz III died unexpectedly in their mid-twenties; the inevitable rumors of poisoning by Queen Bona Sforza were untrue. On taking over Mazovia, Zygmunt I maintained its distinct law code while integrating Mazovia into the Polish economy; Polish nobles, particularly Queen Bona, owned large estates there.

Before incorporation, Mazovia maintained an independent foreign policy and declined to cooperate with Poland on several fronts, particularly concerning Prussia. The duchy avoided fighting the Teutonic Order throughout the fourteenth century, and in 1409 refused to take part in Jagiełło's campaign until the

Polish army entered its territory. The bishop of Płock even told his vassals not to fight. Invading armies, primarily the Poles, devastated Mazovia, and Duke Siemowit IV tried to keep independence until his death in 1426. Mazovia also declined to join Kazimierz IV in 1453 in his fight against the Teutonic Order in order to safeguard trade relations. Exports of timber and other forest products started in the late fourteenth century, transported down the Narew, Bug, and Vistula Rivers to Gdańsk. The Mazovian duchy played an increasingly large role in the Gdańsk grain trade after 1500, contributing almost 30 percent of sales as grain replaced forest products as the province's chief export commodity. Mazovia also benefited from the transit trade that brought Lithuanian furs, wax, and honey through Mazovia to Silesia. In the sixteenth century, cattle drives from Volhynia crossed the duchy on their way to Prussian and Silesian markets; Mazovian farmers added their own stock to the herds. Increasing trade caused Mazovian cities to grow, especially Warsaw, where the number of artisans quintupled between 1427 and 1526 although the duchy remained less urbanized than Great Poland, Little Poland, or Prussia. Warsaw put up stone and brick housing in the sixteenth century as well as defensible city walls. An unusual feature of Mazovian social structure was the large number of knights or lesser nobles (20 percent of the population) due to the numerous wars, the absence of professional soldiers, and the lack of clear social definition. Most soldier-nobles were so poor that they worked the land themselves without serf labor.

The Mazovian central administration remained static during the century before incorporation into Poland. Only the chancellor's office changed by adding a team of ducal secretaries as in Poland-Lithuania. The ducal prefect provided the center of the local authority, supervising estates, administering justice, and directing the police. Like Zygmunt I of Poland, Mazovian dukes relied heavily on senators and rewarded them with appointments to rich offices. The practice restricted choice but ensured expertise. The ducal court and clerical courts, especially the archbishopric at Płock, provided the leading cultural centers for Mazovia with monasteries, schools, and libraries. New schools prepared clergy to assume civil and ecclesiastic posts in Warsaw as it grew; Mazovian graduates of the Jagiellonian University furnished many of the teachers. Mazovia maintained close relations with the royal court in Cracow, and numerous Mazovians worked for the Polish state, particularly in the chancellery.

The Lithuanian State and Identity

Lithuania's independent position weakened in the sixteenth century because of its inability to keep up with the growing economic strength that ensured Polish military dominance. Of course, Poland had no thought of using its strength against Lithuania, but Lithuanian difficulties in defending itself against Russians,

Ottomans, and Tatars made it necessary to appeal to Poland for help. In addition, Polish-Lithuanian monarchs resided far longer in Poland than in Lithuania and considered Polish interests paramount. The population of the Grand Duchy reached about 750,000 by 1528 and spilled out into Ducal Prussia.

Despite Polish influence, Lithuanian political institutions remained distinct from Polish institutions. Lithuanian identity was safeguarded by the continuing prohibition on foreigners (including residents of the Kingdom of Poland) acquiring land by purchase or marriage; even foreign-born daughters and widows were bypassed in favor of Lithuanian heirs. Several celebrated court cases during the sixteenth century upheld this law. Foreigners also had no right to appeal to the grand duke or courts in case of disputes.

Lithuanian lords, who had won the right to elect the grand duke in 1478, gradually transformed the Grand Duchy from a hereditary autocracy into an aristocratic state without opposition from the grand dukes. Like his predecessors, Zygmunt encouraged the Gostautas and Radziwiłł families to monopolize high office and dominate the ducal council, which a 1492 decree had changed from an advisory body into a formal administrative, judicial, and legislative institution. A Lithuanian chamber of deputies evolved, but its membership remained purely appointive and did not represent local noble dietines as in Poland. As a result, no counterpart of the Polish Executionist group emerged in the Grand Duchy. The Lithuanian Statute of 1529 provided a written constitution—written in Ruthenian.

Lithuania lacked the wealth to adopt Polish-style military professionalism, and grand dukes continued to summon the noble levy to fight on behalf of Lithuania but with declining success. A 1492 law required that every ten nobles must supply an armed knight for campaigning, a ratio that increased to 8:1 in 1529. Like Muscovite Russia, Lithuania maintained a register that spelled out the military obligations of each prince, lord, and lesser noble. Great lords supplied many knights while poor nobles jointly supplied only one.

Evolution of the Ruthenian Nobility

Polish institutions began to challenge the domination of the Ruthenian nobility in Orthodox districts of Poland and Lithuania by means of demographic and legal pressures. Polish magnates from Galicia moved into western Podolia in the fifteenth century and displaced some of the native Ruthenians, although the Orthodox element remained strong. Those Ruthenian landowners who lacked proper documentation received life tenure on their holdings instead of ownership, and courts declined to recognize them as nobles, even when their holdings were large. In Podlasie (Grand Duchy of Lithuania), the courts adopted Polish law. Zygmunt I honored his 1516 promise to appoint only local residents as officeholders, but he carefully chose only local Catholics, and Latin soon became the official language. Use of Ruthenian declined to such an extent by the 1560s that local nobles asked the ducal chancellery to correspond with them in Polish or Latin rather than Ruthenian; however, the chancellery honored its legal obligations by using Ruthenian until the 1569 transfer of lands to Poland.

Volhynia remained an Orthodox Ruthenian stronghold. Previous feudal division of lands there left Lithuanian grand dukes little to distribute among their followers when they gained sovereignty in the fourteenth century, and Volhynia barred Polish settlement until 1569. However, polonized nobles from Galicia slowly changed the tenor of life as they acquired land by purchase, lease, or marriage. Volhynia maintained its traditional laws, and Ruthenian remained the official language of the province after 1569.

Some Volhynian magnates strongly defended the traditional rights of the Orthodox nobility and saw themselves as the defenders of Orthodoxy instead of the Church, which was in disarray. The patriarch of Constantinople had officially recognized a Lithuanian-based metropolitanate of Kiev and all Rus in 1458–61, and Lithuanian grand dukes had started nominating the metropolitan of Kiev in 1522, often without regard to training or calling, and metropolitans frowned on efforts by nobles or burghers to act as patrons of devotion and education. Orthodox leaders included the powerful Ostrozsky (Ostrogski) family, which claimed descent from the princes of Kievan Rus. Konstiantyn Ostrozsky the elder (c. 1460–1530) served as grand hetman of Lithuania, starosta of Bratslav, castellan of Vilnius, and palatine of Trakai, making him one of the five wealthiest lords in the Grand Duchy.

FOREIGN POLICY AIMS

Zygmunt I faced a choice among linked but conflicting objectives created by Kazimierz IV's expansion. There were southern objectives (Bohemia, Hungary, and Moldavia), northern objectives (Prussia and the Baltic), and eastern objectives (Russia and Belarus). In the south, Kazimierz's success in placing his sons on the throne of Bohemia and Hungary evoked a challenge from other rivals, particularly from the Austrian Habsburgs, who wanted those thrones for themselves. In addition, the Ottoman Turks reached the borders of Moldavia and Hungary and challenged Polish interests in the region. In the north, the Teutonic Order was not reconciled to the loss of its independence to Kazimierz IV and gained an important new ally by electing Albrecht Hohenzollern, the elector of Brandenburg, as grand master in 1511. In the east, Muscovite Prince Ivan III threw off Mongol overlordship in 1480 and used the title "Tsar of All the Russias," or Russian tsar, sporadically in state documents, laying claim to the Russian, Belarussian, and Ukrainian lands that made up most of the Grand Duchy of Lithuania. Zygmunt I's task was to prevent these enemies from uniting, and he was largely successful, although at a price.

Russia

Zygmunt's most immediate problem lay along the long eastern border with Russia, which had challenged Lithuania through the reign of Zygmunt's predecessor, Aleksander, for possession of the Grand Duchy's Russian territories of Polotsk, Vitebsk, and Smolensk. Zygmunt, as grand duke, prepared a coalition with the Kazan Tatars and the Livonian Order to resist the attack. The new Russian tsar, Vasilii III, recruited the Crimean Tatars and dissident Lithuanian lords, especially Prince Mikhail Glinskii, to attack Lithuania in 1507. The two sides fought inconclusively for two years. Bogdan, prince of Moldavia, took advantage of the fighting to capture Pokuti (Pokucia) province in southern Ukraine and advance on Lviv before he was repelled and signed a peace in 1510. Russia renewed hostilities in 1512. Lithuania was successful at first, regaining its previous losses. However, Russia signed an alliance in 1514 with Austria, which supplied the armaments and technical personnel that permitted it to capture Smolensk. In September 1514, Lithuanian Great Hetman Konstiantyn Ostrozsky blunted the Muscovite offensive with a stunning victory at Orsha but failed to retake Smolensk.

Austria

Zygmunt I neutralized the hostility of Maximilian I, Holy Roman emperor and ruler of Austria, spurred by the Jagiellonian success in winning the Bohemian and Hungarian thrones. Maximilian built a broad coalition including Brandenburg, the Livonian Order, Saxony, and Denmark to combat the Jagiellonian expansion. He also encouraged Friedrich of Saxony, grand master of the Teutonic Order, to renounce the 1466 Peace of Toruń and regain independence. The papacy pressured Poland-Lithuania to abandon war against Russia, make peace with the Teutonic Order, and undertake an anti-Turkish crusade.

Zygmunt found that he had no choice but to come to terms with Maximilian. After promoting pro-Habsburg diplomats to the offices of chancellor and vice-chancellor, Zygmunt traveled to Vienna with his brother, King Władysław of Hungary, to meet Emperor Maximilian for the so-called Treaty of Vienna of July 20–22, 1515. In it, Emperor Maximilian adopted Louis, the Jagiellonian heir to the Hungarian throne, as his son, making him "General Vicar of the Holy Roman Emperor" and heir apparent to the imperial throne—an elected position that Maximilian lacked the authority to confer. Louis became engaged to Maximilian's niece, Maria, and an engagement was arranged between the elderly Maximilian and Louis's sister Anna, although Anna later married one of Maximilian's nephews instead. Maximilian also promised not to support Ducal Prussian efforts to avoid swearing allegiance to Zygmunt and lifted his condemnation of Prussian cities, such as Gdańsk, that had remained loyal to Poland.

The agreement provided substantial immediate gains for Zygmunt at a price of long-term dangers that could not be predicted at the time, but which came to pass. Poland-Lithuania's immediate gain was detaching Maximilian from his alliance with Russia and Prussia. As a result, Ducal Prussia finally swore allegiance to the Polish crown, and Russia stopped attacking Lithuania for several decades. For his part, Maximilian achieved greater influence in Bohemia and Hungary by improving relations with Jagiellonians. The long-term danger to the Polish-Lithuanian crown was the consignment of the Czech and Hungarian crowns to the Habsburg sphere of influence through close marriage alliances. Indeed, due to the unforeseeable accident of Louis's death in the battle of Mohács against the Ottoman Turks in 1526, the thrones passed directly to the Habsburgs. In Hungary, Zygmunt refrained from supporting his son-in-law, János Zápolya, in his unsuccessful effort to take the Hungarian crown, although he did allow him to take refuge in Poland when defeated. The Turks occupied the lands up to and including Buda when Ferdinand Habsburg drove Zápolya out of Hungary, holding them until the late seventeenth century. Queen Bona Sforza unsuccessfully opposed Habsburg influence, mostly out of irritation with Charles V for refusing to assign her valuable family properties in southern Italy. The Habsburg alliance also caused Zygmunt to miss his chance to acquire western Pomerania when Prince Bogusław X of Szczecin offered to accept Polish suzerainty in 1503, proposed complete union in 1513, and suggested an "eternal alliance" in 1518. Nobles from Great Poland favored the proposal, but nobles from Little Poland preferred to stay on good terms with the Habsburgs, who considered western Pomerania within their sphere of influence. A 1529 treaty allowed the electors of Brandenburg to succeed to dukes of western Pomerania. Similarly, Zygmunt ignored opportunities to take Głogów, his former duchy in Silesia, from his nephew Louis, king of Bohemia and Hungary.

Ducal and Royal Prussia

Zygmunt I brought an end to the long conflict between Poland and the Teutonic Order by arriving at another stable compromise. Conflicts between Poland and the Teutonic Order led to war in 1520–21, which the Order survived thanks to the pope's intervention; the Toruń Compromise of April 5, 1521, opened all matters to outside mediation. The conversion of Albrecht Hohenzollern, grand master of the Teutonic Order, to Lutheran Protestantism broke the long-standing deadlock by isolating him from the Order's traditional protectors, the Empire and Rome. Albrecht secularized Ducal Prussia to gain recognition as duke for himself and his direct heirs; his Brandenburg cousins enjoyed no rights of succession at this time. Albrecht acknowledged Zygmunt's suzerainty and returned the Teutonic Order's written privileges that guaranteed greater autonomy. Prussian subjects could now appeal to the Polish king against their duke. Albrecht gained a seat in the Polish senate and a role in royal elections. The Treaty of Cracow of April 8, 1525, went further than the Toruń treaty of 1466, which itself had never been fully implemented. The treaty was publicly celebrated by a ceremony on the Cracow Market Square, which the nineteenth-century Polish painter Jan Matejko imaginatively represented on a vast canvas. Despite its advantages, the treaty created long-term problems by recognizing the hereditary rights of the powerful Hohenzollern family to Ducal Prussia, and Albrecht immediately signaled a desire to include the Brandenburg electoral line of the Hohenzollern family in the Prussian line of succession. In the long run, Zygmunt's decision to accept a compromise with Ducal Prussia proved fateful, but he felt he had no choice, lacking the military and diplomatic strength to force it into Poland.

Zygmunt I and Albrecht got along well, cooperating in suppressing peasant and burgher rebels, but Queen Bona Sforza steadfastly opposed Albrecht's role in the Polish-Lithuanian state, even though he supported the election of her son Zygmunt August as king during her husband's lifetime. Albrecht did not receive regular invitations to senate sessions, and he played no substantial role in the royal election that he attended in 1530.

Royal Prussia, which had joined Poland in 1454, was reorganized according to Polish models, with palatinates and castellanates. In 1526, dietines began to meet to elect deputies to the Prussian Estates as well as to the Polish parliament.

The Ottoman Empire and the Tatars

A central point in Zygmunt's diplomacy was maintaining peace with the Ottomans and avoiding demands by the papacy and the Habsburgs for an anti-Turkish crusade. Zygmunt safeguarded Polish-Lithuanian interests by signing a "perpetual" peace with the Ottomans in 1533, although he had no objection to Hungarian wars with Turkey and urged rival claimants to the throne to cooperate; Queen Bona's favoritism toward her son-in-law, János Zápolya, undermined Zygmunt's policy of unifying the Hungarian factions.

Tatar raids into the Ukrainian lands of the Lithuanian Grand Duchy required constant attention; in 1524, the Tatars even pushed into southern Poland. To deal with this problem, Poland sent specially organized military units to the Ukrainian palatinates to join in local defense. The Polish parliament increased the size of the army in 1528–29 by 2,500 cavalry and 650 infantry, while Lithuania recruited 2,000 troops from peasants and Cossacks and erected or improved fortifications across the southern frontier that also served as magnets for new settlement. Polish-

Lithuanian forces went on the offensive along these border regions. Raids on Crimean and other Black Sea territories, often without the knowledge or approval of the central government, brought back booty and liberated Christian slaves, but these activities invited retaliation. Local authorities organized Cossack units from local residents, regardless of social origin, and used them for self-defense, although the Cossacks sometimes raided Turkish and Tatar lands without authorization. While Poland-Lithuania sought to maintain a presence in Moldavia, its influence steadily declined and the province finally fell to the Ottomans. Military action continued well into the seventeenth century.

CHAPTER 4

Zygmunt II August

Zygmunt II August (1520–72) was the last Jagiellonian king. A remote but attractive personality whose romantic difficulties left a mark on his reign, he presided over the Polish-Lithuanian state at the height of its power. Several paradoxes marked his reign. Zygmunt August disliked sharing his royal prerogatives with increasingly assertive parliamentary deputies, but he reached a compromise with them and carried out important parts of their program. A practicing Catholic, Zygmunt nevertheless respected religious toleration in order to preserve domestic peace. A strong dynast, his last significant act was to use his royal prerogative to give up his dynasty's royal stronghold and force Lithuania into tighter union with Poland by transferring the Grand Duchy's Ukrainian provinces to the Polish Kingdom, with far-reaching effects that turned out to be both beneficial and catastrophic.

Zygmunt II August

Nine-year-old Zygmunt August was elected grand duke of Lithuania in 1529 and king of Poland at the height of his father's reign; several months later, in 1530, he was crowned over substantial opposition. Zygmunt August's mother, Queen Bona Sforza, raised the young heir by her side at court and allowed him to participate at an early age in romances and court festivities such as banquets, balls, and masquerades instead of spending time at his father's side learning political and military affairs. In the eyes of the tradition-minded court marshal, Krzysztof Szydłowiecki, the twelve-year-old's upbringing meant that "the older the king gets, the stupider he gets. He has entirely depraved manners and no one at court respects him in the least." Nevertheless, Zygmunt August married Elisabeth Habsburg in 1543 to cement his father's alliance with Austria.

Grand Duke Zygmunt August and the Radziwiłłs

Zygmunt August finally had a chance to act independently when his father sent him to Lithuania as his representative in 1544, with a generous allowance for court and public expenses. The twenty-four-year-old grand duke quickly took control from his father, the "supreme duke," and, by threatening to divorce his Habsburg wife, gained power over ducal appointive and judicial functions in Lithuania as well as control over ducal castles and estates. Zygmunt August allied himself with the strong Radziwiłł faction headed by a personal friend from the Cracow court, "Black" Mikołaj Radziwiłł (the nickname distinguished him from his cousin "Red" Mikołaj Radziwiłł), who sought to monopolize appointive offices in Lithuania and block Queen Bona from purchasing landed estates there. The Radziwiłłs made useful changes to improve revenues, primarily in the administration of crown lands. They also encouraged the spread of Calvinism in Lithuania, partly to improve educational standards, while carefully avoiding any direct challenge to the Catholic hierarchy. The Radziwiłłs ruled in Zygmunt August's name, as the grand duke devoted himself to an ill-concealed romance with Barbara Radziwiłł, the young and beautiful widow of Stanislas Gostautas (Stanisław Gasztold), palatine of Trakai. Zygmunt August maintained a lavish Polish-speaking court in Vilnius and a second, equally lavish, Lithuanian-speaking court. He also spent much time hunting in the provinces, rarely visiting Queen Elisabeth, who resided at her own court. Her death in 1545, shortly after the Habsburgs paid her rich dowry, gave rise to rumors of poisoning. The grand duke attended the funeral ceremonies in Vilnius, where he indulged his taste for extravagant banquets and built a gallery to connect his palace to the Radziwiłł palace where Barbara lived. He later sent Black Mikołaj Radziwiłł to Vienna to return part of the Habsburg dowry; Emperor Ferdinand I rewarded him by making Radziwiłł a prince of the Holy Roman Empire, presumably to improve relations with Zygmunt August.

The Radziwiłł (Radvilas) family were among the leaders of the Lithuanian magnates who opposed closer ties with Poland. This family descended from Kristinas Astikas (Christian/Krzysztof Ościk), a Lithuanian noble who first appeared in historical sources in 1385 in Duke Vytautas's service and rose to be castellan of Vilnius. His son, Radvilas, whose first name became the family's last name through the patronymic "Radziwiłłowicz," son of Radziwiłł, also served Vytautas and rose to high position even though he took part in a conspiracy to dethrone the young Kazimierz IV in order to protect Lithuanian distinctiveness. Radziwiłł's sons continued to gain importance. Mikołaj II Radziwiłł served as palatine of Vilnius and as Lithuanian chancellor, and gained the title of prince of the Holy Roman Empire from Maximilian as a reward for his part in negotiating the 1515 Jagiellonian-Habsburg Treaty of Vienna. His brother, Jan II, served as castellan of Trakai and fathered Black Mikołaj Radziwiłł, who resisted the Union of Lublin. Another brother, George, served as hetman and castellan of Vilnius; he fathered Zygmunt August's wife, Barbara Radziwiłł, and Red Mikołaj Radziwiłł, who also resisted the Union of Lublin. Barbara's first marriage to Stanislas Gostautas brought her vast wealth in her widowhood.

The Radziwiłł fortune grew dramatically. Krzysztof Ościk owned only a few villages in the 1380s, while his great-grandchildren owned some 14,000 homesteads with 90,000 serfs. Ducal grants and leaseholds provided the main source of landed wealth. Lithuanian dukes (Polish kings) rewarded loyal service with lavish grants of land; when they ran short of land in the sixteenth century, the Radziwiłłs developed their ducal leaseholds by clearing forests and colonizing new areas. The family also had an effective matrimonial policy of marrying rich heiresses and providing their own daughters with rich cash dowries instead of land. Some Radziwiłłs purchased land with money earned by holding office.

Zygmunt August married Barbara Radziwiłł secretly in 1547, thinking she was pregnant, thereby confirming the dominance of the Radziwiłłs in the Grand Duchy. Queen Bona Sforza opposed the marriage energetically, because she had planned an alliance with royalty, and blocked official recognition of the marriage in Poland. Her faction in the Piotrków parliamentary session of 1547 carried on a merciless campaign of vituperation, accusing Barbara Radziwiłł of immorality and her relatives of despotism. Zygmunt the Old refused to recognize his son's marriage, but he still gave him command of Polish forces when war threatened with Prussia. Zygmunt August's organizational abilities improved his reputation even though no combat occurred. The young king returned to parliament, announced his marriage, and departed.

Political Disputes in the Kingdom of Poland

Zygmunt II August had a hard time gaining control of the Polish government after his father's death in 1548, even though he had already been elected king and heir in 1530. He started governing with political support from his father's magnate allies and adopted his father's Habsburg alliance, ignoring the clamor of Executionist deputies seconded by Queen Bona's partisans. He continued to distribute royal leaseholds to his supporters in defiance of the Executionist legislation and satisfied the bishops by condemning Protestants sharply. In foreign affairs, he renewed the Austrian alliance, marrying Katharina Habsburg when Barbara Radziwiłł died in 1553. Successful military action against the Tatars in 1549 won him popularity that helped him weather the storm.

Zygmunt August's critics attacked his marriage to Barbara Radziwiłł as a ploy to gain political influence. It took two years for the new king to bring his queen to court and get her crowned; some opponents went so far as to demand a divorce. The Executionists felt more sure of themselves than they had during his father's reign, and some saw the dispute as a chance to force Zygmunt August to dismiss his father's advisers and "execute the laws," as his father had promised but failed to do. Opponents of the marriage contended the king must acknowledge parliament as the ultimate ruler of Poland. Zygmunt August fought back by threatening to dissolve the Polish-Lithuanian union and relinquish the Polish throne while remaining hereditary lord of Lithuania.

After the dispute over Zygmunt August's marriage passed, Executionists appealed to him to assume more power and rule without his traditional magnate advisers. For example, Rafał Leszczyński, crown court marshal and himself a magnate, told the king, "We do not want anyone other than you to share in your royal power." Antimagnate feeling united the many divisions within the Executionist camp: Catholics and Protestants; richer and poorer nobles; reformers and conservatives; Habsburgists, Hohenzollernists, and Muscovites. The Executionist camp had a Protestant flavor, for its leaders, mostly Calvinists, demanded that the clergy pay taxes, participate in national defense, and give up their court jurisdiction. At the 1559 parliament, they presented numerous complaints to the throne about lack of order and justice and refused to approve taxes for the Livonian War. Zygmunt August rejected their demands and left Poland to spend three years in Lithuania without convening another parliamentary session. He later accepted some of the Executionist demands in order to fight the Livonian War.

The public storm over his marriage also estranged the king from his mother and her powerful faction, which adopted the arguments of antiroyalist parliamentary supremacy to seek dominance at the young king's court. One tactic of Bona Sforza's faction was to criticize her son's use of royal judicial powers and urge parliament to pass a law reducing them. The king ignored these changes ostentatiously. For example, he accused Stanisław Stadnicki of Żmigrod of lèse-majesté for refusing to answer a court summons on the grounds that the king's court lacked authority. Eventually, Stadnicki apologized and was absolved, but had to leave court permanently. Bona's partisans pushed for unification between Poland and Lithuania, a step that Zygmunt August opposed because it would have reduced his independent power. He successfully employed the risky tactic of appointing some of Bona's leading supporters to positions which they failed to handle satisfactorily. Their failure undermined the reputation of the group.

Queen Bona Sforza admitted defeat and went to Italy in 1556 with her large fortune. She left her domestic estates and some cash to her son when she died in Italy in 1557, but changed her will on her deathbed to leave her extensive southern Italian properties to Philip II of Spain. Polish diplomats failed to get her will annulled on the plausible grounds that Ferdinand's agents had forced the change on her in her weakened condition or simply forged a new will. Polish-Lithuanian monarchs tried for centuries without success to reclaim Bona's rich Neapolitan inheritance of lands and cash.

PEACEFUL COEXISTENCE: THE RELIGIOUS COLD WAR

Zygmunt August continued his father's policy of religious toleration in order to maintain domestic peace. A practicing although not exceptionally pious Catholic who corresponded with John Calvin, he saw the value of Church reform and leaned toward creating a national reformed church that would unite Catholics and Protestants. At the 1550 and 1552 parliamentary sessions, many Executionist deputies agreed and urged the summoning of a national synod to endorse use of Polish-language liturgy, communion in two kinds (the wafer and the wine) for ordinary communicants, and clerical marriages. Opposition from Polish bishops led Zygmunt August to send a delegation to Rome in 1555 to ask permission to hold a synod in Little Poland chaired by the papal nuncio, but the pope agreed only to hold a national synod in Rome, making it much more difficult to enact substantial change. Polish bishops began to take a stronger line against the Protestants, endorsing the reforms of the Council of Trent that made few concessions to Protestants. As expected, the 1558–59 parliamentary session failed to create a national church and King Zygmunt August endorsed the Council of Trent in 1564.

Despite his endorsement of the Roman Catholic Church, Zygmunt August took no action against the Protestants of Poland-Lithuania. He consistently rejected the claims of Catholic courts to try religious crimes, and refused to enforce their decrees. He and other Catholic political leaders regarded parliament as the only place to try nobles despite the inclusion of many Protestant deputies. In 1552, the pious Catholic Hetman Jan Tarnowski denounced the bishops' assertions of judicial competence, saying that "this is not a matter of faith, but of liberties which your court violated." A bill endorsing their claims passed anyway, but Zygmunt suspended it for one year and never put it into effect. Mixed marriages were common, if frowned upon.

Protestantism flourished under Zygmunt August, claiming almost one-quarter of all nobles in Poland-Lithuania (half of the nobles in Little Poland, two-thirds in parts of Great Poland, and 15 to 20 percent in Lithuania), generally magnates and richer nobles. Most professed to be Calvinist and formed a synod in 1554, but theological indifference marked Polish Calvinism. Calvinist nobles seemed motivated primarily by anticlericalism, a desire for lower taxes, and freedom from hierarchical control. Mazovia remained immune to Protestant influence.

Protestant groups banded together to secure their position in the Polish-Lithuanian state. The first attempt by the Calvinist Synod in 1555 failed, although its compromise confession gained many adherents. However, Catholic Church reforms stimulated Calvinists and Lutherans to reach a formal understanding in Vilnius in 1570 and join with the Czech Brethren in a union at Sandomierz. Synods of the major Protestant sects coordinated their defense and set common educational and social positions, although they reached no theological compromise. All major groups rejected the religious and social doctrines of the Polish Brethren, who denied the existence of the Holy Trinity. Some endorsed pacifism and radical social egalitarianism as well. In addition to disliking the doctrines of these "Arians" (a reference to early Christianity), most Polish-Lithuanian Protestants resented the prominence of foreigners and burghers among them.

The leading spirit of the Polish Catholic resurgence was Stanisław Hozjusz (Hosius, 1504–79), a Cracow burgher who grew up in Vilnius. Refused permission by his father to join a monastery, Hozjusz attended the Jagiellonian University and worked as secretary for several bishops before studying law and humanities in Italy, where he received a doctorate. He returned in 1534 to work for the bishops and then went on to serve in the employ of a royal secretary, specializing in Prussian affairs. He corresponded with Erasmus and supported Erasmian reform in the Church in the 1530s, but his position gradually stiffened as Protestantism spread and he attacked it strongly. His service in Zygmunt I's royal chancellery brought him Church preferment, and his support for Zygmunt August's marriage to Barbara Radziwiłł gained him promotion to a bishopric.

On instruction from the Piotrków synod, Hozjusz wrote a new Confession of Catholic Faith in 1551 that went through thirty-eight editions in many languages within his lifetime; he also wrote a major treatise on Catholic dogma. His books earned him an appointment as papal legate in the last stage of the Council of Trent in 1562–63 and gained him some supporters as a candidate for pope. Within Poland-Lithuania, Hozjusz rallied other Catholic clergy to defend Church unity, episcopal authority, and the influence of clerical chapters in governing church regions. He opposed breaking with Rome to create a national church under any circumstances. At his suggestion, the papacy sent Francesco Commendoni, who developed a close relationship with King Zygmunt August, to be papal nuncio. The king introduced the decrees of the Council of Trent to the 1564 parliament, and Bishop Hozjusz introduced the Jesuits to Poland-Lithuania, starting with Prussian Warmia. Reforming Catholic bishops like Stanisław Karnkowski replaced the older generation of indifferent and more tolerant bishops, although it still took more than a decade to get the Tridentine reforms passed at a Polish-Lithuanian synod, due primarily to strictures against accumulating benefices. Tridentine practices went into effect progressively throughout the late sixteenth and early seventeenth centuries.

Hozjusz supported the election of Henri Valois and then Maximilian of Austria; he only transferred his allegiance to Stefan Batory when Maximilian died in 1576.

Heightened religious sensibilities contributed to more criticism of Jews by Christians. The first documented ritual murder charge was laid in 1547 in Mazovia and others followed quickly. Zygmunt I, Zygmunt August, and Stefan Batory took these cases under royal supervision in order to quash them, and royal investigations exonerated the accused, although at least one Jew was executed before his appeal from a lower court verdict could be heard. A 1564 edict issued by Zygmunt August allowed accused Jews to be released from prison into the custody of other Jews.

The Livonian War and the Executionist Program

Zygmunt August ended his disputes with parliament in order to fight Russia for control of Livonia on the Baltic coast. Livonia had been established as a missionary state by the mostly German Order of the Livonian Knights that merged with the Teutonic Knights of Prussia in 1237 but lost their expansionist energy after a serious defeat by Alexander Nevskii, the prince of Novgorod, in the battle fought on the ice of Lake Chud (Lake Peipus) in 1242. The Livonian Order converted the Latvian and Estonian pagans with less force than the Teutonic Knights had used in Prussia and established important trading cities along the coast, such as Narva, Tallinn (Reval), and Riga, which connected the Baltic coast to the hinterland by the major rivers. By the mid-sixteenth century the Livonian Order had become very weak, partly due to the spread of Protestantism.

Polish claims to Livonia were first advanced by Albrecht Hohenzollern, former grand master of the Teutonic Knights and now duke of Prussia, who hoped to expand his control over the coast as an autonomous subject of the Polish king, and got his brother Wilhelm appointed archbishop of Riga in 1539. Zygmunt I supported Albrecht's plans in order to gain Livonian support for a war against Russia. Polish sympathizers, headed by Archbishop Wilhelm, objected to an extension of the Livonian-Russian truce by the master of the Livonian Order, Heinrich von Galen, in 1553. The truce would have kept Livonia out of any Polish-Russian conflict. Riga's burghers and the Livonian Order wished to maintain their independence, but Zygmunt August intervened militarily in 1557 to bring Livonia into the Polish-Lithuania sphere of influence.

Russia's search for a foothold on the Baltic coast had important commercial implications that attracted the interest of other Baltic states. Ivan IV of Russia sought to make Narva the commercial entrepôt for Russian trade linking Europe with Central and East Asia, preempting Riga and Gdańsk, which had hitherto monopolized the Russian Baltic trade. Refused extensive commercial concessions, Ivan invaded in 1558, taking Narva and Dorpat in the east while Tallinn turned to Swedish King Erik XIV for protection. The Livonian government could not raise troops for defense, and the Polish-Lithuanian state failed to honor its promise to help, because Zygmunt August could not get parliament's support. In 1561, the master of the Livonian Order, Gotthard Kettler, who still controlled part of western Livonia, put his duchy under Zygmunt August's protection.

In order to pass war taxes to secure and defend the Livonian duchy (really western Livonia), Zygmunt August had to convene parliament once again and come to terms with the Executionist opposition. The king signaled his willingness to come to terms by appearing at the parliamentary session of 1562–63 dressed in a Polish caftan instead of his usual Italian-style clothing, and he received a military commitment from the Polish parliament. In exchange, he enacted legislation to reclaim the vast royal estates that had been alienated to the magnates. Executionist deputies estimated the value of the estates at 700,000 zlotys, a sum sufficient to maintain the court and free up revenue for military expenses, although, in practice, landlords used a variety of delaying tactics to keep many estates in their own hands. Parliament raised new revenues for the army with its "quarter" tax, but even here the 1567 parliament took a step back and limited the number of estates to which the rules applied. Despite his lack of enthusiasm for reclaiming estates, the king cooperated with Executionist deputies to carry out other parts of their program. To avoid friction, he split Livonia in two, giving southern Livonia (Courland) to Poland as a vassal under Gotthard Kettler, who converted to Lutheranism and became duke; northern Livonia went to the Grand Duchy of Lithuania. The Lublin parliamentary session of 1569 rejoined the two parts to make it a joint protectorate. Livonia's status as an independent duchy within the state avoided rivalry between Poland and Lithuania and prevented strain between the Catholic Church and Livonia's Lutheran inhabitants. The extensive lands that had belonged to the Livonian Order became royal estates and were used for royal patronage.

At first glance the incorporation of Livonia seemed beneficial, but the long-term results proved harmful. Poland-Lithuania became involved in wars against Sweden and Russia that were beyond its strength, distracting it from Silesia and Pomerania and leading it to ignore the vital issue of internal cohesion. The most important single mistake was King Zygmunt August's agreement in 1563, with senate concurrence, to extend Prussian succession rights to the electoral line in Brandenburg in exchange for Duke Albrecht Hohenzollern's assistance. This paved the way for Prussia's eventual incorporation into Germany.

The prospect of dividing Livonia attracted other Baltic states and war spread.

Russia defeated the Polish-Lithuanian armies handily in 1563–67, precipitating a change in alliances. Sweden, originally suspicious of Poland-Lithuania, became more concerned that Ivan IV might try to conquer Finland and allied itself in 1568 with Poland-Lithuania through a royal marriage between Johan, duke of Finland, brother of Swedish King Erik XIV, and Zygmunt August's sister, Katarzyna (Catherine). Sweden conquered eastern Livonia (Estonia), with its chief city, Tallinn. Denmark, Sweden's rival, promptly allied itself with Russia and seized all of Livonia temporarily, although it only succeeded in holding the island of Ozylia (Ösel/Saaremaa). Riga remained independent under its archbishop until 1581, when it swore allegiance to Poland-Lithuania.

The Polish Navy and Gdańsk Autonomy

Zygmunt August fought the Livonian War at sea as well as on land. Poland put together a fleet by commissioning privateers that sailed under the flags of several Livonian cities because Gdańsk, which already had its own privateers, stood on its privileges and protected its commerce by refusing to supply ships to the Polish king. Zygmunt August exercised his right to use the city's port facilities, however, and some Gdańsk citizens launched their own privateers under the Polish flag. The seventeen-vessel Polish fleet made serious inroads in Russia's Narva trade. In 1568, Zygmunt August created a Maritime Commission to expand and regularize the fleet. Gdańsk objected strenuously to this infringement of its coastal monopoly, forced the royal fleet to move up the coast a short distance, and even executed Polish sailors who seized some of the city's naval supplies. Zygmunt August sent Bishop Stanisław Karnkowski to force Gdańsk to obey his orders. When the city government refused to admit him, parliament authorized Karnkowski to rewrite Gdańsk's charter. Karnkowski headed a parliamentary commission that gave the crown full control over maritime rights in 1570 and subordinated Gdańsk to Poland. Gdańsk ratified the new charter under military threat but it never went into effect.

Polish naval efforts accomplished little. Denmark protected Russia's Baltic shipping to ensure that revenues did not decrease at its toll station on the Baltic Sound dividing the eastern and western Baltic. Denmark destroyed most of the Polish privateer fleet in 1571 and the remainder fell into disarray; several vessels even mutinied. Zygmunt August ordered construction of a powerful fleet, but finished only one capital ship before the war ended and the effort ceased.

Preparations for Polish-Lithuanian Union

Zygmunt August's reconciliation with Executionist deputies pointed toward another step in national integration, the unification the Kingdom of Poland with the Grand Duchy of Lithuania. The two states had drawn much closer over 180 years of Jagiellonian rule. Polish Executionists raised the issue of unification as early as 1538 in order to limit the power of the Lithuanian magnates who cast a large shadow over the developing Polish noble democracy, to provide more efficient centralized government, and to provide more opportunities for themselves to acquire Lithuanian estates and offices. Lithuanian deputies refused invitations to attend the Polish parliaments of 1550 and 1552 to discuss union. Both Zygmunt I and Zygmunt August opposed closer union because the Lithuanian throne was hereditary and their heirs would have to submit to election to a joint throne after union. However, as Zygmunt August grew older without producing an heir, he felt less strongly about maintaining dynastic privileges. Magnates in both countries opposed union, since it strengthened the hand of the Executionists, but Lithuanian magnates had to yield to get Polish help against a Russia that had grown too strong for Lithuania to fight alone.

Several changes to Lithuanian law foreshadowed the union. Zygmunt August reorganized the Lithuanian ministries and senate on the Polish model. Similarly, Lithuanian nobles abandoned their traditional opposition to union in order to gain the advantages that their Polish gentry brethren enjoyed. In 1562 when the war against Russia was going badly, Lithuanian nobles attending parliamentary meetings in the army camp outside Vitebsk turned on Hetman Red Mikołaj Radziwiłł and demanded union with Poland based on a common parliament, a common election, a common military defense, a common foreign policy, and Polish-style gentry rights. However, they still supported Lithuanian autonomy, Lithuanian exclusivity in officeholding, and Lithuanian military independence. The Lithuanian army broke camp at Vitebsk to present the petition to Zygmunt August in person and sent an unofficial delegation to the Polish parliament. In 1563 the fall of Polotsk to Russia prompted the deeply concerned Lithuanian delegates to attend a joint 1564 parliament in Warsaw, to debate union. Deputies presented a full range of arguments—from Polish maximalism, which demanded such a complete integration of the Grand Duchy that even the name Lithuania would be replaced by "New Poland," to the Radziwiłł position calling for personal union only after the extinction of the Jagiellonian dynasty.

The Radziwiłłs tried to block unification. Black Mikołaj spoke for the Lithuanians and withdrew concessions to Poland after receiving news of a Lithuanian military victory over Russia. Returning home, he rallied opposition to union and blocked further negotiations, perhaps dreaming of succeeding the childless Zygmunt August as grand duke, but he died seven years before his sovereign in 1565 at age fifty. His cousin, Red Mikołaj, succeeded to political leadership and bolstered the anti-union side by courting lesser Lithuanian nobles, voluntarily conceding to them the political rights and social status of Polish nobles at the Vilnius parliamentary session of 1565–66, which also gave the Lithuanian lower house similar powers to the Polish lower house and created electoral dietines in the Polish fashion. Administrative reform created five new districts to replace a multitude of smaller ones; only Samogitia remained unchanged. Lithuanian magnate authority was greatly reduced. The restructuring of the court system deprived palatines of their judicial authority over local nobles, although they retained authority over military affairs, crown lands, and commoners. Army units were reorganized to fit the new boundaries, and individual military service was slightly reduced, but an increasing population produced a larger number of soldiers anyway. Unfortunately, the fighting quality of the noble levy was poor because it lacked training and equipment. The deputies rewarded Radziwiłł by endorsing Lithuanian separatism, including measures keeping it difficult for Poles to buy landed estates. But Radziwiłł was prepared to make minimal concessions to gain the military advantages of union.

The lesser nobility's demand for Polish-style noble rights with political autonomy reflected a broader polonization of the Lithuanian nobility. The court of Zygmunt August in Vilnius was largely Polish speaking and attracted nobles from the entire Grand Duchy. Even when speaking Polish, however, Lithuanian nobles carefully guarded their monopoly of offices and landownership rights against immigrants from the Polish Kingdom. Unlike Poland, where the spread of the Reformation tended to pit the Protestant lesser nobles against Catholic magnates, Lithuanian magnates often demonstrated their ethnic identity by converting to Calvinism. The chancellor and palatine of Vilnius, Black Mikołaj Radziwiłł, converted in 1553, first to Lutheranism and then to Calvinism, even though he married a Catholic and spoke Polish at home. The Lithuanian magnate sponsored a Polish translation of the Bible, and Calvin dedicated one of his works to him. Radziwiłł maintained courts on a royal scale in Vilnius and Brześć staffed with prominent musicians and authors. Late in life, he showed an interest in radical Protestant thought. Many other magnates followed suit and supported Calvinism against the Catholic Counter Reformation well into the seventeenth century. Lutheranism mostly attracted burghers of German origin in Vilnius and other cities.

THE FEDERAL UNION OF POLAND AND LITHUANIA

Deputies from both Poland and Lithuania met together in the border city of Lublin on December 23, 1568, to discuss union, but Red Mikołaj Radziwiłł demanded guarantees of safe-conduct from Zygmunt August before he would take part, because he intended to prevent unification. Firmly in control of the Lithuanian delegation, he advocated only union with minimal changes in the federal relationship of Poland and Lithuania. The ducal throne would become electoral after the Jagiellonian dynasty died out, and Radziwiłł agreed to a joint royal election held at the border by a fixed and equal number of Lithuanian and Polish deputies. A common parliament would meet alternately in Poland and Lithuania to decide common matters, primarily military defense. Local issues would be handled by separate parliaments in the two states and by dietines. The laws, privileges, ranks, and offices of the two states would remain distinct. Only Lithuanians would hold Lithuanian offices, although citizens of both states would be able to migrate freely and naturalize. Coinages would be minted separately, but would be uniform in value. Joint commissions would settle border disputes. The chief sticking point was the insistence of the Lithuanian deputies, dominated by the Radziwiłł family, that royal lands *not* be reclaimed and redistributed in Lithuania as had been done in Poland under pressure from the Executionists. Thus, Lithuanian magnates would maintain the enormous economic power that Polish magnates had lost. Lithuanian deputies abandoned Lublin as a unified group on March 1 when Zygmunt August and the Poles rejected their demands.

Zygmunt August forced union on his terms by taking an unexpectedly hard line and using his ducal authority to "return" the "disputed" Ukrainian palatinates of Volhynia, Bratslav, and Kiev to Poland. He then demanded that Red Mikołaj Radziwiłł and other Lithuanian nobles with Ukrainian estates swear allegiance to him as king of Poland. He further dispatched representatives to Ukraine to elicit oaths of allegiance from local nobles, who gladly complied in order to get Polish military protection against Tatar raids, and replaced recalcitrant local officials. Threatened with sanctions, Lithuanian nobles accepted the Union of Lublin, which was proclaimed June 28, 1569.

The Union of Lublin of July 1, 1569, declared that: "The Kingdom of Poland and the Grand Duchy of Lithuania are one inseparable and indistinguishable body, and there is one united commonwealth put together and joined out of two states, and two nations into one people." The term "Commonwealth" is the English equivalent of *Rzeczpospolita,* itself the literal translation of the Latin *respublica* (republic). It was used to denote the democratic and electoral nature of the new Polish-Lithuanian state and the equal position of the two founding nations.

The Union created a common institution to govern both constituent parts of the Commonwealth and decide all issues regardless of whether they applied to Poland-Lithuania as a whole or to local matters in either Poland or Lithuania. The common sovereign, still called the king of Poland and the grand duke of Lithuania, was to be elected jointly by Poles and Lithuanians. This made it impossible to split the two realms and difficult to play them off against each other as in the past. A common parliament composed of elected representatives and appointed senators from both constituent parts met regularly. Regional dietines continued to exist but no separate Polish or Lithuanian parliaments survived.

The kingship and parliament provided the glue that held the Commonwealth together. The act expressed hope that "with God's will this union will last until the end of the world."

Despite unification, the Union of Lublin prevented the extinction of Lithuanian political identity through retention of separate ministries, armies, treasuries, and legal codes as well as the control of royal estates in Lithuania by the magnate elite. The result was the maintenance of a strong feeling of Lithuanian identity as a political nation among nobles who were, paradoxically, increasingly Polish in speech and culture. Lithuanians were determined to maintain their autonomy, no matter how much they polonized, and full separation remained a possibility. After Zygmunt August died in 1572, Papal Legate Commendoni met with Red Mikołaj Radziwiłł and Jan Chodkiewicz to discuss electing Austrian Archduke Ernst as grand duke with Zygmunt August's sister Anna as his wife as the first step toward getting him elected king of Poland; he promised to reward Lithuania with greater autonomy within the Commonwealth. Habsburg Emperor Maximilian II was not interested, and the scheme came to naught. Lithuanians boycotted the first joint session of the Polish-Lithuanian parliament called to elect a new king, and they accepted Henri Valois only reluctantly after sending a separate Lithuanian delegation to Paris to sound him out. Lithuanians also refused to participate in Batory's election and recognized him only after he confirmed Lithuanian privileges. At his election to the Polish-Lithuanian throne, Zygmunt III had to confirm the Third Lithuanian Statute of 1588 that did not even mention union with Poland. The Polish-Lithuanian parliament refused to approve the statute, but it went into effect anyway. Lithuanian autonomy and even separatism remained a feature of Polish-Lithuanian life until the Partitions and beyond, as symbolized by the opening words of *Pan Tadeusz* (*Sir Thaddeus*) by the great nineteenth-century Polish poet Adam Mickiewicz: "Lithuania, My Homeland."

Closer union with Poland was the price that Lithuania paid for Polish military assistance, and it accelerated cultural polonization. The ducal court and the upper nobility already spoke Polish as their first language, and by the 1570s a Lithuanian court official and historian, Augustinas Rotunda, complained that most nobles spoke Polish even if the peasants still spoke Lithuanian. The poet Mikolajus (Nicholas) Daukša said in 1599: "our Lithuanian nation itself, because of its knowledge of Polish and fluent command of that language, has reduced its own language to an extreme neglect, oblivion, and almost rejection; everybody can see it well, but I do not know whether anybody will praise this as being fair."

Indeed, richer and better-educated nobles spoke good Polish while petty nobles spoke a hybrid of Polish, Ruthenian, and Lithuanian. The Catholic Church acted as a major agent of polonization. Due to a shortage of Lithuanian priests, Polish priests staffed the network of parish churches that developed in the fifteenth century, and Lithuanian peasants increasingly understood Polish—even when they spoke it poorly or reluctantly—since both priests and nobles spoke to them in Polish. Polish immigrants swelled the size of the larger cities. St. John's parish, Vilnius, offered both Lithuanian and Polish-language sermons by 1521. The Ruthenian borderlands proved particularly vulnerable to polonization, since the people already spoke a Slavic tongue. Coastal areas such as Samogitia maintained the Lithuanian language better because its inhabitants had less contact with Poles and Ruthenians. Areas such as Suwałki (Suvalkai), with few nobles, also resisted polonization.

The importance of Orthodox nobles in the Commonwealth as a whole diminished rapidly when the absorption of the Ukrainian provinces legalized Polish colonization. Polish influence became very strong in the Kiev and Bratslav regions, which had been resettled in the sixteenth century by Ruthenians from Volhynia and Poles from Little Poland after warfare devastated the region late in the fifteenth century. Immigrant nobles often took over older latifundia that had fallen to ruin. Some Orthodox nobles cited legal privileges when they tried to safeguard Ruthenian as the official language after 1569, but they had little success. New estates acquired on the East Bank of the Dnieper were turned into magnate latifundia. Orthodox nobles polonized quickly and many converted to Catholicism.

Royal and Ducal Prussia

The 1569 parliament also integrated Royal Prussia fully into the Kingdom of Poland, thereby reducing the Prussian parliament to the status of a provincial assembly (dietine). In 1564, Prussian magnates had been forced to return some leaseholds to the state, and in 1569, Prussian senators at the Lublin parliamentary session cooperated with the crown in removing Prussian separate institutions over the protests of Prussian burghers and nobles who wanted to maintain autonomy. Acquiescence did not signify any diminution of separatist feeling, for Prussians continued to guard their traditional rights and energetically protested infringements, particularly the appointment of non-Prussians to the bishopric of Warmia and other local offices. A few vestiges of separate status remained: the Prussian dietine met in two chambers; a separate Prussian treasury issued coins, although with values that were tied to Polish coinage; nobles could refuse military service outside Prussia; and minor differences in court procedures continued. Gdańsk and the Warmia bishopric retained far-reaching autonomy. Most city delegations lost their traditional rights to participate in the Prussian diet, which became a dietine as in other parts of the Commonwealth, although local dietines took over many of its functions. The small Silesian duchies of Zator and Oświęcim were integrated into Poland in 1564.

Ducal Prussia, a fief of the Polish crown, became increasingly dominated by the nobility as a whole, and ties to Poland generally strengthened, although Zygmunt August granted the Brandenburg line of Hohenzollerns successor rights in Ducal Prussia in 1563. Ducal authority declined as nobles asserted their strength. In 1539, Albrecht abandoned the Teutonic Order's practice of claiming noble properties in the absence of a male heir, and in 1542 he agreed to reserve state offices (except chancellor) for native-born Prussian nobles, although he often evaded that obligation. A supreme council of nobles governed in the duke's absence and during an interregnum. Albrecht Hohenzollern was unpopular with the Estates, due to his choice of advisers from outside Prussia and to his high tax policies; thus nobles looked to Poland for support. In 1566, Albrecht found himself forced to summon the Estates, which condemned three of his advisers to death for corruption and banished a fourth. Albrecht granted Prussian nobles full rights of appeal to the Polish king, gave the Prussian Estates the right to supervise treasury policies, and promised once again to use only local nobles as advisers. A Polish delegation came in 1567 to mediate disputes and reclaim landed estates without much success, partly because the troubles were seen as personal rather than institutional and, at age seventy-seven, Albrecht was not expected to live much longer; he died the following year. His only son, Albrecht Friedrich Hohenzollern (1553–1618), succeeded him on the ducal throne. Well-educated, although uninterested in learning Polish, Albrecht Friedrich grew up with Polish nobles and quickly paid homage to Zygmunt August as his feudal overlord, continuing to support him loyally afterward. Mental illness, described at the time as "melancholy" (perhaps depression and paranoia), prevented the new duke from ruling actively and coming to terms with Ducal Prussia's serious problems. The treasury owed a lot of money, but the Estates refused to authorize taxes without receiving greater political rights for gentry. Albrecht Friedrich prepared to offer himself as candidate for the Polish-Lithuanian throne in 1572 until news of his illness made his election impossible.

Despite the different regimes in Royal and Ducal Prussia, common Prussian consciousness remained. Nobles and burghers who lived in one part were considered native of the other part as well.

Zygmunt August's Last Years

Zygmunt August, who directed foreign affairs himself without leaning heavily on advisers, continued his father's retreat from southern involvement. He renegotiated the truce with Turkey that had expired with his father's death, declined to support the claims of János Zápolya, his sister's exiled husband, to the Hungarian throne (while negotiating to preserve the wealth of his sister's estates), and repudiated the individual initiatives of Ukrainian magnates to maintain Polish claims to Moldavia. This allowed him to keep the peace with Russia after the Livonian War wound down. In 1570 the two countries signed an armistice on the basis of the status quo.

Despite the lack of an heir, Zygmunt August spent his last years alienated from his third wife, Katharina Habsburg, whom he disliked. He could not divorce her because he had remained Catholic, but he avoided her and created a national scandal by trying to produce an heir with different mistresses; he succeeded in fathering only one illegitimate daughter. Katharina's death in February 1572 revived hope, and Zygmunt August rushed off to his palace in Knyszyn, Lithuania, where he planned to marry one of his mistresses. He died of fever unexpectedly on July 5, 1572.

CHAPTER 5

Economics and Society in the Jagiellonian Period

Jadwiga and Jogaila's marriage in 1386 coincided with the start of a long period of prosperity that enabled the Polish-Lithuanian state to emerge as an international power. Technological improvements and superior organization produced agricultural surpluses for sale to local cities and abroad. Prosperity led to the colonization of new farming areas, while more efficient production freed rural residents to become artisans or merchants in cities. Established cities grew and new cities were founded. Trade routes crisscrossed Poland-Lithuania, bringing political unification and defining foreign policy interests. Europe's overseas expansion and the sixteenth-century price revolution increased the rate of economic expansion dramatically, making Poland-Lithuania's commodities and raw materials even more valuable. Polish-Lithuanian cities and urban-based industries shared the prosperity by supplying local needs and taking part in transit operations. Favorable economic trends helped the population of Poland-Lithuania increase. The population in 1386 may have been about 3.5 million (3.8 persons per square kilometer). Better statistics give the population as 7.5 million in 1500 (6.6 persons per square kilometer) and 11 million in 1650 (11.1 persons per square kilometer). The population density was highest in the central Polish districts, slightly lower in ethnic Lithuania, and considerably lower in Belarus and the Ukrainian lands. Population increase came both from natural increase and territorial expansion. Wealth brought social mobility to individuals within the established system.

Improvements in Agriculture

At the end of the fourteenth century, the Kingdom of Poland's population comprised some 2 million people living on about 240,000 square kilometers. Ethnic Lithuania covered some 80,000 square kilometers and counted over 400,000 inhabitants. 1 million to 1.5 million Ruthenians (Belarussians, Russians, and

Ukrainians) inhabited the remaining 820,000 square kilometers of the Grand Duchy of Lithuania. The Kingdom of Poland enjoyed a population density of about eight persons per square kilometer, while ethnic Lithuania held about four persons per square kilometer, and the Slavic portion of the Grand Duchy (Belarus, Ukraine, and western Russia) less than two persons per square kilometer. Immigration from German states continued at a slower pace than at its height in the thirteenth century. The Germans assimilated readily in ethnically Polish interior regions such as Cracow, but some border areas became substantially German speaking, especially Silesia and Ducal Prussia. Germans brought with them and Poles quickly adopted technological improvements in agriculture such as the sturdy wheeled plow required to cultivate heavy clay soils in Poland, and villages switched from two-field to three-field crop rotation to improve their productivity. Now farmers devoted one field to winter grain and a second to spring grain, while a third lay fallow. Planting grain at different times helped safeguard peasants against the effects of drought and other catastrophes. Cultivation of pulse and vetch in the fallow fields improved the soil and provided fodder for livestock; in turn, animal manure improved the soil still further for the next year's grain planting. Villagers grazed their livestock on common lands. Less dramatic changes also had a substantial cumulative effect, such as the introduction of manufactured farm implements with metal parts, including farm wagons, rakes, and hoes. The gradual introduction of the scythe made harvesting quicker and easier, and the spread of water mills increased agricultural production. Polish villages produced more rye and other grains for sale to nearby cities and for export. Peasants also cultivated fruits and vegetables. Dyestuffs earned substantial income in the export trade until New World dyes replaced them after 1500.

"German Law" Villages and Cities

Most Polish peasants enjoyed legal freedom under the so-called German law, a system of clearly defined obligations and rights originally adopted in the thirteenth and fourteenth centuries to settle German immigrants but quickly extended to ethnic Poles as well. Both nobles and peasants gained, because German law offered peasants incentives to produce more and afforded them greater autonomy. Peasant taxes, although low, augmented the nobles' cash revenues considerably, and the establishment of new villages brought in new streams of revenue. While peasants were subject to the lord's court, they enjoyed tax holidays for as much as twenty years after the foundation of a new village or the conversion of an old village to German law. When exemptions expired, peasants paid monetary rent of 30 to 48 groszy per allotment of land (in Poland one *łan,* or field, equaled about 40 acres), a sum that remained the same for decades despite general inflation. Peasants also owed small sums (banalities) for various purposes and more substantial sums for renting additional land. Annual payments in kind to the manor totaled another half-zloty in value and comprised two or three bushels of grain, a hen or two, 20 to 30 eggs, and a few cheeses.

Polish nobles actively recruited tenant farmers to colonize uncultivated lands on their estates. They hired a bailiff or village administrator (*sołtys*) to set up and populate a village in exchange for a relatively large land allotment, usually about 125 acres, the right to operate the local tavern and mill, and the job of judging the peasants in the lord's court. The bailiff collected taxes from the peasants, keeping about one-sixth for himself. On the social scale, the bailiff occupied a place between noble and peasant. He paid symbolic taxes to the noble, remained subject to the lord's court, and provided military service on horseback at the lord's call. Bailiffs also performed minor but useful duties such as transporting the mail and feeding horses. As this era of colonization drew to a close, nobles needed bailiffs less and bought them out. The Warta Statute of 1423 forced bailiffs to sell on demand. Some bailiffs earned recognition as nobles because they performed military service well or married well, while others faded into the peasantry.

Serfdom and Other Peasant Obligations

Polish serfdom began to develop in the late fifteenth and sixteenth centuries. The 1493 and 1496 parliaments limited the peasants' right to leave the village, and the 1520 parliament decreed a minimum peasant labor obligation of one day per week. This was less than the one to two days per week that had already become the norm, while three days per week became common in the second half of the sixteenth century; a few peasants had to put in a four-day week on their lord's land. A typical yeoman with a half or full allotment owned two teams of horses and sent his hired man to work on the lord's land with the poorer one. Peasants normally worked from dawn to dusk with time off for dinner and breaks to rest the animals; the number of hours depended on the season. During the harvest, two harvesters substituted for one worker with a horse. Peasants received time off to go to market, where they traded for the manor as well as for themselves. Additional duties involved a few days spent transporting produce, repairing roads, building walls, and digging ditches.

Peasants were tied to the land, and regulations limiting movement became increasingly strict, reflecting a rural labor shortage, although these measures were rarely enforced. Peasants leaving illegally lost their rights to land, but they generally left to accept offers of more land and lower taxes from other nobles who paid for the expensive transport of the peasant household, including animals and equipment. Practically speaking, peasants who left without equipment could not be stopped, despite the 1496 law that authorized only one son per village per year to move to the city in order to study. In 1501, a law required peasant proprietors to gain their lord's permission to leave, and the law was extended to all peasant sons in 1509. Laws passed in 1490, 1538, 1543, and 1563 aimed at speeding the return of peasants to their original lords. The strictures seem to indicate a substantial degree of movement rather than its cessation.

Despite humanitarian complaints by contemporary publicists, peasants appear to have prospered in the sixteenth century. Rapidly rising prices did not drive up cash taxes, so the real value of taxes declined by at least one-third. As a result, Poland-Lithuania escaped peasant uprisings like those in Hungary (1514), Germany (1525), and England (1536). Peasants retained their legal identity, and the 1518 law removing them from the jurisdiction of royal courts appears to have been motivated by the crush of business rather than growing oppression. Local lords often delegated their judicial tasks to peasant tribunals that even heard complaints against the noble estates; nobles were added to these tribunals primarily for serious criminal cases. In some regions, the authority of peasant tribunals was restricted to common lands such as meadows, roads, and forests. Peasants could appeal decisions to noble tribunals and, in criminal cases, to city courts with investigative facilities (torture) and executioners. Peasants continued to inherit, buy, and sell their land subject to feudal limitations. Their names appeared on tax rolls, and courts accepted their sworn evidence.

Peasants owed small payments to church and state as well as to their noble lords. They delivered every tenth sheaf of grain to church warehouses; the cash value of this tax went up as prices rose. Numerous smaller payments were required for church services. After the Reformation, Protestant nobles still collected church tithes, and many pocketed the difference between more expensive Catholicism and more modest Protestantism. Peasants paid little to the state. Exceptional taxes, when enacted by parliament, reached 10 to 12 groszy in the early sixteenth century and 20 to 30 later; as much as 50 percent was used against the tithe.

Peasant Social Structure

The majority of the peasants lived quite comfortably by the sixteenth century. The yeoman farmer (*kmieć*) farming a full or half allotment supported his family and met his obligations without having to work at a second job. Most peasant proprietors farmed a half allotment (85 percent in the well-studied Korczyń district of Little Poland) with two grown sons, and many peasants leased extra land from noble or royal landlords (one-third in the Korczyń district). Such peasants raised grain, vegetables, and fruit for their own use and for the urban market, where produce fetched high prices. Animal husbandry also provided cash revenues; peasants raised cattle throughout the Commonwealth and sheep in Great

Poland and the Carpathian region. One typical peasant owned four old and two young oxen, five milk cows, six dry cows, four pigs, and five horses. The sale of animals, meat, eggs, butter, fruit, and vegetables gave mid-sixteenth-century yeomen peasants 20 to 30 zlotys annually, a considerable sum. Peasants raised additional cash by transporting and selling wood from the forests, hiring out horses to transport grain, and buying and selling miscellaneous goods. The majority of peasants hired at least one male and one female helper.

Cottagers were the second most numerous group in the village, owning less than a quarter allotment. This group, probably comprising 10 to 15 percent of the peasantry, lived in their own cottages on their own land, tended their own gardens, and owned livestock (sometimes including work animals). But they lacked sufficient land for full economic independence and commonly sought employment from nobles or richer peasants. Sometimes nobles built up a labor pool by settling cottagers on their estates in exchange for one day per week of simple serf labor (without animals). Cottagers provided a tithe to the church and paid state taxes. A third group of peasants were landless cottagers. Many lived in other peasants' homes while some had a house and garden but lived primarily from wages. Some owned animals. They were rarely married or, if married, had lost their spouses.

A fourth category were the peasants who lived in villages and worked as innkeepers, brewers, millers, and skilled artisans such as carpenters who maintained the wooden milling gears. The number of village artisans declined in the sixteenth century when nearby towns and cities took over some of the tailoring and other artisanal work that peasants had been doing part-time to supplement their incomes. Villages also accommodated free laborers and vagabonds who accepted jobs according to whim or circumstance; villages needed additional labor for such seasonal work as harvesting, and sometimes offered excellent wages. During the winter, free laborers often moved to cities to find work. Criminal elements took occasional village jobs.

Hired labor made up a significant portion of the agricultural labor in the sixteenth and early seventeenth centuries. Verbal contracts with the force of law set the terms of employment, and village courts resolved disputes between employers and employees. Since the law saw the employer as a parent and the employee as an underage family member, poor-quality work was no excuse for withholding wages or firing an employee. Employers were required to impose moderate corporal punishment instead. They also had to pay for damage or theft suffered by third parties because of an employee's actions. Employees were required to attend church regularly and refrain from immoral acts as much as possible, although employers rarely troubled themselves with their charges' sexual morality; employers were not entitled to demand sexual favors. Obliged to protect employees' health by providing medical assistance and beating them only lightly, employers could be punished for excessive severity. Most servants were unmarried and usually left service when they married.

Agricultural Reforms in the Grand Duchy of Lithuania

In the fifteenth century, most peasants in the Grand Duchy were tenant farmers who paid rent in kind or money. They furnished some labor for the local noble, generally three days for spring plowing, three days for fall plowing, six days for the grain harvest, and a few days for haying; they also helped with the lord's hunt and provided help in emergencies. Restrictions on peasant movement began with a 1447 charter that forbade migration between noble estates and crown estates. Some household servants were still slaves according to a category established in Kievan Rus, and other slaves farmed large estates as tenant farmers. Slavery officially ended in 1588, except for prisoners of war, and the remaining slaves became serfs.

In the mid-sixteenth century, the resurvey of peasant lands broke up old villages, increasing productivity dramatically. Queen Bona Sforza ordered her estates surveyed in 1547, and royal estates soon followed. Nobles imitated the practice. The survey divided each village into three equal sections and introduced the three-field method of agriculture. Peasants moved from their old residences in extended family units to new individual households and, following the Polish example, received allotments that could be farmed by an independent yeoman. A full allotment (*łan*) in the Grand Duchy covered about 50 acres. Intended to be equal, peasant landholdings soon varied from three-quarters of an allotment to three allotments. Peasants worked two days per week on the lord's land for each allotment, and supplied grain, hay, fowl, eggs, and other payments in kind. The reform quadrupled royal and noble revenues.

Agriculture and Ethnicity in Prussia

Prussia had a population of about 500,000 in the late fourteenth century consisting equally of Germans, Poles, and Old Prussians. By then, these ethnic groups had mixed extensively and Lithuanians also began moving into the region. Ethnic Prussians assimilated with their more economically advanced German and Polish neighbors, although the Prussian language survived with the help of papal instructions to parish priests in 1426 to preach in Prussian (translators were used instead) and the later publication of several Lutheran catechisms in Prussian. The last known Prussian speakers died about 1700. Germanized Prussians and Poles dominated in frontier areas.

Free peasants in the Teutonic Order state generally owned one to six allotments (*hufe*/hook or hide), although a few owned up to forty and could be of any ethnicity so long as they accepted Christianity. The "hook," like the Polish *łan,* represented the amount of land an independent peasant could farm, about 45 acres in Prussia. Free peasants paid land rent directly to the Order and provided services such as repairing castles. They also paid a poll tax and furnished labor services that were, in turn, often commuted to payment in cash or goods such as hay, fish, and wood. Free peasants were particularly common in border areas. They carried arms, fought in the military, and hired peasant labor, generally relatives, if they owned enough land. During the fourteenth century the Order probably preferred Polish settlers to ethnic Prussians because they used more advanced farming techniques and seemed less likely to revolt. Polish villages in Prussia adopted German law.

Serfs owned cottages and small plots which they supplemented by working as servants and laborers for the Order or for nobles. They supplied provisions to the army, worked on Order estates, and paid tithes but remained free to move after they met their obligations. Serfs could pass their land from father to son, although the Order reclaimed the land if the male line died out. The tax records of the Teutonic Order identified some serfs as "Prussians," but this seems to have been a legal category for descendants of thirteenth-century rebels. Ethnic Prussians whose ancestors had not revolted appeared on tax records as Germans.

The Teutonic Order distributed large military fiefdoms to nobles in the thirteenth century, but switched in the fourteenth century to a system of small estates that kept the nobility too weak to challenge its supremacy. The typical noble estate consisted of 200 to 400 acres worked by four to ten peasant families, and supplied one light cavalryman by itself or together with another noble estate. These estates provided a comfortable living, but not enough surplus to export in competition with the Order's own output.

Polish Trade with Prussia

Trade linked northern Poland and Prussia closely despite political conflict. These areas were exploited and eventually cleared of forest products for shipbuilding: timber, pitch, potash. Hemp was cultivated to make rope. Merchants even floated timber down the river system to Gdańsk from the distant Carpathian Mountains in southern Poland. Much of the timber was half finished before export, although raw timbers went abroad too; the bows used by the English at the celebrated battle of Agincourt in 1415 probably came from Carpathian yew trees. Gdańsk handled northern Polish goods such as wax and honey as well as skins from declining local animal stocks.

Poles and Mazovians started selling grain to Prussian cities in the fourteenth century, and sales increased sharply in the fifteenth as exports to western Europe grew rapidly. Prussia sent most of the grain to Amsterdam, where it was distributed throughout the growing Dutch and Flemish cities or transshipped to England, France, and Spain; about 25 percent went to Scandinavia and the eastern Baltic cities. Rather than run the risk of shortages and high prices, Gdańsk merchants traveled deep into the Polish interior to contract for the next year's supplies. Commodities from northern Poland (Great Poland and Mazovia) rarely went through Szczecin, because Brandenburg's control of the New March border region added an additional tariff barrier. Most merchants operated as individuals or in family firms; partnerships, while common, rarely lasted beyond a single endeavor. Merchants usually dealt in all commodities and markets rather than specialize in one branch of trade, and they made contracts face to face and orally, only writing down credit transactions. Early theological objections to lending money had eased and many merchants also acted as moneylenders or bankers.

The independent Prussian state of the Teutonic Order carried on an active Baltic trade that provided the Order's major source of income, supplemented by minting coins and collecting monetary rents from peasants. The Order formally joined the Hanse in 1356 on behalf of its cities and fought Denmark in 1368–70 to win the use of territories in southern Sweden for salting the herring catch. At first, trade was carried on by private merchants and the Order supervised Prussian cities closely, limiting their independence. Tensions developed between the Order and secular elements (knights and city representatives) over the exactions of the Order's fiscal agents. High duties prompted Prussian merchants to contemplate escaping the Teutonic state and seek union with Poland.

Direct trade by the Teutonic Order soon became an important source of income and cut heavily into the profits of private traders. Relying on imperial permission from the Golden Bull of 1226 to purchase products for its own use, the Order established well-staffed trade facilities in Malbork and Königsberg. Order castles throughout Prussia kept their own trade representatives for local business as well. The Order imported goods for local sale, exported goods abroad, and acted as an intermediary in the flow of goods from east to west and north to south. It purchased Baltic amber for sale primarily to Flanders and Lübeck. The Order state collected grain from its peasants as tithes and land taxes, and marketed it through grain halls in the major cites or exported it directly to the West. It purchased timber and grain from Mazovia for resale. Trading employees purchased Flemish cloth, salt, and spices for sale in Prussia; they also exported the goods along the Vistula to Mazovia and Poland. In 1400, the Order handled more than 700,000 bushels of grain (two-thirds rye). It used Hanse privileges to improve its trading conditions in Flanders and elsewhere. Prussian cities had cause to complain about economic competition from its political overlord. The Order paid no tariffs or taxes and occasionally closed ports or limited export licenses to reduce competition from its own subjects. It also set up suburban artisanal workshops to compete with nearby cities for business.

INTERNATIONAL AND DOMESTIC TRADE IN POLAND-LITHUANIA

Poland-Lithuania supplied grain to a hungry Europe, but exports were a small part of total grain production. Fragmentary records indicate that merchants exported an average of 44,000 tons through Gdańsk between 1560 and 1599, mostly rye with modest quantities of wheat, barley, and milled flour. This represented only 4 to 5 percent of the country's grain production, which reached some 970,000 tons of rye annually, 120,000 tons of wheat, and 210,000 tons of barley. Farmers saved another 21 percent as seed grain for the next harvest and left 75 percent for consumption at home. Most grain went to supply rapidly growing cities such as Gdańsk with its burgeoning shipyards, warehouses, and artisanal workshops. Poland produced efficiently in the sixteenth century, lagging slightly behind Britain and France in the ratio of crop yield to seed grain use, and preceding Germany, Denmark, and Russia; the Netherlands remained by far the most efficient producer.

Poland-Lithuania also served as an important link in the international network of transit trade. The mid-thirteenth-century Mongol invasion reoriented east-west trade routes from their previous focal point in Kiev. Poland's eastward expansion into Galicia allowed Kazimierz the Great to control a larger portion of the new route in the mid-fourteenth century, establishing Lviv (Lwów) as a key transit point. From there, trade routes led to Kaffa (Feodosiya) in Crimea and Kiliia or Bilhorod (Akkerman) on the Black Sea coast in modern Moldova. Merchants from Cracow and Sandomierz frequented those ports. Armenians, Jews, and Italians moved to Lviv from the port cities to deal in silks from China, cottons from India and Persia, and eastern spices such as pepper, ginger, and cinnamon. From Cracow and Sandomierz the land route went west to Wrocław. A second route turned north from Lviv to Toruń and Gdańsk for the Baltic trade and western Europe. Another important product that traveled through Poland was copper from Slovakia (Kingdom of Hungary), which was carted across the Carpathians to Cracow and then shipped north by barge on the Vistula to the Baltic coast or, less commonly, traveled west to Wrocław over more expensive land routes. Lithuania took some part in transit trade. Important routes ran through Vilnius in Lithuania to the Russian port city of Novgorod and to Moscow via Smolensk. The main products handled here were furs, hides, and wax from the East in exchange for cloth and metal products from the West. This path led west to Poznań and Frankfurt-am-Oder.

Cities throughout Poland-Lithuania made substantial profits from the transit trade by exercising medieval staple rights that kings and parliaments granted and cities prized highly. The staple system required visiting merchants to offer their goods for sale to locals, who could then take them on the next leg of the voyage. The details varied widely. Sometimes all products were affected and sometimes specific ones; sometimes a proportion (such as half) was indicated. The length of time that the goods would be sold could also be specified. To prevent a merchant from bypassing a city, he might be restricted to certain routes. Many staple rights were established in the thirteenth and fourteenth centuries and revised later as a result of urban lobbying. For example, King Louis the Hungarian granted Cracow a staple right in exchange for its quick allegiance to his candidacy for the royal throne. Merchants traveling from Hungary had to go through Cracow and sell their goods. On becoming king, Władysław Jagiełło extended the requirement to all foreigners. This gave Cracow a monopoly on the lucrative east-west and north-south transit trade, particularly in the export of copper. Similarly, Lviv gained its staple right in 1380. The Polish king and local nobles drew direct profits from internal tariffs, road charges, bridge charges, and similar user fees whichever route the merchants took.

The economy of the Ukrainian provinces was closely tied to the transit trade from the Black Sea. An important route led across Ukraine to Moscow or to the Great Fair in Nizhni-Novgorod. It also brought Ukrainian products such as honey, wax, salt, fish, and various artisanal goods to Russia. Russians sent back furs, saddles, weapons, ornaments, leather goods, and wooden products such as cups. Ukrainians also sold their own products to the Turkish Empire, including wax, salt, cattle, skins, and some textiles. Salt from Black Sea sources and potash from forested Volhynia traveled through Lutsk to Belarus and Poland. The local grain trade gained in significance in time. Instead of exporting all grain from Volhynia north to Gdańsk, some went east to Kiev and other regions devastated by invasions. Cattle was raised in quantity in Ukraine, especially Volhynia, and driven across Poland for sale in Germany. Ukrainian residents sold dried and salted fish to Poland and Germany.

While international trade contributed significantly, the local economy occupied most commoners. Peasants supplied most of their own needs through farming, spinning, weaving, and tanning; many villages had their own blacksmiths and farm implement makers. They supplemented this subsistence economy by selling grain and other farm products in the local marketplace to pay cash rent to nobles. Richer peasants bought metal farm implements and professionally-made clothing from town producers. Peddlers toured the villages to buy and sell, much to the annoyance of guild members. Poland developed a dense network of small cities by the fourteenth century (except in parts of eastern Great Poland and the Lublin province), which in turn linked with larger cities in local, regional, national, and international trading networks.

The Nobility in Poland-Lithuania

By 1386 the Polish nobility had taken form as a unified and privileged estate based on landownership, special tax status, and judicial identity. The nobility comprised as much as 10 percent of the Polish-Lithuanian population, making it by far the largest in Europe. Noble "clans," defined by the coat of arms, controlled admission to the nobility and adopted western European practices in the fourteenth and fifteenth centuries such as wearing the knightly belt, following the knight's code of honor, and fighting in tournaments. Efforts in the late fourteenth century by Little Poland lords to create a legally distinct aristocracy proved unsuccessful. Their political rivals from Great Poland ensured the legal equality of all nobles with the help of lesser nobles from Little Poland. Despite legal superiority over commoners, few nobles enjoyed great wealth at this time. Battlefield spoils and royal salaries or gifts yielded most of their cash income. Landed estates themselves contributed little more than the transit tolls and tariffs that merchants paid.

Since membership in the nobility was not clearly defined, commoners frequently ascended to that status. In addition to the hereditary nobility, persons who gained recognition as nobles included prominent bureaucrats and other state servants, warriors, hereditary bailiffs, landowning burghers, prominent burghers, and richer peasants (especially in Little Poland). Intermarriage also advanced burghers and peasants into the nobility along with their families. Several laws attempted to define noble status in the fifteenth century, such as a 1423 law forbidding peasants to seek patents of nobility, presumably with limited effect. The legal recognition of the dietine (*sejmik*) by the Nieszawa privilege of 1454 made noble identity important, and dietine meetings offered a ready occasion to confirm or deny a person's nobility. The nobility can be considered fully formed after King Jan Olbracht pledged in 1493 to call biennial parliaments with corresponding regular meetings of dietines, but later kings and parliaments still granted numerous patents of nobility to rich burghers and brave warriors.

New commercial possibilities helped transform the Polish nobility from knights into agriculturalists in the fifteenth and sixteenth centuries. By 1550, a typical noble estate covered 200 to 400 acres, with pasture, woods, meadows, and unused land. Buildings included wells, barns, stables, granaries, pigsties, and toolsheds. Most nobles owned 15 to 20 animals, half of them milk cows and the rest pigs, sheep, and chickens. They owned relatively few draft animals (horses and oxen) because peasants worked with their own stock. Male and female hired hands lived in the manor house or in separate buildings. Farming techniques changed little after the early fourteenth-century improvements, and agriculturalists had to cut down woods or appropriate pastureland to increase production. Peasants were rarely expropriated at this time, if only because nobles needed peasant labor to cultivate their estates. Use of hired labor for daily tasks such as caring for animals and tending the fields, especially weeding, was essential.

Although the nobility can be subdivided according to wealth and status, precise definition is impossible on economic, social, or legal grounds. Wealth provided one measure: "magnates" owned perhaps 15 to 20 village estates or more; "rich nobles," 10 to 15, "middle nobles," 5 to 10; "poor nobles," 1 to 5; and "barefoot nobles" owned less than one and generally worked the land themselves. Family status provided a second measure; it depended on marriage with the same or higher social group and appointment to local and central offices over several generations. Polish law made no distinction within the nobility except in terms of parliamentary service after 1493, when senators could no longer participate in elections to the chamber of deputies; the king could appoint any noble he chose to senatorial posts. A consensually recognized Polish aristocracy consisted of magnates with exceptional wealth and status: hundreds of village estates, regular appointment to the highest governmental positions, and intermarriage with similar families. Lacking legal sanction, such families declined when they squandered their wealth, lacked competent members, or failed to produce heirs. Most aristocratic families died out or declined into insignificance within two hundred years. Until the Union of Lublin in 1569, the Grand Duchy of Lithuania maintained a legal aristocracy of Lithuanian and Ruthenian princely families and some nobles (boyars) whose families had achieved prominence under the early Lithuanian dukes. These families enjoyed the exclusive right to serve in the ducal council and hold high office. They held large landed estates, enjoyed exclusive access to leaseholds on royal estates, and served as local judges for lesser nobles and commoners. The admission of new members to this aristocracy was rare.

Cities in Poland-Lithuania

Self-governing cities with written charters established under German law, or transferred to it, provided markets for agricultural produce and supplied manufactured goods such as agricultural implements and textiles. The cities jealously guarded their corporate privileges against merchants from other cities as well as peasant and noble businessmen. As a result of competition, many new cities sprang up just outside the gates of established cities, such as Kazimierz outside Cracow or New Warsaw outside the original Warsaw. In time, the newer cities also gained corporate rights. The number of self-governing cities increased, particularly in the Ukrainian provinces where new cities arose on the frontier and became ghost towns as the tide of settlement moved on. Many self-governing cities were founded on noble estates. In about 1500, 56 percent of the cities in the crown provinces were private. The percentage of private cities was particularly high in Great Poland (65 percent) and low in Prussia (14 percent). Some of the most important cities founded were Sieniawa (1558), Tarnogród (1567), Zamość (1580), and Brody (1584).

Union with Poland brought German law to Lithuanian cities. Vilnius received a charter in 1387 and other cities followed. The new city organizations granted Roman Catholics a privileged position. Lviv and some other cities barred Orthodox Christians from holding office and even from residence for a time. Membership in city governments was usually split evenly between Catholics and Orthodox, even when populations were mostly Orthodox. Lithuanian cities allowed Jewish residence but excluded Jews from municipal citizenship; the closely related Karaites gained citizenship.

Burghers in Poland-Lithuania

A patriciate of rich merchants formed a governing elite, monopolizing the offices of mayor, city councillor, and judge. It awarded itself rich municipal contracts and passed tax burdens on to lower social groups. Cracow's patriciate consisted of 20 to 25 families, many of them foreign in origin although thoroughly polonized by 1500. They mixed relatively little with lesser merchants and artisans whom they considered commoners despite full city citizenship. Cracow patricians of the late fifteenth and early sixteenth centuries included Jan Boner, a royal banker and administrator of royal salt mines; Kasper Ber, a mining entrepreneur, refiner, and money coiner; Paweł Kaufman, a manufacturer of metal wire and tiles; and Leonard Fogelweder, a supplier to Kazimierz IV's court who was connected to the Augsburg Fugger (Fukier) family. Merchants of Italian origin such as Sebastian Montelupi, a merchant and banker who financed King Stefan Batory's Russian wars, joined the elite in the sixteenth century. Polonized Scottish merchants with names such as Karmichel, Frazer, and Dyxon gained recognition in the seventeenth century. Patrician wealth allowed the Cracow city council to purchase control of the legal system from the crown in 1475 and give themselves a monopoly of appointments to the city council and the municipal courts.

The leading burgher of the sixteenth century was Jan Boner, who came to Cracow from Nüremberg to go into business with a relative. Boner acquired Cracow city citizenship in 1483, bought a house on the central square in 1491, married into the patrician Morsztyn family in 1493, and won election to the city council for the first time in 1498. He served in the council continually until he died in 1523. Boner made his initial fortune in the textile business and then started lending money to influential noble and burgher clients. King Zygmunt I relied on him extensively, granting him customs revenues and landed estates in exchange for a flow of loans to finance wars and meet general expenses. Boner also managed the royal salt mines. Serving as the king's personal financial adviser, he separated royal finances from state finances. Boner's fabulous wealth allowed him to buy landed estates for his own use and move into the nobility. Another influential burgher was Jan Turzo, a member of a Hungarian family that made a fortune in copper mining. Turzo came to Cracow to represent his family's interests and took Cracow citizenship in 1464. He made Cracow the hub of his operations as he imported metals from Slovakia and shipped them north to Gdańsk, west to Germany and Austria, and east to Lviv and the Black Sea. He also built a refinery in the outskirts of Cracow whose fiery smokestacks contemporaries compared to eruptions of the Italian volcano, Mount Etna. Turzo's companies mined and refined silver and lead in nearby Silesia, and prospected in the Tatras. The Turzos worked in partnership with the Fugger family of Augsburg, which took over the business when the later Turzos returned to Hungary to marry into the aristocracy. In Cracow, Jan Turzo supported the arts, notably as cosponsor of Wit Stwosz's great carved altar in the St. Mary's Cathedral. Intellectual concerns rather than business interests led him to set up Szwajpolt Fiol in the printing business and protect him against attacks from the Catholic Church.

Since it had not yet become the capital, Warsaw had a more modest patriciate in the mid-sixteenth century. The founders of most major burgher families came to Warsaw in the first half of the century to trade in grain, textiles, herring, and wine. They soon branched out into moneylending and bought real estate, often in the suburbs, which they rented out to lesser merchants and artisans. When they had accumulated enough money, merchants bought landed estates as a secure investment and also to ease their entry into the nobility, usually after marriage with an impoverished noble family from the region. Social ascent took at least a century.

Zygmunt Erkemberger, Warsaw's second richest burgher, offers a concrete example of a burgher who rose into the patrician stratum but had not entered the nobility by the end of the sixteenth century. Born in Silesia, Erkemberger acquired Warsaw citizenship in 1574 and married into the local branch of the Fugger family. In partnership with two other merchants, he owned two shops in Warsaw's Old City that sold imported cloth goods to the royal court, nobles, and rich burghers. He also sold cheaper cloth to lesser burghers and tailors from New Warsaw, often on credit. His frequent trips to Elbląg to buy English cloth led him to diversify his operations and deal in transportation supplies such as sails, rope, and wagons. He played a small role in the grain and salt trade as well. Moneylending became an important part of Erkemberger's business activities. He made consumption loans to nobles on collateral such as swords and jewels, and business loans to merchants. Premature death from plague in 1596 stopped him from using his profits to buy landed estates. At his death, he had a net worth of 60,000 to 70,000 zlotys consisting of inventory (13,366 zlotys), outstanding loans (21,599 zlotys), and his furnished house (30,000 to 40,000 zlotys); he owed 6,056 zlotys for recent inventory purchases. He owned no pictures or books.

In general, lesser burghers sought to join the patriciate individually (a few made it like Erkemberger) or campaigned as a group to share the patriciate's control of urban government and chance to profit. Riots could break out when religious and national rivalries added to economic competition, particularly in better developed areas with richer commoners. Silesia and Prussia endured numerous conflicts. They gained support in their riots from the large number of employees, apprentices, domestic servants, criminals, and prostitutes who comprised the urban plebs and who lacked urban citizenship with its legal protections. After riots in Cracow in 1368, Kazimierz III the Great awarded places on the city council to guild representatives. The award remained a dead letter until Władysław Jagiełło placed such "commoners" on a Committee of Sixteen in 1418 that supervised the city council's financial dealings. The Third Order (Commons) finally won recognition in Cracow, Lublin, Gdańsk, and Warsaw in 1520–30 and in other cities subsequently as a result of riots. This branch of the city government comprised 12 to 100 persons from the lesser merchants and artisans. They supervised city finances and placed occasional members on some city councils. Election procedures varied from election (general or guild) to cooptation by the city council. State authorities stepped in when conflicts threatened to become too severe or, as in Gdańsk, took on an anti-Catholic tone.

Estate lines were fluid in the Jagiellonian era, and rich burghers often became nobles by buying landed estates. The marriage of several members of the Boner family of Cracow with Polish magnates was only the most prominent example of marriage across estate lines. King Louis the Hungarian granted his capital, Cracow, and its burghers the right to buy estates, and Władysław Jagiełło put these land purchases under noble law, in effect granting their owners nobility. Warsaw patricians bought landed estates without difficulty; some achieved recognition as nobles in the sixteenth century, but most had to wait several generations before advancing socially.

Nobles hampered burgher progress even if social advancement never closed down fully. Parliament banned the purchase of landed estates by burghers in 1496 and excluded burghers from high state and church office. A 1543 law required the sale of burgher-owned estates in all but nine leading cities. A law abolishing guilds remained a dead letter, but in 1565 parliament successfully barred Polish merchants from traveling overseas on business, while encouraging foreign merchants to come to Poland. Legislation regulated the price of urban artisanal manufactures, leading to decreased profitability. Nobles exempted themselves from taxes and tariffs on grain exports, and imported goods without charge for their own use.

Cities lost their national political role. After 1505, city representatives stopped attending meetings of the chamber of deputies. Cracow (after 1505), Vilnius (after 1569), and Lviv (after 1658) retained the legal right to speak on urban affairs, but in practice their representatives found that they were not admitted. Several cities sent petitioners, or lobbyists, to parliamentary meetings to work behind the scenes. Larger cities took part in royal elections.

Manufacturing and Mining

As in most of Europe, guilds monopolized urban production by regulating production methods and setting prices. Guild members usually lived and worked side by side on streets with descriptive names such as Shoemakers' Street, Weavers' Street, or Brewers' Street. In addition to sharing economic interests, guild members joined together in religious associations and in fraternal organizations. They also carried out their military obligation to defend the city, usually being assigned a portion of the city walls. Elected "elders" governed the guilds, setting production codes and wages for journeymen, who sometimes struck or rioted for better conditions. Criticism about high prices and business monopolies led Władysław Jagiełło to abolish guilds in 1423, but the law never went into effect and the number of guilds increased. Strikes and slowdowns forced reluctant guild masters to recognize the legality of apprentices' and journeymen's organizations that worked to raise wages and improve conditions.

Many jobs remained open to nonguild members, especially in smaller cities where commercial life was less specialized, and in unincorporated suburbs and villages. Nobles could generally use their own serfs for work on their municipal properties, and guild restrictions did not apply to royalty at all. Even city governments supplemented guild specialists with nonguild labor on special projects such as laying water pipes and constructing town halls. Despite numerous antiguild statements by nobles, kings, and parliaments, owners of private cities generally supported guild organization in order to secure a stable labor market.

Manufacturing increased as regional, national, and international markets grew. Poznań and other cities in Great Poland produced inexpensive cloth that sold throughout Poland, Bohemia, Hungary, and the Hanseatic cities in the late fourteenth century. Prussian cities, especially Gdańsk, emerged as industrial centers in the late fourteenth and early fifteenth centuries with the development of shipbuilding. In the early fifteenth century, Gdańsk became the greatest shipbuilding center in the Baltic, filling orders for England and the Netherlands. Separate guild organizations governed numerous specialties; even the sailmakers guild subdivided into weavers and sewers. The development of masonry construction in cities in the fourteenth century fostered the growth of different construction guilds.

Mining played an important role in the economic life of southwestern Poland. Significant silver and lead deposits existed along the Little Poland–Silesian border, and the Cracow region offered rich salt deposits. Self-governing mining associations similar to guilds worked the mines, paying royalties directly to the crown. Production declined after 1400 as miners exhausted easily accessible sources and failed to raise money to deepen and drain the mines. Iron mining around Kielce and Częstochowa north of Cracow went somewhat better. Here, guild masters employed about a dozen miners and contracted with nobles for access to their lands. Royal administrators directed work at the rich salt mines of Wieliczka near Cracow and Bochnia near Przemyśl in Galicia. Silesia, Moravia, and Hungary provided ready export markets for salt in the fourteenth and early fifteenth centuries. Salt from Cracow area mines was used commercially to preserve the Baltic herring that sold throughout Poland-Lithuania.

Jewish Settlement and Community

Jews made up a small part of the city population when Poland and Lithuania came together in 1386. Jews had lived in Poland since at least the tenth century, although the first written privilege spelling out Jewish communal rights and obligations dates from only 1264. Some Polish Jews moved on to the Grand Duchy of Lithuania by the fourteenth century. Grand Duke Vytautas gave limited privileges to Lithuanian Jews in 1388–89 and Grand Duke Jogaila granted them equality with Polish Jews in 1432. The dozen organized Jewish communities of Poland-Lithuania of 1386 expanded to about sixty comprising 10,000 to 15,000 persons by 1500; only a few Jews lived outside the organized communities. Some Jews may have lived in the eastern reaches of Poland-Lithuania as settlers and even as remnants of the medieval Khazar kingdom, but most came from Germany, Austria, Bohemia, or Silesia, spoke Yiddish, a medieval German tongue, and practiced religion in the Ashkenazy (German) manner. Natural increase was rapid due to economic security, freedom from military service, and lack of religious celibacy.

The Polish-Lithuanian Jewish community was still at an early stage of development in the fifteenth century. There were few Jews who knew Hebrew well and almost no famous rabbis. Communal standards for religious practice were relatively lax and scarcely existed in Lithuania. Strict observers found reason to doubt the kosherness of the meat and wine. Jews often ate and drank non-kosher food together with non-Jews. Some converted to Christianity out of sincerity or opportunism without losing their close ties to other Jews. A surprising example of easygoing attitudes was the conversion of a Lithuanian Jew, Abraham Jósefowicz, who became ducal treasurer but continued to practice tax farming together with his Jewish brothers. One of them, Michał Jósefowicz, acted as communal leader of Lithuanian Jewry and was ennobled. The growing wealth and legal protection of Jews in Poland-Lithuania compared very favorably with expulsions in other parts of Europe.

Charters or privileges defined the conditions of Jewish life and gave the Jews a corporate identity distinct from other groups in Polish-Lithuanian society. While considerable variation existed, most privileges guaranteed religious rights such as ritual slaughter and granted Jews communal right to self-government. The law put them under the king or his representative rather than a Christian municipality. Jews on royal estates or incorporated cities were tried in the Palatine's courts, which included Jewish representatives. As plaintiffs, Jews took their cases to noble, urban, clerical, or feudal courts depending on the identity of the defendant. Jews on private estates became subject to patrimonial courts in 1539. Under royal legislation, Jews paid the same tariffs and duties as other Polish residents, although property taxes may have been higher for Jews than other residents; taxes in autonomous Mazovia were considerably higher. In some places individual taxpayers paid directly, while in others the community or a tax farmer paid on behalf of everyone. The Christian clergy failed in its attempts to collect tithes from Jews, even though they had the legal right to do so at certain times.

Jewish communal organizations were in an early state of development in the Jagiellonian era, and relatively few contained all the facilities and practices of better-established Jewish communities. The Jewish community, or *kehilla,* originated in western Europe based on models from the ancient world. Taxpayers, especially the patriciate, collected taxes and served as higher officials. The Jewish community as a whole maintained the synagogue(s), ritual bath (*mikva*), kosher abattoir, cemetery, hospital, drinking well, and public hall for weddings.

The most important communal official was the rabbi, whose major duty was passing legal judgments based on Jewish law (Talmud), although courts sometimes sat without rabbis. Issues that came before a rabbinic court included family, civil, and minor criminal cases in addition to issues of ritual practice; state authorities took charge of serious criminal cases. Well-known rabbis might be invited to judge cases by correspondence. Rabbis rarely took part in religious services, but they ran the higher religious academies (yeshivas) where the Talmud was studied. A graduate received a rabbinical degree but he had no opportunity to "practice" unless a community hired him. Rabbis sometimes represented the community in dealings with Gentile authorities. The community hired a cantor to lead religious services, a sexton to run the synagogue building, a ritual bath attendant, a kosher butcher, and some office staff.

As Jewish communal organizations stabilized in Poland-Lithuania in the course of the fifteenth century, they began to exercise monopoly controls over the Jewish population similar to those exercised by Christian municipal authorities. Jews ran their communal institutions, regulated economic activity, and collected taxes for their own use as well as for transmission to state authorities; conflicts were common. Jewish communities restricted immigration, often requiring a fee from prospective settlers. Kings or their representatives frequently intervened to settle communal disputes.

Jewish Economic Activities

Monarchs invited Jews to settle in Poland and Lithuania to help develop the economy. The major Jewish occupation in the well-established western portions of the country was moneylending; in the east, which lacked a firm system of municipalities and guilds, Jews also became involved in trading, tax collecting, artisanry, and even farming. Many Jews practiced a variety of occupations at the same time. Levko (Leib) in late fourteenth-century Cracow lent money to kings, nobles, and burghers, managed the royal salt mines, co-managed the mint, dealt in real estate, and owned several breweries. Woloczko (Wolf) acted as tax farmer, royal financial agent, and merchant in early fifteenth-century Lviv. He colonized and later managed several villages for the king. Many other Jews had similar jobs in other parts of the country. On the small-scale level, Jews lent minor sums at 25 percent or less as officially appointed "bankers of students" at the Jagiellonian University. Jews also lent money to regular borrowers who paid 50 to 100 percent annual interest on unsecured loans, while loans secured by land brought 10 to 20 percent in the fourteenth century and less in the fifteenth. Foreclosures made Jews into owners and managers of landed estates but attracted resentment from clients who had trouble making their payments. Church pressure sometimes made Jews sell the properties or hire non-Jewish managers. Decrees issued by the Basel Synod (1434) and others attempted to limit Jewish moneylending and encouraged the Polish parliament to help Christian merchants replace them in economically developed centers such as Cracow. Jewish landowning declined in the course of the fifteenth century, and Jews farmed part-time in towns that were too small to support much trade, like their Christian counterparts.

The Polish-Lithuanian state hired Jews to supplement the primitive Polish-Lithuanian bureaucracy by managing the 250 toll stations on royal roads and bridges in the early fourteenth century (increasing later) and collecting state taxes; nobles sometimes imitated the state by employing Jews to manage their estates. Jewish tax and toll farmers paid the state a fixed amount and recouped the expense in their collections from the public; despite written guidelines, the possibilities for abuse were great. Would-be competitors and the Church vigorously opposed so-called Jewish oppression.

Christian merchants defended their trade and production monopolies against Jewish and Christian competitors alike. Jews generally traded without special restriction in the fifteenth century, although a few large cities such as Cracow, Warsaw, and Lviv barred them from the retail trade. Most cities permitted local Jews to trade. Jews dealt with guild restrictions by setting up competing businesses in locations outside municipal jurisdiction. They assumed a prominent role in international trade, where no guild restrictions existed. The social profile of Jews in the largely Polish city of Wrocław in Silesia in the mid-fourteenth century may reflect Jews in the Commonwealth as well. About 15 percent of economically active persons earned wages while 85 percent ran their own businesses. Tax records identify 10 percent as poor and 7 percent as very rich.

The flow of immigration to Poland-Lithuania continued throughout the sixteenth century as Jews were expelled from German and Bohemian cities and Zygmunt I encouraged them to settle in Poland-Lithuania; few Spanish Jews immigrated to Poland-Lithuania after the 1492 expulsion. The Jewish community grew to 80,000 to 100,000 by 1600, and the focus of population shifted eastward to take advantage of the new opportunities presented by economic development, especially in Ukrainian lands. The majority of Jews continued to live in cities and towns, but one-third of Jews in eastern areas settled in villages. Most peasant villages had one or two Jewish families, who earned their living as tax and rent collectors for the noble proprietors, or as innkeepers, millers, and moneylenders. The Lithuanian Statutes of 1529 and 1566 identified Jews as free persons equal to Christian burghers; indeed the First Lithuanian Statute of 1529 set the fine for killing nobles and Jews alike at eight times the fine for killing burghers.

As cities became richer and more influential in the sixteenth century, they sometimes gained privileges to exclude Jews from commerce, as in Cracow, Poznań, Płock, and Lviv in the 1520s, and the total exclusion from Warsaw and seventeen other cities between 1520 and 1600. Jews still lived and worked nearby or even within the cities on properties owned by nobles and clerics, however. To solve the problem of conflicting privileges secured by burghers and Jews, sixteenth-century kings pressed the two groups to negotiate their relationship. Lviv Jews eventually acquired clearly defined residential and commercial rights but did not achieve total equality. Cracow forced its Jewish community to move to the suburban municipality of Kazimierz in 1495 after a fire touched off anti-Jewish rioting. Polish kings allowed this new Jewish community to expand in 1533 and again in 1550, reconfirming its right to do business, and Jewish merchants still traded in the Cracow marketplace, even if they could not live there.

Similarly, Poznań let Jews increase the number of houses that they owned from 49 to 83, and then to 138 between 1558 and the early 1600s. All these agreements underwent later modification.

Gentile Attitudes Toward the Jews

Gentile attitudes toward Jews varied. Nobles, especially large landowners, supported the kings in granting Jews security and settled them on their estates or in their towns, hiring them in various capacities. Like other nobles, the higher clergy generally maintained extensive commercial dealings with Jews and protected them against attack from Christian business rivals. Lesser nobles favored the Jews less, especially if they had trouble repaying loans, but they tended to support Jews who undercut the monopolies of Christian guild merchants and artisans. Sometimes individual nobles could be moved to protect Jews by arguments or bribes from prominent Jewish moneylenders. King Władysław Jagiełło displayed an ambiguous attitude toward the Jews, supporting them at times and siding with their enemies at others, possibly due to his need, as a convert, to show his piety. Most of the time, relations between ordinary Christians and Jews were good.

Jews suffered occasional violent attacks, persecutions, and expulsions, mostly in Poznań and Cracow. The clergy sought to restrict Jewish activity on religious grounds despite their reliance on Jewish business agents, and the Church followed western European models by seeking to isolate Jews residentially. Some clerics held extreme anti-Jewish sentiments. Violent persecution eased in the sixteenth century as the focus of Jewish settlement shifted eastward, but some dozen charges of ritual murder, profaning the host, and similar character were still laid in the second half of the sixteenth century, and city mobs, especially students, rioted at least a dozen times. The worst persecution occurred in 1399 when the city court of Poznań convicted fourteen Jews of profaning the communion wafer and burned them at the stake. The number of persecutions increased in the later fifteenth century, although Kazimierz IV generally restrained anti-Jewish zeal. He was forced to retract Jewish privileges when the visiting Italian monk, Giovanni Capistrano, whipped up popular anti-Semitism in the 1440s, but Kazimierz IV reissued most of them after a few years and protected Jews against attacks. Even Aleksander, who bowed to pressure and expelled the Jews from Lithuania when he became grand duke in 1496, readmitted them in 1503 when his position became stronger. Typically, Abraham of Bohemia acted as financier and adviser to Zygmunt I in Poland after he suffered expulsion from Austria.

Anti-Jewish attitudes worsened in the mid-sixteenth century, perhaps as a result of increased economic rivalry and heightened religious sensibilities. In a strange episode that probably reflects a reaction to the Protestant Reformation, rumors swept Lithuania in 1539–40 that burghers had converted to Judaism and that Jews had abducted children to convert them. The hysteria contributed to harsh provisions in the Second Lithuanian Statute of 1566 that echoed western Europe's anti-Jewish attitudes, although grand dukes, nobles, and prominent clerics blocked their implementation. On paper, Jews had to identify themselves in public by wearing yellow hats. They could no longer testify in court in real estate cases, hold Christian slaves, hire Christian wet nurses, or collect debts that had not been registered in court. The statute barred the grand duke from rewarding Jews by giving them landed estates.

The Royal and State Treasury

Kazimierz III the Great brought treasury revenues to a high point in the mid-fourteenth century, but his successors failed to maintain the same level. Kazimierz regularized the collection of taxes on his royal estates, reclaiming many that his predecessors had given away to nobles for political support, as well as customs duties, mining royalties, and land use taxes. The development of the elective monarchy prompted Kazimierz's successors to distribute lucrative estates to nobles as leaseholds without any real accounting, mainly to ensure their election as king. Louis of Hungary abandoned all regular taxes except the peasant land tax, which he cut in half. In Jagiellonian times, kings depended on special permission from the nobility to raise funds for war and other state purposes. Regular tax revenues fell from about 85,000 silver grzywnas under Kazimierz before 1370 to 60,000 under Aleksander in 1500.

Nevertheless, the Jagiellonian kings still collected substantial revenues. They enjoyed regalian rights over subsoil wealth. Internal tariffs flowed to the royal treasury as did profits from minting coins, mostly from lowering the quality of the metal. Cities paid property and coronation taxes while Jews paid poll taxes (head taxes) in lieu of property taxes. Władysław II Jagiełło convinced the nobles to pay a special levy based on assessed property values for war against the Teutonic Knights in 1404, and the Church paid extraordinary taxes called "charitable contributions" from time to time. Kazimierz IV had to grant political concessions to collect the levy for his 1454 campaign against the Teutonic Knights, but his successors met little resistance when they demanded the levy later.

Kings made no distinction between the state treasury and their personal treasury in the fifteenth century. Royal expenditures went primarily for national defense. Fortifications were particularly important in Kazimierz's time, and soldiers' pay played an increasing part in the budget when professional soldiers replaced the noble levy; even the levy received wages when the army crossed the border. Diplomatic missions were costly, especially when large delegations went to Church conclaves in distant places or to the papal courts at Avignon and Rome.

Improvements in state financing in the sixteenth century permitted the Polish-Lithuanian state to achieve and maintain great power as annual revenues increased from 104,000 zlotys in 1510, to 185,000 in 1563 and 350,000 in 1569; Stefan Batory collected 800,000 zlotys in the 1580s. Under Zygmunt I, Chancellor Jan Łaski reformed the tax system by raising customs duties and collecting taxes more thoroughly, especially the special military levy. A new poll tax replaced the old peasant land tax that had declined so much in value that it was literally not worth collecting. The poll tax was set at 12 groszy per peasant (less for cottagers); barefoot nobles served in the military levy instead of paying. Zygmunt reformed the mint in 1526–28 and issued new coins such as the zloty (gold piece). Separate Prussian and Lithuanian mints issued coins with the same value as Polish coinage. Clergy paid a "charitable donation" in place of military service, and the papacy agreed to allow Peter's pence to remain at home to finance warfare against non-Christian invaders. As a result of these reforms, Zygmunt I's treasury was healthy and the crown's indebtedness decreased. There would have been a substantial surplus if Queen Bona Sforza had paid taxes on her estates.

This revenue allowed Zygmunt I to reclaim some rich royal estates from disadvantageous leaseholds that brought little return. But the king refused to cooperate with parliamentary reformers who wanted to push the process of reclaiming estates much further. He felt that their program as a whole weakened his prerogatives. Zygmunt's counterproposal of regular taxation for military purposes was approved by parliament in 1509–12 and 1526–27, but sabotaged by the nobles and never carried out. Noble reformers of the Executionist school believed that the king was obliged to pay for national defense from his own resources. They had more success with Zygmunt August, who finally bowed to their pressure in 1562–63 and reclaimed royal estates from his supporters in exchange for passing the so-called quarter tax that granted 25 percent of leasehold revenues to the military and the remainder to the state (actually 20 percent, because the leaseholder kept 20 percent of gross revenues for expenses). The treasury carried out a detailed inventory of the royal domains in 1564, which permitted the state to increase treasury revenues substantially; the tax per land allocation went from 12 groszy to 20 groszy in 1563 and 30 groszy in 1578. Peasants could afford these sums because they were deducted in part from the church tithe. Detailed instructions for officials in 1539 and 1558–60 directed royal officials to prevent exploitative use of royal leaseholds.

The royal treasury absorbed the Mazovian and Prussian treasuries at unification. The Lithuanian treasury remained separate, although it adopted Polish procedures in 1569.

Women and Families in Jagiellonian Society

While men enjoyed a superior legal and social position to women of their same social group, Polish customary and pre-Christian princely law gave women some legal and economic protections; Jews and inhabitants of the Grand Duchy of Lithuania were governed by their own laws. Under Polish law, marriages were arranged by parents who negotiated prenuptial economic contracts except in cases of elopement (consensual "abduction"), concubinage (common-law marriage with a woman of a lower social group), and common-law marriage among the urban poor. Women from all social classes came into marriage with dowries that were turned over to their husbands; by Jagiellonian times, landed dowries had virtually disappeared and women brought movable property such as clothes, jewels, cash, household equipment, and cattle. The wife's family's economic obligations ceased with payment of the dowry, and she received no share of her parents' inheritance. In return for the dowry, the husband gave his wife a morning-gift (*dotalicum, wiano*) approximately twice the value of her dowry, often in the form of a mortgage on his property that was protected against foreclosure in case the husband could not pay his debts. The morning-gift became the wife's property if her husband died or if the marriage ended in annulment, and it passed to her children (both male and female) if she died before her husband; it went to her parents if she died childless. Women were fully legal persons, but courts acted as if they needed special assistance from fathers, husbands, and other custodians. A husband generally administered his wife's property and often spoke for her in court, although women testified in both criminal and civil matters that concerned them directly. Many cases arose out of property disputes between widows and their late husbands' families. Criminal law generally treated men and women the same.

An apparently clear division of labor between men and women masked many overlapping functions within the family. On the whole, men managed family businesses: nobles ran estates, burghers traded or manufactured, and peasants farmed. Women managed the home, but their sphere of activity required considerable independent economic behavior and produced revenues that they used according to their own judgment. Women took charge of cattle, dairy production, and poultry, selling the products on the open market. They looked after gardens and orchards, which produced salable surpluses. Some women brewed beer or cultivated medicinal herbs and practiced village medicine. Some used their profits to buy raw materials for their own market operations and to rent land. Of course, women took charge of traditional housekeeping activities such as cleaning, washing, preserving, and cooking; richer women supervised servants in these activities. Their own independent activities prepared women of all social levels to step in and take over the full management of the family business when their husbands went to war or took an active part in politics. Ill or incompetent husbands relied entirely on their wives.

Motherhood was a woman's essential function in marriage, and peasant property settlements often were not final until the birth of the first child. Nobles accepted infertile marriages but sometimes tailored the size of the morning-gift after the fact to the level of the wife's fertility. Customary law assigned heavier penalties to assaults or even negligent accidents that interfered with pregnancy and childbirth. It punished infanticide with death. Illegitimate children could not inherit or gain recognition as nobles in theory, although in practice many did. Children born to a nobleman and his commoner "concubine" became the father's responsibility and they often worked as servants when they grew up. Early marriage and the lack of birth control resulted in a wide range in the ages of siblings. Mothers generally gave birth to eight children of whom four survived in richer families and two survived in poorer families. Peasant families usually counted four to six persons including one or two servants. Noble families might comprise seven to twenty persons, including the father's mother and unmarried sisters, unmarried adult children, lesser nobles, poor relatives with ill-defined functions in the household, and servants. After a parent's death, the surviving spouse looked after the children with the help of relatives and servants free of any legal obligations to the deceased parent's relatives.

Widows enjoyed full personal, economic, and legal independence, although they had to divide their inheritance with children who reached the age of maturity. Widows retained control over their own property, and widowed noblewomen exercised feudal rights over their husbands' estates and serfs. Peasant widows ran family farms, leased land, and hired farm labor as required. Some leased country mills and inns. Widows of artisans took over their husbands' shops, running them with hired labor; sometimes a widow would marry a journeyman, and he supervised production while she managed the finances. Widows chose their own marriage partners without outside interference.

The age of maturity was fifteen for men and twelve for women in the sixteenth century; judicial practice raised the age to eighteen and fourteen a century later. Noblemen received full political and economic rights at twenty-four. City law recognized boys as mature at fourteen and accorded them full rights at twenty-one.

Increasing religious fervor during the Reformation and Counter Reformation may have provided an additional outlet for women's activity. Since piety was seen as a female characteristic, pious women could undertake organizational activity in the religious sphere without fear of censure. During the Reformation, learned Calvinist and especially Anti-Trinitarian women preached in churches;

and during the Counter Reformation, nuns and abbesses managed convents, directed education, and led cultural activities with token male supervision. Legitimation of women's religious concerns regarding their husbands' and children's behavior may also have moderated male dominance within marriages.

Ideal and Real Family Relationships

The ideal noblewoman was, according to an eighteenth-century memoirist, "beautiful, wise, [and] strong to have heirs"; strong-minded women were also prized. Traditionally, wives looked after the home and took responsibility for raising children. Sons remained under their mothers' direction and were not turned over to their fathers at age seven as in some western European countries. Friendship appeared more common in marriage than romantic love, judging by surviving letters from nobles and burghers alike, and the ideal relationship was based on mutual respect and affection. The sixteenth-century poet Mikołaj Rej enjoined wives to be modest and husbands to set a good example. Village courts tried to reconcile peasants in cases of marital strife, although separations and divorces were easy to arrange on grounds of infertility and incapacitating illness, particularly before church marriage became compulsory in 1577. After that date, the Church supplied annulments for improper blood relationships, impotence, forced marriage, bigamy, and lack of proper documentation. Family influence and wealth compensated for objective weaknesses in individual cases.

Lacking a strong medieval tradition of courtly love, Polish-Lithuanian residents probably enjoyed little romantic love outside of marriage (or within it), even if extramarital affairs were probably common. Mikołaj Rej warned men against love matches that might upset political and family relations (as did that of Zygmunt August and Barbara Radziwiłł). Rej counseled marrying a "companion" of equal social status "with a sagacious upbringing and training, and comely manners." He also recommended "a kind-hearted wife raised in the fear of God." Surviving letters and statements in probated wills show that deep affection and respect often developed between marriage partners.

Most sixteenth-century literature was strongly misogynistic, although social customs appear to have been considerably less so. Andrzej Frycz Modrzewski characteristically declared that "women are born for the spindle and . . . they should be vested with concern for household matters, not public ones," and Piotr Skarga insisted that "learning does not serve women as well as prayer and work." He thought that "silence, piety, handwork, and domestic amusement serve women best," although he conceded that women in rich homes who did not have to work for a living could avoid laziness and increase godliness through study. One dissenter was Andrzej Glaber, who thought that "the girls' constitution is very subtle and their ability to learn and understand all things is sharp and quick." Despite the prevailing opinion that they lacked the capacity for study, women learned to read and write in accordance with their social class. Significant numbers of richer noble and burgher women had private tutors and attended schools. A survey of Cracow documents from 1575 to 1580 showed that 50 to 60 percent of men could sign but only 20 percent of women. Correcting for wealth, as many as half the women in the upper nobility and the urban patriciate may have been literate.

A double standard prevailed in sexual relations. Prostitution was legal and the public executioner's duties involved regulating brothels. Armies drew numerous camp followers; prostitutes flocked to political gatherings and trade fairs. Villages did not tolerate prostitution and women of loose morals were expelled, although casual sex was probably common among hired help, who frequently slept in the same room. Adultery was punishable by death, but courts applied that penalty only when the affair led to infanticide or murder; ordinarily a conviction for adultery brought twenty to thirty lashes and a monetary fine. Extramarital sex seems to have been more common in towns and cities where greater anonymity prevailed. Servant girls were liable to abuse and, at best, received a leaving bonus that allowed them to find a husband from their own social class. But discharged servant girls often descended into prostitution. Male misbehavior rarely drew reprisal.

Child-raising seems to have been based on a mixture of strict discipline and affection. Beatings were the common method of social correction for all ages and classes, and parents were often warned against spoiling their children with excessive indulgence. However, healthy Polish mothers generally nursed their own children, and there are numerous literary examples of parental love. Mikołaj Rej delighted in his children, who, "like little birds run around the table, chirping, playing—what a delight, what a pleasure." Jan Kochanowski's *Laments* for his daughter's death also display deep feeling. The insecurities of life produced numerous orphans, whose rights were safeguarded by the courts, although guardians sometimes abused their positions.

CHAPTER 6

Artistic Culture and Education in the Jagiellonian Period

During the reign of the Jagiellonians, Poland completed its integration into the mainstream of European culture; Lithuania followed the same path at a somewhat slower rate. Both nations shared in the intellectual and aesthetic trends of the day through international Church contacts, university study, foreign tourism, and trade. They contributed to European literature, science, and political thought. With the growing use of the Polish language in all areas of intellectual discourse, they achieved a sense of patriotic distinctiveness without the exaggerated feeling of uniqueness that sometimes characterized Polish-Lithuanian culture in later centuries. Poland-Lithuania reached intellectual and artistic maturity during the Renaissance, most notably through the spread of humanism and the writing of poetry. The Protestant Reformation strongly affected political developments and intellectual trends, but failed to strike a deep emotional chord in the population.

THE JAGIELLONIAN UNIVERSITY OF CRACOW

By 1386, Poland had joined the mainstream of European culture. As elsewhere in Europe, clerics formed the primary educated elite. Polish clergy studied at the university that Kazimierz III the Great had founded in Cracow in 1364, but they also studied abroad, especially in Italy and Bohemia. In 1400, King Władysław Jagiełło refounded and expanded Cracow's university with three aims: Christianizing Lithuania, preparing officials to serve the Polish-Lithuanian state, and raising the intellectual level of the populace. The bishop of Cracow served ex officio as chancellor. The transformation was so complete that the refounded university is commonly called the Jagiellonian University. The four fundamental departments of medieval education comprised the university: liberal arts, medicine, law, and theology. Studies in secular and church law predominated; medicine was particularly weak. The regulations of 1406 dictated a practical emphasis on Aristotle's social philosophy and recognized probable proof based on practical experience instead of waiting for absolute proof. Even theology took on a social cast.

The university's function of serving the state was emphasized by close links with the prenationalist orientation of Czech (Bohemian) education that led to the Hussite revolt. The strong German burgher presence in Cracow added to the urgency of strengthening the state by educating Poles. Silesians linked Poland and Bohemia, and many Polish students studied in Prague in the late fourteenth century; scholarships funded by Queen Jadwiga helped Lithuanian and Ruthenian students attend Prague. Mateuš of Cracow (1345–1410), a noted theology professor from Prague's Charles University and later rector of the University of Heidelberg, visited Cracow in 1398–99, where he probably helped reform the Jagiellonian University, drawing on Czech traditions such as preaching in the local language and condemning clerical wealth. Several Czech theologians came to teach in Cracow's newly opened Theological Faculty, challenging local antireform professors. Most Cracow theologians eventually rejected Hussitism, but they adopted the conciliarist view that saw the pope as subordinate to the Church faithful and to the state, and they defended national rights over papal influence in Church affairs. Cracow theologians enthusiastically participated in synods and only reluctantly acknowledged papal supremacy at the late date of 1449. Jakub of Paradyż (c. 1380–1464), a Cistercian monk who studied in a Bohemian monastery before earning a doctorate in theology in Cracow, called for abolition of clerical celibacy and advocated partial secularization of monastic properties. He saw the pope as the executive arm of synods, not an independent "head of the Church" or "vicar of Christ." Another Cracow theologian, Wawrzyniec of Raciborz (c. 1393–c. 1448), portrayed the pope and college of cardinals as the executive between synods.

The Study of History

The need to present arguments in legal disputes, especially against the Teutonic Knights, prompted rapid growth in Polish historical study. Strong presentations made at international synods by Paweł Włodkowic and others stemmed from half a century of collecting and analyzing documents by scholars who also held state office, such as Stanisław Ciołek (d. 1437), vice-chancellor and bishop of Poznań. The royal chancellery even recorded oral traditions going back one or two generations. In the 1430s, Jan Dąbrówka, professor at the Jagiellonian University, edited a teaching version of Wincenty Kadłubek's late twelfth-century Polish chronicle, adding extensive commentary.

By far the most important fifteenth-century historian was Jan Długosz, whose career illustrates the practical importance of historical study. Długosz

(1415–80) came from the lesser nobility; his father had distinguished himself in the battle of Grunwald (1410). Jan studied at the Jagiellonian University but left before graduation to work in the chancellery of the influential bishop of Cracow, Zbigniew Oleśnicki. As the bishop's secretary and director of the chancellery, Długosz later undertook domestic and diplomatic assignments. After Oleśnicki died in 1455, Długosz became canon of the Cracow chapter and held several benefices. When tensions between the chapter and King Kazimierz IV over the appointment of a new bishop eased, Długosz joined the delegation that negotiated the second Peace of Toruń (1466) with the Teutonic Knights, became tutor to the Jagiellonian princes, and served as royal ambassador. He also became a patron of the Jagiellonian University.

Długosz's major work, *Chronicles of the Illustrious Polish Kingdom*, covered Polish history from its legendary origins to 1480. The work had a contemporary focus and devoted most attention to the war with the Teutonic Knights, especially the battle of Grunwald. Długosz defined Polish nationality as the Polish-speaking peoples of Piast Poland, including the inhabitants of the Pomeranian and Silesian provinces that had been lost to the Polish state, and Christianized Lithuanians, even though they spoke and felt Lithuanian. He turned to the symbols of the White Eagle, national saints such as St. Stanisław, and the national song, "Mother of God" ("Bogurodzica"), sung at Grunwald, to characterize Poland. Despite his intense patriotism, Długosz expressed little hostility toward neighboring states and peoples, and he discussed their histories in a matter-of-fact manner. His presentation of internal Polish-Lithuanian developments reveals his orientation toward the Church and the aristocracy of Little Poland. Długosz wrote in Latin, but he considered the use of Polish as an important identifying mark and he doubted the wisdom of accepting foreign immigrants, particularly the recent German immigrants to Polish cities.

Latin, rather than Polish, was used by most writers. Surviving examples of Polish prose from the late fourteenth and early fifteenth centuries include translations of laws from Latin, oaths sworn by witnesses in court, medical prescriptions, monastic rules, prayers, and correspondence.

RENAISSANCE HUMANISM

The introduction of Renaissance humanism, with its emphasis on classical antiquity and purification of the Latin language, changed Europe's cultural discourse in the fifteenth century. Polish clerics and diplomats first encountered humanists in the early fifteenth century while attending international synods or visiting Germany and Italy. After his return from studying in Italy, Grzegorz (Gregory) of Sanok (c. 1407–77) wrote commentaries on Virgil's *Bucolics* that represent the first clearly humanist writings in Poland. A poor noble who tutored magnate children, Grzegorz studied in Cracow, Germany, and Italy. He later served as royal chaplain to Władysław III in Poland and Hungary, and advanced through the Church hierarchy to become archbishop of Lviv while continuing to write Latin comedies and even romantic verse, little of which has survived. Aeneas Sylvia Piccolomini, papal nuncio and later Pope Pius II, gained a positive impression of Cracow humanism from his extensive correspondence with Bishop Oleśnicki, the university's chancellor.

Italians living in Poland furthered the influence of humanism. Francesco Filelfo gave the oration at the coronation of Władysław II's third wife, Sonia, in 1424 before an audience of princes and emperors, and other Italian humanists also spoke on state occasions. The arrival of Philippo Buonaccorsi (1437–94) accelerated the interest in humanist learning. Kallimach (Callimachus), as he became known in Poland, had fled Rome after taking part in a plot against Pope Paul II and, after stopping on the Greek Isles and in Constantinople, sought refuge in Poland. King Kazimierz IV refused to surrender him to the pope because of his own disputes with Rome over the appointment of bishops. Initially received and protected by Grzegorz of Sanok, Kallimach settled in Cracow and soon played a prominent role in the capital's literary life, where his acquaintance with leading Italians earned him appointment as a royal secretary and tutor to the royal children. Kallimach undertook diplomatic missions for Poland-Lithuania to Rome, Venice, and Vienna after Pope Paul II died, and domestically he proposed policies to strengthen royal power. He helped unite Italian and Polish humanists in an informal "academy" that included bishops, professors, and city officials. Their elegant manners and intellectual discussions contrasted sharply with the lengthy banquets and theological discussions that characterized social discourse for the rest of fifteenth-century Polish-Lithuanian society. Kallimach's beautiful Renaissance Latin writing style provided a model for Poles and Lithuanians. He wrote occasional and romantic poems as well as serious works on political and historical topics, such as a history of King Władysław III's reign and biographies of his first protectors, Zbigniew Oleśnicki and Grzegorz of Sanok.

Other early humanistic groups in Cracow favored a German orientation and attracted scholars such as Konrad Celtes from Würzburg. Celtes (or Celtis, really Konrad Pickel, 1459–1508) came to Cracow in 1488 to complete his studies. He prepared commentaries on Plato, Cicero, Horace, and Seneca, wrote on poetics, and produced plays. His occasional verse commented both favorably and critically on life in Cracow. Together with Kallimach, Celtes established the Vistula Literary Society (Sodalitas Literaria Vistula).

A lively humanist community of native Poles emerged. Maciej Drzewicki (1467–1535) wrote "The Lives of Bishops of Włocławek" in addition to serving as diplomat, chancellor of the Jagiellonian University, and eventually primate of the Polish Church. Biernat of Lublin (c. 1465–c. 1529) wrote about Aesop in Polish. Jan Dantyszek (1485–1548) came from a German-speaking merchant family in Gdańsk and made an outstanding career at the Polish royal court. After studying in Cracow and visiting Jerusalem, Dantyszek gained appointment as royal secretary and represented Poland in Austria and Spain for long periods. He also undertook shorter missions to many other European countries. Zygmunt I rewarded him with the Prussian bishoprics of Chełmno and later Warmia. Dantyszek's literary career began in 1510 when he wrote a collection of moralizing Latin verses on virtue and fortune. His 1517 *Elegia amatoria* offered erotic poetry with a mythological base. Late in life, Dantyszek wrote his autobiography in Latin verse, affirming his hope for salvation after an eventful life, and a collection of church hymns. He sharply condemned the Lutheran revolt in Gdańsk.

Two leading humanist poets represented opposite ends of the social spectrum. Andrzej Krzycki (1482–1537), nephew of Piotr Tomicki, vice-chancellor and bishop of Cracow, studied in Bologna and started his Church career as secretary to Jan Lubrański, bishop of Poznań. Krzycki worked effectively within the Church hierarchy and distinguished himself by his anti-Protestant zealotry, but at the same time he was a drinker and carouser who wrote Latin poems about the joys of fast living. Settling down to respectability, he worked for Queen Bona Sforza as a secretary and gained appointment to the bishoprics of Płock and Gniezno. He was noted for sharp satirical poems against personal and political enemies. In contrast, Klemens Janicki (1516–43) came from a peasant family that sent him to study because he was too sickly to work on the farm. Janicki did so well at the Lubrański Academy in Poznań that Archbishop Krzycki appointed him secretary and later sent him to Padua, where he received a doctorate in philosophy. Janicki wrote student poems in Poland and he continued in Italy with such distinction that Pope Paul III accorded him the title of poet laureate. Janicki returned to Cracow in 1540 and died three years later. His Latin poetry displayed the personal tone of Italian poetry incorporating nature images. At the end of his short life, Janicki wrote eloquent verses in an elegiac tone reflecting on his illness, his friends, and his country. He also wrote history in verse such as "Lives of the Archbishops of Gniezno" and "Lives of the Polish Kings." For the most part panegyrics, these works occasionally touched on sensitive political issues, such as the lack of martial spirit among nobles and some political controversies. The humanists Paweł of Krosno and Jan of Wiślica were also commoners.

Humanist Political Thought

Andrzej Frycz Modrzewski (1503–72), the most important Polish political author of the sixteenth century, was born in Wołborz (Great Poland). He earned a baccalaureate degree at the Jagiellonian University when he was sixteen and continued to attend lectures. Taking low-level holy orders allowed him to work in the chancelleries of Jan Latalski, bishop of Poznań, and Jan Łaski the elder, chancellor and archbishop of Gniezno. Łaski sent Modrzewski to Wittenberg for further studies, and from there used him for missions to humanists such as Melanchthon and Erasmus. Łaski assisted Erasmus by purchasing his library, leaving it for him to use during his lifetime; Modrzewski brought the library back to Poland after Erasmus died in 1536. When he returned to Poland for good in 1541, Modrzewski worked for Łaski as part of the Executionist movement, and he later became a royal secretary. His first polemical work argued for applying laws regarding murder equally to nobles and commoners, a measure that parliament adopted in 1543.

Modrzewski's major work, *On the Reform of the Republic* (*De Republica Emendanda*), boldly addressed fundamental issues of state and church from an Executionist position. It was occasioned by the Council of Trent and stemmed in part from diplomatic missions that Modrzewski undertook for King Zygmunt I while serving as royal secretary. For philosophical underpinnings, Book One, "On Customs," proclaimed the essential goodness of human nature, citing the Old Testament. Echoing humanist concerns, Modrzewski supported the Polish form of government that balanced a monarchical element (royalty), an aristocratic element (senate), and a democratic element (chamber of deputies) to prevent abuses of power. Government as a whole should supervise morality and public education carefully, he argued. He proposed creating an office of censor to intervene in family life and business relations to support morality and even to protect serfs against mistreatment by nobles. Modrzewski displayed an asceticism of manners, criticizing dancing, popular amusements, and fancy dress. Book Two, "On Laws," reiterated his concern for legal equality regardless of social origin, while Book Three, "On War," distinguished between just wars (self-defense) and unjust wars (aggression). The three books appeared in print in 1551.

Books Four and Five came out in Protestant Basel (Switzerland) after the Roman Catholic Church banned them. Book Four, "On the Church," endorsed prevailing Roman Catholic religious doctrines, but declared the supremacy of international Church councils over the pope and papal bureaucracy. Furthermore, Modrzewski demanded social equality in assigning Church offices, calling for election of bishops and other officials by diocesan synods and admission of lay commoners to synods along with noble clerics. Similarly, he thought the pope should be elected by an unspecified group that would be wider than the college of cardinals. In Book Five, Modrzewski advocated taxing church benefices and rich monastic orders to pay for public education.

Humanism and Religion

Humanism contributed strongly to the impulse for religious reform, for the Dutch humanist Desiderius Erasmus convinced many reformers, future Catholics and Protestants alike, that understanding the Bible correctly would lead to perfecting religious institutions. Erasmus was well known and corresponded with both Church leaders and lay humanists in Poland-Lithuania. Polish humanists generally favored creating a national Church within the Roman Catholic Church. As the unity of the movement for Church reform broke into Catholic and Protestant wings, Erasmus's influence declined and Catholics assailed him vehemently in the 1560s. Calvinist interest in Erasmus also declined, and Anabaptists cited him only selectively in the early seventeenth century.

The difficulties that Modrzewski encountered as a result of his bold publication illustrate the degree of tolerance—and its limits—that characterized later sixteenth-century Poland-Lithuania. As a member of the clergy, Modrzewski felt vulnerable to arrest by Tridentine reformers and took refuge with Hetman Jan Tarnowski, a devout but independent-minded Catholic, until King Zygmunt August removed him from the jurisdiction of clerical courts. Modrzewski returned to his hereditary estate, resigned from holy orders, surrendered his benefice, and married. He spent his remaining years in religious polemics. The Catholic activist Stanisław Orzechowski tried without success to trap Modrzewski into taking heretical stands, and Bishop Stanisław Karnkowski, when he became bishop of Kujawy, deprived Modrzewski of a lucrative secular office but had to pay compensation. Although some of Modrzewski's more radical social ideas brought him close to the Arians (Anabaptists), he maintained his loyalty to the Catholic Church. Modrzewski's *Republic* finally appeared in Polish translation in 1577 thanks to Calvinist and Arian publishers.

Stanisław Orzechowski (1513–66) was Modrzewski's unlikely opponent. Orzechowski was born near Przemyśl in Galicia into an Orthodox family from the petty nobility. He studied at the Jagiellonian University and later in Germany and Italy, showing interest in both Protestantism and humanist thought. Returning to Poland in 1541, he reluctantly entered the Roman Catholic priesthood at his father's insistence in order to receive a benefice, but he published a treatise in 1547 opposing clerical celibacy and then married, thereby earning excommunication; political pressure got the excommunication lifted. Although Orzechowski never succeeded in getting his marriage recognized, Church authorities did not pursue him strongly, because his speeches and writings made him a useful ally. Not only did Orzechowski attack Modrzewski and others whose views were not acceptable to the Church, but he enthusiastically joined the papacy in championing an anti-Turkish crusade in speeches that were published throughout Poland

and abroad. An attractive anecdotal account of recent Polish history, which included a description of his own situation, earned him widespread popularity. Orzechowski also published a biography of Hetman Jan Tarnowski, portraying him as an ideal independent noble and staunch Catholic. In fact, Tarnowski leaned toward Catholic reform by protecting dissidents like Orzechowski and Modrzewski.

In his last years, Orzechowski became a leading proponent of the nobility's freedoms and portrayed the Catholic Church as the protector of Polish liberties. His 1563 "Dialogue on the Execution of the Polish Crown" took the form of a one-sided discussion between a Catholic and a Lutheran. His 1564 and 1566 works, "*Quincunx,* or the Model of the Polish Crown" and "The System of the Polish Kingdom Based on Aristotelian Politics," presented his ideas for organizing a post-Tridentine Catholic state. Orzechowski accorded the king a key role in Polish government and relied on the Church to protect the freedoms of nobles, who would continue to lead a privileged existence, paying traditionally low taxes and providing military service only in emergencies. Unlike Modrzewski, Orzechowski showed no concern for the social and legal disadvantages of commoners. He propagated his views in unusually elegant Latin or a Polish prose style that showed strong Latin influence in phraseology and imagery.

SCIENCE IN THE AGE OF HUMANISM

Nicholas Copernicus's heliocentric astronomical theory provides another example of Polish humanism. Copernicus (Mikołaj Kopernik, 1473–1543) was born in Toruń, where his father had settled after growing up in Cracow. Copernicus's mother came from an influential Prussian family; her brother, Łukasz Watzenrode, supervised Nicholas's education after his father's death and assured his career. Nicholas studied at the Jagiellonian University and then completed a law degree at the University of Bologna in 1496 with financial support from his uncle and the Warmia Church authorities. He then studied medicine in Padua and earned a doctorate in canon law in 1503 at the University of Ferrara. Returning to Royal Prussia, Copernicus undertook important and time-consuming duties as treasurer and administrator of Church lands for the Warmia bishopric, published an innovative treatise on money, represented the bishop at the Prussian diet, built fortifications, and supervised wills. Copernicus also practiced medicine and oversaw public health during epidemics. Thus he was a rounded citizen of Poland-Lithuania. He spoke German, Polish, and Latin with equal fluency as well as Italian.

While definitive evidence is lacking that Copernicus studied the subject formally, his studies brought him to universities that offered sophisticated astronomical training and he maintained a serious interest throughout his life. He bought astronomy books in Cracow, assisted a noted professor in making observations in Italy, and continued to study when he returned home, all of which led him to offer suggestions to the Lateran Council of 1512–17 on the proposed Gregorian calendar. Between 1524, when Copernicus wrote a widely circulated letter criticizing current astronomical theory, and 1530, he finished his famous treatise *On the Revolutions of the Celestial Spheres,* which proposed the heliocentric theory. This work stemmed from Copernicus's studies of Greek philosophy and astronomy more than from observing the sky. The work became widely known among astronomers before the first printed edition appeared in Nüremberg in 1543, dedicated to Pope Pius III. The introduction described the work as a mathematical treatise. When Copernicus died, he probably had not seen his work in print.

THE SPREAD OF PRINTING AND POLISH-LANGUAGE LITERATURE

The availability of printing contributed to the spread of literature and the development of vernacular languages, and it established Polish as a viable language for belles-lettres, scholarship, law, and other branches of expression. State documents such as laws and decrees appeared in Polish by the mid-sixteenth century. Despite growing use of the vernacular, Latin remained popular among educated Polish-Lithuanians and retained its vitality well into the eighteenth century.

Johannes Gutenberg printed his Bible in Germany in 1455, and a Bavarian, Kaspar Straub, set up a print shop in Cracow to prepare Latin texts for the Bernadine fathers in 1474. The first known Polish-language text appeared in print in Wrocław in 1475. In 1479 a transplanted German embroiderer and mining investor, Szwajpolt Fioł, established a printing business in Poland that lasted twelve years, but Jan Haller, a German who moved to Cracow at a young age, published more books. Among other works, he put out Chancellor Jan Łaski's compilation of Polish statutes. Itinerant Polish printers working abroad included Jan Polonus in Naples (1478), probably the same person as Jan Lettou (John of Lithuania) who worked in England a few years later. Stanislaus Polonus set up a print shop in Seville in 1491.

Movable type accelerated the process of standardizing Polish orthography that had begun when the first handwritten treatise on the Polish language appeared about 1440. Others followed in rapid succession throughout the sixteenth century. A unidirectional Latin-to-Polish dictionary appeared in 1564 together with a treatise on Slavic languages, which has not survived. A Swiss Frenchman known as Peter Statorius, who studied with Calvin and moved to Poland in 1549 as a religious reformer and teacher, published the first Polish grammar in 1568. Scholars and printers frequently argued subtleties of correct usage; the problem of foreign loan words was particularly acute. The Polish that took form was based on the Great Poland dialect somewhat modified by Little Poland usage and included the characteristic "sh" and "ch" sounds of modern Polish along with the distinctive Polish nasal vowels, "ę" and "ą." Printers tended to simplify grammar, eliminating the special plural for the number two, for example. The number of words tripled, in part due to the introduction of loan words from Italian, German, and other languages, many of which stayed in use (such as *kalafior*, cauliflower) and some of which disappeared (such as *dziardyń*, garden). Polish replaced Latin on some state occasions. The bishop of Cracow, Jan Konarski, welcomed Zygmunt I's queen to Cracow in 1512 in Polish, and his successor as bishop, Samuel Maciejowski, delivered a Polish-language funeral oration on the king's death in 1548.

As elsewhere in Europe, religious subjects contributed to the interest in printing, as Catholics and Protestants rushed to publish their polemics and positions. Lutheran Königsberg in Ducal Prussia provided refuge for Poles such as Jan Seklucjan, from Poznań, whose writings and publications on religion drew such sharp criticism from Church authorities in the 1540s that he feared arrest. The Lithuanian magnate Black Mikołaj Radziwiłł turned Calvinist in the 1550s and established a Protestant print shop. Other nobles set up their own print shops, particularly in Little Poland.

Both Protestants and Catholics translated the Bible into Polish. Catholic translations of the Psalms appeared in the 1520s and 1530s, and even Cardinal Stanisław Hozjusz, an opponent of translating the Bible into Polish, permitted his own writings to appear in translation. Hozjusz objected to using Polish in part because of a humanist predilection for Latin; he voiced no objection to having the Bible translated into Old Church Slavonic for those who did not know Latin. A Polish Lutheran translation of the New Testament from the original Greek appeared in Königsberg in 1551–52 along with other biblical texts. A Catholic translation, prepared from the Latin Vulgate, appeared in Cracow in 1561. The Calvinist Brześć (or Radziwiłł) Bible appeared in 1563 prepared by Jan Łaski the younger, Peter Statorius, and others, and was particularly successful from the literary point of view. The Polish Brethren (Arians) published their more literal and less poetic translation in 1570–72, primarily prepared by Szymon Budny. Jesuit Father Piotr Skarga first published his *Lives of the Saints* in 1579, and Father Jakub Wujek retranslated the Vulgate into Polish. The exceptional poetry of Wujek's Bible, which came out in print in stages between 1593 and 1599, was restrained in places by a Jesuit commission that insisted on a greater literal accuracy.

Both Catholics and Protestants studied Hebrew to understand and translate the Bible better. Bishop Piotr Tomicki introduced Hebrew as a teaching subject in the Jagiellonian University in 1528, and the Jesuits, ignoring fears that studying Hebrew would lead to Protestant influence, stressed its importance. Both Jakub Wujek, the Catholic Bible translator, and Szymon Budny, the Anabaptist Bible translator, were accomplished Hebraists. After Greek, and of course Latin, knowledge of Hebrew marked a well-educated sixteenth-century Pole and Lithuanian. Converted Jews taught Hebrew to Christian students who showed little interest in modern Jews. One author of a Hebrew-language poem, a noble named Stanisław Niegoszewski, had been arrested as a student in Cracow for participating in anti-Jewish rioting.

Along with religious literature, secular literature—especially poetry—achieved a maturity in the sixteenth century that determined the shape of subsequent literature. Polish had emerged as a literary language in the fifteenth century. Anonymous poems on table manners and satires accusing peasants of laziness have survived, as have some bawdy student ditties. The sixteenth-century poets Jan Kochanowski and Mikołaj Rej developed the language much further with works that set the standard for other Polish authors. In the absence of copyright, poets freely imitated their styles and even appropriated phrases from their poems. The genres in which they wrote became standard.

The works of Mikołaj Rej (1505–69), the earlier of the two poets, made a major contribution to establishing Polish as a literary language. Born near Halich (Galicia) into a Catholic noble family, Rej went to school in Lviv and Cracow, but his withdrawal at age thirteen left gaps in his education, particularly an imperfect knowledge of Latin, which he read comfortably but wrote with difficulty. Rej worked for a rich noble in his district until his father died and he then took over the family estate. Achieving local prominence, Rej gained election to parliament several times and received numerous royal and clerical leaseholds from the king. He mostly lived on his country estates, but he also bought a house in Cracow, where he received the royal court in 1545 and entertained them with a performance by his village orchestra. Rej turned Protestant after Zygmunt I died in 1548. After 1560, he closed the Catholic churches on his estates and replaced them with Calvinist meeting houses.

Unlike other poets of the Polish Renaissance, Rej wrote exclusively in Polish. He introduced folk expressions, village words, and Slavonic diction into poetic use, rather than using Latinate phrases, and many of his occasional verses were earthy or bawdy. He was best known in his time for his political and philosophical works. Rej's versified *Short Conversation between a Noble, a Bailiff, and a Village Priest* (1543) articulated his Executionist desire for a stronger national government with less magnate influence. He began to examine religious issues as he grew older, and criticized the Catholic Church for excesses before he left it. Rej translated the Psalms into Polish and wrote a poetic drama, *The Life of Joseph,* in 1545. In 1549 he published another verse play, *The Merchant,* which portrayed a heavenly court in which God passed judgment on sinful humanity, using familiar contemporary court procedures. The conclusion, that the true faith of the merchant eventually saved mankind, took a Protestant approach to religion. Rej's poetic observations in *Postilla* (1557) were in the form of freshly translated Gospel readings and commentaries for general consumption. The book was very popular and went through many editions.

Rej's poetry provided an eloquent endorsement of village life that helped establish the rural myth as an important part of Polish identity. In 1558 he published *A Faithful Image of an Honest Man,* in which a young noble sought wisdom from reading the works of Aristotle, Epicurus, and other ancient philosophers, but found true happiness by settling down on his country estate to raise a family. *The Mirror,* published shortly before his death, summed up Rej's thinking. The most important part is the "Life of an Honest Man," in which he preached a life of moderate and moral worldly enjoyment, along with alertness to philosophical issues. Rej took little interest in social questions, and his religious views were moderate and tolerant.

The foremost poet of the Polish Renaissance, Jan Kochanowski (1530–84), was born near Radom to a middle-stratum noble family that owned five villages and enjoyed good political connections. At fourteen he studied at the Cracow Academy and later went on to Königsberg and Padua, giving him the opportunity for more extensive travel in Europe. Returning to Poland, he considered a military career but accepted appointment as royal secretary under Vice-Chancellor Piotr Myszkowski, bishop of Płock, later Cracow. Kochanowski favored Church reform but remained Catholic and took lower orders so that he could receive clerical benefices; however, he resigned in 1574 to marry and raise a family. Although his early poetry was in Latin and based on classical models, Kochanowski switched to Polish around 1560. His first such literary works voiced political opinions. *Harmony* (1564) called for unity and a peaceful approach to pressing religious and constitutional issues. *The Satyr* (1564) criticized economic development through the words of a satyr who emerges from the woods to complain that Poles had cleared too many forests in order to cultivate grain and buy unnecessary foreign luxuries. Another poem urged nobles to keep their children in Poland-Lithuania instead of sending them to study abroad. *The Banner, or Prussian Homage* (1569) celebrated Poland's status as a great power even while Kochanowski bemoaned the nobility's loss of martial spirit. His efforts at writing epic poetry achieved greatest success in recounting the unhappy history of young Count Jan Tęczyński, who fell in love with a Swedish princess during a diplomatic mission. Upon returning to Sweden to marry, Tęczyński's ship was stopped by the Danish navy and he died in captivity. However, Kochanowski abandoned the epic form after his translation of

Homer failed to suit him and after writing an unsatisfactory heroicomic epic describing a chess game.

As he grew older, Kochanowski spent more time at his estate, Czarnolas (Black Forest). He rarely appeared at court in the 1570s, for both personal and political reasons. He backed the unsuccessful Habsburg candidacy for the royal throne in 1573, but he later offered enthusiastic support for Stefan Batory. Chancellor Jan Zamoyski commissioned Kochanowski to write a play for his wedding, which took place in 1578 near Warsaw with Batory in attendance. Although the audience interpreted *The Dismissal of the Greek Envoys,* set at the Trojan court before the outbreak of war, as showing support for Batory's planned war with Russia, the play really expressed pacifist views as well as doubts that wise statesmen could ever prevent war. Kochanowski's presentation of Trojan politics was modeled after Polish realities and he seemed to support Batory's and Zamoyski's appeal for strong, centralized leadership. The play has been regarded as a classic because of its beautiful use of the Polish language, its clear formulation according to the principles of Renaissance drama, and its message.

Kochanowski's translation and adaptation of the Psalms (1579), on which he worked for many years, is another classic. He primarily consulted the Latin Vulgate in preparing his Polish version, although he referred to other Latin versions and recent Polish translations as well. With nondogmatic Christian humanism, Kochanowski negotiated between Catholic and Protestant interpretations to emerge with a version acceptable to both. The language is exquisite. Kochanowski's *Laments* (1580) yielded his most philosophical work. While expressing the author's personal grief over the death of his thirty-month-old daughter, Urszula, the laments were rigorously constructed according to classical canons to express prescribed emotions of sorrow leading to moral conclusions. In the cycle of nineteen poems, Kochanowski came to terms with his daughter's loss through a mixture of stoic acceptance and belief in a Christian afterlife.

A popular form of writing in both Polish and Latin was the tract that advised rulers and nobles how to behave. Mikołaj Rej's *Mirror* and *Honest Man* addressed noble life; Jakub Górski translated several Italian, German, and Latin works; and both Stanisław Orzechowski and Kallimach wrote works in this genre. Wawrzyniec Goślicki's book *On the Perfect Senator,* which appeared in Latin in Venice in 1568, was translated into English in Elizabethan England although its publication was twice banned; Shakespeare might have had Goślicki in mind when he named Polonius. The most important work in this genre was written by Łukasz Górnicki (1527–1603), who came from a burgher family in Oświęcim. His uncle, a poet who served as royal secretary and royal librarian in Vilnius, helped launch his career. Young Górnicki studied in Italy, returned to Poland as a royal secretary, supervised the royal libraries in Vilnius and Tykocin, and, after taking religious orders, received several benefices. *The Polish Courtier,* a translation and adaptation of Baldassare Castiglione's famous work *The Courtier,* told its readers how to be perfect Renaissance gentlemen. Published in 1566, *The Polish Courtier* presented lengthy fictional discussions by cultured members of society in 1549. Górnicki followed Castiglione in preaching the virtues of elegance, charm, and personal culture, giving Polish examples. He placed a high priority on good use of the Polish language. While recognizing that Polish needed to develop to meet new needs, he warned against overuse of foreign expressions. After ennoblement in 1561, Górnicki endorsed nobility as a positive value, but he did not see it as exclusive to the titled nobility; commoners could achieve true nobility of culture and character with hard work. Afterward, Górnicki settled down to supervise the royal lands in Tykocin and wrote histories and political discussions, most of which appeared in print only after his death.

A wide selection of popular works circulated among a growing readership. These works included religious and historical or pseudo-historical romances, comic and satirical tales, and plays on religious or secular themes. Many were translated or adapted from German originals.

Printing in Other Languages

Printing appeared as early in other languages of the Polish-Lithuanian state as it did in Polish but rarely was accompanied by the development of belles-lettres. The printed Lithuanian language developed in the sixteenth century. Martynas Mažvydas (d. 1563) published the first Lithuanian-language book in 1547, a Lutheran catechism, and later a two-volume Lithuanian hymnal. He grew up in Lithuania, moved to Ducal Prussia to avoid religious persecution, and undertook further studies in Königsberg. Lithuanian-language Calvinist prayer books and tracts appeared in Lithuania in the 1590s. Jesuits and other Catholics also carried their message to congregants in Lithuanian. The bishop of Samogitia, Melchior Giedrojć (Merkelis Giedraitis), emphasized Lithuanian identity strongly in education and publishing. Mateusz Stryjkowski wrote a patriotic history of Lithuania in Polish, based on Lithuanian, Ruthenian, and Polish chronicles. Following the fashion of the day, he traced Lithuanian origins back to ancient Rome. Mikolajus Daukša (c. 1527–1613) argued that language was more important to a nation than land or cities, and complained that the Lithuanian nobles had given up Lithuanian for Polish. He translated Rej's *Postilla* and *Catechism* into Lithuanian.

The first Cyrillic books were printed in Cracow in 1491. Szwajpolt Fioł, an established Cracow printer, produced Orthodox liturgical books for export to

Russia until Church censors accused him of heresy and closed his business. Powerful protection and Fioł's pious Catholicism earned him quick release from prison, but he decided to move to Silesia and go into mining. Short-lived Cyrillic print shops opened in Vilnius in 1525 and Zabłudów, on the estate of Prince Grigorii Khodkevich (Grzegorz Chodkiewicz), where religious works were published. Ivan Fedorovych established Cyrillic printing firmly in Lviv in 1573. Hieronim Wietor printed Hungarian books in Cracow.

Jews also adopted printing right after its invention, and Polish Jews, who imported Hebrew-language books from Italy and Germany, opened their own print shop in Cracow in 1534. Curiously, two of the first three Jewish printers converted to Christianity and carried on missionary work among the Jews; one printed the New Testament in Hebrew characters. The Moravian-born and Italian-trained printer Isaac ben Aaron Prostitz established a Hebrew print shop in Cracow that produced most of the important works by Polish rabbis over six decades. He received a royal monopoly to print the Talmud in 1568. Other Hebrew printers set up shop in Cracow and Lublin, but competition from imports gradually drove them out of business in the seventeenth century.

The spread of printing contributed to the development of the low German Yiddish language that generations of Jewish immigrants had brought to Poland-Lithuania. Jews used Yiddish throughout the Commonwealth, and the boundary between the eastern and western dialects of Yiddish developed along the pre-1569 Polish-Lithuanian border. Religious subjects predominated in Yiddish-language literature. The first books appeared in Cracow in 1535 and provided religious instruction for women, who were presumed not to know Hebrew, as well as a Hebrew-Yiddish Bible concordance. Three more collections of instructions for women appeared in Cracow in the second half of the sixteenth century. Religious aids were also designed to help less educated men understand Hebrew prayers. Isaac Sulkes published a commentary on the Song of Songs in Cracow in 1579. Some Yiddish-language publications popularized simple prayers and songs for home use without the elaborate biblical references that characterized Hebrew prayer books. Other Yiddish books were printed in Lublin, Prague, Basel, and several Italian cities.

Secular literature appeared with the publication of Italian romances, mostly knights' tales, in Yiddish translations and adaptations that eliminated or modified Christian references. *Bova d'Antona* (1543) echoed an Italian adaptation of an English romance (*Sir Bewis of Southampton*) concerning a heroic queen who fled to escape her mother's attempts to kill her; the story remained in Yiddish literature for centuries and was last published in Buenos Aires in 1970. The Yiddish adaptation of *Paris e Vienna* (the names of two lovers) greatly reduced the story's Christian elements while leaving Christian clerics as characters in the story. Translated elsewhere, both works circulated in Poland. At least half a dozen romances achieved popularity in Yiddish.

EDUCATION

Increased literacy rates contributed to the emergence of literature in the fifteenth century. Polish nobles sent their children to schools in larger numbers instead of educating them at magnate courts, and the university in Cracow prepared more school teachers to meet the demand. Study abroad remained popular as well. In accordance with a decree of the 1456 Gniezno synod, parish schools in cities and villages more than doubled their number. Burghers made up the majority of students at the Jagiellonian University in the sixteenth century despite a 1496 law restricting high Church offices to nobles. The university itself was more enlarged than reformed and drew almost half its students from abroad. Mathematics and astronomy were added under the direction of Marcin Król (Marcin z Żurawicy), who had studied in Italy. At the Jagiellonian University he challenged many medieval authorities, introduced the study of trigonometry, and worked on the calendar. His student Wojciech z Brudzewa attracted foreign students. Despite the presence of humanists, theological and historical scholarship remained scholastic in orientation.

Jan Lubrański (d. 1520), bishop of Poznań, founded the Poznań Academy in 1519 to provide a modern, humanistic curriculum. Its five-year program of studies concentrated on classical Latin grammar and literature. Geography, modern history, and law were also studied. Lubrański's humanistic and tolerant attitude prevailed despite such setbacks as the inclusion of theology in the curriculum under pressure from the Church hierarchy and the resignation in 1535 of Christopher Hegendorfer, a German-born professor of Greek and Latin, who was accused of Lutheran sympathies by the bishop and threatened by an angry Catholic mob.

Jewish education remained immune to secular trends in the sixteenth century, the Golden Age of Rabbis, although some utilized secular studies such as astronomy and philosophy to shed light on religious problems. By 1500 the growing wealth and maturity of the Polish Jewish community permitted the establishment of community schools devoted to the study of Hebrew language and sacred literature in the rationalistic rabbinical tradition. Education was widespread as richer communities paid for the education of poor boys. Jacob Pollak established the first Polish yeshiva (higher school) in Cracow around 1510 after he resigned as chief rabbi due to disputes within the Jewish community. An intellectual exercise for his students developed into the *Pilpul* (pepper) method of Talmudic analysis that remained popular in Poland-Lithuania until modern times; this method depended on exploiting seemingly minor textual inconsistencies to uncover hidden meanings. A successor in Pollak's rabbinical line, Moses Isserles, planned to codify Jewish religious law and practice for everyday use, but had to settle for preparing a commentary on Joseph Caro's famous codification, the *Shulhan Arukh,* which appeared in Venice in 1565, before Isserles finished. Isserles and other important rabbis such as Salomon Luria and Mordechai Jaffe rejected many of Caro's Sephardic recommendations or modified them for Polish use. As other rabbis founded new yeshivas, the educational level of the clergy and the laity grew rapidly. Polish-Lithuanian rabbis corresponded extensively with their colleagues in other parts of Europe and traveled widely.

A mystical stream of Polish-Lithuanian Jewish thought developed alongside the dominant rational mainstream. Contact with Italy spread knowledge of the mystical book *Zohar,* and the mystical field of study Cabbala, throughout Poland-Lithuania in the sixteenth and seventeenth centuries. Some rabbis traveled to the center in Safed, Palestine (Israel), to study.

Renaissance Music

Poland shared the wealth of mainstream musical European culture. Polish composers followed prevailing Italian and Netherlands styles with some distinct accents such as the use of folk elements and quotations from earlier composers. Composers set Polish-language texts for songs celebrating kings and battles or marking religious festivals. The best musician at the Polish court was Heinrich Finck (c. 1444–1527), who was born in Bamberg and came to Cracow as a youth to sing in the Royal Chapel. After studying in Germany, Finck returned to Cracow as court musician and followed several Jagiellonians to their capitals, most notably Grand Duke (and King) Aleksander to Vilnius in the early 1500s, where he became so well known that Emperor Maximilian lured him away to Vienna in 1510 to become his court composer. Little has survived from Finck's Polish-Lithuanian period, but he wrote in the predominant style of complicated three-part polyphony with difficult vocal ornamentation. By 1510, Finck had begun to adapt the simpler and more euphonious innovations of the Netherlands school.

Mikołaj of Radom (dates unknown) composed Italian-style three-part sacred motets for the Royal Chapel in the early fifteenth century. Sebastian of Felsztyn (c. 1485–1543), a priest who studied theology at the Jagiellonian University, became one of the first Polish composers to write four-part sacred motets in the Netherlands style; he wrote primarily for his church in Sanok, but the Royal Chapel in Cracow also performed his music. Sebastian also wrote treatises on the ethical and therapeutic nature of music based on Plato and Boethius, and on music notation. Other Cracow music professors wrote theoretical works that attracted foreign students such as Heinrich Finck. Marcin Leopolita (d. 1589) came from Lviv to study in Cracow and remained there as a court composer for Zygmunt August. He is best known for his Easter Mass based on Polish hymns, but he also wrote five-part motets that survive only in organ transcription. Another priest educated in Cracow, Tomasz Szadek (d. 1612), sang in the Royal Chapel choir while serving as a curate in the Cathedral. He wrote compositions for male choir in the Netherlands style, based on a plainsong *cantus* drawn from Polish or foreign sources. Wacław of Szamotuły (c. 1524–c. 1560) studied in Poznań and Cracow. He started his career in Cracow as court poet and composer of a cappella polyphony in the late Netherlands style. Turning Protestant around 1550, Wacław moved to Brześć as court composer for the Calvinist magnate Mikołaj Radziwiłł. Much of Polish music was written for the Rorantist Choir in Cracow, which was founded in 1543 after the style of the Sistine Chapel choir in Rome. This eight-voice male choir remained active until the First Partition in 1772, performing music by Polish and foreign composers.

The most important Polish Renaissance composer was Mikołaj Gomółka (c. 1535–c. 1595), who was also a performer and a successful lawyer. After studying and performing at the royal court in Cracow as chorister and wind player, Gomółka moved to Sandomierz to became a town councillor and president of the municipal court. Returning to Cracow as a musician, Gomółka worked for Bishop Piotr Myszkowski and Chancellor Jan Zamoyski, among other nobles. Gomółka's only known work is a masterpiece (suggesting that other works have been lost). The "Melodies for a Polish Psalter" (1580) set Kochanowski's psalms to four-part choir music as simple hymns in homophonic style that could be sung at home by both Catholics and Protestants. The psalms were presented in the Hebrew (Protestant) sequence rather than the traditional Catholic sequence, and the use of popular dance rhythms made the works particularly appealing. Gomółka matched musical sounds to the mood of the words and utilized adventurous harmonies. The publication of this work was the first substantial music publication using Polish.

Cracow was a center for instrument making. Craftsmen supplied the growing local market and even exported lutes, viols, and wind instruments.

Architecture and Urban Design

Renaissance elements penetrated more slowly into the visual arts than into music. The dominant style in the late fifteenth and early sixteenth centuries remained Gothic, expressed in brick construction in the north and stone construction in the south. Following international trends, Polish architecture and urban design developed more regular streets and city squares. Court architecture introduced Renaissance elements while leaving the basic Gothic structures intact. The result melded the Late Gothic of northern Europe with new elements of Italian origin, reflecting the breadth of Jagiellonian contacts. Architecture in particular demanded compromises between self-conscious artists and traditional guild artisans, who came from several nationalities and backgrounds.

Italian elements filtered through Hungarian intermediaries at first; King Zygmunt I had lived in Buda and imported artists from there. For example, Slovak stonecutters came to Cracow when the Hungarian court reduced its building program and introduced Hungarian variants of Renaissance ornamentation. Italian craftsmen came from northern Italy and Italian Switzerland, areas that lagged somewhat behind the latest developments in Florence and Rome. Italian artists who started up workshops in Polish-Lithuanian cities had to cooperate with the German artists and craftsmen who dominated the artistic and building trades and adapt their ideas to guild traditions. The Chamber of Deputies that met in Cracow's Royal Castle (Wawel) provides an example of stylistic synthesis. A famous collection of thirty carved heads (there were probably more originally) installed in squares on the ceiling of the parliamentary chamber evoked the Renaissance style emphasizing the individuality of each portrayal. The philosophical meaning of the total composition by an anonymous Wrocław artist of the 1530s has been lost, but it seems to have more in common with late Gothic commentary on society and cosmography than with Renaissance messages.

Wawel, the Royal Castle in Cracow, underwent reconstruction and redesign after a major fire in 1499. In 1507–17, Francesco of Florence improved access to apartments by adding an Italianate three-story arcade looking into the courtyard. Similarly, local guild craftsmen such as Benedykt from Sandomierz redecorated damaged rooms in late Gothic style by adding Renaissance highlights including painted friezes, polychromatic doorways, and multicolored ovens to heat the rooms. After Francesco's death in 1516, King Zygmunt's new chief architect, Bartolomeo Berecci, constructed a Renaissance chapel and mausoleum next to the palace. The so-called Zygmunt Chapel used a square form covered with a Renaissance dome. Grave statuary in brown and white marble displayed symbols drawn from contemporary Christianity, neo-Platonism, and antiquity. Berecci created similar chapels for several dignitaries such as Bishop Tomicki. The Renaissance practice of installing sarcophagi with sculpted portraits was incorporated in all major churches throughout the realm. Santa Gucci added tombs for Zygmunt August and his sister Anna. A Gothic chapel was redone as a tomb for King Stefan Batory.

New construction adopted a more complete Renaissance approach, mostly after 1550. The destructive fire of 1555 forced the Cracow Cloth Guild to rebuild its Gothic hall (Sukiennice) in the vast market square. The designers were more concerned with technical improvements to its use than with aesthetics, but they took advantage of the opportunity to construct a pseudo-arcade with columns and install a manneristic roof facade adorned with gargoyles that set a widely imitated style; an eclectic 1870s reconstruction produced the Guild Hall that tourists see today. The Cracow Guild Hall provided the model for the Poznań City Hall, built by Giovanni Battista Quadro, with three levels of arcades, a large central tower, and several smaller turrets. As in Tarnów and Sandomierz, Renaissance features lightened the monumental construction that city councils deemed necessary to defend against riots. Many buildings featured an elaborate roof-level facade of carvings and crenellations that hid the roof itself.

The construction of an entirely new city, Zamość, by Chancellor Jan Zamoyski in the 1590s contributed the only full example of Renaissance city planning with squares and perspectives. The architect, Bernardo Morando of Padua, put Zamoyski's castle on one side of the city and the commercial burgher buildings on the other, with an intermediary public space consisting of the town square, cathedral, and academy. The magnificent late Renaissance church in the Mannerist style is the only building to survive in its original form; others were modified over time. Burgher apartment blocks are harmonious and probably originate in an assigned model. Modern walls and fortifications surrounded the city. The actual construction, however, included Mannerist elements of the late Renaissance and moved away from strict classicism.

Polish vernacular architecture appeared around 1600 as provincial builders imitated classical and Mannerist styles with their own distinct flair and errors. Poor space composition and overelaborate ornamentation characterized local work, which paradoxically rose on occasion to a new art form. The best example is Kazimierz Dolny (Lower Kazimierz), a market city on the Vistula River about halfway between Warsaw and Cracow, which boasts a town square of remarkable appeal. The Przybyła brothers' residence offers an arcaded sidewalk, irregularly placed windows, oversized parapets with immense crestings, and extensive bas-relief sculpture mixing Christian symbols, saints' images, Italian candelabras, and grotesque faces, all dominated by a giant St. Christopher who carries a small child on his shoulder.

Wooden churches are another distinctive feature of Polish-Lithuanian architecture. They spread from Silesia across Poland to the Grand Duchy of Lithuania in the fifteenth century, and generally imitated stone Gothic styling in overall form and in details around the doors and windows. They were built by guild carpenters.

Sculpture and Painting

The exceptional wood sculpture of Wit Stwosz (Veit Stoss) provided another link between Gothic and Renaissance styles. Born in Germany, Stwosz studied wood sculpture with Nicholas of Leiden and came to Cracow in 1477 at the invitation of the Cracow city council. His greatest accomplishment was the three-part altarpiece for St. Mary's Cathedral that presents a panorama of biblical scenes from the lives of the Virgin Mary and Christ, with many details drawn from late fifteen-century Cracow life. Numerous individualized portraits suggest an early Renaissance style, as does the free-flowing elegance of the robes. Stwosz worked in other media as well. He carved a stone crucifix for the cathedral that betrayed precise anatomic knowledge typical of Renaissance artists, as might be expected since Stwosz associated with humanist circles in Cracow. Stwosz designed the grave of King Kazimierz IV, which commented on death with unusual frankness, and cast a bronze bas-relief wall plaque for Kallimach. Stwosz's successors were competent, but lacked his genius. He was only one of many German artists who worked in Cracow.

The leading stone sculptor of late sixteenth-century Poland-Lithuania was Giovanni Maria il Mosca, known as Padovano, who came from Padua around 1530. He was known in Italy for his elegant jewelry, but he undertook major sculptural projects in Poland such as the tombs of Queen Elisabeth (Zygmunt August's first wife) in Vilnius, Bishop Piotr Gamrat in Cracow, and the Tarnowski brothers in Tarnów. Padovano's greatest work is the ciborium in St. Mary's Cathedral in Cracow. In this vaulted altar canopy, he introduced a Venetian classicism linking monumentalism with small, detailed figures. Hieronim Canavesi from Milan, who worked with Padovano before launching out on his own, was also known for his tombs. Canavesi's growing use of emotional exaggeration brought criticism from some patrons for sloppy workmanship and inaccurate anatomy.

Painting lacked widespread popularity in sixteenth-century Poland-Lithuania, although fourteenth- and fifteenth-century churches included elaborate iconography on the walls and ceilings. While most churches had plaster walls, some wooden churches were also painted well into the sixteenth century. Władysław II Jagiełło brought artists from the Grand Duchy of Lithuania who introduced Russo-Byzantine elements in Cracow, Gniezno, and especially Lublin. Noteworthy was the important Icon of the Madonna (Matka Boska Częstochowska), an Italian painting housed in the Jasna Góra monastery in Częstochowa that acquired Orthodox characteristics when restored by Russian and German artists around 1400. There were many other religious paintings on wooden panels, mostly altarpieces, a style that spread to Poland from Bohemia in the fourteenth century and remained popular in southern Poland for two hundred years. Churches in northern Poland (Prussia and Great Poland) adopted Netherlands styles in the late fifteenth century as contact grew through the international grain trade. The most famous single work was a Last Judgment painted by Hans Memling for the altar of St. Mary's Cathedral in Gdańsk, with its finely drawn portraits, dramatic scenes from the Bible, and romantic landscapes. Secular subjects were occasionally portrayed, and Gdańsk wall paintings of the early fifteenth century incorporated individualizing elements foreshadowing Renaissance techniques.

The tapestries portraying Old Testament stories ordered by King Zygmunt August from Michael Coxcie of Flanders displayed Italian influence, particularly of the Raphael school. Gdańsk artwork made some impact, particularly the tomb of Zygmunt August, which was ordered from that city. Artistic metalwork was well developed in altarpieces, candlesticks, and other symbols.

CHAPTER 7

First Interlude: Henri Valois and Stefan Batory

The extinction of the Jagiellonian dynasty represented another step in the long process of reducing royal power that began when the Piast dynasty died out in 1370. The Jagiellonian monarchs shared power with representatives in a developing parliament, but their traditional authority, prestige, and longevity allowed them to retain a dominant position in political disputes. The Jagiellonians' successors lacked these advantages. Polish-Lithuanian nobles viewed them with suspicion as newcomers and foreigners, and insisted on their own rights as nobility. Much of this suspicion was generated during the short and unhappy reign of Henri Valois. While far more successful, Stefan Batory made no lasting impact on political structures because he reigned for only ten years and left no heir to seek election to the Polish-Lithuanian throne.

HENRI VALOIS AND THE ROYAL ELECTION OF 1573

Zygmunt August's death in 1572 concluded the reign of the Jagiellonian dynasty that united Poland and Lithuania in 1386. The principle of elective monarchy had been established after the death of Kazimierz the Great in 1370 and continued through the Jagiellonian era, subject to the understanding that parliament would choose a Jagiellonian, normally the eldest son of the previous monarch. Thus prior to 1573, parliament had always elected the new king. The only attempt to designate an heir during his father's lifetime raised such a storm that the dynasty promised never to try again.

Three outstanding issues dominated the royal election of 1573. First, disputes over the form of the election helped determine its result. The conflict between the chamber of deputies and the senators continued, closely linked with the question of whether Poland-Lithuania would remain religiously tolerant. Lacking a king or regent, nobles banded together throughout the Commonwealth in regional confederations to form local governments, protect internal order, and prevent foreign invasion. Senators took the initiative in forming a national government. Magnates from Great Poland gathered at Łowicz, the estate of Primate Jakub Uchański, while Little Poland magnates gathered in Cracow under the direction of a Calvinist, Crown Great Marshal Jan Firlej. The two groups met at Knyszyn, Lithuania, where Zygmunt August lay in state. Deputies from the Executionist bloc proposed that the election be held in Lublin, near Protestant strongholds in Little Poland, Lithuania, and Ruthenia, with an enlarged parliament that they could dominate. They proposed that Marshal Firlej act as regent during the interregnum. However, bishops and secular senators got the archbishop of Gniezno approved as regent, and he ordered that the election be held near Warsaw with all nobles entitled to participate. Nobles from staunchly Catholic Mazovia attended the election in the village of Kamień on the east bank of the Vistula in substantial numbers, and Protestant nobles from more distant regions found it difficult to get there. The primate ran the election and crowned the new king.

Second, the religious issue was addressed. The Catholic victory on the form of the election was partly balanced by a Catholic promise to enact a law guaranteeing freedom of worship and political rights to all nobles. Catholics accepted the proposal in order to keep the peace and maintain their control over the election.

Third, the nation had to choose a foreign policy orientation, because rivalry between the Austrian Habsburgs and the French was spilling over into Poland-Lithuania. A Habsburg orientation meant helping the Austrians reconquer Hungary from the Ottoman Turks in the hope that Poland-Lithuania would make gains in Moldavia and push eastward along the Ukrainian Black Sea coast against the Tatars. However, this strategy would bring Poland into conflict with the very dangerous Turkish army, provoke Tatar depredations, and run the risk of initiating competition with Hungary for control of Moldavia. In contrast, a French orientation meant peace with Turkey so that Poland-Lithuania could concentrate on extending its Baltic and Muscovite frontiers. But alliance with France threatened to revive the Habsburg-Muscovite alliance that had bedeviled Zygmunt I, menacing Poland-Lithuania from the east and south. These issues remained current into the eighteenth century. In general, most senators were Catholics and favored a Habsburg orientation, while many deputies were Protestants and favored a French orientation.

Electing a King

Several European monarchs offered themselves as candidates to the Polish throne. Catholic arguments in favor of a Habsburg proved surprisingly unpopular even though agents distributed gifts liberally and Catholic clerics energetically supported Archduke Ernst, son of Emperor Ferdinand. The bishop of Płock, Piotr

Myszkowski, eloquently supported Archduke Maximilian, whom he described as knightly in character with an extensive knowledge of foreign languages. Myszkowski stressed that Maximilian was a cousin to the Jagiellonians through the double marriage of 1515. He promised that electing him would improve trade with the Habsburg lands of Silesia and Bohemia-Moravia. The wine tax would be abolished and Maximilian would pay for Polish students to study in Vienna. Nonetheless, Bishop Myszkowski's arguments were outweighed by the general desire for peace with Turkey and fears of Habsburg sponsorship of the Catholic Counter Reformation. The candidacy of Johan (John) III of Sweden, Zygmunt August's brother-in-law, attracted attention only briefly.

The French candidate, Henri Valois (1551–89), brother of King Charles IX of France, won the election. Jean Montluc, bishop of Valence, attractively presented Henri as a candidate who would guarantee the liberties of the average noble. Montluc also tried to clear him of the stain of the St. Bartholomew Massacre of Protestants in Paris on August 24, 1572, by claiming inaccurately that Henri bore little direct responsibility and that the Protestants were really rebels. The prospect of gaining French military and diplomatic support for Poland-Lithuania was attractive and French royalist traditions seemed less dangerous to the nobility than nearby Habsburg practices. Protestant nobles supported Henri despite the massacre but imposed constitutional conditions on him to prevent similar outrages in Poland-Lithuania, a condition that Montluc accepted without hesitation. Montluc reminded Polish-Lithuanian electors that Henri was wealthy and promised that the new king would marry the aging Anna the Jagiellonian, Zygmunt August's sister, to maintain the dynastic tradition. Montluc gained important support from Jan Zamoyski, who had risen to prominence under Zygmunt August. Zamoyski's interest in France stemmed mostly from foreign policy considerations, since he saw Austria as Poland-Lithuania's rival for control of the rich lands to the southeast. Having studied in France and Italy, he liked the atmosphere that he encountered at the French court and he approved the moderate anti-Protestantism that he had observed during his sojourn before the St. Bartholomew Massacre. Zamoyski was an effective speaker whose attacks on Habsburg absolutism gained Valois considerable support.

Thousands of Polish nobles attended the election that took place on an open field near Warsaw. Votes were taken by province amid demonstrations. As Henri's popularity grew and his supporters became more vocal, the declining opposition quit the field, agreeing to make the election unanimous only when offered a prominent role in setting the conditions for Henri's election. Primate Uchański nominated Henri formally and the nobles elected him on May 16, 1573.

Lithuanian nobles boycotted the proceedings to emphasize their independence but recognized Henri's election as a fait accompli. The Lithuanian ducal council confirmed the election, overcoming a few voices in favor of abandoning union with Poland. Previously, magnates had generally favored Archduke Ernst's election provided that he marry Anna, return the Ukrainian provinces to Lithuania, and guarantee a monopoly of officeholdings to Lithuanians. A few Lithuanians had planned to propose a Russian candidate to the throne who would guarantee Lithuania's autonomy and return conquered territories until Ivan IV the Terrible demanded the creation of a hereditary throne linked to Russia, coronation by the Orthodox Church, and the return of Kiev. Ivan proposed to elect his son Fedor to the joint Lithuanian-Russian throne.

A magnificent delegation headed by the experienced diplomat Adam Konarski, bishop of Poznań, went to Paris to negotiate the terms of acceptance with the king-elect. Reflecting the balance in the country, the delegation included nine Catholics and four Protestants, eight senators and five lesser nobles (all of whom eventually gained promotion to the senate). All were well educated and several had diplomatic experience. The quality of the delegation made a deep impression on a French observer who commented: "There was not a single one of them who did not speak Latin fluently and many expressed themselves in Italian and German; some spoke our language so accurately and beautifully that they seemed to come from the banks of the Seine rather than the Vistula or Dnieper."

The Polish delegation made a spectacular entrance to Paris in a procession of fifty carriages through the crowded streets. The Polish style of wearing long beards surprised Parisians, and their ermine-trimmed robes and bejeweled swords dazzled them. However, negotiations proved difficult, as the French court resisted Polish demands for religious toleration and constitutional limitations on royal power until news arrived from Poland that Habsburg supporters were gathering to take power. Polish negotiators bluntly told Henri that he would not rule without endorsing toleration, and he gave in.

On September 10, 1573, Henri took an oath in Notre Dame Cathedral to respect traditional Polish liberties and the law on religious freedom that had been passed during the interregnum. His brother Charles IX, the king of France, also took an oath to recognize Polish liberties and promised to offer toleration to the French Protestants. A ceremony took place before the Paris law court (*parlement*) on September 13 confirming the election. Polish representatives handed Henri a certificate of election to the throne of Poland-Lithuania.

THE POLISH-LITHUANIAN "CONSTITUTION"

The election of Henri Valois set clearly written terms establishing the main elements of the Polish constitution. Henri agreed to two documents, the Henrician articles and the *pacta conventa* (sworn articles). In them, the king recognized the principle of free election and abandoned all succession claims. He agreed to make war, conclude peace, or summon the military levy only with parliamentary agreement. He further promised to pay nobles if the levy went outside Poland-Lithuania's borders and raise professional army detachments at his own expense. Henri accepted the requirement to meet with elected senators-residents to discuss business between parliamentary sessions and summon parliament at least every second year. He acknowledged the nobility's right to disobey if the king violated laws and privileges. All Polish-Lithuanian kings until 1795 had to swear obedience to the Henrician articles before they were crowned as well as agree to specific articles tailored to the political exigencies of the day.

The Henrician articles included a pledge of religious toleration enacted by the Convocation Parliament, known as the Union of Warsaw, in January 1573. The bill was sponsored jointly by Calvinists, Lutherans, and Czech Brethren, who had sunk their differences in the Union of Sandomierz (1570), although they still refused to permit the Anti-Trinitarians to join. The primate of the Catholic Church and other leading bishops agreed to religious pluralism in order to forestall the wars that racked most of Europe. Freedom of religion was limited to nobles and other free persons while, in law, peasants and residents of private cities could be compelled by the feudal lords to accept their religion, although in practice they rarely were. The zealously Catholic Mazovians tried unsuccessfully to abolish the act by parliamentary means, but even they rejected extra-parliamentary moves by Counter Reformation bishops to abolish religious toleration by excommunicating its Catholic proponents. Almost alone in early modern Europe, Poland-Lithuania accepted religious pluralism until 1795 even if some kings evaded its spirit.

Henri as King of Poland-Lithuania

Henri left for Poland after many delays occasioned by his concern over his brother's ill-health; Henri was heir apparent to the French throne. He finally reached the Polish border in late January 1574 and came to Cracow in mid-February to be crowned. The twenty-four-year-old monarch made an unfavorable impression on the traditionalist Poles, who saw him as an overdressed fop, dripping with jewelry and using perfume. Rumors of homosexual relations with painted courtiers reached Poland as well. The young king spent his time with his French attendants eating, drinking, and playing cards—losing large sums drawn from the treasury. He paid little attention to state business and even less to the late king's fifty-year-old spinster sister, Anna, whom the French ambassador had previously flattered with thoughts of marriage to the handsome young king. For their part, the French courtiers complained of the cold winter trip, bad food, and long formal Polish feasts with tedious speechmaking in Latin, a language few of them understood.

Poles indulged in much politicking. Particularly active was the Church, which tried to reverse the newly minted guarantee of religious toleration. After unseemly public disputes at the royal coronation on February 21, 1574, a compromise formula retreated somewhat from the strong guarantees of Protestant rights that Henri had accepted in Paris. Arguments continued the next day when parliament opened and the king offended both sides of the debate by his indifferent and haughty attitude. Deep divisions revealed themselves in the decision to put off confirmation of the Henrician articles to a future session. Some deputies claimed that the king had violated the constitution, a failure that absolved them of their oath of allegiance. The parliament dissolved bitterly on April 2, 1574, without accomplishing anything beyond the formal coronation. There was no formal closing.

Henri Returns to France

In mid-June, when Henri received news from France that his brother Charles IX had died, he rushed home to claim the throne. Constitutionally, Henri probably should have called parliament into session to seek permission to go abroad, but instead he slipped out of Cracow in the middle of the night in disguise and set out with a few retainers. Poles who had been his guests at a magnificent feast the night before awoke to find their king was gone. Servants had seen him leave and Castellan Jan Tęczyński managed to catch him shortly after he crossed the border into Czech Silesia, but could extract only a promise to return in three or four months. Checking the royal apartments in Wawel Castle later, Poles found that Henri had taken all his jewels and gold. They also found a letter addressed to parliament justifying his absence and explaining that he intended to continue as king of Poland-Lithuania after he became king of France.

Henri's flight provoked a constitutional crisis that weakened royal authority and strengthened the nobility. Since it was not clear whether Henri was still king, the executive authority was paralyzed and dietines gathered as if there were an interregnum, to administer justice, taxation, and defense. The primate summoned parliament despite the dubious legality of his unauthorized action; Lithuania, Prussia, and several palatinates refused to take part. Parliament adopted a compromise resolution that neither endorsed Henri's kingship nor ended it, but notified him that he would lose the throne if he failed to return by May 12, 1575, and formed a confederation to govern the country. Lithuania and Prussia refused to join the confederation, citing their constitutionally separate status. Henri failed to return by the deadline given him, and sent only a single representative with promises to come in the future. Parliament declared the throne vacant, but serious disagreements prevented an immediate election. Meeting on a field outside Warsaw as for an election, senators continued to debate what they should do.

The mass of nobles, led by members of the chamber of deputies, moved to another field, where they called for new provincial dietine meetings to prepare for a new election. The senators objected on constitutional grounds.

KING STEFAN BATORY OF TRANSYLVANIA

A poorly attended parliamentary session in October 1575 set the royal election for November 7 at the village of Wola, well within twentieth-century Warsaw's city limits. Most senators, along with Lithuanian and Prussian delegates and the papal nuncio, supported the candidacy of Emperor Maximilian II Habsburg. Lesser nobles had enough of foreign candidates and demanded the election of a "Piast," or Polish candidate, to the throne. This allegedly Polish candidate became Stefan Batory (István Báthory), prince of Transylvania, who promised to recognize the Polish constitution and marry Anna the Jagiellonian. French and Turkish diplomats supported him in order to deny the throne to the Habsburgs. The actual election became chaotic. On one field near Warsaw, Maximilian was elected on December 12, 1575, while Anna was elected king three days later on another field together with her fiancé, Stefan Batory, as co-ruler. The double election unleashed a short, sharp war to determine who would sit on the Polish-Lithuanian throne.

Batory contrasted sharply with Valois. He came from a modest principality and could be expected to take Polish affairs seriously. He was a mature man and a proven warrior. Like Valois, however, he was a staunch anti-Habsburg, because as prince of Transylvania he claimed the Hungarian throne that the Habsburgs occupied. Batory publicly advocated peace with Turkey, which the Polish nobles fervently wished, but privately planned to reconquer the Hungarian lands.

Stefan Batory (1533–86) was the youngest of three sons of a powerful Transylvanian magnate, also named Stefan Batory. He became prince of Transylvania in 1571, when the Zápolya line died out. Transylvania was an independent principality in eastern Hungary (now western Romania) that bore considerable resemblance to the Polish-Lithuanian Commonwealth. Its population comprised three nations (Hungarians, magyarized Szeklers, and German burghers), and the state recognized four major religions (Roman Catholicism, Lutheranism, Calvinism, and anti-Trinitarianism). Peasants and shepherds practiced Orthodox Christianity without interference. As in Poland, the parliament enjoyed wide prerogatives while the prince directed internal administration, military affairs, and foreign policy; the principality suffered little interference from its nominal overlord, Ottoman Turkey. Batory put his experience to good use in Poland-Lithuania, applying the political and military techniques that he had developed at home.

Batory won election to the Polish-Lithuanian throne because he had demonstrated outstanding military capacities in 1571 by defeating a rival claimant to the Transylvanian throne who had Austrian troops under his banner. Leaving the government of Transylvania to his younger brother Christopher, who governed effectively, Batory quickly defeated the Habsburg challenge and secured the Polish-Lithuanian throne. He was crowned in Cracow on May 1, 1576. Maximilian of Habsburg died in November, but some diehards still refused to recognize Batory because he had promised in his *pacta conventa* to keep peace with Turkey and would not allow them to expand to the southeast.

Batory and Gdańsk

Batory subordinated Polish interests in Gdańsk and Prussia to his ambitious Russian plans and allowed this region to slip further from Poland's grasp. Hoping to force revision of the Karnkowski Statutes of 1570 that limited the city's autonomy, Gdańsk refused to recognize Batory's election and resisted him militarily. Batory reacted strongly. He besieged the city, blocking the flow of trade and redirecting it to neighboring Elblag. After Gdańsk put up stiff resistance with financial and military assistance from Denmark, Batory made a drastic mistake that cost Poland dearly. He weakened his authority over Gdańsk by abolishing the Karnkowski Statutes in exchange for a payment of 200,000 zlotys; Vice-Chancellor and Hetman Jan Zamoyski personally received 20,000 zlotys from Gdańsk for arranging the deal. Additional concessions in 1585 gave Gdańsk tax relief, the ability to close the port, and a promise that the Commonwealth would not build its own fleet. Furthermore, while preparing for war against Russia in 1577, Batory appointed Elector Georg Friedrich of Brandenburg as administrator for his cousin, the ailing Duke Albrecht Friedrich, in exchange for another 200,000 zlotys, fulfilling an earlier promise by Zygmunt August. Batory ignored the protests of the Prussian Estates, which actually offered to pay 100,000 zlotys annually in perpetuity to keep the Berlin Hohenzollerns out, as well as protests by the Polish-Lithuanian parliament. After Georg Friedrich helped Batory fight Russia, he received permission to change the ducal title from duke *in* Prussia to duke *of* Prussia, a change that implied succession rights. Batory ignored complaints from the Prussian Estates about Georg Friedrich's methods of collecting taxes and declined to support the head of the noble opposition, Frederick von Aulack, when he took refuge in Poland to avoid retaliation.

Batory was free to make war against Moscow, but he had paid a high price.

Batory and Jan Zamoyski

Stefan Batory built up a strong faction in parliament headed by Jan Zamoyski, who became a virtual co-ruler of the realm. A noble from a moderately wealthy family, Zamoyski (1542–1605) studied in Cracow and Padua, where his fellow students elected him rector. On his return to Poland, Zamoyski entered public service as royal secretary to Zygmunt August. His first important mission was to reclaim royal estates leased to Jan Starzechowski, palatine of Podolia, while his subsequent work on an archival commission gave him detailed knowledge of old laws, which he used to great advantage in parliamentary maneuvers. Zamoyski also discovered and utilized Jan Długosz's century-old forgotten monumental *History of Poland,* although he left it unpublished.

Zamoyski rose to prominence during Henri Valois's election by stressing the political rights of the lesser nobility. Batory gave Zamoyski a high position because of his efficiency, breadth of knowledge, and popularity, appointing him crown vice-chancellor in 1576, chancellor in 1578, and crown great hetman in 1581 with life tenure, a precedent that eventually led to lifetime tenure for all ministers and a serious diminution of royal power. Zamoyski accumulated ministries and estates until he became the richest and most powerful man in the Commonwealth after the king. Despite his pro-French orientation, Zamoyski recommended that Batory cultivate his pro-Habsburg opponents with patronage appointments even though this course alienated Batory's electoral supporters, especially the Zborowski family. In office, Zamoyski reformed the chancellery and ended major fraud (although he enriched himself with gratuities) and replaced enough personnel to make the secretariat loyal to himself. He was a particularly good propagandist whose "flying press" operated while he traveled with the army, printing state documents, descriptions of battles, and belles-lettres. However, Zamoyski sometimes neglected small, but important, business matters, such as the appointment of translators, the use of secret codes in diplomatic mail, and the regulation of salt mining. Political success permitted him to marry into the powerful Radziwiłł family in 1577, and, after his first wife died, he married Batory's niece Gryzelda in 1583.

Zamoyski became very rich from royal favor. He drew income from leaseholds on royal estates and used the money to purchase his own estates in the developing southeast, where he built the private city of Zamość with an official incorporation privilege granted by parliament in 1580 and confirmed by King Stefan in 1583. Zamoyski granted the inhabitants self-governing rights with reduced taxation for twenty-five years; he established commercial fairs and markets to help his burghers prosper. King Stefan augmented these privileges by granting Zamość the staple right and permitting it to hold a regional fair soon after the well-established Iaroslav (Jarosław) fair. The city's most important economic activity was trading with the East and it also served as a formation point for cattle drives to Germany. Rugmaking was the only major manufacturing activity. Zamoyski intended at first to permit only Roman Catholic settlers but he soon included Armenians, Sephardic Jews, and Greeks in 1588–89; later all settlers were welcomed. Zamość also became a showplace of architecture and urban design for its patron.

Zamoyski's wedding to the king's niece permitted him to show off his importance. He arranged for knightly tournaments and Roman-style processions with prisoners of war and booty, and he commissioned and staged Jan Kochanowski's play, *The Dismissal of the Greek Envoys*. Since Batory had no children, Zamoyski hoped to put himself into consideration for the throne even if he never offered himself formally as candidate. Zamoyski's promotion was only one of numerous promotions of noble leaders to the senate that stripped the Executionist movement of its leadership and made Batory a senatorial king.

Batory's Aims as King

Batory's ultimate goal was to use Poland-Lithuania to win the Hungarian throne for himself, and he used royal power effectively without challenging the drift toward parliamentary power. Indeed, he agreed without hesitation to the Henrician articles that his predecessor had never confirmed, and he accepted new limitations on his authority to receive foreign ambassadors and hire foreign mercenary soldiers. Batory created noble tribunals in 1578 (Poland) and 1581 (Lithuania) as the highest courts of appeal in order to win popularity and get the deputies to vote military taxes, even though this change abandoned a vital symbolic function of kingship as the source of justice; now the dietines that elected the tribunal judges would seem sovereign. Batory asserted his royal authority while dealing with parliament, however. When the 1576, 1582, and 1585 parliamentary sessions dissolved without completing their business, Batory gained tax approval by reviving the old practice of meeting separately with dietines. He encouraged Lithuanian senators, deputies, and other important citizens to prepare for parliamentary sessions by meeting in Vilnius despite the risk of implicitly approving their separate status.

Batory used his power to its fullest in punishing the magnate Samuel Zborowski. Banished for brawling in the presence of King Henri, Zborowski spent time in Transylvania in Batory's service. As king, Batory winked at Zborowski's visits to Poland until Zborowski and his brothers began to stir up domestic opposition to Batory and push the Commonwealth into a premature war with Turkey. Then Zamoyski personally arrested and executed Samuel in 1584 with Batory's approval. Another brother, Krzysztof Zborowski, was convicted of treason by a parliamentary court and banished, forfeiting his estates. The powerful Zborowski family and other magnates launched a public relations offensive against royal "tyranny" and laid the foundations for the nobility's common action against royal power. This political crisis led Batory to distance himself from Zamoyski, whom the Zborowskis attacked unmercifully at dietines and in parliament. Batory also suspected that Zamoyski was not fully devoted to his plans for Hungarian expansion.

Batory's foreign policy depended on regaining the support of the pro-Habsburg magnate and Catholic factions that had opposed his election. He achieved this by helping the Catholic Church organize a national council in 1577 to confirm the Tridentine reforms and by supporting the Jesuit order's growth. A Jesuit, Marcin Laterna, became Batory's confessor in 1579, and Batory founded three Jesuit academies in Lithuania. The oldest, the Vilnius Academy (1578), which enjoyed substantial revenues and tax privileges, served as a counterpart to the Jagiellonian University in Cracow. The noted preacher and scholar Piotr Skarga headed the new school. At first, Vilnius taught only theology and liberal arts, primarily to train priests. Batory introduced the controversial Gregorian calendar in 1582.

War with Russia

Batory's first steps in foreign policy focused on reversing Ivan IV's gains on the Lithuanian and Livonian fronts in accordance with his coronation oath, and this required costly military reforms. Batory greatly accelerated the introduction of professional heavy cavalry, the Hussars, who replaced the lightly armed and poorly disciplined noble levy. He improved the infantry by hiring Hungarian, German, and Scottish mercenaries before he gained permission from parliament in 1578 to form infantry units with soldiers from the royal domains and pay for them with a new tax. Batory also recruited Cossacks. Zygmunt August had left the artillery in good condition and Batory merely improved its financing, but he had to import foreign engineers to build bridges and fortifications. He started a cartography service.

Batory gathered 56,000 troops to launch an attack on Polotsk (Russia), which he captured quickly on August 30, 1579; 30,000 of his troops came from the Lithuanian levy. He did not have to face Ivan's reserves, which remained in Pskov and Novgorod to protect against a possible Swedish attack. The following year, Batory sent Zamoyski with 48,000 troops (25,000 from Lithuania) to attack the strong fortress of Veliki Luki, which guarded the road to Pskov, and captured it on September 5, 1580. Neighboring fortresses quickly surrendered.

The 1581 military campaign started slowly and ended with a compromise. After convincing a reluctant parliament to fund his campaign, Batory finally moved toward Pskov in July and reached it in late August. He lacked sufficient infantry and artillery to carry the well-fortified and well-supplied city by storm, but hoped to force the Muscovites to send a relief column from Livonia that he could defeat in open battle. The Muscovites sat tight, however, and November's frosts brought the Polish forces into danger from hunger and disease. Not realizing how desperate the Polish situation was, Russia offered favorable terms in January 1582. After prolonged negotiations, Batory gained Livonia and Polotsk for the Commonwealth, but he returned Veliki Luki. Parliament declined to grant Batory all the taxes he wanted for another war against Russia when Ivan died in 1584.

Not content with his Russian victories, Batory carried on far-reaching diplomatic negotiations to prepare for war against Turkey to liberate Hungary or even conquer Constantinople. Pope Sixtus V promised financial subsidies, the Italian city states were enthusiastic, and alliance with Russian Regent Boris Godunov seemed possible. Batory returned to Lithuania beforehand to deal with Sweden's opportunistic expansion into eastern Livonia (Estonia) and its encouragement of Livonian cities to revolt against Batory's governors, particularly in Riga, where the governor followed strong anti-Protestant policies.

Batory died suddenly on December 12, 1586, before his grand plans went into effect. He had covered up his poor health for several years, maintaining his usual energetic military and hunting activities. Modern doctors diagnose kidney failure touched off by excessive use of alcohol to control the pain of his condition.

PART TWO

The Vasa Period, 1587–1697

CHAPTER 8

Zygmunt III Vasa (Waza)

The long reign of Zygmunt III Vasa from 1587 to 1632 represents the peak of Polish-Lithuanian wealth, power, and culture, and yet it also marks the beginning of the Commonwealth's decline toward destruction. Paradoxically, although King Zygmunt III was one of the most hard-working and farseeing of all Polish-Lithuanian rulers, his errors provoked the erosion of his own cause. Overconfident about his royal power and the strength of his realm, he tried to do too much on too many political and military fronts instead of making hard choices. He stubbornly pursued his rights in Sweden as well as the conquest of Russia and Moldavia, neglecting simpler and less spectacular consolidation in Prussia. Convinced that he was right, he alienated many of his subjects so that the existing gulf between parliament and royalty became a chasm. He tried to achieve Church union and started many of his Orthodox subjects on the road to revolt.

The Election of Zygmunt III Vasa

Zygmunt III Vasa was born in 1566 in a Swedish prison to Katarzyna (Catherine) the Jagiellonian, sister of Zygmunt August, and Johan (John) Vasa, duke of Finland, whom King Erik XIV had imprisoned. Katarzyna raised Zygmunt in prison as heir to the throne of Lutheran Sweden, but she entrusted his education to Jesuits, who made him an ardent Catholic and more suitable for the Polish throne. Zygmunt was intelligent and cultured. He spoke Swedish, German, Italian, Latin, and Polish. He was an accomplished musician, painter, goldsmith, and alchemist and he also played court tennis so well that only his royal dignity kept him out of tournament play. As a Jagiellonian, he offered himself as a candidate to the Polish-Lithuanian crown when Batory died.

Royal electors in August 1587 selected two rival kings, as they had in 1573. When hope faded that he might attract support as Batory's relative by marriage,

Chancellor Jan Zamoyski rallied a majority of the nobles to elect Zygmunt Vasa. Negotiations over the terms of the election proceeded slowly because Polish-Lithuanian delegates insisted that eastern Livonia (Estonia) be ceded to Poland. Despite Zygmunt's refusal, Polish-Lithuanian senators eventually accepted his candidacy, officially postponing the resolution of the Livonia issue until Zygmunt inherited the Swedish throne. Habsburg supporters refused to recognize Zygmunt's election and proclaimed the election of Archduke Maximilian of Austria, who promised large subventions for the Polish-Lithuanian military, assistance against Turkey, and peace with Russia. Maximilian led an army toward Cracow to claim the throne, but Zamoyski successfully defended the city, personally leading a charge that broke the besieging force. Then Zamoyski went on the offensive and, driving Maximilian back into Silesia, captured him and his leading Polish supporters at the battle of Byczyna on January 24, 1588. Aided by the papal envoy, Maximilian gained his release and returned to Vienna, where he refused to renounce the Polish-Lithuanian crown as he had promised.

The new king spoke little, offered few compliments, and irritated his more expansive Polish subjects by both his personality and his artistic and sporting interests. From the start of his long reign in 1587, Zygmunt III lacked sympathy for the nobles who had put him in power and preferred the magnates who had supported his rival. He particularly disliked Chancellor Zamoyski, who patronized the young king and took personal charge of dealings with the Habsburgs. Zygmunt's hostility prevented Zamoyski from reforming the royal electoral procedures that had resulted in two double elections. The king rewarded Zamoyski at first by granting his patronage requests, but he soon turned to other advisers so he could rule on his own. The rift between king and chancellor encouraged leading Habsburg supporters to join forces with Zamoyski's political enemies, the Zborowskis, to block his plans to decide royal elections by majority vote after preliminary balloting in dietines. The use of armed force would be prohibited at royal elections and foreign diplomats would be barred from attending. The interregnum would be shortened by abolishing the convocation parliament that met after the election. This useful reform failed because Zamoyski wished to limit the electoral choice to descendants of Zygmunt Vasa or Slavic candidates, thus eliminating Habsburgs from consideration. The Catholic hierarchy refused to go along unless legislation specified that the king be Catholic. Zamoyski and his Protestant allies refused.

Zygmunt's Relations with Parliament

Shortly after his election, Zygmunt went to Tallinn (Reval) to meet his father, Johan III of Sweden, to discuss the relationship between the two kingdoms. Johan feared that Zygmunt would promise control of Estonia to Poland and allow his uncle, Johan's brother, Duke Karl of Sodermanland (the region near Stockholm), to seize control of the Swedish throne. With promises of Habsburg assistance, Johan proposed that his son abandon Poland in return for a substantial cash gift, marry a Habsburg princess, and retire to an Italian duchy. Zygmunt rejected the idea, but it became known and many Poles suspected him, like Henri Valois, of indifference to Poland-Lithuania: Zygmunt's marriage with Habsburg Archduchess Anna in 1592 only seemed to confirm Polish fears and offended the anti-Habsburg Zamoyski faction.

King Zygmunt III faced substantial opposition, since few Poles were inclined to trust the young foreigner. Following agitation at dietines, deputies to the so-called Inquisitional Parliament of 1592 questioned the king at length in a hostile manner about his alleged plans to leave Poland-Lithuania. Zygmunt's reliance on Catholic senators made even his electoral supporters suspect absolutist designs, particularly when Queen Anna died in 1598 and he married another Habsburg archduchess, Constance, over heated objections from advisers. Zamoyski sharply criticized Zygmunt, and Zygmunt responded in kind. When Zamoyski died in June 1605, a printed version of his final speech to parliament circulated in a truncated and exaggeratedly antiroyalist edition.

Zygmunt had no thoughts of dismissing parliament and ruling absolutely, but his first two decades as Polish-Lithuanian king convinced him that change was essential. He asked the parliamentary session of March 1606 for the authority to form a strong standing army funded by regular tax revenues. Later in the 1620s, Zygmunt developed a more comprehensive reform program to solve the problems he had encountered in fighting wars against Russia. He sought permanent taxation, a large standing army, and swift, regularized parliamentary procedures. He proposed a reform of royal electoral practices to allow election of a successor during his lifetime. The dietines rejected his ideas, fearing loss of autonomy and strengthening of royal power. Rather than improve Poland's capacity to make war by improving the central government, dietines increasingly chose to hamper the central government. Pacifist views spread.

An outspoken warrior king such as his predecessor Stefan Batory, or his successor Władysław IV, might have won over the opposition with bold plans, but Zygmunt turned increasingly to patronage and outright bribery or acted on his own when he failed to convince parliament to carry out his wishes. In 1606, he ignored individual protests by opposition nobles and relied on majority votes without waiting for the traditional consensus to form. In 1615, he tried, and failed, to convince senators to proclaim as law a tax bill that the chamber of deputies had rejected. Then he instructed the chamber of deputies not to introduce any new bills and forbade it to initiate legislation. In 1627, Zygmunt ordered the marshal (the speaker) not to read certain bills for discussion, and the parliamentary session ended without enacting any legislation. He used his control over appointments to the parliamentary Editing Commission to change wordings and delete acts that he thought ill-advised. For example, the 1626 final printed version included four substantial textual changes that the commission had not authorized.

Zygmunt bears part of the blame for the failure of reform during his reign because his personality and methods irritated many Polish nobles and brought their fears to the surface. His disregard for parliamentary tradition alienated politically active society, even though it was motivated by a desire to strengthen the Commonwealth militarily and fiscally. He needed to make the choice either to cooperate with parliamentary reformers or to ignore parliament and rule on his own like Henri IV of France.

THE ZEBRZYDOWSKI REVOLT OF 1607

After Zamoyski's death, Mikołaj Zebrzydowski assumed leadership of the Zamoyski faction and opposed the king even more strongly than his predecessor had. He demagogically accused the king of planning to destroy the Polish constitution during the parliamentary session of March 1606, which gathered under protest and finished without approving any legislation. Zebrzydowski was Catholic, but Protestant nobles featured prominently among the opposition as a result of Zygmunt's refusal to appoint them to high positions and his toleration of anti-Protestant riots in Polish and Lithuanian cities. A flood of polemical literature advocated republican constitutional changes such as parliamentary control of ministerial and other appointments, local election of officials, ministerial (rather than royal) control of the treasury, and recognition of the binding character of instructions that dietines wrote for their parliamentary deputies. The proposals ignored the problems of running parliament and the welfare of the common people. Sensing that public opinion was turning against them, royalists acknowledged noble supremacy and moderated their own demands.

Not content with verbal protests, Zebrzydowski led his supporters in an open revolt in 1607. The rebels declared that they no longer owed allegiance to Zygmunt because he had allegedly violated his coronation oath by opening negotiations with several candidates to replace him on the throne, particularly Gabriel Batory of Transylvania. Army detachments led by two distinguished commanders, Stanisław Żółkiewski and Jan Karol Chodkiewicz, met the rebels at Guzów near Jędrzejów in Little Poland on July 7, 1607, defeating them easily. Zygmunt failed to capitalize on his victory, doubtless feeling a lack of full support from the royalist faction, and accepted apologies from the rebel ringleaders. He avoided direct constitutional clashes with the opposition deputies, who increasingly dominated the chamber of deputies, until the end of his reign. As his long life drew to a close and factions maneuvered for position, Zygmunt at the 1631 parliamentary session revived Jan Zamoyski's plans to introduce majority rule into the royal elections, but could not pass them. He succeeded only in passing legislation to give his landed estates to his children at the price of reconfirming the ban on electing a successor during the king's lifetime.

Jakub Sobieski and Senatorial Proposals for Reform

Despite these conflicts, the chamber of deputies worked more effectively during Zygmunt's reign than at any other time in Polish-Lithuanian history. It dealt with as many as 130 acts in a single parliamentary session, debating a few and passing the rest on the basis of recommendations from the marshal. Laws were passed by consensus rather than by majority vote. A single negative voice did not kill a bill automatically, and thus a clever marshal could avoid putting matters to a vote until he had negotiated a compromise. The reason that Zygmunt accomplished many of his domestic and foreign policy aims during his reign was his successful cultivation of the senate and its reemergence as parliamentary leader under the direction of new aristocrats promoted by Zygmunt August, Stefan Batory, and Zygmunt III. Like their political forebears in the Executionist movement, the new senators worked to ensure effective central government in which kings and parliament would share power. They, rather than the king, handled relations with the chamber of deputies.

Jakub Sobieski (1588–1646), father of the future King Jan III Sobieski, was a leading proponent of this cooperative reform. As a deputy, he cooperated with the senators and earned a place in their ranks. Born in 1588 to Marek Sobieski, a middle-rank noble who entered the senatorial elite because of his military abilities, Jakub finished his schooling with three and one-half years' residence in western Europe. Returning to Poland, he took part in the successful Khotyn campaign of 1621 against the Ottomans, and his role in negotiating peace earned him appointment to several diplomatic delegations in the 1620s and 1630s. Sobieski achieved public prominence by delivering popular eulogies at funerals of notables such as Hetman Stanisław Żółkiewski and Hetman Jan Karol Chodkiewicz. He served as parliamentary deputy twenty times and parliamentary marshal four times before Władysław IV elevated him to the senate in 1639 as palatine of Belz, later palatine of Rus (1641).

Sobieski advocated a series of reforms to provide more effective central government. He recommended making royal elections more efficient by declaring a three-quarter majority sufficient and limiting the number of participants. While supporting the unanimity rule in parliament, Sobieski aimed to prevent deputies who came late from challenging legislation passed before their arrival, and he wanted the senate to keep a record of debates and decisions. He also sought to increase parliament's powers by giving it control over the royal mint; his proposals for free trade in salt and potash would have diminished royal income substantially, although the intent was to lower prices. To limit the use of royal patronage, Sobieski demanded that Zygmunt III fill senatorial vacancies promptly and he objected to the king's nomination of underage relatives to high positions. Sobieski wished to prohibit Zygmunt from keeping foreign advisers and even suggested that kings remain unmarried in order to avoid prejudicing the freedom of royal succession.

Sobieski's political confidence reflected the economic success that made him feel capable of guiding the enterprise of state. Many of his fellow nobles felt the same way. He amassed a substantial fortune, starting with one large inherited estate and adding others through marriage or by purchase with the salary he collected from holding office. At the end of his life, Sobieski owned estates containing 13 cities and 150 villages. He gained royal privileges for his cities to hold trade fairs, staple rights for some products, and tariff relief. An active manager, Sobieski supervised city properties, set up city governments, and rebuilt houses after fires so that business could continue. After 1638, he resided in his private city, Żółkiew, near Lviv, where he rebuilt the city walls to protect against Tatar raids. Sobieski invited Jewish merchants to settle there and used his office as the palatine of Rus to protect them against discrimination in the royal city of Lviv. His estates yielded grain that he sold on the Gdańsk market. He raised cattle, established commercial fish ponds, and logged his heavily forested estates. Sobieski was a good husband and father who carefully supervised his four sons' physical and intellectual education. He spent money liberally on their education and also contributed generously to Cracow Academy, which he preferred to Jesuit schools, as well as local Catholic churches and monasteries, Orthodox churches, and synagogues. A fervent Catholic, Sobieski still regarded the papal nuncio with suspicion as a representative of a foreign power.

Counter Reformation

Distressed by the loss of his native Sweden to Protestantism, Zygmunt followed a Catholic policy in Poland. His strong Catholicism brought quick reconciliation with the Catholic Church, which had opposed his election. He respected his oath of toleration and refrained from persecuting Protestants, but he gradually stripped them of influence by appointing only Catholics to ministerial and senatorial positions, and favored them in allocating leaseholds on royal estates. At Zygmunt's election, the appointive Polish senate included thirty-eight Protestants, but when he died there were only two. Ambitious nobles had to be Catholic to succeed.

The king also winked at persecution of Protestant commoners by Catholic commoners, although Protestants did far better in Poland than in France or Catholic Germany, not to mention Italy or Spain. He tolerated mob attacks on Protestant minorities in royal cities such as Cracow (1591), Poznań (1606 and 1616), Lublin (1627), and Vilnius (at several different times), which destroyed Protestant churches, prevented religious services in private homes, and desecrated cemeteries. For the first time in a century, Zygmunt used state authorities to enforce religious decrees issued by Catholic bishops, including several executions for blasphemy and slandering the Catholic Church. On dubious grounds and with little effect, he also forbade Protestant sects to convoke synods. Jews and Muslim Tatars also suffered.

In return, Catholics, especially the Jesuits, supported royal claims to constitutional power. The king's influential confessor, Jesuit Piotr Skarga, published his Polish-language *Parliamentary Sermons* in 1597 in which he advocated stripping parliament of its sixteenth-century gains, restricting it to voting on taxes and presenting petitions. Similarly, Krzysztof Warszewicki published a Latin work, "On the Best State of Freedom," in 1598 openly calling for a hereditary throne. Both authors expressed the hope that a powerful king could protect peasants from feudal excesses.

The Zebrzydowski revolt of 1607 showed the Jesuits that royal power had its limits and that they needed noble support to roll back Protestantism. They had come to Poland in 1564 and had rapidly opened a network of schools that provided an excellent education in the humanist tradition. Growth followed rapidly. The number of Jesuit priests increased from 500 in 1608 to 1,000 in 1626. There were twenty-five Jesuit colleges in 1608 and forty-two in 1634, located in most political, social, and cultural centers, particularly those under Protestant threat in places like Royal Prussia. The crowning point was the Vilnius Academy, which drew students from all over Lithuania and Poland as well as from Livonia, Prussia, Scandinavia, and Germany. Even Protestants and Orthodox Christians attended because the schooling was modern and tuition-free. Most students were nobles, but some burghers and peasants studied there, too.

THE UNION OF BREST, 1596

Union with Ruthenian Orthodoxy in 1596 appeared to strengthen the Roman Catholic Church, but in the long run it aggravated conflict between the Catholic and Orthodox nations. The Roman Catholic Church had achieved a short-lived union with the Greek Orthodox Patriarchy in the last days of the Byzantine Empire, and it resumed its drive for Church union in 1573 by opening a Greek College in Rome and a Congregation for Eastern Churches. Catholics met willing partners in conscientious Orthodox bishops such as Gedeon Balaban, the Orthodox bishop of Lviv, and Ipatii Potii, the Orthodox bishop of Lutsk, who saw clearly that the Orthodox Church within Poland-Lithuania had fallen into disarray. Orthodoxy owed allegiance to the patriarch of Constantinople, who drew substantial revenues in fees and patronage charges while Polish-Lithuanian sovereigns appointed Orthodox bishops for political reasons with little regard for religious devotion or administrative skill. The Orthodox Church also found itself increasingly subject to demands for subordination by the newly formed Moscow Patriarchate (1589). The clergy were poorly educated and many Orthodox nobles turned Calvinist to meet their spiritual needs or reduce their payments to Church hierarchies; some adopted Anabaptist beliefs. At Church synods in Brest-Litovsk (Brześć) in 1595–96, most Orthodox bishops agreed to recognize the Roman Catholic pope's authority if they could keep their Slavonic liturgy, their separate Church hierarchy, and Orthodox traditions such as married clergy. They also demanded the admission of Uniate (Greek Catholic) bishops into the Polish-Lithuanian senate. The Union of Brest did in fact solve the immediate problems of the Orthodox Church in Poland-Lithuania. The reform of the Eastern-rite Basilian monastic order along Jesuit lines provided a well-educated and devoted clergy until the end of the Commonwealth. For more than two hundred years, most Uniate bishops were Basilians and many studied in the Greek College in Rome. Nevertheless, the Roman Catholic hierarchy in Poland-Lithuania never fully accepted Greek Catholics as their equals, preferring to convert them to Roman Catholicism and opposing the reception of bishops in the senate.

The Union of Brest proved unacceptable to much of the laity. Many Orthodox nobles, Orthodox burghers, and the Cossack Host rejected it and continued to follow Orthodox practices; thus the Union deepened the struggle between these important groups and the Polish-Lithuanian state. The single most important opponent of Church union was Prince Konstiantyn Ostrozky the younger, of Volhynia (c. 1526–1608), who had worked since 1577 for a full union of all Roman Catholics with all Orthodox Christians, including the Russians. Ostrozky maintained good relations with the Catholic Church, arranging with the pope to send Greek teachers to his Orthodox academy at Ostrih and supporting the controversial introduction of the Gregorian calendar. However, Ostrozky vehemently rejected the limited Union of Brest and mobilized Orthodox clerics and nobles to fight it. As a patron of the Orthodox Church who had nominated many sitting Orthodox metropolitans, he was bitterly offended by the Orthodox Church discussions that ignored him. Forming a confederation in 1599, Orthodox nobles and their Protestant allies pledged to organize common synods, while their parliamentary deputies hampered parliament's efforts to expand Church union or implement important promises such as seating the Uniate bishops in the Polish-Lithuanian senate. In 1600, Ostrozky's efforts were rewarded by a call from Volhynian and Kievan deputies to cancel Church union and, in 1603, the parliamentary session failed when Orthodox and Protestant deputies demanded that parliament discuss religious issues before dealing with other business. Brotherhoods, or urban associations of Orthodox merchants and artisans, remained Orthodox and redoubled their efforts to support the old Orthodox Church, even though it was technically illegal after 1596. Cossacks and peasants rejected the Uniate Church because it seemed to be subject to Polish overlords.

Like the Jagiellonians, Zygmunt considered the interests of the Catholic Church less important than the unity of the realm. He eschewed political retaliation against Ostrozky and other non-Catholic nobles, and he supported a parliamentary bill in 1609 that restored a quasi-legal status to the Orthodox Church by explicitly recognizing the rights of Orthodox nobles to remain in office. Zygmunt III made no effort to carry out provisions of the Union of Brest that admitted Uniate bishops to the senate, at least in part to avoid confrontation with Orthodox deputies.

Zygmunt III Loses the Swedish Throne

The election of Zygmunt III to the Polish throne came in part as an extension of the common interests between Poland-Lithuania and Sweden, but the link turned into a disastrous rivalry that weakened Poland-Lithuania profoundly and aggravated Zygmunt's relations with the Polish-Lithuanian nobility. In the late sixteenth century, close ties between the two countries developed in common opposition to Denmark's control over Baltic shipping to the west and Russia's effort to gain a foothold on the Baltic coast to the east, and they took the concrete form of the marriage that produced Zygmunt III. Already king of Poland-Lithuania, Zygmunt was crowned king of Sweden in 1594, but he had to recognize Lutheranism as Sweden's state religion and leave government in the hands of a regency council, headed by his uncle Duke Karl of Sodermanland, when he was not present in Sweden.

Two major issues prevented the Polish-Swedish union from being successful. First, Zygmunt's Swedish representatives had promised in 1586–87 to turn eastern Livonia (Estonia) over to Poland-Lithuania, expecting Sweden to make additional gains during its war with Russia, but the regency council concluded peace rather than risk losing the gains that Swedish armies had already made. By the terms of the treaty of Tiavzin (Teusina) in 1595, Narva became the dividing point between Swedish possessions to the west and Russian possessions to the east, leaving no room for Poland-Lithuania. Second, Zygmunt's Catholic devotion aroused the suspicion of Lutheran Swedes who feared that he would reimpose Catholicism on their country.

In order to gain control over Sweden, Zygmunt raised a fleet and invaded the country in 1598. After initial successes on Swedish soil, he lost the decisive battle of Linköping on November 5, 1598, and was captured. To regain his freedom and return to Poland, he surrendered his most prominent Swedish supporters to the regent, his uncle Karl, who tried them before the Swedish parliament in 1600 and executed them. The same parliament formally dethroned Zygmunt and offered the throne to his young son Władysław, if he would come to Sweden within six months and convert to Lutheranism. After receiving the expected refusal, Zygmunt's uncle assumed the Swedish throne as King Karl IX. Poland-Lithuania formally incorporated Livonia, but had to conquer it from Sweden. War dragged on inconclusively, despite Lithuanian Hetman Jan Karol Chodkiewicz's stunning victory at Kirchholm, near Riga, when a well-timed charge by heavy cavalry units completely destroyed the much more numerous Swedish army. Sweden and Poland-Lithuania suspended hostilities in 1608 in order to intervene in Russia's Time of Troubles.

Russia and the Time of Troubles

Poland-Lithuania saw possibilities of regaining lost territories and expanding Catholic influence in the east when Russia fell into disarray after the death of Ivan IV in 1584. Some Lithuanian magnates and Jesuits accepted the claims of a Russian émigré to be Dmitrii, Ivan IV's son, the rightful heir to the Muscovite throne. The youth had really died in 1591. One magnate, Jerzy Mniszech, married his daughter Marina to "Dmitrii" in exchange for promises of vast grants of land and money after he regained his throne. Polish Jesuits supported Dmitrii when he secretly converted to Catholicism and promised to convert Russia. Late in 1604, he led an invasion force consisting primarily of Mniszech's well-trained private regiments and crossed into a famine-racked Russia to meet a favorable reception from peasants and Cossacks. When Tsar Boris Godunov died unexpectedly in April 1605, many boyars rejected his son in favor of Dmitrii, who reached Moscow and was crowned tsar in June 1605. The prominent role of Jesuits and Polish nobles at the new tsar's court made him unpopular very quickly, and an uprising overthrew him in May 1606. Mobs killed Dmitrii, and many Polish and Lithuanian advisers were killed or imprisoned by his successor, Tsar Vasilii Shuiskii. A second false Dmitrii came forward in 1607 with Polish-Lithuanian support and encamped outside of Moscow. Shuiskii asked for Swedish help, as he was also faced with popular revolt in the provinces. Despite Shuiskii's efforts to maintain good relations with Poland-Lithuania, Zygmunt invaded in 1609. Hetman Stanisław Żółkiewski destroyed the major Russian army, which included western European mercenaries, at the battle of Klushino in July 1610, and Smolensk fell in April 1611 after a long siege.

Hoping to avoid chaos and social unrest, Russian boyars invited Zygmunt's son Władysław in August 1610 to be tsar of Russia and invited Żółkiewski to occupy the Moscow Kremlin in Władysław's name. Discussions for the union of the two realms had already been going on for more than a decade. The most far-reaching proposal came in 1600 when a Commonwealth delegation to Moscow heard a recommendation from a Russian boyar to chose a common sovereign for the two realms when either the Vasa or Godunov dynasty died out. The sovereign would split his time evenly among Poland, Lithuania, and Russia and grant religious freedom to Catholics and Orthodox Christians, but not Greek Catholics (Uniates). Free trade and personal mobility would be assured and the two realms would share a uniform currency. Russia and Poland-Lithuania would retain their separate governments, but they would maintain a common treasury against the Tatars and a common Baltic fleet. Polish-Lithuanian delegates never had to weigh the merits of this proposal because other Russian boyars let it be known that they did not wish to allow Polish-Lithuanian nobles to compete for offices and estates in Russia. They also objected to the prospect of mixed marriages and the establishment of Catholic churches in Moscow. In 1610, without reopening the question of union, Żółkiewski agreed on Władysław's behalf to convert to Russian Orthodoxy, to protect Russia's Orthodox character, to return recent Polish-Lithuanian conquests in western Russia, and to retake Swedish conquests on the Baltic coast and in Novgorod.

Neither Władysław nor any of the other candidates who stepped forward won the Russian throne. King Zygmunt III declined to recognize his son as Russian tsar under these terms and claimed the throne for himself, intending to annex western Russian lands and introduce Catholicism. The Swedes nominated their own candidate to the Russian throne. Former supporters turned on the second false Dmitrii after a military defeat and killed him. Russian nobles, burghers, and peasants rallied together, formed new armies, and retook Moscow in November 1612. The Russian Assembly (Zemsky Sobor) chose Mikhail Romanov as the new tsar in February 1613. The Russians continued to fight the Swedes until 1617, when the Peace of Stalbovo awarded the coast to Sweden and returned inland cities to Russia. Polish-Lithuanian forces headed by Prince Władysław and Hetman Chodkiewicz occupied much of western Russia for several years but could not reconquer Moscow. A fourteen-year armistice signed in January 1619 at Deulino gave Poland-Lithuania control of Smolensk and other western regions and allowed Władysław to retain his claim to the tsarist throne.

Zygmunt made concessions to the Hohenzollerns in order to secure their help in the long war with Russia.

Renewed Conflict with Sweden

Sweden took advantage of Zygmunt's continued involvement with Russia to make significant gains in Livonia. Karl IX died in 1611, leaving the throne to his warlike son Gustav Adolf, who conquered small but strategic points in Livonia in 1617 that gave him control over river transport, and, in 1621 when Poland fought a campaign against the Turks, temporarily took Riga. Counterattacks by Lithuanian Hetman Krzysztof Radziwiłł limited Swedish acquisitions and left the Commonwealth in control of most inland Livonian territory, but Sweden collected tariffs when Polish-Lithuanian nobles sent their agricultural produce to the seacoast. When the short Polish-Swedish truce expired, Gustav Adolf renewed operations in Livonia and occupied Dorpat in 1625. He retook Riga in 1629 and held western Livonia (Courland) as a Swedish fief for the remainder of the century, theoretically as a vassal of Poland-Lithuania. Only the inland region of southeastern Livonia near Daugavpils/Dyneburg became a Polish-Lithuanian province.

Two major factors encouraged the Swedish king to expand his war with Poland. First, the Thirty Years' War began in 1618 with the consolidation of Habsburg control over Bohemia and transformed itself into a war between Catholic and Protestant states. Gustav Adolf was aggressively Protestant and later conceived of forming his own empire, a league of German Protestant states. His principal enemy was the Catholic Habsburg emperor, Ferdinand, but he found it also worthwhile to attack Zygmunt III of Poland-Lithuania, Ferdinand's brother-in-law and Gustav Adolf's rival for the Swedish throne. Despite his Catholic zeal and the Habsburg alliance of 1613, Zygmunt had no intention of intervening in the war, but Polish-Lithuanian control over Prussia on the Baltic coast prevented Gustav from consolidating his conquests to the east and west. By attacking the Commonwealth, Gustav strengthened his own position for further attacks on the Empire. Equally important, Swedish national interest lay in controlling the entire Baltic coast in order to profit from the lucrative trade in grain and forest products as well as the Russian transit trade.

In July 1626, Gustav Adolf unexpectedly attacked Royal Prussia, weakening Poland's wavering hold on the Baltic coast. He occupied Elbląg and several of Gdańsk's suburbs, beginning a naval blockade of that city which remained loyal to the Commonwealth. Gustav wintered in Prussia, supporting his army by charging merchant ships a 30 percent duty on the value of their cargos. The Polish-Lithuanian parliament understood the gravity of the situation and supplied ample means, but the Polish army could not defeat the Swedes in the field.

A six-year truce signed in September 1629 at Old Market (Altmark, Stary Targ) retained Gdańsk and Königsberg for Poland, but it accorded Sweden most of the coast. A separate agreement with Gdańsk permitted Sweden to collect a 3.5 percent tariff on Gdańsk's shipping (more than the combined Polish, Prussian, and Gdańsk duties) and demilitarized the city, forcing the Polish fleet to set up a less protected base where it fell into Swedish hands two years later. Gustav Adolf was now free to carry his war against the Habsburg Empire deep into Germany, and he had additional means to do so.

Ducal Prussia Passes to Brandenburg

Zygmunt's preoccupation with foreign wars, like Batory's, led him to neglect real opportunities to tighten links with Ducal Prussia. Prussian nobles wanted protection against their dukes, but Polish-Lithuanian kings ignored their overtures for two reasons: they wanted the support of the Prussian dukes in their military ventures, and they feared that dealing with the noble opposition in Prussia would strengthen the noble opposition in the Polish-Lithuanian parliament. As a result, both Batory and Zygmunt III made deals that allowed Ducal Prussia to slip into Brandenburg's orbit instead of launching an aggressive policy that might have brought the duchy into the Polish-Lithuanian state.

The opportunities for intervention came from the loose suzerainty that Polish kings still exercised over Ducal Prussia. They could hear appeals from Prussian nobles against their dukes and they could intervene when the line of succession was in doubt. As mentioned in the previous chapter, while preparing for war against Russia in 1577, King Stefan Batory appointed Elector Georg Friedrich of Brandenburg to replace his ailing cousin Duke Albrecht Friedrich Hohenzollern as administrator in exchange for a payment of 200,000 zlotys. After Georg Friedrich helped Batory fight Russia, he was allowed to change the ducal title from duke *in* Prussia to duke *of* Prussia, a change that implied succession rights. When Georg Friedrich died in 1603, Prussian nobles, especially those of Polish ethnicity, attacked what they saw as Hohenzollern tyranny and urged Zygmunt III to find another administrator for their ailing duke. Zygmunt honored their requests for greater appeal rights to Poland (although not to the crown tribunal), but he appointed the new elector of Brandenburg, Joachim Friedrich, as administrator in 1605 and permitted his son, Johann Sigismund, to replace him in 1611. The Polish-Lithuanian parliament ratified these decisions with obvious reluctance in order to get Prussian help for war with Russia. When the long-lived but mentally ill Albrecht Friedrich finally died in 1618 without a son, Johann Friedrich, the new elector of Brandenburg, ruled over Royal Prussia by hereditary right subject only to the obligation of supplying military assistance to Poland

and an annual payment of 30,000 zlotys. His successor, Georg Wilhelm, took over in 1620 after making a final payment of 200,000 zlotys to the Polish-Lithuanian state. Prussia remained a Polish fiefdom and Georg Wilhelm promised that he would permit his subjects to appeal to Polish courts, but its relationship with Poland became increasingly tenuous.

CRIMEAN TATAR SLAVE RAIDS AND WAR WITH THE OTTOMAN TURKS

Zygmunt III's cooperation with the Habsburgs led to renewed warfare against Turkey. Relations between the Commonwealth and the Ottomans were already touchy as a result of continuous cross-border raids by vassals of the two states. The Crimean Tatars carried on damaging slave raids into the Commonwealth's southeastern lands, penetrating as far as Galicia. The Tatars were descendants of Genghis Khan's Mongols who had conquered the prosperous trading cities of Crimea inhabited by Genoese and other Italians, Franks, Armenians, and Jews. Like other post-Mongol states on caravan routes, the Tatars established an urban way of life administered by a well-educated and cultured Islamic bureaucracy. The khans built handsome palaces and public buildings in their thriving cities. The Tatar khan and his governing council exercised suzerainty but incomplete control over their nomadic cousins the Nogay Tatars, who lived in northern Crimea and whose military prowess prevented their Polish-Lithuanian and Russian neighbors from expanding to the shores of the Black Sea. The Giray dynasty established the Crimean Tatar state firmly in 1440, but struggles among Tatar clan leaders led the Ottomans to take over vassalage after a 1478 agreement made the Crimean khans into Ottoman officials who received salaries and land grants in Anatolia and Rumelia. Nonetheless, the Crimean khans still ruled as hereditary sovereigns over the Nogays, and, as successors to Genghis Khan, they claimed the right to collect tribute from Poland-Lithuania and Moscow. The slave trade supplanted other forms of trade as the mainstay of the Crimean economy after 1450, for the Nogays carried off hundreds of thousands of Christians from Poland-Lithuania and Russia and sold them to Crimean merchants, who resold young men to the Ottoman army and women to harems. Prisoners of high rank were held for ransom. Textile and metallurgical manufacturing also contributed to the Crimean economy. Zaporozhian Cossacks responded to Tatar raids by crossing the Black Sea in small boats to attack Turkish towns.

Open warfare developed when Hetman Żółkiewski tried to detach Moldavian Prince Gaspar Graţiani from Turkey in 1619 and dispatched specially recruited Cossack regiments against another Turkish vassal, Prince Gábor Bethlen of Transylvania. The Ottomans destroyed Żółkiewski's army as it entered Moldavia in September 1620 at Ţutora (Cecora) on the Prut River in Moldova, killing

Żółkiewski and capturing many officers. The Tatars then raided deep into Podolia, Volhynia, and Galicia to carry off more slaves. In 1621, Lithuanian Hetman Jan Karol Chodkiewicz gathered a strong army that included many Zaporozhian Cossacks and intercepted an Ottoman expedition on its way to invade Poland. Chodkiewicz heroically barred the way at Khotyn on the Dniester River. Unable to pass and exposed to harsh weather, the Ottomans negotiated a peace in November 1621 that set the border at the Dniester, but failed to solve the problem of cross-border raids by Tatars and Cossacks.

Emergence of the Zaporozhian Cossacks

The growing prominence of Cossacks in Poland-Lithuania stemmed from the development of the southern Ukrainian region within the borders of the Polish-Lithuanian state. The word "Cossack" derived from a Turkic word for hero or warrior, and referred to fighters within two separate groupings. Adventurous young men of all classes and estates joined both groups and transferred from one to the other freely.

First, Royal Cossacks emerged when Polish and Lithuanian armies recruited Cossack units for campaigns largely in the south and east. King Stefan Batory assumed supervision of Cossacks in 1583 and put 500 Zaporozhians on a register for regular pay; the 1590 parliamentary session raised the limit to 1,000 while attempting to restrict the freedoms of self-proclaimed, unregistered Cossacks. Because poor finances prevented the Commonwealth from paying Cossacks and other soldiers regularly, they revolted in 1591 under the leadership of their commander, Krzysztof Kosiński, a Catholic noble. The revolt attracted many peasants but was suppressed in 1593. Another revolt erupted in 1594 under Severyn Nalyvaiko, a Cossack officer, and spread into Belarus. Hetman Stanisław Żółkiewski suppressed this revolt in 1596 with regular army troops and private magnate levies (which must have included Cossack soldiers). Nevertheless, the need for Cossack troops kept growing. Polish-Lithuanian armies used as many as 30,000 to 40,000 Cossack troops against Russia and Sweden during the Time of Troubles, and Cossack troops figured significantly in the Moldavian fighting of 1621. Attempts to restrict Cossack activities in 1614 and 1617 had only a temporary effect, because the Commonwealth itself required them.

Cossacks also found ready employment in the rapidly growing towns and cities of the Kiev and Bratslav palatinates as magnates and city governments recruited them to defend against Tatar raids and other enemies. Transfer of the area from the Grand Duchy of Lithuania to the Kingdom of Poland by the Union of Lublin in 1569 spurred their economic development. Both Catholic and Orthodox nobles moved into the region with thousands of peasants whom they transferred from their old estates or whom they recruited with promises of easy terms. Over 200 new cities were founded in the Kiev palatinate alone. About 60 percent of the population lived on noble estates in small towns protected by wooden stockades. Unlike Poland proper, relatively few petty nobles could establish themselves, and vast estates became characteristic. The richest magnate, Jeremi Wiśniowiecki, who converted to Roman Catholicism in 1633, acquired about 250,000 serfs by 1648; other nobles such as the polonized Ostrozky, Zbarazky, and Koretsky families as well as the Polish Zamoyski, Koniecpolski, and Potocki families also enjoyed great fortunes. Magnates hired Jews to act as estate agents, tax collectors, and leaseholders on their estates. Other Jews came to work as artisans and merchants. Some Jews lent money to nobles and peasants.

Second, the Zaporozhian Cossacks comprised a powerful, independent military force drawn from a variety of sources. They elected their own officers, made their own military decisions, and conducted their own foreign affairs. Throughout the 1500s, adventurers from all estates and classes set up camps along the Dnieper to attack the Crimean Tatars and Ottoman possessions around the Black Sea to win booty and to liberate Christian slaves. In the 1550s, Dmitri Wiśniowiecki, the Orthodox prefect of Kaniv, established the first fortress (*sich*) below the great Dnieper rapids (*za porohamy* in Ukrainian) as his base of operations and led Cossacks on raids. Cossacks maintained the permanent base after Wiśniowiecki's death in 1561, and a self-governing Cossack society emerged beyond the reaches of the Commonwealth, Russia, and the Ottomans. The hetman was the highest officer; his staff consisted of adjutants, a chancellor, quartermaster, and judge. Cossack military units lived in barracks and elected their own officers. About 5,000 to 6,000 Cossacks usually lived at the *sich*, although the majority may have been absent at any one time. They campaigned and, in peacetime, hunted, fished, kept bees, made salt, and traded. Cossack raids against the Ottomans reached a high point in the first quarter of the seventeenth century when they sacked the important Ottoman cities of Trebizond (Turkey), Perekop (Crimea), Varna (Bulgaria), Bilhorod (Moldova), Izmail (Moldova), and Kiliia (Moldova). In 1615 and 1620, Cossacks penetrated the Istanbul harbor and burned ships. These raids prompted the Ţutora campaign of 1620 and the Khotyn campaign of 1621.

While the Zaporozhian Cossacks often acted as if they had established an independent country, individual Cossacks continually shuttled back and forth to the Commonwealth. Some, tired of frontier life, settled in and around Ukrainian cities and lived with their families until they chose to undertake military service again. Richer Cossacks bought landed estates. Early in the seventeenth century there could easily have been 40,000 to 50,000 self-described Cossacks with military experience. The Commonwealth found this unsettled element dangerous. It often attempted to deprive the Cossacks of arms and force them into permanent settlements as burghers or peasants, but the need to recruit large numbers for military service undermined these efforts.

Their importance led the Cossacks to demand a clear and privileged definition of their status within the Polish-Lithuanian state. They emphatically refused to be relegated to the servile peasantry when they returned to civilian life. Cossacks who had purchased land often sought recognition as nobles, especially those who came from the lesser Ruthenian gentry and had failed to document their claims to noble status. Hetman Koniecpolski attempted to solve the problem in 1625 by creating a register of 6,000 free Cossacks; the rest would have to accept peasant or burgher status. Armed revolts by nonregistered Cossacks brought minor increases in the register. Cossacks residing in the "Wild Fields" around the Zaporozhian Sich remained Polish-Lithuanian subjects in theory but kept their independence in practice. The situation was explosive and Zygmunt failed to develop a long-term policy.

Revival of the Orthodox Church

The Cossack situation was part of an economic, social, and religious revival of the Orthodox regions of the Commonwealth, especially in the Ukrainian lands. The Orthodox revival began shortly after the Ukrainian provinces were transferred from the Grand Duchy of Lithuania to the Kingdom of Poland in 1569. Prince Konstiantyn Ostrozky served as palatine of Kiev and became a senator after the Union of Lublin. One of the Commonwealth's richest magnates, Ostrozky offered himself as candidate for the Polish-Lithuanian throne in 1573 and also for the Russian throne in 1594. He defended the political rights of Orthodox nobles and acted as their leader in seeking an equal partnership with Polish and Lithuanian nobles. After failing to stop the Union of Brest, Ostrozky organized a second synod that kept the Orthodox Church going despite lack of official recognition. At about the same time, fraternities organized by Lviv guilds established other Orthodox schools and supported Orthodox learning, supplementing Ostrozky's own patronage. Objections to the Union of Brest of 1596 appeared in print and circulated widely. For instance, Ivan Vyshensky, a Galician Orthodox monk who lived mostly at Mount Athos in Greece, wrote works such as "A Letter to the Bishops Who Abandoned Orthodoxy" in which he demanded moral and political reform of the Orthodox Church, particularly the abandonment of "pagan" innovations such as the study of grammar and rhetoric.

The Orthodox Monastery of the Caves in Kiev began publishing religious books in the 1620s, and a Kievan brotherhood (fraternity) sprang up as well. Zaporozhian Cossacks, who considered themselves the defenders of Orthodoxy, formally joined the Kievan brotherhood as a group in 1620. Teofan, patriarch of Jerusalem, consecrated Yov Boretsky as Orthodox metropolitan of Kiev and ordained several bishops in order to renew the Orthodox Church hierarchy that the Union of Brest had decapitated. Zygmunt III did not recognize the new bishops but neither did he take action against them, because he needed to recruit Cossacks for the Turkish war. Orthodox Christians struggled with Uniate Catholics for control of church buildings. In 1632, Władysław IV ended the conflict by convincing parliament to recognize the Orthodox Church and divide church property between Orthodox and Uniate Catholics.

Continued Lithuanian Separatism

The Union of Lublin was only a few decades old when Lithuanian leaders threatened to dissolve it if Poland failed to recognize their needs. Most Lithuanian leaders strongly opposed Zygmunt III's involvement in war against Russia during the Time of Troubles because they knew the Grand Duchy could not withstand Russia's inevitable retaliation. Lithuanian Grand Chancellor Leon Sapieha said that Lithuania would have to go its own way if Poland did not discuss defense against Russia, and he opposed Zygmunt's use of force to relieve the Polish garrison in the Kremlin in 1612. Similarly, Krzysztof Radziwiłł, later palatine of Vilnius and Lithuanian grand hetman, at first a firm advocate of close union with Poland, turned against Zygmunt III's aggressive policy toward Sweden in order to focus on defense against Russia. Radziwiłł engineered an armistice with Sweden in 1622 against Zygmunt III's wishes, as did Lithuanian Grand Hetman Sapieha in March 1626. The subsequent truce with Sweden in 1627 evoked countercharges from Jerzy Zbarski, castellan of Cracow, among others, that the Lithuanians had violated the provisions of the Union of Lublin.

CHAPTER 9

Władysław IV

Władysław IV (1595–1648) succeeded to the Polish-Lithuanian throne in 1632 when Zygmunt III Vasa died after a forty-five-year reign. Despite his abilities and popularity, Władysław failed to accomplish much, and his short reign left Poland on the verge of collapse. His military reforms proved to be his most lasting legacy, effectively ensuring the Commonwealth's survival for another generation. He understood the need to strengthen central authority in Poland-Lithuania, but he failed to adhere to consistent domestic or foreign policies. Władysław also failed to recognize the enduring opposition of the Orthodox nobility to their inferior place within the Polish-Lithuanian state. His failure to build a political structure that recognized their needs led to the Cossack uprising of 1648 and the loss of vast southeastern territories under his successors. The failure remains surprising in view of Władysław's personal sympathies for Orthodox and Protestant nobles as well as Cossacks.

Władysław IV

Władysław was born in 1595 in Lobzów near Cracow to Queen Anna of Habsburg and raised in the Polish language by Polish officials. Well-educated, Władysław also spoke Latin, German, Italian, and Swedish. He loved art, literature, music, and theater, and he read widely. He took a vital interest in military affairs, sharing in the campaigns that Polish-Lithuanian armies fought for his claim to the Russian throne and participating in Zygmunt's Turkish and Swedish wars. His father sent him on a long European tour when he was twenty to visit western courts and meet leading artists of the day such as Peter Paul Rubens and Guido Reni. As the eldest son, Władysław did not automatically succeed Zygmunt III, but he was the only candidate. The nobles who came to Wola field near Warsaw acclaimed him immediately, in part because of his personal popularity. Even nobles who were suspicious of Vasa royalism and the dynasty's Swedish orientation liked him.

When healthy, Władysław was energetic and spent his days campaigning or hunting, but illness interfered with political and military activity throughout his adult life. He probably suffered from kidney disease and experienced occasional spells of weakness as a young man, losing consciousness for over an hour on one occasion in 1625. Later in life, he was confined to bed for several weeks at a time, and had to attend the 1641 parliament in his sickbed. Władysław's condition was aggravated by feasting and heavy drinking. He died at age fifty-three from an overdose of medicine prescribed to combat an attack of kidney stones.

Władysław married twice for political reasons: first, to the Habsburg Archduchess Cecilia Renata in 1637 and, after her death, to a French princess of Italian origin, Louise Marie Gonzaga, in 1646; the marriages signaled Władysław's foreign policy orientation. He was poor marital material. His relaxed attitude toward morality and religion offended his strict father, and his numerous sexual dalliances earned him a reputation for loose morals. His one prolonged romantic attachment was with Jadwiga Łuszkowska, a burgher, whom he took to Warsaw and who appeared with him in public on occasion. Władysław IV married off his mistress to a court official to please his wife, Cecilia Renata, but continued to visit her at her husband's country estate. He had several short-lived affairs after his first wife's death and at least one illegitimate child.

Władysław and Cecilia Renata lived together quite properly for the first year of their marriage. He presented her with valuable leaseholds and made some minor patronage appointments at her request. Relations cooled as the pious queen lent her support to the Catholic faction at court and Austria failed to support Władysław's plans to gain the Swedish crown. The birth of a son and heir, Zygmunt Kazimierz, in 1640 restored her to favor briefly, but she never recovered from giving birth to a stillborn daughter in 1642 and died in 1644. Cecilia Renata owed some of her isolation to her inability or unwillingness to make allies at court.

Władysław's ability to carry out his plans was not helped by his poor economic management. Heavy expenditures on the military brought good results but his spending on palaces, furnishings, artists, and musicians gave value at too high a cost. He wasted a lot of money on his favorite pastimes: casual love affairs and hunting. He pursued wild boar, elk, and bear in Lithuania on long hunting trips with numerous companions, and when business kept him in Warsaw, he hunted rabbits and other small game. As early as the first year of his reign Władysław had to pawn his jewels to pay his bills, and he still had to beg parliament for emergency assistance ten years later; parliament allocated the large sum of 4 million zlotys.

Military Reform and War with Russia

Władysław's main interest throughout his life was military affairs. Elected tsar of Russia at age fifteen during the Time of Troubles, he became an accomplished and enthusiastic military leader during the campaign of 1616–18 to win the Russian throne. He fought Turks at Khotyn in 1621, where he got to know and like the Cossacks personally, and took part in the war against Sweden in 1626–29. Long campaigning helped him develop unusual rapport with ordinary nobles and common soldiers. Contemporary reports note his directness in speaking with soldiers and other commoners and their ease in relating to him, such as the account of his shaking hands with the Swiss peasant (a descendant of William Tell) who guided him through the Alps during his tour of western Europe in 1624–25. Władysław studied western European military methods, especially those of Spain, at that time.

Polish-Lithuanian difficulties when fighting the Swedes during the 1620s showed him that the Polish military needed a substantial overhaul, and his foreign tour suggested remedies. Unable to hire German mercenaries because they were involved in the Thirty Years' War, Władysław formed a Polish "foreign style" (*cudzoziemski autorament*) army based on German models. He recruited foreign officers to set up the units and trained Polish officers to replace them. Free volunteers from royal and clerical estates and incorporated cities in Poland-Lithuania made up the rank and file; parliament exempted noble estates from recruiting. Foreign style regiments comprised mixed formations of muskets and pikes that could fight off cavalry charges and attack the enemy. Intensive drill ensured the maximum rate of fire. The army expanded the artillery and provided standardized equipment by melting down old cannon and recasting them. Mobile field artillery was introduced. Regular storage and repair facilities were established. Władysław mixed these innovations with Poland-Lithuania's mobile yet hard-charging cavalry that still ruled the eastern European plain, even if it could no longer win battles on its own against modern infantry.

Technical services also received their share of attention. Engineering officers joined artillery units to direct fortification, sapping, and bridge building. Royal engineers directed construction of coastal fortifications and built a major fort at Kodak on the lower Dnieper to guard against attacks from the south by Tatars, Turks, and Zaporozhian Cossacks. Imitating Władysław, magnates used professional engineers to fortify their estates, especially in Ukrainian lands. The king also built a Baltic fleet, starting practically from scratch since his father's fleet had fallen into Swedish hands. Gdańsk could not be pressured into allowing him to construct and anchor the new royal fleet, so he reactivated the Commission for Royal Ships under Hetman Stanisław Koniecpolski, who refitted eleven merchant ships at newly constructed shipyards on the Hel peninsula near Gdańsk and purchased a twelfth. A chain of fortifications protected important coastal sites.

The military reforms demonstrated their efficacy quickly in a victorious war against Russia, which hoped to take advantage of Władysław's inexperience to regain Smolensk and western Russia at the start of his reign. The Polish parliament supported Władysław with generous grants. He took 20,000 troops to relieve the besieged city, and displayed the value of his modernized services as well as the skill of his generals in combining them with substantial cavalry formations. He coordinated his attack with an army formed from magnates' private forces that entered Russian territory from Ukraine as well as with Tatars who raided southern Russia. Władysław and Lithuanian Hetman Krzysztof Radziwiłł raised the siege of Smolensk, cut off Russian general Mikhail Shein, and forced him to surrender on February 25, 1634. Despite their initial success, Polish forces lacked the strength to push into Russia and the two sides signed a peace agreement at Polianovka (Polanów) on June 14, 1634, that confirmed the Deulino armistice of 1619. In this agreement, Władysław renounced his claims to the tsarist throne. Polish forces under Hetman Koniecpolski repelled a simultaneous attack by the Crimean Tatars, and wider war with Turkey was avoided when Murad IV made some minor gestures toward restraining them.

Łukasz Opaliński and Parliamentary Reform

While Władysław avoided major conflicts with parliament, the two sides did not get along easily despite his appointment of an experienced and popular parliamentarian, Jerzy Ossoliński, as vice-chancellor in 1638 and chancellor in 1643. To gain the throne, Władysław reluctantly accepted greater parliamentary control over military appointments and royal estate leases. Once elected, he ignored the senatorial constitutionalists and missed opportunities to enact their positive program. Instead, he sought foreign adventures. Parliamentarians came to suspect him of trying to introduce royal "absolutism" and frustrated his efforts, whether they would have strengthened the Commonwealth, as in the Baltic, or weakened it, as in Moldavia. For example, Jerzy Lubomirski blocked the extension of the parliamentary sessions in 1639 and in 1645, and both parliaments expired without accomplishing anything.

Łukasz Opaliński (1612–62) was the major theorist of senatorial constitutionalism. He came from a leading Great Poland family that had supplied nine generations of senators; only the Leszczyńskis surpassed them. His father, Piotr, the palatine of Poznań, had studied at Polish and foreign universities and maintained scholarly interests throughout his life. Piotr regularly attended dietines at Środa and gained election as deputy to the 1613 and 1616 parliamentary sessions. Out of patriotism, he funded and led two regiments in the 1621 Khotyn campaign. A fervent Catholic, he founded religious establishments and went on numerous pilgrimages. His son, Łukasz, was born in 1612, attended the Lubrański College in Poznań, and went to university at Louvain, Belgium, in 1626–29. He was influenced by Justus Lipsius, a Renaissance scholar who wrote about civic virtue and the rule of law. Lipsius's books had been translated into Polish and appealed to senatorial families. Opaliński also studied in France and Italy.

Opaliński and other senators built on the constitutionalist position that Jakub Sobieski and others had broached under Zygmunt III. Like the king, the constitutionalist senators sought to modernize the government, but they based reforms on senatorial power and sought to restrict the king's independence. For example, Jan Zamoyski had proposed to elect kings by majority vote in 1598. Jan Ostroróg in 1607 had proposed more efficient parliamentary procedures and attacked decentralization in a 1613 speech. In 1626, Krzysztof Zbaraski had advocated internal restructuring of the army with power exercised by parliament, not the king. The most comprehensive statement of reform came during the 1632 interregnum when Jakub Sobieski and Krzysztof Radziwiłł proposed measures to improve parliamentary procedures. They wanted deputies to swear an oath of allegiance to the central government rather than to the palatinates that they represented. They promoted adherence to strict parliamentary procedures and insisted that the parliamentary marshal refuse to discuss matters that were put forward at the last minute. They sought to design a procedure for casting protest vetoes that would not disrupt further deliberations. To improve the army, they recommended establishing more efficient units supported by regular finances. Finally, they wished to improve the treasury by assuring good record keeping supervised by a parliamentary audit. In 1638, the group of senatorial constitutionalists urged the creation of a permanent drafting commission that would regularize laws and record private petitions from the palatinates. They also supported some immediate reforms that would have given the king's agenda primacy in parliament and would have ensured a senatorial role in making decisions about the army. At the 1639 parliament, constitutionalists put forward additional reform proposals. Stanisław Szczucki suggested that the marshal maintain a team of aides to draw up an agenda. He proposed that public matters be discussed first and private matters second. He sought to outlaw the introduction of new material that had not been submitted to dietines previously for approval. The senatorial group supported the unanimity rule but insisted that latecomers to parliament could not veto bills approved before their arrival and that bills rejected early in a parliamentary session could be resubmitted when the full complement of deputies arrived. The proposals did not pass and parliament was broken by a *liberum veto*.

Following the 1639 parliament, Opaliński wrote an extensive tract (published in 1641) entitled *Conversation of a Village Priest with a Noble* in which he presented his reform package. He advocated turning all instructions from the dietines over to the marshal of parliament, who would form an agenda with the help of a regionally balanced committee of deputies. The agenda would group issues under the four headings for consideration in the following order: grievances, public order, security, and private matters (on a single day at the end). He wanted to refer technical matters to experienced commissioners to speed deliberations. Deputies who arrived two or more weeks late would be barred from voting on matters discussed before their arrival. No clients of wealthy nobles or candidates shown to have taken bribes were to serve as deputies.

Opaliński retired from active politics shortly after the 1641 parliament, perhaps disillusioned by his failure to effect reform. In retirement, he unsuccessfully sought to persuade Władysław IV to use his existing powers instead of seeking new ones. Opaliński had other reasons to avoid public life. He had married Izabela Tęczyńska in 1639 and spent years putting her rich but neglected estates in order. Living the life of a country gentleman, Opaliński devoted himself to collecting a large library of Greek, Latin, Hebrew, French, Italian, and Polish books, and writing tracts about taxation, military affairs, and history that have not survived. *Polonia Defensa,* an extant Latin tract aimed at a European readership, justified the Polish mixed political system and masked its defects. Opaliński returned to politics for the 1648 and 1649 parliamentary sessions to work on taxation and military affairs, and he spoke up for parliamentary reform during the reign of King Jan Kazimierz.

Władysław's Failed Baltic Policy

Like his father, Władysław aimed to reclaim his Swedish heritage and win the throne after Gustav Adolf died at the battle of Lützen in 1632 without leaving a male heir; the Swedish king had designated Princess Kristina as his successor, however. Władysław entered into negotiations for a Protestant wife, Elizabeth, grandniece of England's Charles I and daughter of the Winter King, Elector Friedrich V of the Palatinate. Charles I endorsed Władysław's right to the Swedish throne, and Władysław hoped to gain it by provoking a war against Sweden that he would fight with English, Dutch, and other Protestant allies. He gathered a fleet of eleven naval vessels plus some Cossack *chaiki,* and moored them in Gdańsk; new fortifications on the nearby Hel peninsula protected them. Władysław came to Prussia with 24,000 well-armed troops. However, parliament wanted peace because it distrusted the king's motives. To Władysław's fury, in Sztumska Wieś (Stumsdorf) on September 12, 1635, his negotiators agreed on a twenty-six-year peace. By that treaty, Poland regained control of Ducal Prussia while Livonia remained in Swedish hands. Sweden returned the Polish ships that had been confiscated years earlier and promised free trade. Władysław proposed to take over the 3.5 percent customs duty from Gdańsk that Sweden had collected and extend it to other coastal ports in order to build up his navy, but he abandoned the scheme in exchange for substantial payments in 1636. When Władysław revived plans to collect customs duties the following year, Gdańsk invited the Danes to come and attack Polish ships. Later, the Gdańsk city council bought off the king's plan to punish the councillors. Gdańsk had support from senators who did not like Władysław's ambitions. In general, his failure to subjugate Gdańsk reflected his lack of support among parliamentarians and his lack of firm policy. Willing to consider any approach, Władysław then listened eagerly to French proposals for an anti-Habsburg alliance that might earn him Silesian conquests, but he recognized the plan as unrealistic and dropped it. He decided instead to deepen the Habsburg alliance and marry the emperor's daughter, Cecilia Renata, who brought the Silesian duchy of Opole-Raciborz as part of her dowry. It reverted to Habsburg ownership in 1666, however.

ALLIANCE WITH FRANCE

The unexpected death of Queen Cecilia Renata on March 24, 1644, created new political possibilities for Władysław. After proposing to his cousin Christina of Sweden, who turned him down, Władysław found a second wife in Louise Marie Gonzaga de Nevers, an exiled princess of Mantua who grew up in France as a member of the French royal family. The marriage brought Władysław a substantial dowry of 2 million zlotys, which probably attracted him more than the marriage itself or the implied alliance with France. Illness prevented him from attending her gala reception in Gdańsk when she arrived by ship, and she reached Warsaw in March 1646 to find an aging, sick husband who had had many lovers since his first wife's death. Thirty-four-year-old Queen Louise Marie was rich, intelligent, and more interested in politics than romance. The political tie with France had no immediate foreign policy significance, although Władysław may have hoped that France would put pressure on its ally, Sweden, to make concessions to Poland-Lithuania. He might also have hoped that Louise Marie's distant relationship with the Byzantine imperial family, Paleologus, would help him carry a Turkish campaign into the Balkans.

The marriage led to increased tension with parliament because the nobility disliked France for both political and moral reasons, but the queen brought important intellectual and cultural activity to Warsaw that helped expand Poland-Lithuania's intellectual horizons.

RELIGIOUS POLICY

Unlike his father, Władysław IV consistently followed a path of religious toleration, partly from temperament and partly from policy. He was a strong but not a crusading Catholic who got along well with members of other religions. His religious policy was also dictated by his need for the support of Orthodox and Protestant nobles to gain the royal throne. Even though he tended to ignore them when he did not need them, Władysław demonstrated good relations with Polish Protestants to impress Swedes and potential Protestant allies in his quest for the Swedish throne. To this end, he appointed numerous Protestants to senatorial positions, increasing their number to eleven. At the urging of Polish Calvinists, he reluctantly agreed to close the Anabaptist academy at Raków in 1638, taking this as an opportunity to restate the principle of religious freedom for less controversial Protestant groups. In addition, Władysław sought support from Orthodox nobles in Ukraine and Belarus. He restored the legality of the Orthodox Church, removing some churches from Greek Catholic (Uniate) control and returning them to Orthodoxy. He appointed Petro Mohyla as metropolitan of Kiev and supported Mohyla's Academy as it modernized and expanded Orthodox scholarship in the Commonwealth. This favorable policy made it easier for Władysław to deal with the Zaporozhian Cossacks, who often claimed to protect the Orthodox religion, and to recruit Cossacks for his ambitious political policies.

ADAM KYSIL AND THE RUTHENIAN QUESTION

Good personal relations blinded Władysław to the need for institutional changes to recognize the Orthodox nobility and the Cossacks. Although Cossacks had been valuable troops, they had also staged dangerous uprisings for greater pay and status. Shortly before Władysław came to the throne, an uprising led by Taras Fedorovych in 1630 had increased the register to 8,000. Following his father's example, Władysław pacified the Cossacks by building a fortress at Kodak to cut the Zaporozhian Cossacks off from Kiev and other settled areas of Ukraine; a Cossack detachment destroyed the fortress within months, but registered Cossacks turned the leader, Ivan Sulyma, over to Polish authorities for trial and execution. When a new revolt broke out early in Władysław's reign, Hetman Mikołaj Potocki destroyed the Cossack armies in 1637 at Kumejki (Kumejky), near Chyhyryn. This victory allowed the 1638 parliamentary session to lower the number of registered Cossacks to 6,000, reduce their military independence, and force peasant status on all nonregistered Cossacks. Cossack officers now had to come from the nobility, and laws threatened Cossacks with harsh punishments if they left the Ukrainian palatinates for the Sich. Magnates of both Catholic and Orthodox religions took bloody reprisals against former rebels on their estates. A final rebellion under Cossack Hetman Yakiv Ostrianin was quickly suppressed. For the next ten years, a "golden peace" prevailed with only local unrest, and noble estates expanded unhampered. Władysław mistakenly concluded that he could tap the Cossacks' military abilities without running the risk of upsetting the social system. He counted on support from the increasingly important Orthodox element.

Adam Kysil (Kisiel in Polish), an Orthodox noble who rose to prominence under Władysław to help him develop his eastern ambitions, illustrates the opportunities available to Orthodox nobles under Władysław, and their limitations. Kysil (1600–1653) came from a moderately wealthy Volhynian family that proudly traced its origins to the princes of Kievan Rus. He married into a similar family from the Kievan palatinate and acquired considerable wealth by buying and leasing estates in both areas, exploiting the forest reserves of the Volhynian estates to manufacture potash for sale. He became rich enough to field a small private army and gave gifts to Cossack leaders. The military abilities Kysil displayed against the Turks and Tatars and the diplomatic talents he showed with the Cossacks and Russians opened the way to his political advancement. Władysław IV appointed Kysil castellan of Kiev in 1646 and palatine of Chernihiv in 1648.

Kysil achieved high office without forgetting his Orthodox identity. Basing his arguments on guarantees included in the acts of 1569 that transferred new Ukrainian lands to the Kingdom of Poland, he energetically defended the rights of the Orthodox Church to control church properties and carry on its religious activities as well as the rights of Orthodox nobles to keep their land and gain political preferment. Ironically, Władysław found Kysil's Orthodox assertiveness a useful check on demands from the papacy and ultra-Catholic Poles.

In 1646–48, Kysil worked hard on two projects for Władysław IV. First, with Metropolitan Mohyla's help, he carried on protracted negotiations to unify the Orthodox and Greek Catholic Churches and then unify the resulting all-Ruthenian Church with the Roman Catholic Church. Many Uniates and Orthodox were interested because they saw Roman Catholicism gaining ground at their expense, and some Catholics favored the idea in order to unify Christendom against the Turks. The Vatican rejected Kysil's proposals because they did not give the Vatican enough power; lay nobles like Kysil would have too much influence. The possibility of Church union died with the 1648 Cossack revolt. Second, Kysil worked to conclude an alliance with Russia against the Turks. He had to overcome opposition from Lithuania, which feared concessions to Russia, and from Ukrainian border nobles who did not wish to hand over portions of their estates to settle Russian claims. Kysil finally succeeded in negotiating a defensive alliance with Russia against the Tatars in 1647, and later said that the Russians had agreed verbally to fight against the Swedes to win control of the Baltic coast. Again, the Cossack revolt made the plan irrelevant.

Władysław's Plans for War against Turkey

Władysław's last chance to achieve glory lay in an energetic campaign against the Ottomans. The king began talking about war with Turkey in 1640. He stopped paying tribute to the Tatars in 1645 to provoke them to attack. When they failed to oblige him, he proposed war against them at the 1645 parliamentary session. The senate approved but the commons, more concerned with Russian relations, ignored the appeal. Władysław asked the papacy, Venice, and Russia for subsidies. Only Venice offered a little help.

Władysław decided to evade parliament and go to war on his own. Hetman Stanisław Koniecpolski proposed concentrating on the Tatars with Russian assistance and arranged for combined campaigns by Russia and Poland in 1647 that proved unsuccessful. Władysław planned to launch a major attack on Turkey to regain the Black Sea coast (especially Moldavia) and suppress the Crimean Tatars, and he dreamed of capturing Constantinople. He mounted an ambitious diplomatic offensive that reached as far as Persia (Iran) and Morocco and enlisted Balkan Christians. After the death of Hetman Stanisław Koniecpolski, Władysław named new generals who were more amenable to aggressive action and planned to increase the Cossack register from 6,000 to 12,000.

His reckless plans to attack Turkey were blocked by Chancellor Ossoliński and other senators who insisted that Władysław consult parliament. But parliament rejected the idea in 1646, complaining that the king was breaking the *pacta conventa* by recruiting soldiers without permission, and it asked him to disband his new forces. It was soon obvious that the army was maintaining its readiness anyway and tempers became so hot that one deputy introduced a bill to renounce obedience to the king. Parliament passed a law requiring him to disband the army, limit the royal guard to 600 soldiers, and dismiss his foreign advisers. Władysław did not ask for war taxes, of course, and had to agree to summon an extraordinary parliamentary session to check that he was carrying out his promises. Political gatherings during the summer of 1647 saw opposition to Władysław's plans grow. With greatly reduced finances, he tried to provoke the Tatars and Turks to attack by sending Jeremi Wiśniowiecki south at the head of 20,000 men; Aleksander Koniecpolski made a similar move toward Ochakiv (Ochakov). The Tatars failed to react.

Death put an end to Władysław's plans. The king lost interest in public affairs after his seven-year-old son, Zygmunt Kazimierz, unexpectedly fell ill and died. Władysław IV also died unexpectedly on May 20, 1648, without publicly abandoning his plans for war. His death left the Cossacks prepared for dramatic increases in recruitment and eager to fight.

CHAPTER 10

Jan Kazimierz

The reign of Jan Kazimierz is a watershed in Polish-Lithuanian history that separates the era of greatness from the era of decline and collapse. Decades of unresolved constitutional problems, overly ambitious territorial expansion, ethnoreligious conflicts, and economic decline caught up with the Commonwealth in the dramatic episode known in Polish tradition as The Deluge, when Cossack, Russian, and Swedish forces poured across the borders to conquer everything but a few islands of resistance. The period of foreign invasions and civil wars that plagued the Cossack state after it seceded from Poland-Lithuania is known to Ukrainians as The Ruin. Jews still remember seventeenth-century massacres with horror.

King Jan Kazimierz and his noble opposition failed to avert these catastrophic developments and, despite cooperating impressively to overcome them in the short run, failed to create structures to resolve long-term issues. The king's personality and royalist policies made it difficult for him to work with parliamentarians who opposed him with even greater vigor and less responsibility than they had opposed his predecessors. Traditional Vasa insistence on regaining the Swedish inheritance touched off the disaster. Nevertheless, the strength of the Polish-Lithuanian state can be seen in its ability to defeat the Swedes and fight the combined Cossack and Russian armies to a standstill.

JAN KAZIMIERZ

Władysław IV was succeeded on the Polish throne by his younger brother, Jan Kazimierz (1609–72), who was born in Cracow. Jan II Kazimierz was as adept at military affairs as Władysław but far more religious. Relations between the two brothers were uncertain, perhaps because of the difference in temperament and age and perhaps because Jan Kazimierz was being groomed for the Polish throne after 1612 when Władysław IV expected to become tsar of Russia. Like his father and brothers, Jan Kazimierz enjoyed a cultivated upbringing and particularly loved music. He played the lute and theorbo.

The failure of Zygmunt III's grand plan for dynastic expansion left the Polish Vasas underoccupied. Lacking Swedish or Russian estates, all of Władysław's younger brothers went into the Church, but not before Jan Kazimierz spent his early years as a military commander. He took part in the Smolensk campaign at age fifteen. Sent to Vienna to prepare for a war against Turkey that did not materialize, he entered Austrian service and commanded a 4,000-man light cavalry unit of Ukrainian Cossacks (Lisowczycy) in battle against the French. Władysław recalled him to Poland but gave him little to do, so Jan Kazimierz went off to serve in the Spanish navy in 1638. France interrupted his journey and held him prisoner for two years to punish King Władysław for his political alliance with Austria, France's rival. Returning to Poland for only three years after his release, Jan Kazimierz proceeded to Italy, where he surprised everyone by taking holy orders as a Jesuit. When the Jesuits insisted that he return home to bolster the Catholic faction, he quit in order to stay in Rome, where he was appointed cardinal, but he resigned and returned to Poland after Władysław's only son died. When Władysław also died, Jan Kazimierz offered himself as candidate for the throne and gained election with the support of Chancellor Jerzy Ossoliński and Władysław's widow, Louise Marie, who expected him to follow Władysław's policies and negotiate with the Cossacks. Cossack Hetman Bohdan Khmelnytsky's endorsement of Jan Kazimierz's candidacy proved decisive, and he was crowned January 17, 1649, marrying his brother's widow in May with papal dispensation. Royal commissioners headed by Władysław's principal adviser on Cossack affairs, Adam Kysil, traveled to Ukraine to appoint Khmelnytsky officially as hetman.

BOHDAN KHMELNYTSKY AND THE GREAT COSSACK REVOLT OF 1648

Jan Kazimierz assumed the throne in the midst of an unparalleled disaster. In the spring of 1648, Khmelnytsky (Bogdan Chmielnicki in Polish) led a large Cossack army out of the Sich to attack Polish nobles in Ukrainian lands. Khmelnytsky (c. 1595–1657) came from a minor Ukrainian noble family of Orthodox religion that gave him a good education at a Jesuit school in Iaroslav. Serving as a Cossack officer in the Polish army as a young man, Khmelnytsky was captured at Ţutora in 1620 and spent two years in Turkish captivity. Upon release, he returned to his estate at Subotiv, married, and devoted himself to building up his property. Władysław IV rewarded him for his loyalty during the Cossack risings of 1625 and 1638 by appointing him chancellor of the Zaporozhian Host. Khmelnytsky also served as a member of the Cossack delegation that went to Władysław IV in 1646 to discuss preparations for war with Turkey.

This loyal Orthodox Ruthenian noble and cossack revolted in 1648 in order to pursue a private grievance against his Catholic neighbor, Daniel Czapliński, who had raided Khmelnytsky's estate to settle a land dispute and possibly to settle a personal grudge as well. Czapliński's powerful protectors, who disliked Khmelnytsky as a royalist, thwarted his efforts to obtain justice in the courts and threatened to arrest him. He fled to the Zaporozhian Cossacks in January 1648. Appeals fell on fertile ground among the large numbers of Cossacks who had gathered to prepare for Władysław IV's planned—and canceled—war against Turkey. Khmelnytsky convinced the Cossacks to expel the Polish garrison, elect him hetman, and rise up against the Poles. Since the Cossacks lacked cavalry, Khmelnytsky negotiated an agreement with the Crimean Tatar khan to join the campaign with his light cavalry. The combined army won a string of victories against Polish forces. Khmelnytsky destroyed the Polish advance guard at Zhovti Vody (Żółte Wody, Yellow Waters) on May 16, 1648, assisted by the desertion of registered Cossacks to his side. The inexperienced generals in charge of the main Polish force abandoned their fortified positions and retreated. Khmelnytsky caught up with them near Korsun on May 26, 1648, and destroyed their army, taking them prisoner.

A vast popular uprising erupted throughout the Ukrainian lands as the news spread. Thousands of volunteers flocked to Khmelnytsky's banners, and local leaders formed armed groups to attack Poles and Jews, both of whom were savagely murdered regardless of age or sex. Catholic churches and other buildings were destroyed and their contents looted. Polish magnates and private armies retreated, escorting lesser nobles, Catholic priests, Jews, and other refugees to safety, and they committed similar atrocities against Ruthenian men, women, and children. The richest landlord of Ukraine, Jeremi Wiśniowiecki, a Catholic descendant of an Orthodox noble family, kept the largest private army, 6,000 men, and distinguished himself by his cruel reprisals.

The convocation parliament that gathered at Warsaw in July 1648 to elect a new king had to deal with this emergency. It sent an army of 40,000 men, including 8,000 German mercenaries, against 40,000 Cossack regulars and more than 40,000 Cossack militia. Headed once again by incompetent and disunited generals, the Polish army fled from the battlefield at Pyliavtsi on September 23, 1648. Khmelnytsky met no significant resistance as he followed. He allowed the cities of Lviv and Zamość to pay huge sums to avoid conquest and made moderate demands from his position of strength. He proposed to make peace with the Polish-Lithuanian state in exchange for recognition of traditional Cossack privileges, exemption from local noble control, abandonment of Polish forts impeding Cossack access to the Black Sea, abolition of the Union of Brest, and amnesty. Khmelnytsky paused to allow Poland-Lithuania to elect its new king, and returned to Kiev in triumph.

The Election of Jan Kazimierz

Disputes about the Commonwealth's Ukrainian policy dominated the royal election. Jan Kazimierz represented the accommodationist faction headed by Chancellor Jerzy Ossoliński and Adam Kysil. Ossoliński sought to follow Władysław IV's policy of harnessing the Cossacks to the royal cause in order to provide the court with leverage against a reluctant noble parliament. Kysil wished to achieve full equality for Orthodox nobles and full recognition of the Greek Catholic bishops, particularly giving them seats in the senate. Władysław's widow, Louise Marie, also supported Jan Kazimierz. The peace party convinced parliament to bypass the warlike Wiśniowiecki and elect accommodationist generals to face the Cossacks, but they fought poorly and the Cossacks spread into Volhynia, forcing Kysil, who had been sent to negotiate with Khmelnytsky, to take refuge in a Polish army camp in September 1648. Negotiations resumed in January 1649, but went nowhere because Khmelnytsky, after returning to Kiev, came to think of himself as the head of a sovereign hetman state and lost interest in reconciliation with Poland-Lithuania.

Hard-line magnates from Ukraine and anti-Orthodox Catholics demanded an all-out assault on Khmelnytsky's forces. They favored the election of a younger brother, Karol Ferdynand, the bishop of Płock.

The Royal Couple

Once elected, Jan Kazimierz and Louise Marie sought to gain political freedom of action by creating a royal faction within the senate and, since neither had a significant independent income, by building up their personal fortunes. They put many high government positions up for sale at high prices and filled other vacant posts on the basis of personal loyalty demonstrated by marrying the queen's "nieces"—really favored ladies-in-waiting. For example, the queen's French lady-in-waiting, Marie Casimire d'Arquien, contracted two political marriages. Her first, to Jan Zamoyski the younger, proved unsuccessful because he lost interest in politics as he got older. After he died, Marie Casimire married Jan Sobieski, who proved an important ally for Queen Louise Marie. The marriage started him on his ascent to become King Jan III.

Although initially successful, the policy of building an independent royalist faction made Jan Kazimierz and Louise Marie unpopular with many Polish-Lithuanian nobles. The prices they charged were so high that few nobles could afford them, while some nobles with ample means simply refused to pay. Similarly, nobles who were already married or could not compete for the queen's wards for other reasons saw that they had no chance of attaining political preferment and drifted into opposition. Some responded to the political and military crises of Jan Kazimierz's reign by supporting foreign invaders in the hope of placing a more amenable king on the throne.

The royal couple's personalities alienated many nobles as well. Just as his brother Władysław IV had possessed a facility for being liked, Jan Kazimierz had a facility for antagonizing people. The new king had become prickly from living much of his life in his brother's shadow without proper recognition of his status. He never gained the love of the army even though his bravery in battle earned respect from officers and soldiers under his command. His Catholic piety and numerous pilgrimages alienated Protestants and Orthodox nobles. His marriage to Louise Marie and his subsequent pro-French policies attracted ridicule and hostility. For her part, Louise Marie offended traditionalists who resented her influence on patronage appointments and policy. Foreign ambassadors heard complaints that she led the king around "as a small Ethiopian leads an elephant" or as a zookeeper "leads a bear by the nose." The royal couple frequently argued in public, particularly when the king pursued sexual liaisons at court.

French manners and women's fashions further affronted traditionalists. The greater presence of women at court and their greater interaction with men seemed to lower moral standards. Conservative Polish-Lithuanian society, which had been comfortable with Habsburg queens, took offense at fashions such as the deep décolletage and elaborate ornamentation in lace and jewels. The noted poet Wacław Potocki complained in verse: "Women lost all shame . . . as women show off their breasts and naked arms." He was also unhappy that fashionable married and unmarried women dressed the same way and wore makeup. A widely circulated anonymous satirical verse proclaimed as Louise Marie lay gravely ill: "We all say at the hour of your death—Devil, take your own for your praise."

Moral objections to French fashions took on added political significance because of the large French presence in Warsaw. Of the 134 foreigners at the royal court, 100 were French, and some 1,000 French lived in Warsaw, comprising 8 percent of the 13,000 residents. Most of the French brought their families to Warsaw, but unmarried soldiers and clerics lived there as well. The Poles greeted the French enthusiastically at first but cooled to French involvement in politics. Nevertheless, they remained well disposed to Queen Louise Marie's active support for the arts. She sponsored poets and playwrights, and theater remained active until the Swedish invasion of 1655; it continued sporadically afterward. A thirty-six piece royal orchestra played for banquets, ballet, and special religious events. Throughout the 1640s and 1650s, the queen supported scientific experimentation by the French diplomat and Italian Capuchin monk Valeriano Magna, who performed early experiments with vacuums, and Tito Livias Burattini, who experimented in optics and brought a copy of Pascal's adding machine to Warsaw. The queen's secretary, Pierre Des Noyers, kept in close touch with French and other astronomers.

THE COSSACK WARS

Jan Kazimierz won the throne without much difficulty and moved in 1649 to regain control of rebel-held lands. He gave Wiśniowiecki command of an army of 15,000 regulars that found itself besieged at Zbarazh by 80,000 Cossacks and Tatars. Jan Kazimierz allowed himself to be surprised at the head of a 25,000-man relieving army, but he fought well and saved his army by reaching an agreement with the Tatar Khan Islam Giray to withdraw from the war. Left alone, Khmelnytsky negotiated terms with the king at Zboriv on August 18, 1649, that made the hetman's conquests an autonomous part of the Polish-Lithuanian state. The agreement set the Cossack register at 40,000 soldiers and barred the Polish army and Jews from the palatinates of Kiev, Bratslav, and Chernihiv. Public office was reserved for Orthodox nobles and Cossack senior officers. The Orthodox metropolitan of Kiev gained a seat in the Polish-Lithuanian senate. Rebels were amnestied, but Polish nobles reclaimed their estates, and peasants had to return to serfdom. Kysil went back to Kiev to be reinstalled as castellan of Kiev and represent Poland-Lithuania in carrying out the agreement. He had some successes, such as punishing some Cossack rebels for murder and opening negotiations for Church union, but both Polish nobles and Cossacks criticized him sharply for the inevitable failures.

Many on both sides, regarding the peace as merely a truce, prepared for war. Khmelnytsky yielded to appeals from Kievan Metropolitan Sylvester Kosiv to protect the entire Orthodox world, and began to call himself "autocrat of Rus" in discussions with Kysil. He conceived a grandiose scheme to form a coalition of Orthodox and Protestant powers such as Cromwell's England to force Poland-Lithuania to admit Rus as a third, equal partner and replace Jan Kazimierz as king with Transylvanian Duke György II Rákoczy. Similarly, the Polish-Lithuanian war party gained the upper hand, sensing that they could subdue the Cossacks. Chancellor Jerzy Ossoliński was hotly criticized for the Zboriv agreement, which he had concluded in order to press his plans for war to conquer Moldavia, and even Jan Kazimierz found it expedient to repudiate him. Ossoliński died in August 1650 while traveling to Italy to raise support for an anti-Turkish crusade. Wiśniowiecki gained a temporary appointment as hetman, and the king added two rich royal leaseholds to his immense holdings (although he irritated Wiśniowiecki by giving richer rewards to a personal friend and musical associate). Marshal Jerzy Lubomirski concluded that Jan Kazimierz was to blame for the dangers that beset the Commonwealth and plotted to overthrow him. Queen Louise Marie negotiated Lubomirski's reconciliation with Jan

Kazimierz, allowing Lubomirski to keep his ministerial post, but word failed to reach one of the noble conspirators, Aleksander Kostka Napierski, before he launched an abortive rebellion in the mountains south of Cracow that touched off a peasant rebellion. A noble levy easily defeated the rebels.

A 100,000-man Polish army raised from state forces, provincial militias, private armies, and a noble levy defeated an equal number of Cossacks and Tatars at Berestechko in Volhynia on June 30, 1651. Seeing no gain to themselves in the fierce fighting, the Tatars withdrew and carried off Khmelnytsky as a prisoner. Despite loss on the battlefield and heavy casualties, the Cossacks continued to put up a stubborn defense and Khmelnytsky soon rejoined them with fresh forces. The Polish levy dissipated as nobles withdrew to look after their estates. After some inconclusive fighting around Bila Tserkva (Biała Cerkiew), Poles and the Cossacks reached an agreement restricting the area under Khmelnytsky's control from three palatinates to one, the Kievan Palatinate, and reducing the Cossack register to 20,000. Once again, Kysil tried to administer the agreement but had to flee when the fighting resumed in 1652; he died in 1653. Khmelnytsky tried to conquer Moldavia for his son, Tymish (Timothy), and defeated the Polish forces that sought to hold him back. Jan Kazimierz raised another large army and invaded the Cossack Hetmanate only to find himself besieged once again by the more mobile Cossacks. Another Tatar withdrawal forced the Cossacks to accept the status quo.

THE COSSACK-RUSSIAN ALLIANCE

Khmelnytsky turned to Russia to break the military deadlock after briefly considering alliance with the Turkish sultan. The hetman had opened negotiations with Moscow as early as 1648, but the cautious Russians waited until the time was ripe. In October 1653, the Russian Assembly (Zemsky Sobor) in Moscow approved the incorporation of Ukrainian lands into the Russian Empire, and Tsar Aleksei Mikhailovich sent Vasilii Buturlin to Khmelnytsky to negotiate an agreement. Late in 1653, Buturlin met with the leadership of the Cossack Host in Pereiaslav, near Kiev. On January 18, 1654, the Pereiaslav agreement was proclaimed, joining the territory of the Cossack Hetmanate to Russia. Khmelnytsky swore allegiance to Tsar Aleksei while Buturlin promised the Cossacks autonomy; following Russian protocol, he refused to take an oath in the tsar's name. Shortly thereafter, 127,000 Cossacks and burghers swore allegiance to Tsar Aleksei in 117 Ukrainian cities. Khmelnytsky saw this as a tactical alliance rather than a permanent relationship, as did the Russians, who put more emphasis on expanding into Belarus than on solidifying their control over the Ukrainian palatinates.

The Pereiaslav agreement made the Cossack Hetmanate an autonomous part of the Tsarist Empire. Cities elected their own officials, who collected taxes for local needs and for the tsar's treasury. Tsarist officials supervised tax collections but could not impose new taxes. The Cossack leadership received salaries from local revenues, ranging from 1,000 Polish zlotys annually (secretary-general of the Host) to 30 zlotys (regimental standard bearer). Each ranking officer also received a flour mill that yielded further income. Artillery and artillery officers were supported from local revenues for the winter. The hetman continued to have the right to receive envoys, provided they "meant well" (i.e., were friendly to Russia). In practice, this meant that Russian agents opposed the reception of envoys from the Turkish sultan and the king of Poland-Lithuania, and the Cossacks were required to detain other envoys who intrigued against Russia. The metropolitan of Kiev was confirmed in office and in his Church lands. The Cossacks insisted that Russian troops be stationed at key points to defend Ukraine and Belarus against the Poles, and requested large subsidies for Cossack troops. The Russian negotiators could not meet all the Cossack demands, but they promised to pay what they could afford and to restrain the Don Cossacks from stirring up the Crimean Tatars, who might vent their rage against the hetmanate. Zaporozhian Cossacks received permission to garrison the border fort at Kodak, which the Russians supplied with munitions. The Host was set at 60,000 registered Cossacks. A Charter of the Zaporozhian Host issued by Tsar Aleksei Mikhailovich assured Cossacks of their traditional freedom to elect their officers and rule themselves.

The Pereiaslav agreement touched off another round of disastrous fighting. Polish forces invaded Ukraine to take bloody revenge for their losses, while Cossacks and Orthodox peasants responded in kind. Tatars plundered at will, driving peasants into slavery and killing those who were too young, too old, or too sick to march to Crimea. Polish forces in Ukraine pushed the Cossacks back and, once again with Tatar allies, undertook "pacification." However, Khmelnytsky led his Cossacks into Belarus to annex the region and Moscow sent a Russian army that destroyed Lithuanian forces at Szepielewicze on August 24, 1655. When Aleksei added "Tsar of Belarus" to his list of titles, Khmelnytsky became uneasy and sought to regain his independence through alliance with the Swedes, Prussians, and Transylvanians. This policy ultimately failed and led to tensions between the Cossack leadership and the tsar.

"THE DELUGE": THE SWEDISH INVASION OF 1655

Suddenly, the Polish-Lithuanian Commonwealth, which scarcely had enough troops to withstand one major enemy (Cossacks) let alone two (Cossacks and Russia), found itself overpowered by a third, Sweden. Sweden saw that Russia's conquests in Belarus threatened its possessions in Livonia and proposed an alliance with Poland-Lithuania, but negotiations foundered over Jan Kazimierz's refusal to abandon his claim to the Swedish throne and Sweden's demands for more territory along the Baltic coast. Swedish Queen Kristina's abdication in 1654 brought the matter to a head. Her energetic successor, Karl X Gustav, seized the opportunity presented by Poland-Lithuania's involvement with the Cossacks.

Many Polish and Lithuanian nobles refused to support Jan Kazimierz at this critical juncture because they felt he was seeking personal and dynastic advantage at the Commonwealth's expense. The extraordinary parliamentary session of June 1655 could only respond to the Swedish invasion by providing a few additional troops. After seven years of paying high taxes to finance the Cossack wars, Polish and Lithuanian nobles preferred to rely on the noble levy to meet military needs. Only Royal Prussia, which had seen the Swedish army in action, voted to hire mercenaries. As a result, Poland fielded only 7,000 regular cavalry and 6,500 trained infantry as well as another 33,000 undisciplined noble cavalry to meet the new threat.

Sweden attacked with a superbly trained army, mostly veterans of the Thirty Years' War, supported by excellent artillery. They attacked from an unexpected direction, too, because Brandenburg allowed Swedish General Arvid Wittenberg to bring his garrison troops from Germany to attack. The Polish commander, Krzysztof Opaliński, was not a professional soldier and had no hope of withstanding the 14,000 Swedish professionals who brushed aside his 13,000 noble cavalry and 1,400 professional infantrymen with minimal effort. The Polish army hastily surrendered at Ujście on July 24, 1655, although the overwhelming majority of nobles fled rather than sign the capitulation.

Swedish King Karl X Gustav arrived in person at the head of a new corps and led the combined army into the Polish interior. The Swedes easily defeated Polish armies at Piątek in Great Poland and marched to Warsaw, which Jan Kazimierz left undefended. The Swedes beat him again in Little Poland, and Jan Kazimierz withdrew to his possessions in Silesia. After Karl X defeated the remaining Polish field army, General Stefan Czarniecki surrendered Cracow, and won the right to withdraw with his Polish regulars who had defended the city tenaciously.

Polish armies did no better in the East against the Russians and Cossacks, and, in retreat, they accepted Swedish sovereignty. Lithuanian Grand Hetman Janusz Radziwiłł, who was on bad terms with Jan Kazimierz because the two blamed each other for military failures against the Cossacks, signed the Kejdany accord of August 18, 1655, recognizing King Karl X Gustav as king of Lithuania, thereby breaking the Lithuanian Union with Poland. Karl rejected Radziwiłł's efforts to establish Lithuania as an equal partner in union with Sweden and make himself grand duke, but he confirmed noble privileges and promised to appoint a Lithuanian as viceroy. Prince Bogusław Radziwiłł, a cousin, made a separate agreement and fought for Poland-Lithuania's enemies until the end of the war;

after receiving amnesty, he held several important political positions in Poland-Lithuania. Not everyone followed the Radziwiłłs, however. One group of nobles recognized Tsar Aleksei Mikhailovich as king of Lithuania in exchange for Aleksei's promise to confirm Lithuanian laws and liberties. Another group remained loyal to King Jan Kazimierz. The Swedes tried to round out their success by expanding their control of the Baltic coast. After they captured Malbork, Friedrich Wilhelm, elector of Brandenburg, allied himself openly with Sweden to protect Königsberg.

The Swedish victory seemed so complete that contemporaries termed it a flood, or deluge, that covered the land. Only a few islands of resistance remained, such as Gdańsk and the fortified monastery of Jasna Góra, near Częstochowa.

Victory Against the Swedes

Resistance against the Swedes never entirely ceased, and it grew in strength as the Swedes financed their occupation with heavy confiscations and requisitions. The occupation forces further antagonized Poles and Lithuanians by systematically looting Catholic churches, and sometimes Lutheran zealots damaged holy objects out of hatred for Catholicism. Nobles, burghers, and peasants formed partisan units to attack the Swedes, liberating outlying regions and cities in the fall of 1655. On December 29, 1655, Hetman Stanisław Potocki renounced his oath of allegiance to Karl Gustav and formed an anti-Swedish confederation of nobles at Tyszowce; the Swedish failure to pay his soldiers was an important factor in his decision. Jan Kazimierz spread propaganda from Silesia and recruited Tatar assistance. The success of Jasna Góra in holding out against the Swedish general Burchard Müller and forcing him to withdraw gave the anti-Swedish movement confidence. When both Swedish and Russian troops levied requisitions and despoiled Lithuania, peasant rebels helped Lithuanian Field Hetman Wincenty Gosiewski expel the Swedes in 1659–60.

Jan Kazimierz returned from Silesia to reconquer his country and to take charge of the Tyszowce confederation. He swore an oath to improve peasant conditions and summoned a general levy of Poles from all estates and classes. The remnants of the royal army under Stefan Czarniecki avoided battle with the Swedes and attacked their lines of communication. Partisans made the countryside so dangerous that the invaders shut themselves away in fortified cities. As Polish-Lithuanian forces won more victories, the regular army grew to almost 60,000 troops (30,000 regulars and a volunteer levy of similar size). Jan Kazimierz liberated Warsaw on June 30, 1656, after a short siege; some unpaid Polish soldiers celebrated by plundering civilians. The king later lost a three-day battle outside Warsaw on July 28–30, 1656, against the major Swedish forces when his army failed to push home a successful cavalry charge, but the Swedes continued to retreat into Pomerania. Karl Gustav hoped to retain Swedish conquests along the Baltic by enticing György II Rákoczy, prince of Transylvania, to attack by promising him the Polish-Lithuanian crown. He also reached separate agreements with Brandenburg, the Cossacks, and Bogusław Radziwiłł of Lithuania, to partition the Commonwealth, but these never went into effect. Rákoczy invaded in January 1657 with 40,000 troops, conquering southern Poland and relieving the besieged Swedish garrison in Cracow. Unsupported by Sweden and defeated in battle on July 24, 1657, at Medzhybizh (Międzybóż) in Right Bank Ukraine, Rákoczy renounced his claims to the Polish throne and withdrew. Tatars destroyed his army on the way home and Hetman Jerzy Lubomirski, who commanded forces in Little Poland, plundered Transylvania.

Sweden's enemies joined forces with Poland-Lithuania to end the war. Austria sent troops to fight along with Jan Kazimierz, although Poland-Lithuania had to pay the costs. A joint Danish-Commonwealth army invaded southern Sweden and forced Karl Gustav to bring his troops home to prevent the Danes from regaining the contested province of Skania (Skåne). Friedrich Wilhelm of Brandenburg abandoned Sweden and switched to the Polish side in exchange for recognition of his full sovereignty in Ducal Prussia at the Treaty of Wehlau (Welawa) on September 19, 1657, and the supplementary Treaty of Bromberg (Bydgoszcz) on November 16, 1657; he agreed to supply Poland-Lithuania with 1,500 infantry and 500 cavalry in wartime. Russia had already negotiated peace with Poland-Lithuania at Vilnius on November 3, 1656.

Peace was at hand. Parliament gathered in Warsaw in 1658 to enact new taxes to build up the infantry and artillery needed to reconquer Swedish-held cities along the coast. Toruń, which Polish cavalry had blockaded for about a year, fell to a Polish-Austrian army in mid-November 1658, and the remaining Pomeranian cities were taken in 1659. Sweden met with Poland-Lithuania to negotiate a settlement with France's assistance as mediator. Karl Gustav's death eased negotiations. Signed near Gdańsk, the Treaty of Oliwa (May 3, 1660) reaffirmed territorial possessions held at the beginning of the war; Poland-Lithuania renounced claims to Swedish Livonia and Jan Kazimierz renounced his claims to the Swedish throne. Friedrich Wilhelm of Brandenburg returned his conquests to Sweden but the Oliwa treaty reaffirmed the legal independence of Ducal Prussia, a situation that Jan Kazimierz found preferable to making the territorial concessions that Friedrich Wilhelm sought. Sweden signed separate treaties with Denmark in 1660, and Russia in 1661.

Ducal Prussia

Prussian nobles and burghers still looked to Poland-Lithuania for support after the Treaty of Wehlau accorded full sovereignty to Friedrich Wilhelm I, the elector of Brandenburg. Even before he had been sworn in as duke, Friedrich Wilhelm collected more taxes in Prussia than the Estates had authorized and named a viceroy with broad military and civilian powers instead of working through local officials. Seeing that he intended to restrict their political and economic freedoms, Prussian nobles and the capital city of Königsberg avoided taking an oath of allegiance. Friedrich Wilhelm overawed them by building new fortifications and deporting Königsberg's mayor, Hieronymus Roth, to a Brandenburg prison, where he died sixteen years later. Two leading Prussian nobles, Lieutenant-General Albrecht Kalkstein and his son Christian Ludwig Kalkstein, came to Warsaw to ask Jan Kazimierz for help. The Polish-Lithuanian king lacked military strength and hoped mistakenly that Friedrich Wilhelm would support him in his Russian campaigns, so he told his representatives in Königsberg to welcome the new duke. When the Estates gave up and swore allegiance in October 1663, Poland-Lithuania's chance to regain influence in Ducal Prussia was lost.

HADIACH AND THE PARTITION OF UKRAINIAN LANDS

Poland-Lithuania regained the upper hand in the Ukrainian lands when the Swedish threat declined. Despite the Pereiaslav agreement, Russian-Cossack cooperation was full of problems, such as in 1655, when the Cossacks failed to capture Lviv because Tsar Aleksei demanded that they surrender it to him. There were similar disagreements over control of reconquered parts of Belarus, and the Russians objected when Khmelnytsky designated his sixteen-year-old son Yurii as heir to the Hetmanate without consulting them. When he died in 1657, his senior officers ignored his wishes and named one of their number, Ivan Vyhovsky, as hetman. The new hetman reversed Khmelnytsky's course and signed the Treaty of Hadiach with Poland-Lithuania on September 16, 1658.

The Hadiach treaty would have reshaped eastern European history by maintaining the size and strength of the Commonwealth and preventing Russian expansion, but it proved unpopular with both the Cossacks and Polish-Lithuanian nobles, and it never went into effect. According to the terms of the treaty, the Kievan, Pereiaslav, and Chernihiv palatinates would have become an autonomous grand duchy of Ruthenia within a tripartite Polish-Lithuanian-Ruthenian state. The grand duchy would have been governed by a hetman with life tenure, elected in the Polish-Lithuanian parliament from four candidates presented by a Ukrainian assembly and confirmed by the king. Nobles and senior Cossack officers would have received equal status with Polish and Lithuanian nobles. Dietines in the new grand duchy would have elected deputies to the parliament in Warsaw, and territorial officers (palatines and castellans) would have regained their seats in the senate along with six Orthodox bishops who would have been seated for the first time. The grand duchy would have enjoyed separate courts, treasury, currency, and its own army consisting of 30,000 registered Cossacks as well as 10,000 mercenaries. Polish and Lithuanian armies would have been barred from entering the grand duchy without permission and, if summoned, would have fallen automatically under the hetman's command. Orthodox Christians would have received equal religious rights, and the Greek Catholic Church would have been abolished within the duchy. In exchange, the grand duchy would surrender the right to conduct separate diplomacy, allow Polish nobles to regain their landed properties, and abandon its claims to other provinces with substantial Orthodox populations such as Volhynia, Galicia, and Podolia. A general amnesty was proclaimed. The Polish-Lithuanian parliament ratified the treaty on May 22, 1659.

Hadiach was the product of the polonized Orthodox nobles and the Cossack senior officers who wished to achieve equality with Polish and Lithuanian nobles as serf owners and participants in Polish-Lithuanian noble democratic institutions. The career of its major proponent, Ivan Vyhovsky (d. 1664), is typical. His date of birth is unknown. He studied at the Kievan Mohyla Academy, joined the Orthodox brotherhood of Lutsk, and worked for the Polish government in minor capacities before serving in the Polish army at the outbreak of the Cossack uprising of 1648. After being captured, Vyhovsky joined the Cossacks. Khmelnytsky recognized his diplomatic abilities and appointed him military chancellor, later general chancellor, as well as Yurii Khmelnytsky's guardian. The Treaty of Hadiach was drafted by another polonized Ruthenian, Yurii Nemyrych (Jerzy Niemirycz, 1612–59), an exceptionally well-educated magnate who owned 14 cities and 50 villages on his estates in Volhynia and the Kievan Palatinate. An Arian, Nemyrych defended Anti-Trinitarians in court and in parliament, and supported György II Rákoczy as candidate for the Polish-Lithuanian throne in 1648. He fought against the Cossacks as colonel-general of the Kievan Palatinate's noble levy but switched to the Swedish side in 1655 in hopes of improving the Protestant position in the Commonwealth and reconquering his estates in the Ukrainian palatinates. Karl Gustav assigned him important military and diplomatic duties. After the collapse of Swedish and Transylvanian efforts in the Commonwealth, Nemyrych converted to Orthodoxy, became a regional governor, and reclaimed the estates that he had lost in the Cossack revolt. He helped engineer Vyhovsky's election as hetman, drafted the Hadiach treaty, and, as chancellor, headed the Ukrainian delegation to the Polish-Lithuanian parliamentary session for ratification. Nemyrych fought with Vyhovsky against the Russians but lost his life to Cossack opponents.

Vyhovsky lost control of the Hetmanate, and the Hadiach treaty never went into effect. Even though it ratified the treaty, the Polish-Lithuanian parliament did not wish to acknowledge Cossack supremacy in Ukrainian lands and forbade Jan Kazimierz to support Vyhovsky militarily. Unchallenged, Russia sent in troops and spread anti-Catholic religious propaganda among ordinary Cossacks, who were already anti-Polish. The Russians had the support of the Zaporozhian Host, which refused to recognize Vyhovsky as hetman on the grounds that he had failed to present himself there for election. The outbreak of Cossack insurrections throughout the Hetmanate forced Vyhovsky to flee to Poland-Lithuania, where he served the state until a Cossack rival accused him of treason and succeeded in having him executed.

With Vyhovsky gone, the Hetmanate became a battleground for rival factions. Russia sponsored Ivan Bezpaly and then Yurii Khmelnytsky as hetman in exchange for modifications of the Pereiaslav agreement that further limited Cossack autonomy. After Polish Field Hetman Jerzy Lubomirski reconquered the Hetmanate briefly, Russia turned to Ivan Briukhovetsky, who fell in line with Russian policies after executing his chief Cossack rival, marrying into an aristocratic Russian family, and expelling the Poles.

The Russo-Polish treaty of Andrusovo, signed near Smolensk on January 30, 1667, brought an end to the Russo-Polish war by partitioning the Hetmanate along the Dnieper River. Poland-Lithuania gained the Right (West) Bank except Kiev, which fell to Russia along with the Left (East) Bank. Zaporozhia was placed under joint protection. Many Cossacks resented the settlement, and fighting continued to bring desolation and ruin to the region for decades.

The Hetman State

The borders of the Hetmanate shifted with the fortunes of war, but its institutions remained constant. When Bohdan Khmelnytsky died in 1657, the Hetmanate comprised about 1.5 million people living in the former Kievan, Bratslav, and Chernihiv provinces. Orthodox and partially Orthodox Galicia, Volhynia, Podolia, and Belarus remained in the Polish-Lithuanian state. An elected king, the hetman enjoyed unrestricted authority over military, civil, and judicial matters. His staff of military and civil advisers included a secretary or chancellor, a treasurer or quartermaster general, a chief judge, and several lesser officers who carried out special assignments. Kiev was the official capital, but each hetman used cities on his own estates as functional capitals (Chyhyryn after 1649; Baturyn and Hlukhiv in the eighteenth century). The sixteen regiments of the Cossack Host provided civil and judicial administration to the Hetmanate's sixteen districts. Local administration was supplied by smaller military units. The hetman had little authority over the Zaporozhian Host, which acted like an independent state.

The Hetmanate granted privileges to a new nobility formed by Cossack officers and Orthodox nobles. Ordinary Cossacks returned to their villages in the vast crown-owned lands that made up 50 percent of the Hetmanate to farm as free peasants who owed taxes in cash and kind to the state and provided minor services such as transportation. Cossack officers and Orthodox nobles owned two-thirds of privately held land, while the Orthodox Church owned the remaining third. Peasants on private estates still owed full feudal obligations as before. Over time, many Cossack officers made crown lands into private property and enserfed the peasants. The Cossack state recognized the self-governing privileges and guild monopolies of major cities such as Kiev, Chernihiv, and Poltava, although in practice Cossacks often infringed on those privileges the way Polish nobles had.

The Orthodox Church regarded the Cossack leadership with suspicion and rarely supported it against opponents. It avoided endorsing the Cossack revolt of 1648 out of its traditional social conservatism, although it did not condemn it, and it opposed Khmelnytsky's alliance with Russia in 1654 for fear of subordination to the Muscovite Patriarchate. Bohdan Khmelnytsky suspected the higher clergy of welcoming Lithuanian Hetman Janusz Radziwiłł's brief conquest of Kiev in 1651, but Cossack authorities left the Church alone until 1658, when Metropolitan Dionysii Balaban supported Hetman Ivan Vyhovsky's pro-Polish policies and fled to the Polish-controlled Right Bank when he lost. Most Orthodox clerics preferred Tsar Aleksei Mihailovich to Vyhovsky, and accepted the tsar's appointment of a temporary replacement for Balaban. Nor did they object to the Moscow patriarch's assertion of authority over the Left Bank Orthodox Church in 1686. Like ordinary Cossacks, most Ruthenian clergy viewed the Moscow Patriarchate as an additional guarantee that pro-Polish policies would never succeed.

The Hetmanate declined quickly from its position of strength under Khmelnytsky, as the new institutions proved too fragile to survive the complicated domestic and foreign situation. Cossack disunity and Russo-Polish rivalries touched off more than a decade of civil war, leaving the Ukrainian lands desolated and partitioned.

Jewish Settlement in Ukraine and the Catastrophe

Jews flocked to Ukrainian territories after the Union of Lublin threw Podolia, Bratslav, and Kiev open to colonization by Polish and polonized Orthodox nobles. Polish kings extended existing Jewish legislation and issued new privileges to immigrants. Jews also moved in smaller number to the Grand Duchy, where endemic border warfare left them open to harsh treatment from Russian commanders who expelled or slaughtered them, along with Catholic clerics, when they captured Lithuanian cities. The Cossack revolt that began in 1648 and the Swedish invasion of 1655 brought to a close the expansive growth of the Jewish population in the Polish-Lithuanian Commonwealth, although natural increase continued to be substantial.

While earlier uprisings had seen attacks on Jews and their property, the Cossack uprising of 1648 brought unparalleled horror. In addition to religious anti-Judaism, Cossack and peasant insurgents hated Jews because they acted as agents of the nobility. Jewish artisans were tarred with the same brush even though the local economy badly needed their manufacturing skills. Nevertheless, neighborly relations were often friendly in peacetime and some Jews served in Cossack regiments, probably after conversion to Christianity. The statistical reports of seventeenth-century Jewish chroniclers, who made Khmelnytsky the most significant villain in Jewish tradition since the biblical Haman, appear greatly exaggerated, but at least ten thousand Jews were certainly killed and whole communities were wiped out. When towns fell, insurgents killed Jews and Poles (especially Roman Catholic priests) with exceptional cruelty; some victims were literally cut into pieces or flayed alive. Rape, murder, and destruction of property were commonplace. Rather than save themselves by conversion, Jews fled before the approach of Cossack armies when they could, often falling victim to attacks during their flight, and on several occasions protected themselves by asking the Tatars to accept them as slaves. Jews also fought back militarily, providing guild militia units to defend the walls of cities such as Bar, Lviv, Niemiriv (Niemirów), and Żółkiew, and fighting in Polish-Lithuanian armies. Separate Jewish detachments appear to have fought in the battle of Berestechko and some lesser engagements.

The Swedish war of 1655–57 brought additional death and destruction to the Jews of Poland-Lithuania. Significant massacres occurred in at least thirty cities and towns. In addition to the usual confiscatory requisitions, Swedish armies (the lower ranks included many foreign mercenaries) occupying Poznań, Cracow, and several smaller cities singled out Jews for attack. Catholics in Cracow joined the Swedish soldiers in looting Jewish stores, in part because they blamed Poland-Lithuania's non-Catholic population for the unparalleled disasters that befell the Commonwealth. Some Polish partisan forces also attacked Jewish communities and accused numerous Jews of treason. King Jan Kazimierz confiscated the real property and goods of Cracow Jews and turned them over to the Polish commander, Jerzy Lubomirski, because of their alleged collaboration with the Swedes.

Royal Reform and the Lubomirski Revolt

The disastrous flood of invasions convinced both royalists and republicans of the need to make significant constitutional reforms, but the two groups could not agree on a common policy and the chance was squandered. King Jan

Kazimierz sought to strengthen the power of the monarchy by electing a successor during his lifetime in order to avoid the compromises that candidates always made during royal elections. He and Queen Louise Marie sought to make Henri Jules duc d'Enghien heir to the Polish-Lithuanian throne, since they had no children and their Swedish cousins were obviously unacceptable. France had become popular after mediating an end to the Swedish war. There had been some possibility of electing the French duke as heir apparent while the Swedish war was still going on, but it could not be done in peacetime. Courtiers suggested that Jan Kazimierz provide military support for the duke's election, and then abdicate.

Concentrating on electing a new king prevented Jan Kazimierz from cooperating with the significant group of parliamentarians that still advocated reforms to make parliament more effective. They saw the *liberum veto,* which had been first cast in 1652, as a dangerous practice that had to be modified or abolished. Primate Andrzej Leszczyński sought to abolish or severely limit it. An anonymous pamphlet entitled "Points Submitted to Parliament" boldly called for the abolition of the *liberum veto,* recognition of majority rule (qualified on some issues), and secret voting. It offered a suspensive veto for the king and the senate. Parliament would meet annually and a residents' council composed of senators and deputies would advise the king between sessions. At the 1661 parliament, Chancellor Mikołaj Jan Prażmowski advocated abolishing the unanimity rule, but gained little support from deputies, who saw recent military victories as confirmation that the existing system worked.

Łukasz Opaliński, who had been a leading spokesman for senatorial reform in the previous two reigns, returned to parliament as crown court marshal to work on treasury reform and again addressed constitutional issues. His 1657 letter called for changes in parliamentary procedures, executive practices, and treasury policies. Opaliński sought to hold parliamentary sessions without convoking dietines in advance; instructions from previous meetings would become suggestions instead of binding obligations. Parliament's agenda would be based on royal proposals, rather than deputies' priorities. All private matters would be discussed elsewhere. Majority voting would prevail, and the *liberum veto* would apply only to decisions contrary to established laws or measures changing the existing system of government. Opaliński wanted to expand the role of the senate council, adding elected deputies to allay republican suspicions. The treasury would get permanent taxes for military needs. His proposals made parliament the key state institution, reducing the power of the dietines. He insisted on retaining the elective kingship and rejected Jan Kazimierz's plans for electing a successor during his reign.

The king did not support parliamentary reform efforts, in part because he could use the veto to head off interference, and his continued efforts to achieve royalist reform led ultimately to armed revolt. A confederation of antiroyalist nobles dominated the parliamentary sessions of 1661 and 1662 and rejected the king's plans, demanding the execution of the leader of the Royal Party in Lithuania, Vice-Chancellor Krzysztof Pac. Hetman Jerzy Lubomirski, who had renounced his wartime acceptance of a royal election while the king was still alive, perhaps in the hope of gaining election to the throne himself, was particularly vocal in opposition. Lubomirski's refusal to take part in the Russian campaign gave an excuse for King Jan Kazimierz to have him condemned for treason by a parliamentary court and sentenced to death. Lubomirski's friends saved him by casting a *liberum veto* before the case was entirely wound up, but some of his supporters were actually executed. Lubomirski fled to Silesia and sought foreign help. Claiming that Jan Kazimierz had broken his coronation oath, Lubomirski returned to Poland and raised an insurrectionary army that defeated the king's forces in the battle of Mątwy. As a compromise solution, Lubomirski asked the king's forgiveness—in exchange for Jan Kazimierz's abandoning his policies and restoring Lubomirski to office.

Jan Kazimierz Abdicates

Jan Kazimierz had no hope of improving his political position after he compromised with Lubomirski and he fell in with French schemes to place Philip Wilhelm, duke of Neuburg, a French ally and relative of the Polish king by marriage, on the Polish-Lithuanian throne. The king received 150,000 livres to abdicate and Neuburg promised to pay his debts if he were elected. Jan Kazimierz went through with the plan in 1668 and moved to France, where Louis XIV granted him seven rich monasteries including St. Germain des Prés, even though Neuburg lost. The ex-king led the life of a private gentleman in France. He talked about returning to Poland-Lithuania and made some diplomatic efforts to gather allies against the Ottoman invasion of Podolia shortly before his death on December 16, 1672. Jan Kazimierz's heart was buried in St. Germain des Prés, but his body was transported to Poland and laid to rest in the Wawel Cathedral in Cracow.

CHAPTER 11

Noble Democracy as a Political System

The distinctive noble democracy of Poland-Lithuania began during the Jagiellonian era and reached its high point of development during the Vasa dynasty. Sharing power with parliament, Kings Zygmunt III, Władysław IV, and Jan Kazimierz brought the Commonwealth to its apex of political and military strength. Yet the system of checks and balances between kings and parliaments held within itself the seeds of decline and led eventually, although not inevitably, to the paralysis and destruction of the Polish-Lithuanian state in the eighteenth century.

THE KING AND HIS MINISTERS

Polish-Lithuanian kings dominated politics because of their position and wealth. They formulated both domestic and foreign policy, subject to the approval of parliament, proposed legislation, and vetoed bills that they found unacceptable. When strong criticism made it difficult to act, kings built royal parties in parliament by patronage and flattery, and, if all else failed, a royal supporter could be instructed to end opposition by casting the *liberum veto*. Kings could also use patronage to get their way at the dietines where deputies were elected and instructions were written. Even though officeholders enjoyed lifetime tenure, kings controlled the senate and ministerial ranks through a graduated hierarchy of appointments. Disloyal appointees could be left stranded on a relatively low rung of the ladder or moved up, if they cooperated, from one position to another within the ranks of castellan, palatine, and minister. Appointments as prefect (*starosta*) of crown lands offered recipients substantial revenue.

Jerzy Ossoliński provides an example of the ascent to high position that gave kings so much power along the way despite life tenure. He began his career as a royal courtier and gained appointment as under pantry-master in 1628. He advanced to crown court treasurer in 1632, palatine of Sandomierz in 1630, crown vice-chancellor in 1643, and crown chancellor in 1650, accumulating nine different prefectures between 1629 and 1650. Clerics also won graduated promotions to higher offices and richer benefices. Andrzej Leszczyński started as canon of Cracow in 1623 and abbot of several monasteries (1636, 1643, 1644). He became bishop of Kamieniec (1640), bishop of Chełm (1646), crown vice-chancellor (1645), crown chancellor (1650), and finally primate (archbishop of Gniezno) in 1652.

Kings appointed their ministers: marshals, chancellors, treasurers, and hetmans. The crown great marshal governed the king's court, dictating ceremony, setting food prices, and supervising judicial proceedings. The court marshal assisted him. After about 1550, marshals published security regulations for parliaments and royal visits. They controlled the Marshal's Guard. Chancellors and vice-chancellors supervised government operations and carried on domestic and foreign correspondence. After 1504, they made sure that crown decrees were constitutional on the basis of careful records that have generally survived to the present day. The crown chancellors took charge of foreign relations with the West while the Lithuanian chancellors directed foreign relations with Russia. Chancellors supervised the assessorial courts. The great treasurers and court treasurers (vice-treasurers) supervised the treasuries of Poland and Lithuania, and administered expenditures under parliamentary supervision.

Professionalization of the army led to the appointment of trained commanders—the crown great hetman in the 1520s and, as second-in-command, the field hetman. Lithuania adopted the same system. A regimentary took the place of a hetman who could not serve in a given campaign. The office of hetman formally gained ministerial rank and life tenure in 1581. In addition to exercising command, the hetman formulated military policy and maintained diplomatic missions in Turkey, Crimea, Wallachia, and Moldavia. The office did not gain senatorial status until 1764, but kings generally appointed the generals to the senate as palatines or castellans.

The office of referendar developed in the sixteenth century to present cases to the crown courts. Local offices bearing antiquated titles such as chamberlain, master of the hunt, ensign, and pantry-master offered their holders no power and little income, but candidates sought them eagerly for the honor they bestowed and because they served as stepping stones to ministerial positions. Sale of offices and military commissions began in the sixteenth century and became general in the seventeenth. Both the king and the outgoing officeholder received payment.

Parliament

Parliament achieved coequal status with the king by the mid-sixteenth century. The king took a direct part in parliamentary proceedings, forming one of three equal parliamentary estates: the king, the senate, and the chamber of deputies. After 1569, parliaments met in Warsaw; after 1673, every third session met in Grodno, Lithuania. The king met separately with the senate and chamber of deputies to discuss the issues of the day, and all three estates met together at the end of the parliamentary session to ratify legislation. The ruler appointed a parliamentary Editorial Commission to prepare the final texts for publication.

Parliament became increasingly important in the sixteenth and seventeenth centuries. Only parliament could pass new laws after 1505, except that the king could still issue decrees in areas under royal jurisdiction such as royal cities, matters concerning Jews, and mines. Parliament summoned the military levy. A 1538 law prevented the king from pardoning in cases of murder among nobles, and in 1543 parliament denied him the right to exempt royal officials and supporters from prosecution. Kings lost the ability to protect serfs in their dealings with noble landlords, although royal courts continued to provide due process to peasants on crown estates. After 1578, parliament controlled all ennoblements except those awarded on the battlefield. The treasurer reported to parliament, not to the king. Parliament alone enjoyed the right to issue pardons and grant amnesties. After 1607, parliament assigned sixteen senators-residents (twenty-eight after 1641) to attend the royal court (four at a time) to advise the king and supervise his activities.

Parliament met frequently. In addition to regular biennial sessions, numerous extraordinary sessions lasting two or three weeks dealt with emergencies such as external dangers or financial crises, usually shortfalls in army pay. The details were often worked out during regular parliamentary meetings, and deputies went home to consult their constituents during the period between the two sessions.

Senate

Originally a royal council of advisers and territorial officials, the senate acquired more formal character after 1500. It shared decision-making informally with Polish-Lithuanian kings and provided them with experienced personnel. In 1526, the senate consisted of 95 members: 2 archbishops, 7 bishops, 5 ministers, and 81 territorial officials. The number increased to 140 in 1569 as the Union of Lublin added Lithuanian ministers, bishops, and territorial officials. Territorial expansion further increased the number of senatorial positions to 150 in 1638, although the number of senators was usually slightly smaller due to double officeholding.

Senators debated issues in parliament and voted on them in joint session with the chamber of deputies. Senior members spoke first by position (starting with the castellan of Cracow), and others generally joined the emerging consensus. Although senators did not initiate bills, they influenced their development because the senate mediated between hostile groups in the chamber of deputies and drafted compromise proposals. They made up most of the Editorial Commission that kings appointed at the end of parliamentary sessions to prepare the official texts of new laws. Eloquent speeches by experienced senators in joint sessions influenced the course of debate in the chamber of deputies. On occasion, the senate exercised veto power—for example, blocking the king's proposals on religious disturbances in 1606. The senate also acted as a parliamentary court under the chairmanship of the king or his court marshal to try accusations of lèse majesté, embezzlement of state funds, and violence at parliamentary gatherings. Between parliamentary meetings, a *senatus consultus* advised the king on appointments, marriages, finances, taxes, foreign policy, and military affairs. Zygmunt III wanted to regularize senatorial procedures by establishing a published record of discussions. Senators may have been trying to increase their powers when they broke precedent in 1615 and 1623 by proposing legislation. If so, they failed.

Most kings considered the senate a friendly body because they controlled membership through their power of appointment. The senate contained both aristocrats (senatorial families for several generations) and "new men" whose families had never gained preferment to the senate before. Some had been strong republicans whom the king appointed to win them over to his side—or at least to get them out of the chamber of deputies. Jan Zamoyski was the archetypical "new man" who reached the highest state offices during the reigns of Stefan Batory and Zygmunt III. A more typical new man was Wojciech Baranowski, a noble from a comfortable but not rich family, who rose from royal secretary to progressively higher benefices until he became bishop of Przemyśl and vice-chancellor in 1585. Paradoxically, his political opposition to Zygmunt III's policies won him promotion to the rich Płock bishopric because rules against multiple officeholding forced him to resign as vice-chancellor. Renewed support for Zygmunt III during the Zebrzydowski rebellion gained him promotion to archbishop of Gniezno.

Chamber of Deputies

All nobles enjoyed the right to participate in dietines to elect parliamentary deputies to the chamber of deputies, which represented the several lands of Poland. The number of deputies was originally set by custom, ranging from one to six based on the size of the district, and later regulated by law. After 1569, the chamber of deputies consisted of 122 deputies from the Polish crown provinces and 48 from Lithuania.

Despite democratic electoral procedures within the noble constituency, the chamber of deputies contained a narrow political elite, and senators regularly gained election to the chamber of deputies until the rules differentiating the two bodies became fixed. About half the deputies usually held provincial office. In the seventeenth and eighteenth centuries, about one-third of the deputies came from magnate families while, on average, 15 percent gained promotion to the senate as a result of their service as deputies. The chamber of deputies contained numerous professional politicians—that is, deputies elected to five sessions or more. Most were rich nobles who could afford the time and expense of political activity. Many deputies looked for promotion to the highest ranks of the central government. In 1572–1655, 47 percent of deputies were wealthy nobles and magnates owning more than fifteen villages, many of whom later won promotion to senatorial rank. Aristocrats filled the office of marshal (speaker) in 26 percent of parliaments. They provided 50 percent of the marshals during electoral parliaments.

The original function of the chamber of deputies in the fifteenth and sixteenth centuries was to ratify decisions made by the king and senate, but assertive members of the Execution of the Law movement (Executionists) in the mid-sixteenth century proposed new legislation as well. In the later sixteenth century and throughout the seventeenth century, the members of the chamber of deputies generally confined their activities to amending proposals made by the king and proposing alternatives with the help of the more experienced senators. Final votes took place only in joint session between the chamber of deputies and the senate at the end of parliament.

Parliamentary Practice and the Unanimity Rule

At the start of a parliamentary session, deputies elected a marshal and heard the king's "Propositions from the Throne." The marshal took and recorded straw votes during debates to guide discussion and incline minorities toward making concessions. The end of a six-week regular session or a short extraordinary session came with formal enactment of legislation that had been agreed upon informally.

The custom of making parliamentary decisions unanimously began as a reasonable drive for consensus and ended as a damaging practice that paralyzed the Polish parliament for about one hundred years; it contributed materially to the Partitions. The practice of awaiting unanimity arose in the fifteenth century in order to respect the decisions made by local and regional authorities; instructions from dietines were considered binding because parliamentary deputies were held to represent the views of their constituents. Like other Europeans during the late Middle Ages, Poles disliked mechanical majority voting. Father Piotr Skarga, a noted royal adviser, argued that parliament should respect the common good and that the majority should convince the minority instead of outvoting it. Parliamentary efficiency was also hampered by many other practices, such as the need to obtain special permission before holding evening sessions.

Parliamentarians generally found ways to overcome or evade procedural restraints. Serious differences of opinion among large blocks of deputies were resolved by extensive consultation involving the king, senate, and chamber of deputies. Sometimes deputies and senators met without the king. When no resolution could be reached, the issues were left for a later time. Small minorities were simply ignored by marshals who declared decisions by acclamation, allowing the majority to shout their opponents down. In addition, small minorities frequently respected the preponderant view voluntarily; in 1611, for example, the minority group consented to the passage of legislation that it opposed. In 1629, deputies from four palatinates withdrew their protest to the principle of a proposed hearth tax when the proposed tax rate was reduced. In 1632, the marshal added a paragraph to a law stating that a prominent deputy had disagreed. In 1633, a deputy temporarily walked out in protest to suspend the operations of parliament but returned later to allow deliberations to resume. Royal and magnate patronage could be enlisted to convince recalcitrants. Protests generally affected only a specific bill and ended when the deputy withdrew his protest. Parliament rarely broke down and failed to pass legislation before 1650, although the handwriting was on the wall. Parliament failed in 1637, 1639, and 1645, among other years.

LIBERUM VETO

Even before 1600, deputies came to accept the idea that a parliamentary session might end without passing any laws, even though they did not necessarily like the prospect. After the stormy and unsuccessful parliament of 1605 failed to pass a single bill, Jan Ostroróg said that "this kind of government is a great shame if the Republic can be brought to ruin through the stupidity or stubbornness of a single individual." Jan Szczęsny Herburt observed in 1593 that a majority vote provided a "great likelihood of something good being decided for the Commonwealth, especially in matters over which there are some doubts." But he reluctantly accepted the unanimity rule because of the dangers posed by factionalism when the "majority was turned to evil purposes, because one side tried to win over and enlist supporters" instead of judging issues on their merits. Political pressure and royal patronage could generally secure a majority regardless of right and wrong, he feared.

After 1600, deputies accepted fewer polite fictions and required unanimity more strictly as they grew more suspicious of the central government and fearful of cooptation by the king or senate. The idea that parliamentary deputies owed their primary allegiance to their constituents was bolstered by the right of disobedience proclaimed by the *pacta conventa* of 1573 and echoed in the Zebrzydowski revolt in 1607. Dietines met more frequently and drafted more detailed instructions for their representatives. It became almost impossible to pass laws, since the deputies could not maneuver or compromise in parliament.

The unanimity rule developed into the *liberum veto,* or free veto, in 1652 when all the accomplishments of an entire parliamentary session were wiped out by a single protest on a single issue. Under instructions from Hetman Bogusław Radziwiłł, deputy Władysław Siciński cited his dietine's instructions, protested against the king's tax proposals, and left Warsaw. His absence made it impossible to confirm legislation that had received preliminary acceptance by the chamber and senate. The *liberum veto* developed still further in 1669 when parliament came to complete standstill eight days before the end of the six-week parliament because one deputy protested on behalf of a group and left Warsaw so that he could not be convinced or coerced into returning. And finally, a protest ended the 1688 parliament before it even elected its marshal on the first day. From 1573 to 1763, approximately one-third (53) of all parliamentary sessions failed to pass a single law, mostly after 1650. Deputies cast the *liberum veto* in order to frustrate the king or the parliamentary majority on a specific issue. Despite theories of local supremacy and genuine respect for provincial instructions, there was little thought of decentralizing Poland-Lithuania. The ease with which the veto could be invoked simply made its use irresistible in factional fighting.

PARLIAMENTARY REFORM

The defects of unanimity and the *liberum veto* were obvious to many contemporaries, such as the Ruthenian deputy to the 1627 parliament who rejected the binding nature of instructions on the grounds that one province's instructions should not dictate policy to the entire country. As he put it, binding instructions made a single deputy into "the entire parliament." Similarly, he argued that "there is no reason why we should all perish because of the obstinacy of one palatinate." He was not alone. Parliamentary procedures were continually reviewed in the early seventeenth century, largely at the initiative of members who served many terms in the chamber of deputies before gaining appointment to the senate. One line of approach was to permit the senate to initiate legislation; royalists supported this approach because the king generally controlled the senate. Republicans in the senate supported a second line of approach, that of making the chamber of deputies more efficient, in order to keep political control in noble hands. Zygmunt III made notable efforts to reform parliament as well. Interest in parliamentary reform continued to grow in the eighteenth century.

CONFEDERATIONS

In the late Middle Ages, confederations comprised leagues of nobles or cities that took up arms to meet specific emergencies, but they came to represent the will of the noble nation during the interregna of the 1570s when oaths of allegiance to Polish-Lithuanian kings lapsed. Confederations were organized in a single province but became "general" if other provinces joined in. The federal nature of the Polish-Lithuanian state was reflected in the need to organize separate confederations for Poland and Lithuania. Confederations elected a "generality," or government, consisting of a marshal, councillors, and military commanders. A General Council constituted a legal parliament if joined by the king. The *liberum veto* was suspended during confederations and majority rule prevailed. In the eighteenth century, some parliaments were confederated without forming a general confederation. "Hooded" parliaments (named for the dark hooded capes worn as a sign of mourning) met under the auspices of confederations to govern Poland-Lithuania during interregna; the primate of the Catholic Church acted as regent. Some confederations met "with the king" to help him govern more effectively. Using the legal right to disobey kings who violated their oaths of office, nobles also formed confederations "against the king"; such a confederation was called a *rokosz* (rebellion) after Rákos field, where Hungarian nobles gathered to assert their will in the fourteenth century. A king could organize his supporters in a counterconfederation to respond. Confederations recorded their acts in local court registers.

Dietines

The traditional meetings between kings and local nobles grew increasingly important during the reign of Kazimierz IV, who found them useful allies against the magnates in his royal council. After 1493, these local assemblies, or dietines (*sejmiki*), elected deputies to parliamentary sessions of the chamber of deputies on a regular basis. Dietines were considered the sovereign base of the nation, and all local nobles could attend. After 1569, when Lithuania adopted Polish procedures, there were forty-six dietines in the crown provinces and twenty-four in Lithuania (the number underwent minor change over time). The parliamentary process began when the king formulated his legislative program with the help of his ministers and senators, and the royal chancellery convoked dietines by messages that were read out in parish churches and town fairs. Dietines usually met in churches because of their large size. The senior senator started the dietine by arranging the election of a marshal, who directed the discussions, counted votes, presented conclusions, and edited resolutions. District marshals served as dietine marshals in Lithuania. The dietines also drafted detailed instructions for deputies. All local nobles could participate in dietines except lawyers, litigants, and tax collectors. Dietines recognized majority voting in electing parliamentary deputies, although other resolutions generally required unanimity.

Since dietines did not allow protests to paralyze their activities, dissenters sometimes moved to another location and elected their own deputies. When parliament met, a credentials committee decided which delegation it would recognize.

Dietines met for so many local functions, in addition to national ones, that participation in and travel to all of them could easily fill several months each year; only relatively wealthy nobles could afford the time and expense. Electoral dietines met infrequently to elect life-tenured judges to district courts, and deputational dietines met biennially to elect judges for the tribunals. Relational dietines met after parliamentary sessions to hear the deputies' reports. "Hooded" dietines met during interregna to form confederations and govern the country. Economic dietines allocated local tax responsibilities, created tax machinery, distributed funds for local expenses, and recruited soldiers for the local militia.

As the *liberum veto* and other practices hampered central government operations after 1650, dietines took on many of its functions. They collected taxes, disbursed funds, recruited local army detachments, and exercised police functions. The 1717 parliament abolished the jurisdiction of dietines in these matters, but they still carried on these necessary functions from time to time when the central government failed.

Participants at dietines generally obeyed regulations to leave their firearms at home, but they wore swords and got into fights despite penalties for obstructing debate. In addition to settling personal grudges, belligerent nobles used their numbers and weapons to suppress political opponents in a rough and ready form of majority rule. But they avoided pitched battles, and the number of deaths and serious injuries was small. The marshals bore the responsibility of repairing damage to local property from dietine funds.

CITIES AND PARLIAMENT

Polish cities lacked representation in parliament. Their exclusion in the sixteenth century stemmed from three main sources. First, nobles did not want to share their exclusive parliamentary rights with cities and burghers, although they understood the productive role that cities played and did what they could to strengthen both the local and national economies. Second, the cities themselves relied on royal privileges and wished to avoid the risks of sitting in parliament, where they might be outvoted. Large cities strongly protected their legal status against parliamentary reformers in the Executionist movement of the sixteenth century who demanded political centralization and uniformity of treatment. Economic competition between cities prevented them from acting together. Third, kings wished to see cities excluded from parliament in order to weaken that institution. National sentiment had some bearing as well, particularly in the fourteenth and fifteenth centuries when city governments often consisted of German speakers, and several parliaments and provincial assemblies demanded that only ethnic Poles serve as city councillors. Smaller cities were mostly Polish by ethnicity.

Treasury

Polish-Lithuanian kings drew their revenues from vast estates that made up one-third of the Polish Kingdom and half of the Grand Duchy of Lithuania. At one extreme, Polish kings inherited more than 60 percent of Royal Prussia from the Teutonic Knights while at the other extreme they inherited only 15 percent of Mazovia and their original patrimony in Great Poland. Elective kings renounced or distributed much of this wealth in the form of long-term leaseholds to secure their election and win continuing political support. These leaseholds produced little revenue for the crown. The royal treasury and the state treasury were one and the same until the sixteenth century, and parliament demanded that shortfalls in revenues be made up by more intensive exploitation of the royal estates. Zygmunt I and Zygmunt August both bowed to pressure and reclaimed some estates, although both would have preferred to use the estates for patronage and acquire revenues from taxation.

A variety of ingenious taxes and tariffs provided additional sources of income, but the state lacked the bureaucracy to collect them efficiently. It enjoyed the greatest success when national emergencies made the population most willing to pay taxes, such as special levies for defense that usually varied from two to ten times the value of the outmoded fourteenth-century peasant land tax; in 1661, the state collected fifty times the value to recover from the midcentury invasions. A misleadingly named "quarter" tax, enacted in 1577, was originally successful but declined in value over time. After allowing the leaseholder to keep 20 percent of revenues, this tax on leased crown lands allocated 25 percent to the army and 75 percent to the crown. After the first flush of enthusiasm, parliament neglected its responsibility to oversee the tax and noble leaseholders found excuses to appropriate most of the revenues for themselves. Poor tax collecting caused King Zygmunt III such trouble when he assumed the throne in 1587 that the treasury designated certain royal estates for the king's personal use only. The major tax on burghers was the road tax, really a tax on assessed property values, while Jews paid a per capita poll tax without undergoing a formal census.

Seventeenth-century monarchs raised substantially larger revenues than their predecessors had, but only Zygmunt III accumulated a surplus through sound administration of his royal estates and cutting expenditures. Liquor and excise taxes yielded much revenue. Tariffs and special transit charges also provided some income, at the cost of hampering trade. A wintering tax on peasants supported the army for part of the year. Under the impact of the Great Northern

War, all civilian control over taxation disappeared and armies extorted money at will from dietines and citizens. In 1717, parliament regained control and centralized taxation, although it collected revenues at too low a level to permit effective government.

The last half of the eighteenth century saw a systematic improvement in treasury operations and government revenues. The central administration functioned more efficiently, the number of taxes and tariffs was reduced in order to collect the remaining charges more effectively, and exemptions for nobles were reduced or eliminated. The Four Year Parliament (1788–92) achieved some success in improving the revenues from the royal estates, but its greatest success came in assessing a 10 percent permanent "voluntary offering" on revenue from noble estates as well as a 20 percent tax on clerical estates. It also introduced special tobacco and other excise taxes to raise money for the army.

Tax revenue climbed very substantially in absolute terms during the Polish-Lithuanian state's 409-year history, but not enough to maintain the state's existence. Although inflation explains much of the increase, the treasury's achievements should not be undervalued. Annual state revenues amounted to 400,000 zlotys under Kazimierz III in 1360–70 but declined over the course of the fifteenth century to less than 300,000 zlotys in 1500 and averaged about 150,000 zlotys under Zygmunt I. Zygmunt II August increased them to 350,000 in 1569, but he still had to fight the Livonian War on borrowed money. Stefan Batory boosted revenues to 800,000 zlotys and Zygmunt III expanded them to 1,400,000 in 1629. Jan Kazimierz collected the remarkable sum of 19,217,000 zlotys in 1664, but revenues fell catastrophically to 2,400,000 for Jan III Sobieski in 1690. August II collected 5,200,000 in 1717. Stanisław August Poniatowski collected 16,400,000 in 1775 and 50,100,000 in 1791.

Law Courts

Like other European states in the early modern era, the Polish-Lithuanian state maintained separate courts for nobles, burghers, Jews, and peasants. Clerical courts held jurisdiction only over strictly religious matters by 1500; they could not hear civil and criminal cases. Noble court cases started in land courts or castle courts and followed Polish customary law based on decrees issued by medieval rulers as modified by later decrees and legislation; unlike Poland, Lithuania codified its law. Dietines elected judges to the land courts, but ironically they ceased functioning effectively in the seventeenth century when the dietines held the most power. Noble castle courts, where judges were named by the royal prefect, became more popular, perhaps because they kept official records of real estate transactions, business dealings, and even political statements that nobles wished to record.

Noble tribunals supplanted the royal courts as the highest courts of appeal in Poland (1578) and Lithuania (1581). The crown tribunal met twice yearly in Little Poland and twice yearly in Great Poland. Dietines elected twenty-seven nobles as judges; six nobles sat with six clergymen to hear cases involving clerics. Decisions were made by consensus, if possible, or by majority rule. In the mid-seventeenth century, the tribunals began accepting cases directly that had not been heard at lower levels. Decisions were usually final, but they could be appealed to a parliamentary court or to the next seating of the tribunal on the grounds of serious legal error. Tie votes sent cases to the royal court. Accusations of corruption and political interference were constant. Noble courts followed customary law; parliament expressly rejected Roman law in 1532.

Noble courts, including the tribunals, found it very difficult to enforce their decisions, and nobles essentially had to be convinced to accept a court decree. Courts gained the right to seize real estate in civil settlements in 1522, but court procedures required three different methods of assessment and discussion before a court decree would be issued. Even then, courts lacked their own officers and called on local citizens to help out. This paved the way for self-interested vigilante action, particularly in the late seventeenth and early eighteenth centuries. In practice, the guilty noble could usually bargain his penalty down to lesser financial terms or a period of banishment.

A parliamentary court functioned while parliament was in session to hear cases of lèse majesté, treason, corruption, use of force during parliament or legal proceedings, capital charges against nobles, and serious civil cases involving the treasury. Originally composed of senators meeting under the direction of the king or his court marshal, members of the chamber of deputies were added in 1588. The parliamentary court declined as parliamentary activity slackened in the late seventeenth century.

Royal courts consisted of the assessorial court, the relational court, and the marshal's court. Chancellors supervised the assessorial court, which heard cases involving royal finances and estates as well as cases between royal cities and nobles (including the king and the clergy); it also acted as an appeal court for burghers. The court enjoyed a good reputation for fairness and professionalism. The king issued judgments in cases involving feudal dependencies, such as Prussia and Livonia, in the relational court, as well as cases involving the Orthodox Church; this court ceased hearing appeals from the assessorial court late in the seventeenth century. The referendary court judged cases involving peasants in the crown domains, often protecting them from excessive demands by leaseholding prefects.

Professional lawyers represented both the prosecution and the defense in noble courts. Serving as a lawyer (*palestra*) was a common profession for poor nobles, particularly since training generally involved apprenticeship rather than formal schooling. Many burghers served as lawyers, too. Judges generally lacked professional qualifications and depended on political favoritism for royal appointment or election by fellow nobles.

Incorporated cities maintained their own courts. The judges were chosen by the city government and generally came from the wealthier citizens. They lacked professional expertise. Cities followed German legal practices rather than Polish customary law, and larger cities employed professional executioners whose job included extracting confessions by torture. Smaller cities contracted for these professional services relatively rarely because they were expensive. Owners of private cities usually imitated royal cities in setting up courts and city governments.

Jews maintained their own courts to settle internal disputes. The royal assessorial court judged disputes between Jews and Christians.

CHAPTER 12

Economics and Society in the Vasa Period

The so-called little ice age of the 1590s ended the long-term prosperity of the sixteenth century and ushered in a general seventeenth-century crisis that affected Poland-Lithuania along with the rest of Europe. Population growth slowed and the money supply declined as the flow of precious metals from the New World dwindled. Commodity prices decreased, especially in agriculture; grain prices began to fall around 1580. Agricultural improvements in western Europe, especially Holland and Britain, lowered demand for Polish-Lithuanian grain and cattle. Real wages and industrial prices declined while food and fuel costs increased, although they rose and fell in sharp surges. Overall, real wages fell behind the cost of living, and the rich got richer while the poor got poorer.

Poland-Lithuania maintained general prosperity throughout the first half of the seventeenth century, but signs of decline abounded such as falling profits and the replacement of wage labor by serf labor. The disastrous midcentury wars delivered a sledgehammer blow to this weakening economy, which, battered by another half century of warfare, did not recover until well into the eighteenth century. The Polish-Lithuanian Commonwealth held about 10 to 12 million persons in 1600 with a density of 10 to 12 persons per square kilometer. The Polish lands (excluding the sparsely populated Ukrainian provinces) exceeded a density of 20 persons per square kilometer, while the population of ethnic Lithuania reached 1.3 million with 15 persons per square kilometer. Together with Belarussian portions, the Grand Duchy had 4 million inhabitants with an average 13 persons per square kilometer.

MARKET AGRICULTURE, HIRED LABOR, AND THE RISE OF SERFDOM

Polish-Lithuanian agriculturalists depended on world markets and responded to changing circumstances in different ways according to the nature of their landholdings (noble or peasant), the size of their farms, and their distance from markets. In general, both noble and peasant agriculturalists near the Baltic coast increased production by buying more land and hiring more labor, while nobles in more distant regions substituted unpaid serf labor for wage labor or, if peasants, spent more time performing serf labor. Both groups sold all they could on local, national, and international markets. Whenever possible, agriculturalists diversified their activities to earn more money. Peasants diversified their crops and activities by entering the transport business and related enterprises, working part-time in nearby cities, and hiring themselves out as agricultural laborers. Rich nobles founded private cities and managed their agricultural trade with increasing care, while the poorest nobles sought employment with their richer neighbors or in cities. Vagabondage grew.

Proximity to ports in the Baltic basin from Prussia to Livonia created favorable economic conditions for agriculture that allowed both nobles and peasants to expand the monetarized market agriculture that characterized the sixteenth century. The short distance to the point of sale meant low transportation costs, which made up as much as 40 percent of grain prices. Landlords recruited Dutch settlers, after the great floods of 1540 and 1543 devastated the low-lying Vistula delta, in order to gain their expertise in drying the land and building dykes and levees. Colonization of the Vistula delta continued well into the seventeenth century as nobles (including royal and clerical estate managers) saw the advantages of settling peasants in "Dutch villages," where peasants paid rent instead of providing labor dues; despite the name, many of the settlers came from the Germanies or other parts of Poland-Lithuania. Peasants in Dutch villages held unusually high land allocations averaging four full land units (*łan/hufe*) which they farmed with hired labor. As many as half of the peasants in Royal Prussia performed only 10 to 15 days unpaid labor per year. Peasants in adjacent regions of Great Poland provided full labor dues to their noble landlords, but they earned enough from selling their produce on the open market to send hired men to the nobles' fields in their stead. Nobles also hired labor to work their estates.

Polish and Lithuanian agriculturalists who lived farther from markets maintained their incomes by increasing production, lowering costs, and diversifying their businesses. Many nobles cultivated previously fallow land and found pretexts to take over fields from peasants, shifting them onto poorer lands. Forced to adopt a short-term strategy by declining market prices, nobles used agricultural practices that degraded the land such as sowing more profitable wheat on lands that were more suitable for rye or fodder crops. The number of livestock declined, and consequently the amount of manure for fertilizer diminished. Nobles invested less money in stables, barns, and pigsties.

The use of serf labor rose in the course of the seventeenth century because of economic pressures more than legislated noble action, as serfs, rather than hired laborers, gradually came to carry out the daily labor in the fields. Estate owners often hired fewer farm workers and increased the amount of serf labor to cut costs, mainly by pressing into service small farmers who came to work without animals. Serf labor varied from place to place, but typical peasants at the end of the sixteenth century contributed three days per week, except during the sowing and harvesting seasons, when they worked an extra day. The peasants also supplied farm produce to the noble household and spent time transporting the noble's produce to market. By 1650, a typical peasant with a full landholding (*łan*) spent about two-thirds of his time working for the lord with his horse and team. A peasant still met these obligations easily if he had sons to work the landlord's fields, but a peasant without sons had to hire labor to meet his feudal obligations or spend more time in person fulfilling labor dues. Such a peasant probably lost his land as a consequence or traded down to a lesser allotment. The number of full and half allotment peasant farms decreased sharply in the first half of the seventeenth century (from 70 percent to 44 percent in the Cracow area, for example) and the number of small farms grew commensurately. Sources fail to describe the situation of landless peasants because they owed no obligations.

In addition to raising more grain, both rich and poor nobles made short-term gains by harvesting trees as a cash crop at the expense of long-term losses from a degraded environment. In the late sixteenth century, authors of political and economic tracts had already noted the need to reduce forest use or at least rationalize forestry. The Carpathian and Holy Cross Mountains were heavily logged along with Lithuania, Podlasie, and the Kurpie region in northern Mazovia. As a result, Poland-Lithuania exported more wood and wood by-products instead of using them at home. Wood exports shifted from Gdańsk to Prussian and Livonian ports as the Polish Kingdom used up its forests. Deforestation proceeded particularly rapidly along navigable rivers, causing soil erosion and flooding as far away as the Lublin area and the foothills of the Carpathians. Some species, such as yew trees, disappeared; and, among forest animals, the aurochs became extinct. Design efficiencies permitted saltworks to adapt to fuel shortages, but previously profitable foundries and glassworks could not change and had to reduce their operations.

Cattle raising declined in Poland as grain cultivation extended to more land, but the Ukrainian lands picked up the slack; some Moldavian cattle crossed Poland as well. About 30,000 head of cattle were driven across Poland yearly. Sheep were widely cultivated, especially in Great Poland, Pomerania, and the Carpathians. Wool exports to well-established textile manufactures further west continued to be significant well into the seventeenth century.

The Reemergence of the Magnate Elite

Large estates had a greater ability than smaller ones to sell products in the falling market, and they withstood the uncertainties of the weather better. In the late sixteenth century, magnates supplied about 55 percent of grain to the market in Mazovia and over 70 percent upriver in Little Poland, Ruthenia, and Volhynia. They were able to invest time, resources, and cash in organizing the transport of their grain by raft to Gdańsk to take advantage of higher prices instead of selling it to local merchants. As these profits were used to acquire more land from poorer nobles and peasants, the concentration of landownership changed noticeably. In the Cracow district, for example, the percentage of peasants living on large estates (more than ten villages) increased from 9 percent to 25 percent between 1581 and 1629 and the percentage of peasants in medium estates (five to nine villages) increased from 14 percent to 20 percent. The decline of the lesser nobility is indicated by the consequent fall in the percentage of villagers on small estates (less than one complete village) from 20 percent to 7 percent. Outstanding examples of the trend are provided by Sebastian and Stanisław Lubomirski, whose holdings grew from 4 to 91 villages (as well as 23 royal villages on leasehold), and Jeremi Wiśniowiecki, whose holdings in Left Bank Ukraine grew from 600 hearths in 1630 to 38,460 in 1647.

Because poorer nobles (owning one to five peasant villages) could not cut costs as easily as richer nobles, they often became economically and politically dependent on neighboring magnates (owning more than fifteen villages). While poorer nobles often succeeded economically for a time, their small cash reserves meant that one bad harvest or a fire could push them to the edge of bankruptcy. Nobles borrowed from their richer neighbors and lost their estates if they failed to repay the loans. The luckier ones found jobs for themselves or their children as estate administrators, lawyers, and soldiers. At the very least, they could count on expensive presents and invitations to feasts from their richer neighbors during the numerous political campaigns for dietines, parliaments, and tribunals.

A distinct magnate social layer reemerged in the seventeenth century after a period of greater equality in the mid-sixteenth century. For example, Chancellor Jan Zamoyski accumulated vast landed estates by 1600 that included more than two hundred villages and eleven cities. He also leased royal estates with twelve more cities and six hundred villages. Other magnates included the Ostrozky and Zaslavsky families in Volhynia. The Koniecpolski and Wiśniowiecki families in Ukraine and the Radziwiłłs and Sapiehas in Lithuania were only slightly less rich. Potockis and Lubomirskis held extensive estates throughout all regions of the Commonwealth. Professional managers increased profits by keeping careful inventories and receipts, and handled the export-import trade themselves.

Magnates founded "private" cities to facilitate local exchange and bring in cash rent. The Radziwiłłs (1586) and Zamoyskis (1589) also perpetuated their wealth by convincing parliament to create entailed "ordinations."

At the height of their power, Polish-Lithuanian magnates spent vast sums on building and furnishing palaces, supporting large numbers of retainers, and entertaining in a princely style. These expenditures may have been excessive by the standards of other European nobilities, but they kept the political machine operating smoothly. In keeping with the expectations of Polish-Lithuanian noble democracy, magnates needed to cultivate support among local nobles by providing patronage appointments as well as the proverbial bread and circuses. Mastery of the local machine laid the basis for political success on the national level, where magnates acquired high state office and rich leaseholds of crown lands. The richest noble families comprised a well-recognized power elite that monopolized high state offices and married among themselves. A subgroup of magnate aristocrats owned hundreds of villages and enjoyed princely incomes. Like other European aristocrats, they spent wealth conspicuously on elegant palaces and artistic furnishings; their patronage established the cultural tone of the Commonwealth.

While distinctive, the magnate elite lacked the legal privileges that established clearly defined aristocracies of barons, dukes, and counts in other European countries, and it remained open to new members. Membership in this ill-defined noble subgroup depended on wealth and talent almost as much as birth. Magnate families rarely survived for more than two hundred years, because they died out, lost their property, or suffered other exceptional reversals, and new families rose through their abilities and connections. The fabulously wealthy Ostrozky family of Volhynia died out in the seventeenth century, and the Czartoryski family rose in the early eighteenth century from titled obscurity to wealth and high political office. The princely titles enjoyed by some descendants of the Lithuanian and Ruthenian royal houses and, more rarely, bestowed by the Holy Roman emperor or the pope remained purely honorary.

As their economic fortunes dropped, poorer nobles put more stock in their legal identification. The declining rate of intermarriage between nobles and commoners did not stop nobles such as Walerian Nekanda Trepka from proclaiming the sanctity of the nobility. This déclassé noble who had lost his fortune collected information throughout Poland-Lithuania about mismarriages, misalliances, and pretenders, and published it in his *Book of Plebeians*. Trepka searched out and identified would-be nobles by speech, manners, and dress. He even included individuals who had received patents of ennoblement on the grounds that the king "can give a village, but only God can make a noble." Trepka thought education important for nobles, but urged that it be practical rather than academic, and he considered formal degrees superfluous. Travel rather than formal study provided the knowledge of languages, foreign countries, architecture (especially forts), and religion that he demanded.

The Economic Development of Ukrainian Lands and Lithuania

The economy of the Ukrainian lands developed rapidly after the Union of Lublin threw them open to colonization. Grain was cultivated as a cash crop in the long-settled western regions of Galicia and Volhynia where river routes led to Gdańsk. Landlords raised cattle on a large scale in less accessible areas and drove them across Poland to sell in Silesia and Germany. Newly settled areas along the Dnieper River were still in a formative stage and lacked economic stability. Landlords were anxious to see profits from their heavy investments of cash, equipment, and serfs, whom they transferred from their estates further west or attracted with promises of fifteen to twenty years freedom from feudal dues. Imposition of feudal obligations when the grace periods expired, as well as milling charges, liquor charges, and other incidental fees, made peasants bitterly resentful. Urban development was rapid.

Hetman Stanisław Koniecpolski typified the new landlords of Ukraine. Made rich from rewards for his long and distinguished military career, Koniecpolski bought vast estates near Brody in western Ukraine. He hired a French architect and engineer, Guillaume de Beauplan, to build his major palace at Podhorce in Italian style with arcades and galleries. The efforts of his Hungarian vintner failed because the climate was not good enough, but Koniecpolski succeeded economically with his private city of Brody, where he settled Ruthenian, Armenian, and Jewish merchants, and encouraged the manufacture of rich oriental-style fabrics such as silks, brocades, and carpets. Factories on his estates produced iron goods, powder, and bricks.

Economic growth in the Grand Duchy of Lithuania slowed after the Union of Lublin of 1569. Labor dues gradually increased from four to six days, and monetary rent, still common, often doubled, although favorable market conditions allowed both landlords and peasants to sell all they produced. The number of incorporated cities continued to grow.

The Economic Impact of the Mid-Seventeenth Century Wars

The Cossack wars and invasions by Russians, Swedes, and Transylvanians devastated Poland-Lithuania between 1648 and 1657. The government lost the capacity to keep records, but fragmentary reports suggest that less than half of agricultural fields could be planted in the 1660s. Animal husbandry declined by almost half and grain production by two-thirds. Peasants suffered considerably more than nobles. Perhaps one-third of all cities were burned to the ground, usually by one or another invader but sometimes by the Polish or Lithuanian armies; the suburbs were also destroyed in the course of military operations. Invaders carried off much of the accumulated wealth of the Polish-Lithuanian state and its citizens. Swedish armies systematically pillaged churches, palaces, private homes, and workplaces. Other armies and a host of thieves from all nationalities took what they could.

New catastrophes such as the Great Northern War (1698–1721) continued to afflict the Commonwealth and cause further losses. These losses amplified the structural weaknesses that had been visible before 1650. Loss of accumulated capital and inventory deepened the nobility's reliance on serf labor instead of hired labor, and lack of money made it difficult for merchants and artisans to reestablish their businesses. On the positive side, labor shortages forced nobles and other employers to moderate their treatment of dependents.

Urban Growth and Stagnation

City life continued to be an important component of Polish-Lithuanian social and economic life despite the economic slowdown, but the focus of urban life gradually shifted to private cities, which became increasingly important and dynamic. At the end of the sixteenth century, burghers comprised about 25 percent of the Polish crown population of 3 million, and their number continued to grow during the first half of the seventeenth century, although at a slower rate except in the eastern Ukrainian palatinates of Bratslav, Kiev, and Chernihiv, where they increased rapidly. Legal privileges defined city identity, but almost all cities (88 percent) numbered only 600 to 2,000 inhabitants and corresponded to our idea of towns. Towns were characteristic of urban life in Mazovia, Galicia, and the eastern Ukrainian provinces at the end of the sixteenth century. Small cities (2,000 to 10,000), particularly numerous in Great Poland and Little Poland, made up 11.5 percent of the total number of cities. Large cities included Gdańsk (40,000), Cracow (22,000), Lviv (20,000), Vilnius (20,000), Poznań (18,000 to 20,000), Elbląg (15,000), Toruń (12,000), and Warsaw (10,000 to 12,000),— but together they made up only 0.5 percent of the total number of cities. The most urbanized province was Royal Prussia, where 37 percent of the population lived in urban areas and the major cities were exceptionally large compared with other provinces.

The queen of Poland-Lithuania's cities remained Gdańsk, which reached its high point at this time. The import-export trade and manufacturing sustained a metropolitan population that grew from 40,000 in 1550 to over 70,000 in 1650. The size and prosperity of Gdańsk maintained a social structure and civilization that disappeared from other parts of the Commonwealth where burghers became fewer and less powerful. The patricians continued to run the municipal government and manage the city properties that gave them profitable opportunities for investment. They rebuilt the city between 1575 and 1625 in the Dutch manner, often with Dutch architects. City regulations separated the patricians from ordinary residents, listing how many servants a citizen could hire, how many guests he could invite, and what refreshment he could provide at funerals, weddings, and christenings. Only the rich enjoyed the legal right to ride to church in a coach; lesser residents had to walk. Patricians had the exclusive right to wear rich fabrics such as satin, brocade, and damask; women could wear gold jewelry and imported white lace. Poorer groups had to dress more simply and wear cloth produced in Gdańsk.

The "national" character of Gdańsk is typical of the early modern period, when many people felt overlapping loyalties to different political centers. First, the majority of the population, particularly the patriciate, consisted of German-speaking Lutherans and Calvinists who considered themselves primarily citizens of Gdańsk and defended Gdańsk's legal privileges. Second, they thought of themselves as part of Royal Prussia and insisted that Poland-Lithuania respect Prussian legal privileges. Third, Gdańsk considered itself a loyal part of the Polish-Lithuanian Commonwealth and defended the power of the realm to which it was closely linked through trade and intellectual exchange. Like other groups in society, Gdańskers sought to increase the economic and political privileges that the Polish-Lithuanian state had granted them or at least to prevent their reduction when Warsaw tried to centralize power. After the 1620s, Lutheranism was the city's dominant religion, based on the legal privileges issued by Zygmunt August in 1557 and Stefan Batory in 1577, but Catholics and Calvinists enjoyed legal equality. Other groups, notably Mennonites and Jews, did not possess legal rights and lived outside the city.

Despite the glamor of late sixteenth- and early seventeenth-century Gdańsk, signs of decline abounded. The grain trade (mostly rye) went into decline after reaching its peak in 1618. Ship captains carried at least 60,000 to 80,000 cartloads (*last,* a volume measure averaging one to two tons of grain) in peak years between 1550 and 1650, but export volumes declined in the 1630s and 1640s because Gdańsk merchants could not find more grain to purchase in the countryside. Merchant ships bringing supplies to Gdańsk increasingly returned with only ballast in their holds after unloading their imported consumer goods. Profits fell for both merchants and producers as grain prices declined. Gdańsk merchants still did well as intermediaries with the interior in the grain trade and as importers, but they abandoned the shipping business to Dutch and English merchants instead of sinking their capital into building larger ships to compete with them.

Even with these beginnings of decline, Gdańsk's port remained active and this helped make it the largest manufacturing center in the Commonwealth. Nobles and merchants came there from all over to sell their produce and bring manufactured goods back for use or resale. Metallurgical manufacturing covered the spectrum from ships' anchors and church bells to delicate work such as clocks, needles, and wire sieves; refining and casting came to an end in midcentury when Swedish armies carried off the equipment. Leatherworking ranged from tanning to manufacturing shoes, purses, and harnesses. Woodworking similarly varied from ships and carriages to barrels, boxes, and birdcages. Building trades supplied the expanding local market. Food trades such as milling, baking, and butchering supplied rations to ships' crews as well as to the city population.

Industrial expansion put pressure on the guild system, which gradually yielded to more capitalistic forms. Enterprising guild masters evaded restrictions by purchasing raw materials for resale at a profit, sometimes to poorer artisans on credit. Manufacture of small items for sale in shops and stalls also led to the emergence of an independent (nonguild) distribution system of fairs and markets. Masters in some trades divorced themselves from production and concentrated on trading or organizing production. For example, bricklayers and carpenters often turned into contractors, and some brewers hired salaried brewmasters to prepare the beer so they could work in sales. The positions of journeyman and apprentice deteriorated as numerical quotas and high fees kept 25 to 50 percent from advancing to the rank of guild master. Separate journeymen fraternities sprang up in some trades, and some organized strikes.

The trade in timber and timber products also declined in the course of the seventeenth century. The peak occurred in 1610, when 10,000 cartloads of ash were exported to England and the Lowlands for manufacturing blue dye and potash fertilizer; the number of cartloads declined to 1,599 in 1640 and 205 in 1650. Exports of finished planks fell from a high of 600,000 in 1610 to less than 100,000 in 1640 and only 5,000 in 1650. Destruction of Polish-Lithuanian forests and war damage in eastern Poland-Lithuania caused the decline.

Unlike Gdańsk, which continued to grow rapidly, the medieval capital, Cracow, reached its peak around 1550 and stagnated while the suburbs grew slowly. Cracow remained a major international trading center despite the transfer of the royal residence and parliament to Warsaw in 1595. In the early seventeenth century, its trading sphere extended to England in the west, Russia in the east, and the Black Sea coast in the south, but competition and warfare gradually reduced operations to central Poland and the Ukrainian provinces. The city's population grew by only about 1,000 residents between 1550 and 1650, while the Christian section of suburban Kazimierz, a substantial incorporated city, held steady at 5,000. However, the Jewish section of Kazimierz grew from 2,000 to 4,500. Guild organizations were common among both Christians and Jews. Two additional small incorporated suburbs, Kleparz and Stradom, and several unincorporated villages provided homes for 2,000 to 3,000 residents who supplied the metropolitan area with services such as baking, brewing, and building. Nobles and clerics took advantage of their exemption from city law to establish residential and business properties inside incorporated cities as well as in the suburbs.

Urbanization in Private Cities and Suburbs

While royal cities stagnated, economic growth continued in city suburbs and private cities. The establishment of cities on their properties near or even inside royal cities allowed nobles to diversify their economic operations and increase their revenues. Businesses started up outside the walls of major cities such as Gdańsk, Cracow, and Warsaw in order to avoid the rigidities and expenses of the guild system and to make use of cheaper land. Independent artisans worked for less money and paid their employees lower wages than guild artisans received inside the walls. City residents flocked to suburban shops and marketplaces, which provided space for rural craftsmen as well as suburban workers. Nobles and clerics built residences in the suburbs. Some used their exemption from city jurisdiction to establish commercial enterprises inside the city walls and lease space to nonguild artisans. Peasants and occasionally poor nobles sought work in these suburbs. In Royal Prussia, migration from rural areas made the suburbs Catholic while the cities remained Protestant.

Private city development reached its peak in the late sixteenth and early seventeenth centuries. Laws passed after the mid-sixteenth century exempted them from parliamentary jurisdiction, leaving them subject to the fiscal, juridical, and religious policies of their owners. Some owners acted arbitrarily and capriciously, but most regarded cities as investments and, wishing to see them prosper, allowed their residents personal freedoms, elected self-governments, and municipal courts. Although most private cities counted fewer than 2,000 inhabitants, many carried on specialized trading and manufacturing operations that produced great wealth. Polish historians traditionally consider the bifurcation of private and incorporated cities one of the major sources of the political weakness of the Polish bourgeoisie and, given the role of the Third Estate in western European development, one of the sources of weakness in the Polish state.

Some new cities established by nobles on their estates displayed imaginative urban design influenced by Italian models. The outstanding example was Jan Zamoyski's Zamość, which has survived almost intact to the present day. Bernardo Morando of Padua designed it along two axes intersecting in a city square that served as a recreational piazza and also as a buffer separating the burgher city from Zamoyski's palace. Subsidiary market squares provided space for artisans and farmers to sell their goods. Morando carefully placed public buildings such as the town hall, churches, and synagogues along boulevards to provide vistas. Burgher apartment houses lined the city streets harmoniously, presumably based on a model design. Earth fortifications in the modern irregular polygon shape formed part of the urban design. Similarly, the city of Brody was founded in 1586 on a functional grid with two large market squares, probably intended to separate Polish merchants from Armenian and Ruthenian competitors.

The needs of the age created new urban forms. First, larger cities needed earth bulwarks some distance outside the city to defend against improved artillery. These defenses were expensive because their construction required engineering expertise and a large unskilled labor force. Some cities adjusted by tearing down buildings (Brody and Toruń); others expanded and made new land available for development inside fortifications (Gdańsk and Warsaw). Secondly, the Catholic Reformation brought new features to Polish and Lithuanian cities. Jesuits and other religious orders built attractive churches in accessible locations within cities while numerous monasteries sprang up in the suburbs. Some smaller cities developed as "calvaries" or procession routes with chapels, such as Góra Kalwaria and Ujazdów near Warsaw. Such centers were shaped in the form of a long cross. The high road formed the long part of the cross, which a street bisected at right angles; both held chapels and churches. Inns and shops, often owned or managed by Jews, supplied pilgrims' needs, and a permanent population eventually built residences.

Noble Attitudes Toward Cities

Polish noble theorists generally held favorable attitudes toward cities because they recognized that cities played an important part in the economic life of the Polish-Lithuanian Commonwealth and in their own personal fortunes. For example, Anselm Gostomski pointed out in the 1560s, in his pioneering manual on noble estate management, that cities purchased and distributed grain from noble properties. In parliament and dietines, noble deputies devoted considerable attention to passing legislation that provided tax relief for cities that had suffered from fires, floods, and war. Other laws encouraged the construction of infrastructure, particularly warehouses. Acts designed to lower prices, such as price-fixing and antiguild measures, were passed in order to make the cities more competitive and not just to please noble consumers or show contempt for burghers, as historians have often argued. Noble politicians sought to increase tax burdens on cities but tried not to strangle them.

Nevertheless, nobles thought of their own well-being first and granted themselves exemptions from staple rights, tariffs, and internal customs duties so that trade was increasingly concentrated in their hands. In about 1600, more than 70 percent of the goods transported on the Vistula were owned by nobles. They took most of the grain and forest products to Gdańsk, where they bought clothes, furniture, wines, and other consumables for the entire year, but they also made space available (at a price) to merchants from their private cities to import supplies for the local market. Such imports included dried fish, metal goods, and textiles. Relatively few theorists criticized Polish-Lithuanian nobles for abusing tax exemptions to compete unfairly with merchants.

In addition, some measures were counterproductive, if well intentioned. Andrzej Ciesielski's 1572 manual advocated supporting city prosperity by keeping the merchants at home; he thought this policy would spur foreign investment and encourage foreign merchants to immigrate. In 1632, Jan Grodwagner recommended banning commodity exports and imports of manufactured goods in order to encourage the local manufacture of common goods such as textiles (wool and linen) and metalware (knives and locks). Similarly, Krzysztof Opaliński advocated stimulating industrial growth by fixing local prices lower than the prices of imported goods. Opaliński also wanted cities represented in parliament, in part to keep burghers from seeking ennoblement. Several other authors suggested ways of supporting manufactures and excluding foreign competition.

Burghers

The burgher economic system was still organized, as in previous centuries, into guilds, supported by social and religious fraternities, but the guild system was beginning to fray around the edges. Rich merchants organized themselves into larger firms with several agents and assistants. Traditional apprenticeships prevailed, but private business schooling operated outside the guild system in Gdańsk and Toruń. The "factor" system expanded substantially. Factors, or agents, usually signed a written contract with their employers and received up to 2 percent of the proceeds of sales; they took part in some transactions as minor partners. Gdańsk firms maintained factors in major Commonwealth cities such as Warsaw, Lublin, Cracow, and Poznań. Special postal facilities allowed them to keep in regular contact, particularly throughout Prussia, Great Poland, and Silesia. The largest firms maintained factors in Holland and other foreign commercial centers. Dutch, British, French, Italian, and other factors worked in Poland. Merchant profits remained high. In the late sixteenth and early seventeenth centuries, Gdańsk merchants made almost 30 percent profit on grain exports, 40 percent on potash exports, and up to 100 percent on imported colonial and western goods; some of the profit came from commodity and currency speculation. Prosperous Gdańsk merchants and patricians plowed some of their profits into banking and moneylending. They lent substantial sums throughout the Commonwealth, particularly to Polish kings, and tied up as much as 30 percent of their capital in credit operations.

Nonguild competition cut into burgher profits. Nobles, peasants, and burghers from other cities who did not have the monopoly privileges of citizenship shared an interest in opening up business opportunities. Ethnic and religious minorities such as Jews, Scots, Armenians, and Protestants were particularly noteworthy here. Kings, nobles, and clerics used their exemption from municipal law to hire "servitors" to work in and around cities. City governments tried to restrict the development of nonguild competition with little success. The most thriving centers such as Gdańsk, Lviv, Warsaw, and maybe Cracow, saw nonguild workers outnumber guild workers.

Despite changes, most production throughout the Commonwealth was still performed by a single master working with two or three journeymen and apprentices. Artisanal profits were low, and artisans prospered mostly by having secondary occupations such as credit, trade, and alcohol manufacturing or sale.

Jewish Trade, Artisanry, and Other Occupations

Burghers met increasing competition from Jews as trading and artisanal manufacturing supplanted moneylending as the most important Jewish occupations by about 1600. International trade played a large part in the new Jewish economy. Acting as agents for Polish nobles, Jewish merchants often took advantage of noble tariff exemptions to claim relief for their own goods as well. As a spin-off, Jews became active in long-distance and short-distance transport both as contractors and carters. Jews participated in trade fairs in such numbers that the Jewish community often designated its own market judge to resolve disputes.

Profits from banking and trading were often placed in industries such as fur manufacturing and tanning which had low start-up costs because artisans supplied their own simple and inexpensive tools. Like their Christian neighbors, Jewish artisans formed guilds to regulate and monopolize production. Jewish guilds included organized apprenticeships paid by the parents, journeyman laborers, and masters. Most guilds produced everyday goods and services; they organized glaziers, carpenters, metalworkers, barbers, dice makers, musical instrument makers, and many other workers. Two distinctive Jewish guilds were kosher butchers and tailors; the latter upheld Talmudic proscriptions against mixing fabrics.

Litigation between Christian and Jewish guilds was endless, as was litigation between Catholic guilds and rival guilds organized by Protestants, Armenians, and Orthodox Ruthenians; sometimes the principals fought it out, too. Jewish artisans worked more cheaply than Christian artisans and incorporated cheaper work methods such as the domestic or putting-out system of subcontracting to urban and rural women who wove at home. The Jewish practice of drumming up business by using runners to approach customers on the street or even on the road outside of town was particularly irritating to staid Catholic guild masters.

Jewish leaseholding and estate management also played a large part in economic activities, particularly in Ukraine. Nobles licensed potentially profitable activities to create a local monopoly and collected high rent from lessees. Jews bid successfully on many such leases and hired local craftsmen, often peasants, to operate them. Flour milling was a profitable leasehold. Jews also become prominent in the timber trade, directing logging operations on estates and making rafts or barges to ship grain to Gdańsk (after which the rafts were broken up and sold as timber). The liquor trade provided another important Jewish rural industry. Agricultural surpluses in grain-growing regions with poor river transportation such as Ukraine were brewed into beer or later distilled into vodka; mead was also brewed from local honey. Noble-owned taverns, operated by Jewish leaseholders, sold alcoholic drinks to travelers and local residents to whom their noble masters increasingly assigned purchasing quotas to discourage them from brewing their own liquor at home. Dairy production also became a Jewish specialty, probably growing out of the cattle drives that took noble-owned beef cattle to market in Germany, Austria, Bohemia, and Russia. Jewish religious requirements (the need to separate meat and meat implements from milk and dairy implements) may have played a role, too.

Jews played a prominent part in administering the nobles' agricultural activities. Contracted managers (the *arenda* system) may have managed as many as half of the estates in the Grand Duchy of Lithuania and Ukrainian lands. Jewish agents collected rents and tolls, administered labor dues, and served as judges in civil and criminal cases. As agents of the nobility, they probably had the right to condemn criminals to death, although that right does not appear to have been used often, if ever. Jewish supervisors probably hired a largely Jewish staff to work in far-flung villages. The 1620 inventory shows that Prince Konstiantyn Ostrozky, the palatine of Kiev, employed 4,000 Jews in his vast estates in Volhynia. Many lived in his private city of Ostrih, which became a important Jewish religious and cultural center. Jewish communal governments in Ukraine exercised control over individual Jewish activities and worked to maintain good Jewish-Christian relations, especially with their noble employers. There were very few recorded complaints against Jewish administrators, but anti-Jewish violence in the Cossack uprising revealed the deep hostility that pervaded the Ruthenian peasantry and Cossacks. Minor administrators at the bottom of the hierarchy undoubtedly farmed the land for their own subsistence.

Christian rivals such as Renaissance merchants and Jesuit Banks of Piety took over much of the moneylending that Jews had handled before, and Jews became net borrowers by 1600. Communal organizations seemed a good risk because they collected taxes, so nobles and Christian clerics lent them money at favorable rates and often required them to guarantee loans to individual Jews as well.

As a rule, Jews used these loans for investment. Interest rates varied enormously, but common interest rates in the mid-seventeenth century were 20 to 25 percent except during fairs, when short-term loans could reach 50 percent. The use of credit instruments made long-distance business easier.

Jewish Self-Government

Jewish life in Poland-Lithuania achieved new heights of self-government under the Vasa monarchs and made Jews virtually a state within a state, but they also faced increased hostility. The center of Jewish life moved to the eastern regions of the Polish-Lithuanian state and remained there despite the population losses and dislocations of the mid-seventeenth-century wars. Jewish cultural institutions continued to grow, although the community lacked the outstanding personalities of the sixteenth century.

Immigration to Poland ebbed in the early seventeenth century because persecution declined in the German lands and because Polish Jewish communities viewed immigrants as unwelcome competition. But natural increase was substantial, partly due to early marriage (generally financed by parents), military exemptions, and the absence of clerical celibacy. Ritual injunctions may have contributed to a higher standard of hygiene, particularly with food handling. Jews enjoyed greater access to trained physicians and hospital care than most Christians. The Jewish population of the Commonwealth numbered about 30,000 in 1500, 150,000 in 1576, over 500,000 in 1650, and declined to about 450,000 in 1658 as a result of death and emigration during the Cossack and Swedish wars. As a percentage of total population, the Jews increased from 0.6 percent in 1500, to 2.0 percent in 1576, and 4.5 percent in 1648.

A series of state privileges ensured the integrity of the Jewish community and the personal safety of individual Jews in the early seventeenth century, partly because the state needed a strong communal government to collect taxes and turn suspected criminals over to royal courts. Jewish testimony was accepted in court against accused Christian murderers, while courts required the testimony of Jewish witnesses to prove Jewish guilt in assault and murder cases. Jewish residential rights were defined primarily by communal regulations.

Jews bolstered their identity as a separate community and also as a constituent part of the Polish-Lithuanian Commonwealth through the extension of self-government. The Council of the Four Lands (Great Poland, western Little Poland, eastern Little Poland, Volhynia) received royal recognition in 1580 and the Council of Provinces in Lithuania in 1623; they functioned until 1764. The state relied on the councils to collect the Jewish poll tax instead of using state tax collectors, and the Jewish councils took it upon themselves to make decisions regarding Jewish life throughout the entire Commonwealth at a time when

Christian burghers could influence only their city of residence. The councils grew out of regional gatherings of community leaders in the early sixteenth century; in the late sixteenth and seventeenth centuries, the Council of the Four Lands generally met twice a year, at the Lublin and Iaroslav trade fairs, while the Lithuanian Council met about once every five years. Procedures and membership remained flexible. About half of the twenty to thirty delegates in the Council of the Four Lands represented Jewish communities in major cities, while the remainder represented smaller communities; the Lithuanian Council was smaller. Only the richest 1 percent of Jewish householders elected delegates to regional gatherings, analogous to Polish dietines, which in turn elected delegates to the councils; Lithuanian voting was more democratic. A Rabbinical Council met at the same time.

The councils allocated responsibility for state taxes to Jewish communities throughout Poland and Lithuania, and also decided a wide variety of economic, social, and religious issues. They confirmed residential restrictions in cities, minimized competition among Jewish businesses, and supervised credit operations, among other activities. In the social sphere, the councils maintained local oligarchies by condemning criticism as sedition, but they also supported charitable and medical services for the poor and supplied dowries for poor women. They fulfilled religious obligations by ensuring that each community maintain a yeshiva for higher religious study and compelled sabbath observance. The councils enforced their decisions by collective social and economic pressure and, if all else failed, by excommunicating recalcitrants. The Rabbinic chamber acted as a supreme court for local Jewish courts, judging disagreements between constituent members or between the constituents and the council. It sometimes acted as a court of appeal for Rabbinical judges in other countries.

The councils elected an executive consisting of a chairman, a combination secretary-treasurer, several clerks, and assessors. The executive chose a chief lobbyist (*shtadlan*) to represent the Jewish community at the royal court and at parliamentary sessions. The lobbyist had to speak Polish eloquently and have keen political sense. To gain favorable privileges from Polish-Lithuanian authorities, or at least avoid unfavorable decisions on economic and residential questions, the Jewish community relied both on argumentation and the presentation of lavish gifts, often in cash. Individual communities also chose lobbyists to speak for them locally.

Repeated denials that Jews committed ritual crimes against Christianity (ritual murder and profanation of the host) by high state and clerical officials, including the pope, did not entirely protect Jews against false accusations in the decentralized Polish-Lithuanian legal system, and Jewish communities frequently had to protect their members; this defense prevented attacks on Jewish communities as a whole. Jewish communities spent a lot of money to convince court officials that Jews did not commit ritual crimes against Christianity and to look for the real motives behind the false accusation, usually some economic dispute between the Christian accuser and the Jewish defendant. Some accusations came from converts who became Christian missionaries and accused other Jews of ritual crimes.

JEWS AND THE STATE

Noble officials gradually replaced the Jews as tax collectors for the Polish-Lithuanian state. In 1548, the Polish parliament passed a resolution demanding that only Christian nobles collect taxes from Christians; the resolution was reissued in 1562 and 1563. The newly created Council of the Four Lands tried to reduce friction by advising Jews to leave the collection of liquor taxes to Christians, a self-imposed prohibition that was irregularly observed by Jews in Great Poland and Little Poland and ignored in Ukrainian lands. A similar self-imposed prohibition on leasing royal salt mines was also observed irregularly. Jews continued to collect royal tolls on internal transportation, an occupation which left them open to charges of abuse and countercharges of mistreatment. Magnates often imposed tolls within their estates and hired Jews to collect them. In contrast, a Jewish ban on minting coins was strictly observed; Jews did not want to be blamed for the constant decline of specie value.

Jews paid regular taxes plus a special Jewish poll tax, although they were exempted from urban property taxes that Christian burghers paid. Normal taxes often included taxes on ownership or management of land, liquor taxes, tolls, and customs duties. Revenues from the poll tax amounted to 10,000 zlotys in the crown provinces and 3,000 zlotys in Lithuania in 1579. The growth of tax receipts to 20,000 zlotys in the crown provinces and 12,000 zlotys in Lithuania in 1649 reflected the growth of Lithuanian Jewry from 23 percent to 38 percent of the total Jewish population in the Commonwealth. Kings and royal officials demanded onerous special levies and payments as well. For example, Władysław IV demanded 60,000 zlotys in 1643 to pay his debts. Palatines and subpalatines received substantial regular payments (4,000 and 1,000 zlotys annually in Poznań), as did many other officials, including churchmen. Jewish communities made regular payments to student groups to protect themselves against attacks. The Cracow Jewish community supplied officials of the Jagiellonian University with 189 pounds of sugar, 86 pounds each of pepper and ginger, 68 pounds each of rice and raisins, substantial amounts of nuts and spices, plus cash before Christmas and Easter each year.

Frequent tax disputes engaged Jewish and Christian municipal authorities and led to lawsuits, administrative judgments, and constant renegotiation.

Municipalities often tried to tax Jews on their own authority or impose payments for land and facilities used by the Jewish community. Jewish communities cited privileges establishing their separate legal status to refuse payment. The two communities usually achieved a compromise solution, although not necessarily to anyone's satisfaction.

CRIMES AND PUNISHMENTS

Considerable criminal activity went on in Poland-Lithuania, although it is not clear whether the situation was better or worse than in other countries, and the country was subject to depredations by ill-disciplined soldiers, especially between 1648 and 1720. In peacetime, small bands of highwaymen sought out potential victims and likely places to attack them. Professional thieves traveled from city to city to pursue their activities, frequenting known underworld taverns where they met local fences and disposed of their loot. Pickpockets abounded, and breaking-and-entering crimes were common. Underpaid soldiers could be a danger in any setting. Quarreling and brawling were common at all social levels and might lead to serious injury, particularly among nobles who carried arms. Women were convicted in half the cases of brawling in cities. However, crime was low in the villages, as peasants committed few offenses other than appropriating firewood or other disputed items from their noble masters and retaliating against neighbors for the death of livestock. They committed petty moral crimes such as failing to attend church and smoking tobacco.

Punishments for crimes were harsh and aimed at scaring criminals into behaving properly. As elsewhere in Europe, torture was commonly used in investigating crimes, although nobles, city patricians, doctorate holders, children, pregnant women, and the elderly were spared except in serious cases. All levels of government applied corporal punishment to convicted criminals instead of keeping them in prison. Priests and local nobles often intervened in village courts to reduce penalties from death or mutilation to fines or whipping. Banishment was a common penalty. The medieval custom by which a virgin could release a criminal from the death penalty by marrying him declined and disappeared by the late seventeenth century.

A survey of late sixteenth-century and early seventeenth-century crime in five Polish cities reveals that many crimes resulted in the death penalty. Murderers, arsonists, sodomists, and robbers were invariably put to death, as were most counterfeiters, rapists, bigamists, and persons convicted of sacrilege. Significantly fewer adulterers, fences, petty thieves, and gamblers were executed. Courts generally executed men by hanging or beheading, and women by beheading or drowning. The application of penalties was uneven and depended on the personality of the judge.

Execution of civil judgments was unusually difficult because the courts lacked links with the police.

The Treatment of Perceived Deviance: Witchcraft, Ritual Murder, and Homosexuality

Although estimates differ widely, witchcraft trials probably occurred less frequently in Poland-Lithuania than in western European countries. Poland-Lithuania's relative intellectual backwardness luckily restrained officials from attributing great significance to minor village practices. The Catholic Church lacked an inquisitional office in Poland-Lithuania; religious toleration eroded concern about heretics; and the political system of noble democracy prevented the struggle between bureaucracy and the royal court that contributed to witchcraft trials further west. Polish-Lithuanian Catholicism followed devotional rituals, especially the cult of the Virgin Mary, without the rational base in theology and demonology that figured prominently in western witchcraft trials. Convictions and executions were most common in northern and western Poland.

Belief in witches and spirits was common at all levels of society. Following western European practice, witch trials were transferred from clerical to secular courts in the fifteenth century, and some cities bordering the Germanies showed misguided zeal in punishing alleged witches; but most regarded witchcraft as a minor offense, particularly in the sixteenth and early seventeenth centuries. Convictions, generally based on accusations of causing the death of farm animals, often resulted in a simple oath by the "witch" not to harm anyone. In 1636, one court threatened to fine anyone who brought the issue up again. By the late seventeenth and early eighteenth centuries, trials became more common, and courts assessed fines, floggings, and even death. Accused witches were examined by ducking or torture; if tried and convicted, they were often imprisoned in specially built barrels, which did not touch the ground, or burnt at the stake. The height of witchcraft trials came in 1675–1725 and declined quickly after that, leading a mid-eighteenth-century memoirist to claim, with some exaggeration, that "no one believed in witchcraft." Both August II and August III attempted unsuccessfully to stop city courts from trying witches. King Stanisław August Poniatowski met no opposition in the Polish-Lithuanian parliament in 1776 when he moved to abolish the use of torture and death penalty in witchcraft cases. As in other European countries, these measures effectively ended all persecution of alleged witches.

Ritual murder trials of Jews for allegedly killing Christian children to use their blood for making matzo also occurred along with trials for profaning the host. Late sixteenth-century kings required that such cases be heard in royal courts in order to dismiss them, but in the seventeenth and eighteenth centuries the lower courts heard cases and often took them seriously. Torture was used in examinations, and convicted Jews were burnt alive. The number of cases is hard to establish because few court records have survived and ritual murder cases are known primarily from obviously unreliable contemporary anti-Jewish tracts. The first known accusation in Poland-Lithuania was launched in the mid-sixteenth century and estimates vary from 80 to 150 cases in the Vasa period.

Homosexuality itself was not a crime but sodomy was punishable by impalement or another method that caused maximum pain. Historians have not yet studied how often charges were brought; there are indications that offenders from higher social levels escaped punishment, although they may have endured disapprobation.

Social Ceremonies and Their Importance

Life was full of ceremony for all levels of society. Even though idleness was frowned on, saints' days and other religious holidays filled half the calendar year. Carnival (before Lent) saw elaborate festivities such as masquerades when nobles dressed up as picturesque commoners, although commoners did not imitate their betters as in some western countries. Zygmunt III and his courtiers often dressed as Gypsies, Jews, peddlers, priests, and peasants. The ceremonial character of life was emphasized by gesture and ritual such as kissing the hands or feet of social superiors. Taking off hats as a sign of respect was very important and led to occasional diplomatic incidents; for example, Emperor Leopold's failure to remove his hat while greeting Polish troops after the 1683 Battle of Vienna contributed to alienation between Austria and Poland-Lithuania. Tadeusz Rejtan's celebrated effort to block the Polish Parliament's ratification of the First Partition in 1773 by throwing himself on the floor in front of exiting deputies represented this symbolic and theatrical approach to life. The imitative effort by Jan Sucharzewski to prevent passage of the May 3, 1791 Constitution seemed anachronistic, however. Cities put on great shows for visiting dignitaries with triumphal arches, fireworks, skilled teams of dancers from local guilds, and even professionals. Gdańsk was particularly famous for its festivals; Cracow celebrations were somewhat more modest, but more numerous.

Food, Drink, and Disease

Seventeenth-century Poles from all social classes ate much the same food in such quantities as they could afford. Magnates and urban patricians consumed 6,000 to 7,000 calories daily with a wide variety of smoked and fresh meats served in spicy sauces; flour dishes such as bread, noodles, and groats; and eggs and dairy products. Vegetables such as cabbage, beets, mushrooms, and carrots were served mainly as soups and pickles. Lettuce, cauliflower, and other Italian vegetables that Queen Bona Sforza introduced in the sixteenth century achieved only modest acceptance. Fruits such as apples, plums, and sour cherries were cooked as garnishes and made into soup. Fish was served on Fridays and other fast days, frequently in luxurious culinary preparations with imported spices. The first published cookbook appeared in 1544, a translation from Czech, and the first original Polish cookbook appeared in 1682. Regional foods that made their way into the national mainstream included bigos from Lithuania, pierogi from Ukraine, and gingerbread from Pomerania. Beer was the common drink for all classes, since water was correctly regarded as unhealthy (town water supplies were mostly contaminated). Distillation of spirits began in the late sixteenth century in Ukraine; Gdańsk merchants imported Dutch spirits and made their own. French, German, and Hungarian wines partially replaced mead as the popular drink among the gentry; heavy sweet Spanish wines were highly prized. Diaries and court records commonly mention excessive alcohol consumption fostered by practices such as forcing guests to drink heavily. Tobacco and coffee entered general use in the seventeenth century. For the most part, the lower classes ate plainer varieties of the same foods in smaller quantities. Servants in rich households may have eaten 3,000 to 4,000 calories daily; peasants less; urban workers still less. During bad harvests, the poor tried to survive on nettles, bran, straw, leaves, nuts, seeds, wild fruit, and birch bark.

The rich suffered the diseases of excess consumption (high blood pressure, heart disease, stroke, gout, gastric distress) while the poor experienced those of insufficient consumption (malnutrition, rickets, anemia, low resistance to disease). Both groups ate too little fresh fruit and vegetables and suffered eczema, boils, and scurvy. The level of hygiene was low, as in the rest of Europe. Poor sewage disposal, contaminated water supplies, and infestation of vermin caused the spread of dysentery, tuberculosis, typhoid, and smallpox, among other diseases. Venereal disease was common. Like other cities in Poland-Lithuania, Warsaw suffered outbreaks of plague in 1569, 1572, 1591, 1592, 1600, 1601, 1605, 1620, 1622–31, 1639, 1646, 1652–4, 1657–58, 1660–63, 1674–75, 1677–79. The streets of Polish-Lithuanian cities, towns, and villages were filled with persons disabled by genetical problems as well as victims of accidents, badly set bones, and malnutrition. Many children died in infancy, and overall life expectancy was only thirty years at all social levels. Only the very rich had access to the medicine of the day. Most turned to traditional herbal medicines or cures such as bed rest, blood letting, and purgatives. Dubious potions were made from pearls and precious stones or from excrement and urine. Housewives and local healers provided most of the care and gained their knowledge from family tradition or published literature. Hospitals looked after the indigent while servants and innkeepers treated travelers.

CHAPTER 13

Culture in the Vasa Period

During the Vasa period, the juxtaposition of greatness and decline opened a curious bifurcation of Polish-Lithuanian culture between pan-European trends and a unique "Sarmatian" variant that expressed the distinctive values and experiences of the noble elite. While producing colorful features that unified the nobility and integrated some nonnoble elites into the culture, the Sarmatian ideology became xenophobic and blinded its proponents to the grave problems affecting the Polish-Lithuanian state. Religion also played a vital role in defining national and artistic culture. The resurgence of Roman Catholicism brought the Polish majority together, but it had a centrifugal effect on the Commonwealth as a whole and alienated other members of this polyglot, multiethnic society. Not wishing to become Catholic, the Ruthenians, Jews, Prussian Germans, Karaites, and Tatars clung to their own religiously based particularisms. Only Lithuanians safeguarded their identity within the Catholic orbit. Non-Catholics with legal privileges to protect, such as Prussian German burghers and Jews, identified with the Polish-Lithuanian state and came to terms with its elite.

Sarmatianism coexisted with European cultural forms, and both nobles and intellectuals moved from one cultural style to the other without hesitation as the situation required. The European Baroque provided the fashions, artistic expressions, and ideas for court circles and richer nobles. Sarmatianism provided the basis of provincial life. The political ideology of noble democracy was not exclusively Sarmatian and it pervaded noble society, whatever cultural forms the nobles embraced. Not all proponents were conservative. Some recommended reformist variants.

SARMATIAN DISTINCTIVENESS

A complex of historical, artistic, political, and social characteristics came together to form the Sarmatian civilization of Poland-Lithuania of the seventeenth and early eighteenth centuries. "Sarmatian" refers to the historical myth created by Renaissance scholars who claimed that Polish-Lithuanian nobles descended from a third-century warrior people who lived on the steppes north of the Black Sea. According to this myth, Sarmatian national practices evolved into the political system of Polish-Lithuanian noble democracy with its civil liberties for nobles, elected kingship, and parliamentary near-supremacy protected by the *liberum veto*. The large size of the Polish-Lithuanian nobility (7 to 10 percent of the population) and the deep conviction of noble superiority reflected the gulf between the so-called Sarmatian conquerors and the rest of the population. Religious factors were added. After the mid-seventeenth-century wars against the Lutheran Swedes, the Orthodox Russians and Cossacks, and the Moslem Turks and Tatars, Sarmatians considered the Polish-Lithuanian elite to be an exclusively Catholic nation although commoners might worship differently if they accepted their inferior social position.

While the Sarmatian ideology primarily benefited nobles, it spread widely among the Polish-Lithuanian population, creating a powerful sense of distinctiveness and superiority to other nations that bears comparison with modern Russian and American messianic tendencies. Polish-Lithuanian nobles were absolutely convinced that they lived in the freest and best society in the world and that these institutions had enabled the Polish-Lithuanian state to achieve its vast size. Their resistance to reform came from love of liberty and xenophobia. Polish-Lithuanian nobles identified France with sexual immorality and royal absolutism after Henri Valois's brief reign and the reign of seventeenth-century kings with French wives. Machiavelli brought Italy into permanent disrepute. The German states raised no moral distaste, but conflicts with Prussia and Austria made them seem hostile. The Orthodox religion made Russia seem alien, and its prolonged conflict with Poland-Lithuania made it appear hostile. The Sarmatian ideology spread to burgher scholars and jurists, who cited it approvingly out of a shared sense of national consciousness and a desire to protect their legal privileges within the Commonwealth.

A variant of the Sarmatian ideology developed in Royal Prussia, contradicting Polish-Lithuanian xenophobia by embracing the ideals of a multinational Commonwealth with religious tolerance and providing support for Prussian political and economic liberties. Prussian scholars, patronized by the city councils, presented their own fanciful historical theory that the ancient Sarmatian empire included Polish, Lithuanian, and Prussian branches. The purest form of Sarmatianism survived in Prussia, granting an equal place to nobles and the burgher elite. This ideology had no influence outside Prussia.

The World of the Sarmatians

A network of customs acted as a daily reminder of the Sarmatian civilization's distinctiveness. Many practices stemmed from the expressiveness of the pan-

European Baroque, but they developed a unique form in the Polish-Lithuanian Commonwealth in part because of its extensive contact with Russian and Ottoman civilization. In addition, the Baroque persisted longer in Sarmatian Poland-Lithuania than further west. The religious calendar was the basis for social life and afforded more than a hundred days of rest during the year. Roman Catholics followed the reformed Gregorian calendar after 1582, but Orthodox Christians continued to schedule events according to the Julian calendar. Jews observed their own religious calendar and holidays.

Extensive contact with the Turkish Empire lent visual and artistic distinctiveness to Polish-Lithuanian nobles who collected and utilized opulent Turkish caftans, carpets, and jewel-incrusted weapons. Some shaved their heads, leaving only a Turkish-style scalp lock. Noble manners were effusive. A lesser noble showed his subordination to a magnate or other patron by kissing his hands, chest, stomach, knees, or feet. Some occasions demanded prostration on the floor. A superior might hug the head of a favored subordinate at his departure; children kissed their parents' feet when leaving or returning home, or when asking important favors such as permission to marry. Sons knelt on one knee before either parent; daughters knelt on both knees. Sarmatians cried in public to express grief or joy. For example, King Jan Kazimierz cried at the news of a military victory until "tears as big as peas poured down his cheeks," according to the memoirist Jan Pasek. Deputies wore swords in parliament and demonstrated their approval by throwing their hats in the air or their opposition by literally cutting up proposed legislation. The Roman Catholic Church fostered emotive customs, sometimes borrowed from the Orthodox Church, such as sighing, crying, and groaning at the mention of Christ and the Virgin Mary, or even at a pious phrase. During Mass, participants beat their face, forehead, cheeks, and chest, and banged their head against the earth when the celebrant held the host aloft. Flagellation was a Good Friday custom followed by both greater and lesser nobles. Other ascetic practices included prostration, standing in cruciform position for long periods, and attending Mass in full armor.

Showy excess marked the culinary life of the rich. Cooks prepared banquet foods such as fowl garnished with colorful feathers, and whole deer, wild boar, or suckling pigs on platters. Food was sometimes dyed and gilded, and shaped into elaborate landscapes. The rich provided for the poor by serving them coarser cuts of meat in another hall or outside. Among themselves, court circles and the Europeanized aristocracy usually avoided excesses and emphasized good manners.

The memoirs of Jan Chryzostom Pasek (c. 1636–c. 1701) provide a uniquely intimate picture of this Sarmatian world from the point of view of a lesser noble. Born in Mazovia and educated at a Jesuit academy, Pasek wrote his memoirs in his later years. Although they are a factual record of his part in the military and political campaigns of 1656–88, the memoirs are more noteworthy as a collection of tales about everyday events. Through his stories of military, political, and domestic life, Pasek uncovers the motivations of the average Sarmatian noble. At his best, Pasek is idealistic, loyal, and generous; at his worst, he is rapacious, brutal, petty, quarrelsome, and superstitious. Some modern literary critics see him as an unredeemably negative figure in moral and political terms, but others consider him a comic author who exaggerated his actions in the Falstaffian tradition for literary effect. Despite these significant differences, critics universally praise the lively, spoken quality of his prose and appreciate the insights that it provides. Two of the tales which historians and literary critics retell are the story of the pet otter who caught fish for his master and the account of nobles who grew so angry at the behavior of a theatrical character that they killed him on stage.

The Catholic Resurgence

Polish-Lithuanian culture was closely intertwined with religion, and reflected the triumph of Catholicism in the era of the Counter Reformation. Instead of confronting Protestantism head-on, Polish-Lithuanian kings adopted a long-range policy of winning back the nobility and securing the enthusiasm of the masses, who had been neglected by both Catholics and Protestants in the past. As elected foreign-born kings, Stefan Batory and Zygmunt III bowed to local toleration and pursued their Catholic goals by peaceful means such as ignoring Protestants when assigning state positions. Many nobles reconverted out of self-interest, while Catholic reform brought others back to the Church out of conviction. The Council of Trent eliminated many corrupt practices within the Church, and the Jesuits led an expansion of schooling that played an important part in rebuilding Catholicism.

The Catholic Reformation transformed Catholicism into an evangelical mass religion. Benedictine monks and both professors and students from Jesuit schools undertook extensive missions across the Commonwealth to make nominal Christians into devout ones. They worked with local priests to teach prayer and catechism as well as to administer the sacraments, spreading the word through powerful sermons. Special attention was devoted to Protestant areas and eastern areas that had been neglected in the past. New practices such as greetings ("Let Christ be praised") were established to reinforce religiosity, and congregational singing became part of worship. Mass pilgrimages to churches in freshly named Calvaries, such as the Holy Cross Mountains near Kielce, became popular. Religious demonstrativeness soon surprised foreigners. Canonized Polish saints such as Jadwiga and Stanisław Kostka gradually replaced the Spanish saints as life models. Patriotism focused strongly on the Virgin Mary of Częstochowa, who was seen as the Queen of Poland. Paintings and sculpture in Catholic churches provided instruction for the illiterate worshippers. After the Council of Trent, the Catholic Church made sure that priests were properly prepared to perform their duties, which now included keeping parish records of births, deaths, and attendance at Easter confession. Local clergy revived or founded new parish schools, charitable hospitals, and orphanages.

In addition to the Jesuits, new orders emerged to replace the declining older ones. Begging orders included the Carmelites (1605), Bonifraters (1609), Reformers (1622), and Pijars (1642); the older Dominican and Bernardin orders remained prominent. The number of monasteries more than doubled from 227 in 1600 to almost 500 in 1650. Female orders, such as the Augustinians, Carmelites, and Benedictines, devoted themselves to the education of girls and to charitable work. There were 21 cloisters in 1550 and 95 in 1650; 840 nuns took orders in 1600 and 2,760 in 1650.

Religious literature played an important role in Catholicism's triumph. The Jesuits took the lead, printing 344 items between 1564 and 1600. The Bible translation by Jakub Wujek (1540–97) was so accurate and so eloquent that some Protestants preferred it to their own. Mikołaj Sęp Szarzyński (1550–81) wrote expressive sonnets to the Virgin Mary imbued with Baroque and Counter Reformation imagery of human weakness and fear of death. The *Lives of the Saints of the Old and New Testament for Every Day in the Year* by Piotr Skarga (1536–1612) proved so popular that it remained in print for over three hundred years. Skarga introduced a religious dimension to politics, portraying national dangers as God's punishment for Poland's sins. Virtually all poets discussed religious themes in the early seventeenth century, although the best poetry generally followed other genres. Piotr Kochanowski (1566–1620) successfully translated popular epics by Tasso and Ariosto. Samuel Twardowski (c. 1595–1661) wrote epics describing Polish military activities.

Anna Alojza Ostrożska (Ostrozky) was a model figure of the Catholic Reformation. She was born in 1600 to an Orthodox magnate father and a devout Roman Catholic mother. In 1620 she married the elderly but active General Jan Karol Chodkiewicz, only to be widowed the following year. Anna did not remarry. She turned over her father's Ostrih Academy to the Jesuits and founded other Catholic institutions. Saying that it was his wish, Anna ordered her father's remains to be reburied in a Uniate cemetery and, when the reburial touched off a riot that the Catholic-dominated courts punished harshly, she intervened to reduce the sentences. However, new riots ensued when the courts ordered other Orthodox institutions to be handed over to the Uniates. Ostrozka founded hospitals for the poor and lame, often personally worked on the wards, and was known for prolonged praying and harsh practices to mortify the body; she may have been a virgin in her brief marriage and certainly had no further close relations before her death in 1654. She made vast donations to Jesuits and other Catholic orders in her will, which her cousins contested unsuccessfully.

Active persecution of Dissidents (non-Catholics) came principally in the early eighteenth century, when parliament passed laws preventing the building or rebuilding of churches (1717) and barring Dissident nobles from parliaments, courts, and other public offices (1733 and 1736).

The Decline of Protestantism

The absence of serious resistance from Protestantism suggests that it sank only shallow roots in Poland-Lithuania except in ethnic German regions such as Prussia. Polish and Lithuanian nobles had turned to Protestantism in the mid-sixteenth century to get a better education and press their political point of view, especially in the Execution of the Laws movement, as well as to meet their religious needs. Religious issues aside, seventeenth-century Catholic schools now outstripped Protestant schools except in mathematics and science, two subjects that concerned nobles little. Thus many Protestant nobles sent their sons to the Jesuits who both educated and converted them. In addition, the rising tide of noble assertiveness demonstrated during interregna showed clearly that noble rights and freedoms could be articulated through Catholicism. Tridentine reforms and the polonization of the Catholic Church counteracted many of the causes of the Reformation, while Protestantism lost its attractiveness as a result of sectarian feuding, censorship of nonconforming thought, and persecution of religious opponents. Protestant nobles also found it expensive and troublesome to maintain churches on their estates. Both nobles and commoners found Protestantism lacking in color and proved receptive to resurgent Catholicism.

Calvinism disappeared from its Little Poland stronghold during the seventeenth century and maintained itself primarily in Lithuania. The Third Lithuanian Statute of 1588, which incorporated statutes on religious toleration, helped nobles maintain the religion of their choice on their estates and also gave Protestant Churches the legal right to buy landed estates. Protestantism, especially Calvinism, became a manifestation of Lithuanian autonomy. Lithuanian deputies in parliament defended their coreligionists in Poland against attacks by Catholic mobs by threatening to dissolve parliament if Zygmunt III failed to punish the rioters; they often made common cause with Eastern Orthodox nobles. The powerful Radziwiłł family acted as the chief patrons of Protestantism, maintaining it on their vast estates and protecting it throughout the Commonwealth, but their attempts to dominate Lithuania with Swedish and Transylvanian assistance in the mid-seventeenth century fatally compromised Calvinism and exposed it to

Catholic retaliation. Pockets of Calvinism remained in Lithuania into the eighteenth century.

The Polish Brethren provided an unusually interesting variant of Polish Protestantism. Founded by followers of the Italian Anabaptist, Faustus Socinus, these so-called Arians, a reference to early Christianity, had great difficulty reconciling their religious beliefs with their identity as Polish-Lithuanian nobles. Early enthusiasts challenged the legitimacy of private property, but most Polish Brethren accepted the existing social system and satisfied their Christian conscience by treating serfs and other commoners humanely. Sixteenth-century Polish Brethren generally maintained that Christianity forbade them to perform expected noble duties as warriors in the military levy and officeholders who administered local criminal justice. Irritants like these, combined with their radical religious denial of the Holy Trinity, made them very unpopular among other Protestants as well as among Catholics. By the 1630s, most Arians had abandoned radical social viewpoints, rationalizing fighting in defensive wars and administering justice to miscreants, but they remained unpopular. Never numerous, they gained considerable influence because of their high level of solidarity and education. The leading Arian magnate, Jakub Sieniéński, established a high school in his private city of Raków, halfway between Cracow and Lublin, that provided excellent instruction in Latin, Polish, ethics, natural science, and mathematics, and attracted students from Calvinist as well as Arian homes. Raków became a leading intellectual center for religious and rational thought for all of Europe until the state ordered it closed in 1638. Most Arian synods took place in Raków, as Sieniéński poured much of his fortune into Church affairs, including funding propaganda trips to Germany, Holland, France, and England. Protestant and Catholic parliamentary deputies voted to expel the Arians in 1658 at the end of the Swedish invasion, even though many had fought patriotically in the Polish and Lithuanian armies.

THE EUROPEAN CULTURE OF POLISH-LITHUANIAN ELITES

Polish-Lithuanian royal, magnate, and burgher elites coexisted with Sarmatian culture when dealing with provincial society but preferred to follow the models provided by western Europe. The Vasas brought the richness of European culture to their courts. They maintained personal artistic interests and invited numerous foreign artists, especially Italians, to Poland; other foreigners came in the wake of the Vasas' foreign-born wives. The Polish-Lithuanian magnate elite assimilated European Baroque culture and learning at court, and introduced them in their palaces throughout the Commonwealth, where provincial nobles encountered them. Royal and Ducal Prussia, especially Gdańsk, became another contact point between pan-European culture and provincial Sarmatianism. The foreign tour became an essential part of a wealthy Polish noble's upbringing, supplementing or supplanting university study. Upwardly mobile lesser nobles acquired European polish in the provinces, the capital, and abroad, if they could afford it. Urban patricians had the wealth and contacts to participate in this cultural style.

While the royal court and provincial manor houses may have reflected polar opposites in cultural styles, most members of the Polish-Lithuanian Commonwealth kept a foot in both camps. They moved back and forth in dress, furnishings, and manners as the situation required. Latin grammar, still a link to classical culture and sixteenth-century intellectuals, provided the basis for seventeenth-century education, and many Sarmatians spoke Latin fluently. The development of Latin-incrusted Polish speech illustrates the ambiguities of an apparent xenophobic isolationism.

LITERATURE, SCIENCE, AND EDUCATION

Cultural life remained vigorous in the Vasa era. Polish-Lithuanian printers published books in Polish and Latin; printing in Gdańsk was even more varied. Sebastian Petryca translated Aristotle into Polish, providing commentary. G. Knapski published a Polish-Greek-Latin thesaurus in 1621 (expanded edition 1643). Latin-language studies of the classics continued, spurred by feelings of common interest with the Roman Republic. Eastern contact stimulated Polish translations of the Koran in 1640 and *Gulistan* (*Rose Garden*) by the Persian poet Sadi. Scientific interests stimulated Szymon Syreniusz's study of medicinal herbs. Agricultural subjects were studied by Teodor Zawadzki (1616), who also wrote several books about raising horses. In addition to buying published books, many nobles kept handwritten books, which included political materials from parliament, family records, medical advice, and gossip. Such collections also listed social duties such as models for expressing thanks, letters for specific gifts (oranges and marzipan, for example), letters for visiting, and letters asking favors. Printing flourished in Gdańsk, and the work was often of high artistic quality. Books were published in German, Dutch, Polish, French, Latin, Greek, and Hebrew. Important Polish political tracts often appeared first in Gdańsk, and Gdańskers engaged in and published research on a large variety of topics from natural science to the history and geography of Prussia. Polish Protestant literature continued to come out in Königsberg in Ducal Prussia.

The Jagiellonian University in Cracow took some steps to adapt seventeenth-century educational methods with help from Anna the Jagiellonian and Władysław IV, as well as bishops, nobles, and burghers. Old-fashioned scholastics dominated the theological and law faculties, but new funds allowed the creation of modern university faculties. Anatomy and botany were added to the medical faculty in 1602, although it took many years to fill the posts and enrollment was poor. Between 1612 and 1615, the university created chairs in Greek and Latin rhetoric; Hebrew studies were established on a less permanent basis. Other new fields of studies included modern history, surveying, military engineering, geography, geometry, moral philosophy, civil law, and music. Some progress was made in the library, and a printing shop was founded. Ethnic Poles filled most professorial posts; about half had studied abroad. The university was fully Catholic, even though some professors had studied in Protestant universities (especially in the Netherlands) and Jansenism made an impact. As before, the Jagiellonian University supervised a network of high schools throughout the Commonwealth. About 40 percent of students in the Jagiellonian University came from burgher homes.

Zygmunt III preferred to support the Jesuits intellectually and financially, and two Jesuit academies provided the Jagiellonian University's main rivals. The Jesuits also opened schools in Prussia to keep the nobility and peasantry Catholic. Cardinal Hozjusz founded the first academy at Braniewo in 1565; it became a papal seminary in 1581. Additional Jesuit schools opened in Toruń (1605), Gdańsk (1621), and Grudziądz (Graudenz, 1647). The Vilnius Academy, founded by Stefan Batory in 1578 to protect Catholicism in the eastern Commonwealth, comprised two faculties: the faculty of liberal arts and philosophy, and the faculty of theology. Well-developed humanistic studies were bolstered by the presence of notable foreign scholars from Germany, Sweden, Portugal, Spain, and England. The Vilnius Academy reached its height in the mid-seventeenth century when it attracted noble youth and prepared them for careers in public life. The faculty of theology trained nobles and commoners for the priesthood. Władysław IV also supported this academy handsomely, and he restrained the students' anti-Protestant demonstrations. Chancellor Jan Zamoyski founded and endowed another major academy in his private city, Zamość, in 1595. The Zamoyski academy aimed ambitiously to establish humanism by introducing subjects such as classical philology and history, and to prepare nobles for public service. Szymon Szymonowic, a noted poet who helped organize the Academy, emphasized the importance of studying the Stoics and late Greek medical writers. He collected old Greek manuscripts and maintained extensive contacts with foreign universities. Links with the Padua medical school were particularly close. Some foreigners taught in Zamość, too. Zamoyski's death in 1605 led to the academy's decline. Conflicts among his heirs weakened the school's élan, and professors drifted away to Cracow and elsewhere despite better pay in Zamość. Noble students switched to Cracow as well. The situation improved during 1635–46, as more students attended and additional subjects, especially law, were added.

Stimulated by the Protestant Reformation and close ties to Germany, Prussian cities provided their citizens with impressive educational and cultural facilities that also attracted Protestant nobles from across the Commonwealth. The Gdańsk Gymnasium, founded in 1558, functioned as a university, offering a full program of religious, humanistic, legal, and medical studies. The high level of medical studies was reflected in the appointment of the entire faculty as doctors to the Polish-Lithuanian royal court. Gdańsk introduced anatomy into the curriculum in 1568 and epidemiology was extensively studied in the 1620s. Medical literature appeared in several languages, including books by Sebastian Śleszkowski on bleeding (1615), fevers (1616), poison (1618), and plague (1623). After 1589, the Polish language was taught by such distinguished instructors as the poet Jan Rybiński. Gdańsk merchants sent their children to perfect their Polish by living with associates in the interior according to rank: patricians with magnates or upper gentry, lesser merchants with lesser gentry or burghers. University study abroad was common and the municipality offered grants to poorer citizens. The Toruń Gymnasium, renewed in 1583–1600, also adopted a comprehensive program of instruction on a high level. The early seventeenth-century philosopher Benedykt Keckermann gained European-wide renown for publications on theology, moral philosophy, logic, politics, history, and other subjects. Many Lutheran and Calvinist churches established schools, and numerous private schools provided instruction in Polish, French, and Dutch. The overwhelming majority of the students and scholars were burghers.

The Protestant Reformation stimulated the formation of public libraries in Prussia. Albrecht Hohenzollern opened his large collection of books and manuscripts to professors, students, and other members of the educated public in 1540. Gdańsk opened the library of a former Franciscan monastery to the public in 1596 and added private collections to round out the sophisticated literary, philosophical, and religious collection. Elbląg and other cities opened public libraries, too. Traveling actors presented a wide variety of theatrical works in several languages in Prussian cities, while guilds and urban schools established theater programs that had themes of local and national interest. Urban festivals included artistic and shooting competitions. Satirical literature met the needs of literate but unsophisticated readers.

The Fine Arts

Interest in the fine arts developed rapidly after Zygmunt III's assumption of the Polish-Lithuanian crown, and centered in the new capital, Warsaw. The king took few furnishings from Wawel Castle when he left Cracow other than a series of Flemish arrases with biblical scenes, and he built and furnished his Warsaw residence with proper monarchical flair and expense. The new Royal Castle contained a magnificent Senate Chamber with ten windows looking out over the Vistula River and the main courtyard. Multicolored painted designs adorned some walls while others displayed tapestries, and the ceiling had two large oil paintings by Tomassio Dolabella celebrating recent military victories against Russia. The Marble Room was also magnificent. Zygmunt furnished these and other rooms with paintings by contemporary masters such as Rembrandt, Rubens, Jordaens, and Brueghel. He employed three agents in western Europe to buy art for him and arranged for Rubens to paint his portrait from sketches that his heir, the future Władysław IV, brought to Antwerp. Zygmunt supported court painters such as Pieter Stoutman, one of Rubens's more prominent students, and especially Dolabella, who created a portrait gallery of Polish kings. His son Władysław also took a serious interest in painting. He visited Rubens in Flanders and Reni in Italy during his 1624 trip to western Europe, commissioning important paintings. Most of Zygmunt's fine collection was taken by Swedes or destroyed in the mid-seventeenth-century wars that swept Poland; some were sold in the aftermath. Polish and Lithuanian magnates developed artistic interests after a time. Chancellor Jerzy Ossoliński purchased original works by Raphael, Titian, and Dürer, for example. Elegant new palaces went up throughout the country.

The burghers of Gdańsk and other Prussian cities took a prominent role in creating impressive works of art. City halls and churches met high architectural standards, and patrician homes were indistinguishable from magnate palaces. In Gdańsk, the Arsenal, Golden Gate, Artus Court, and Neptune Fountain were all constructed or renewed between 1580 and 1620. Fine art flourished and a painters' guild formed in 1612. Leading painters such as Daniel Schultz spent part of their careers at the court of Zygmunt III, a notable patron, and executed commissions for magnates and churches in the interior. Close contacts with the Netherlands brought Dutch painters to Gdańsk and made the Netherlands' artistic style most popular, although Italian art had its supporters, too. Gdańsk craftsmen were also famed throughout the Commonwealth, supplying fine furniture, ornate locks, gold medallions, and church statuary, among other artistic products, to rich nobles and burghers. Rich burghers put up ornamented houses across the Commonwealth; an idiosyncratic jewel was built in the grain transportation center, Kazimierz Dolny, along the Vistula River. Lesser burghers shared these artistic interests on a more modest scale.

Architecture and Urbanization

One of Zygmunt's innovations was to make Warsaw the real capital of Poland-Lithuania. The Union of Lublin (1569) had declared that the joint Polish-Lithuanian parliament would meet in Warsaw, but King Zygmunt August failed to start building a palace or parliament building there before his death. Henri Valois lacked time and interest; Stefan Batory was too busy campaigning. In contrast, Zygmunt III hastened to act, in part to assure himself easier access to Sweden. The economic significance of Warsaw in trade with Lithuania grew too, and a serious fire in Cracow's Wawel Castle in 1595 made Zygmunt take action. Rather than start from scratch, the king added to existing structures. The Warsaw Royal Castle contained parliamentary chambers in the older, Gothic section; the lower chamber met on the ground floor while the senate met on the second floor. Zygmunt installed his royal apartments and chapel along with the ministerial offices near the Senate Chamber. Despite the move to Warsaw, Zygmunt kept Wawel up. His Italian court architect lived in Cracow for a while to complete structural repairs and refurbish the royal apartments with expensive furniture and wall coverings.

Władysław IV continued to beautify Warsaw, and rich nobles built palaces both there and throughout the Commonwealth. The number of churches increased. Architecture became professionalized and guild traditions were abandoned, allowing foreigners to design innovative new structures following international models. Władysław's Italian architects, Jan Baptist Gisleni and Constantine Tencalli, built in a softer style than Zygmunt had used for the Warsaw castle. The column built to honor Zygmunt III outside the Royal Castle, still a Warsaw landmark, imitated contemporary Roman construction. Elegant magnate palaces in the Italian style built or faced with stone were constructed along Cracow Suburb Street (Krakowskie Przedmieście) with gardens sloping down toward the Vistula River. Rural construction used wood, which was cheaper and easier to get.

Building activities resumed in and around Warsaw when Poland-Lithuania recovered from the Swedish wars. Jan III Sobieski, as magnate and king, practiced artistic patronage on a grand scale. His finest building was Wilanów (Villa Nuova), near Warsaw, designed by Augustino Locci the younger, a polonized Italian. He first built a rectangular two-story palace, but then rebuilt it in Italian style with elaborate symbolically decorated facades as Sobieski's ambitions grew. The surrounding area was carefully landscaped in the French manner. The palace wings that modern tourists see were added in the eighteenth century. Tylman van Gameren, a Dutch architect and engineer, built more than a dozen palaces, making him the leading Polish architect of the late seventeenth century. He mostly used northern late Baroque style, and his buildings resembled contemporary Dutch and Swedish construction. He adopted a monumental style softened by decorations and leaning toward early classicism. His imposing three-story Krasiński Palace (1677–82, now a branch of the National Library), for the palatine of Płock, Jan Dobrogosta Krasiński, included ornamental windows designed by the Gdańsk sculptor and architect Andreas Schlüter. He also designed the Marywil (Marie-Ville) palace and trade complex on what is today Theater Square (Plac Teatralny). This elegant money-making urban development outside the city limits was shaped in an uneven pentagon with shops on the ground floor and apartments upstairs. One side, a simple gallery, contained a chapel; the courtyard was open. Queen Louise Marie, who gave her name to the commercial development, also hired van Gameren to build a church in New Warsaw that displayed classical elements.

Music

Music flourished at the royal court and spread throughout the Commonwealth. Italian musicians set the tone during the Vasa period, and local musicians learned to write in the Italian style while providing some specifically Polish accents through the use of native religious melodies, such as Christmas carols and Gregorian chant variants, as a base for their polyphonic constructions. Composers utilized the Polonaise in both secular and sacred works. Regional dances of Polish, Ukrainian, Hungarian, Turkish, and other origins can also be found in seemingly Italian music along with borrowings from older Commonwealth composers. Regional musicians used native elements more openly than musicians at the sophisticated center of the Commonwealth's musical life.

At the start of his reign, Zygmunt III expanded the royal choir from fourteen to sixty voices to perform an international and local repertory that included such works as Krzysztof Klabon's "Songs of the Slav Muse Praising the Present Victory at Byczyna." Zygmunt later established his own chapel choir directed by Asprilli Pacelli, who was followed by other Italian composers. By about 1600, large-scale works in the ornate Venetian style replaced the simple homophonic music of the Reformation and Counter Reformation. The major court composer was Vencentius Lilius (Gigli), whose "Sacred Melodies" for five to twelve voices were published in Cracow in 1604. Zygmunt III maintained sixty instrumentalists and singers directed by Italian musicians. Mikołaj Zieliński (c. 1550–1615) is known only from two surviving collections published in 1611 dedicated to Wojciech Baranowski, archbishop of Gniezno, whom he served as music director. Zieliński composed in monumental polychoral style. His two cycles for the Church year included twelve works for seven voices, forty-three works for eight voices, and a twelve-part *magnificat* for three choirs. In addition to voices, the works required instruments and organ continuo. More intimate pieces for solo instruments or voice featured Italianate embellishments. Zieliński's works were dramatically expressive and chromatically adventurous. Marcin Mielczewski (d. 1651) was a an internationally known musician at the Warsaw royal chapel and later at the court of Karol Ferdynand Waza (Vasa), bishop of Płock. He wrote most of his large output in concertato style (solo voices over a basso continuo accompaniment), and his Masses for large choir and orchestra sometimes quoted folk melodies or rhythms. Popular religious songs also appeared in his more complex Masses. Mielczewski probably composed madrigals and instrumental pieces that have not survived. The future Władysław IV introduced a visiting Italian opera troupe in 1625 and established a royal opera company at court in 1628 that premiered twelve operas and three ballets between 1635 and 1648, more than in Paris. This company functioned until 1655 and performed a substantial repertoire, some of it written for special occasions such as the royal wedding of 1637. Magnates quickly imitated the royal court, and even nobles with more modest incomes followed suit. An indication of the widespread musical interest was the publication of musical adaptations for general use. The Pelplin Organ Tabulature compiled in the 1620s transcribed many contemporary works, especially motets, and Aleksander Gorczyń's 1647 publication *Musical Tablature* presented popular tunes of the day.

The most interesting musical personality of the era was Adam Jarzębski (c. 1589–c. 1648), a composer, instrumentalist, poet, and businessman. Jarzębski started his musical career in 1612 as a violinist at the court of the elector in Berlin, but after visiting Italy, he moved to Warsaw to play in the Royal Chapel orchestra; he earned extra money by teaching music to the children of rich nobles. Jarzębski turned to composition. His two-part instrumental *canzoni e concerti* adapted and transformed works by noted composers such as Giovanni Gabrieli, Palestrina, and Lassus. His works featured richly ornamented melodies and rich harmonies with chromaticism and dissonance using popular tunes and dance rhythms. Jarzębski succeeded in business as well as in music. Zygmunt III rewarded him for his musical accomplishments with leaseholds on crown properties, especially mills, which he managed well; and Władysław IV hired him in 1635 to construct the royal palace at Ujazdów as well as the theater in the main Royal Castle. Jarzębski invested his profits in Warsaw real estate. Always ambitious, when newly selected Crown Court Marshal Adam Kazanowski suggested that he write a guidebook to Warsaw, he provided a book-length description in verse that gave an excellent description of buildings, particularly his patron's property. The verses were not aesthetically satisfying.

Cracow became a music center once again after the mid-seventeenth-century wars devastated Warsaw. Bartłomiej Pękiel left the Royal Chapel in Warsaw for Cracow and, as kapellmeister, developed the Cracow Cathedral Choir to a high level. Musical activity continued strongly even after Pękiel returned to Warsaw.

The Catholic Reformation influenced musical styles. Jesuits actively developed religious songs and musical plays in the German style. They staged religious operas full of pomp and splendor and introduced music to religious processions. The use of folk dance tunes made productions more attractive. For example, one Carnival dialogue showed Bacchus dancing with Polish mountaineers. Other orders such as the Piarists followed suit.

Changing Lithuanian Cultural Identity

Lithuanian patriotism appeared in the cultural as well as the political sphere. Use of the Lithuanian language gradually slowed. Calvinist prayer books and tracts were published in the Lithuanian language late in the 1590s, and the Vilnius Academy trained priests to preach in Lithuanian as well as Polish so they could carry their message to the people. Constantine Sirvydas published a trilingual Lithuanian-Polish-Latin dictionary in 1629 and the first Lithuanian grammar in 1630. However, publication in Lithuanian remained rare.

Educated Lithuanians used the Latin and Polish languages by preference but remained conscious of their national identity. The Lithuanian nobility, like the Polish, stressed local control, and their political program slowed centralization. For example, the 1614 Polish-language translation of the Third Lithuanian Statute replaced the Ruthenian original in juridical practice, but the nobles of the Grand Duchy continued to reject Polish law. Mateusz Stryjkowski, a Pole living in Lithuania, wrote a Latin-language history of Lithuania compiled from Lithuanian, Ruthenian, and Polish chronicles. Following the fashion of the day, he traced Lithuania's origins back to ancient Rome. Andrzej Rymsza wrote a powerful description in Polish verse of Prince Karol Radziwiłł's successful military campaign against Russia in 1581; Jan Radwan and Jan Kozak described other Radziwiłł military victories in Latin verse. All three authors were graduates of the Vilnius Academy, where Polish-Lithuanian student relations were occasionally tense.

Orthodox Revival and Ruthenian National Consciousness

The transfer of Ukrainian lands in 1569 from the Grand Duchy of Lithuania to the Kingdom of Poland accelerated the process of polonization and also stimulated a conscious Orthodox revival that defined a Ruthenian national consciousness. As Lithuanian protectionist barriers against Polish settlement lifted, more ethnic Polish nobles entered the newly acquired territories and gained land grants from the king. They mixed with the local Ruthenian nobility, transforming it from the Lithuanian nobility of Russian tradition—wealth without legal rights—into a Polish nobility with extensive, defined individual and corporate rights. The sudden integration of the eastern palatinates into the Polish Kingdom gave rise to religious and ethnic tensions that the Polish state failed to discern, let alone solve. Separation from Orthodox Belarus in the Grand Duchy of

Lithuania also laid the basis for the later development of a specifically Ukrainian, rather than general Ruthenian, consciousness.

The nobility of the Ukrainian palatinates had taken form before their annexation by the Polish Kingdom in 1569. Nobles had a keen awareness of indigenous nobles and newcomers; long-established Catholics were accepted as indigenous nobles. Both Orthodox and Catholic nobles shared noble privileges even if snobbery tended to make Catholics feel superior. Catholic schooling produced numerous conversions, and Catholicism gave better access to high office, although Orthodox nobles held some secular senatorial appointments. The Greek Catholic (Uniate) Church attracted few nobles after its founding at the Union of Brest (1596), and it soon acquired the reputation of a church for peasants; Orthodox nobles preferred to convert to Protestantism or Catholicism. The new eastern Ukrainian palatinates had a more Lithuanian and less Polish social structure. They lacked the large number of petty and middle nobles found in Poland, although where they existed they remained traditionally attached to Orthodoxy. Nobles held mixed attitudes toward the Cossacks. Adventurous nobles, especially poorer ones, often joined or led the Cossacks against the Turks and Tatars. Some Orthodox and Catholic nobles accepted Cossack officers as nobles if they were wealthy and bought landed estates. Others regarded Cossacks as little better than peasants, even when the king ennobled them.

Nobles maintained their allegiance to their home provinces by insisting on the use of Ruthenian in legal documents. Nobles from Kiev and Bratslav petitioned the king in the 1570s to keep Ruthenian scribes at court to provide Ruthenian documentation. Religious works stated that the Christianization of Rus by Vladimir established the Ruthenian nation. Most nobles rejected the Union of Brest for violating ancient Ruthenian liberties and laws. For example, a polemic entitled "The Warning" (c. 1610) reproached the Poles for granting Jews and Muslims more religious freedoms than Orthodox Christians. Some of these works even appeared in Polish, especially after the 1620s. Other works by Meletii Smotrytsky and Jan Szczęsny Herburt also defended Orthodox Christianity.

Nobles and burghers kept Orthodoxy vigorous while the Church went into decline in the fifteenth and sixteenth centuries. The patriarch of Constantinople paid little attention to his Ruthenian provinces after 1453, and the Roman Catholic Lithuanian grand dukes generally appointed Orthodox bishops for political reasons with little regard for the needs of the faithful. But Prince Konstiantyn Ostrozky opened a primary school on his estate at Ostrih in 1570 and added an academy in 1578 where Ruthenian and foreign scholars taught. The Ostrih Academy stressed Orthodoxy's Byzantine roots, using Greek as the main language of instruction; it taught Latin, too. Some professors taught in Ruthenian; it is not clear whether Church Slavonic was used. The academy's printing press published two dozen books in 1578–1612, particularly the first complete text of the Bible in Church Slavonic, translated from the Greek by a team of scholars headed by Herasym Smotrytsky.

Burghers from Lviv and other cities took an active role in the Orthodox revival. The Brotherhood of Holy Dormition Church in Lviv founded a school in 1585 and campaigned against local clerics who neglected their duties. Jeremiah II, patriarch of Constantinople, removed the Brotherhood from the authority of local bishops and placed it under his direct control, instructing it to report on abuses in local churches and supervise other brotherhoods. The Brotherhood school's own curriculum made Church Slavonic an equal partner with the Greek language. Brotherhoods founded eight more schools between 1584 and 1591 with a conservative Greco-Slavonic curriculum that emphasized the use of these languages in Bible study. The schools had not yet absorbed Renaissance scholarly innovations.

Pushed by the laity, the Orthodox Church itself revived. Continuity in the Orthodox Church was ensured by Theophanes, patriarch of Jerusalem, who, while returning from a trip to Moscow in 1620, consecrated new bishops in Kiev to replace those who had defected to the Greek Catholic Church. The ordinations were carried out in secret without the approval of the Polish-Lithuanian state that law required. King Zygmunt III expelled Theophanes as an Ottoman spy and outlawed the new bishops, but Władysław IV legalized the Orthodox Church again in 1632 and appointed new Orthodox bishops himself, since he refused to recognize the 1620 ordinations. Orthodox schools, presses, and brotherhoods gained legal recognition, and the Orthodox received permission to build new churches. The revival of Orthodoxy was signaled also by Archimandrite Elisei Pletenetsky, a Galician noble, who built up the Monastery of the Caves in Kiev (1599–1625) and purchased a printing press that published forty books including a Ruthenian lexicon and grammar.

Meletii Smotrytsky (1577–1633) was an outstanding figure in Ruthenian letters in the early seventeenth century who defined the nature of the Ruthenian people. His *Threnos* (1610) reflected the strong anti-Catholic attitudes of his Orthodox upbringing, but he became much more moderate in the 1620s and converted to Ukrainian Catholicism in 1625 in the hope of bringing both branches of the Ruthenian nation together while winning support among Roman Catholic nobles. Smotrytsky is best known for his Church Slavonic grammar and religious tracts. He supported the use of Slavonic language in the liturgy and limited the Ruthenian vernacular to popular religious works such as postils, homilies, and the catechism. He defended Ruthenian religion and traditions because he considered the Ruthenian people to be an equal partner with Poles and Lithuanians within the Polish-Lithuanian state. Like his noble contemporaries, he used the term "nation" to refer to the nobility with its rights, freedoms, and liberties, and rejected its application to Ruthenians as a whole. For him, faith (*religia ruska*) defined the Ruthenian people, and he appealed to lapsed Orthodox nobles such as the Sapiehas, Chodkiewiczes, and Wiśniowieckis to return to their ancestral traditions.

As the newly appointed metropolitan of Kiev, Petro Mohyla (Petru Movilă, 1597–1647) modernized Orthodox education and sought equality for the Ruthenian (Orthodox) nation within the Commonwealth. A member of a Moldavian ducal family with long-standing ties to Poland-Lithuania, he was a polyglot who studied in Lviv and Paris and used Ruthenian, Latin, Polish, Greek, Slavonic, and Romanian easily; he wrote his will in Polish. Many Orthodox clerics considered him too friendly to Roman Catholics, too pro-Polish, and possibly Uniate in inspiration. His successor as metropolitan, Sylvestr Kosiv, continued his loyalist tradition. As metropolitan, Mohyla improved the organization and administration of his see, reformed monastic orders, and gathered scholars to revitalize Orthodox religious thought.

Mohyla received royal permission to establish a new school in 1631 along the lines of Polish Jesuit schools. After the first year, he merged it with the Kiev Epiphany Brotherhood school in the Podil district with the aim of creating a higher school; it finally gained official status as an academy in 1694. The Kievan Mohyla Academy taught liberal arts (Greek and Latin) to prepare students for the Church; it was not authorized to prepare students for state service. The curriculum was based on the study of Greek, Latin, Slavonic, and Polish. Students received instruction in poetics and rhetoric as well as catechism, church music, and arithmetic. Much of the instructional material was Polish in origin, translated into Latin. Some Russian Orthodox Church material was also used. The Cossacks were suspicious of the school at first, but later offered it their protection. Cossack leaders such as Ivan Samoilovich and Ivan Vyhovsky studied there.

Ruthenian historical consciousness emerged in the early seventeenth century from the Orthodox Church revival and a growing Ruthenian national awareness. Kiev's role as the intellectual center of the Ruthenian nation drew Orthodox Galicians and Volhynians, creating a proto-Ukrainian national feeling. Around 1620, it became commonplace to identify the Cossacks with the warriors of old. Metropolitan Yov Boretsky called them "Remnants of Old Rus" in 1621, and similar statements appeared in the Latin and Polish languages from the pens of Ruthenian scholars. The *Hustyn Chronicle,* written in the 1620s by Zakharia Kopystensky, archimandrite of the Caves Monastery, provided a local history that found the roots of the Ruthenian nation in the early medieval state of Kievan Rus. However, the work concentrated on recent history to provide the background to the author's rejection of the Union of Brest. The *Lviv Chronicle,* written by

Mykhailo Hunashevsky, a well-educated lesser noble from Bratslav palatinate who had fought in the Cossack revolt of 1638 before taking holy orders, started in the fourteenth century and emphasized the relationship between the medieval Galician principality and the modern Ruthenian nation. Both these works and others appealed to the past to establish the existence of a Ruthenian nation that included all Orthodox Christians in the Kingdom of Poland and the Grand Duchy of Lithuania. Chroniclers used the term "Ukraine" only in reference to the "wild fields" along the Dnieper. The works implicitly recognized the sovereignty of Polish and Lithuanian rulers.

By the end of the seventeenth century, a clear concept of distinctiveness pervaded the educated elite centered in the Ukrainian palatinates, and distinguished that region from Belarus and Russia. Seventeenth-century scholars identified two separate Ruthenian languages: Lithuanian Slavonic in Belarus and Little Russian, or Rossiacam, in Ukraine. The Hetmanate used the Ukrainian vernacular as its administrative language, and the term "Cossack" became the common identifying adjective for the region, state, and language. Ukrainian clerical scholars brought their expanded consciousness to St. Petersburg in the late seventeenth and early eighteenth centuries, linking the new Russian Empire firmly to Kievan Rus and applying the traditional name Rus, or the alternative Rossija (Russia), to the united East Slavs rather than the traditional Muscovite appellation Moskva.

Despite its limited acceptance by Ruthenians, the Greek Catholic Church shared in the Ruthenian revival and even led in educational development. Much of Greek Catholic education was provided by the Basilians, a monastic order founded by St. Basil which had been fundamentally overhauled in Ukraine and Belarus in 1617 by Metropolitan Yosyf Rutsky. He modeled his reforms on the Jesuit order and gave the Basilians additional tasks of providing pastoral missions and establishing print shops. The Basilian order grew rapidly. With assistance from nobles, the Roman Catholic hierarchy, and the pope, they founded several high schools to teach local nobles. The best students received scholarships to complete their studies at the Greek College in Rome or in other foreign schools.

Jewish Thought and Literature

Like Ruthenian culture, Jewish culture was dominated by its clerical tradition. Mainstream rabbis gradually abandoned their predecessors' opposition to Caro's *Shulhan Arukh* and accepted it as definitive. Rabbis themselves became culture heroes to Polish-Lithuanian Jews, who eagerly chronicled their lives and deeds for an admiring public, and mysticism gained adherents after the disastrous mid-seventeenth-century wars. Influenced by misfortune, Hebrew language authors, themselves rabbis, detected a greater influence of evil spirits in the supernatural world that they studied through the Cabbala, and popularized millenarian fears of Judgment Day. Some rabbis were celebrated for their ascetic practices and submissiveness to fate. Historical accounts described the Cossack massacres.

A popular stream of Yiddish literature arose for the general public. Biblical, Talmudic, and Jewish historical stories appeared in Yiddish adaptations starting with a paraphrase of the Book of Esther published in Cracow in 1589. The most substantial single collection came from the pen of Jakub ben Abraham of Mezhirech (Międzyrzecz) who published a collection of 257 stories in Basel in 1602. Biblical translations also appeared; Samuel, Kings, Daniel, Joshua, and Psalms were all published in Yiddish between 1578 and 1594, but did not spread widely because many rabbis frowned on the use of the vernacular for religious subjects. Nevertheless, a full translation of the Pentateuch and Rashi's commentaries appeared in Lublin in 1623–27 in a handsome and rigorously prepared edition. In 1597, the German novel *Dietrich von Bern* came out in a Yiddish adaptation that changed Christian references or eliminated them altogether. Other German and Italian romances appeared in Yiddish translation and were imported to Poland-Lithuania. Yiddish theater began with the performance of plays for Purim holiday, some of which have survived in manuscript. Mummers performed these plays, which were full of broad humor and even impropriety, in private homes.

Increased Hostility to Jews

Catholic hostility toward Jews sharpened during the Counter Reformation, although Protestants remained the main target. The noted preacher Piotr Skarga was only one of many clerics who judged Jews guilty of crimes such as ritual murder and who generally considered them undesirable inhabitants of the realm. The worst decades for ritual murder trials were 1590–99, when nineteen accusations were made, and 1610–19 with eleven. Court records from 1610–19 show some acquittals but more convictions resulting in fines or executions. There were many physical attacks on Jews and Jewish property, usually by students, notably from the Jagiellonian University in Cracow, who enjoyed lenient treatment from the Church authorities; noble status helped shield many from judgment. In addition to religious enthusiasm, students were often motivated by poverty or greed to loot Jewish shops. Young artisans joined them enthusiastically. Jewish communities found it necessary to pay off student groups on a regular basis to prevent attacks. As time went on, escalating demands for ransom became increasingly difficult to meet. The worst attack of this period took place in Cracow in 1637 and cost seven Jewish lives; thirty-three saved themselves by promising to convert.

The Karaite Community

A dissident Jewish community, the Karaites were closely associated with the Tatars. Karaism took form in the ninth century among Babylonian-Persian Jews who rejected the Rabbinic tradition and the Talmud. The Karaites codified their religious practices in sixteenth-century Turkey before the Turkish Karaite community declined and leadership passed to the Tatar-speaking Crimean community, which had been founded in the twelfth century. Lithuanian Grand Duke Vytautas probably brought some Crimean Karaites to Trakai and other Lithuanian cities, where they continued to live until the Holocaust. Karaites followed a Jewish religion based entirely on Torah without Talmudic interpretation. Leaders insisted on following biblical precepts literally; individuals interpreted the Torah freely and communal consensus defined practice. Karaite scholarship defined strict observance of the Jewish calendar, marriage practices, and dietary ritual purity, areas in which they generally found Rabbinic traditions too lax.

Karaites developed a religious literature of their own. An early work of Lithuanian Karaite scholarship by Isaac ben Abraham Troki (1533–94) was an anti-Christian treatise that later appeared in Latin translation. Some minor pieces stressed Karaite differences with the larger Jewish community in the hope of avoiding Christian persecution, to no avail; the Cossacks persecuted Karaites as Jews in 1648. The Karaite scholar Solomon ben Aaron Troki wrote treatises on Karaism and its difference with Rabbinic Judaism in the early eighteenth century. A minor flowering of Karaite scholarship at this time prompted several Christian scholars to write about them.

The Evolution of the Tatar Community

Census figures showed that the number of Tatars swelled to 3,500 in 1528, 7,000 in 1550, and 9,000 in the seventeenth century; the actual numbers may have been larger. The Tatar population declined somewhat in the late seventeenth and early eighteenth centuries as several thousand Tatars sought refuge in Turkish lands from the wars and economic miseries that devastated Poland-Lithuania. About half the Tatars were Ducal Tatars, whom Lithuanian grand dukes had settled on their lands in exchange for military service. Ducal Tatars enjoyed the same rights as Lithuanian nobles except that Tatars did not take part in politics. So-called Cossack Tatars enjoyed similar privileges but held smaller land grants. In peacetime, they delivered the mail and performed other services for grand dukes. Some worked as carters and followed trades such as tanning. The other half of the community were Common Tatars who worked as artisans or petty traders. They were free persons but not nobles. Use of the Tatar language declined by 1550 and was generally replaced by Ruthenian. Most Tatar speakers were recent immigrants. Polish language use spread among Tatars along with the polonization of Ruthenian nobles. Some Tatars probably spoke Lithuanian in areas of Lithuanian ethnicity such as Samogitia.

The Islamic religion in the Sunni variant defined the Tatars as a nationality and kept them from fading into the Ruthenian or Polish national groups. Tatar communities maintained mosques and clerical personnel. Several higher Islamic schools trained clerics, clerks, and lay persons in religion, religious literature, and Arabic script, but Tatars rarely made pilgrimages to Mecca or other holy sites, and they generally ignored Koranic strictures against drinking alcohol. The men often married Belarussian women in the first centuries when few Tatar women lived in Lithuania, and treated them more in the Slavic than in the Islamic manner. Male children were raised as Muslims.

CHAPTER 14

Second Interlude: Michał Wiśniowiecki and Jan III Sobieski

WIŚNIOWIECKI

Michał Korybut Wiśniowiecki (1640–1673) was elected to the vacant Polish-Lithuanian throne on June 19, 1669. The new king was born in 1640 to the richest magnate of Ukraine, Jeremi Michał Wiśniowiecki, who died only months after his son's birth, and Gryzelda Zamoyska, granddaughter of Chancellor Jan Zamoyski. Young Michał was raised by his mother at Zamość and later at the royal court in Warsaw. He learned to speak eight languages while studying at home as well as in Prague, Dresden, and Vienna, but he acquired no interest in politics, philosophy, literature, or the arts. He returned to Poland to lead the life of a passive country gentleman, taking no part in political or military affairs. When Jan Kazimierz abdicated, this unlikely candidate was put forward by pro-Habsburg and anti-French factions as a native son, or "Piast," because of his famous father—in order to prevent a foreigner from taking the throne. There was strong opposition to the French candidates whom Jan II Kazimierz had tried to advance during his kingship: Louis, duc de Condée; his son, Henri d'Enghien; and Philip Wilhelm, duke of Neuburg. As before, Polish-Lithuanian nobles suspected the French of absolutist ambitions and immorality. The Habsburgs promoted Duke Karl of Lorraine as king, but the nobles also feared Habsburg absolutism and involvement in wars against Turkey. Numerous minor candidates came forward, including Tsar Aleksei Mikhailovich of Russia, Kristina, the former queen of Sweden, and James Stuart of Great Britain.

The pro-Habsburg vice-chancellor, Bishop Andrzej Olszowski, advanced Wiśniowiecki's name in order to prevent a French victory, arguing that Piasts understood the Polish constitution and respected noble liberties. As an unambitious young noble, unmarried, Catholic, and relatively poor after the loss of the family's vast Ukrainian estates in the Cossack rebellion, Michał posed no threat to the nobility. Olszowski won over masses of petty nobles and many intellectuals who were convinced of the perfection of Poland's constitution. They included men like the popular senator Stanisław Warszycki, castellan of Cracow, who insisted that future parliaments be held on horseback "to safeguard those freedoms which our ancestors won through bloody conduct." Some nobles shouted: "We don't need a rich man, for after he becomes the king of Poland he'll be rich. We don't need anyone related to other royalty, because it is a danger to liberty. But we need a strong man, a military man." Jan Chrysostem Pasek, soldier and memoirist, knew that Michał was not a military man, but he supported his candidacy out of respect for Michał's father and out of dislike for the leaders of the French and Habsburg parties. In the same spirit, the poet Wacław Potocki called the young king an "eagle"; poet and historian Wespazjan Kochowski called him "Great Michał." At the election, 80,000 of his noble supporters used force to overawe the supporters of the other candidates: Philip Wilhelm, duke of Neuburg, who enjoyed French, Austrian, Prussian, and Swedish support; the duc de Condée, France's real favorite; and Duke Karl of Lorraine, Austria's real favorite.

An anti-Michał opposition group of "malcontents" from the French Party, including Primate Mikołaj Prażmowski and the future king, Jan Sobieski, abandoned efforts to block Wiśniowiecki's election. To protect their political position in opposition, they reversed their constitutional views and championed the very institutions they had been trying to modify when Jan Kazimierz held the throne—the *liberum veto* and the nobles' right to revolt. The parliamentary session following the coronation was broken when nobles who wanted compensation for the estates that they had lost in Left Bank Ukraine cast a *liberum veto*. The French Party began plotting to dethrone Michał as soon as he married young Eleonora Maria Josefa, sister of Habsburg Emperor Leopold I. The malcontents attempted to censure the king at the spring 1670 dietines, claiming that he had broken his coronation oath by marrying without parliament's permission. They stopped only when Chancellor Olszowski mobilized armed supporters and threatened to summon a full levy to support Michał (who did little). The queen proved a valuable political ally for the king, because she won personal loyalty from nobles and solidified the support of the Habsburg Party for the king; she played no direct role in politics, however.

Prussia

The Habsburg orientation prevented the government from taking advantage of discontent in Ducal Prussia that might have brought that rich and strategic province back under Polish control. Jan Kazimierz had ignored the protests of the Prussian opposition in the early 1660s, and likewise Wiśniowiecki ignored them in 1667 when Christian Ludwig Kalkstein-Stoliński, now a Prussian general, succeeded to his father's estate and leadership of the dissident nobles. His brother, who wanted to take over the family property, denounced him for allegedly trying to overthrow Duke Friedrich Wilhelm. Christian was quickly convicted and sentenced to one year's imprisonment on a diet of bread and water. The court increased the sentence to life imprisonment and then commuted it to a 5,000 thaler fine and exile to his estates for two years. Kalkstein fled in 1670 to Warsaw, where he worked with Vice-Chancellor Bishop Andrzej Olszowski to regain control of Ducal Prussia. Friedrich Wilhelm arranged for Kalkstein's abduction from Warsaw, imprisonment in Klaipėda, and execution in 1672. King Michał protested, but took no action because of imminent war with the Cossacks and Turkey. In 1674, Friedrich Wilhelm felt free to bombard Königsberg to force it to pay excise taxes that the Estates had not approved, and charged the city for military expenses.

The Ottoman Turks and the Cossacks

Despite King Michał's passivity and the country's deep political divisions, Poland-Lithuania turned back a serious threat to the remaining Ukrainian lands, although it lost the Left Bank forever. Hetman Petro Doroshenko (1627–98) tried to reunite both banks of the Dnieper in a single Cossack state under Turkish protection. Succeeding to the office of Left Bank hetman in 1668 after a Cossack mob murdered his predecessor, Doroshenko took his army across to the Right Bank and defeated a Polish-backed Cossack army. He demanded that Poland-Lithuania recognize the enlarged boundaries of his Hetmanate including Ukrainian, Belarussian, and some Polish lands, and that it grant special economic privileges to Cossacks in exchange for a promise to support the Commonwealth militarily. The sultan proclaimed a formal Cossack-Turkish alliance in 1669, and the Ottoman armies invaded Podolia in 1672, capturing it without major resistance other than the strong defenses of Kamianets-Podilskyi. This garrison city (the name means Fortress of Podolia) was located by the deep gorge of the river Smotrych and protected by a sophisticated moat and modern artillery placed by French technical specialists. Despite the apparent triumph of his policy, Doroshenko found himself distrusted by the majority of the Cossacks, who rejected the idea of an alliance with their traditional Muslim enemy and supported Russian-backed rival candidates for hetman. Doroshenko was forced to abdicate and went into exile in Russia, where he died on an estate that the tsar gave him.

Poland-Lithuania failed to resist the Turkish-Cossack alliance effectively because of political divisions. At the beginning of the war, King Michał mobilized a part of the Polish-Lithuanian army and raised provincial levies but ingloriously failed to lead them out of camp. Efforts to raise new armies failed when both royalists and their opponents broke two parliamentary sessions within a single year with the *liberum veto*. The pro-French group demanded that Michał abdicate in favor of a French candidate. Their leader, Crown Hetman Jan Sobieski, proved himself as a military leader at this time, saving the Polish Right Bank with a brilliant campaign of fast maneuvering. He defeated Tatar raiding parties and freed thousands of prisoners destined for Turkish slave markets. Unable to exploit his victories for lack of reinforcements, Sobieski signed a treaty at Buchach on October 18, 1672, that halted the Turkish advance at the price of surrendering Podolia to Turkey and paying the sultan an annual "gift" of 22,000 zlotys.

Having failed to reconquer the Cossack state on the Right Bank Ukraine and having lost Podolia, the discredited King Michał Wiśniowiecki clung to power with the help of a military confederation. Sobieski threatened to challenge him with his army, but Queen Eleanor, the papal nuncio, and several senators mediated the dispute. The two sides were reconciled for the time being at the parliamentary session of April 1673. The Polish-Lithuanian parliament refused to ratify the treaty of Buchach and voted new taxes to raise an army of 50,000 soldiers with which Sobieski defeated the Ottomans at Khotyn (Moldavia) in November 1673. The victory safeguarded the Commonwealth against further attacks and allowed it to regain control of the Right Bank, subjugating the Cossacks. Sobieski lacked the strength to recapture Podolia, partly due to political rivalries, and the Polish-Turkish border remained 75 miles from Lviv until 1699. Determined to lead a military campaign in person, Michał came to Lviv and reviewed the troops, but he suffered an attack of stomach ulcers and died on November 10, 1673, at the age of thirty-three, shortly before Sobieski's great victory.

Sobieski

King Jan III Sobieski (1629–96) was the first Polish king since Stefan Batory to be elected as a mature, experienced political leader. He came from a major political family. His father, Jakub Sobieski, had been an important general and parliamentary leader, and his maternal grandfather was Hetman Stefan Żółkiewski. Jan and his older brother Marek attended the Jagiellonian University in Cracow before going to western Europe for more than two years' residence and private study. There, the future king laid the foundations for his excellent, well-used library, one of the largest in Poland-Lithuania, which reveals his strong interest in history, military affairs, and philosophy as well as classical poetry, art and architecture, natural science, and estate management. In addition to Polish, Sobieski learned Latin, French, German, and Turkish. Polish literary historians regard his correspondence with his wife Marysieńka, an affectionate diminutive form of Marie/Maria, among the outstanding published letters of the seventeenth century. Marysieńka was unusually intelligent, well-educated, and beautiful. She had a lively personality, faced wartime risks bravely, and loved the arts, especially music and dance. A French-born protegée of Queen Louise Marie, she came to Poland young enough to learn to speak excellent Polish. Marysieńka played a small part in politics for such a strong-minded person, even during the period of French alliance.

Sobieski's palaces at Wilanów, Żółkiew, and Jaworów reflected his sophistication and good taste. The papal nuncio reported that Wilanów was filled with "a large number of fine paintings" including five Rembrandts, but his heirs sold most of his collection after his death. Sobieski started an academy for aspiring Polish artists. He was a careful estate manager for whom, in later life, acquiring wealth became a fixation. Like many other magnates, he enjoyed good relations with "his" Jews, protecting their mercantile interests and giving them financial assistance in difficult times.

Jan Sobieski and his brother Marek returned to Poland after Władysław IV's death and fought against the Cossacks; Marek died and Jan was severely wounded. Except for a brief diplomatic mission to Turkey in 1654, Jan spent the whole decade of 1648–58 fighting. He joined Swedish King Karl X Gustav in 1655 when his regiment switched sides, and he learned Swedish infantry tactics. Sobieski left Swedish service in March 1656, for which the Swedes condemned him to death in absentia, and rejoined King Jan Kazimierz to serve as Polish commander of a Tatar detachment at the unsuccessful battle of Warsaw in July 1656. After the Swedish war, King Jan Kazimierz rewarded Sobieski with the office of crown flag-bearer, a stepping stone to appointment as hetman. Sobieski spent a lot of time at the royal court, where he met Marie Louise d'Arquien, one of the queen's ladies-in-waiting. The two fell deeply and lastingly in love, but politics took the upper hand and the queen married Marie Louise to Jan Zamoyski the younger. Nevertheless, Sobieski's romantic attachment helped tie him to the reformist Royal Party, and, after initial hesitation, he turned against his former commander, Jerzy Lubomirski, during his brief rebellion. King Jan Kazimierz rewarded Sobieski's loyalty with appointment to Lubomirski's vacated posts of crown field hetman and crown great marshal, and Sobieski fought against Lubomirski, losing badly at the battle of Mątwy. Sobieski finally married Marie when Zamoyski died in 1675. Because of his French ties, Sobieski shared Jan Kazimierz's unpopularity until he successfully repelled a Cossack-Tatar invasion in November 1667 and was rewarded with the vacant post of crown great hetman.

THE FRENCH PARTY AND PLANS FOR REFORM

A rich magnate, thanks to his father's success and his own efforts, Sobieski played a major role in Polish-Lithuanian politics, but he needed French subsidies to win the Polish crown and raise troops for foreign wars. Sobieski had half-heartedly supported the French candidate during the 1669 royal election and only joined the pro-French Malcontents who called for Wiśniowiecki's abdication after the Turkish invasion of 1672. During the parliamentary sessions of 1672 and 1673, Sobieski favored an alliance with Russia and Austria in order to repel the Turks. Although he also advocated forming an alliance with Persia against Turkey, Sobieski saw his alliance system primarily as a Christian crusade and called on Balkan Christians to revolt. He backed his view with a great military victory over the Ottomans at Khotyn (Moldavia) in 1673. Wiśniowiecki's death brought Sobieski's election as king of Poland-Lithuania with little opposition except in Lithuania, where nobles opposed his plans for a Russian alliance.

Like the Vasas, Sobieski hoped to strengthen the throne and make it hereditary, and like them, he failed. He also hoped to abolish the *liberum veto,* make parliamentary debate more efficient, and strengthen the central executive offices. He started promisingly enough by recentralizing the treasury, which he had helped put into provincial hands (dietines) in 1667 to hamper Wiśniowiecki, but lost control again in 1679.

To carry out his broader reform aims, Sobieski planned to reconquer Ducal Prussia from Brandenburg, turn it into a private duchy for his family, and use its wealth as a springboard to strengthen the Polish-Lithuanian crown. The king and his friends acquired estates in Prussia to take advantage of a future change in sovereignty. Sobieski negotiated a secret treaty with France in 1675 that provided lavish subsidies for war against Brandenburg and, if necessary, Austria. Louis XIV also promised to finance Sobieski's existing war against Turkey to bring it to a negotiated conclusion in 1676 so that he could concentrate on the Baltic. The city of Gdańsk paid Sobieski handsomely to reconfirm its privileges when he came there in 1677 to prepare for war, expecting to coordinate action with a Swedish invasion from Livonia.

Sobieski abandoned his ambitious plans because the Swedes failed to launch their invasion and parliamentary opposition to his allegedly absolutist aims was rising rapidly. In addition, Lithuanians, who feared any increase in Swedish power, had to be mollified. Cuts to his military budget made him pass by the opportunity that arose the next year when the Swedes attacked Ducal Prussia from Livonia, investing Klaipėda and taking Tilsit. Rather than join the Swedes as he had originally intended, he reversed his position and allowed Friedrich Wilhelm of Prussia to send troops across Polish Royal Prussia to force the Swedes out of Ducal Prussia. The international situation had become less favorable, as well. Turkey threatened to attack in the south, and Louis XIV signed peace agreements with his opponents in western Europe in 1678–79, withdrawing his support from Sobieski.

Lithuanian Autonomy

Lithuanian nobles maintained their separate political consciousness despite acculturating fully to Polish culture. They identified with the Polish-Lithuanian federated state, but defined their interests differently from the Poles. Even though separation was no longer a real option, Lithuanian leaders threatened to dissolve the Union with Poland to bolster their political position. For example, Lithuania forced the Poles to promise that every third Polish-Lithuanian parliamentary session would be held in Grodno, Lithuania. Following the expulsion of the Russians from the Grand Duchy in 1661, Lithuanian magnates competed for political domination in order to control important ministries, acquire crown land leases, and attain decisive influence over decisions in the tribunals. Chancellor Krzysztof Zygmunt Pac led his extended family and connections to dominate Lithuania in the late seventeenth century. In 1668, Lithuanian Great Hetman Michał Pac supported a Russian candidate to the Polish-Lithuanian throne, promising to mobilize the Lithuanian army in support. The Russian candidate was not elected, but the Pac family maintained good relations with Russia, especially with resident-envoy Tiapkin. The Pac faction also supported the election of Tsar Feodor in 1674. When King Jan III Sobieski considered allying himself with Sweden to reconquer Prussia, Lithuanian Great Hetman Pac took Prussian subsidies to fight the Swedes. Lithuania's military weakness was made painfully obvious by the ease with which the Swedes brushed the Lithuanian army aside on their way to attack Ducal Prussia in 1676. The lower classes, which played no role in politics, maintained their ethnic heritage, chiefly Lithuanian or Ruthenian.

The Vienna Campaign and Turkish Wars

After failing to make gains on the Baltic coast, Sobieski returned to the anti-Turkish policy that eventually made him famous. When the Ottomans invaded Austria in 1683, Sobieski signed a treaty with the Habsburg emperor to work together against Turkey. Austria was to fight in Hungary, and Poland in Podolia and Moldavia. Poland-Lithuania and Austria also agreed to come to each other's aid if Cracow or Vienna were threatened. The Polish-Lithuanian parliament voted new taxes to increase the army from 18,000 to 48,000 men. A Turkish invasion in force aimed at Vienna made Sobieski come to Austria's relief, both because of the terms of the alliance and out of conviction that Turkey would attack Poland next.

As the Turkish siege of Vienna was nearing a critical phase, Sobieski reached Vienna with 27,000 soldiers to link up with 18,000 Austrian and 30,000 German troops. They opposed over 100,000 Ottomans encamped beneath Vienna's city walls. As the most experienced commander, Sobieski took overall command.

The combined armies made a difficult approach through the Vienna woods and attacked the Ottomans. Around 6 P.M. on September 12, the second day of fighting, Sobieski personally led a charge by 20,000 heavy cavalry, mostly Polish, that broke through the Turkish lines, killing 15,000 soldiers and capturing 117 guns. The allied forces lost about 3,500 men. They stopped to loot the rich Turkish camp, and the Turks withdrew when darkness fell. The allies followed up this success with a victory near Párkány in northern Hungary in which most of the 35,000-man Turkish army was killed. Polish-Lithuanian infantry and artillery shared military honors with the cavalry. Nevertheless, Poland made no specific gains and the army was considerably weakened through casualties and disease. The Cossacks took advantage of the Vienna campaign to clear the Turks from Ukraine and occupy Moldavia, but the Tatars counterattacked, allowing the Turks to keep Kamianets-Podilskyi and regain several other fortresses.

Sobieski spent the remainder of his reign trying to defeat the Ottoman Turks along the borders of the Commonwealth without much success, while his Austrian, Russian, and Venetian allies made progress along their borders. Sobieski's campaigns showed that Poland-Lithuania lacked the resources and will to support a strong army on a regular basis. He failed to recapture Kamianets-Podilskyi, the key to Podolia, since he lacked the expensive artillery and infantry needed in siege operations. In 1685, he created four Cossack regiments on the Right Bank, appointing the officers himself instead of allowing them to be elected democratically according to tradition. Sobieski invaded Moldavia in 1686 and 1691, but eventually withdrew when he failed to lure the Turks into a decisive battle.

To continue the fight, Sobieski signed an "eternal peace" in 1686 with Russia. It made permanent the terms of the Andrusovo agreement (1667) partitioning the Ukrainian lands and relinquishing to Russia sole control of Zaporozhia, the southern Ukrainian steppes, as well as the Black Sea coast—in order to put an end to punishing, if militarily insignificant, slave raids by the Tatars. The peace treaty was so unpopular among Poles with eastern Ukrainian estates that parliament refused to ratify it until 1710. However, Lithuanians provided much of the impetus for negotiating the peace, to avoid war with Russia. The Commonwealth was rewarded for its efforts against the Ottomans by regaining Podolia, including Kamianets-Podilskyi, in the Treaty of Karlowitz signed in 1699, three years after Sobieski's death. Poland was considerably weakened by decades of fighting.

Military Successes and Failures

Jan III Sobieski owed his military success to his training in the Swedish wars. He learned cavalry tactics from General Stefan Czarniecki while fighting the Swedes, infantry tactics from the Swedes, and combined tactics from Hetman

Jerzy Lubomirski during the 1660 campaign against Russian and Cossack armies. The tactics that Sobieski used successfully during his military career depended on quick action in pitched battles to destroy the enemy army with minimal losses, often after bold maneuvers in difficult terrain such as the hilly Vienna woods. Lacking financial resources, Sobieski often used delaying tactics to gain time to mobilize. He polonized the army by introducing Polish as the language of command even though many western Europeans and soldiers from the East, such as Romanians and Tatars, still served. The leading military theorist of the day, Andrzej Maksymilian Fredro, wrote several tracts in which he also called for polonization and improvements in the infantry and artillery.

Many of Sobieski's military problems stemmed from financial difficulties caused by low levels of taxation and inadequate methods of collection. Treasury operations became a provincial responsibility exercised by dietines for much of Sobieski's reign. A new wintering tax (*hiberna*) on royal and clerical estates kept the cavalry intact, but no similar provisions were made for the infantry, artillery, or dragoons, which consequently declined in discipline and preparedness. A decline in the number of nobles who served in the army, particularly in the artillery and infantry, did not interfere with military efficiency, but it presaged the lack of tax support needed to maintain effectiveness. Even the traditionally noble cavalry found its lower ranks filled with commoners. The number of hussars (heavy cavalry) declined and the army replaced them with less expensive, but less effective, light cavalry. French influence led to the introduction of modern flint and steel muskets with bayonets, although at a slower pace than elsewhere in Europe, for financial reasons.

THE LAST YEARS

Sobieski's difficulties resulted, in part, from his growing unpopularity among Polish nobles. The Vienna victory renewed fears of royal absolutism, especially because of Sobieski's evident plans to secure the Polish-Lithuanian throne for his son Jakub, and his former supporters slipped into opposition. The parliamentary sessions of 1685, 1688–89, and 1692 were wasted in angry debates, sometimes featuring attacks on Sobieski's Jewish business agent, Jacob Bezalel, in order to get at the king. Sobieski's supporters in the army, and some new senators he had appointed, urged him to stage a coup d'état, but he declined, probably out of respect for the unwritten Polish constitution. Feeling isolated, Sobieski aged rapidly and built his personal fortune greedily. He died of a lingering illness.

PART THREE

The Eighteenth Century

CHAPTER 15

August II

Friedrich August I (1670–1733), elector of Saxony, succeeded Jan Sobieski as king of Poland-Lithuania with the royal title of August II. He was a systematic and effective ruler with a commitment to reform, but since he had no common political language with his Polish-Lithuanian subjects, his actions were counterproductive. Like his predecessors, he hoped to make Poland-Lithuania a dynastic possession of his family, the Wettins. Just as the Jagiellonians had used hereditary Lithuania to strengthen their position in Poland and the Vasas had hoped to use hereditary Sweden to strengthen theirs, so August planned to use hereditary Saxony to expand royal power in the Polish-Lithuanian Commonwealth. Like the Vasas, August II aimed to overcome parliamentary opposition, improve taxation, increase the army, and provide more effective government. The strategy had worked poorly for the Vasas, and it failed to work for August.

SAXONY

August II grew up in Saxony, a medium-sized but wealthy and industrialized state in southeastern Germany. Saxony had a well-developed agriculture based on rent-paying peasant production, artisanal manufactures, mining and metallurgy in southern mountain regions, and international trade centered in Leipzig. Major centralized manufactures, such as Europe's first porcelain factory at Meissen, also emerged. August's tutors instructed him in foreign languages and state matters, and he took a particular interest in military affairs, especially fortification. He also was keenly interested in art and imitated Louis XIV by using high culture, especially collecting paintings and sculpture, to symbolize his political aspirations. He was indifferent to religion and dabbled in fashionable mystical practices like alchemy and astrology.

Domestically, August hoped to strengthen royal power and evade the restrictions of the Saxon Estates (Landtag), which voted taxes and passed legislation by majority vote, a far more effective procedure than the Polish-Lithuanian unanimity rule. The throne was hereditary. In both Saxony and Poland-Lithuania, monarchs collected substantial revenue from regalian rights such as landed properties and mining revenues. The Polish-Lithuanian king enjoyed more freedom in making ministerial appointments than his Saxon counterpart. The Saxon Estates made major bureaucratic appointments up to and including the Secret Cabinet (or council). In contrast, rapidly increasing tax revenues from excise taxes allowed Johann Georg II, elector of Saxony and August's grandfather, to establish a standing army under his command in 1682 to fight against the Ottoman Turks, while Polish-Lithuanian state revenues declined and the Polish and Lithuanian hetmans effectively controlled the Polish-Lithuanian armies.

August's Character and Aims

Friedrich August was very ambitious, even though he was a second son and not expected to succeed to the electoral throne. He became elector of Saxony in 1693 at age twenty-four when his older brother, Johann Georg IV, died after only two years in power. As king, Friedrich August sought to increase his authority by appointing a series of viceroys to collect taxes and administer the country, starting with his cousin Christian August, a Catholic bishop who was not generally accepted in Lutheran Saxony. The Saxon Estates opposed the innovation in principle. In 1706, August created a Secret Cabinet appointed by himself instead of the Estates, but had to curtail its functions, once again because of parliamentary opposition. As the head of a strong, prosperous state, he hoped to win election as Holy Roman emperor, in place of the Habsburgs.

Religious issues reflected the political needs of the Saxon electors. The Saxon state was closely tied to Lutheranism. Saxony had been a leading Protestant power and its elector led the Protestant forces at the imperial diet during the Thirty Years' War (1618–1648). Nevertheless, several electors had flirted with Catholicism in order to gain greater political freedom. Johann Georg III, Friedrich August's father, staffed his standing army with Catholic and Calvinist officers. As elector, Friedrich August followed his father's policies. He replaced older, Saxon officers and bureaucrats with men of his own age from other German states who owed him personal allegiance. The most important was Jakob Heinrich Flemming, a Pomeranian noble whose family had served Brandenburg for several generations. Friedrich August sent him to Poland for the royal election as his personal representative, and later arranged for his naturalization so that he could hold office. Starting as a Saxon colonel, Flemming gained the rank of general in the Polish army and took part in several campaigns, although his major activities were diplomatic. He fostered close cooperation with Austria and Prussia, and opposed alliance with Russia.

August used state power to develop trade and industry. He sponsored the Leipzig trade fair and encouraged the immigration of highly productive Calvinist Huguenots whom France expelled in 1685. General August Christopher von Wackerbarth, another immigrant to Saxony, acted as August's economic and cultural adviser. As director of buildings, he constructed fortifications in Saxony and the Commonwealth, as well as elegant palaces such as the Zwinger in Dresden, capital of Saxony. Pursuing his military occupations, August served without notable success as commander of the imperial armies in Hungary during the 1695–96 campaigns. He displayed bravery in battle but lacked leadership qualities.

August was known in eighteenth-century Saxony as August the Strong because he overcame many obstacles to make Saxony influential, prosperous, and cultured. August's personal habits are little known, except that he had several mistresses-in-title who gave birth to children, most notably Maurice de Saxe, who achieved fame as a marshal of the French army. Following eighteenth-century practice, August accorded public recognition to his mistresses and their children, but he married Christina Eberhard in 1693 to provide an heir to the Saxon and Polish-Lithuanian thrones. Christina refused to convert to Catholicism along with August and lived apart from him, although they never divorced. He took their son, the future August III of Poland-Lithuania, from his mother and raised him at court with due propriety. His court was a showplace. He built palaces, collected art, and organized lavish celebrations with street festivals and processions. There is only one contemporary reference to August II's exceptional strength, and widely repeated colorful accounts of his drunkenness and lechery appear to be exaggerations or inventions by nineteenth-century Prussian historians to discredit him and justify Prussia's campaign to unify Germany.

August's Election as King of Poland-Lithuania

Friedrich August declared his candidacy for the Polish-Lithuanian throne at the last minute after careful preparations. He won over the Vatican by converting to Catholicism in private so as not to offend the Lutheran Saxons, and sent proofs to Warsaw to impress the Poles. Vienna supported him against the French candidate, François, duc de Conti, a cousin of Louis XIV. Friedrich August sketched out reform plans for himself in notes entitled "How to Transform Poland into a Flourishing Country That Enjoys the Respect of Its Neighbors." He advocated making all social estates equal before the law, expanding trade, importing artisans to improve manufactures, reorganizing the army, collecting funds for diplomatic activities, and creating four universities.

On June 26, 1697, on Wola field near Warsaw, a gathering of nobles elected Conti to be king of Poland-Lithuania in the preliminary vote, but a concerted effort by the Austrian Party to stop him gave the final victory to Friedrich August in the second, official, vote. The Habsburgs enjoyed financial and political support from the papal nuncio and the Jesuits. Russian diplomats also used their influence to support Friedrich August. Cardinal-Primate Michał Radziejowski declared Conti elected while Stanisław Dąbski, bishop of Kujawy, declared Friedrich August elected. The final decision came by force of arms.

Friedrich August took strong action to win the crown but abandoned his reformist aims to keep it. Quickly assuring the Saxon Estates that his conversion was personal and would not affect Saxony, he gained their congratulations and permission to take Saxon troops to Poland to secure the throne. Austria allowed him transit through Silesia, even hinting that it might be willing to surrender territory permanently, and he was crowned in Cracow on September 15. The duc de Conti reached Poland at the same time with a French flotilla, which Gdańsk refused permission to anchor. He waited passively for two months at the nearby small port of Oliwa, but when no armies gathered to support his claims, he ingloriously returned to France. Conti's Polish and Lithuanian supporters accepted the Saxon accession and garnered high positions in the new regime. Primate and Chancellor Radziejowski, who had previously declared Conti king, became the spokesman for the Polish-Lithuanian nation in negotiations over the *pacta conventa*, and August accepted his demands to limit the royal prerogatives. August settled in Warsaw, restoring the royal castle that Sobieski had neglected in favor of his suburban palace, Wilanów. He attempted to conform to Polish mores by celebrating Carnival modestly. His wife Christina remained in Dresden, for as a Lutheran she could not be crowned queen of Poland, and the presence of August's mistress-in-title offended the more straightlaced Warsoviennes. The king enjoyed unofficial, short-term romantic liaisons during his later sojourns in the Commonwealth.

First Steps as King

August modeled his new court after Louis XIV's, combining political centralization with artistic culture and merging the two royal courts of Dresden and Warsaw as much as possible while honoring the political systems of the two countries. French served as the common language. Polish musicians, including Sobieski's music director, Jacek Różycki, came to Dresden. Italian theater, popular in Warsaw, also reappeared there. August staged lavish balls, theatrical performances, and hunts. Sobieski's sons took part in knightly tournaments. Amateur theatricals involved the king and leading nobles.

August began his activities as king of Poland-Lithuania by reopening hostilities with Turkey with visions of partitioning the Ottoman Empire and gaining Constantinople, but he made little progress. Polish and Saxon troops squabbled over logistics, and neither fought well until the generals paid the troops out of their own pockets. Lithuanian troops arrived only after the minor battle of Podhajce, in which Hetman Feliks Potocki defeated a Tatar column on September 8–9, 1698. August failed to lay siege to Kamianets-Podilskyi, but his diplomats acquired that fortress city and all of Podolia through the Treaty of Karlowitz in 1699 in exchange for relinquishing small conquests that Sobieski had made in Moldavia. August celebrated peace in Warsaw with a spectacular fireworks display.

August then looked northward for glory but found disaster. Meeting Peter I of Russia in August 1698 at Rava Ruska near Lviv, he formed an anti-Swedish coalition with Russia and Denmark, aiming to make Livonia a Wettin fief not subject to the laws of Poland-Lithuania and Saxony, although he also considered briefly the opposite plan of conquering Ducal Prussia from Brandenburg with Swedish help. Livonia looked promising because Livonian nobles and merchants were violating Swedish regulations by selling their grain and forest products through Lithuanian ports to avoid high Swedish tariffs. The Livonian émigré spokesmen Johann Reinhold von Patkul and two other Livonian nobles who served as colonels in the Saxon army assured August of Livonian support. August signed a secret agreement with them that recognized the Wettins as hereditary monarchs.

The Great Northern War Begins

The resulting Great Northern War brought catastrophe to Polish-Lithuania. Denmark, Russia, and Saxony concluded agreements in 1698 and 1699 to attack Sweden, seize her Baltic empire and, in Denmark's case, regain Skania. The campaign was a disaster from the start. The Saxons invaded without sufficient preparation and the Livonian Estates remained loyal to the sixteen-year-old Swedish king, Karl (Charles) XII. Polish-Lithuanian nobles refused to support August's dynastic ambitions militarily or financially, and Cardinal Radziejowski tried to mediate the conflict, stressing Polish-Lithuanian neutrality. The Saxons invaded Livonia, laying siege to Riga, but gave up when they heard that Karl XII had forced the Danes to sign a peace treaty. Sweden refused to make peace with August because he continued military activities during negotiations and even achieved some minor success. Karl destroyed Peter I's Russian army at Narva on November 20, isolating August, who now tried desperately to make peace, but Karl crushed the Saxon forces in Livonia in July 1701 and demanded August's abdication from the Polish-Lithuanian throne. The Polish-Lithuanian parliament declared itself neutral and asked August to withdraw Saxon troops from Lithuania. Friedrich Wilhelm of Brandenburg took advantage of the moment to crown himself king in Prussia and extend the informal use of his title to his entire realm.

Poland-Lithuania had to join August in the war in order to protect against the Swedish armies that entered the Commonwealth to force August's withdrawal. Before they invaded, August gained temporary control of Lithuania by allying himself with the enemies of the Sapieha faction, which had dominated Lithuania in the 1690s after Michał and Krzysztof Zygmunt Pac died. Nobles who were excluded from the distribution of patronage denounced the Sapiehas' "tyranny" and supported August's efforts. Lithuanian Great Hetman Jan Sapieha lost the battle of Olkienniki in 1700 to a magnate levy stiffened with Saxon regulars. The subsequent division of power among leading families, including the Czartoryskis, Radziwiłłs, Ogińskis, Massalskis, and Kossakowskis, prevented Lithuania from speaking with one voice.

Since dietines could not be held under wartime conditions to elect deputies to parliament, an extralegal gathering at Sandomierz in September 1702 committed the Commonwealth to support August with an army of 30,000 men, financed by 8 million zlotys in taxes. The Lublin parliamentary session of June-July 1703 promised even more ambitiously to raise 13.5 million zlotys to provide 48,000 troops. In fact, when they eventually met, the dietines declined to collect new taxes. August still raised a 30,000-man army in February 1704, but the troops were too poorly paid and poorly trained to stand up to the Swedes in battle. Karl pursued August into Lithuania and Poland, devastating the countryside along his line of march. Efforts by August and Primate Radziejowski to negotiate peace failed. Nobles in Little Poland abandoned him after he lost Cracow.

Swedish sympathizers, who had been verbally abused in Lublin, gathered in January 1704 in Swedish-controlled Warsaw, and formed a confederation that declared the Polish throne vacant because August was planning to cede territory to conclude peace with Sweden. The confederation proposed to replace August with Jan III Sobieski's son Jakub, but August captured him and the confederation elected Stanisław Leszczyński instead.

Election of Stanisław Leszczyński as Counter-King

Stanisław Leszczyński came from a Great Poland magnate family that had filled high senatorial and ministerial positions for several generations. The Leszczyńskis were rich and famous for their support of culture and the arts. Rafał Leszczyński had settled Czech Brethren on his estates in the mid-sixteenth century even before he himself converted. Most of the family remained Protestant until the mid-seventeenth century, when they opportunistically reconverted to Catholicism, but they still held ideals of toleration. Stanisław's father, also named Rafał, achieved prominence as a political and military leader, and Stanisław's maternal grandfather, Stanisław Jan Jabłonowski, had fought with distinction against the Turks.

Born in 1677, the future king, Stanisław, received a careful education from Jesuit tutors at home and then in a Lutheran high school in Leszno before he traveled to western European courts as a teenager. He emerged as a cultivated, polished young man who was unusually well read, but curiously less accomplished in foreign languages than many of his contemporaries; while fluent, his French was filled with errors. His father engineered young Stanisław's election as deputy to the 1699 parliament. The Leszczyńskis favored Jakub Sobieski's candidacy for the Polish-Lithuanian throne but switched quickly to the victorious Saxon side. Stanisław became palatine of Poznań as a reward. As August's rule crumbled, twenty-seven-year-old Stanisław Leszczyński was elected king of Poland and grand duke of Lithuania on July 12, 1704.

POLAND-LITHUANIA UNDER TWO KINGS

Leszczyński's youth and lack of independent strength made him a Swedish puppet. Breaking with tradition, the Swedes had Leszczyński crowned in Warsaw (instead of Cracow) on October 5, 1705, with Lviv Archbishop Konstanty Zielinski officiating (instead of the archbishop of Gniezno). Leszczyński signed the Treaty of Warsaw on November 28, 1705, making Poland-Lithuania a vassal state, permanently allied with Sweden. Poland-Lithuania agreed to join the war against Russia. The Commonwealth would take Russia while Sweden would be free to expand along the Baltic. Leszczyński also made religious and economic concessions to Sweden, promising to guarantee personal religious freedoms to Protestant commoners (nobles already enjoyed religious freedom) and to funnel overland Russian transit trade through Swedish-controlled Riga instead of Gdańsk. As in 1655–57, the Swedes supported their large army entirely at the expense of occupied Poland-Lithuania. Leszczyński continually intervened with Swedish authorities to reduce the financial exactions on his noble supporters—usually without success. With his own estates in Great Poland devastated by punitive Saxon raids, Leszczyński had no income and had to beg Sweden for personal and political expense money.

The Saxon and Russian armies attempted to expel Leszczyński by invading from both sides, and August recaptured Warsaw briefly on September 6, 1704, after a four-day battle that reduced the Royal Castle to ruins. Anti-Swedish nobles gravitated toward Peter I and August II, particularly after they signed a political and military alliance in 1704 at Narva, which Peter had recaptured. Peter promised to recapture Livonia for the Commonwealth and subsidize the Polish-Lithuanian army. He arranged for Cossack Hetman Ivan Mazepa to arrest a Cossack rebel against Polish authority, Simon Palij. Poles and Lithuanians loyal to August formed a counterconfederation at Sandomierz in May 1705.

The new alliance did not prevent Karl XII from quickly defeating the Saxon army in February 1705 near Wschowa in Great Poland. Faced with the entire Swedish army, Peter retreated so precipitately that Karl invaded Saxony rather than pursue him. Helpless, August signed the Treaty of Altranstadt (near Leipzig) on September 24, 1706, in which he relinquished the Polish-Lithuanian crown, paid a large penalty to Karl, and agreed to billet the Swedish army in Saxony. He also surrendered the Livonian émigré Patkul to the Swedes to be executed as a traitor. Ironically, August II defeated a Swedish detachment near Kalisz before the terms of the treaty went into effect in 1707. Despite August II's concessions, members of the pro-Russian Sandomierz Confederation refused to recognize Leszczyński as king and some dreamed of claiming the throne themselves. Crown Great Hetman Adam Sieniawski won a major victory in 1708 against Leszczyński's Crown Great Hetman Józef Potocki.

Russia Defeats Sweden

Karl XII's attempt to finish off his Russian enemy led to his downfall along with that of King Stanisław Leszczyński, his client. Karl reentered Poland in September 1707 and marched east throughout 1708 as the Russians retreated without offering battle. Leszczyński wanted to come to terms with his opponents, especially Hetman Adam Sieniawski, but Karl XII insisted on a military solution and, forbidding Leszczyński to summon parliament to reconcile the factions, invaded Russia. Sieniawski proved to be a dangerous enemy when he stopped a Polish-Swedish force (Leszczyński commanded the Polish troops) from invading the Russian Ukraine to meet King Karl's army and his new ally, Cossack Hetman Ivan Mazepa. For their part, the Russians kept a Swedish force under General Adam Ludwig Lewenhaupt from reaching Karl with fresh troops and supplies. Cossack Hetman Mazepa succeeded only in bringing a few thousand Cossacks to Karl XII's camp on the eve of the decisive battle.

Peter I's great victory over Karl XII's smaller Swedish army at Poltava on July 8, 1709, allowed August to reclaim the Polish-Lithuanian throne and sent Leszczyński into exile. August continued to fight in the anti-Swedish coalition in order to gain international recognition rather than conquer new territories. However, Karl's defeat did not permit August to call parliament and enact reforms, since Leszczyński still had supporters throughout the country. The would-be king hovered around Poland's western borders, mostly in Swedish-controlled western Pomerania, hoping to reconquer his throne. He finally renounced all authority in Poland-Lithuania in exchange for keeping the empty royal title and gaining financial compensation from August, but the agreement needed Karl XII's approval. Leszczyński traveled to Karl's refuge in Ottoman Moldavia and spent almost two years there before returning to western Europe without ever meeting the Swedish king or receiving his written approval.

Pacification of Poland-Lithuania

A General Council held in Warsaw in February–April 1710 confirmed August as king of Poland-Lithuania and pledged unrealistically to maintain a 64,000-man army. August's plans for major reforms, such as the centralization of taxation and three new appointments as hetman, renewed noble suspicion of "absolutism" and were decisively rejected. Parliament bowed to Russian pressure and finally ratified the so-called eternal peace of 1686 assigning Left Bank Ukraine to Russia in exchange for the promised return of Livonia. Russia also gained the right to protect Orthodox Christians throughout the Commonwealth.

August's control over Poland-Lithuania remained tenuous, and war raged throughout the realm. Polish-Lithuanian support for the Russian war against Turkey attracted Tatar raids that devastated the southern provinces. Leszczyński's supporters attacked August II from Moldova, crossing the entire Commonwealth from Podolia through the Cracow and Poznań regions to reach Swedish Pomerania. Russian troops, garrisoned in Lithuania, pursued the Swedish troops and devastated the land. The Saxons were little better when they attacked the estates of Swedish supporters, and ill-paid Polish-Lithuanian soldiers did not spare their fellow countrymen, either. The situation eased in 1713 when the Treaty of Adrianople brought an end to the Russo-Turkish War, although Cossack uprisings in Ukraine lasted until 1715. August committed most of his 25,000-man Saxon army to pacifying the Commonwealth. Its presence led to widespread resentment. Peasants rebelled to resist fresh requisitions after disastrous harvests in 1713–15.

Fighting left Poland-Lithuania in desperate shape, and famine loomed. Statistical evidence is unreliable, but the population of Poland-Lithuania probably decreased by more than 25 percent as a result of death and emigration during August's Great Northern War. Swedish, Russian, Saxon, and rival Polish armies crisscrossed the Commonwealth from 1702 to 1720. They levied large, official contributions in order to finance their activities: Swedes in 1702, 1706, and 1709; Saxons in 1704, 1706, 1713, 1714, and 1715; Russians in 1707, 1709, 1710, 1717, 1718, and 1719; Poles in 1716. Soldiers ruthlessly looted for personal profit as well. Swedes were systematic and forceful, although not unnecessarily brutal, while the Russian troops, particularly from the Caucasian nationalities, gained a fearsome reputation. Under wartime conditions, plague killed 25 to 50 percent of the populations of urban centers such as Gdańsk, Toruń, and Cracow in 1708–10. Villagers fell victim, too. Agricultural productivity declined sharply.

Renewed Reform Efforts

August made significant reforms in Saxony after the Swedes left in the summer of 1707, but he failed to do the same in Poland-Lithuania when he regained the throne. In Saxony, he enacted an excise tax that enriched the treasury and encouraged manufacturing, especially for export. The Leipzig fair played a large role in marketing Saxony's new products. August reformed and expanded Leipzig University, recruiting commoner-graduates into public service. The Estates regained their influence in exchange for paying 1 million thalers, and within the Estates the number of noble deputies increased. To gain their support, August limited the activities of the appointive Secret Cabinet that he had organized once again in 1706. His improved finances allowed August to rebuild the Saxon army and join Austria to fight against Louis XIV. He also resumed artistic patronage such as expanding his collection of paintings and building the Zwinger pavilions in Dresden to display them. Few Polish artists and musicians took a role at August's court after the Great Northern War.

In Poland-Lithuania, August launched unsuccessful plans to abolish the *liberum veto* and ensure the succession of his son after Leszczyński renounced the throne in 1713. August bolstered his position through his cultural policy. In Warsaw, he planned the reconstruction of the Royal Castle and encouraged private development east of the Saxon Palace along Royal Street (Ulica Królewska), although the work was not carried out until the 1720s. The palace gardens contained a second theater, supplementing the theater in the Royal Castle.

Ideas put forward at the parliamentary sessions of 1712–13 aroused noble fears of an absolutist coup d'état. When August began using Saxon troops to take control of Poland-Lithuania and force the Commonwealth to pay for Saxony's military expenditures in the Great Northern War, dissident nobles formed the Tarnogród Confederation with the goal of forcing the Saxon troops to leave Poland-Lithuania, dethroning August, and introducing reforms based on parliamentary supremacy. They excluded senators from leadership (few wished to join, anyway) because they seemed greatly compromised by collaboration with Sweden or Russia. Despite Saxon military victories, the number and determination of the Confederates, some of whom had received military training in the Saxon Cadet School, forced August to retreat to Gdańsk, where he negotiated an agreement with them in 1716.

The resulting Warsaw Treaty between August and the Confederates made the relationship between Poland-Lithuania and Saxony a personal union only. Saxon ministers could play no role in Commonwealth politics and the Saxon army departed, leaving behind only a 1,200-man royal guard. Peter I did not officially guarantee the loosened relationship, but Russian policy kept Poland-Lithuania whole—and weak. The 1717 parliament reaffirmed the bargain, since Russian troops ensured the absence of dissent. The parliamentary session was held on one day (February 1) and became known as the Silent Parliament because the leaders agreed not to debate issues, thus avoiding the possibility of a dissident casting a *liberum veto*. Despite the use of unconstitutional means, the passage of a reform package helped restore order to Poland-Lithuania. Several significant measures reaffirmed the central government's power in collecting taxes and running the army. A peacetime army of 24,000 men was authorized, although tax revenues were too small to reach even that small size. The reformist spirit ran out at this point, and no further progress took place during August's reign. Indeed, discrimination against non-Catholics deepened. August managed to gain a certain amount of freedom of maneuver from Russian control in the following years by agreement, first with France and later with Austria. However, he could not oppose Russia's annexing of Livonia through the Treaty of Nystad with Sweden in 1721 or Brandenburg-Prussia's annexing of Swedish Pomerania.

Continuing Cossack Rebellions

Major revolts put the Russo-Polish settlement in Ukrainian lands into question throughout August II's reign. The Polish parliament ordered the dissolution of Right Bank Cossack regiments in 1699 at the end of the Turkish War. In 1702, after Karl XII of Sweden defeated August II, Simon Palij (c. 1640–1720), a Right Bank Cossack colonel, revolted against Poland-Lithuania with 12,000 soldiers, hoping to create a Cossack state out of Polish territory; other units joined. Poles and Jews fled west, fearing massacre, before the Polish army suppressed the revolt. Palij had studied at the Kievan Mohyla Academy and served at different times as a Zaporozhian Cossack and a registered Cossack in the Polish army. Ivan Mazepa, hetman of the Left (Russian) Bank, rejected overtures to join in the fight to recreate the independent Hetmanate, and united with the Poles to suppress the revolt in 1703–4. He turned Palij over to the Russians, who exiled him to Siberia in 1705. Palij was allowed to return after Mazepa broke with Moscow and took command of the Bila Tserkva Cossack regiment shortly before his death.

Hetman Ivan Mazepa (c. 1644–1709) was born near Bila Tserkva and went to school in Kiev and Warsaw before serving at the court of Polish-Lithuanian King Jan Kazimierz, who sent him to western Europe for further humanistic and military studies. Mazepa served Jan Kazimierz until his father died, when he returned to Ukraine to take over the family estates and become an officer in Hetman Petro Doroshenko's army. Mazepa later switched to Hetman Ivan Samoilovich and may have denounced him to the Russians who installed Mazepa as hetman in 1687.

Mazepa owed his election as hetman of Left Bank Ukraine to his diplomatic skills and cooperation with foreign powers rather than to popular support, but he hoped to build a strong state and he used his wealth and position to support the arts, education, and industry. Mazepa aspired to restore a united Right and

Left Bank Hetmanate supported by a Russia that would recognize local autonomy. He sought support among senior Cossack officers by guaranteeing their landed estates, among Orthodox churchmen by promoting its autonomy, and among ordinary Cossacks by guaranteeing their free status. He also limited service by serfs to two days per week. Mazepa promoted the spread of education and rebuilt neglected or war-damaged churches, especially the St. Sophia Cathedral in Kiev, in late Baroque style. Despite his efforts, the Cossack officers distrusted Mazepa because of his Russian connections, while ordinary Cossacks lacked faith in him because of his aristocratic tendencies. Mazepa's influence in the Orthodox Church in the Hetmanate was limited by increasing Russian control. Assuming ecclesiastic supremacy, the patriarch of Moscow installed his own appointee whenever an Orthodox bishop died. The last Kievan metropolitan appointed by the patriarch of Constantinople died in 1675, and a Moscow-dominated synod finally elected a successor in 1685. The Ottomans pressured the patriarch of Constantinople into recognizing the election to keep Russia from joining Sobieski's planned invasion of Moldavia.

The approach of Swedish armies and concerns about Russian intervention in domestic affairs led Mazepa to revolt against Russian control of the Left Bank in 1709. He established secret contacts and came to terms with Stanisław Leszczyński to recreate the Hadiach treaty making Ruthenia the third element in the Polish-Lithuanian Commonwealth. Karl XII offered armed support when he entered Ukraine with his army in April 1709. Russia retaliated quickly by arresting and torturing Cossack officers suspected of disloyalty, capturing the Zaporozhian Sich, and burning Mazepa's capital at Buturlin. Mazepa still managed to join Karl with 4,000 of his own troops plus 8,000 Zaporozhians. When Peter I of Russia won at Poltava, he also secured Russia's control over the Hetmanate, even though the Ottoman Turks forced Peter to return the Right Bank to Poland-Lithuania by the 1711 Treaty of Prut. Links between Right and Left Bank Ukraine weakened as the Left Bank Ukraine underwent rapid economic development based on trade with Russia, while the Right Bank integrated with Poland-Lithuania and only gradually recovered from years of fighting.

Reform by Administrative Measures

August II's diplomatic maneuvers, as he switched alliances continually in order to gain support, left him completely isolated, and after the Great Northern War concluded, he pursued economic and administrative progress in Poland-Lithuania without seeking bold political gains. The king applied the same measures to Saxony and Poland-Lithuania, achieving much greater success in the former. Improved administration increased the profitability of the royal estates, as did careful attention to breeding stock and regularizing the collection of peasant rents.

The saltworks at Wieliczka, near Cracow, and other mines were reconstructed and modernized. These reforms had a limited effect on the general economy in Poland-Lithuania and tax revenues remained low. In contrast, Saxon manufacturing grew rapidly. Europe's first porcelain factory in Meissen ran at a loss, but military reconstruction stimulated the growth of the textile and armaments industries. A system of patents both encouraged and protected new inventions.

August II bureaucratized the governmental structure of both realms, limiting his personal involvement in day-to-day administration. The secretaries of the Saxon Secret Cabinet now reported to ministers, who presented issues to the elector for final decision. August kept brief, regular hours, meeting Polish ministers on Mondays and Thursdays from 8 to 9 A.M. and Saxon ministers on Tuesdays, Wednesdays, Fridays, and Saturdays. He continued his cultural policies in both countries.

August abandoned his Polish-Lithuanian ambitions and contented himself with providing decent administration. A brief rapprochement with the nobility in the mid-1720s accomplished little positive. The Lutheran mayor of Toruń and nine city councillors had been condemned to death by a royal commission for their actions in suppressing a riot in the city; August confirmed the sentence. Diplomatic intervention by Russia and a coalition of Protestant countries made August popular in Poland-Lithuania as defender of the faith. His popularity increased when he stood up to the Vatican and dismissed the papal nuncio in order to maintain his right to appoint Church officials. Nevertheless, good will extended only far enough for the 1726 parliamentary session to accept August's proposals to reform the tribunals. His effort in 1727 to place his illegitimate but acknowledged son Maurice de Saxe on the Ducal Throne of Courland strained relations once again; many Polish nobles saw this as a revival of the king's ambitions in Livonia. The king's ability to act in Poland-Lithuania for the remainder of his reign was reduced by the death of his previous advisers and their replacement by a new generation that had no interest in royal reforms. Maneuvers between the two leading magnate families, the Potockis and the Czartoryskis, for political influence dominated the political life of the Commonwealth until the Partitions.

August gathered a court party, generally by allying himself with The Family (the Czartoryskis and their close relatives, the Lubomirskis), whom he strengthened by marriage alliances with some of his former mistresses or their daughters. He also gained supporters through Masonic connections. The first lodge opened in Warsaw in 1728 and attracted the aristocracy throughout the country. Scholarly societies in Gdańsk, Elbląg, and Warsaw linked up with the Masons. Prominent members took part in informal and far-ranging discussions at the Royal Castle in Warsaw. Young Poles trained at the Polish Officers School that August established in 1730; after graduation, most served in the Saxon army, which grew to 30,000 men as tax revenues expanded. The small Polish army received new weapons and adopted new tactics. August hoped to use his influence to enact reforms at the 1733 parliament but abandoned his plans when he fell seriously ill.

August accepted these disappointments with resignation. Gangrene set in after he underwent a minor operation in late 1732. On his deathbed in Warsaw, he neither recommended nor refused permission for his son to seek the Polish-Lithuanian crown, saying that he had found it more trouble than it was worth. His dying words asked God's forgiveness, because "my whole life was one sin." He died on February 1, 1733.

CHAPTER 16

August III

August III was a weak but intelligent and systematic king whose failures resulted from his willingness to forgo reform in order to avoid the kind of trouble that had ruined his father's reign. He preferred doing nothing to taking action that might antagonize his Russian patrons or his Polish-Lithuanian subjects. Apart from some minor improvements that his Saxon ministers made in organizing his estates in the Commonwealth, August let the ship of state drift until it nearly ran aground. Left to themselves, Polish-Lithuanian nobles squabbled over patronage. Almost all recognized the need for major reform, but could not or would not cooperate to achieve it.

THE ELECTION OF 1733 AND THE WAR OF POLISH SUCCESSION

The royal election of 1733 was the most hotly contested election since 1596, when Jan Zamoyski fought the Austrians to ensure the election of Zygmunt III Vasa. The young elector of Saxony, Friedrich August, enjoyed little popular support because of his father's military defeats and reputed absolutist goals. His marriage to Maria Josefa of Habsburg gave him Austrian backing, but did not gain him much support in Poland-Lithuania. In contrast, the exiled Stanisław Leszczyński, held in contempt in 1704–9 as a Swedish puppet, now found himself extremely popular. The rival Czartoryski and Potocki factions united behind him, each convinced that its members would enjoy the lion's share of patronage appointments.

The convocation parliament of April–May 1733 created a General Confederation to elect a "Piast," or Polish, candidate to the throne and excluded all "Dissidents," or non-Catholics, from participating in this or future parliaments as well as other public offices. The confederated parliamentary session failed to increase military preparedness or raise more troops, even though the 15,000-man Polish-Lithuanian army could not defend the country against the 30,000

Russian troops stationed in Lithuania. Leszczyński left his exile in Chambord in late August, traveled through the Germanies in disguise, and on September 8 reached Warsaw, where he evoked wild enthusiasm with a surprise appearance at Holy Cross Church wearing the Polish caftan instead of western European clothes. On September 13, an enthusiastic crowd of 13,000 nobles gathered on the electoral field at Wola outside Warsaw to acclaim him king of Poland-Lithuania. The French ambassador, Antoine Felix de Monti, openly orchestrated Leszczyński's candidacy, and the French court declared war on Austria and Saxony in October to support him. France had spent fifteen years preparing for this moment. Living in poverty-stricken exile in Alsace in 1719, Leszczyński had been flabbergasted to receive representatives of the young King Louis XV, who requested the hand of Leszczyński's daughter, Maria. The aim of the marriage was to increase French influence in Poland and provide Louis XV with a wife who would bear children without seeking to play a role in court politics. Pious to a fault, Maria Leszczyńska satisfied these requirements. The French court regarded Saxony as an Austrian dependency and wanted to elect Leszczyński to restore France's traditional anti-Habsburg coalition of Poland-Lithuania, Sweden, and Turkey. Paris was wary of committing resources to distant Poland, however, and gave Monti limited funds.

Leszczyński's rival for the Polish-Lithuanian throne, Friedrich August of Saxony (1696–1763), had been groomed as a teenager to rule Poland-Lithuania, although his education had been neglected at the height of the Great Northern War and he never learned to speak Polish. He spent his childhood with his Lutheran mother and shared her indifference, or even hostility, to the Catholic Polish-Lithuanian Commonwealth. August II abruptly removed his heir from the queen's care in 1711, ostensibly to have him meet Peter I of Russia, and later sent the youth traveling throughout Europe under the care of Catholic tutors. After a year, Friedrich August broke his oath to his mother and converted to Catholicism; he became pious. In 1719, he married Maria Josefa, daughter of Austrian Emperor Joseph I, becoming so deeply devoted to her that some observers thought that she dominated him. The couple had eleven children, the eldest of whom succeeded Friedrich August as elector of Saxony and was appointed heir to the Polish-Lithuanian throne by the Constitution of May 3, 1791, although he never accepted the position.

Despite initial reservations, Russia, Austria, and Prussia endorsed Friedrich August's candidacy to the Polish-Lithuanian throne when France championed Stanisław Leszczyński. Friedrich August also made concessions to win their favor by abandoning thoughts of reforming the Polish constitution and renouncing his claim to the Austrian succession, recognizing Maria Theresia's rights to the Austrian throne. He also agreed to let Empress Anna of Russia appoint her favorite, Ernst Biron (Bühren), as duke of Courland. Russian armies entered Poland to stage a second royal election at the village of Kamień, near Warsaw, on November 5, 1733, with only 1,000 Polish nobles in attendance. Ironically, the scene paralleled Stanisław Leszczyński's election in 1704. Friedrich August was crowned in Cracow on January 17, 1734, as August III; Maria Josefa was crowned queen.

The War of the Polish Succession lasted from 1733 to 1735, but France was least interested in its ostensible cause, the Polish throne, and sent only enough troops to Poland to defend Gdańsk, leaving the rest of the country to August. France committed most of its forces to gaining territory along the Rhine. As Russian armies approached Warsaw, Leszczyński fled to Gdańsk with his guards regiments. Despite receiving Leszczyński hesitantly without the usual parades and fireworks, Gdańsk recognized him as king and defended him for five months. France belatedly sent a fleet with 1,500 soldiers to help, but they did not want to fight, and surrendered to the Russian besieging army as quickly as they could. Seeing the end approach, King Stanisław escaped in peasant clothes. French ambassador de Monti surrendered and Leszczyński's leading Polish supporters, such as Stanisław Poniatowski and Prince August Czartoryski, swore allegiance to August III. Russian and Saxon armies easily overpowered the partisan bands that sprang up throughout the country to support Leszczyński, who abdicated in January 1736 at Louis XV's request, receiving in exchange the newly conquered duchy of Lorraine for his lifetime. He set up an attractive court at Lunéville, where he received Polish travelers and preached reform.

The Pacification Parliament held in July 1736 turned out to be the only parliamentary meeting in August III's reign that was not broken by a *liberum veto*. The two-week session ratified his accession and proclaimed amnesty for his opponents, some of whom received official positions, although naturally most posts went to Saxon supporters.

August III

The newly elected King August III showed little interest in his new realm and came there primarily for short parliamentary meetings. August's long absences and lack of serious political initiatives allowed the Polish-Lithuanian nobility to enjoy their liberties without interference, and they celebrated his reign as "sweet." The eighteenth-century Polish memoirist Andrzej Kitowicz wrote that "Poland never had and never will have so good, magnificent, and generous a king as August III." Kitowicz exemplified the noble attitudes of the age, criticizing the nobility for paralyzing government with the *liberum veto* while applauding August's willingness to leave the practice in place. Political and military disasters had impressed many Polish and Lithuanian political leaders of the need for reform, but reform held a lower priority than the ordinary business of politics—holding office and distributing estates.

August III gloried in the bureaucratic machine that his father had created and left business in the hands of the ministers who reported to him in the Secret Cabinet. Factional politics prevented the Polish-Lithuanian state from addressing the problem of constitutional reform, which in turn would have allowed action on pressing issues such as financial reconstruction and military expansion. The Polish-Lithuanian royal court, the unsuccessful driving force for reform from 1600 to 1735, only pressed gently and intermittently for change under August III, who was content to let ill-enough alone. The ultimate reality of politics was patronage appointments to rich ministerial and senatorial posts, tribunal offices, and local positions. All offices drew salaries and allowed their holders to make decisions that influenced the wealth and status of other nobles, thereby allowing officeholders to elicit favors or bribes. The vast Ostrozky entail in Volhynia provides an example of the interplay of politics and wealth. Its owner, Prince Janusz Sanguszko, the eighteenth-century heir to the sixteenth-century magnate Konstiantyn Ostrozky, was badly indebted but could not break up the entail to sell off sections. The Czartoryskis gathered a coalition of magnate families, including political enemies such as the Potockis, to ignore the law and buy pieces of the estate. The Radziwiłłs and Jan Klemens Branicki blocked the patently illegal transactions only because they had been excluded.

August III's first important adviser was Aleksander Józef Sułkowski, a childhood friend who quickly lost his position to a Saxon, Heinrich Brühl, a lesser noble who served August for many years and became rich in the process. Brühl arranged to be naturalized as a Polish noble to take part in Polish-Lithuanian politics. He attempted to introduce minor reforms to centralize and regularize both tax collections and military affairs, and he improved the economic organization of the royal estates. Like his father, August III paid considerable attention to cultural affairs. He enjoyed and understood the arts; Italian painting and opera were his great loves. August made opera available in Warsaw and brought artists, architects, and musicians there, particularly when he had to escape Dresden during the Seven Years' War.

"The Family"

Brühl and the Saxon Court leaned toward a political alliance with The Family, an extended family and political faction headed by August and Michał Czartoryski, that formed the single most powerful grouping in the Commonwealth. August's marriage to Zofia née Sieniawska provided the fortune that financed The Family's political activities, and the Czartoryskis increased their strength with the help of other judicious alliances. The marriage of their sister Konstancja to Stanisław

Poniatowski provided them with their first day-to-day leader. Poniatowski was an able general, politician, and pamphleteer who had supported Leszczyński and the Swedes until 1719, when he finally made peace with the Saxons. The Czartoryskis also arranged a marriage with Georg Flemming, the respected grand treasurer of Lithuania. The marriage alliance between Izabela Poniatowska and Jan Klemens Branicki served them well for about twenty years. In the 1730s, Poniatowski went into semiretirement, accepting promotion to castellan of Cracow and abandoning policy leadership to Lithuanian Chancellor Michał Czartoryski. Poniatowski continued to write influential reform pamphlets.

Like other political families, the Czartoryskis aimed primarily to win power and, if possible, introduce reforms. During the Russo-Turkish War of 1736–39, they opposed the transit of Russian armies through the Commonwealth to the Balkans and stopped August III from bringing Poland-Lithuania into the war on Russia's side. In 1746, they allied themselves with Brühl and the Saxon court, endorsing military and fiscal reform in a confederated parliamentary session. Chancellor Andrzej Załuski helped block this move on constitutional grounds. The Czartoryskis engineered Brühl's naturalization as a Polish noble through the use of fraudulent documentation and received, as a reward, the appointment of Michał Czartoryski as Lithuanian chancellor. The Czartoryskis' failure to arrange for the election of a Saxon heir as king during August III's lifetime and a subsequent refusal to allow Brühl's daughter to marry Kazimierz Poniatowski led to a break.

In opposition to August III after 1752, the Czartoryskis used the traditional techniques of noble democracy to paralyze government even while they planned political reforms in conjunction with the Russian Young Court of Peter III and Grand Duchess Catherine in St. Petersburg. The Czartoryskis even cast a *liberum veto* to end the 1761 parliamentary session in order to protect Prussian currency as a favor to Russian Grand Duke Peter, a confirmed Prussophile. In 1762, the Czartoryskis plotted to dethrone August III with the help of Russian troops, but Catherine II, who had just dethroned her husband, Peter III, drew back at the last minute out of concern for possible diplomatic repercussions. Civil war might have broken out in Poland-Lithuania or the Czartoryski faction might have collapsed, had not August III and Brühl died.

The Czartoryskis drafted a comprehensive reform plan to create a powerful and effective noble parliament as they prepared to take power. They planned to replace the *liberum veto* with majority voting, allow parliament to meet whenever necessary (not just for six weeks every second year), and abolish the dietines' binding instructions for parliamentary deputies. Parliament was to take over formerly royal powers such as appointing officeholders and distributing landed estates, as well as appoint parliamentary committees to assume powers exercised by royal ministers. Landless nobles would lose their political rights in order to prevent magnates from packing the dietines. The number of local dietines and the number of parliamentary deputies would increase.

Anti-Czartoryski Forces and Their Sources of Power

The Czartoryskis' rivals were a group of smaller magnate factions calling themselves Republicans. The extensive Potocki family was the most important, although it was far less cohesive than the Czartoryskis. Józef Potocki, crown great hetman after 1736, planned confederations to overthrow August III and looked to foreigners for support. He hoped that France would help him elect the duc de Conti or even Charles Stuart, the Scottish Old Pretender, to the Polish-Lithuanian throne, and to abolish the *liberum veto*. Antoni Potocki discussed similar ideas in pamphlets that circulated in manuscript. Primate Teodor Potocki prepared a proposal for the 1738 parliamentary session for a 30,000-man army paid by indirect taxes and a revised tax on crown lands, but found himself blocked by his cousin Hetman Józef Potocki, who feared loss of political influence after such a reform. The Ukrainian magnate Franciszek Salezy Potocki married his daughter to Alojzy Fryderyk Brühl, son of Heinrich Brühl, as a mark of cooperation with the court. The Radziwiłł family remained very important in the Grand Duchy of Lithuania. In the 1740s, the last significant Wiśniowiecki princes died, leaving their fortunes to Prince Michał Radziwiłł, who controlled the Lithuanian tribunals. Michał's son, Prince Karol Radziwiłł, lacked his father's balance and acted so arbitrarily that some supporters turned to the Czartoryskis for protection. In August III's last years, Brühl constructed a new court faction through marriage alliances to perpetuate his own political influence.

Magnates backed up their influence with armed force. The largest private army in the mid-eighteenth century belonged to the Radziwiłł family. It varied between 1,000 and 2,000 peasant soldiers from the Radziwiłłs' Belarussian estates trained by foreign officers; local nobles took command in the 1760s after the Radziwiłłs set up their own cadet school to provide professional training. The Radziwiłł forces were more modern than the Polish and Lithuanian armies; almost half consisted of infantry and the remainder of sharpshooters, artillery, and dragoons. Units were quartered in garrison cities across Radziwiłł's estates. This army was a significant force in the Polish-Lithuanian context.

With parliament paralyzed by frequent use of the *liberum veto*, political rivalry was often played out in the tribunals. In 1743, a Potocki or "Republican" partisan, Adam Tarło, beat up opposing deputies at a meeting of the crown tribunal in Piotrków, Great Poland. The following year, Kazimierz Poniatowski challenged him to a duel and killed him. The 1749 tribunal broke up before it started to sit, and the Potockis wrecked the special sitting of parliament in 1750 called to discuss judicial reform. By the 1750s, armed clashes became common and civil war seemed possible.

THE WAR OF THE AUSTRIAN SUCCESSION

In foreign policy, August III clung closely to Russia, which had put him on the Polish-Lithuanian throne. He attempted to increase his prestige by sending troops to fight with the Russians and Austrians in the 1736–39 war against Turkey, but the opposition cast a *liberum veto* at the 1738 parliamentary session to stop him. Far more important was the War of the Austrian Succession (1740–48), in which Friedrich II (the Great) of Prussia seized Silesia from Austria. Silesia had once belonged to the Polish crown, and many ethnic Poles still lived there. Much of Polish trade flowed through Wrocław and other Silesian cities. In December 1740, August allied himself with Empress Maria Theresia of Austria in return for promises of Prussian territory in Lusatia that would provide a direct link to Poland. August renounced the unratified agreement and deserted his ally when the Austrians lost the battle of Mollwitz in April 1741. He joined the anti-Austrian coalition of Prussia, France, and Bavaria in hopes of winning part of Upper Silesia or even gaining the Czech crown. However, the Austrians beat the Saxon army in Bohemia, and Friedrich II declined to share his territorial gains with his hapless ally when he negotiated the Treaty of Berlin that confirmed Prussia's annexation of Silesia. Saxony signed a separate treaty with Austria in 1742 without making any territorial gains. In 1743–45, August switched sides again and allied himself with Austria in exchange for the promise of a corridor across Silesia. There was also talk of acquiring Ducal Prussia in exchange for relinquishing part of Ukraine and Belarus to Russia if she joined the alliance. However, Prussia prevailed militarily and kept its recent Silesian conquests.

Since August III fought only as elector of Saxony, the Polish-Lithuanian Commonwealth remained neutral despite the importance of the main prize—neighboring Silesia with its historical and economic ties as well as its large Polish population. Through their intense maneuvering with foreign powers, the Czartoryski and Potocki factions canceled each other out and prevented the Commonwealth from taking a stand. August tried to enact financial and military reforms at the 1744 session of the Polish-Lithuanian parliament, having made a secret agreement with Austria and Russia, whose side he planned to join in the Second Silesian War (1744–45). But the Czartoryski opposition blocked his efforts by casting a *liberum veto*. Further attempts to strengthen the government after the war at the 1746 and 1748 parliamentary sessions also failed due to the use of the *liberum veto,* this time cast by the Potocki "republican" faction.

The Seven Years' War

Poland-Lithuania also avoided involvement in the Seven Years' War of 1756–63, passively waiting to see who would hold power in East Central Europe. Russia, allied with Austria and France against Prussia and Britain, established military headquarters in Great Poland for its attacks on Prussia. At the high price of foreign occupation, the Russian presence effectively shielded the Commonwealth from Prussian aggression as Friedrich II quickly conquered Saxony. However, the Russians could not prevent Prussian officials from issuing large quantities of debased Polish coins from the seventeenth-century stamping dies that they found in the Leipzig mint. Prussia financed its military activities in part by releasing the debased currency into Poland, melting down authentic coinage and skimming off the profits. Export traders protected themselves by insisting on payment for grain and other products in foreign currencies, but most petty nobles, burghers, and peasants had to take their chances with the coinage that came their way. Friedrich's military victories forced August III to flee to Warsaw, leaving his wife in Saxony to moderate Prussian behavior.

Saxon control over Poland-Lithuania was protected by Empress Elizabeth until she died in 1762. She even allowed Prince Karl of Saxony to take the ducal throne of Courland, a position that was expected to help his chance of succeeding to the Polish-Lithuanian throne. Elizabeth's nephew and successor, Peter III, reversed her policy, taking the fatally unpopular step of allying himself with Prussia and pulling Russia out of the Seven Years' War just as it was about to win. He paid for his policy by losing his throne, and later his life, to his wife, Catherine II the Great. As empress, Catherine supported the Czartoryskis in Poland-Lithuania and expelled Karl from Courland. When peace was signed at Hubertusburg, August returned to Dresden, where he died a few months later.

Haidamak and Peasant Rebellions

The weakness of the Polish-Lithuanian state and the underdeveloped economy that had not yet recovered from the ravages of the Great Northern War contributed to the outbreak of several noteworthy rebellions. The most important ones involved ethnic and religious issues as well.

Cossack groups continued to link Right and Left Bank Ukraine. Cities and rural nobles still employed Cossacks in their militias, frequently in self-governing, semiautonomous units. Numerous Cossacks followed time-honored practices by leaving their units occasionally to join the independent Cossack forces of the Zaporozhian Sich or attacking and robbing nearby social and religious enemies, often with peasant help. While the primary focus of these gangs was banditry, times of social conflict and international tension gave their acts social and political significance and permitted them to involve up to 1,000 men. Haidamak rebellions swept the region as the tax exemptions granted peasants after the Great Northern War expired in the early 1730s. Cossack-led bands of dissatisfied peasants and bandits plundered and burned towns and estates, killing Roman Catholic and Uniate clerics, Polish nobles, and Jews, especially innkeepers. Another Haidamak revolt broke out in 1734 during the War of the Polish Succession. Centered on the Right Bank in the Kiev region, Podolia, and Volhynia, the revolt could be felt as far away as Lviv and Kamianets-Podilskyi. Russian and Polish troops crushed the rebellion, but outbreaks continued sporadically for years. Another revolt broke out in 1750 without external stimulus. Much of Right Bank Ukraine was involved and rebels captured several cities.

An armed revolt in the Kurpie region north of Mazovia capped several decades of resistance to the imposition of feudal labor duties on royal estates that had previously required only monetary rent. After resistance in 1700 brought military repression, the peasants appealed to royal courts against new demands. Supporters of Stanisław Leszczyński's royal candidacy organized partisan bands to attack August III's soldiers and Russian detachments in 1735, and local peasants turned against their overlords after the struggle for royal succession concluded. It took a substantial military effort to defeat them. Authorities hanged the leaders and flogged other participants or suspected participants.

Bands of bandits infested well-forested mountains along Poland's southern border, and several leaders achieved fame as local Robin Hoods. Janosik was active in Podhale, southeast of Cracow, on both the Polish and Slovak sides of the border; Proćpak led bandits around Żywiec and Ondraszek near Cieszyn (Teschen).

CHAPTER 17

Stanisław August Poniatowski

Stanisław August Poniatowski (1732–97), the last king of Poland, was a hard-working and effective political leader with a firm commitment to reform, but he failed to unify a badly split nation until it was too late to forestall the Partitions. He bears a share of the responsibility for the political miscalculations that allowed Poland-Lithuania's neighbors to partition her. Nevertheless, his political, educational, and cultural leadership in cooperation with other noble reformers allowed the state to make greater progress than it had under any king for over 150 years.

THE LAST KING OF POLAND

The last king of Poland was the second son of Stanisław Poniatowski, whose marriage to Konstancja née Czartoryska made him a leader of The (Czartoryski) Family and one of the most influential politicians of his generation. Young Stanisław received an exacting education at home from his parents and tutors, learning French, German, English, and Latin and reading the works of the philosophes. His father intended to send sixteen-year-old Stanisław to observe the War of the Austrian Succession at close quarters, but the war ended and he went on the Grand Tour instead. During this and other trips in the next few years, Stanisław gained a close acquaintance with the political and intellectual life of western Europe. English constitutional politics and French culture impressed him most. When they came of age, Stanisław and his brothers plunged into politics as junior members of the Czartoryski faction in the early 1750s. Kazimierz, who liked army life and joined the Austrian army later, achieved prominence by killing a political opponent, Adam Tarło, in a duel. Stanisław more modestly acted as orator and political organizer for his uncles. Andrzej became a professional soldier in the Austrian army while Michał, the youngest, joined the Church. In order to give young Stanisław international experience and have an agent at the Russian court, the Czartoryskis placed him as secretary to Charles Hanbury Williams, the British ambassador to Russia in 1756.

Poniatowski's Russian experience changed the course of Polish history. Britain supported Prussia and opposed Russia in the Seven Years' War that had just broken out, and Ambassador Williams approached the Young Court of Grand Duke Peter and Grand Duchess Catherine in the hope that it would moderate Tsarina Elizabeth's anti-Prussian policy. Stanisław became Catherine's lover and intellectual tutor as they read the philosophes together, but Elizabeth discovered the liaison and expelled him for political rather than moral reasons. Stanisław Poniatowski returned to Poland as a noteworthy personality whose importance grew when Elizabeth died and the incompetent Peter III lost the imperial throne to his wife, Catherine II (the Great), in 1762.

As empress, Catherine launched a more aggressive policy to wrest control of Poland-Lithuania from Saxony and was prepared to support a coup d'état by the Czartoryskis when August III died in November 1763. She acceded to Czartoryski requests and dispatched 30,000 Russian troops to secure the throne for Poniatowski, who took the name Stanisław II August on his election. In preliminary discussions, Catherine agreed to support modest reforms but demanded in exchange that Poniatowski recognize Russia's right to "guarantee" the antiquated Polish-Lithuanian constitution (i.e., prevent major reform) and support Orthodox Christians. The empress's foreign minister, Nikita Panin, coordinated Russia's policy with Prussia in the so-called Northern System of alliances. The powerful Czartoryski faction ensured Poniatowski's success in the election at Wola, outside Warsaw, with the help of Russian troops. The Republican faction unsuccessfully backed the elderly crown great hetman, Jan Klemens Branicki, Poniatowski's brother-in-law, who fled to Hungary after a short campaign.

Political and Social Reform, 1764–67

Poniatowski and the Czartoryskis launched an ambitious reform program before the royal election in 1764, organizing a confederation that allowed them to suspend the *liberum veto* and use police measures against opponents. The confederation lasted until 1766. At the preelection convocation parliament of May–June 1764, Chancellor Andrzej Zamoyski voiced The Family's plan to make parliament more effective and limit the power of the senatorial elite by creating a supreme executive council. The new regime intended to abolish private armies, codify the law, and end appeal rights to Rome in Church law. Zamoyski also urged extensive educational reforms. To pay for increased state activities, Zamoyski advocated reclaiming crown lands and leasing them out again at higher prices, increasing taxation, reestablishing the mint, and instituting protective tariffs. New state commissions would improve trade and restore cities to prosperity. Zamoyski expressed sympathy for the plight of the serfs, but only proposed that serf-soldiers in the tiny Polish-Lithuanian army receive their freedom after ten years' service.

The postelectoral parliamentary session of 1764 enacted part of the ambitious reform program, most importantly creating military commissions in the crown provinces and Lithuania that superseded the independent hetmans. Limited finances permitted a modest increase in the well-disciplined foreign-style detachments, replacing the ill-disciplined and outmoded national cavalry, composed mostly of nobles. In 1765, Poniatowski opened a Cadet School in Warsaw to provide military training and modern secular education to members of the lesser nobility. As chancellor, Andrzej Zamoyski organized noble Commissions of Good Order to supervise royal cities and restore them to financial health. Interest in economic reform was also signaled by the construction of the Ogiński Canal in Lithuania and the formation of the Wool Manufacturing Company, a joint stock partnership of nobles and burghers. A new journal built support for further reform among the educated public. Published by two Enlightened priests, Franciszek Bohomolec and Ignacy Krasicki, *Monitor* advocated a wide spectrum of social, political, and economic measures.

Left to themselves, the Czartoryskis and Stanisław August would have overhauled the Polish-Lithuanian state, but they encountered vociferous domestic opposition, lost Russian support, and fell out among themselves. Russia aimed above all to create a fully dependable Russian Party and turned from the Czartoryskis to disenfranchised Orthodox nobles, whom Catherine intended to restore to political activity; she extended her protection to Protestant nobles in deference to her Prussian ally. The Catholic Church and most nobles objected vehemently on political grounds; they were perfectly willing to grant religious liberties to commoners in order to encourage economic development. Poniatowski wavered, but the Czartoryskis followed their political nose and lined up with the conservative opposition. The elder Czartoryskis also deferred to conservative complaints about their nephew's royal pretensions. Poniatowski had surrounded himself with unpopular foreign advisers, especially Italians, and failed to make politically expedient gestures toward old Polish customs. Many nobles never forgave him for appearing at his coronation in French-style knee breeches and jacket instead of the traditional Polish caftan. They certainly noticed that Poniatowski's head was too small for the Polish crown, which had to be adjusted for the ceremony.

The Russian Alliance with Polish Conservatives

Russian Ambassador Nikolai Repnin, nephew of Russian Foreign Minister Panin, had already decided that the Czartoryskis were the principal obstacle to Russian control before they changed course. To build a new base of support, Repnin forced the election of Gabriel Podoski, a corrupt priest who lived openly with his mistress, to the fortuitously vacant position of archbishop of Gniezno (primate) and blocked reform at the 1766 parliamentary session, demanding that Chancellor Zamoyski withdraw his bill to abolish the *liberum veto* and dissolve the confederation. The 1766 parliamentary session ended quickly after enacting minor improvements in executive authority, for Russia and Prussia jointly threatened to declare war on Poland-Lithuania if their demands were not met. Zamoyski resigned as chancellor in 1767, seeing no hope for additional reform.

New Russian military units entered Poland-Lithuania in March 1767 to sponsor confederations that would follow Russian orders. They backed the formation of a confederation of Protestant nobles in Toruń and a confederation of Orthodox nobles at Slutsk (Słuck), but Repnin put his main hopes in the Confederation of Radom, formed in June 1767 by the Catholic leaders of the anti-Czartoryski opposition who had opposed Poniatowski's election in 1764. The marshal of the Confederation was Prince Karol Radziwiłł, whom the Russians had forced into exile in 1764 for opposing Poniatowski's candidacy. Hetman Jan Klemens Branicki and Hetman Wacław Rzewuski joined the Radom Confederation along with Kajetan Sołtyk, bishop of Cracow, and other magnates.

The Russian-Conservative alliance did not work. The conservative nobles wanted to dethrone Poniatowski, which Russia would not allow, and Russia wanted to grant Protestant and Orthodox nobles political rights, including ministerial positions, measures which the noble opposition rejected. Poniatowski regained some credit with Repnin, and under military pressure from the Russian troops remaining in Warsaw the 1768 parliamentary session enacted legislation restoring political rights to Dissident nobles (which never took effect) and passed Fundamental Laws that could be modified only by unanimous vote. These laws guaranteed traditional noble liberties of free royal elections, *liberum veto,* right to revolt, and noble monopolies on both state officeholding and ownership of landed estates. However, the Fundamental Laws accepted some reforms from 1764 such as majority voting on "economic and state matters" including taxation, military affairs, and parliamentary procedure. Catherine II "guaranteed" the constitutional settlement and withdrew her troops from the Commonwealth, leaving Poniatowski in place. Ambassador Repnin arrested and sent into Russian exile several of his former allies who threatened to revolt against the slender reforms enacted at the 1768 parliamentary session.

THE WAR OF THE BAR CONFEDERATION

Russia's renewed sponsorship of Poniatowski only hastened the formation of a new confederation at Bar, Podolia (near the Ottoman Moldavian border), that aimed to dethrone Poniatowski, expel Russian troops, and repress Dissident nobles. The revolt spread throughout Ukraine and eventually the entire Commonwealth. Bitter conflicts raged in the countryside as Confederate appeals to religious and patriotic sentiment, reminiscent of the Swedish war of 1655–57, brought noble, burgher, and peasant sympathizers to their ranks. As soon as Russian and Polish-Lithuanian troops suppressed one Confederate unit, fresh levies of noble cavalry and units of magnates' private armies sprang up elsewhere as partisans. Russian and Polish regular troops almost always held the upper hand militarily, although the Confederates succeeded in capturing and holding Cracow and the Jasna Góra monastery at Częstochowa for several weeks. They were encouraged by Turkey, which declared war on Russia, while France provided the Confederates with financial assistance and military training; Saxony also provided subsidies. A Confederate government-in-exile met in Prešov, Slovakia (Kingdom of Hungary), and declared Stanisław August dethroned on October 22, 1770. Confederates kidnapped Poniatowski in Warsaw on November 3, 1771, but the king convinced his captors to let him go after a few hours. Nevertheless, this assault on the royal person undermined foreign support for the revolt and led the Habsburgs to expel the government-in-exile from their territory. Fighting quickly wound down and concluded during the summer of 1772.

The brightest event produced by the Bar Confederation came after its defeat, for its ideologist Michał Wielhorski commissioned Jean-Jacques Rousseau and Gabriel Mably to comment on the Polish-Lithuanian constitution. Knowing Poland-Lithuania primarily through the information provided by Wielhorski, these philosophes praised the Commonwealth's noble democracy for its civic involvement and republican zeal and overlooked its inefficiencies, commenting only briefly on social injustice. Within Poland, the War of the Bar Confederation caused widespread destruction. It also gave military experience to a new generation of Poles and laid the foundation for the patriotic Insurrections of 1794, 1830–31, and 1863–64. Only one Bar Confederate showed outstanding military talent, Kazimierz Pułaski, who fought and died in the American Revolutionary War.

THE HAIDAMAK REBELLION OF 1768

The largest and bloodiest Haidamak rebellion occurred in 1768 during the Russo-Turkish War and the Polish War of the Bar Confederation. A small band under Maksym Zalizniak, a Zaporozhian Cossack, marched into the Right Bank Ukrainian lands calling on the peasants to revolt against feudal obligations. As towns fell to the rebels, another 2,000 men joined the rebels for the siege of Uman (Humań), a fortified city. Cossack guard units commanded by Ivan Honta (Gonta) defected to the rebels and Uman surrendered to the Cossacks, who mercilessly slaughtered several thousand Jewish and Catholic men, women, and children. Uniate clergy were also attacked. Other Right Bank Cossack units joined the rebellion in the Kiev, Bratslav, Podolia, and Volhynia palatinates, especially in the Carpathian Mountains. Russian troops harshly suppressed the revolt with assistance of Polish units in a prolonged campaign.

The First Partition

The War of the Bar Confederation opened the door to the First Partition. Russian troops pursued Bar Confederates onto Ottoman territory in June 1768, and Turkey, which never recognized Poniatowski as king and objected to Russian domination of Poland-Lithuania, declared war in November. Russia won victories at sea and on land, eventually occupying Crimea, Moldavia, and Walachia. Austria sought to minimize the extension of Russian power by diplomatic means. Prussia feared the loss of Silesia in a renewed general European war and proposed that all three powers satisfy their appetites at Polish expense. France, Turkey's ally, also preferred to redirect Russia toward Poland. Austria touched off the partition by opportunistically reviving medieval Hungarian claims to Carpathian border territories and occupied Spiš (Szepesség, Spisz, Zips) in 1769. In 1770, Austria moved further into Polish territory with less justification, an act that provided an excuse for Prussia and Russia to grab territory. Negotiations took more than a year. A Prusso-Russian accord was signed in St. Petersburg in February 1772, and Austria joined in August 1772.

In the First Partition, Poland-Lithuania lost almost 30 percent of its territory and 35 percent of its population. Prussia obtained the rich and well-developed territories of Royal Prussia (without Gdańsk or Toruń), including more than 580,000 inhabitants and 36,000 square kilometers. Austria acquired Galicia with 2,650,000 inhabitants and 83,000 square kilometers while Russia took northeast Belarus with 1,300,000 inhabitants and 92,000 square kilometers. The three partition zones were theoretically equal, and indeed the small but economically well-developed Prussian acquisitions equaled or exceeded the other two zones in value. Russia, which agreed to partition only in order to concentrate on its Turkish war, clearly gained the least valuable territories, but it maintained its domination over the rest of Poland. Poland-Lithuania could do nothing to stop the Austrian, Prussian, and Russian armies from moving in.

The three allied ambassadors demanded that the Commonwealth hold a confederated parliamentary session to ratify the Partition. Deputy Tadeusz Reytan protested dramatically in parliament while Poniatowski and the Czartoryski camp worked behind the scenes to delay ratification, but the Partition gained official approval on September 30, 1773. Afterwards, Russia and Austria followed liberal trade policies toward Poland while Prussia enacted harsh protectionist measures that allowed it to export manufactured goods extensively to Poland-Lithuania at high prices and buy Polish agricultural produce at low prices.

Reform Activity at the Partition Parliament

Parliament continued in session until April 1775 to enact legislation that would ensure the Commonwealth's stability. Russia planned to keep post-Partition Poland intact as a dependent state, so it gradually came to view King Stanisław August Poniatowski as the only political leader who would be both subordinate and effective. Russian Ambassador Otto Magnus Stackelberg ruled the Commonwealth from 1772 to 1788 like a Roman proconsul, as Poniatowski put it, and the ambassador kept corrupt Polish nobles on his payroll to control the king. Stackelberg allowed Poniatowski to build up his own powerful political "party" through effective use of royal patronage—distribution of rich leaseholds on crown lands and income-bearing offices. Poniatowski's chief lieutenants were Lithuanian Vice-Treasurer Antoni Tyzenhauz (after 1780, Vice-Chancellor Joachim Chreptowicz) and his brother, Michał Poniatowski, bishop of Płock and later primate-archbishop of Gniezno. The king showed great skill in grass-roots politics by carrying on a large volume of correspondence with ordinary nobles throughout the Commonwealth and helping them with their personal concerns.

The Partition Parliament of 1773–75 created the Permanent Council as an orderly executive authority operating between parliamentary sessions. Composed of eighteen senators (including ministers) and eighteen deputies elected by parliament, the institution was originally intended to limit the king's power still further, but Poniatowski filled it with his supporters and used it effectively. The full council coordinated the five departments (foreign affairs, police or good order, military, justice, and treasury), which determined policy and supervised executive activity by ministers with life tenure. In practice, much of the work was done by Poniatowski's private secretaries and advisers. Parliament also enacted a law limiting royal patronage by requiring that crown land be auctioned off to the highest bidder for fifty-year leases. In practice, this measure improved national finances somewhat without hampering unduly Poniatowski's ability to control patronage. Parliament also made banking easier, altered social legislation to allow nobles to pursue trade and commerce, restored the general tariff, and unified tax administration. Discussions about reforming serfdom failed to lead to concrete action.

Parliament also created the National Education Commission to administer the large network of Jesuit schools that were threatened with collapse when Pope Clement XIV abolished the Society of Jesus in 1773. The commission supervised schools established by other religious orders as well. Unfortunately, the Russian clique that parliament put in charge of selling off ex-Jesuit properties operated in an extraordinarily corrupt manner and greatly reduced the funds available for schooling. Nevertheless, the commission kept many Jesuit schools functioning while reforming their curriculum and welding them into an effective network. The commission itself, originally eight and later twelve members, included both royalists and anti-royalists who worked with rare harmony even during times of bitter political conflict. A subsidiary body, the Society for Elementary Books, sponsored the writing and publishing of Polish textbooks.

Reform and Opposition between the Partitions

Poniatowski's hopes of enacting further reforms faced strong opposition after 1775 from a new generation of nobles headed by the younger Czartoryskis and Potockis. Stanisław Lubomirski, August Czartoryski's son-in-law, took charge of the Czartoryski faction because August Czartoryski's son Adam Kazimierz refused to assume the mantle of leadership, just as he had declined to compete with Poniatowski for the throne in 1764. Lubomirski mobilized The Family's far-flung connections and amplified them through marriage alliances between his three daughters and members of formerly anti-Czartoryski families: two brothers, Ignacy and Stanisław Potocki, and Seweryn Rzewuski. The two Potockis came from a less wealthy branch of the noted family, but they were well educated and politically active. This opposition group received some support from Catherine's favorite, Count Grigorii Potemkin, in Petersburg, despite the empress's support for the king through Ambassador Stackelberg. Poniatowski's former friend, Crown Great Hetman Franciszek Ksawery Branicki, opportunistically joined the opposition to prevent further erosion of his office's power. Opposition plans failed when Ambassador Stackelberg permitted Poniatowski to organize the 1776 parliamentary session as a confederation so that the *liberum veto* would be suspended and opponents could be excluded. Parliament approved minor improvements in the power of the Permanent Council, giving the council full control over the army and restoring the king's power to make military appointments. It also appointed ex-Chancellor Andrzej Zamoyski as head of a new law commission that would introduce reforms in the guise of codification.

Russia desired tranquillity in Poland rather than additional reform and permitted no new significant initiatives after this. International politics played a part in that decision. Austria supported the Czartoryskis and Lubomirskis, who owned estates in Austrian Galicia as well as in the Commonwealth, in order to force Russia to join future military campaigns against Turkey. To mollify these oppositional leaders, Stackelberg refused to allow Stanisław August to confederate parliamentary sessions in 1778, 1780, 1782, 1784, and 1786; they reached successful conclusions by avoiding contentious issues. Poniatowski feared to introduce Zamoyski's reformist law code at the 1778 parliament and opponents shouted down efforts to discuss it in 1780. The draft law code attempted to strengthen municipal jurisdiction over noble and clerical properties within city limits, and reintroduce city representatives to parliament, if only to present their ideas. It would have made Jews subject to municipalities and expelled indigent Jews from the Commonwealth. The proposed code divided the peasantry into two groups: feudal peasants who remained subject to nobles and rent-paying peasants who could appeal their contracts to royal courts and leave their farms at the expiration of their contracts. Clerical decisions could no longer have been appealed to Rome had the code passed. In 1782, the opposition complained vehemently about the confinement of Kajetan Sołtyk, bishop of Cracow, who had become insane, primarily because the king appointed his own brother, Bishop Michał Poniatowski, to administer the bishopric's vast estates and use the revenues to finance the king's political activities. Poniatowski also granted wealthy offices and estates to his unusually capable nephews, Stanisław and Józef Poniatowski; Józef later became a marshal in Napoleon's army. The 1786 parliamentary session was wasted on false accusations by Ignacy Potocki and Adam Czartoryski against the king's closest advisers for allegedly plotting to poison Prince Adam.

The Permanent Council and the king's agents carried on constructive work behind the scenes. Poniatowski built a reliable network of diplomatic agents throughout Europe who kept him well informed about international developments. General Jan Komarzewski, the king's adjutant-general, made some progress in modernizing the Polish and Lithuanian armies by purchasing new muskets and introducing new infantry tactics. Infantry and artillery replaced ill-armed, ill-disciplined national cavalry units as much as possible, although budget problems prevented the combined armies from reaching even the ludicrously low statutory limit of 24,000 men; in fact, the army did not even reach 20,000 men. Military administration improved and the army could be called upon to enforce court decrees. On the civilian front, the Polish-Lithuanian state exercised greater administrative control over cities, not without objections from some self-governing cities. The crown treasury collected taxes more efficiently, and a new treasury police helped implement new taxes and tariffs.

THE RUSSO-TURKISH WAR AND THE GREAT PARLIAMENT

The imminent outbreak of another war between Russia and Turkey in 1787 broke the stalemate between Poniatowski and the opposition, and produced a major overhaul of Polish institutions. Unable to leave Polish-Lithuanian soil without parliament's permission, Poniatowski waited at Kaniv, near Kiev, to pay court to Catherine II during her triumphal tour of the Dnieper regions lately absorbed into the Russian Empire. His political opponents traveled a few miles further to attend her at greater leisure in Kiev. Count Potemkin, Catherine's governor in the region, conducted the tour and showed both real accomplishments and pseudo accomplishments that gave rise to the term "Potemkin villages." Poniatowski proposed to join Russia and Austria in the imminent Turkish war by raising an expeditionary corps at Russia's expense and receiving Moldavia as a reward. He asked permission to confederate the 1788 parliamentary session to quiet the opposition, which tried to convince Catherine that they would make better allies in Poland-Lithuania and, by raising noble cavalry regiments, in the field against the Turks. The empress, who met Poniatowski for the first time since 1758 on the imperial barge anchored in the Dnieper River between the two countries, accepted a minimal version of Poniatowski's offer, in order to to prevent political agitation at the 1788 parliamentary session. She agreed to confederate parliament to enact an alliance and raise some new troops, but she declined to offer any immediate cash subsidy, rejected all constitutional reforms, and refused to allow Poland-Lithuanian any territorial awards at Turkey's expense.

THE FIRST PHASE OF THE GREAT PARLIAMENT, 1788–90

The confederated parliamentary session (Great Parliament, Four Year Parliament) began in October 1788. Despite Stackelberg's and Poniatowski's electoral preparations, the opposition showed unusual strength. Calling themselves Patriots to imply that Poniatowski was a Russian hireling, Prince Adam Czartoryski and others dressed in Polish caftans at political gatherings in the provinces instead of their usual knee breeches and jackets, and commissioned literary works on patriotic themes. They turned for support to Prussia, which felt threatened by the Russo-Austrian alliance. One week after parliament began, Prussian deputy Ludwig Büchholtz (soon replaced by Girolomo Lucchesini) formally protested against the proposed Russo-Polish treaty on the spurious grounds that it was aimed against Prussia. Prussia voluntarily withdrew its guarantee of the 1768 Fundamental Laws, opening the door to constitutional reform and an increase in the size of the Polish-Lithuanian army. Russia voluntarily abandoned the proposed alliance before the matter came to a vote, but the newly assertive Polish parliament rubbed salt in Russia's wounds by demanding that Russia withdraw its troops from Right Bank Ukraine. Russian compliance hampered communications with troops in the Balkans throughout the war.

Prussian support and Russian withdrawal allowed the opposition to take control of parliament and enact significant political changes. It abolished the Military Department of the Permanent Council on the grounds that it was a tsarist imposition, returning control to the parliamentary Military Commission. Then, in January 1789, it abolished the entire Permanent Council. On March 29, 1790,

Prussia and Poland-Lithuania concluded a military alliance in which the two countries promised to come to each other's aid if attacked. Prussia's aim was to build an international alliance with Poland-Lithuania, Great Britain, and the Netherlands to fight another war with Austria and acquire Gdańsk and Toruń from Poland while Poland regained Galicia from Austria. The alliance lost its meaning when Prusso-Austrian disputes were solved peaceably in July 1790 and the Polish parliament declared that it would never cede Gdańsk and Toruń. Opposition leaders Prince Adam Czartoryski and Ignacy Potocki had agreed in principle to the cession as the price of regaining independence from Russia, but most deputies refused categorically.

Opposition leaders helped gain control of parliament by proposing enlargement of the Polish-Lithuanian army to 100,000, four times the Russian-inspired legal limit; even royalists agreed enthusiastically and the act passed in November 1788. Nobles patriotically agreed to pay a 10 percent tax, euphemistically called a "voluntary contribution," from their own revenues. They also imposed a 20 percent annual "voluntary contribution" in lieu of taxes on the clergy, appropriating the vast estates of the recently vacated Cracow bishopric and allocated only 100,000 zlotys annually for the next bishop. Parliament used the additional funds to increase the army from 25,000 soldiers in 1788, to 56,000 in 1791, and 65,000 in 1792. Members of the opposition clashed over whether the new army would consist of well-armed infantry with artillery and engineering support as in other European armies, or ill-armed, ill-trained noble cavalry according to Polish tradition. The progressive and conservative factions compromised on a 50-50 split; the heavy expense of setting up modern regiments also played a role. Professionally trained officers returned from foreign armies and from premature retirement to take up commissions.

Cities entered the political equation with the Black Procession of November 23, 1789. Inspired by noble reformers, Jan Dekert, mayor of Warsaw, invited representatives from all incorporated cities of the Polish-Lithuanian Commonwealth to gather in Warsaw and prepare a petition to parliament. In response, 294 representatives from 141 cities joined in; only Cracow stood on its dignity as the old capital and submitted a separate, more conservative, petition. The burghers marched in formal black attire from the Warsaw City Hall to the Royal Castle to present their petition to the king and parliamentary officials. The document, edited by Hugo Kołłątaj, reforming rector of the Jagiellonian University and political publicist, requested the creation of a house of burgesses in parliament, full control over noble properties and Jewish residences in and around cities, freedom from arrest without due process, the right to buy landed estates (allegedly for manufacturing), and abolition of supervision by royal governors. Despite the burghers' respectful presentation and moderate demands based on old legal precedents, some parliamentary deputies interpreted their activism as an extension of French Revolutionary violence and threatened military counteraction—or hid. However, the majority saw the need for social change and established a parliamentary commission to draft a reform bill. As an interim measure, parliament ennobled several hundred prominent burghers from the army, city governments, business, and education, either to reward them for their achievements or to separate them from their constituents. The burghers' petition and parliament's sympathetic reception prompted Jews, who feared that they would lose their trading rights, to send representatives to Warsaw to present their own ideas for change. Jewish groups received support from some nobles as well.

Parliament began to plan the total renovation of the anachronistic Polish-Lithuanian constitution. In September 1789, parliament established a Deputation to Draft Proposals on the Form of Government. As head of the commission, Ignacy Potocki set out "Principles to Improve the Form of Government" in December 1789, mostly aimed at giving parliament supremacy over royalty, although he also showed some interest in improving the status of commoners. A more complete draft in August 1790 took the radical step of proposing to make the throne hereditary in the Saxon (Wettin) line after the death of childless Stanisław August and to give the Saxon kings, instead of parliament, the power to appoint high officials. It also lifted widely ignored prohibitions against the purchase of landed estates and military commissions by burghers.

The Second Phase of the Great Parliament, 1790–92

As the deputies' term in office drew to a close after two years of unprecedented activity, parliament broke with past practice to enact a law prolonging its mandate for another two years, thereby maintaining the confederation that had suspended the *liberum veto,* and simultaneously called elections for a second set of deputies to join them in a doubled parliament. Both republican and royalist reformers did well as candidates to parliament in the dietine elections that preceded the next parliamentary session, although the proposals for an hereditary throne proved unpopular. Conservative Patriots such as Szczęsny Potocki and Seweryn Rzewuski broke with their former colleagues who supported the hereditary throne.

Reform-minded Patriots formed a surprising alliance with King Stanisław August Poniatowski, who was ably assisted by Hugo Kołłątaj and his Italian secretary, Scippione Piattoli. After several months of secret discussions, the two groups joined forces to pass a law on dietines on March 24, 1791. The new statute stripped landless nobles, about half of the nobility, of political rights, and left them freemen who might work as free peasants or apply for city citizenship. Although the new law decreased the number of voters by half and disenfranchised families who later showed their patriotic merit in nineteenth-century insurrections, the measures were needed to separate great magnates from their dependent followers and restore democracy to the countryside, and ultimately to parliament.

A Law on Cities passed on April 18, 1791, redefining the rights of incorporated royal cities; it did not apply to the large number of private cities on noble and clerical properties that contained more than half of the Polish-Lithuanian urban population. The law offered burghers significant gains for which they felt deeply grateful, even though the gains fell far short of equal citizenship. Noble and clerical properties within cities became subject to municipal law, and burghers gained full legal protection, the right to buy landed estates, greater access to state offices, and freedom from supervision by regional state officials. It provided cities with some parliamentary representation by creating twenty-four parliamentary "plenipotentiaries" authorized to discuss urban issues in parliament and giving them seats on the three commissions (Treasury, Police, and Courts) that governed urban affairs. However, plenipotentiaries were not full parliamentary deputies and could speak only to burgher issues before parliament. Burgher improvements threatened their business rivals, the Jews, who lost noble and clerical protection and became subject to municipal authorities without gaining the right to take part in municipal politics themselves.

The Constitution of May 3, 1791

The reforming coalition worked in strict secrecy to prepare a new constitution that was enacted on May 3, 1791, by a kind of coup d'état. Reform leaders quietly notified favorable parliamentarians to return early from Easter recess. After preliminary rallies, 182 of 504 deputies and senators attended parliament on May 3. Army units commanded by the king's nephew, Prince Józef Poniatowski, surrounded the Royal Palace where parliament met, while thousands of burghers put pressure on opposition deputies by lining the streets and shouting their approval for the proposed constitution. Citing the pressing demands of international affairs, parliament's leaders ignored parliamentary procedure and enacted the new constitution by acclamation without distributing it to the deputies in print as required by law or discussing it in detail. One hundred ten voted in favor of the Constitution of May 3, 1791. Seventy-two voted against.

The final document had been edited and reedited by Ignacy Potocki, Hugo Kołłątaj, and King Stanisław August Poniatowski to reconcile conflicting republican and royalist elements. The Constitution abolished the *liberum veto* and reaffirmed that parliament could meet at any time and for any length within its two-year mandate. A cabinet (Guardian of the Laws/Straż Praw) chaired by the king and composed of the primate, marshal of parliament, and five ministers (police, chancellery, foreign affairs, war, and treasury) appointed by the king exercised executive authority. Decisions required the signature of both the king and any minister, regardless of jurisdiction. Parliament held both legislative power and a measure of executive authority, blurring the lines of authority. As before, the king made legislative proposals to 204 parliamentary deputies sitting in the lower house along with 24 nonvoting city plenipotentiaries. The chamber of deputies could also initiate legislation; its decisions on important political, legal, and financial issues were limited only by a suspensive veto from the 132-man senate. The two houses met together to vote on lesser matters. In addition, parliament could dismiss ministers by two-thirds vote and try them for abuses of power before a parliamentary court. Since the cabinet was seen as a stronghold of royal power, the Constitution checked it by limiting the king's patronage powers and granting the parliamentary marshal the power to call parliament into session. The chamber of deputies exercised executive functions through the parliamentary commissions, chaired by ministers who were not members of the cabinet. The constitution reaffirmed previous legislation disenfranchising landless nobles and granting burghers limited political rights. Peasant contracts with landlords became enforceable in state courts. The Constitution also abolished Lithuanian autonomy and centralized the Polish-Lithuanian state.

Controversial in its inception, the Constitution of May 3 became the most celebrated single document in Polish history and acquired the same significance to later generations as the near-contemporary American Declaration of Independence and the French Declaration of the Rights of Man. While future generations acknowledged the Constitution's limitations, particularly its failure to abolish serfdom, they saw in it proof that Poland was capable of reform and was worthy of statehood in the modern world. The Second Republic (1919–39) celebrated the anniversary of the May 3 Constitution as a national holiday, as does post-Communist Poland. Many Polish cities named major streets May 3 Boulevard, although the Communists frequently renamed them May 1 Boulevard to celebrate socialism. Polish émigré communities make May 3 the focus of their activities.

Stripped of patriotic rhetoric, the Constitution replaced the unworkable constitution that had evolved in the seventeenth and eighteenth centuries with a reasonably efficient constitutional monarchy in which parliament would have gained supremacy over Stanisław August Poniatowski's successors. Checks and balances in the system might have made it prone to gridlock, but the abolition of the *liberum veto* and the diminution of authority of ministers with lifetime tenure meant that the new system could not be completely paralyzed. Social progress was less definitive, but it was significant. Burghers moved several steps closer to full citizenship, and gestures, at least, were made toward the peasantry. Further legislation was intended to round out the new system. Reformers planned to change the anomalous status of Polish-Lithuanian Jews. A so-called Economic Constitution was supposed to create a national bank and give peasants more autonomy.

The New Constitutional Regime

The Constitution came into effect immediately upon passage of the constitutional bill of May 3, 1791, and lasted until the Targowica Confederation superseded its authority on July 14, 1792. The May 3 Constitution's not completely legal adoption gained a mixed reception, and the new regime worked hard to increase its popularity. City governments supported it without reservation and were encouraged to organize festivities in its honor; their Jewish competitors imitated them. Poland's first political club, the Society of Friends of the Constitution, consisting of 214 members, mostly parliamentary deputies, took the case for reform to the nobility. Club statutes established equal membership regardless of social origin, and some prominent Warsaw burghers also joined. As in French Revolutionary clubs and modern political parties, members pledged themselves to support positions adopted by majority vote. Dietines met in February 1792 and most swore allegiance to the Constitution. No dietine even protested the provision making the throne hereditary. Moderate legislation, friendliness to opponents, and lavish distribution of patronage won over many potential antagonists. Stationing army units near dietine meeting places ensured that opponents could not mobilize their armed followers; the army did not intervene to force acceptance of the government position.

The governing coalition of Royalists and Patriots passed new legislation limiting the effectiveness of the May 3 Constitution in order to mollify opponents. Parliament gained greater power to oversee and overrule the executive, since new laws required weighted majorities of two-thirds and three-quarters to carry a wide variety of political and fiscal matters, instead of a simple majority. Dietines gained the power to appoint senators, instead of future kings. Leasehold prices for crown land, intended to become an important source of state revenue after reform, were set so high that only rich nobles could bid for them; past abuses were ignored. Nobles successfully avoided full subordination of their urban properties in municipal jurisdictions and continued to disregard guild monopolies. No Jewish reform bill passed, because insufficient common ground was established among competing interest groups.

Lithuanian Identity in 1791

Separatist rhetoric faded in Lithuania throughout the eighteenth century, but autonomist sentiment remained. Lithuanian dietines objected strenuously to the proposed Zamoyski law code which would have supplanted the Third Lithuanian

Statute. Several dietines protested that the 1569 Union of Lublin had guaranteed Lithuania's use of its own law code. The dietines attacked Polish interference in Lithuanian affairs rather than the contents of the Zamoyski code.

Lithuanian assertiveness forced the authors of the May 3 Constitution to abandon plans to unify Lithuania with Poland fully. The Constitution had abolished Lithuanian autonomy, uniting the Lithuanian and crown armies and treasuries, and merging the separate ministries of chancellor and marshal. Lithuanian deputies led by Kazimierz Nestor Sapieha, Lithuanian marshal of the confederated Great Parliament, forced passage of an act entitled "Mutual Obligation of Both Nations" in October 1791 that reasserted the federal nature of the state. Concretely, the act reestablished a separate Lithuanian treasury headed by its own treasurer as part of a national treasury, and ensured that Lithuanian tax money would remain at home. Popular sentiment for the Grand Duchy's autonomy prompted Lithuanian deputies to insist on establishing a separate commission to draft a new law code, instead of joining the commission of the Polish crown provinces. The desire to maintain Lithuanian autonomy contributed to the active role in the Targowica Confederation played by some Polish-speaking Lithuanian nobles.

THE ISSUE OF JEWISH EMANCIPATION, 1788–92

Conservative and progressive elements mixed strangely to debate the future path of the Jewish community. Some Christian progressives and a few Jewish progressives judged that only coercive measures would force the Jewish community to abandon autonomy and accept integration. Most Jews rejected forced acculturation and worked to expand their commercial opportunities with the support of Polish nobles who disliked and distrusted the increasingly assertive Polish burghers. Anti-Semites, especially burghers, favored restricting Jewish activities without offering any new opportunities. Resolving the issue took on increasing importance as several thousand Jews settled in Warsaw during the exceptionally long life of the Great Parliament, and Christian guild members reacted with a violent anti-Jewish riot in 1790. Throughout the four-year sitting of parliament, city representatives worked to uphold and extend urban privileges that restricted competition from nonmembers, including Jews. The Jews of Poland-Lithuania took an active role in pushing for reform legislation. Individuals published pamphlets in Jewish, Polish, and western languages advocating various kinds of reform legislation. In late 1791, Jewish communities across the Commonwealth sent more than a hundred representatives to Warsaw to prepare the final reform legislation that they expected parliament to enact. Their spokesmen reached agreement with the king's secretary, Piattoli.

As the matter came before parliament, a reformist committee proposed granting Jews citizenship and allowing them to reside anywhere in the country with full economic and political rights. However, Jews would have to adopt Polish dress, language, and customs, give up their communal government, and place their schools under the jurisdiction of the National Education Committee. Influenced by Jewish promises to pay his large debts, King Stanisław August Poniatowski expressed his willingness to grant Jews equal rights without requiring their acculturation. Vice-Chancellor Hugo Kołłątaj attempted to square the circle and introduced a bill on the last day of the Great Parliament that granted Jews only limited residential rights in previously forbidden cities, but opponents shouted him down. The Prussians and Austrians abolished Jewish autonomy after the Third Partition, and the Russians abolished it in 1844.

The Russo-Polish War and the Second Partition

Some opponents of the new regime could not be mollified. Count Szczęsny Potocki and Hetman Seweryn Rzewuski traveled to Kiev to conspire with Potemkin and, after his death, went to St. Petersburg. Hetman Branicki joined them there and together they reached an agreement with Empress Catherine II to overthrow the new regime. An act, signed in St. Petersburg on April 27, 1792, but released on May 14 at the border town of Targowica, annulled legislation of the Great Parliament, including the Constitution of May 3, on the grounds that it violated the Fundamental Laws of 1768. The Targowica Confederation claimed to be the lawful authority and called on Polish nobles to join. In fact, the success of this confederation depended entirely on Russian armed might, which Catherine provided to restore her control over Poland-Lithuania and to keep the spirit of the French Revolution, with which she identified moderate Polish reform, far from her borders.

The Polish army, which had grown to 65,000 men in 1791–92, faced 97,000 Russian troops who crossed the border on May 18. In Ukraine, Prince Józef Poniatowski's 17,000- man army stood against 64,000 Russian troops, while 14,000 Polish and Lithuanian troops faced 33,000 Russians in Lithuania. The Russian armies were more modern, too. Following standard European military practice, Russian infantry outnumbered cavalry 3:1, while the Polish-Lithuanian proportion was 1:1. Polish and Lithuanian forces fought well and won a number of minor victories, but the weight and experience of the Russian army ceaselessly pushed them back. The inexperienced Prince Józef Poniatowski and the veteran of the American Revolutionary War, Tadeusz Kościuszko, won the first victories for Commonwealth forces in decades.

King Stanisław August Poniatowski, the supreme commander of the Polish-Lithuanian army, never believed in the possibility of military victory despite brave public promises to fight to the end, and he regarded the war as an armed demonstration to improve his negotiating position with Catherine. Poniatowski immediately opened discussions with Russian ambassador Jakob Bulgakov offering to make Catherine's son, the Grand Duke Constantine, heir to the Polish-Lithuanian throne under the May 3 Constitution. Catherine rejected the offer and demanded that Poniatowski join the Targowica Confederation. The majority of the Polish cabinet agreed on July 24, hoping that negotiations could continue, and Poniatowski acceded, telling the army to lay down its arms. Some military leaders such as Józef Poniatowski and Tadeusz Kościuszko, and some political leaders such as Ignacy Potocki and Adam Czartoryski, emigrated rather than capitulate. Targowica rejected Hugo Kołłątaj's application to join, seeing him as a dangerous radical.

Prussia, which renounced the Polish alliance on the grounds that the May 3 Constitution violated the Prussian guarantee of 1773, abandoned its war against Revolutionary France and signed an agreement with Russia in January 1793 to intervene. In the Second Partition, Prussia took 58,000 square kilometers of territory including Great Poland, Gdańsk, and Toruń, while Russia took 250,000 square kilometers in Ukraine and Belarus. Austria continued to fight France and missed taking a share in the Second Partition. The Partition violated Catherine's promise to the Targowica leaders, and Potocki, Rzewuski, and Branicki resigned their positions. This left the leadership to Russian dependents such as Lithuanian Hetman Szymon Kossakowski, a Russian general.

Parliament convened under duress in Grodno, Lithuania, in June 1793, and deliberated until November. Deputies resisted passively until the Russian army surrounded the parliament building, arrested leading opponents, and forced ratification of the Second Partition. The Grodno parliament annulled the May 3 Constitution, but Russia allowed some modest reforms. Royalists reestablished the Permanent Council, provided qualified majorities to decide some issues while restoring the *liberum veto* on constitutional questions, and changed the procedures to have special sessions of an enlarged parliament elect new kings instead of mass gatherings of Polish-Lithuanian nobles. Burghers retained personal freedoms but lost their political role. Compared to the constitutional system before the Four Year Parliament, Grodno represented progress. Compared to the May 3 Constitution, Grodno represented a major step back.

THE 1794 INSURRECTION

Émigrés gathered in Dresden to plot an insurrection and chose General Tadeusz Kościuszko as commander, supporting his policy of mobilizing able-bodied men from all social classes as in the American and French Revolutions. Kościuszko had far more wartime experience than other Polish officers as a result of his service in American Revolutionary armies, where he displayed outstanding talent as a military engineer by building field fortifications at the crucial battle of Saratoga (1777) and permanent fortifications at West Point. He had enjoyed minor battlefield success in 1792 at Dubienka against the Russians. Kościuszko was also politically more suitable than the king's nephew, General Józef Poniatowski, his superior officer, who chose to sit out the 1794 Insurrection anyway. Kościuszko visited Poland secretly in September 1793 and postponed the insurrection until better preparations could be made.

The 1794 Insurrection began in March when General Antoni Madaliński refused orders to disband his cavalry unit. When the Russian garrison left Cracow in pursuit, Kościuszko appeared and proclaimed a revolutionary government on March 24. He took command of local forces and raised several thousand additional soldiers by calling a military levy. Kościuszko defeated a Russian column at Racławice on April 4, thanks to an heroic last minute charge by peasants armed with scythes, but he could not fight his way to Warsaw until Polish troops and Warsaw guilds revolted on April 17 and 18, expelling the Russian garrison.

To underline the break with all previous governments, Kościuszko was declared a dictator, but by prearrangement he shared power with the Supreme National Council headed by Ignacy Potocki and Hugo Kołłątaj in Warsaw. To spur enlistment and to promote social justice, Kościuszko took the radical step of abolishing personal serfdom and reducing labor obligations by 50 to 75 percent; an armed peasantry would not easily be refeudalized afterwards. The Połaniec Decree of May 7 formalized these initial steps for the duration of the insurrection and guaranteed the peasants' right to till the land they worked under serfdom. Kościuszko encountered substantial resistance from nobles when he tried to ensure that they paid their taxes without passing the burden on to the peasantry. Warsaw radicals, headed by some of Kołłątaj's former associates, demanded intensification of the insurrection and broke into Warsaw's prisons on the night of May 8–9 to hang four Targowica leaders after an appearance before an improvised revolutionary court. Prussian troops intervened, defeated Kościuszko at Szczekociny with Russian help, and took Cracow on June 15. As they approached Warsaw in early July, the Polish army, bolstered by guild recruits and even a small detachment of Jewish cavalry, offered steadfast resistance. The siege was relieved by the outbreak of the insurrection in Great Poland, which forced the Prussians to withdraw in haste but not before another Warsaw crowd hanged several more Targowica leaders on June 28 and threatened a general insurrection. Kościuszko sent troops into Warsaw to arrest about a thousand participants and restored control by the insurrectionary authorities.

Kościuszko went down to defeat against overwhelming Russian force. Russia introduced new units when the Russo-Turkish War ended and Turkey declared neutrality in the Polish uprising. Kościuszko was defeated, wounded, and captured at the battle of Maciejowice on October 10, 1794. General Alexander Suvorov captured Praga on the east bank of the Vistula River (now part of Warsaw), on November 4 after a short siege, looted the largely Jewish suburb, and slaughtered several hundred civilians. Insurrectionary authorities left Warsaw and the remainder of the army pulled out, effectively ending the struggle.

Lithuanians took an active part in the 1794 Insurrection and displayed more social radicalism than their Polish counterparts. Conspirators drove the Russian garrison out of Vilnius on April 22–23 and hanged Hetman Kossakowski. The insurrectionary Lithuanian Supreme National Council called on Lithuanians from all social strata to rise up to achieve equal citizenship and even published an appeal in the Lithuanian language. The insurrectionary *Vilnius National Gazette* praised French Jacobins and their policies. As national commander in chief, Kościuszko transferred the radical Lithuanian commander, Jakub Jasiński, to a command near Warsaw and installed a more moderate government, the Central Deputation of the Grand Duchy of Lithuania. Peasants in the Grand Duchy maintained their radical spirit, refusing to perform feudal obligations and attacking manor houses. The Russian army took Vilnius on August 11 and Lithuanian armies retreated to join Kościuszko.

The Insurrection of 1794 accomplished much in its brief life. It gave the Commonwealth an opportunity to demonstrate political and military determination that had been lacking since Sobieski or even the Swedish War of 1655–57. At its height, the army reached about 70,000 men, and at least another 70,000 served as replacements and local militia. Appeals to townspeople and peasants, particularly promises of ending serfdom made in the Połaniec Decree, showed a social vision appropriate for the French Revolutionary era. These qualities captured the Polish imagination and made the 1794 Insurrection a potent legend for the nineteenth and twentieth centuries. Nevertheless, the odds were overwhelming and the inevitable failure led directly to the Third Partition, which ended the First Republic of the Polish-Lithuanian Commonwealth. The insurrection also played an important role in protecting the French Revolution by keeping Prussian and Austrian forces occupied. French Revolutionary leaders ignored appeals and diplomatic approaches from Kościuszko and refused to grant Poland-Lithuania financial assistance despite their common enemies.

THE THIRD PARTITION

Catherine II rejected appeals by all Polish leaders and refused to maintain a rump Polish-Lithuanian state as a buffer. Austria intervened militarily to prevent Prussia from taking southern Poland. Austria, Prussia, and Russia agreed to divide up what was left. Austria acquired the rest of Little Poland and domination over the newly created Free City of Cracow, which it finally annexed in 1846. Prussia took Warsaw, the rest of Great Poland, and Mazovia. Russia took the rest of Ukraine, Belarus, and Lithuania. Stanisław August Poniatowski abdicated on November 25, 1795. He died on February 12, 1797, as a prisoner-pensioner in St. Petersburg.

CHAPTER 18

Economics and Society in the Eighteenth Century

Poland-Lithuania took more than half a century to recover from the extraordinary devastation caused by seventy years of warfare in the late seventeenth and early eighteenth centuries. The slow pace of recovery was dictated by unfavorable economic trends. While poorer nobles, peasants, and burghers stagnated at a low level of economic activity, new forces sprang from the concentration of wealth in the hands of magnate elite and the expansion of metropolitan areas surrounding the older, decaying cities, leading eventually to a revival in agriculture and manufacturing in the second half of the century.

WARTIME DEVASTATION

Wars and civil wars raged across the Commonwealth from 1648 to 1715, devastating the economy as armies marched across fields, laid siege to cities, confiscated goods, stole livestock, requisitioned food, and levied contributions—often violently. Famine and epidemics accompanied war and occupation. The population of the Commonwealth, allowing for loss of territory, decreased by 30 percent from 1650 to 1720. The area under cultivation decreased by half across the Commonwealth, and peasant landholdings declined in size. Grain production declined by almost two-thirds immediately after the Swedish War of 1655–57. Western Poland recovered quickly, but parts of Mazovia remained only half settled in the mid-eighteenth century and parts of Galicia (Sanok region) remained up to 75 percent unsettled. Marauding soldiers targeted royal estates during the Great Northern War of the early 1700s. Cities suffered as badly. About 60 percent of urban Great Poland was destroyed, and other regions were also hit hard. Governments levied taxes harshly and arbitrarily throughout the period in order to pay military expenses. The currency was debased.

The Commonwealth recovered from wartime destruction slowly, because unfavorable structural changes had occurred in the Polish-Lithuanian economy.

Grain exports averaged only about 20,000 tons from 1660 to 1760, although they exceeded 100,000 tons in a few years, since competition from western European and Russian grain as well as American rice weakened demand in western Europe. Domestic demand for grain, meat, skins, and butter also declined. Wartime destruction in cities lowered the burghers' ability to buy textiles, clothing, shoes, bricks, and iron. Production declined.

The Grand Duchy of Lithuania suffered even more than the Kingdom of Poland. Much of the Grand Duchy lost 30 to 40 percent of its population, more from hunger, disease, and flight than from direct military action. In 1718, a special decree tried to stem the exodus by forbidding peasants to leave noble estates under any circumstances. Lithuanian peasants retreated from border regions, including Vilnius itself, where Lithuanian-language preaching at the Church of St. John ceased in 1737.

ECONOMIC STAGNATION AND RECOVERY

When peace finally came, landlords rebuilt their estates by replacing farm animals, equipment, and buildings when they had cash or access to credit. They relied on serf labor to perform most of the work except when the serfs were too poor to supply the customary farm equipment, and then the landlords paid cash. The peasants had a harder time rebuilding their farms, since almost none had money and they fell into greater dependence on landlords. The technical level of production declined. Peasants often had to share draft animals and even plows, forcing them to cultivate their land less efficiently. They also lacked fertilizer. Peasants harvested less than three grains for every one sown and, of these, one had to be saved for seed. Livestock inventory declined, and slower oxen replaced horses as primary draft animals because they cost less to maintain. On the estates of the archbishop of Gniezno, peasant households generally owned six head of cattle and 1.3 horses in the first half of the seventeenth century, but only 4.1 cattle and 0.5 horses in 1685. They undoubtedly owned even fewer after the Great Northern War of 1698–1721. Millponds could rarely be restored, and mills worked less effectively in the lazy flow of Poland-Lithuania's slow-moving streams.

Milling and other manor monopolies replaced the free market that had characterized village economies in the sixteenth and early seventeenth centuries. Landlords took up the liquor trade to replace falling grain sales and found that it could contribute as much as 50 percent of manor revenues in the late seventeenth century. Typically, a landlord employed professional brewers, often Jews, as leaseholders and granted them a monopoly within a given village but required them to purchase his grain to make beer. They also forced peasants to buy specified quantities of liquor, to keep them from buying on the open market or brewing their own. Village taverns also sold salt, herring, and metal products that peasants had previously bought in towns and cities. Peasants had to supply new products to the manor as feudal dues, including textiles and wood products, and were also obliged to sell grain, flax, and fowl to the manor, which resold them at higher prices.

Farming methods improved in the later eighteenth century. A German immigrant, Wawrzyniec Mitzler de Koloff, published a series of articles in 1758–61 reporting recent improvements in stock breeding and cultivation techniques, the first round of an ongoing discussion in print aimed at stimulating technical and administrative innovations. About 85 books on agriculture appeared between 1765 and 1795, more than had been published in 1650–1765. The prolific scientific writer Father Krzysztof Kluk published *Necessary and Useful Plants* in 1777–79, a four-volume study of *Domestic and Wild Animals* in 1779–80, and a *Plant Dictionary* in 1786–88, as well as several textbooks for school use.

Some of Kluk's recommendations found their way into practice on the estates of enterprising magnates. New plows, hoes, and harrows with iron parts worked more effectively. Scythes gradually replaced sickles, and simple machines separated grain from chaff. Farmers used more fertilizer and plowed more carefully. The multifield system replaced the three-field system, and, less frequently, farmers introduced full crop rotation with nitrogen-fixing crops such as clover and alfalfa to replenish the soil. Dutch cattle and other new breeds improved milk production, and merino sheep furnished more wool than older varieties. However, only the richest landlords could afford such improvements and overall yields remained low. Peasants grew more industrial crops such as rapeseed, flax, buckwheat, and peas. Cultivation of potatoes began in the late eighteenth century in western Poland, mostly for personal use. Magnate latifundia improved management. A central office often directed the network of estates and drafted detailed instruction for local officials. Bookkeeping was improved. Work was better organized and duties equalized. Some estates parceled out the land among the peasants in exchange for monetary rent.

Recovery in Lithuania and the Ukrainian Lands

Economic recovery in Lithuania began around 1730. The population doubled over the next sixty years, reaching 1.3 million in 1790, 15 percent of the Commonwealth's population. Vilnius had over 20,000 residents but city dwellers made up only 13 percent of Lithuania's largely rural population. Grain exports rose rapidly after 1750, encouraging landowners to cultivate more land and increase peasant feudal work obligations. For example, Lithuanian Vice-Treasurer Antoni Tyzenhauz raised peasant obligations and burgher rents on royal estates sharply and used the profits to control Lithuanian politics for the king.

When numerous petitions brought no relief, a young schoolteacher of noble origin led 300 armed peasants near Šiauliai (Szawle) in 1769 to seize the crown lands on which they worked and restore the former level of feudal obligations. The Lithuanian army retook the area with Russian help and executed the rebel leaders. Tyzenhauz also launched an ambitious industrialization project near Grodno that employed over 1,300 workers in twenty-two factories at its height in 1780. These enterprises were not economically viable, however, and collapsed when Tyzenhauz could no longer provide subsidies.

Ukrainian lands had to be reorganized and recolonized following decades of invasion and civil war. After the partition of Ukrainian lands between Poland-Lithuania and Russia in 1667, almost all nobles in Right Bank territories adopted Roman Catholicism and Polish culture, while the Greek Catholic (Uniate) Church and Cossacks helped keep a separate Ruthenian consciousness alive among commoners. Cossack officers continued to provide a focus of revolt against Polish nobles and the Catholic Church, although the decline of Cossack regiments within the Polish-Lithuanian army marginalized them and deprived them of political focus. Cossack revolts degenerated into banditry as the eighteenth century progressed.

The state distributed crown lands in Volhynia, Podolia, Bratslav, and Kiev provinces to magnate families who settled their latifundia with peasants from other estates and attracted new peasants with reduced obligations. After a long grace period, nobles reimposed labor dues in the northern areas where good transportation made cash markets available and collected monetary rent in the less accessible southern areas. As elsewhere in the Commonwealth, Ukrainian cities revived very slowly from wartime devastation. Trade and industry (mostly service to noble and peasant agriculture) concentrated in villages and towns on nobles' private estates. Once again, nobles invited Jews to settle on their estates as leaseholders, business managers, traders, and artisans. With support from Polish nobles and the state, the Greek Catholic Church gradually replaced the Orthodox Church and took over most of its congregants.

PEASANT AGRICULTURE

Agriculture continued on a market basis in Royal Prussia and in adjacent areas of Great Poland, Kujawy, Kurpie, and Mazovia as well as the distant Carpathian foothills. In 1719, for example, the city of Poznań introduced monetary rents on its farmlands with great success due to the ready market for agricultural produce. Other cities also rented vacant lands to peasants. The percentage of rent-paying peasants increased steadily throughout the eighteenth century, reaching 85 percent by the 1760s on some estates. Monetary rent suited landlords far more than peasants where the market conditions were poor, as in parts of Ukraine, Belarus, and Lithuania. Sometimes peasant resistance to feudal labor service inclined nobles to institute monetary rent. A few landless nobles rented land and worked it themselves. Jews who rented or leased village inns and mills added to the free village population. Renting often coexisted with feudal practices such as liquor and other monopolies based on sales to local peasants. Inns become general stores.

In other regions of Poland-Lithuania, most peasants worked the land as serfs under somewhat worsening conditions. The lack of cash meant that they could no longer commute their labor obligations into cash payments or hire help to carry out those obligations, which probably increased slightly to an average of four days for a peasant with a full or half allotment. Peasants who had provided less than average labor dues were forced up to the norm. On a noble estate in Great Poland, a yeoman had to send his hired worker(s) to work five to eight man-days a week with draft animals and equipment. Poorer peasants sent family members, including children, to work in the fields to make up for their lack of animals and equipment. Clerical estates might require one day less, and royal estates two days less. Labor obligations were sometimes measured by piecework, rather than time, and might encompass tasks such as clearing fishponds, shearing sheep, and repairing roads. Peasants often had to transport their landlords' beer and other products as much as 50 to 100 miles, without pay, or stand guard over the landlord's fields and woods. Families wove cloth, made baskets, cut wood, and performed numerous other petty services. Peasants on royal estates also paid a new tax to support the army through the winter. While peasants found paying the tax preferable to quartering soldiers in their homes, military detachments collected the tax directly and sometimes abused their authority. The multiplicity of obligations tied peasants more closely to the manor and made it difficult, even for landless peasants, to leave. Taxes probably made peasants reluctant to improve their properties for fear of increasing their obligations. They raised poultry and sheep instead of cattle and cultivated garden vegetables instead of grain. In addition, the improving international grain market after 1750 encouraged landlords to reinstate labor dues in many regions.

Eighteenth-century publicists devoted extensive attention to peasant issues for a mixture of humanitarian and economic reasons. Progressive authors such as the ex-king, Stanisław Leszczyński, and the future vice-chancellor, Hugo Kołłątaj, advocated replacing feudal labor with monetary rents. They also wanted serfs recognized as full legal persons whose rights and obligations would be determined by state courts instead of feudal justice. Chancellor Andrzej Zamoyski introduced monetary rents on his estates in 1765, but the peasants failed to earn enough cash and asked him to reestablish labor dues. In 1769, Prince Paweł Brzostowski successfully introduced monetary rents and granted peasants full ownership of their buildings. Several leading magnates followed his example. Chancellor Zamoyski attempted to write some of these reforms into his proposed law code in 1778. The Constitution of May 3, 1791, made peasant-landlord contracts enforceable in court. Tadeusz Kościuszko went much further during the 1794 Insurrection. His Połaniec Decree accorded peasants legal freedoms and reduced their labor obligations by almost one-half for the duration of the fighting.

Peasants resisted economic pressure in a variety of ways. Royal peasants could appeal adverse decisions by local officials to the referendary court, a procedure that Church estates and some magnates imitated. Since serfs had no legal means of appealing against a ruling by their masters, discontented peasants resisted passively by working poorly on manorial land and using inferior draft animals. Unusually bad economic conditions, particularly in wartime, or harsh treatment by bailiffs prompted peasants to flee to other estates that offered better terms. The poorest peasants made up about 50 percent of the escapees. Other peasants fled to cities and joined the urban poor, or fled abroad.

Armed resistance broke out from time to time, although Poland-Lithuania did not experience major serf rebellions outside the Ukrainian lands. Still, several thousand peasants rose up at different times in ethnically Polish districts such as the Carpathians, Great Poland, and Kurpie. Numerous lesser revolts and local demonstrations occurred in response to changes in feudal dues, usually involving several hundred peasants from a single village. Banditry was endemic in mountain and forest regions, so nearby landlords had to treat their serfs well. However, the bandits robbed from the poor as well as the rich.

In addition to feudal dues, peasants paid taxes to church and state. The taxes were often collected in kind due to lack of cash.

Rich and Poor Nobles

As a result of economic stagnation, land passed out of the control of poor nobles and into the hands of magnates who had greater access to credit for restoring productivity. In Wieluń, for example, petty nobles held 34 percent of the noble villages in the mid-sixteenth century but only 8 percent in the late eighteenth. Conversely, nobles with multiple villages increased their holdings from 39 percent to 71 percent of total land in the same period. Credit was crucial to maintaining landownership. In the early seventeenth century, magnates had borrowed from gentry, while in the late seventeenth and early eighteenth centuries gentry borrowed from magnates and declined from independent landholders into leaseholders. Some magnates, notably in Galicia, offered credit to peasants at nominal rates.

Great noble families such as the Radziwiłłs, Sapiehas, Potockis, and Czartoryskis towered over their neighbors at this time. Administering their estates bureaucratically, they employed landless nobles as secretaries, bailiffs, and soldiers. They lent money to poorer nobles, used their influence on local officeholders, and formed private military detachments to control their estates. In return, their noble employees and other dependents offered political support at dietines that enabled magnates to achieve prominence and gain valuable patronage appointments.

Magnates stimulated economic activity. Their residences provided a market for luxury goods such as cloth, silks, colonial products, and wine as well as a market for everyday goods and services for themselves, their dependents, and their numerous employees. The construction and renovation of impressive palaces on estates scattered throughout the Commonwealth stimulated business activity. Magnate armies and other retainers bought uniforms, arms, and other supplies. In addition, many churches were built or rebuilt; in Cracow, for example, twenty-two churches were rebuilt in 1661–90.

Warsaw was the single most important center of the construction industry, providing many jobs and mobilizing financial resources. The Krasiński Palace went up in 1677–99 along with a new real estate development near the royal palace called Marywil (Marie-Ville) in 1691–95, and Saxon army barracks. Numerous magnate palaces were built at the end of the seventeenth century, such as the Potocki Palace on Senator Street (Ulica Senatorska) and the Radziwiłł Palace on Krakowskie Przedmieście. Reconstructions included the Kazimierz Palace (now Warsaw University). The late Saxon period between 1740 and 1760 proved particularly busy as the Saxon Theater, Załuski Library, and Collegium Nobilium were erected, among other buildings.

Incorporated Royal Cities

Cities suffered even greater devastation from wars than the countryside. Many suffered direct damage during sieges, including spoliation of the suburbs and surrounding countryside; all were subjected to levies, requisitions, and loss of trade. Warsaw, Poznań, and Cracow lost about 50 percent of their population in seventeenth-century wars; some smaller cities such as Inowrocław and Leszno were completely destroyed. Oświęcim declined from 500 to 20 houses and from 200 to 6 artisans. Mazovian cities, one-third of which were burned during the fighting, lost 60 to 70 percent of their population, most of whom took refuge in nearby villages. Cities such as Cracow and Poznań also lost heavily in early eighteenth-century fighting as they changed hands and suffered numerous requisitions. Plague killed almost half the population. Even Gdańsk, which the Swedes never captured, lost its prosperity due to the interruption of the Vistula trade, and one-quarter of its population died, mostly from plague.

While Warsaw and Gdańsk recovered fairly quickly, most royal cities stagnated as manufacturing and trade shifted to private cities and villages. Royal cities saw a decline in the number of artisans and guilds. In Cracow, the number of taxpayers declined by 62 percent in 1646–1720 and still had not recovered fully by 1760. Guild masters cut costs by lowering the wages and allowances (especially food) for apprentices and journeymen, as well as restricting promotion to master status.

In order to keep themselves afloat in hard times, city dwellers rented and farmed undeveloped lands owned by the municipality, or moved to smaller cities and villages. Many city dwellers, particularly in smaller centers, worked part-time at their professions and part-time on the land. Part-time town artisans supplied village needs, undermining full-time services in larger cities. The same was true for petty merchants, who settled in small towns to compete with the traditional Jewish and Scottish peddlers to supply needles, knives, ribbons, and other petty goods to peasants. Some Jews settled permanently in villages, especially tavernkeepers on noble estates.

Suburbs and the Development of Metropolitan Areas

Economic development increasingly took place in suburbs that surrounded stagnant or even declining royal cities. Nobles and clerics developed their properties in and around cities, leasing shops to Jews and other individuals who worked for less money or used cheaper and more efficient production methods than guild members. Warsaw saw the number of noble properties increase from twelve to eighteen in the eighteenth century. Most notably, Crown Great Marshal Franciszek Bieliński founded Bielino in 1757 as a self-governing private city subject to his authority. Its main streets, Świętokrzyska (Holy Cross) and Marszałkowska (Marshal) streets, met in the center of today's Warsaw. Toward the Vistula River, elite residential neighborhoods developed, such as Mariensztat (Mary's City) near the Royal Palace and Stanisławów, King Stanisław August Poniatowski's own development. The king later exchanged these with the city of Warsaw for unimproved grounds on which he built his elegant summer palace, Łazieńki, with its man-made lake, theater, and conservatory. He also donated the Kazimierz Palace, now the site of Warsaw University, to the state for use as the new Cadet School. Greater Warsaw also expanded to the west (Wola), north (Żoliborz from "jolie bord"), and east (Praga) across the Vistula River with noble palaces, shops, and industry. Nobles and clerics developed the Vistula River floodplain for industrial uses. Poor artisans and domestic servants threw up wooden shacks and workshops near river shipyards, docks, warehouses, mills, tanneries, and breweries. The incorporated city of New Warsaw opened its agricultural lands to development and doubled its population. Only the Old City stagnated.

Warsaw's population climbed rapidly from about 24,000 in 1754 (although this figure is probably too low because it includes only incorporated areas) to

63,000 in 1784 (Greater Warsaw, somewhat unsystematically), to 110,000 in 1792 (Greater Warsaw). During the 1794 Insurrection, the presence of the army and refugees swelled the size of the population to 150,000. Greater Warsaw's population included many recent immigrants, as indicated by the greater number of men than women. Many Germans settled in Warsaw as artisans, merchants, and professionals, and German names outnumbered Polish names in 28 of 35 Warsaw guilds in 1791, but their number included many polonized descendants of earlier immigrants. A French colony composed of tutors, artists, artisans, merchants, and professionals maintained itself. Smaller numbers of Italians, Greeks, Hungarians, and polonized Armenians could be seen as well.

Some Warsaw burghers took advantage of this growth to acquire great fortunes as bankers, merchants dealing in luxury goods, and, occasionally, manufacturers. Most of this new elite, the first concentrated burgher elite since the Renaissance, was ennobled in 1790. Piotr Tepper, a Lutheran, built a palace in 1763 on ul. Miodowa (Honey Street), an elegant avenue near the Old City where the richest magnates lived, and later gained permission to buy three suburban landed estates. His nephew and heir, Piotr Tepper Fergusson, continued banking and established a luxury department store nearby. He also acted as one of King Stanisław August Poniatowski's financial agents, founded an import-export agency at the Black Sea port of Kherson, furnished supplies to the Russian army, and co-managed the state lottery. He built his own palace near the Old City and several in the countryside. The collapse of his business in 1793, when foreign bankers refused credit to Poles because the Partitions made them poor risks, led to a national banking crisis. Piotr Blank, a French immigrant, bought suburban and rural palaces with monies acquired through banking, leasing the tobacco monopoly, and co-managing the state lottery.

Jews provided many of the new immigrants. Formally excluded from residing in the Old City of Warsaw except during parliamentary sessions, Jews settled in nearby noble and clerical properties when the province of Mazovia annulled its ban on Jewish settlement in 1768 and did business in the Old City on day passes. By 1792, the Jewish population probably exceeded 10,000 persons or 10 percent of the city's population. Most were artisans, storekeepers, peddlers, and workmen, although a small elite of bankers, industrialists, and professionals also existed. Shmuel Zbytkower was their informal leader, since he was the most important of numerous royal "servitors" whose business was exempt from guild regulations. Zbytkower made a great deal of money from the cattle trade (transport, slaughter, tanning) and enjoyed lucrative contracts with the royal court, the Polish state, and foreign armies. King Stanisław August Poniatowski sold Zbytkower the long-term rights to develop part of Praga, enabling him to set up milling operations and breweries as well as permitting him to build a palatial home. Similarly, Prince August Sułkowski invited so many Jewish artisans and merchants to one of his nearby suburban properties that it became known as New Jerusalem in the early 1770s. The Warsaw city government prevented this development from taking root, but the name survives in modern Warsaw's Jerusalem Boulevard (Aleje Jerozolimskie).

Cracow also grew outside its legally recognized boundaries. The population of the medieval city shrank slightly from 10,200 in 1699 to 9,872 in 1791, but greater Cracow grew to almost 25,000 inhabitants. Much of the population lived in seventeen satellite properties owned by clergymen, nobles, and even the City of Cracow itself. More artisans than merchants lived there.

Polish nobles recognized the need for metropolitan area institutions before the burghers, who wanted to protect their local privileges. The crown marshal had jurisdiction over the Warsaw area because the king lived there and he made urban planning decisions including development, markets, and police. Marshal Bieliński established the Paving Commission in 1740 and built streets to link separate settlements into one metropolitan area. The 1765 parliament created noble Commissions of Good Order to clean up the finances of burgher-run cities that suffered badly from confusion, mismanagement, and corruption. The Warsaw Commission of Good Order forced a union of Old and New Warsaw, but left the noble-owned suburban properties untouched. Parliament soon established commissions for Lviv, Cracow, Poznań, and Wschowa. City governments recognized their common interests for the first time in 1789 when the Warsaw city government, urged by progressive noble politicians, organized a joint petition to parliament with 140 other cities. The Urban Act of 1791 unified most incorporated cities with their suburban areas, made noble residents into city citizens, and gave cities limited representation in parliament.

PRIVATE CITIES: THE KEY TO NOBLE ENTERPRISES

The growing number of private cities in the eighteenth century testifies to the growth of economic activity in the Commonwealth as a whole. Private cities comprised 66 percent of all cities in the Polish provinces (88 percent in Ukrainian provinces), but most were small. As in previous centuries, private cities functioned as income-producing real estate developments for wealthy nobles and clerics. They provided marketplaces for agricultural produce and industrial goods such as agricultural implements and clothing. Liquor production and sale were also concentrated there. Noble landlords took a cut of all economic transfers in the form of taxes, license fees, and lease payments. Better landlords took care to ensure the prosperity of their client city dwellers with fair treatment. More than half of the merchants in private cities were Jewish, and they developed a symbiotic relationship with their noble patrons.

Like other magnates (as well as lesser nobles), Elżbieta Sieniawska dealt extensively with Jewish merchants from her private cities and employed many Jewish agents to look after her personal economic interests. The operations of the Sieniawski-Czartoryski estates, particularly in Podolia, provide a good example of private city operations throughout the Commonwealth. In the early eighteenth century, Elżbieta Sieniawska (née Lubomirska) personally managed her family's vast estates, including more than twenty private cities that enjoyed self-governing rights subject to appeal to herself, as owner. She kept a close eye on her cities, including Shklov (Szkłów), Puławy, and Medzhybizh (Międzybóż), encouraging settlement and protecting market operations. When necessary, she lent money to town merchants to set up their businesses or to recover from fires and natural disasters. Sieniawska's employees handled the large-scale export of agricultural goods from her estates as well as business operations within her estates.

Sieniawska used her merchants as a buffer between her economic enterprise and the vagaries of the marketplace, particularly in the grain trade. Only magnates like her had the resources to build fleets of grain barges and send them to Gdańsk. She permitted local merchants to rent space on them for their smaller quantities of produce and to bring supplies for the local market. These cash payments tipped the balance between profit and loss for Sieniawska's annual grain trade. Merchants in her cities also provided an alternative market for noble-produced grain when low prices or wartime dislocation made sale to Gdańsk imprudent. On occasion, Sieniawska required them to purchase surplus grain, salt, poultry, fish, livestock, cloth, lime, saltpeter, and liquor. In turn, the merchants had to find local outlets or take the risks of selling them in distant markets.

A minority of private cities took part in national and international trade links. The Lubomirskis and Sanguszkos owned the private city of Opatów (Apt), 125 miles southeast of Warsaw, throughout the eighteenth century. In addition to providing regional services, merchants from Opatów traveled regularly to Germany and Silesia to sell textiles and furs, and to purchase luxury goods for the magnate court. Opatów merchants also traded extensively with Russia through the merchants of the private border cities Shklov and Brody. Financial records indicate that some merchants operated on as large a scale as better-known merchants in major cities.

The Revival of Domestic and International Trade

Foreign trade and mining revived slowly in the eighteenth century. Early in the century, Polish-Lithuanian trade suffered from the Great Northern War and the development of St. Petersburg, which took over the export of Russian forest products, skins, and furs that had previously transited through Poland-Lithuania. The

Swedish, Cossack, and Turkish wars interrupted the transit trade with the Black Sea as well. Grain exports improved after 1720, and other aspects of international trade revived in the second half of the eighteenth century despite Prussia's control over the Vistula and Silesia. After the First Partition gave Prussia a stranglehold on the lower Vistula, it levied prohibitive transit tolls in order to reroute Polish exports to Prussia. Scandinavia replaced western Europe as the Commonwealth's major customer for grain after Lithuania developed the port of Palanga. Poland also increased exports along land routes to Bohemia and Austria, and pressed southeast to reach the Black Sea port of Kherson. Despite difficulties, exports improved sufficiently to give Poland-Lithuania a positive balance of trade. The low point of grain exports through Gdańsk came in 1715 (4,800 tons), but the peak figures of 1768 (114,000 tons) and 1770 (124,000 tons) equaled the best times of earlier centuries. The grain trade flourished during the years of the Great Parliament of 1788–92. Forest products and linen cloth also contributed to export earnings.

Communications improved throughout the Commonwealth and assisted the growth of trade. The Ogiński Canal linked the Dnieper and the Niemen. Designed to convey products to the Baltic, it also served to transport grain to the Black Sea after the First Partition. The Royal Canal linked the Vistula and the Dnieper basins, also aiding exports to the Black Sea in the 1780s and 1790s. Portions of rivers were dredged and regulated to ship heavy goods such as grain and iron. In 1764, all internal tariffs and duties were abolished, and uniform weights and measures adopted. Large regional markets facilitated internal distribution such as the sale of textiles from Great Poland to cities in Little Poland. Agriculturalists in Little Poland depended heavily on importing iron agricultural implements from Styria, Hungary, and Moravia, as well as raw steel that Cracow manufacturers used for their products. Northern sections of the Commonwealth depended more on Swedish ironware imported through Gdańsk, which also imported ore for manufacturing. Trade links between the Grand Duchy of Lithuania and Poland remained weak.

Silesian mining declined sharply under the impact of eighteenth-century wars, and the transit trade across Poland fell correspondingly. Copper, lead, and silver mines suffered wartime destruction, and iron mines in the Old Polish Basin reached the limit of profitable exploitation with available technology. Refining did considerably better, particularly in the late seventeenth century when Jan III Sobieski subsidized munitions manufactures. Mining and refining revived in the mid-eighteenth century and became profitable on the lands of ecclesiastic and noble lords. Jacek Jezierski, later the castellan of Łuków, owned several refining ovens and manufactured agricultural implements. The salt mines in Wieliczka and Bochnia retained their importance.

The Magnate-Jewish Symbiosis in Poland-Lithuania

Jews had come to Poland in the late Middle Ages and early modern times under royal protection and had worked extensively for the Polish-Lithuanian state, but that long tradition came to an end in the eighteenth century as the Saxon monarchs employed German Jews as their business agents while the state gradually adopted more bureaucratic procedures and employed poor nobles. Luckily for Jewish merchants, Polish and Lithuanian nobles made up the slack by deepening their reliance on Jewish agents.

At the end of the seventeenth century, King Jan Sobieski used Jewish financiers to administer Polish-Lithuanian state revenues as well as his personal wealth. He assigned the collection of all royal tariffs in Podolia and Ukraine, more than 500,000 zlotys annually, to Jacob Bezalel ben Nathan. How much he kept for himself is unknown. At times, Bezalel also collected royal tariffs in Lithuania and Little Poland and, in turn, sublet collection to numerous Jewish subcontractors. He hired a private guard of thirty soldiers to protect himself against angry taxpayers. Sobieski made Jezue Moszkowicz his prime agent for exporting raw materials such as forest products from the royal estates. However, Sobieski's Saxon successors turned more to German court Jews (Hofjude) such as Berend Lehmann of Saxony and Samuel Oppenheimer of Vienna. Foreign Jews financed the revival of the Polish export trade starting in the 1660s, when Marx Schlesinger of Vienna exported zinc, copper, saltpeter, and powder. Other Austrian and German Jews joined in the trade. Salt and military supplies (munitions, food, and clothing) were popular export items. However, at the end of the eighteenth century, King Stanisław August Poniatowski turned to local Jews such as Shmuel Zbytkower to supply to his court and the Polish-Lithuanian army; Zbytkower also provided supplies to the Russian and Prussian armies as well as to foreign diplomats in Warsaw.

Most, perhaps all, Polish magnates resembled Sobieski in employing Jewish agents with numerous Jewish subagents to administer their vast wealth. Elżbieta Sieniawska provides the best documented example. She employed Yisrael Rubinowicz for four decades as general manager (*ekonom*) on her western estates because she usually resided on estates east of the Vistula that she managed herself. While reporting regularly to Sieniawska, Rubinowicz collected rents and taxes from her estates, made and administered contracts with nobles, townspeople, and peasants, and intervened with local authorities in her name. He derived sufficient income as her agent and from his own business enterprises, which frequently piggybacked on hers, to buy a landed estate and live like a midrank noble who owned three to five villages. His wealth made Rubinowicz a figure to be reckoned with in local Jewish politics. Sieniawska also used another Jew, Moses Fortis, as her personal physician and business agent who purchased luxury goods such as gems for her and conducted land negotiations when he was called to minister to other great nobles across the Commonwealth.

The career of Shmuel Itsakowicz (Samuel ben Isaac) as estate manager for Anna Radziwiłł and her son, Hieronim Florian Radziwiłł, between about 1720 and 1745 resembles Rubinowicz's relationship with Sieniawska. The major difference was that after more than twenty-five years of service, Itsakowicz found himself accused of and eventually confessed to defrauding his employers of 6 million zlotys, more than the entire state budget for most years during the Saxon dynasty. He signed his entire fortune over to Radziwiłł to stay out of jail. Lesser nobles also employed Jews as their business agents even while some attempted to introduce special taxes on Jews or bar Jewish leaseholding outright. Johann Joseph Kausch, an eighteenth-century traveler to Poland-Lithuania, reported seeing a constant threesome of a noble, his Roman Catholic chaplain, and his Jewish business agent. While this may be an extreme example, such groupings symbolized the spiritual and material world of the Polish nobility.

Royal and "Private" Jewish Urban Settlements

Many Jews, especially the rich, emigrated to Germany, the Netherlands, Italy, and Turkey to escape the mid-seventeenth-century Cossack uprising and Swedish wars. Others, including poorer Jews, moved west and north within the Commonwealth. Both groups lost most of their savings, making it difficult to continue business operations. Formerly rich merchants left war-torn cities and settled in villages that offered only limited opportunities. Structural changes affecting the entire Polish-Lithuanian economy, particularly the decline of grain and forest product exports, contributed further to impoverishing the Jewish population. Competing for declining opportunities, Christian burghers worked harder to exclude Jews from living and working in cities, although, as in the past, nobles often protected individual Jews or whole communities. As business opportunities revived in the 1670s, Jewish merchants traveled regularly to markets and fairs in Silesia and eastern Germany. The liquor trade, which depended on licenses and monopolies from cities and nobles, took on great importance in Jewish economic life. Podolia and the Ukrainian region revived quickly when Cossack rebellions and the Polish-Lithuanian part of the Great Northern War ended around 1710.

Private cities often overtook incorporated cities as the centers of business activity. The largely Jewish city of Leszno (Lissa), founded by the Leszczyńskis and later sold to the Sułkowski family, replaced Poznań as the center of Great Poland trade. Leszno specialized in importing cloth and skins from Silesia and Saxony, and selling them to both Jewish and Christian merchants throughout the Commonwealth for domestic use or export to the east. Leszno merchants also handled silks, spices, wool, cotton, and metal goods. Similarly, Jan Sobieski settled Jews in his private cities, especially Żółkiew (Zholkva) near Lviv, giving them tax relief for ten years and other concessions. Sobieski also developed his private city of Brody as a center for the Turkish trade, including the manufacture and sale of Turkish-style embroideries and metalwork. In 1704, Sobieski's heirs sold Brody to the Potockis, who helped it develop further. After major fires in 1742 and 1753, Crown Hetman Józef Potocki invested 1 million zlotys at 7 percent yearly in the Jewish merchants. This exceptionally large sum allowed them to travel as far as England and Russia to trade on world markets. Under the Czartoryski owners, the modest city of Medzhybizh in Podolia increased 50 percent between 1720 and 1740 and reached a size of about 5,000 persons, one-third of them Jews.

Noble and clerical owners took an active role in managing their Jewish populations in person and through their agents. They confirmed the appointment of Jewish civic officials, including rabbis, and provided a court of appeal for both Jewish and Christian municipal courts. Owners heard petitions from individuals who complained that the communal authorities mistreated them. For example, a poor Jewish shopkeeper in Medzhybizh complained that he had been assessed the same amount of tax as international merchants, and the Jewish butchers' guild complained that the Jewish communal authorities had confiscated their newly refurbished synagogue and turned it over to the tailors' guild. The resolution of these cases was not noted.

Jewish guilds gained official recognition from the Jewish community and sometimes from Christian city governments as well. Communal representatives generally sat on guild boards and helped establish their regulations. Jewish guilds often resented communal restrictions and tried to free themselves by appealing to Christian political authorities; in Berdychiv (Berdyczów), for example, the Jewish tailors' guild successfully appealed for relief to the city's noble owner in 1732. More commonly, the communal authorities asserted control over the guilds and enacted restrictive regulations limiting membership, in one typical case, to married applicants who had apprenticed for three years and worked as a journeyman for one year; three years probationary membership was required. Elections to guild councils were indirect. Guilds were most common in the clothing trades and kosher butchering, although they also existed in the building trades and music. Tailors and furriers, grouped into numerous subspecialties, made up more than half the Jewish artisans.

Although widespread, Jewish guilds were few in number and small in size. Consequently, many Jews failed to gain the economic security that membership provided or found themselves confined to journeyman status. Failed masters, journeymen, and free-lance artisans worked on their own, facing opposition from both Jewish and Christian guilds in securing raw materials, renting workplaces, and marketing goods. These independent artisans tried to cut costs and undersell their guild competitors by lowering their overhead, accepting lower wages, or even selling lower-quality goods that the poor could afford to buy—hence the contemptuous term "bunglers" (*partacze*) applied by Christian competitors. The lowest category of Jewish workmen consisted of intermediaries who roamed the streets and markets looking for customers and offering to take them to a good shop or provide other services for a fee. Most Jews lived close to the margin of existence. Leaseholders usually controlled only a small facility such as a single mill, inn, or customhouse and collected only enough money to get through the day. In about 1750, 39 percent of all Jews lived in small villages as petty innkeepers.

General improvements in the Polish-Lithuanian economy permitted Jews to better their situation after 1764. The number of Jewish merchants traveling to German fairs increased dramatically. Many of the goods destined for the Russian and Turkish markets were exchanged in the Ukrainian city of Berdychiv. Jews also exported grain, wool, skins, honey, and horses. Part of the revival of the grain trade, which also had the effect of raising domestic prices, originated in the activity of Jewish merchants who opened overland exports to Russia, Galicia, and Germany. Hides were often shipped to Prussian manufacturers. The trade in horses primarily comprised sales to the military forces of neighboring countries. Richer merchants such as Shmuel Zbytkover also lent money to the Polish-Lithuanian state and to King Stanisław August Poniatowski. Jewish artisans supplied goods for export, such as the tailors who prepared ready-made clothing for sale in Russia. In Great Poland, hundreds of Jewish women did fine lacework and embroidery on order from Prussian merchants.

In contrast, the Jewish role in the liquor trade declined. Deepening peasant poverty and the revival of the grain trade made nobles reduce this element in their local economy. Humanitarians interested in peasant welfare blamed Jews, the immediate sales agents, for peasant drinking, and some Jewish writers also urged their fellow countrymen to find other occupations. After the 1768 Haidamak massacres, the Polish parliament and several dietines restricted Jewish tavern ownership, and some magnates stripped Jews of tavern leaseholds. More than half of the inns and taverns passed from Jewish to Christian hands in the Kiev and Bratslav palatinates in 1778–84 alone; a lesser change probably occurred in other parts of the Commonwealth. Some of the dispossessed Jews found alternative employment in petty manufacturing. Numerous clothing and munitions factories were founded by Jews after 1785. Efforts to settle

Jews on the land as farmers were unsuccessful, however. Many Jews could not find work in the changing economy and became beggars or vagrants, attracting unfavorable attention of the police and hostile publicists.

Communal Debt and the Decline of Jewish Communal Government

Internal decay and outside attack caused the effectiveness of Jewish self-governing institutions to decline. While poor business conditions reduced income, Jewish communities faced the need to assist refugees from the mid-seventeenth-century wars and reestablish communal services such as hospitals, cemeteries, synagogues, schools, and aid to widows and orphans. Communal authority was increasingly divided among central cities, which declined, and successful new towns or cities that magnates developed on their land. For example, the Lviv Jewish communal authorities lost political and taxing authority over the Sobieskis' city, Żółkiew, which had formerly been a satellite.

The same phenomenon occurred on a broader scale as the previously subordinate regions within the Four Lands refused to accept established authorities and insisted on separate representation. The General Council found it increasingly difficult to allocate taxation. Similarly, the quality of the council officials declined as political maneuvering replaced careful scrutiny of qualifications as the basis of selection. Ideological divisions within the Jewish community, such as Shabbateanism and Hasidism, further challenged political cooperation.

The Council of the Four Lands found itself in continual financial difficulty as it paid significantly higher taxes to the state, bribes to officials, and social assistance benefits to the Jewish poor. Communal and central Jewish authorities raised taxes to unprecedented levels and added new consumption taxes. They borrowed extensively from richer monastic orders such as the Jesuits, Franciscans, and Bernardins, as well as from nobles.

Jewish communities across the Commonwealth accumulated huge debts without increasing productivity. Starting in the sixteenth century, nobles and clerics had invested surplus capital with individual Jewish businessmen and, if loans were not repaid, often collected from communal authorities. In the early seventeenth century, the Council of the Four Lands and the Lithuanian Council paid the debts of several Jewish communities and required that individual businessmen receive approval from communal authorities before contracting new loans from non-Jews. After 1650, in declining economic circumstances, the richer members of the community who dominated the communal authority monopolized credit and provided a 7 to 10 percent return to non-Jewish investors. Business opportunities increased more slowly than debts, and the elders often spent money on political lobbying, especially against ritual murder charges, instead of on economic investments. As a result, Jewish communities amassed millions of zlotys of debt by the mid-eighteenth century with little chance of repayment. Interest on the debt was paid through taxes on the community as a whole, including the artisans and poorer merchants who had no possibility of profiting from the credit. Class tensions grew rapidly.

The debt issue drew Christians into Jewish communal affairs. Complaints that communal funds and contracts for communal services were administered for the personal benefit of the governing elite became increasingly common in the eighteenth century, and, as in royal cities two hundred years earlier, protests and even riots by artisans and lesser merchants broke out. A few larger Jewish communes created the Tribunes of the People to supervise elections and finances, but they found it difficult to act for their constituents. For example, the Cracow tribune, Simon ben Zarach, and the Leszno tribune, Samuel ben Moses, were jailed by Christian authorities at the request of Jewish officials. Nevertheless, disadvantaged groups had greater success in convincing Polish authorities to roll back taxes and fees than they had in convincing the Jewish communal authorities.

State officials asserted greater control over Jews, who had previously enjoyed autonomy, for several reasons. First, it was easier for the state to apply centralizing methods to Jews than to nobles. Second, deepening concern about communal debts made some political leaders think of instituting closer supervision over Jewish financial affairs. Third, anti-Jewish attitudes, especially accusations of Jewish financial dishonesty, made Jewish tax autonomy seem less desirable. State treasury officials attended meetings of the regional and national Jewish councils in the eighteenth century and approved financial decisions; noble dietines and Christian city governments were not subject to the same controls. Unfortunately, the state officials often represented the private interests of rich creditors or extorted bribes from Jewish participants instead of doing their jobs conscientiously.

In 1729, the provincial dietine of Kujawy first demanded that the Jewish tax autonomy be abolished and reiterated the demand in 1736. The parliamentary sessions of 1746 and 1748 discussed this measure at length but took no action, in part because the deputies feared that Jews would emigrate. In 1764, the government of the new king, Stanisław August Poniatowski, abolished national Jewish autonomy and refused to recognize the Council of the Four Lands or the Lithuanian Council as representing the Commonwealth's Jews. The state took over administration of the Jewish poll tax, although as a practical matter some Jewish communities continued to act as tax collectors. The councils never met again.

A special parliamentary Liquidation Commission examined the debts of Jewish communal governments and concluded that they amounted to 2.5 million zlotys; 60 percent was owed to monastic orders and the remainder to nobles. Many Jewish communities had no immediate prospect of repaying.

Industrialization

Magnates took much of the initiative to industrialize Poland-Lithuania in order to reduce their outlays of scarce cash and for patriotic motives, such as improving the technical and industrial level of the Commonwealth, but their enterprises rarely turned a profit. Magnates founded factories to produce goods for their own courts ranging from luxuries (porcelain, glassware, silks, ornamental belts, and playing cards) to military goods (uniforms and small arms) and clothing for everyday use. They used unpaid serf labor to prepare buildings for production and haul materials, but hired free labor to operate the factories. Faced with a lack of willing workers, city administrations arrested vagrants and forced them to work. When there were not enough Christian beggars, Jewish community leaders could be asked to supply Jewish beggars. Needless to say, impressed laborers often worked poorly, since the pay was low and they were not accustomed to regular work discipline. Nevertheless, the work trained some supervisors and laid the basis for a future industrial working class. Few factories achieved economic viability because there was limited demand for luxury goods and because it was very expensive to hire western European technical experts. Impressive but unprofitable factories included the Radziwiłł glassworks, porcelain manufactures, clothing factories, and Potocki ornamental textiles.

In contrast, entrepreneurs made profits from food processing and textile manufacturing for the local market. Grain milling, brewing, and distilling took place in the countryside. Seed mills pressed flax, hemp, and rapeseed for oil as well. Nobles set up sawmills and brickyards to serve their estates and sell to nearby cities. Peasants produced textiles through the putting out system as part of their serf obligations or for small payments. They made coarse hemp linen for local use, and some flax linen was made too. Weaving became an important source of income for poorer peasants, particularly in the Carpathian foothills. Jewish merchants often financed cottage industries as an outgrowth of their wool marketing. Burghers formed partnerships, occasionally with nobles, as in the Company of Wool Manufacturing founded in 1767 and the Society of Domestic Linen Manufacturing in 1787, two firms that enjoyed royal endorsement. Credit facilities emerged, primarily operated by magnates; some burghers also lent money. A Warsaw burgher of Scottish origin, Piotr Tepper the elder, was the richest of six bankers who were ennobled in 1790. He also ran a store that sold luxury items, mostly imported, ranging from candelabras to carriages. His heir, Piotr Tepper Fergusson, owned a palace in Warsaw and lived in a showy, magnate style. He and several other leading burghers received special parliamentary permission to buy landed estates. Prot Potocki was the first banker from the nobility. Most of the banks collapsed in the Crash of 1793, following the Second Partition.

TAXATION AND CURRENCY

August II tried to restore central control over finances after the destruction and dislocation of the Great Northern War left tax collection in the hands of dietines and the army. In 1717, parliament broke with tradition by establishing regular taxation to support the army instead of relying on special levies. It also eliminated the practice that had developed over the previous half-century by which the army received its funds directly from dietines. These positive steps toward stability still left the Polish-Lithuanian treasury badly underfinanced, because tax levels were low, economic activity was slow, and privileged groups, chiefly nobles and clerics, remained largely untaxed.

Parliament enacted several new taxes at the start of Stanisław August Poniatowski's reign and collected them effectively. Revenues increased from 1.5 million zlotys in August II's last years to over 3 million in 1765 and kept climbing. Parliament enacted a new hearth tax in 1764 and increased the Jewish poll tax. The military "quarter tax" went up 25 percent and the wintering tax was commuted to a 50 percent surtax on the existing hearth tax. Alcohol taxes went up as did the Church's annual "voluntary contribution." A general customs duty was intended to bring in another 5 million zlotys, but Friedrich II of Prussia complained that the duties violated the Treaty of Wehlau of 1657 and started collecting his own duties from Polish boats on the Vistula. Poland-Lithuania had to withdraw the duty.

Another significant step in improving revenues came after the Great Parliament voted to raise a 100,000-man army. It required all clergy except poor rural parish priests to pay a 20 percent tax on revenues and confiscated the bishop of Cracow's vast estates, leaving him only a salary. Nobles accepted a 10 percent income tax (called a "voluntary offering"), although technicalities and passive resistance restricted the amount collected. A law passed late in the parliament applied the tax to crown estates. Other taxes paid by commoners also increased.

Lack of a stable currency hampered trade. The zloty declined in silver content by two-thirds in just six years (1659–65), and the mint turned out more copper shillings. The Saxon kings minted good money in Dresden and suspended operations in Warsaw, with the result that the country suffered from lack of specie. The issuance of new, high-quality coins after 1766 helped to reestablish price stability.

CHAPTER 19

Culture in the Eighteenth Century

The devastation of war and the xenophobic tendencies of Sarmatian distinctiveness left Poland-Lithuania a heritage of cultural isolation that was gradually overcome during the eighteenth century. Throughout the period, royal and magnate courts as well as Royal Prussian cities generally remained current with European trends, but in earlier decades they stood out like islands in a sea of increasing backwardness. At first, schools taught an obsolete curriculum while educators criticized new trends in western European thought. Popular works concentrated on saints' lives and political speeches in a literary language that mixed Polish with Latin phrases. Almanacs and encyclopedias such as Benedykt Chmielowski's midcentury opus, *The New Athens of the Academy of All Science*, presented astrological predictions along with accurate scientific information and repeated old superstitions. Early newspapers such as the *Polish Courier* (1729–74) provided political, social, and incidental information, although richer readers often preferred receiving handwritten newsletters that were tailored to their needs by professional editors.

As they emerged from decades of relative isolation after 1750, inhabitants of the Polish-Lithuanian state found the new dominant trend in European thought, Enlightenment, somewhat surprising. Polish art, music, literature, and philosophy adopted the new thought system with some sense of foreignness, particularly since the fundamental libertarian values of Polish public life differed from the primary value of greater efficiency that characterized other European countries, especially the Enlightened monarchies.

COMING OF THE ENLIGHTENMENT

While individuals throughout the Commonwealth displayed an interest in Enlightenment culture, the first phase of the Enlightenment in Poland-Lithuania concentrated in Royal Prussia where Gdańsk and Toruń formed part of the north

German cultural scene, exchanging schoolteachers and scientists with cities such as Lübeck and Hamburg. Gdańsk organized a literary society in 1720 and a society for natural science in 1742. The Gdańsk Academy, a higher school, also played an important role in expounding the ideas of the German Enlightenment. Astronomy, physics, chemistry, and other natural sciences attained European standards. Ethnic Poles were also involved. Inspired by his friend, Bishop Józef Załuski, Catholic bishop of Kiev, Rector Peter Jaenichen of the Toruń Gymnasium developed an interest in history and wrote several works on Prussia's place in the Polish-Lithuanian Commonwealth. Jeanichen introduced new courses on civil law, international law, medicine, physics, and modern languages to his school. Most Prussian teachers knew Polish and some of them published studies on Polish subjects, including Johann Daniel Hoffmann, who researched Polish etymology and the history of the Polish Reformation. The *Toruń Weekly News* published information on recent Polish books.

Ethnic German scholars from Royal Prussia maintained ties with the Polish interior and considered themselves part of the Polish-Lithuanian Commonwealth. The Gdańsk historian and lawyer Gottfried Lengnich (1689–1774) may be considered typical. Born into a merchant family in Gdańsk, his family sent him to Gniew to study Polish to prepare him to work in the family business. He finished his studies in Gdańsk and did so well that his family allowed him to continue in Halle. Lengnich returned to Gdańsk to take up an academic career, teaching and researching Gdańsk history. In 1718, he published *The Polish Library,* a historical study of early Prussian history criticizing the Teutonic Order and gaining him employment at the Gdańsk Athenaeum. Additional publications of medieval chronicles and other source material won him appointment as a member of the Imperial Academy of Sciences in St. Petersburg (1738). His appointment as Saxon royal councillor gave him a substantial salary of 1,200 thalers a year. Lengnich published a history of Poland in Leipzig in 1740 dedicated to Stanisław Poniatowski the elder. At the request of two leaders of the early Polish Enlightenment, Bishops Józef and Andrzej Stanisław Załuski, Lengnich researched and published his Latin-language book *Public Law of the Polish Realm,* in Gdańsk in 1742–46 (extended and republished 1765–66), which expounded a Prussian position favoring the Polish king and supporting freedoms based on law while criticizing the Polish-Lithuanian parliament for anarchic tendencies. The book quickly appeared in Polish translation (1761), and Polish schools adopted it as a text. The National Education Commission later prepared a textbook derived from Lengnich's original work.

German thought influenced the early Enlightenment in Warsaw and other Commonwealth cities. Serving as chancellor of the Jagiellonian University in Cracow, Bishop Andrzej Stanisław Załuski introduced the rationalist educational views of Christian Wolff but had less success in introducing courses in Polish law, natural law, mathematics, and physics. His brother, Bishop Józef Andrzej Załuski, opened the capital's first public library in Warsaw in 1747 with 300,000 books and 10,000 manuscripts. He died in 1771, leaving it to the state, which entrusted it to the National Education Commission in 1780. Russia commandeered the library after the Third Partition and took it to St. Petersburg, where it became the core of the Saltykov-Shchedrin Library. Bishop Józef Załuski also published the *Volumina Legum,* a complete collection of Polish laws, and tried to organize a scientific society. The German physician and musicologist Wawrzyniec Mitzler de Koloff came to Poland in 1743 to tutor the children of Jan Małachowski, later crown great chancellor. Moving to Warsaw in 1746, Mitzler de Koloff sought wealthy sponsors to organize a modern medical school in Warsaw. He gained royal assent but failed to raise adequate funds. Mitzler de Koloff published several short-lived scholarly journals in various languages on literary, economic, and scholarly subjects.

Educational Reform

Polish-language schooling began to modernize and expand during the reign of August III. The schools, which taught an outmoded curriculum unsuited to the Age of Enlightenment, needed a major overhaul. Furthermore, schooling left large sections of the population untouched. Virtually all peasants and poor nobles were illiterate along with almost half the burghers. Almost half of middle nobles and more than one-quarter of rich nobles lacked basic skills. Educational reform started at midcentury in schools for the elite and progressed downward slowly.

The Italian Theatine order opened the Collegium Varsaviense for rich nobles in 1737 along the lines of the Italian Knights' Academies to prepare nobles for careers in public service. The high school taught modern and classical languages, history, geography, and mathematics. Also in 1737, the émigré King Stanisław Leszczyński established his own Knights' Academy in Lunéville (Lorraine), which lasted until his death in 1776 and taught 564 students, including 167 Poles. Students took a three-year course in military and academic subjects, including modern languages, modern history, philosophy, law, physics, mathematics, and military architecture. Leszczyński educated the students without charge and found jobs in the French army for graduates. The most important new school was Piarist Father Stanisław Konarski's Noble Academy, which opened in Warsaw in 1740. Konarski had studied in Italy and France before returning to Poland to work for Bishop Józef Załuski on the publication of Poland's collected laws, and he assisted Stanisław Poniatowski the elder in formulating his reformist politics. Konarski's Noble Academy replaced a heavily Latin and classical curriculum with a program based on modern languages, modern history, and experimental science.

Latin was taught from Konarski's own short textbook. The elite student body also studied the history, politics, and geography of Poland-Lithuania at length from a program that advocated social and political reform. A student theater prepared one tragedy in Polish and one comedy in French each year for public presentation. Students visited the royal court and also magnate residences to prepare for careers in public life. Konarski's success won over reluctant Piarists, and other Piarist schools undertook reform in the same spirit after 1750.

The Jesuits imitated the Piarist innovations throughout their vast school system. They corrected the faults of their old system based on classical education in which relatively few students stayed long enough to achieve an adequate level of knowledge. Between 1749 and 1755, the Jesuits founded five new colleges that attracted a large number of students, especially in Warsaw. New Jesuit schools taught foreign languages (the number of schools teaching French increased from 40 in 1740 to 199 in 1777), and adopted new methods of teaching Latin. Franciszek Bohomolec, who taught rhetoric at the Jesuit academy in Warsaw, published a treatise in Latin advocating use of the Polish language and wrote Polish-language plays for student presentation. The Jesuits sent students to Vienna, Prague, and Paris to study science and mathematics, which gained a prominent place in the new curriculum. The Jesuit Vilnius Academy built an observatory in 1753 and taught modern astronomy. Jesuit cartographers prepared the first Polish atlas at King Stanisław August Poniatowski's request. The universities in Cracow and Vilnius changed more slowly due to faculty resistance.

Educational reform initiated under August III became dominant after 1764, with active sponsorship by King Stanisław August and reformist magnates. The king created his own Cadet School in Warsaw in 1765, entrusting the command to his cousin, Prince Adam Czartoryski. This partnership continued long after the two became political enemies. The Cadet School accepted poorer nobles who could not pay the high fees at noble academies, providing them with a four-year course in military studies (drill, mathematics, fortifications, drawing) and civilian studies (modern languages, Polish and other history, geography, philosophy). Students specialized in military preparation or chose law courses for work in the civil service. Polish became the language of instruction after the first few years when courses had to be offered in French and German for lack of trained Polish teachers. Czartoryski paid for much of the 10,000-volume library and collections of scientific equipment, minerals, and medals. Instructors prepared new textbooks and printed them in the school's print shop. Prince Adam Czartoryski wrote a Cadet Catechism, which spelled out his high ideals of public service and patriotism. The most famous graduate of the school was Tadeusz Kościuszko, and generals Jakub Jasiński, Karol Kniaziewicz, and Andrzej Mokronowski also studied there. Julian Ursyn Niemcewicz, soldier, novelist, and poet, attended. The curriculum adopted an openly reformist political program.

THE NATIONAL EDUCATION COMMISSION

The abolition of the Jesuit order by Pope Clement XIV in 1773 created an educational crisis in Poland because Jesuits ran more than two-thirds of Poland-Lithuania's schools, but it also presented an opportunity to modernize education further. The Partition Parliament rose to the occasion by creating the National Education Commission to operate the former Jesuit schools in 1773, although widespread corruption in the sale of Jesuit properties limited the finances and forced almost half of the Jesuit schools to close. The commission included many well-educated political leaders devoted to cultural and political reform, such as Ignacy Potocki, Adam Czartoryski, Andrzej Zamoyski, Bishop Michał Poniatowski, and, in later days, Julian Ursyn Niemcewicz, as well as prominent academics. King Stanisław August Poniatowski was deeply interested and met frequently with the commission, which hired a French physiocrat philosophe, Samuel Dupont de Nemours, as its first secretary. After 1775, ex-Jesuit Grzegorz Piramowicz replaced him and also served as secretary of the Society for Elementary Books.

The National Education Commission divided Poland-Lithuania into six departments (Great Poland, Little Poland, Mazovia, Rus/Ukraine, Lithuania, Belarus). In all, it governed sixty-four schools including thirty-eight former Jesuit schools, nineteen Piarist schools, and six Basilian schools, grouped into three academies, twenty-two provincial schools, and thirty-nine district schools. In the first years, 208 teachers were clerics, including 180 ex-Jesuits. The Piarist schools followed commission guidelines and directives, but they functioned under the direct supervision of the Piarist order as before. The commission sent regular inspectors to check the level of training of instructors, the curriculum, the educational materials, and the work of the students. School inspections indicated that teachers needed further training and students needed new textbooks. After 1780, lower schools came under the direction of the Jagiellonian and Vilnius Universities. By 1788, more secular teachers graduated from the universities and replaced clerics within the lower schools. Girls were included in educational plans, although they were expected to study in private schools for girls or with tutors.

The Society for Elementary Books prepared pedagogical works for the National Education Commission. The membership consisted primarily of professional educators who set out pedagogical methods and educational materials. New textbooks were prepared in such subjects as Latin, history, Polish grammar, moral science, botany, and zoology. The society could not find competent Polish authors to write textbooks in geography, chemistry, and farming.

University reform was needed as the capstone to the general school reform. Hugo Kołłątaj, a Cracow canon, was appointed rector of the Jagiellonian University in 1777 and instructed to modernize the school. He quickly put the school's finances in good order and reorganized the philosophy department as a school of analysis to prepare students for work in other fields as well. He introduced studies of the sciences, economy, and natural law as teacher training for the National Education Commission's schools. In 1782, the university was reorganized from four colleges (theology, medicine, law, and science) into two divisions—moral (theology, law, literature) and science (science, mathematics, medicine). Kołłątaj's secularizing reforms, including symbolic gestures such as wearing knee breeches instead of clerical robes, provoked strong opposition from conservative faculty members and Cracow clerics, who asked Rome to discipline him. Bishop Michał Poniatowski's support permitted Kołłątaj to continue his work and launched him on his meteoric political career during the Great Parliament. Feliks Oraczewski briefly succeeded Kołłątaj as rector, but he resigned after only three years (1787–90) when he failed to carry reform forward fast enough. The Vilnius Academy improved its scientific and medical facilities under the astronomer Marcin Poczobutt, who became rector in 1780, although the humanities faculty remained a stronghold of older clerics until the end of the century.

Lack of funds slowed the progress of the National Education Commission in organizing parish and other lower schooling. Bishop Ignacy Massalski energetically set up 300 parish schools in Lithuania, but the number fell to 252 after he left the commission in 1777. He organized a teachers' seminar at Vilnius University with thirty students who learned surveying, agriculture, and music. The much larger crown provinces of Poland were less receptive. They supported 175 parish schools in 1775 and 300 in 1791. In 1785, the National Education Commission published a textbook for parish schools with reading, writing, arithmetic, catechism, and customs (family life and patriotism), and a teacher's guide that instructed parish school teachers on their moral and pedagogical duties. The Great Parliament required each parish to support instruction in reading, writing, and arithmetic. In 1791, the commission appealed to Rome for permission to abolish monastic establishments and use the funds for schooling; the political crises of the Partitions freed Rome from the need to reply.

Despite its enormous service in saving Polish schooling from collapse, the National Education Commission was distrusted by many nobles who preferred clerical schooling. They were suspicious of secularization and feared that the schools would introduce free-thinking and free-living. Proposals to give the commission absolute power over all schools evoked an avalanche of criticism and contributed to the short-lived popularity of the Targowica government, which petitioned the Vatican to recreate the Society of Jesus to take over Polish schooling. The 1793 Grodno Parliament placed the National Education Commission under the supervision of a new government department and instructed it to abolish innovations. Monastic orders gained supervisory powers over schools, and teachers were forbidden to study abroad.

THE STANISLAVIAN AGE

Poniatowski's coronation as King Stanisław August brought such important new patronage to Enlightenment trends that the Stanislavian age is often seen as a distinct period in Polish cultural history. Like more powerful European monarchs of his day, Poniatowski saw culture as a way of convincing the educated and influential members of society of the need for reform. The king left a very strong mark on the Polish Enlightenment. He did not write himself, but he surrounded himself with writers, stimulated their output, and harnessed them to the education of society. The king initiated Thursday Dinners at the castle attended by leading authors, mostly nobles, and he proved a genial and informal host with a gift for encouraging lively and provocative discussion. At the dinners, writers presented excerpts from their recent works on a wide variety of personal, social, and political issues. French influence was marked, but native issues and native viewpoints were expressed.

JOURNALISM AND REFORM

The king helped establish *Monitor,* a weekly journal of mores and politics modeled after the English *Spectator.* The editor, Franciszek Bohomolec, set forth a balanced cultural and social criticism that criticized the old-fashioned Sarmatians for ignorance, social prejudice, and cupidity, while also ridiculing fops who dressed in the latest French fashions but had no understanding of French philosophy. Other articles proposed moderate peasant reform, stressing the moral need to treat peasants humanely, and argued for religious toleration. *Monitor* devoted considerable attention to purifying the Polish language by removing Latin survivals and French encroachments. Stanisław Kleczewski wrote "About the Beginning, Age, Changes, and Perfection of the Polish Language" in 1767. Franciszek Ksawery Dmochowski adapted Boileau's *L'Art poétique* into Polish, and the Piarist Father Onufry Kopczyński wrote a *Grammar for National Schools* for the National Education Commission. The Cracow Academy introduced philological studies in 1780, which became part of the Moral College of the Literary School. Bishop Ignacy Krasicki later served as editor of *Monitor,* and Mitzler de Koloff assisted. A second journal, *Pleasant and Useful Delightful Amusements,* achieved a more limited circulation. Edited by Father Jan Albertrandi and later by Bishop Adam Naruszewicz, it confined its pages to literary subjects. The journal published works by the king's literary circle in 1769–77. Several short-lived magazines concentrated on scientific, legal, and economic subjects.

Ex-Jesuit Stefan Łuskina's newspaper, the *Warsaw Gazette,* held a monopoly on newspaper publishing in the Kingdom of Poland that helped it to last from 1774 until 1791. The newspaper came out weekly and provided systematic news coverage to 500–1,000 customers. Łuskina based his reports of international affairs on foreign newspapers. Domestic coverage focused on doings at the royal court, activities of leading magnates, and Church matters. Advertisements for books, services, and runaway servants provide an interesting insight on daily life. While the editor's conservative attitudes were obvious, particularly his hatred of the philosophes, he applauded the American Revolution and its libertarian ideals. In contrast, Łuskina harshly condemned the French Revolution, and his strenuous objections to the reforms of the Great Parliament led him to support the Targowica Confederation. Reformers founded a rival newspaper, the *National and Foreign Gazette,* in 1791 to promote domestic reform. They offered sympathetic coverage of the first years of the French Revolution. This *Gazette* introduced novel features such as a larger format, quicker publication, and more careful attention to language. Several newspapers appeared in Lithuania, most notably the *Vilnius Gazette* (1761–92).

Father Piotr Świtkowski's monthly magazine, *Historico-Political Memoir,* provided information and opinions on a wide variety of subjects to the educated public in 1782–92. He republished substantial articles from the western press on agriculture, trade, economics, inventions, and industry. Many of these articles argued for peasant and burgher reform. Literary articles popularized Shakespeare and introduced new literary trends such as the German Sturm und Drang. Świtkowski also published short-lived papers such as the *Warsaw Magazine* (with Joachim Chreptowicz), the *Polish Patriot,* and *Selected Economic News.* During the Great Parliament, Świtkowski engaged in political polemics, providing a forum for the radical group Kołłątaj's Forge, to call for major social and political reform. Targowica closed the *Memoir* and other progressive papers. Tadeusz Podlecki published the *Commercial Daily* from 1786 to 1794.

The 1794 Insurrection government presented its views through the *Government Gazette* and also permitted private parties to present other opinions. A radical priest, Józef Meyer, published his own *Warsaw Gazette* during the 1794 Insurrection, along with the *Newspaper of the National Insurrection* and *Friend of the People.* Many other short-lived papers appeared in Polish, French, and German in both Warsaw and the provinces. Lithuanians published the Polish-language *Vilnius National Gazette.*

Reform and the Concept of the Nation in Political Literature

Reforming authors, some of whom played a notable role in politics, redefined the concept of the Polish "nation" from the Renaissance and Baroque ideal of the "noble republic" to a modern concept of universal citizenship embracing commoners. They all saw burghers and peasants as Polish-Lithuanian citizens, although most, as in the 1791 French constitution, restricted political rights to property owners. Many, but not all, reformers accepted Jews as citizens if the Jewish community polonized its outward behavior. The Constitution of May 3, 1791, and the 1794 Insurrection endorsed this new view of the Polish nation in part.

Józef Wybicki's *Patriotic Letters to Ex-Chancellor Andrzej Zamoyski* (1777–78) provided the most important political tract of the inter-Partition period. Born in 1747 in Pomerania and educated at a Jesuit school in Gdańsk, Wybicki supported the patriotic but conservative Bar Confederates as a young parliamentary deputy. He changed his mind when he studied natural and civil law at Leiden University in 1770–71, and, on his return to Poland, joined Andrzej Zamoyski's committee to draft a reformist law code. In lengthy anonymously published letters, Wybicki advocated ending personal serfdom (with compensation for landlords) and substituting monetary rent for peasant labor obligations. Wybicki supported strong governmental action to stimulate and supervise agricultural and industrial development. He also advocated limiting the degree of Vatican control over the Polish Church, particularly prohibiting appeals from Church courts to Rome. Wybicki presented his views attractively and comprehensively in good literary language.

The Great Parliament opened the door to two particularly distinguished political pamphleteers, Stanisław Staszic and Hugo Kołłątaj. Staszic was born in Piła, Great Poland, in 1755 to a burgher family. He became a priest and went abroad to study natural science, eventually translating Buffon's *Epoques de la nature* into Polish (1786). Staszic returned to Poland-Lithuania in 1781 as tutor to Andrzej Zamoyski's children, a position in which he showed more literary than pedagogical skill. Staszic used his patron's famous ancestor as a takeoff point to discuss current problems. His *Observations on the Life of Jan Zamoyski* (1787) advocated a republican program giving parliament executive power, abolishing the *liberum veto*, and raising a 100,000-man army. He hoped to protect Polish independence by offering the throne, with reduced powers, to a powerful foreign royal house. Staszic adopted Rousseauist rhetoric about sovereignty of the people, and advocated burgher and peasant reform. He presented his views passionately, with a generous admixture of sentimental and theatrical rhetoric. A few years later, Staszic demanded quick action in his *Warnings for Poland* (1790).

He put even more emphasis on popular sovereignty, denouncing Polish-Lithuanian magnates for political and economic selfishness. He also reviled Jews for their allegedly harmful economic activities. Despite his literary involvement, Staszic played no part in political developments and left the country during the later stages of the Great Parliament. After 1815, Staszic became a high state official in the Congress Kingdom, a successful industrialist, and the author of both scientific and political literature.

Hugo Kołłątaj, the educational reformer, politician, and author, was born in 1750 to a poor noble family in Volhynia. Unusually gifted academically, Kołłątaj received his doctorate from the Jagiellonian University at age eighteen before entering the priesthood. His brother's financial assistance allowed him to study canon law and theology in Vienna, Naples, and Rome, where he came to the pope's notice. When Kołłątaj returned to Poland, Bishop Michał Poniatowski brought him to Warsaw to work for the National Education Commission, where his work gained such approval that he was sent to Cracow as rector of the Jagiellonian University. Ten years of successful work in educational reform earned Kołłątaj the Order of St. Stanisław and appointment to a well-paid subministerial position in Warsaw in 1786. He took an independent line at the start of the Great Parliament, publishing a two-volume collection of *Anonymous Letters to Marshal Stanisław Małachowski* (1788), which comprehensively discussed the need for major political and social reform. He added his *Political Law of the Polish Nation* in 1790 to flesh out some of his ideas.

Kołłątaj's views generally resembled Staszic's, but they were presented at greater length and in thoroughly practical terms that could be translated easily into legislation. Kołłątaj called for a gentle revolution by parliamentary means. In politics, he advocated reconstructing an effective executive authority, ending the *liberum veto,* and replacing the aristocratic senate with a house of burgesses. He hoped to raise a 60,000-man army of patriotically trained and motivated soldiers, end personal serfdom, substitute rent contracts for feudal labor obligations, and integrate Jews within the body politic. He saw the need for economic development and planned to use the state to regulate and support it, employing measures such as state construction of roads and canals. A practical politicians as well as an author, Kołłątaj rose to become Lithuanian vice-chancellor in 1791 and a leader of the 1794 Insurrection.

Kołłątaj gathered additional writers, known as Kołłątaj's Forge, who took more radical positions than his own. His closest associate, Franciszek Salezy Jezierski (1740–91), also came from a poor noble family and became a priest. After studies in Italy, Jezierski worked for the National Education Commission as a school inspector and served as rector of two different high schools. He moved to Warsaw in 1788 to earn a living as a free-lance writer. His best-known work is his

Catechism on the Secrets of the Polish Government, ostensibly a translation of an 1735 English work but really an original satire with overtones of the French Revolution aimed at Polish conservatives. A fictional biography of *Jarosz Kutasiński, Noble from Łuków* traces the life of a poor noble forced by poverty to work in commoner occupations. The satire aimed to break down rigid social barriers. He also wrote a novel about early Polish history that described a virtuous society before conquest by Sarmatians. Humorously known as the "twelve apostles," a dozen other associates poured out literary works, political pamphlets, and satirical verses to press their case for change. Several members adopted radical "Jacobin" strategies to fight the 1794 Insurrection.

ROYALIST THEATER

Theater played an important role in Poniatowski's cultural policy. In addition to maintaining an Italian opera troupe and arranging for presentations by French and Italian traveling actors, Poniatowski opened Warsaw's first public theater in 1765. The theater continually suffered from financial problems, in part due to sharp competition from the visiting troupes, and lacked a permanent home. Nevertheless, the existence of a Polish theater allowed Bohomolec to contribute seven enjoyable, if didactic, plays in the style of Molière, satirizing both old-fashioned and trendy nobles. His plays featured clearly labeled one-dimensional characters such as Sir Old-Fashioned or Sir Idler. Prince Adam Czartoryski revealed a more subtle theatrical skill in adapting French and English comedies for private presentation in magnate palaces. He directed the plays and trained the amateur actors himself.

The repertory of the 1780s included comedies of manners and bourgeois dramas. Franciszek Zabłocki adapted sixty comedies in the 1770s and 1780s from Italian and French authors. He used recognizable local characters for his satires on old-fashioned nobles (*Sarmatianism*) and superficial westernization (*The Fop in Love*). Zabłocki wrote his plays in elegant classical verse enlivened by common idioms. While his plays dealt with the nobility, "bourgeois drama" brought commoners into view. The anonymous author of *Beverly* polonized an English play to show the inner nobility of an unjustly imprisoned merchant. Similarly, *The Deserter Who Loved His Family* showed the virtue of a peasant soldier caught while deserting the army to protect his parents against exploitation by a ruthless official. The play added political to social propaganda by having the king learn of the incident, pardon the soldier, arrange just treatment for the parents, and reprove, but not punish, the official. Józef Wybicki wrote the most successful play in this genre. His *Mayor of Poznań* appeared during the Great Parliament and portrayed the social and political integration of nobles and burghers. Other important theatrical productions came out of Adam Czartoryski's republican circle.

Ignacy Krasicki and Polish Literature

Polish Enlightenment poetry, centered around the royal court, displayed great variety. The foremost poet of the Polish Enlightenment, Ignacy Krasicki (1735–1801), took part in Thursday Dinners, but his major contributions began after the First Partition, primarily between 1775 and 1780. Born into a moderately rich family with magnate connections, Krasicki studied in Poland and rose rapidly in the Church. His large fortune as prince-bishop of Warmia allowed him to collect fine wines, exotic plants, and rare books while conscientiously fulfilling his clerical obligations. He was noted in salon society for his urbanity and wit, even though the loss of his estates to Prussia in the First Partition reduced his activities greatly. Krasicki is best known for his short satires and fables in clear, concise, yet elegantly classical language such as the following fable with its obvious allusion to the First Partition:

Two wolves suddenly fell upon a lamb in the wood.
They were about to tear it apart;
It asked, "By what right?"
"You are tasty, weak, and in the wood." Soon they had eaten it all.

The Polish original is in rhymed verse.

Krasicki's heroicomic epic *The Mouse-iad* (1775) drew on a legend of early Polish history to present a battle between cats and mice. Another, *The War of the Monks* (1778), satirized monastic orders for ignorance, bigotry, corruption, and especially drunkenness. The poem described a dispute between Dominicans and Carmelites in a small town that ends amicably in a drinking bout. Krasicki's sequel, written in 1780 to deflect criticism, was full of irony. He wrote little poetry after 1780.

The first Polish novel was Krasicki's *The Adventures of Nicholas Experience* (1776), about a young man raised in Sarmatian ignorance and corrupted by a French tutor who had fled Paris to avoid arrest. Nicholas is shipwrecked on a Utopian island inhabited by wise philosophers in a just society based on natural law. His story parallels Voltaire's *Candide,* except that Nicholas returns to Poland to undertake reform while Candide quietly cultivates his garden. The novel also introduced Polish readers to themes drawn from popular works such as Defoe's *Robinson Crusoe* and Rousseau's *Emile*. A second novel in the form of conversations, *Sir Chamberlain,* published in three parts (1778, 1784, 1803), presents a treatise on the virtues of country living and the importance of dealing fairly with peasants. The lesser known *History Divided into Two Books* (1779) offers readers an early glimpse of time travel. The protagonist, Grumdrypp from

Gulliver's Travels, recounts his personal experience among defeated nations such as the ancients Gauls and finds them more civilized than the Romans, a heartening conclusion for Poles after the First Partition. Bishop Józef Kossakowski, later a leader of the Targowica Confederation, was another novelist of the day.

The court historian, Bishop Adam Naruszewicz (1733–96), attended the king's Thursday Dinners and wrote both effective panegyrics and conventional pastoral poems. His satires in the style of Boileau offered a biting picture of Warsaw life, focusing on old-fashioned nobles with antiquated ideas. Stanisław Trembecki wrote libertine poetry, odes, and fables as well as historical works in the classical style in which he praised the king and reforming magnates. He also translated Tacitus and Horace. A drunkard, troublemaker, and Don Juan, Trembecki fought duels across Europe, but he also discussed philosophy in Paris with Diderot, d'Alembert, and Holbach. King Stanisław August appreciated his wit and invited him to Thursday Dinners. Later, Trembicki resided on the estate of Szczęsny Potocki, an organizer of the Targowica Confederation, where he wrote his longest poem celebrating Potocki's wife, Zofia, and paid homage to the natural beauties of Ukraine; the poem finally appeared in print in 1806.

Two radical poets died young. Deist and libertine, Kajetan Węgierski admired the philosophes and argued extreme positions in verses that offended influential social and political leaders. Forced to flee Poland, he visited the United States in 1783 and praised the infant republic highly. Węgierski died of tuberculosis in France in 1787 at thirty-two leaving a body of concise verses, mostly satirical, and Polish translations of such works as Alexander Pope's *Rape of the Lock.* Jakub Jasiński attended the Cadet School and served in the Polish army. He commanded the Vilnius Insurrection of 1794 end died defending Praga. Jasiński wrote light poems until the French Revolution and the Targowica Confederation inspired him to address patriotic subjects. One verse derided Stanisław August for mourning Louis XVI's execution and another poem declared optimistically on the eve of the insurrection that "wherever people have said 'I want to be free' they have always become free!"

Republican-Oriented Literature

Adam Czartoryski formed a second literary center on his estate at Puławy that was less classically oriented and more sentimental. His wife, Izabela Czartoryska née Poniatowska, fostered a cult of patriotism that linked Poland's past greatness with feelings for its future. This approach to poetry was both a foretaste of nineteenth-century romantic nationalism and part of the opposition's political program. A Czartoryski dependent, Franciszek Karpiński enjoyed the benefits of a Jesuit education and considered taking orders as a youth before residing at Puławy for several years and finally settling down on his own estate. Karpiński's religious verse drew upon the imagery of Polish Baroque poetry to celebrate God and nature while his secular poems spoke of pastoral love. Poland's leading sentimental poet, Karpiński wrote a treatise *On Speech and Poetry* (1782) that broke with rationalistic limitations and advocated writing poetry based on feelings. Dionizy Kniaźnin lived at Puławy as a tutor. He wrote plays for the palace theater, notably *The Spartan Mother*, which was staged on the eve of the 1788 parliamentary elections. The play drew analogies between old-fashioned classical virtues and the virtue of Polish opposition to Poniatowski's Russian alliance. Princess Izabela Czartoryska appeared in the title role. Kniaźnin also wrote delicate poems, whose charms lay in their subtle meter. He translated extensively to and from Latin, as well as from German and English (Ossian). A devoted patriot who dressed in the old Polish style, Kniaźnin became so depressed after the failed 1794 Insurrection that he went mad.

Another Czartoryski dependent, Julian Ursyn Niemcewicz (1757–1841), wrote the most famous play of the Stanislavian period. *The Deputy's Return* appeared in 1791 as part of the propaganda leading up to the enactment of the May 3 Constitution. In it, a deputy to the Great Parliament returns home during the holidays and wins the hand of a daughter from a wealthy noble family. The deputy favors reform while his more old-fashioned parents are willing to make reasonable accommodations to change. The young lady's father represents an unthinking and ignorant Sarmatian. The mother, with equal lack of thought, embraces fashionable French sentimental literature and supports the suit of a Frenchified idler who is only looking for a large marriage settlement. A noble of modest means, Niemcewicz gained his education and traveled widely thanks to Prince Adam Czartoryski's patronage. He translated French novels into Polish in 1781–82, introducing medieval themes to Polish literary consciousness. Niemcewicz gained election to the Great Parliament as a Czartoryski supporter and served as Kościuszko's aide-de-camp in the 1794 Insurrection, subsequently spending two years in Russian prison with Kościuszko. After his release, Niemcewicz accompanied Kościuszko to America, married a widow, and lived in New Jersey until 1807, when he returned to Europe by himself. Niemcewicz wrote important plays, poems, novels, and memoirs in the nineteenth century.

Music and the Polonaise

The Polish-Lithuanian Commonwealth followed the mainstream of European musical styles and the number of musical ensembles continued to grow, although it remained lower than in neighboring states. August II found music politically useful. He maintained an orchestra in Warsaw, directed by Jacek Różycki, who wrote vocal and instrumental music in a mixture of Roman, Venetian, and other Italian styles. After Różycki died in 1703, the orchestra was staffed mostly with

German musicians. August II also maintained a largely Polish so-called Jannissary Orchestra that played Turkish music and which he brought to Saxony to entertain participants at important political gatherings. August II kept a sixteen-piece bagpipe and fiddle orchestra in Dresden that dressed in Polish folk costume to fascinate guests and visiting musicians. August III was more interested in opera. The only noted composer of the period, Stanisław Szarzyński, was a Benedictine monk who lived in Warsaw around 1700, writing motets and instrumental compositions for small ensembles.

Cracow was a second center of musical activity. The Jesuit church of St. Peter organized musical teaching in the mid-seventeenth century and established a fine permanent choir and orchestra, used a century later by Jacek Szczurowski and Antoni Miłwid, who helped introduce the symphonic form to Poland-Lithuania. Both incorporated Polish dance melodies in their works. After the Jesuit order was abolished in 1773, the musicians scattered to other churches and magnate courts. Some joined the Wawel Castle choir and orchestra, which hired itself out to magnates to play at banquets and weddings. Wacław Sierkowski, a Wawel canon, founded a new music school that taught commoners as well as nobles. He was particularly fond of Italian cantatas, which he performed in his own Polish translation. Poznań and Lviv had orchestras as well.

Musical activities also flourished in magnates' palaces, particularly among the fabulously rich magnates of Belarus and Ukraine. Prince Karol Radziwiłł, known for his eccentricities, maintained two ensembles—the usual court orchestra and a Jewish band that Radziwiłł dressed in Turkish clothing. The Jewish band was famous for playing Polish dances, but Radziwiłł even had them accompany Church services. Antoni Tyzenhauz maintained a large orchestra and also founded music and ballet schools. A French ballet master conducted the latter, which included serf children among its students. In 1778, the school moved to Warsaw, where it eventually became part of the National Theater. Prince Janusz Sanguszko maintained two small classical orchestras plus a dozen mountaineer bagpipe players who were charged with waking up drunken guests after banquets. Hetman Wacław Rzewuski and Franciszek Sułkowski maintained the largest orchestras in Poland-Lithuania.

International Italianate and German styles predominated in composition. Foreign-born musicians directed the most important ensembles, but the Commonwealth's economic troubles opened new opportunities for local musicians at the courts of lesser nobles and in the Church. Church musicians such as Grzegorz Gorczycki, the director of the Cracow Court Cathedral, used folk rhythms and melodies in their religious music. The development of musical plays for Christmas and Easter led to the widespread introduction of Polish and Ukrainian folk dance material.

Growing interest in national dances by European composers led to the adoption of the polonaise as a national musical form in Poland-Lithuania. Professional composers adapted the distinctive Polonaise rhythm from the simple folk form, usually sung, and recast it as a processional dance. Instrumental settings encouraged more complicated rhythms and melodies. In the late seventeenth and early eighteenth centuries, the "noble polonaise" found favor with Couperin, Handel, Bach, Telemann, and others. A more ornate "court polonaise" appeared at the end of the eighteenth century and won popularity among such nineteenth-century composers as Chopin, Moussorgsky, and Tchaikovsky. Józef Kozłowski, Count Andrzej Ogiński's music director, popularized the polonaise at the Imperial Court at St. Petersburg when he became court composer. He also wrote a requiem for Poniatowski's funeral in St. Petersburg. In 1792, his first employer's son and music student, Michał Kleofas Ogiński, the last Lithuanian treasurer, wrote the first of many polonaises to be played on the piano. Works such as the "Polonaise for the Partition of Poland" possessed an elegance and elegiac quality that paved the way for Chopin. A variant of the genre was the patriotic song, written by obscure professional musicians, for the Bar Confederation. The "May 3 Polonaise" and "May 3 Mazur" celebrated the 1791 Constitution while other songs commemorated triumphs and defeats of the 1792 war, the Targowica Confederation, and the 1794 Insurrection. A 1797 mazur (or mazurka), another folk dance adopted by court musicians, "Poland Has Not Died" ("Jeszcze Polska nie zgineła"), became the Polish national anthem.

Opera

King Stanisław August Poniatowski had very little appreciation for music but supported opera as an extension of his theatrical interests. Earlier monarchs had encouraged the growth of opera, especially August II, who sponsored performances at his Warsaw court until he erected an opera house in 1724 and opened performances to the public. When August III took up residence in Warsaw, he brought along his orchestra and singers as well as his opera master, Johann Adolf Hasse, and his wife, a leading mezzo-soprano. Warsaw burghers displayed little interest at first despite free admission; on occasion, the royal guard compelled passersby to fill the house. Warsaw's public found Italian opera incomprehensible at first, but gladly attended biblical musical plays organized by Jesuits in churches and imitated later by other orders. Warsaw's public came to appreciate French and Italian opera when King Stanisław August reintroduced them in the 1760s. The first Polish-language opera with spoken dialogue, *Misery Made Happy* by Maciej Kamieński, modeled after the Viennese *singspiel*, was staged in 1778. Others followed, written by the king's Polish-born court composer Kajetan Gaetano, the Czech-born Jan Stefani, and others. Polish opera also came to Lviv (1780), Cracow (1781), Lublin (1782), Poznań (1783), Dubno (1784), and Vilnius (1785). Increased musical activity permitted the organization of instrumental concerts, and music became sufficiently important to warrant the commissioning of music pedagogy books by the National Education Commission.

The most important opera personage was Wojciech Bogusławski (1757–1829), a noble who served briefly in the army before becoming an actor, director, playwright, and producer. He adapted his first opera from a popular play by Franciszek Bohomolec, *Misery Made Happy,* and had it set to music by Maciej Kamieński, a Slovak who settled in Warsaw after completing his studies in Vienna. Bogusławski's repertoire soon included twenty Polish operas and forty operas translated from French, Italian, and German originals. As the first director of the newly formed National Theater in Warsaw, he staged Niemcewicz's play *The Deputy's Return,* in January 1791. During Targowica, Bogusławski adapted another play, *Henry VI at the Hunt,* from an English novel that had some undercurrents of political discontent. Bogusławski joined the anti-Targowica underground and guardedly voiced his opinions in his 1794 operetta, *A Supposed Miracle, or Cracovians and Mountaineers.* This ostensibly nonpolitical work, with music by Jan Stefani, a Czech, dealt with a conflict between the two groups which ended when a supposed miracle, really an electrical demonstration by a university student, brought them together. Bogusławski staged this play after the Cracow insurrection but before the Warsaw insurrection, and the audience enthusiastically responded to the play's allusion to the power of the people, especially when the actors ad-libbed political rhymes. Targowica censors closed the show in Warsaw after three performances. Bogusławski worked in Austrian Lviv after the Third Partition, returning to Warsaw in 1799 to revive the National Theater. He started preparations to construct the huge National Theater building that finally went up shortly after he died.

Scientific Collections

As well as patronizing the humanities, the Polish-Lithuanian elite enthusiastically supported educational institutions such as the Cadet School, the National Education Commission, and reformed universities in developing natural science studies based on their collections. Poniatowski collected and familiarized himself with geological and biological specimens, and planned to establish a natural science museum. He also collected scientific books and hired foreign scholars, Filip Carosi and J. J. Ferber, to manage the collections. Several scientists performed important educational reform work, such as mathematicians Michał Hube, director of the Cadet School, mathematician Jan Śniadecki, professor at the Cracow and Vilnius universities, and astronomer Marcin Poczobutt, rector of the Vilnius University. Among other scientists were the chemist Jan

Jaskiewicz, an early adherent of Lavoisier, and Krzysztof Kluk, the village priest who wrote numerous books on Polish plants and animals. The Jagiellonian University in Cracow reformed its medical studies along Viennese lines. In 1767, local Germans and Poles, nobles and burghers alike, formed the Warsaw Physics and Chemistry Society, which published a program of studies but closed in 1769. Jean Dubois de Jacigny, a professor at the Cadet School, founded a short-lived Physics Society in the late 1770s.

HISTORICAL SCHOLARSHIP AND ECONOMICS

Historical scholarship played a role in the cultural revival. An outgrowth of the Thursday Dinners was the loosely organized Society of People Loving the Public Good and Science (1771). Discussion bore fruit in a *Political History of Ancient Countries* (1772) by two participants. A planned second volume never appeared, but an anonymous short work "On the Establishment of Order in Civil Law and the Basis of Societies of Law-Abiding People" came out in the royalist magazine, *Amusing and Useful Entertainments,* in 1772 after a reading at a Thursday Dinner. Bishop Adam Naruszewicz wrote a biography of Hetman Jan Chodkiewicz that went unpublished until 1881 and planned to write other biographies for a book modeled on Plutarch's *Lives,* but King Stanisław August convinced him in 1775 to write a general history of Poland, agreeing to pay the costs. Poniatowski's chancellery collected documents from sixty state, Church, and private archives for Naruszewicz's use. Six volumes of his *History of the Polish Nation* appeared in 1780–86, reaching only 1386.

Kajetan Skrzetuski wrote the *Political History of the French Kingdom* (1773) and a two-volume general history of Europe entitled *Political History for Noble Youth* (1773–75). Wincenty Skrzetuski wrote a *History of the Swedish Kingdom* (1772) and Karol Wyrwicz produced a popular *Short World History* that appeared in French (1766) and Polish (1787). Feliks Łojko, a treasury official, collected seventy large files of data from the state archives for use in current political and economic debates. He wrote treatises, such as a 1773 work attempting to prove Poland's rights to the provinces of Pomerania and Spiš that Prussia and Austria claimed in the First Partition. Łojko was also a pioneer of economic statistics.

Physiocratism dominated economic thought. Based on French philosophy, it appealed to Polish nobles because it emphasized the importance of agriculture to the national economy rather than trade or manufacturing. Wealthier nobles and intellectuals supported the mixture of economic and moral arguments based on natural law. Physiocratism encouraged several magnates to reform their landed estates and it inspired political measures to help peasants during the Great Parliament and the 1794 Insurrection. The National Education Commission published several physiocratic textbooks, notably Hieronim Stroynowski's *The*

Science of Natural Law, Political Law, Political Economy, and the Law of Nations (1785). Few Polish authors wrote from a cameralist point of view stressing the need to develop industry, but for pragmatic reasons government officials and landed nobles understood the need to subsidize and protect manufactures whenever possible.

ARCHITECTURE

The Saxon accession changed the architectural landscape little. August II entertained far-reaching plans to build a magnificent palace rivaling Versailles, but the failure of his political plans put his ambitions on permanent hold. He had hoped to expand Warsaw along a monumental axis featuring a great Court of Honor with a monumental gate opening into a park in the form an elongated pentagon. The axis was to start at Krakowskie Przedmieście with radial avenues providing a focus for additional development. The forty-year building project was never completed in its entirety because funds ran out, but both Saxon monarchs added pieces to it and some magnates located their palaces nearby. The Saxon palace provided a model for magnates' palaces with open spaces in the suburbs, such as Ujazdów, which was linked to the religious processional center through tree-lined boulevards. Modern names like Saxon Gardens and Saxon Fields recall the building achievements of the eighteenth century. Similarly, Jan Klemens Branicki used a Saxon architect to design a magnificent palace near Białystok in 1728–58. In all, more than forty private cities benefited from urban planning by their magnate owners.

Italian and Italian-trained architects built churches in Warsaw and other cities. Following the trends of Prague and Vienna, northern Italian models became popular in Poland with their monumental styles, complicated decoration, use of perspective, and light/dark effects. Among the most interesting buildings from the period was an Evangelical Lutheran Church with its enormous dome. Paradoxically, Church architecture influenced the construction of large synagogues in Poland-Lithuania, reflecting the growing integration of Jews with Christian society. Both wooden and stone synagogues featured cupolas designed to provide the illusion of a heavenly tent. The size and complexity of the structures indicate that sophisticated engineering was involved, probably by court architects on loan from the Jews' magnate patrons. The basic form and function remained traditionally Jewish, of course, and Jewish craftsmen put up the buildings, decorating them with lavish wood carvings and decorative paintings of plants and animals.

Royal and magnate residence construction fueled Warsaw's late eighteenth-century growth and filled suburban Warsaw with new palaces, mostly in the classical style. Stanisław August Poniatowski purchased the Ujazdów palace and linked it to nearby Warsaw with a new network of roads, attractively designed to provide pleasing vistas framed by rows of trees. His beautiful summer palace in the classical style, Łazieńki ("The Baths"), was flanked by an artificial lake with an island and romantic ruins, a conservatory, and a theater. The king also added a classical style wing to the Baroque style Royal Castle to house his library, and rebuilt much of the rest to his classicist taste. Princess Izabela Czartoryska constructed a family palace at Powązki in suburban Warsaw in the English style with a natural garden housing antique "ruins." Elegant palaces were built for other nobles including the kings' brothers, Hetman Franciszek Ksawery Branicki, and the king's Swiss adviser Maurice Glaire, among many other figures.

Painting

Royal patronage dominated painting. Marcello Bacciarelli and Bernardo Belotto (Canaletto) came from Italy as court painters to August III and remained at Stanisław August's court, where Bacciarelli distinguished himself as a portraitist and Canaletto painted urban scenes with such detailed realism that engineers used them to reconstruct Warsaw after World War II. A French artist, Jean Pierre Norblin, is known for his drawings of peasants and street scenes.

King Stanisław August collected art avidly. He acquired fifteen paintings by Rembrandt and his workshop, including *The Polish Rider,* as well as numerous paintings by Brueghel, Rubens, Watteau, Fragonard, Leonardo, Reni, Cranach, Holbein, and others. He also collected 30,000 drawings. Many rich nobles and burghers were also art collectors, most notably Count Stanisław Potocki and Josef Kabrun, a Gdańsk burgher, who made their major purchases shortly after the Third Partition.

The Enlightenment in Lithuania

The Lithuanian language ceased having any influence on the nobility, and use of the Ruthenian language (Belarussian) also declined in the eighteenth century. In 1697, polonized Lithuanian nobles introduced and passed a bill in Parliament requiring the use of Polish in all official documents; the same bill reaffirmed the independence of Lithuanian ministries. The cultural level declined, despite the presence of several important professors, such as Zygmunt Lauxmin at the Vilnius Academy, whose book on rhetoric first appeared in Vilnius in 1648 and was republished in thirteen foreign editions, mostly in Germany, and Józef Naronowicz-Naroński, a Ruthenian citizen of the Grand Duchy who wrote on military fortifications. In general, the Vilnius Academy and other schools taught religious subjects almost exclusively. Religion was taught in a narrow manner, expressing fear of witches and evil spirits, though actual witchcraft trials were rare after 1725.

Interest in the Lithuanian language revived during the eighteenth century among the literati. Lithuanian folk materials were collected but did not appear in print until the nineteenth century. Some literary works were published in Lithuanian, such as the 1706 translation of Aesop's fables by Jan Szulc, a Protestant pastor from Tilsit. The major Lithuanian poet Kristijonas Donelaitis (1714–80) lived in Klaipėda (Prussia) and, in the 1760s, wrote an epic poem called *The Seasons* that described Lithuanian village life and customs in elegant hexameters. It circulated among a narrow circle of enthusiasts in manuscript, appearing first in print in German translation in 1818 and subsequently in many other European languages, including Polish. Ducal Prussia modernized the Lithuanian legal vocabulary by publishing official documents. Church sermons were published in Lithuanian, and Lithuanian was used in some schools in Ducal Prussia. Filip Ruhig (Ruigys) compiled his Lithuanian dictionary in 1747 in part to purify Lithuanian and eliminate Germanisms. In all, 304 books appeared in the Lithuanian language in the eighteenth century, mostly on religious subjects. The language showed strong Polish influence except for prayer books, which maintained relatively pure Lithuanian usage.

Polish-language Lithuanian culture revived along with the economy. The *Vilnius Courier* started publishing in 1760 with *Literary Information* as a supplement. When it folded after three years, other papers took up the slack, notably the *Vilnius Gazette* in 1761. Schools staged plays based on Lithuanian history, especially great battles and other deeds of medieval Lithuanian dukes. Vilnius entered a period of magnificent building in the late seventeenth and eighteenth centuries, including a reconstruction of the Cathedral of St. Stanislas, a refurbishing of the Church of St. Peter and St. Paul, a reconstruction of altars and chapels of St. John's Church, and a rebuilding of St. Anne's. The Tyzenhaus, Radziwiłł, and Sapieha families were among those magnates who put up grand residences. Wojciech Bogusławski opened Vilnius' first public theater in 1785 in the Oskierek Palace. Baroque style predominated, although some construction adopted classical canons.

The Emergence of Separatism in Royal Prussia

The trend toward Enlightenment uniformity and centralization threatened Prussia's autonomous position within the Polish-Lithuanian Commonwealth and stimulated some Prussian scholars to advocate separatism. While the Saxon monarchs had ignored the Prussian Estates in collecting taxes, the 1764 Convocation Parliament struck directly at Prussian stability by reducing the number of deputies that it could send to parliament and centralizing administrative agencies. Reform efforts to abolish the *liberum veto* affronted Prussian patriots no less than Polish conservatives. The leading Prussian scholar and jurist, Gottfried Lengnich, substituted historical documentation for fanciful Sarmatian theories in his proof of Prussia's right to autonomy. Going beyond the historical evidence, he claimed that Prussia had thrown off the yoke of the Teutonic Order on its own in 1454 and voluntarily associated itself with Poland. He called the 1569 Union of Lublin an illegal assault on Prussian liberties and considered the 1764 reforms to be worse. Embittered, Lengnich refused to help King Stanisław August prepare arguments against the First Partition. Lengnich was not alone, as the large volume of treatises shows. Toruń's lobbyist at the 1764 parliament, Samuel Luther Geret, went so far as to propose establishing a duchy of Prussia, with Catherine II's brother as grand duke.

Prussian opposition to Polish reform came from autonomist sentiments rather than German nationalism. German-language Prussian scholars associated Germany with the absolutist policies of the Teutonic Order, and the emergence of Enlightened absolutism in Brandenburg-Prussia only confirmed Prussia's hostility to Germany. Nevertheless, hostility to Poland grew and left Prussians few resources to withstand German efforts to integrate them after the Partitions.

Sarmatian Anti-Semitism and the Enlightened Response

Jews gained a reputation as being anti-Polish among seventeenth-century Catholics who blamed the Commonwealth's disasters on Protestant, Orthodox, and Jewish religious dissent. Anti-Jewish actions became increasingly common as students attacked Jews in the streets and led guild members in riots against them. Despite Jan III Sobieski's good relations with individual Jews, anti-Jewish riots broke out in Brest Litovsk (1680), Cracow (1682), Vilnius (1682), and Poznań (1687); in Poznań, Jewish self-defense repulsed the attackers. The Great Northern War brought persecution from Saxon, Swedish, Russian, and Polish-Lithuanian armies. Only heavy ransom payments saved many Jewish communities from danger. The 1717 Silent Parliament doubled the size of the Jewish poll tax, but it also restored order to the cities and prevented anti-Jewish attacks. Violent outbreaks in 1734–39, 1750, and 1768 in Ukraine by Haidamaks saw cities attacked and Jews slaughtered.

Jews faced legal persecution even though kings and other noble protectors prevented most cases from coming to trial and the number of ritual murder cases declined in the eighteenth century. The Piotrków tribunal in 1663 condemned Matthew Kalahore, a Cracow pharmacist and communal official, for dishonoring the communion wafer, burned him at the stake, and fired his remains out of a cannon. At least twenty-eight accusations of ritual murder were brought in 1698–1761, and most resulted in convictions and executions; some defendants won acquittal. As in other criminal matters, investigators used torture during interrogation and the penalty for a conviction was death. A sudden spate of cases around 1750 sent the Jewish community to seek protection from Pope Benedict XIV, who condemned the concept of ritual murder. The pope's report was entered into state records and the Jewish community circulated it in Latin, but anti-Semitic literature and popular superstitions persisted. Bishops often blocked synagogue construction and repair.

Despite the prevalence of anti-Jewish attitudes, the Polish-Lithuanian parliament and kings passed special legislation to help Jews recover from the disastrous mid-seventeenth-century wars, because they saw Jews as an essential element in the Commonwealth's economic life. While Mazovian dietines sought to expel Jews in the 1670s, the Cracow dietine voted to give the Jews tax relief and directed local officials to protect them against rioting. In subsequent years, other dietines extended similar protection to their Jews and helped individual communities recover from fires and plagues. Jews gained exemption from quartering soldiers in 1683 and the right to pay taxes in current, depreciated money in 1685. Persecution of Jews through the courts ceased almost entirely as soon as Stanisław August Poniatowski assumed the Polish-Lithuanian throne. Mob action declined quickly.

As elsewhere in Europe, Polish Catholic publicists debated the possibility of emancipating the Jews and integrating them into the body politic. In 1785, an anonymous pamphlet advocated incorporating Jews into the burgher estate with full economic and political equality. Interestingly, a Jewish doctor translated the Polish-language work into German and dedicated it to King Stanisław August. Piotr Świtkowski, an otherwise enlightened journalist, responded with a program to settle Jews in agricultural colonies, because he viewed Jewish merchants and artisans as a destructive element in Polish-Lithuanian cities. The matter was hotly debated during the Great Parliament. The leading advocate of emancipation was Mateusz Butrymowicz, a deputy from Pińsk, whose 1789 pamphlet "On the Method of Forming Polish Jews into Useful Citizens" advocated granting Jews equal urban citizenship, requiring them to adopt Polish as their primary language, removing them from the liquor trade, and settling them on the land.

Hasidism and the Jewish Enlightenment

The presuppositions that dominated Jewish life in the Commonwealth began to shift during this period of intellectual, economic, and political ferment. Rabbinical Judaism flourished in Poland-Lithuania and rabbis such as Elijah, the Gaon (Great Scholar) of Vilnius, led European Jewry, but new religious trends emerged as well as the beginnings of Jewish secularization.

The would-be Jewish messiah from the Ottoman Empire, Shabbetai Zvi, won over many followers in the 1660s among the Jews of Podolia and nearby regions who shared Shabbetai's desire to replace the rabbinic and communal establishment. The way was prepared in part by the mysticism of the Cabbala that spread from Palestine to Poland-Lithuania in the sixteenth century. Small circles of mystics combined study of esoteric tracts with meticulous observance of the commandments; some practiced fasting and self-mortification while others developed ecstatic practices. Communal authorities frowned on innovations because they tended to fragment the community but later came to accept and support these "hasids," or pious ones, as part of the communal elite. Hasids included both Rabbi Elijah of Vilnius, the exemplar of Rabbinic Judaism, and the Besht, the founder of Hasidism.

Israel ben Eliezer (c. 1700–1760), called the Ba'al Shem Tov (literally, the Good Master of the Divine Name), or the Besht, an anagram, was born in Podolia and orphaned at a young age. While he did not study long enough to become a rabbi, he received sufficient education to earn a living at various times as a teacher, deacon, ritual butcher, and ritual circumciser. To increase his spiritual powers by communing with God and nature, the Besht moved into the Carpathian Mountains, where he earned his living by digging clay that his wife sold in nearby towns. Later, she ran an inn. When the Besht left the mountains at age thirty-six, he became a traveling healer (commonly called *ba'al shem*), effecting cures and exorcizing demons with prayer, religious amulets, and herbal medicine. In 1740, his growing reputation earned him an invitation from the Jewish communal authorities in the nearby prosperous market city of Medzhybizh (Międzybóż) to become the town doctor and teacher. They provided him with a house on the market square for the rest of his life. The Ba'al Shem Tov led a cabbalistic study group where he explained his visions and dreams, and told parables. He also took a role in disputes among local Jews as well as between Jews and Christians. In particular, he tried to save Jews from depredations of bandits, rebels, and Tatars.

The Besht appears to have nudged existing Hasidic elitism in a more popular direction, particularly through his mystical prayers, his efforts at spiritual communion with God, his use of magic (practical Cabbala), and his teachings of numerology (letter substitution). Hasidism, whether through the Besht's own doctrines or those of his followers, emphasized individual salvation before world salvation. Hasids believed that God is literally everything and that prayer pierces through illusion, allowing Jews to see the essence of the universe. Valid prayer depended on individual devotion and took the form of sudden insights during mundane activities outside the synagogue. When an individual transcended ego ("annihilates selfhood"), the sorrows of the world no longer existed and sin lost significance. Besht considered melancholy spirits a hinderance in reaching true understanding; joy and optimism were more helpful. The Tsaddik (Holy Man) acted as an intermediary between God and ordinary people, who were obliged to support him and his family. A widespread popular Hasidic movement developed shortly after his death which reinterpreted the requirements for kosher slaughter and demanded the introduction of Sephardic prayers. Meeting apart from the established community due to ritual differences, Hasids prayed ecstatically, expressing their feelings through song, dance, shaking, and clapping. Rabbi Dov Ber of Mezhirech became the leader and Rabbi Jacob Joseph of Polonnoe published the Ba'al Shem Tov's sayings in 1780. After the First Partition, missionaries spread Hasidism to Jews in Central Poland and Belarus as well as to Galicia and Hungary. Their success challenged the authority of rabbinic and secular leadership within the Jewish community and encouraged the emergence of Hasidic rabbinic dynasties in the nineteenth century.

Opponents of Hasidism such as Rabbi Elijah of Vilnius considered Hasidic ecstasy and talk of miracles to be both delusion and idolatry, seeing Hasidic emphasis on prayer as contrary to traditional Torah learning and intellectual endeavor. In 1772, the Hasidim were excommunicated in Vilnius and their written works burned. After attempts to mediate the dispute failed, the Vilnius Jewish authorities issued another ban in 1781, declaring that hasids "must leave our communities with their wives and children . . . and they should not be given a night's lodging; their kosher slaughter is forbidden; it is forbidden to do business with them and to intermarry with them, or to assist at their burial." The ban was unenforceable, and conflict between the two Jewish communities led to mutual denunciations to secular authorities, who generally sided with the official Jewish communities. Nevertheless, many Jewish communities and rabbis coexisted with Hasidism without difficulty.

Another sign of the transformation of Polish-Lithuanian Jewry was the career of Jacob Frank (1726–91), who aspired to lead the Jews to a new religion but converted to Christianity with several thousand followers. Born in Podolia to a pious, middle-class family, Frank became a merchant in the Ottoman Empire and returned to Poland-Lithuania in 1755 claiming to be a prophet. When the Polish authorities arrested Frank and many followers at the request of Jewish communal authorities, Frank appealed to Bishop Mikołaj Dembowski for help, and rewarded this fanatically anti-Jewish cleric by holding a public disputation in 1757 with learned rabbis. As judge, Dembowski declared the Talmud to be worthless and corrupt and publicly burned all available copies. Frank attempted to consolidate his position with another disputation in 1759, in which he charged Judaism with ritual murder, but higher Church authorities intervened to stop Dembowski's successor from declaring Judaism guilty. Although Frank and some 500 followers converted to Christianity, his claims to be a new Messiah led to his imprisonment in the Jasna Góra monastery in Częstochowa in 1760. After his release in 1773, Frank's unusual brand of Christianity attracted several thousand new converts. He still claimed to be God's prophet and maintained

Jewish practices such as the Saturday Sabbath, but he also led pseudo-religious orgies. Polish authorities forced him into exile in Bohemia, where the Austrians tolerated his presence because of his supposed political influence in the Ottoman Empire. Frank's followers included both rich merchants and poor artisans. Their response to his charismatic leadership implies an interest in escaping the confines of Rabbinic Judaism and reaching out to the Christian world. This episode coincided with a concerted missionary effort among Jews by some Catholic religious orders.

A more direct response to changing conditions was the growth of intellectual interest in the non-Jewish world known as the Jewish Enlightenment (Haskalah) that began in the late eighteenth century. Individual Jews from Poland-Lithuania sought to move beyond Talmudic scholarship and acquired a knowledge of European languages to study philosophy, history, and science. Lacking a critical mass of Jewish philosophes at home, young scholars like Isaac Satanower, Mendel Levin Satanower, and Salomon Maimon went to Berlin, where they played a role in the emerging circle of Moses Mendelssohn. Some remained in Germany, but others returned home to continue their studies and publish works on a variety of subjects, often aided financially by Polish noble patrons such as Prince Adam Czartoryski. For example, Mendel Levin, who lived in the chief city of Czartoryski's Podolian estates, translated the Bible into Yiddish and wrote anti-Hasidic comedies that have been lost. Moses Marcuse of Słonim adapted and polonized a famous Swiss medical handbook, adding a strong attack on traditional education, and an Enlightenment commentary about the need for productive labor. He combatted superstition and folk medicine such as that practiced by the Ba'al Shem Tov. Several medical doctors who had studied abroad played a prominent role as publicists and interpreters for the Jewish community during the four years of the Great Parliament.

The Consolidation of Greek (Ukrainian) Catholicism

The 1720 Zamość Synod, the first since 1626, laid the foundations for the modern Greek Catholic Church just as the Council of Trent had redefined the Roman Catholic Church in the sixteenth century. Called by Metropolitan Leon Kiszka, Papal Nuncio Jerome Grimaldi presided, and the Armenian Catholic Archbishop, Jan Tobias Augustynowicz, also participated. The synod set Church dogma, organized pastoral care, and defined the duties of priests and hierarchs. It reorganized clerical seminars and monasteries. Pope Benedict XIII confirmed and published the synod's decisions in 1724. The network of parishes expanded and the area of Greek Catholic parishes in the heavily populated areas of southwestern Ukraine (Przemyśl, Lviv, Lutsk) was kept under 20 square kilometers, allowing careful pastoral supervision. Elsewhere, parishes were significantly greater, ranging up to 300 square kilometers in the center of the Grand Duchy of Lithuania (Belarus). The metropolitan of Kiev headed the Greek Catholic Church and resided in Vilnius. The metropolitanate of Kiev made up almost half of the Church, and the metropolitanate of Polotsk made up another fifth. Both metropolitanates covered much of the north, where few Greek Catholics lived.

After 1740, secular authorities and the Roman Catholic hierarchy made a concerted effort to help the Greek Catholic Church improve education. The number of schools increased rapidly, and standards were high although the curriculum was old fashioned. It took several decades to catch up with the newest trends in Piarist and Jesuit education. The Basilian order ran most Greek Catholic schools, and it became one of the largest monastic orders in the Commonwealth. Improvements in schooling and intensive pastoral activities ensured the continued existence of the Uniate Church. The Basilians' bold offer to take over all schooling in southeastern Poland-Lithuania in 1774 in exchange for ex-Jesuit properties received support from the papal nuncio, Giuseppi Garampi. Not surprisingly, new Roman Catholic schools were organized instead, but existing Basilian schools enthusiastically implemented the curriculum put forward by the National Education Commission. Basilian schools proved popular, even enrolling Catholic students and a few Jews along with the sons of Uniate nobles and priests. Some students went on to study at Cracow and Vilnius universities. Latinization of prayers and customs caused some complaint and contributed to the decline of the Uniate Church in Belarus, but the concentration of faithful and the number of churches remained high in Ukrainian lands.

The separate Armenian Catholic Church faded away as Armenian Catholics polonized and used Polish-language prayers in Church, although a small hierarchy continued to exist.

CHAPTER TWENTY

Epilogue

The Partitions put an end to the Polish-Lithuanian state after 409 years. The adventure that began with Jadwiga's marriage to Jogaiła and made Poland-Lithuania into the second largest state in Europe was over, but its legacy endured. During the Commonwealth's long existence, a culture developed that expanded East Central Europe into new regions—modern Belarus, Lithuania, Prussia, and Ukraine.

The reasons for the collapse of the large and once-powerful Polish-Lithuanian state are complex. They involve a combination of constitutional weakness, economic decline, and predatory behavior by Poland-Lithuania's neighbors. A host of institutions defining Poland-Lithuania's "golden liberties" (especially the elective kingship and the *liberum veto*) caused the state to wither away, while adherence to the Sarmatian ideology of noble democracy held off reform far too long. The economic decline experienced by Poland-Lithuania in the seventeenth and eighteenth centuries also affected neighboring states, but the Commonwealth's political weakness prevented proper use of available resources to protect the state. The predatory behavior of Poland-Lithuania's Russian, Prussia, and Austrian neighbors in 1772, 1793, and 1795 outstripped normal aggressive behavior of European states in the early modern period and stopped the recovery that had recently begun.

The Polish-Lithuanian legacy left its imprint on the Polish mentality. Four hundred years of success instilled in the Poles the self-confidence of a Great Power and a sense of their historical destiny. The institutions of noble democracy nurtured a love of freedom and independence that produced the remarkable record of national uprisings in the nineteenth and twentieth centuries and the equally remarkable record of resistance to Communism. Unfortunately, some Poles also acquired a feeling of superiority to other nationalities which infuriated minority groups even in periods when positive traditions of toleration predominated—and toleration did not always predominate. The strong sense of Polish-Lithuanian tradition accounts for later efforts to restore the broad borders of the pre-Partition state despite the emerging national movements of its former coresidents—Lithuania, Belarus, Ukraine. At the start of the twenty-first century, the negative remnants of Poland's earlier role appear to have declined to the point of extinction.

The Lithuanian heritage of the Polish-Lithuanian state should not be overlooked. The Lithuanian elite accepted Polish cultural identity in the Commonwealth, but jealously guarded Lithuanian autonomy and political identity before and after each successive political union with Poland, a characteristic that preserved Lithuania as a separate political unit and prepared the way for future independence. Some of Poland's greatest writers, such as the national poet of the nineteenth century Adam Mickiewicz, and the Nobel laureate Czesław Miłosz, came from Lithuania and celebrated their Lithuanian homeland in the Polish language. Lithuanian speakers, mostly of lower-class origin, rejected Polish speakers as members of the Lithuanian nation in modern times and ignored them or fought them in their search for national independence. As a result, Polish-speaking Lithuanians became a minority in the country they had once dominated. The conflicts between the Polish and Lithuanian states were often bitter when they regained their independence in 1918, especially over borders and the capital city of Vilnius/Wilno. Happily, they have not reappeared since the fall of Communism.

Membership in the Polish-Lithuanian state separated Ruthenians, or at least their significant political and intellectual elites, from Muscovites or Russians, so that their emergence into full-fledged nationalities in later years became possible. Two separate nationalities, the Ukrainian and the Belarussian, evolved in prenational form before the end of the eighteenth century. In Poland-Lithuania, the nobility, the Cossacks, and the Ukrainian churches (both Orthodox and Catholic) developed a self-conscious identity that helped define Ukrainian nationality in the post-Partition period in both the East and the West. Their participation in the Polish-Lithuanian parliament and army, on the one hand, and their conflicts with the Polish-Lithuanian state, particularly in the Cossack uprising, on the other, provided the core of Ukrainian identity. Anti-Polish elements predominated in the emergence of modern Ukrainian nationalism during the nineteenth and twentieth centuries, as is illustrated in the works of the national poet Taras Shevchenko. Some Ukrainian thinkers acknowledged, however, that participating in the Polish-Lithuanian state had at the very least kept Ukraine out of Russian hands for several centuries. Polish-Ukrainian relations since the fall of Communism reflect the more favorable attitudes. Lacking the high drama of the Cossack revolts, the Belarussian experience was less clearly delineated. As a result, the outlines of Belarussian identity remain less firm, although here, too, separate historical experience distinguishes Belarus from Russia.

Jews achieved a cohesiveness and institutional identity in the Polish-Lithuanian Commonwealth that defined them in modern times. While they shared Jewish identity with coreligionists in other lands, their Polish-Lithuanian experience as a large autochthonous group laid the foundation for modern Jews of Eastern Europe. Through mass migration in the late nineteenth and twentieth centuries, they became a significant and sometimes dominant part of the the largest Jewish communities throughout the world—in North and South America, Israel, Western Europe, and South Africa. Rabbinic Judaism, Hasidism, and, above all, communal institutions all reached a remarkably high level of development in Poland-Lithuania.

In contrast, Prussians and Prussian Germans underwent assimilation by the German nation in the nineteenth century, even if a few contemporary historians are beginning to look at the past with different eyes and recover the mixture of nationalities that Prussia once enjoyed. Tartars, Karaites, and other smaller groupings have also faded from the scene.

In sum, the Polish-Lithuanian state played a vital role in European politics, diplomacy, warfare, economics, and intellectual life over its four centuries of existence. Its unique institutions enriched Poland's European identity and rippled through the Ukrainian, Belarussian, Lithuanian, and Jewish elements of the Commonwealth. Effects can still be felt today.

BIBLIOGRAPHICAL ESSAY

This bibliographical essay provides references to English-language works and a limited number of other sources, mainly in French. Like the preceding chapters, the bibliography is organized by dynasties to accommodate political history. Unfortunately, because long-term trends in constitutional, economic, social, and cultural history follow their own patterns and do not fit easily within such borders, readers should check adjacent periods to ensure that they do not miss important references. This is particularly important for Polish material in translation, since modern Polish historians generally discuss cultural topics over a broad period labeled "Old Polish Culture" and group many issues, including politics, according to economic criteria. Ukrainian and Jewish national histories follow their own periodization. Full book citations are only given once in the following bibliographical essay. Second and subsequent references list only the full title.

GENERAL

While there is no substitute for knowing the languages of East Central Europe, English-language historiography on the Polish-Lithuanian state is substantial. It includes major national histories, monographic studies, and numerous articles that appear in varied and scattered publications. Polish-language readers should look at recent accounts, particularly Jerzy Topolski, *Polska w czasach nowożytnych (1500–1795)* [Poland in Modern Times, 1500–1795] (Poznan: Wydawnictwo Naukowe UAM, 1994), and the interpretive study by Andrzej Wyczański, *Polska Rzecz Pospolita Szlachecka* [The Polish Noble Republic], 2d ed. (Warsaw: PWN, 1991); both include substantial bibliographies. Topolski's work appears as part of a five-volume series. Jörg K. Hoensch, *Geschichte Polens* [History of Poland], 2d ed. (Stuttgart: UTB, 1990), provides an introduction to German-language historiography. There is no recent French equivalent.

Polish and Ukrainian history are well served by well-researched and well-written large-scale national histories in English. Volume 1 of Norman Davies, *God's Playground: A History of Poland*, 2 vols. (Oxford: Oxford University Press, 1981; New York: Columbia University Press, 1982), offers a brilliantly written interpretive account of Polish history to 1795. Leading Polish historians of the postwar period present their views more systematically in the older collective work, Aleksander Gieysztor et al., *History of Poland* (Warsaw: PWN, 1968). Volume 1 of *The Cambridge History of Poland*, 2 vols. (Cambridge: University Press, 1941) includes chapters by English and Polish historians of the 1930s and is still useful. Adam Zamoyski's *The Polish Way: A Thousand-year History of the Poles and Their Culture* (London: John Murray, 1987) provides an attractively written account. Popular accounts written by a Polish journalist have now been translated into English: Pawel Jasienica, *Piast Poland, Jagiellonian Poland, The Commonwealth of Both Countries,* and *A Tale of Agony,* trans. by Alexander Jordan (Miami, Fla.: American Institute of Polish Culture, 1983–92). Manfred Kridl provides *A Survey of Polish Literature and Culture* (Hague: Mouton, 1956), and the Nobel-prize winning poet Czesław Milosz gives his personal interpretation of *The History of Polish Literature*, 2d ed. (Berkeley: University of California Press, 1983). Grzegorz Michalski et al. provide *An Outline History of Polish Music* (Warsaw: Interpress, 1978). A sketch of legal systems can be found in Wenceslas J. Wagner, ed., *Polish Law Through the Ages* (Stanford: Hoover Institution, 1970). Basic historical information appears in George J. Lerski et al., *Historical Dictionary of Poland, 966–1945* (Westport, Conn.: Greenwood, 1996). Jacek Jędruch's *Constitutions, Elections and Legislatures of Poland, 1493–1977* (Washington, D.C.: University Press of America, 1982), is a handbook of information on parliaments and parliamentary processes; the section covering the period 1493–1795 is substantial.

Paul Robert Magocsi, *A History of Ukraine* (Toronto: University of Toronto Press; Seattle: University of Washington Press, 1996), offers an unusually broad interpretation of Ukrainian history showing its Polish-Lithuanian context and covering the histories of major ethnic groups living in Ukrainian territories. Orest Subtelny, *Ukraine: A History* (Toronto: University of Toronto Press, 1988), concentrates more exclusively on the Ukrainian ethnic element. Nicholas L. Chirovsky, *An Introduction to Ukrainian History,* 3 vols. (New York: Philosophical Library, 1981–86), gives much interesting detail. Bernard D. Weinryb, *The Jews of Poland* (Philadelphia: Jewish Publication Society, 1973), contributes an expert introduction to this subject; and a classic work, Simon Dubnow, *History of Jews in Poland and Russia,* 3 vols. (Philadelphia: Jewish Publication Society, 1916–20), can still be used. Much useful information about Jewish thought in Poland appears in a major prewar Yiddish work, Israel Zinberg, *A History of Jewish Literature,* trans. and ed. by Bernard Martin, 12 vols. (New York: Case Western Reserve University Press, 1972–78). Belarus is described in Nicholas P. Vakar, *Belorussia: The Making of a Nation* (Cambridge, Mass.: Harvard University Press, 1956). Albetas Gerutis, ed., *Lithuania 700 Years* (New York: Manyland Books, 1969), gives a very short introduction to that country. Alfred Bilmanis, *A History of Latvia* (Princeton: Princeton University Press, 1951), devotes ample space to the period before 1800. Two regional histories put Poland-Lithuania in a broader context: Piotr S. Wandycz, *The Price of Freedom* (New York: Routledge, 1993), and Philip Longworth, *The Making of Eastern Europe* (New York: St. Martin's Press, 1994). Henryk Litwin emphasizes the multinational character of the Commonwealth in his article, "The Nations of the Polish-Lithuanian Commonwealth: Controversial Questions," Acta Poloniae Historica 77 (1998): 43–58.

National historical narratives are amplified by journal articles, historiographical reflections, encyclopedias, and historical atlases. *Acta Poloniae Historica* (cited hereafter as *APH*) publishes significant Polish articles, book reviews, and reports of scholarly colloquia in translation, mostly in English. Every few years, *APH* also provides exhaustive bibliographies of Polish scholarship in translation, including little-known journals and anthologies. The *Polish Review* concentrates on Polish studies with an increasingly broad perspective. *Harvard Ukrainian Studies* (cited here as *HUS*) and the *Journal of Ukrainian Studies* provide a forum for international scholarship on Ukraine, while *Polin: a Journal of Polish-Jewish Scholarship* publishes articles by scholars from Britain, Israel, North America, and Poland.

A recent account of Polish historiography appears in Piotr S. Wandycz, "Historiography of the Countries of Eastern Europe: Poland," *American Historical Review* 97:4 (1992): 1011–25. Multilingual bibliographical information is available in Gershon Hundert and Gershon Bacon, *The Jews in Poland and Russia: Bibliographical Essays* (Bloomington: Indiana University Press, 1984). Murray J. Rosman offers "Reflections on the State of Polish Jewish Historical Study," *Jewish History* [Israel] 3:2 (1988): 115–30. Bohdan S. Wynar, *Ukraine: A Bibliographic Guide to English-Language Publications* (Englewood, Colo.: Ukrainian Academic Press, 1990), provides a guide to the subject. A "Discussion," *Slavic Review* 54:3 (1995): 658–719, examines fundamental questions in Ukrainian historiography. Stephen Velychenko looks at how historians of several nations understood Ukrainian history in *National History as Cultural Process: A Survey of the Interpretations of Ukraine's Past in Polish, Russian, and Ukrainian Historical Writing to 1914* (Edmonton: Canadian Institute of Ukrainian Studies, 1992) and *Shaping Identity in Eastern Europe and Russia: Soviet-Russia and Polish Accounts of Ukrainian History, 1914–1991* (New York: St. Martin's Press, 1993). Irena Gieysztor reports on "Research into the Demographic History of Poland: A Provisional Summing-up," *APH* 18 (1968): 159–86.

Specialist encyclopedias offer articles by noted scholars on all aspects of the Polish-Lithuanian state, including personalities and institutions. See the recent edition of the *Encyclopedia of Ukraine,* 5 vols. (1984–93), *Encyclopedia Lituanica,* 6 vols. (1970–78), and *Encyclopedia Judaica,* 16 vols. (1971–72). The

Modern Encyclopedia of Russian and Soviet History, 61 vols. (1976–97), is also useful. *The New Grove's Dictionary of Music,* 20 vols. (1980), provides a short article on Poland and numerous articles on leading Polish musicians. *The Dictionary of Art,* 34 vols. (1996), provides a long article on Poland with extensive cross-referencing to other articles. A volume in this series, Paul Robert Magocsi, *Historical Atlas of East Central Europe* (Seattle and Toronto: University of Washington Press and University of Toronto Press, 1993), offers useful and attractive maps along with expert explanations of the eras portrayed. Magocsi's *Ukraine: A Historical Atlas* (Toronto: University of Toronto Press, 1985) covers Ukrainian history. I. C. Pogonowski, *Poland: A Historical Atlas* (New York: Hippocrene, 1986) and *The Historical Atlas of Poland* (Warsaw: State Cartographical Publishers, 1986) provide numerous maps of Poland and surrounding territories.

THE POLISH-LITHUANIAN STATE IN THE JAGIELLONIAN ERA

Political History

The leading figures have been little studied in English. A late book by a major historian of interwar Poland is Oscar Halecki, *Jadwiga of Anjou and the Rise of East Central Europe* (Boulder, Colo.: East-European Monographs, 1991), which can be supplemented by articles by Anna Brzezińska, Paul Knoll, and Thaddeus V. Gromada in *Polish Review* 44:3 (1999). A reliable general introduction to mid-fifteenth-century Poland-Lithuania, including the political system, appears in a translated work, Maria Bogucka, *Nicolas Copernicus: The Country and Times* (Wrocław: Ossolineum, 1973). The best-studied part of political history is the evolution of the parliamentary system. Several contributions by leading Polish historians (Henryk Samsonowicz, Andrzej Wyczański, and Antoni Mączak) in J. K. Fedorowicz, ed., *A Republic of Nobles* (Cambridge: University Press, 1982), delineate the political authority held by kings, parliaments, and dietines. James Miller underscores parliamentary activity in "The Sixteenth-Century Roots of the Polish Democratic Tradition," in M. B. Biskupski and James S. Pula, eds., *Polish Democratic Thought from the Renaissance to the Great Emigration: Essays and Documents* (Boulder: East European Monographs, 1990). A comparative view appears in Stanisław Russocki, "The Parliamentary Systems in 15th-Century Central Europe," *Poland at the 14th International Congress of Historical Sciences in San Francisco* (Wrocław: Ossolineum, 1975), 7–22. Papers by leading Polish historians (Antoni Mączak, Andrzej Walicki, and Waldemar Voisé) appear in Samuel Fiszman, ed., *The Polish Renaissance in Its European Context* (Bloomington: Indiana University Press, 1988): on issues of political theory and practice.

Harry E. Dembkowski, *The Union of Lublin: Polish Federalism in the*

Golden Age (Boulder: East European Monographs, 1982), studies this fundamental act. Ukrainian aspects of the Union of Lublin are discussed in Jaroslaw Pelenski, "The Incorporation of the Ukrainian Lands of Old Rus into Crown Poland," *The Contest for the Legacy of Kievan Rus'* (Boulder: East European Monographs, 1998), and Jerzy Borzęcki, "The Union of Lublin as Factor in the Emergence of Ukrainian National Consciousness," *Polish Review* 41:1 (1996): 37–61.

International politics draw limited attention. William H. McNeill, *Europe's Steppe Frontier, 1500–1800* (Chicago: University of Chicago Press, 1964), presents a pioneering study of a geographical region rather than the histories of the states that comprise it. David Kirby, *Northern Europe in the Early Modern Period: The Baltic World, 1492–1772* (New York: Longman, 1990), includes the Polish-Lithuanian region.

Both Lithuanian and Ruthenian aspects of the Grand Duchy of Lithuania have been investigated. Jonas Žmudzinas, *Commonwealth polono-lithuanien où l'Union de Lublin (1569)* (Hague: Mouton, 1978), provides a Lithuanian perspective on the developing relationship between Poland and Lithuania. Joseph Jakstas asks "How Firm Was the Polish-Lithuanian Federation?" *Slavic Review* 22:3 (1963): 442–49, in response to Oswald P. Backus, "The Problem of Unity in the Polish-Lithuanian State," 411–31 and 450–55. A Polish scholar, Jerzy Ochmański, describes "The National Idea in Lithuania from the 16th to the First Half of the 19th Century: The Problem of Cultural Linguistic Differentiation," *HUS* 10:3/4 (December 1986): 301–15. The role of Ruthenians in the Grand Duchy is discussed by Oswald Prentiss Backus, *Motives of West Russian Nobles in Deserting Lithuania for Moscow, 1377–1514* (Lawrence: University of Kansas Press, 1957), and, in more general terms, by George Vernadsky, *Russia at the Dawn of the Modern Age* (New Haven: Yale University Press, 1959). George Shevolov, "Byelorussia versus Ukrainian: Delimitation of Texts before AD 1569," *Journal of Byelorussian Studies* 3 (1974): 145–56, discusses language use in the Grand Duchy. Jaroslaw Pelenski, *The Contest for the Legacy of Kievan Rus'*, reprints significant articles.

Old stereotypes of German-Polish conflict are reinterpreted in B. Zientara, "Nationality Conflicts in the German Slavic Borderland in the 13th and 14th Centuries and Their Social Scope," *APH* 22 (1970): 207–25. Aspects of the classical work by F. L. Carsten, *The Origins of Prussia* (Oxford: Oxford University Press, 1954), are updated in Michael Burleigh, *Prussian Society and the German Order: An Aristocratic Corporation in Crisis, c. 1410–1466* (Cambridge: University Press, 1984).

The thorny question of distinguishing between modern nationalism and less clearly defined Renaissance attitudes is studied by Konstantin Symons-

Symonolewicz, "National Consciousness in Medieval Europe: Some Theoretical Problems," *Canadian Review of Studies in Nationalism* 8:1 (1981): 151–166, and Paul W. Knoll, "National Consciousness in Medieval Poland," *Ethnic Studies* 10 (1993): 65–84. The problem is studied more generally in a special issue by I. Banac and F. E. Sysyn, *Concepts of Nationhood in Early Modern Eastern Europe, HUS* 10:3/4 (December 1986). See also Peter F. Sugar and Ivo John Lederer, eds., *Nationalism in Eastern Europe,* 2d ed. (Seattle: University of Washington Press, 1995).

Cultural History

Articles in the *Dictionary of the Reformation,* 4 vols. (1996), survey the Reformation in Poland-Lithuania. A full account appears in Ambroise Jobert, *De Luther à Mohila: La Pologne dans la crise de la chrétienté. 1517–1648* (Paris: Institut d'Études Slaves, 1974). Janusz Tazbir boasts of religious toleration in his translated work, *A State without Stakes: Polish Religious Toleration in the Sixteenth and Seventeenth Centuries* (New York: Kosciuszko Foundation, 1973). Antanas Musteikis covers *The Reformation in Lithuania* (Boulder: East European Monographs, 1988) as does Marceli Kosman, "Programme of the Reformation in the Grand Duchy of Lithuania and How It Was Carried Through (ca. 1550–ca. 1650)," *APH* 35 (1977): 21–50. George H. Williams, "Erasmianism in Poland," *Polish Review* 22:3 (1977): 2–50, describes Erasmus's strong influence on the early stages of both Catholic and Protestant reform in Poland and the declining interest in later periods. Jill Raitt, ed., *Shapers of Religious Traditions in Germany, Switzerland, and Poland, 1560–1600* (New Haven: Yale University Press, 1981), supplies short biographies by George Huntston Williams, "Stanislas Hosius," 157–74 and "Piotr Skarga," 175–94, and a biography by Zbigniew Ogonowski of the Anabaptist, "Faustus Socinus," 195–209. Analysis and documents are found in George Huntston Williams, *The Polish Brethren,* 2 vols. (Missoula: Scholars Press, 1980). Oscar Halecki discusses the efforts of the Catholic Church to bring Orthodox Christians under its wing in *From Florence to Brest, 1439–1596,* 2d ed. (Hamden, Conn.: Archon Books, 1968). David A. Frick, *Polish Sacred Philology in the Reformation and the Counter-Reformation* (Berkeley: University of California Press, 1989), discusses translations of the Bible into Polish.

Harold Segel takes a biographical approach to *Renaissance Culture in Poland: The Rise of Humanism, 1470–1543* (Ithaca: Cornell University Press, 1989). Nicholas Copernicus's career is described in Angus Armitage, *Copernicus: The Founder of Modern Astronomy* (New York: Thomas Yoseloff, 1957), and Paul Knoll, "The World of Young Copernicus," in Nicholas H. Steneck, ed., *Science and Society, Past Present, and Future* (Ann Arbor: University of Michigan Press, 1975), 19–44. Szczepan K. Zimmer discusses *The Beginning of Cyrillic Printing, Cracow 1491: From the Orthodox Past in Poland* (Boulder:

Social Science Monographs, 1983) against a general background of early printing in Cracow. Several translations of Polish-language literature are available to English-language readers: Bogdana Carpenter, ed., *Monumenta Polonia* (Ann Arbor: Slavica, 1989); Michael J. Mikos, ed., *Medieval Literature in Poland* (New York: Garland, 1992); Michael J. Mikos, ed., *Renaissance and Baroque Literature in Poland* (New York: Garland, 1994); and Jan Kochanowski, *Laments,* trans. Stanisław Baranczak (New York: Farrar, Straus and Giroux, 1995). An abridged version of Jan Długosz's monumental fifteenth-century history of Poland has been published by Maurice Michal, ed., *The Annals of Jan Dlugosz* (Chicester, UK: IM Publication, 1997).

Artistic trends are presented and interpreted in a handsomely illustrated volume by Helena and Stefan Kozakiewicz, *The Renaissance in Poland* (Warsaw: Arkady, 1976). Jan Białostocki describes Poland-Lithuania in *The Art of the Renaissance in Eastern Europe* (Ithaca: Cornell University Press, 1976) and more briefly in "Renaissance Sculpture in Poland in Its European Context: Some Selected Problems," in Fiszman, ed., *The Polish Renaissance in Its European Context,* 281–90. Thomas DaCosta Kaufmann places Polish-Lithuania art in context in *Court, Cloister, and City: The Art and Culture of Central Europe, 1450–1800* (London: Weidenfeld and Nicolson; Chicago: University of Chicago Press, 1995). Urbanization is discussed in Wojciech Kalinowski, *City Development in Poland Up to the Mid 19th Century,* trans. Agnieszka Glinka (Warsaw: Institute for Town Planning and Architecture, 1966). Brian Knox describes *The Architecture of Poland* (New York: Praeger, 1971). Art collecting is addressed in W. Tomkiewicz, "Le Mécenat artistique en Pologne à l'époque de la renaissance et du début du baroque," *APH* 16 (1967): 91–108, and, more broadly, in Andrzej Wyrobisz, "The Arts and Social Prestige in Poland between the Sixteenth and Eighteenth Centuries," in Fedorowicz, ed., *A Republic of Nobles,* 153–78.

The New Grove's Dictionary of Music provides articles on leading Polish musicians by Polish specialists. Tomasz M. Czepiel describes *Music at the Royal Court and Chapel in Poland, c. 1543–1600* (New York: Garland, 1996).

Economic and Social History

There is no comprehensive picture of Polish-Lithuanian economic development in English for this period, but a good deal of information can be gleaned from studies on the grain trade and others with a regional focus. Stanisław Hoszowski wrote a seminal article on the "The Revolution in Prices in Poland in the 16th and 17th centuries," *APH* 2 (1961): 7–16. Contributions to *Poland at the XIth International Congress of Historical Sciences in Stockholm* (Warsaw: PWN, 1960) by Marian Małowist and Stanisław Hoszowski amplify the picture of Baltic trade. Edmund Cieslak and Czesław Biernat, eds., *History of Gdańsk* (Gdańsk: Wydawnictwo Morskie, 1988), report the highlights of their multivolume Polish-language work. The American sociologist, Immanuel Wallerstein, makes the Polish experience an important part of his controversial interpretation of *The Modern World-System*, 2 vols. (New York: Academic Press, 1974–80), based on Dependency Theory. His view is challenged by Jerzy Topolski in "Economic Decline in Poland from the Sixteenth to the Eighteenth Centuries," in Peter Earle, ed., *Essays in European Economic History, 1500–1800* (Oxford: Clarendon Press, 1974), 127–42, and in other works. F. W. Carter provides a detailed study of trading patterns in *Trade and Urban Development in Poland: An Economic Geography of Cracow, from Its Origins to 1795* (Cambridge: Cambridge University Press, 1994). More narrowly focused studies include articles such as Antoni Mączak, "Money and Society in Poland and Lithuania in the 16th and 17th Centuries," *Journal of European Economic History* 5:1 (1976): 69–104; Mączak, "Wool Production and the Wool Trade in East Central Europe from the 14th to the 17th Century," *La Lana Come Materia Prima: Atti della prima "Settimana di studio" 18–24 Aprile 1969* (Florence: Leo S. Olschki, 1974), 353–67; and Danuta Molenda, "Investments in Ore Mining in Poland from the 13th to the 17th Centuries," *Journal of European Economic History* 5:1 (1976): 151–69.

A broad context is provided in Marian Małowist, "Problems of the Growth of the National Economy of Central Eastern Europe in the Late Middle Ages," *Journal of European Economic History* 3:2 (1974): 319–57, and Jerzy Topolski, "Sixteenth Century Poland and the Turning Point in European Economic Development," 3:2 (1974): 70–90. Similarly, Antoni Mączak et al., *East-Central Europe in Transition: From the Fourteenth to the Seventeenth Century* (Cambridge: University Press, 1985), includes articles by Andrzej Wyrobisz, Eric Fugedi, Leonid Żytkowicz, Marian Małowist, and Jerzy Topolski on agriculture and commerce in comparative perspective.

The magnate grouping within the nobility receives careful scrutiny in Henryk Litwin, "The Polish Magnates, 1454–1648: The Shaping of an Estate," *APH* 53 (1986): 63–92. Social mobility is discussed in W. Dworzaczak, "Perméabilité des barrières sociales dans la Pologne du XVIe s.," *APH* 24 (1971): 20–50.

Cities and city dwellers are examined in a variety of works. Paul W. Knoll discusses "The Urban Development of Medieval Poland, with Specific Reference to Krakow," in Barisa Krekic, ed., *Urban Society in Eastern Europe in Premodern Times* (Berkeley: University of California Press, 1987), 63–136. More generally, Andrzej Wyrobisz discusses "Small Towns in 16th and 17th Century Poland," *APH* 34 (1976): 153–64, and, more recently, "Power and Towns in the Polish Gentry Commonwealth: The Polish-Lithuanian State in the Sixteenth and Seventeenth Centuries," in Charles Tilly and William P. Brockmans, eds., *Cities* and the Rise of States in Europe, A.D. 1000–1800 (Boulder: Westview, 1994), 150–67. Maria Bogucka describes "Polish Towns between the Sixteenth and Eighteenth Centuries," in Fedorowicz, ed., *A Republic of Nobles*, 135–52, and "The Towns of East-Central Europe from the Fourteenth to the Seventeenth Century," in *East-Central Europe in Transition: From the Fourteenth to the Seventeenth Century*, 97–108.

The evolution of the Jewish community and the role of the Jews in Poland-Lithuania are described in detail in volume 16 of a fundamental study by the distinguished Polish-Jewish-American historian, Salo Whittmayer Baron: *A Social and Religious History of the Jews*, 16 vols. (New York: Columbia University Press, 1952). Jacob Goldberg, *Jewish Privileges in the Polish Commonwealth* (Jerusalem: Israel Academy of Sciences and Humanities, 1985), publishes original sources together with a substantial introductory discussion. Masha Greenbaum describes *The Jews of Lithuania, 1316–1945* (New York: Gefen, 1995). Maurycy Horn analyzes "Jewish Jurisdiction's Dependence on Royal Power in Poland and Lithuania Up to 1548," *APH* 75 (1997): 5–18. The views of a noted prewar historian of Jewish economic life are summarized by a devoted student in Jacob Litman, *The Economic Role of Jews in Medieval Poland: The Contribution of Yitzhak Schipper* (New York: University Press of America, 1984). Mark Wischnitzer explores artisanal activities in *A History of Jewish Crafts and Guilds* (New York: Jonathan David, 1965). Selected topics are discussed by articles in Antony Polonsky et al., *The Jews in Old Poland, 1000–1795* (New York: I. B. Tauris, 1993). *Polin* devotes volume 10 to social and cultural aspects of "Jews in Early Modern Poland" (1997), including articles by Elimelech Westreich, Zenon Guldon, and Jacek Wijaczka. G. D. Hundert discusses "Jewish Urban Residence in the Polish Commonwealth in the Early Modern Period," *Jewish Journal of Sociology* 26:1 (1984): 25–34.

Research on women's history in Poland-Lithuania begins with Aleksander Gieysztor, "La femme dans la civilisation des peuples slaves," in Pierre Grimal, ed., *Histoire mondiale de la femme*, 3 vols. (Paris: Nouvelle Librairie de France, 1967), 3:45–95. Maria Bogucka summarizes and interprets recent research in "The Foundations of the Old Polish World: Patriarchalism and the Family, Introduction to the Problem," *APH* 69 (1994): 37–54. She addresses "Gender in the Economy of a Traditional Agrarian Society: The Case of Poland in the 16th–17th Centuries," *APH* 74 (1996): 5–19, and her general discussion of "Women and Religion in the Early Modern Period," *APH* 77 (1998): 5–26, includes material on Poland. Andrzej Wyrobisz analyzes "Patterns of the Family and Woman in Old Poland," *APH* 71 (1995): 69–82. Andrzej Karpiński studies "Female Servants in Polish Towns in the Late 16th and 17th Centuries," *APH* 74 (1996): 21–44. Bogucka continues her pioneering work in new aspects of history in "Space and Time as Factors Shaping Polish Mentality from the 16th until the 18th Century," *APH* 66 (1992): 39–52.

THE POLISH-LITHUANIAN STATE IN THE VASA ERA

Political History

The earlier years of the Vasa dynasty have not received much attention in English, although Antoni Mączak paints them as "The Conclusive Years: The End of the Sixteenth Century as the Turning-Point of Polish History," in *Politics and Society in Reformation Europe: Essays for Sir Geoffrey Elton on His Sixty-Fifth Birthday* (New York: St. Martin's Press, 1987), 516–32. Kazimierz Lepszy discusses "The Union of the Crowns Between Poland and Sweden in 1587," *Poland at the XIth International Congress of Historical Sciences in Stockholm* (Warsaw: PWN, 1960), 157–82. The dramatic finale of the period is reported in Robert I. Frost, *After the Deluge: Poland-Lithuania and the Second Northern War, 1655–1660* (Cambridge: University Press, 1993), which analyzes both domestic politics and international relations. The events can be viewed briefly from the Swedish side in Michael Roberts, *The Swedish Imperial Experience, 1650–1718* (Cambridge: University Press, 1979). The whole period is surveyed in Robert I. Frost, *War, State and Society in the Baltic* (London: Longman, forthcoming). The hero of Vienna is investigated by Zbigniew Wójcik, "Jean Sobieski—du politicien a l'homme d'État," *APH* 47 (1983): 5–32.

Trends in constitutional development have come under considerable scrutiny. Władysław Konopczyński, *Le Liberum veto* (Paris: Champion, 1930), is still the definitive history of this distinctive institution. Robert I. Frost discusses "Liberty without License? The Failure of Polish Democratic Thought in the Seventeenth Century," in Biskupski and Pula, eds., *Polish Democratic Thought from the Renaissance to the Great Emigration,* and Polish historians present their views in Władysław Czaplinski, ed., *The Polish Parliament at the Summit of Its Development (16th–17th Centuries)* (Wrocław: Ossolineum, 1985): Władysław Czaplinski, Juliusz Bardach, Jan Seredyka, and Stefania Ochmann. Henryk Olszewski provides "Reflections on the Theory and Practice of Seym Debate in Poland from the 16th to the 18th Centuries," *APH* 48 (1983): 57–75. Stanisław Plaza analyzes "Changes in the Political System of the Polish Commonwealth After the Extinction of the Jagiellonian Dynasty," *APH* 52 (1985): 65–86. Andrzej Kaminski challenges long-standing interpretations when he emphasizes the constructive role of the senate in "The *Szlachta* of the Polish-Lithuanian Commonwealth and Their Government," in Ivo Banac and Paul Bushkovitch, eds., *The Nobility in Russia and Eastern Europe* (New Haven: Yale University Press, 1983), 17–45, and in Andrzej Sulima Kamiński, *Republic vs. Autocracy: Poland-Lithuania and Russia, 1686–1697* (Cambridge: Harvard Ukrainian Research

Institute, 1993), along with an extensive discussion of Polish-Lithuanian diplomatic practice. Henryk Olszewski, "The Political System and Political Thought in Poland During the Reign of Jan Sobieski," *APH* 52 (1985): 87–104, takes the story beyond the Vasa period.

The noted Russian émigré historian George Vernadsky discusses the great Cossack revolt of 1648 in the outdated but still useful biography, *Bohdan, Hetman of Ukraine* (New Haven: Yale University Press, 1941). The historiography of the Cossack revolt is analyzed in John Basarab, *Pereiaslav 1654: A Historiographical Study* (Edmonton: Canadian Institute of Ukrainian Studies, 1982). George Gajecky scrutinizes *The Cossack Administration of the Hetmanate*, 2 vols. (Cambridge, Mass., 1978). Frank E. Sysyn, *Between Poland and the Ukraine: The Dilemma of Adam Kysil, 1600–1653* (Cambridge: Harvard Ukrainian Institute, 1985), portrays the career of an Orthodox noble who worked within the Polish-Lithuanian Commonwealth. Peter J. Potichnyj, ed., *Poland and Ukraine: Past and Present* (Edmonton: Canadian Institute of Ukrainian Studies, 1980), includes thoughtful, wide-ranging discussions of the Polish-Ukrainian relationship by Ivan L. Rudnytsky, Andrzej Kaminski, Frank E. Sysyn, and Orest Subtelny. Andrzej Sulima Kaminski examines "The Cossack Experiment in *Szlachta* Democracy in the Polish-Lithuanian Commonwealth: The Hadiach (*Hadziacz*) Union," *HUS* 1:2 (1977): 178–97. The Cossack revolt and the Hetman State are further examined in L. R. Lewitter, "Poland, the Ukraine and Russia in the 17th Century," *Slavonic and East European Review* 27 (1948–49): 157–71 and 415–29.

The Prussian passage from Polish to German rule is analyzed in the classic study, F. L. Carsten, *The Origins of Prussia* (Oxford: University Press, Oxford 1954), and in Anna Kaminska, *Brandenburg-Prussia and Poland, 1669–1672* (Marburg/Lahn: Herder Institute, 1983). Prussian views of the Polish-Lithuanian Commonwealth are discussed in Karin Friedrich, *The Other Prussia: Poland, Prussia and Liberty, 1569–1772* (Cambridge: University Press, 1999). Wiesław Majewski, "The Polish Art of War in the Sixteenth and Seventeenth Centuries," in Fedorowicz, ed., *A Republic of Nobles*, 179–97, introduces Polish military tactics. Lithuanian attitudes are discussed in Zbigniew Wójcik, "The Separatist Tendencies in the Grand Duchy of Lithuania in the 17th Century," *APH* 69 (1994): 55–62, and Kazimierz Piwarski, "Lithuanian Participation in Poland's Baltic Politics, 1650–1700," *Baltic and Scandinavian Countries* 3 (1937): 21–26.

Social and Economic History

The complexity of economic decline was raised in Andrzej Kaminski in "Neo-Serfdom in Poland-Lithuania," *Slavic Review* 34:2 (June 1975): 252–68, and, more recently, in Jacek Kochanowicz, "The Polish Economy and the Evolution of Dependency," in Daniel Chirot, ed., *The Origins of Backwardness in Eastern Europe* (Berkeley: University of California Press, 1989), 92–131. Domestic elements are stressed in Jerzy Topoleski, "La régression économique en Pologne du XVIe au XVIIIe siècle," *APH* 7 (1962): 28–49, and "La dynamique de court terme et la dynamique de la longue durée dans l'explication de l'évolution agraire en Pologne du XVIe–XVIIIe siècle," *Studia Historiae Oeconomicae* 17 (1982): 15–27. A fundamental analysis against which several of these authors were reacting is Witold Kula, *Economic Theory of Feudalism* (London: NBL, 1976), originally published in Polish in 1962. Local studies are discussed in Jerzy Ochmański, "Polish Studies on the Economic History of Byelorussia in the Period of Feudalism," *Studia Historiae Oeconomicae* 16 (1981): 81–94. J. K. Fedorowicz, *England's Baltic Trade in the Early Seventeenth Century* (Cambridge: University Press, 1980) adds a detailed treatment of trading links with Poland.

Defining the magnate elite dominates writing on social classes. Adam Kersten delineates "Les Magnats—élite de la societé nobiliaire," *APH* 36 (1977): 119–34, as does A. Pośpiech with W. Tygielski, "The Social Role of Magnate Courts in Poland from the End of the 16th up to the 18th Centuries," *APH* 43 (1981): 75–100. Henryk Olszewski analyzes "The Essence and Legal Foundation of the Magnate Oligarchy in Poland," *APH* 56 (1988): 29–50. A subperiod is discussed in E. Opaliński, "Great Poland's Power Elite under Zygmunt III, 1587–1632," *APH* 42 (1980): 41–66. Włodzimierz Dworzaczak points in another direction with his article, "La Mobilité sociale de la noblesse polonaise aux XVIe–XVIIIe siècles," *APH* 36 (1977): 137–62. Maria Bogucka addresses "Social Structures and Custom," *APH* 68 (1993): 99–114, with particular reference to issues of social mobility.

Analysis of criminal behavior and punishment is a relatively new field in Polish historiography. Maria Bogucka discusses "Law and Crime in Poland in Early Modern Times," *APH* 71 (1995): 175–95, and Marcin Kamler reports "Penalties for Common Crimes in Polish Towns 1550–1650," *APH* 71 (1995): 161–74. More narrowly, Marcin Kamler deals with: "Infanticide in the Towns of the Kingdom of Poland in the Second Half of the 16th and the First Half of the 17th Century," *APH* 58 (1988): 33–50; "The Role of Torture in Polish Municipal Judicature in the Second Half of the 16th and the First Half of the 17th Century," *APH* 66 (1992): 39–52; and "Robbery in the Polish Lands During the Second Half of the Sixteenth and the First Half of the Seventeenth Century," *APH* 68 (1993): 59–77.

Contemporary descriptions of the emerging Cossack group are provided in Lubomyr R. Wynar, ed. *Habsburgs and Zaporozhian Cossacks: The Diary of Erich Lassota von Steblau, 1594,* trans. Orest Subtelny (Littleton, Colo.:

Ukrainian Academic Press, 1975), and Guillaume du Beauplan, *A Description of Ukraine* (Cambridge: Harvard University Press for the Ukrainian Research Center, 1993).

Cultural History

The Old Polish way of life is recreated in Maria Bogucka, *The Lost World of the "Sarmatians": Custom as the Regulator of Polish Cultural Life in Early Modern Times* (Warsaw: History Institute, Academy of Sciences, 1996). The Sarmatian mentality of Polish-Lithuanian nobles is analyzed in Stanisław Cynarski, "The Shape of Sarmatian Ideology in Poland," *APH* 19 (1968): 5–17. Jan Chrysostem Pasek, *Memoirs of the Polish Barogue,* trans. Catherine S. Leach (Berkeley: University of California Press, 1976), offers an example of that mentality. Janusz Tazbir emphasizes pan-European elements in his article, "Culture of the Baroque in Poland," in *East-Central Europe in Transition: From the Fourteenth to the Seventeenth Century,* 167–80. Maria Bogucka shows its relevance for commoners in "L'Attrait de la culture nobiliare: Sarmatisation de la bourgeoisie polonaise au XVIIe siècle," *APH* 33 (1976): 23–42.

Religious culture is analyzed in Aleksander Witkowska, "The Cult of the Jasna Gora Sanctuary in the Form of Pilgrimages till the Middle of the 17th Century," *APH* 61 (1990): 63–90. Religious issues are described by a participant in Stanislas Lubieniecki, *History of the Polish Reformation and Nine Related Documents,* translated and interpreted by George Huntston Williams, Harvard Theological Series 37 (Minneapolis: Fortress Press, 1995). For texts and interpretations, see George Huntston Williams, *The Polish Brethren.* 2 vols. (Missoula: Scholars Press, 1980). Janusz Tazbir describes "The Fate of Polish Protestantism in the Seventeenth Century," in Fedoyowicz, ed., *A Republic of Nobles,* 198–217, and H. Hans traces "Polish Protestants and Their Connections in England in the XVII and XVIII Centuries," *Slavonic and East European Review* 37 (1958): 196–220. John Friesen discusses "Mennonites in Poland: An Expanded Historical View," *Journal of Mennonite Studies* 4 (1986): 94–108. Peter J. Klassen provides a short description of *A Homeland for Strangers: An Introduction to Mennonites in Poland and Prussia* (Fresno: Center for Mennonite Brethren Studies, 1989).

The emerging Orthodox and Cossack groups in Ukraine come under scrutiny. Articles by Omeljan Pritsak, Frank Sysyn, and Orest Subtelny in Ivan L. Rudnytsky, ed., *Rethinking Ukrainian History* (Edmonton: Canadian Institute of Ukrainian Studies, 1981), analyze the rediscovery of the past and the evolution of the nobility. Teresa Chynczewska-Hennel discusses "The National Consciousness of Ukrainian Nobles and Cossacks from the End of the Sixteenth to the Mid-Seventeenth Century," *HUS* 10:3/4 (1986): 377–92, and Frank E.

Sysyn analyzes "Concepts of Nationhood in Ukrainian History Writing, 1620–1690," *HUS* 8:3/4 (1985): 393–423. A special issue devoted to the Kiev Mohyla Academy came out in *HUS* 8:1/2 (1984). A special issue of the *Journal of Ukrainian Studies* (Summer-Winter 1992) 17:1–2 was devoted to Early Modern Ukraine and includes articles on Ukrainian political and cultural identity, mostly in the seventeenth century, by: Zenon E. Kohut, Iaroslav Isaievich, Mikhail Dmitriev, Shmuel Ettinger, and Frank E. Sysyn, among others. David A. Frick, *Meletij Smotryc'kyj* (Cambridge: Harvard Ukrainian Research Institute, 1995), explores the ambiguities of Ruthenian national consciousness and religious identity in the early seventeenth century.

The evolution of the Tatar group is presented in Andrzej B. Zakrzewski, "Assimilation of Tatars within the Polish Commonwealth, 16th–18th Centuries," *APH* 55 (1967): 85–106, and Piotr Borawski, "Religious Tolerance and the Tatar Population in the Grand Duchy of Lithuania: 16th to 18th Centuries," *Journal* (Great Britain): 9:1 (1988): 119–33. The history of the Crimean Tatar state is described in Alan Fisher, *The Crimean Tatars* (Stanford: Hoover Institution, 1978).

Marius Karpowicz, *Baroque in Poland* (Warsaw: Arkady, 1991), analyzes artistic trends and illustrates them with handsome color plates. Delma Brought, *Polish Seventeenth-Century Church Music* (New York: Garland, 1989), provides an entry into Polish music of the period.

The Polish-Lithuanian State in the Eighteenth Century

Political History

Unlike earlier periods, the eighteenth century has been studied in considerable detail by foreign scholars. Jean Fabre's monumental account of *Stanislas-Auguste Poniatowski et l'Europe des lumières* (Paris: Les Belles Lettres, 1952) shows the links between culture and politics, and a popular introduction is provided by Adam Zamoyski, *The Last King of Poland* (London: Jonathan Cape, 1992; New York: Hippocrene, 1997). Kościuszko is known in English primarily through the work of an amateur scholar, Miecislaus Haiman, *Kosciuszko in the American Revolution* (New York: Kosciuszko Foundation and the Polish Institute of Arts and Sciences in America, 1975 [reprint of the 1943 edition]) and *Kosciuszko: Leader and Exile* (New York: Kosciuszko Foundation and the Polish Institute of Arts and Sciences in America, 1977 [reprint of the 1946 edition]).

Jerzy Lukowski, *Liberty's Folly: The Polish-Lithuanian Commonwealth in the Eighteenth Century, 1697–1795* (London: Routledge, 1991), provides a reliable general interpretation of political, economic, social, and cultural developments. R. R. Palmer *The Age of the Democratic Revolution,* 2 vols. (Princeton: Princeton University Press, 1956–64), draws on Polish scholarship to place developments in international context. Józef Andrzej Gierowski discusses "The

International Position of Poland in the Seventeenth and Eighteenth Centuries," in Fedorowicz, ed., *A Republic of Nobles*, 218–38. John L. Sutton describes *The King's Honor and the King's Cardinal: The War of the Polish Succession* (Lexington: University Press of Kentucky, 1980), relatively little of which deals with Poland. Herbert H. Kaplan analyzes *The First Partition of Poland* (New York: Columbia University Press, 1962) and finds Austria to be primarily responsible. G. T. Lukowski examines *The Szlachta and the Confederacy of Radom, 1764–1767/68: A Study of the Polish Nobility* (Rome, 1977). Daniel Stone discusses *Polish Politics and National Reform, 1775–1788* (Boulder: East European Monographs, 1776). Robert H. Lord wrote a brilliant, pioneering work on both domestic and international history on *The Second Partition of Poland* (Cambridge: Harvard University Press, 1915). Diplomacy is studied in Jerzy Lukowski, *The Partitions of Poland: 1772, 1793, 1795*. (New York and London: Addison; Wesley, Longman. 1998). Larry Wolff sheds light on the little known issue of *The Vatican and Poland in the Age of the Partitions* (Boulder: East European Monographs, 1988). English-language papers by Józef Gierowski, John Stanley, and Daniel Stone appear in the proceedings of the multinational, multilingual conference commemorating the bicentenary of the 1794 Insurrection in Heiko Haumann and Jerzy Skowronek, eds., *"Der letzte Ritter und erste Burger im Osten Europas"* (Basel: Helbing & Lichtenhahn, 1996).

Constitutional issues and the Constitution of May 3, 1791, are discussed in detail. The bicentenary of the Constitution was celebrated with the publication of a facsimile edition of an eighteenth-century book, *New Constitution of the Government of Poland Established by the Revolution, the Third of May, 1791* (Warsaw: Zamek Krolewski w Warszawie, 1991). Numerous articles by leading scholars reflect on aspects of late eighteenth-century Polish history in a large anthology by Samuel Fiszman, ed., *Constitution and Reform in Eighteenth Century Poland: The Constitution of May 3, 1791* (Bloomington: Indiana University Press, 1997). A reevaluation of the role of magnate factions in achieving reform is contributed by Janusz Duzinkiewicz, *Fateful Transformations: The Four Years' Parliament and the Constitution of May 3, 1791* (Boulder: East European Monographs, 1993). Daniel Stone provides British views in "Daniel Hailes and the Polish Constitution of May 3, 1791," *Polish Review* 36:2 (1981): 51–63, and analyzes the new constitutional regime in "The First (and Only) Year of the Constitution of May 3, 1791," *Canadian Slavonic Papers* 35:1–2 (June–March 1993): 69–86.

Papers presented mostly by leading Polish historians during a three-year colloquium at Brooklyn College provide broad general coverage of Polish-Lithuanian military problems in the Partition era. Gunther E. Rothenberg et al., *War and Society in East Central Europe in the Pre-Revolutionary Eighteenth Century*

(Boulder: Social Science Monographs, 1982), vol. 2, includes articles by Emanuel Rostworowski, Marian Zgórniak, Jerzy Kowecki, Leonard Ratajczyk, Józef Andrzej Gierowski, and Daniel Stone. Béla K. Király et al., *War and Society in East Central Europe in the Era of Revolutions, 1775–1856* (New York: Brooklyn College Press, 1984), vol. 4, includes contributions by Daniel Stone and Andrzej Zahorski. See also Daniel Stone, "Patriotism and Professionalism: The Polish Army in the Eighteenth Century," *Studies in History and Politics* 3 (1983/1984): 61–72.

Political and social thought are analyzed in Andrzej Walicki, *The Enlightenment and the Birth of Modern Nationhood: Polish Political Thought from the Noble Republic to Tadeusz Kosciuszko* (Notre Dame: Notre Dame University Press, 1989). Barbara Grochulska discusses "The Place of the Enlightenment in Polish Social History," in Fedorowicz, ed., *A Republic on Nobles*, 239–57, and Daniel Stone examines "Democratic Thought in Eighteenth Century Poland," in Biskupski and Pula, eds., *Polish Democratic Thought from the Renaissance to the Great Emigration*, 55–72.

Continuing efforts by Cossacks to attain statehood are shown in I. S. Mazepa, *On the Eve of Poltava* (New York: Ukrainian Academy of Arts and Sciences, 1975), and Orest Subtelny, *The Mazepists: Ukrainian Separatism in the Early Eighteenth Century* (Boulder: East European Monographs, 1981). Ukrainian national consciousness is examined in Zenon E. Kohut, "Problems in Studying the Post-Khmelnytsky Ukrainian Elite (1650s to 1830s)," in Rudnytsky, ed., *Rethinking Ukrainian History*, 103–19, and in "The Development of a Little Russian Identity and Ukrainian Nationbuilding," *HUS* 10 (1996): 559–76. John-Paul Himka discusses the role of the "The Greek Catholic Church and Nation Building in Galicia, 1772–1918," *HUS* 8:3/4 (1984), 426–52, and "The Conflict between the Secular and Religious Clergy in Eighteenth-Century Western Ukraine," *HUS* (1991): 15:1/2. David Saunders, *The Ukrainian Impact on Russian Culture, 1750–1850* (Edmonton: Canadian Institute of Ukrainian Studies, 1985), shows the importance of Polish-influenced Ukrainians in an unexpected context.

Economic and Social History

Late eighteenth-century social changes and their political significance are discussed in Daniel Stone, "The End of Medieval Particularism: Polish Cities and the Diet, 1764–1789," *Canadian Slavonic Papers* 20:2 (June 1978): 194–207. Bogna Lorence-Kot, *Child-Rearing and Reform: A Study of the Nobility in Eighteenth-Century Poland* (Westport: Greenwood Press, 1985), presents an introduction to gender roles and family structures. Cezary Kuklo uses archival sources to explore "The Family in 18th Century Warsaw: Demographic Studies," *APH* 61 (1990): 141–60.

Two recent books clarify aspects of Jewish life in eighteenth-century Poland-Lithuania. M. J. Rosman, *The Lords' Jews: Magnate-Jewish Relations in the Polish-Lithuanian Commonwealth during the Eighteenth Century* (Cambridge: Harvard Ukrainian Institute, 1990), explores the important economic role that Jews played on the estates of great nobles, and Gershon David Hundert, *The Jews in a Polish Private Town: The Case of Opatow in the Eighteenth Century* (Baltimore: Johns Hopkins University Press, 1992), describes political, economic, social, and religious life. Hillel Levine, *Economic Origins of Anti-Semitism: Poland and Its Jews in the Early Modern Period* (New Haven: Yale University Press, 1991), relies on ideal types. Articles by Peter J. Martyn, Marian Marek Drozdowski, Artur Eisenbach, and Krystyna Zieńkowska in *The Jews in Warsaw,* ed. Władysław T. Bartoszewski and Antony Polonsky (Oxford: Blackwell, 1991), discuss the place of Jews in eighteenth-century Poland-Lithuania. The same issues are discussed more broadly in Krystyna Zieńkowska, "Citizens or Inhabitants? The Attempt to Reform the Status of the Polish Jews During the Four Years' Sejm," *Polin* 10 (1997): 31–52. Cultural and political issues are linked in Daniel Stone, "Jews and the Urban Question in Late Eighteenth Century Poland," *Slavic Review* 50:3 (Fall 1991): 531–42.

Cultural History

Richard Butterwick, *Poland's Last King and English Culture* (Oxford: Clarendon Press, 1998), adds an English dimension to the French orientation of Fabre's biography. Ambroise Jobert undertook major studies of cultural issues in *Magnats polonais et physiocrates français, 1767–1774* (Paris: Droz, 1941) and *La Commission d'éducation nationale en Pologne (1773–1794)* (Paris: Droz, 1941). Jacek Staszewski discusses the decentralized nature of the Polish Enlightenment in "La culture polonaise pendant la crise du XVIIIe siècle," *APH* 55 (1987): 107–32. Jerzy Jedlicki shows that eighteenth-century Poles understood themselves to be catching up to the West in "Native Culture and Western Civilization," *APH* 28 (1974):63–86. Daniel Stone adds a note on Sarmatian stereotypes in "The Cultural Life of Conservative Polish Nobles in the Partition Era," *East European Quarterly* 9:3 (1975): 271–75. The visual arts are analyzed and handsomely illustrated in Stanisław Lorentz and Andrzej Rottermund, *Neoclassicism in Poland* (Warsaw: Arkady, 1986). Władysław Tomkiewicz describes "Les Rapport des peintres françaises du XVIIe siècle avec la Pologne," *Biuletyn Historii Sztuki* 20:2 (1958): 174–85.

Jewish cultural and religious evolution are traced in several studies. Two frequently reprinted eighteenth-century Jewish memoirs are Moses Hadas, ed., *Solomon Maimon: An Autobiography* (New York: Schocken Books, 1975), and M. Vishnitzer, ed., *The Memoirs of Ber of Bolechow (1723–1805)* (London: Oxford University Press, 1922). The background to the Jewish Enlightenment is presented in Moses A. Shulvass, *From East to West: The Westward Migration of Jews from Eastern Europe during the 17th and 18th Centuries* (Detroit: Wayne State University Press, 1971). David E. Fishman presents *Russia's First Modern Jews: The Jews of Shklov* (New York: New York University Press, 1995) building on his earlier article, "A Polish Rabbi Meets the Berlin Haskalah: The Case of R. Barukh Schick," *AJS Review* 12:1 (1987): 95–121. The new eighteenth-century religious movement is presented and interpreted in Gershon David Hundert, ed., *Essential Papers of Hasidism* (New York: New York University Press, 1991), and Ada Rapoport-Albert, ed., *Hasidism Reappraised* (London: Littman Library of Jewish Civilization, 1996). Moshe [M. J.] Rosman gives new biographical information on the Besht in *Founder of Hasidism* (Berkeley: University of California Press, 1996). Another religious figure is examined in Jan Doktór, "Jakub Frank, a Jewish Heresiarch and His Messianic Doctrine," *APH* 75 (1997): 53–74; this special issue devoted to Jewish studies also includes Jakub Goldberg, "18th Century Memoirs of Polish Jews: Memoirs of Mojżesz Wasercug from Great Poland," 19–30. Volume 10 of *Polin,* a special issue devoted to Jews in Early Modern Poland, includes articles by Jacob Goldberg on marriage, Thomas C. Hubka on wooden synagogues, and Daniel Stone on knowledge of foreign languages.

INDEX

Adrianople, treaty of, 253
Aesop, 97, 329
Agincourt, battle of, 73
Agriculture: improvements in, 68; in German law villages, 68–69; and serfdom, 69–70, 190–92; in Lithuania, 72; in Prussia, 72–73; and settlement of Ukrainian lands, 195; and mid-seventeenth-century wars, 195–96, 256, 289–90; eighteenth-century recovery of, 290–92; peasant, 292–94; noble, 294–95. *See also* Peasants; Trade
Albert of Brandenburg, 30
Albertrandi, Jan (John), 315
Albrecht Friedrich, 123, 143
Aldona, 4
Aleksander: Grand Duke of Lithuania, 23, 26, 33; Polish King, 33–35; Jewish regulations, 87; supports music, 110
Aleksei Mikhailovich, 168, 170, 233
Alembert, Jean Le Rond d', 321
Algirdas, 3, 4
Alsace, 260
Altranstadt, treaty of, 252
America, 272, 284, 285, 316, 321, 322
Anabaptists. *See* Arians; Protestantism
Andrusovo, treaty of, 172, 240
Anna (daughter of Zygmunt I), 37
Anna (Russian empress), 260
Anna Habsburg (wife of Zygmunt III), 133, 149
Anna the Jagiellonian (Habsburg wife), 47
Anna the Jagiellonian (wife of Stefan Batory), 118, 119, 122
Antwerp, 221
Architecture, 111–13, 221–23, 327–28
Arenda. *See* Jews
Arians, 42, 43, 104, 120, 156, 217
Ariosto, 215
Aristotle, 95, 101, 105
Armed forces: noble levy, 7; Teutonic Knights, 15; Lithuanian, 44–45; reorganized against Tatars, 49–50; Batory's reforms, 126; Cossack units, 145–47, 292; Władysław IV's reforms, 151–52; partisan units, 168, 272; Sobieski tactics and reforms, 240–41; Radziwił private army, 264; military commissions, 270, 277; Komarzewski reforms, 276; Great Parliament, 278, 308, 317, 318; 1794 insurrection, 285–87
Armenians, 39, 43, 75, 124, 144, 195, 200, 202, 297, 334, 335
Astikas, Kristinas (Christian/ Krzysztof Ościk), 52, 53
Astravas (Ostrowo) Agreement, 10
August II (Friedrich August I of Saxony): revenues under, 187; and Saxony, 245–46; cultural interests of, 245, 248, 254, 322–23, 324, 327; character and aims of, 246–47; election of, 247–48; first steps as king, 248–49; and Great Northern War, 249–50; and election of Stanisław Leszczyński, 250–52; and Russia's defeat of Sweden, 252–53; reform efforts of, 253–58; and Cossack rebellions, 255–56; death of, 258
August III (Friedrich August II of Saxony): early years, 247, 254; election of, 259–61; as king, 261–62; cultural interests of, 262, 324, 328; and "The Family," 262–64; and anti-Czartoryski forces, 264–65; and War of Austrian Succession, 265; and Seven Years War, 266; and peasant rebellions, 266–67; educational reforms of, 312
Augustynowicz, Jan Tobias, 334
Aulack, Frederick von, 123
Austria: and Jagiełło, 8; and Kazimierz IV, 23; and Zygmunt I, 37, 46–49; and Zygmunt II, 51, 52, 53, 63, 66; trade with, 80, 203, 300, 301; Jews in, 83, 87, 284, 301, 334; and Henri III, 106, 117–18; and Batory, 122; and Zygmunt III, 131–33, 142–43, 144, 155, 212; and Władysław IV, 149, 150, 155; and Jan Kazmierz, 160, 169; and Sobieski, 209, 234, 238, 239–40; and Michał Wiśniowiecki, 233–34; and August II, 246, 247–48, 254, 255; and August III, 259–60, 265–66; and Stanisław II and August Poniatowski, 268, 272, 273, 275, 277, 285, 287–88

358 INDEX

Ba'al Shem Tov. *See* Israel ben Eliezer
Bacciarelli, Marcello, 328
Bach, Johann Sebastian, 324
Balaban, Dionysii, 273
Balaban, Gedeon, 138
Baltic. *See* Ducal Prussia; Prussia; Royal Prussia
Bamberg, 110
Banking and moneylending, 80, 81, 85, 201, 202, 203–4, 282, 294, 297, 305–6, 308
Bar, 174, 271–72, 317, 324
Baranowski, Wojciech, 223
Baroque: music, 149, 160, 223–25; culture, 212–13, 217–18; literature, 213–14, 218, 322; religious literature, 215; printing, 218; fine arts, 220–21; architecture and urbanization, 221–23. *See also* Sarmatianism; Science and medicine
Basel synod, 85
Basilian order. *See* Greek Catholic Church
Báthory, István. *See* Batory, Stefan
Batory, Christopher, 123
Batory, Gabriel, 134
Batory, Gryzelda, wife of Jan Zamoyski, 124
Batory, Stefan (Stephen), 57, 79, 106, 112, 131, 133; revenues under, 89; background of, 122–23; and Gdańsk, 123, 197; and Jan Zamoyski, 123–25; policies of, 125–26; and war with Russia, 126–27; death of, 127; Prussian policy of, 143; forms Cossack units, 145; and Warsaw, 222
Baturyn, 172
Beauplan, Guillaume de, 195
Belarus (Bielorussia). *See* Ruthenian territories
Belotto (Canaletto), Bernardo, 328
Belz, 135
Benedict XIII, 334
Benedict XIV, 331

Benedykt from Sandomierz, 112
Ber, Kasper, 79
Berdychiv (Berdyczów), 303, 304
Berecci, Bartolomeo, 112
Berestechko, battle of, 165, 174
Berlin, 334
Bethlen, Gábor, 144
Bezalel, Jacob, 241, 301
Bezpaly, Ivan, 172
Białystok, 327
Bieliński, Franciszek, 296
Bielski, Fedor, 26
Biernat of Lublin, 98
Bila Tserkva (Biała Cerkiew), agreement of, 165
Bilhorod (Akkerman), 32, 146
Blank, Piotr, 297°
Bochnia, 83, 300
Boethius, 110
Bogdan, Prince of Moldavia, 47
Bogusław X of Szczecin, 48
Bogusławski, Wojciech, 325, 329
Bohemia. *See* Czech Kingdom
Bohomolec, Franciszek, 270, 312, 315, 319, 325
Boileau, Nicolas, 315, 321
Bologna, 101
Boner, Jan (John), 38, 79
Boretsky, Yov, 148, 228
Brandenburg: controls Pomerania, 7, 246; conflicts with Poland, 16, 30, 47, 74. *See also* Prussia
Branicka, Izabela née Poniatowska, 263
Branicki, Franciszek Ksawery, 275, 284, 285, 328
Branicki, Jan Klemens, 262, 263, 327
Braniewo, 219
Bratslav, 46, 173, 196, 226, 273, 292, 304
Braunsberg, 18
Breughel, Pieter, 221, 328
Briukhovetsky, Ivan, 172
Brody, 79, 195, 200, 299, 303
Bromberg (Bydgoszcz), treaty of, 169

Brühl, Alojzy Fryderyk, 264
Brühl, Heinrich, 262, 263, 264
Brześć (Brest-Litovsk), 24, 138, 330
Brzostowski, Paweł, 293
Buchach (Buczacz), treaty of, 236
Büchholtz, Ludwig, 277
Bucovina, 33
Buda, 36, 48, 112
Budny, Szymon, 104
Buffon, George-Louis Leclerc, 317
Bug (Buh) River, 44
Bulgakov, Jakob, 285
Buonaccorsi, Philipo (Kallimach), 32, 97, 114
Burattini, Tito Livias, 163
Burghers, 79–82; in seventeenth century, 201–2; in Ruthenian revival, 226–27; in 1794 insurrection, 286; Enlightenment attitude towards, 317–19. *See also* Cities; Jews
Butrymowicz, Mateusz (Matthew), 331
Buturlin, 256
Buturlin, Vasilii, 165
Byczyna, battle of, 132, 223
Bydgoszcz, 40, 169

Calvin, John, 55, 102
Canals, 300
Canavesi, Hieronim, 114
Capistrano, Giovanni, 87
Caro, Joseph, 110, 229
Carosi, Filip, 325
Carpathian region, 73, 292, 294
Castiglione, Baldasarre, 107
Catherine II (the Great), Empress of Russia, 263, 266, 269, 271, 276, 284, 285, 287, 330
Catholic Church: role in state formation, 5–6; independence from Rome, 26–27, 35; wealth of, 42; and Zygmunt II, 55–57; and Catholic resurgence, 56–57, 214–16; and humanism, 100–1; and Counter Refor-

mation, 136–39, 224–25; and appeal rights, 269, 276, 317; taxed, 278, 308
Cecilia Renata Habsburg (first wife of Władysław IV), 150, 155
Cecora. *See* Ţuţora
Celtes, Konrad (Konrad Pickel), 97
Cerekwica, 28
Cesarini, Julian, 22
Chamber of Deputies, 180–81. *See also* Parliament
Chambord, 260
Charles I, 154
Charles V, 39, 43
Charles IX, 119, 121
Charles Stuart, 264
Charles University, 95
Chartoryski (Czartoryski), Aleksander Vasilievich, 26
Chartoryski family. *See* Czartoryski family
Chełm, 30
Chełmno, 18, 98
Chernihiv, 157, 170, 196
Chmielnicki, Bogdan. *See* Khmelnytsky, Bohdan
Chmielowski, Benedykt, 309
Chocim. *See* Khotyn
Chodkiewicz, Grzegorz. *See* Khodkevich, Grigorii
Chodkiewicz, Jan Karol (John Charles): defeats Zebrzydowski, 134; funeral of, 135; victory at Kirchholm, 140; and war with Russia, 141; victory at Khotyn, 145; husband of Anna Ostrożska, 215; biography of, 326
Chojnice, 28
Chopin, Fryderyk, 324
Chreptowicz, Joachim, 274, 316
Christina Eberhard of Saxony, 247, 248
Chronicle of the Grand Duchy of Lithuania, 13
Chud, Lake, 57
Chyhyryn, 156, 172
Cicero, 97

Ciesielski, Andrzej (Andrew), 201
Cieszyn (Teschen), 267
Ciołek, Stanisław, 95
Cities: established under German law, 78–79; private, 79, 199–200, 298–99; lack parliamentary representation, 82, 185–86; and mid-seventeenth-century wars, 194–95, 289–90; in seventeenth century, 196–200; noble attitudes toward, 200–1; and Zamoyski's reforms, 269, 276; and Black Procession, 278–79; laws concerning, 280; and May 3 constitution, 281; and suburbs, 296–98. *See also* Burghers; Industry; Jews
Clement XIV, 274, 313
Commendoni, Francesco, 56
Commissions of Good Order, 270, 298
Conciliarism, 95
Confederation of Radom, 271
Confederation of Slutsk, 271
Confederation of Toruń, 271
Confederations, 116, 168, 183–84, 251–52, 254, 271–72, 282
Constance, Council of, 19
Constance Habsburg (wife of Zygmunt III), 133
Constantine (Russian Grand Duke), 285
Constantinople, 248, 256
Constitutional reform: and Zygmunt II, 58–64; and Zygmunt III, 132–34, 135–36; and Władysław IV, 152–54; and Jan III Sobieski, 237–38, 241; and August II, 245–46, 248, 253–55; and August III, 259, 261, 263, 265; and Czartoryski initiative, 269–70; and fundamental laws, 271, 277; and partition parliament, 274–75; and May 3 constitution, 277–83; and concept of the

nation, 317–19. *See also* Elective Kingship; Enlightenment; Liberum veto; Parliament
Conti, François, duc de, 247–48, 264
Copernicus, Nicholas (Mikołaj Kopernik), 101–2. *See also* Science and medicine
Corvinus, Matthias, 31
Cossacks, 50, 144–45, 160; Zaprozhian, 145–47; and Orthodox Church, 147–48; and Władysław IV, 156–58; great Cossack revolt, 160–61; wars, 164–65; Russian alliance of, 165–66; and Hadiach treaty, 170–72; and Hetman state, 172–73; attitudes towards Jews, 173, 174, 203, 267, 330; as term, 229; alliance with Turks, 236; and Russian control of Zaporozhia, 240; and Ivan Mazepa, 251–53, 255–56; Haidamak and other rebellions, 255–56, 266–67, 272–73, 292, 304. *See also* Education; Greek Catholic Church; Orthodox Church; Ruthenian Territories
Council of the Four Lands, 204, 305. *See also* Jews
Council of Trent, 55, 56, 100, 215, 334
Counter Reformation. *See under* Catholic Church
Couperin, François, 324
Courland, 58, 142, 257, 266
Courts: and law codes, 38–39, 45; and contracts, 71–72; and noble tribunals, 125, 264; system of, 187–89; Jewish, 204; and Zamoyski's reforms, 275, 276; referendary, 294
Coxcie, Michael, 115
Cracow: governmental affairs, 6, 10, 40, 117, 123, 149, 137, 165, 167, 169, 176, 179, 239, 248, 250, 251, 272, 276, 278, 286, 288;

Cracow *(continued)*
and urban development, 68, 79, 83, 86, 196, 198–99, 202, 295, 296, 298, 308, 318; Jews, 85–86, 174, 198, 230, 330, 331; cultural life, 97–114, 209, 217, 220, 223, 224, 323, 325, 335. *See also* Jagiellonian University
Cracow Academy. *See* Jagiellonian University
Cranach, 328
Crimea, 144, 178, 273. *See also* Tatars
Crimes and punishments, 207–9
Cromwell, Oliver, 164
Czapliński, Daniel, 161
Czarniecki, Stefan, 167, 240
Czartoryska, Izabela née Poniatowska, 321, 322, 328
Czartoryska, Konstancja, 262
Czartoryska, Zofia (née Sieniawska), 262
Czartoryski, Adam: oppositional politics of, 276, 277; foreign policy of, 278; emigrates, 285; cultural and educational interests of, 312, 313, 319, 321–22, 334
Czartoryski, August, 261, 262
Czartoryski, Michał, 262, 263
Czartoryski family, 13, 250, 294, 303; under August III, 257–59, 263; reform plans of, 263–64, 268–70. *See also* Chartoryski, Aleksander Vasilievich; Stanisław II August Poniatowski
Czech Kingdom, 3, 5, 7, 22, 23, 31, 43, 117, 142, 334
Czerwiński Privilege, 10
Częstochowa, 83, 114, 168, 215, 272, 333

Dąbrowka, Jan (John), 95
Dąbski, Stanisław, 248
Dantyszek, Jan (John), 37, 98
Danube River, 32
Daugavpils (Dyneburg), 142

Daukša, Mikolajus (Nicholas), 63, 107
Defoe, Daniel, 320
Dekert, Jan (John), 278
Dembowski, Mikołaj (Nicholas), 333
Denmark, 47, 74, 123, 139; wars with Poland-Lithuania, 59, 105, 155; alliance with Poland-Lithuania, 169
Deulino, armistice of, 141, 152
Diderot, Denis, 321
Dietines (*sejmiki*): under Kazimierz IV, 27–28; powers of, 184–85, 279. *See also* Taxation
Długosz, Jan (John), 8, 31, 36, 95–96, 124
Dmitrii, false, 140
Dmochowski, Franciszek Ksawery, 315
Dnieper River, 151, 195, 276, 277, 300
Dniester River, 32
Dobrzyń, 16–17
Dolabella, Tomasso, 221
Donelaitis, Kristijonas, 329
Doroshenko, Petro, 235, 255
Dorpat, 58, 142
Dov Ber of Międzyrzecz (Mezhirech), 333
Dresden, 247, 248, 254, 266, 285, 308, 323
Drzewicki, Maciej, 97
Dubieńka, battle of, 286
Dubno, 325
Ducal Prussia: established, 42–43; subordination to Poland, 48–49; Brandenburg succession rights granted to, 58; reorganized, 64–65, 89; German settlement of, 68; language and literature of, 107; Brandenburg acquires hereditary control of, 143–44; Poland regains control of, 155; Brandenburg gains full sovereignty of, 169–70; as cultural center, 217; discontent in, 234; Sobieski's plan to reconquer, 238; August II considers conquering, 249; and August III, 265; and Lithuanian cultural revival, 329
Dürer, Albrecht, 221
Dyxon, 79

Education: Lubrański Academy (College), 98, 153; Renaissance, 109–10; Vilnius Academy, 137, 219, 225, 312, 313, 314, 328; Mohyla Academy, 156, 171, 228, 255; Raków academy, 156, 217; Baroque, 215; Arians, 217; Zamość Academy, 219; Prussian schools, 220, 310; Ostrih academy, 226; brotherhood schools, 227; National Education Commission, 274–75, 284, 310, 311, 313–15; Collegium Varsaviense, 311; Knights Academy, 311; Noble Academy, 311–12; Jesuit schools, 312; Royal Cadet School, 312–13, 325, 326, 296; noble attitudes toward, 314–15; scientific collections, 325–26; Greek Catholic schools, 335. *See also* Jagiellonian University; Jesuits
Elbląg (Elbing), 17, 18, 196, 257
Elective Kingship: established, 5–6, 24, 32, 34, 39, 41, 119–20, 177–78; election of Henri III Valois, 116–19; election of Stefan Batory, 122–23; election of Zygmunt III, 131–32; election of Władysław IV, 149; reform proposals, 153, 175; election of Jan Kazimierz, 162; election of Michał Wiśniowiecki, 233–34; election of Jan III Sobieski, 236–37; election of August II, 247–48; election of Stanisław Leszczyński, 251; election of August III, 259–61; elec-

INDEX 361

tion of Stanisław II August, 269; abolition proposed, 279; importance of, 336
Eleonora Maria Josefa, wife of Michał Wiśniowiecki, 234, 236
Elijah, the Gaon of Vilnius, 331, 332
Elizabeth, Russian Empress, 266
Enghien, Henri Jules duc d', 175, 233, 234
England: landed estates, 42, 70; cultural contacts, 102, 106, 217, 219; political issues, 154, 164, 268, 269, 278, 303. *See also* Trade
Enlightenment: coming of, 309–11; and educational reform, 311–15; journalism, 315–16; and concept of nation, 317–19; and royalist theatre, 319; literature, 320–22; music, 322–25; scientific collections, 325–26; historical scholarship and economics, 326–27; architecture, 327–28; fine arts, 328; in Lithuania, 328–29; response to anti-Semitism, 331; Jewish, 334. *See also* Science and medicine
Epicurus, 105
Erasmus, Desiderius, 38, 56, 99, 100
Erik XIV, 58, 59
Erkemberger, Zygmunt, 80–81
Erlichshausen, Konrad, 29
Ernst, Archduke of Austria, 117, 118
Estonia, 4, 59, 127, 132, 139
Eugene IV, 22
Execution of the Laws: under Zygmunt I, 34, 37, 40–41, 45; under Zygmunt II, 54, 58–64, 181; election of Henri Valois, 117; stripped of leadership, 125

Fedorovych, Ivan, 108
Fedorovych, Taras, 156

Ferber, J. J., 325
Ferrara, 101
Filelfo, Francesco, 97
Finck, Heinrich, 110
Fine arts. *See under* Baroque; Enlightenment; Renaissance
Finland, 59
Fioł, Szwajpolt, 80, 102, 107
Firlej, Jan (John), 117
Flemming, Georg, 263
Flemming, Jakob Heinrich, 246
Florence, 112
Fortis, Moses, 302
Four Year Parliament. *See* Great Parliament
Fragonard, Jean-Honoré, 328
France: election of Henri Valois, 117–18; policy toward Władysław IV, 155; policy toward Jan Kazimierz, 160; influence with Wiśniowiecki and Sobieski, 163–64, 233–34, 235; challenges election of August III, 260–61; cultural influence of, 268, 272, 313, 317, 319, 320, 321, 322, 327, 328; interest in Bar Confederation, 272; concern over first partition, 273; French revolution, 279, 285, 287, 316, 317, 321
Francesco of Florence, 112
Frank, Jacob, 333–34
Frankfurt-am-Oder, 75
Frazer, 79
Fredro, Andrzej Maksymilian, 241
Friedrich II, Holy Roman Emperor, 14
Friedrich II (Frederick the Great), 265, 266, 308
Friedrich III Habsburg, 29, 31
Friedrich V, 154
Friedrich of Saxony, 30, 47
Friedrich Wilhelm I, 168, 169, 235, 238, 249
Fryderyk (son of Kazimierz IV), 35
Fugger (Fukier) family, 79

Gabrielli, Giovanni, 224
Gaetano, Kajetan, 324
Galen, Heinrich von, 57
Galicia, 4, 8, 16, 25, 45–46, 83, 100, 144, 171, 172, 195, 196, 227, 273, 294. *See also* Partitions of Poland
Gameren, Tylman van, 222
Gamrat, Piotr, 114
Garampi, Giuseppi, 335
Gasztold. *See* Gostautas
Gdańsk (Danzig), 14, 16, 17, 18, 29, 30, 44, 58, 59, 64, 73, 114, 115, 123, 136, 168, 199, 200, 201, 202, 209, 217, 219, 238, 248, 251, 257, 261, 273, 278, 285, 295, 299, 309, 310; political life, 59, 123, 154–55, 197; economic activities, 74, 75, 82, 196–98; cultural life, 220, 221, 328; *See also* Burghers; Cities; Prussia; Royal Prussia
Gediminas, 3, 4
Gedyminovichi, 13
Genghis Khan, 144
Genoa, 32
George of Poděbrady, 31
Georg Friedrich, 123, 143
Georg Wilhelm, 144
Geret, Samuel Luther 330
Giedrojć, Melchior (Merkelis Giedraitis), 107
Gierowski, Józef Andrzej (Joseph Andrew), xii
Giovanni Maria il Mosca (Padovano), 114
Giray, Islam (Tatar Khan), 164
Giray dynasty, 144
Gisleni, Jan Baptist, 222
Glaber, Andrzej (Andrew), 92
Glaire, Maurice, 328
Glinskaia, Elena, 26
Glinskii, Mikhail Lvovich, 26, 47
Głogów, duchy of, 31, 36, 48
Gniew, 29, 310
Gniezno, 6, 7, 23, 98, 114, 117, 251, 271, 274, 290
Godunov, Boris, 140
Golden Bull, 74

Golden Horde. *See* Mongols
Gomółka, Mikołaj (Nicholas), 111
Góra Kalwaria, 200
Gorczycki, Grzegorz, 323
Gorczyń, Aleksander, 224
Górnicki, Jakub, 106
Górski, Jakub, 106
Gosiewski, Wincenty, 168
Goślicki, Wawrzyniec, 106
Gostautas family, 45
Gostautas, Stanislas (Stanisław Gasztołd), 52, 53
Gostautas, Jonas (John/Jan Gasztold), 23–24
Gostomski, Anselm, 200
Graţiani, Gaspar, 144
Great Northern War. *See* August II
Great Parliament, 187, 276–83, 300, 314, 316, 317, 322, 334
Great Poland (Wielkopolska), 6, 44, 117, 167, 196, 201, 252, 266, 285, 286, 292, 293, 294, 302, 313
Greek Catholic Church: and Union of Brest, 137–39; restricted, 156, 215, 226; revival of, 229, 292, 313, 334–35. *See also* Ruthenian territories
Gregorian calendar, 102, 126, 138, 213
Grimaldi, Jerome, 334
Grodno, 285, 292, 315
Grodwagner, Jan (John), 201
Groicki, Bartłomiej (Bartholomew), 39
Grudziądz, 219
Grunwald, battle of, 14, 16–17, 96
Grzegorz (Gregory) of Sanok, 96, 97
Gustav II Adolf (Gustavus Adolphus), 142–43, 154
Gutenberg, Johannes, 102
Guzów, battle of, 134

Habsburg, Albert, 22
Habsburg, Elisabeth (wife of Zygmunt II), 52, 114
Habsburg, Elizabeth (wife of Kazimierz IV), 23
Habsburg, Ferdinand (Holy Roman Emperor), 48, 52, 55, 117, 142
Habsburg, Katherina, 66
Habsburg, Maria, 47
Habsburg, Wilhelm, 8
Habsburgs. *See* Austria, Hungary
Hadiach, treaty of, 170–72, 256
Haidamak rebellions. *See* Cossacks
Halle, 310
Haller, Jan (John), 102
Hamburg, 310
Handel, George Frederic, 324
Hanseatic League, 18, 74
Hasidism. *See* Jews
Hasse, Johann Adolf, 324
Health, 209–10
Hegendorfer, Christopher, 109
Hel peninsula, 154
Helena, wife of Aleksander, 33
Henri III Valois, 57; elected king, 116–19; as king, 120–21; returns to France, 121–22; Batory compared to, 122; Zygmunt III compared to, 133; reputation, 212; and Warsaw, 222
Henrician Articles, 119
Herburt, Jan Szczęsny, 182, 226
History, study of, 95–96, 228, 326, 329
Hlukhiv, 172
Hoffmann, Johann Daniel, 310
Hohenzollern, Albrecht, 42–43, 57, 65, 220
Hohenzollern, Albrecht Friedrich, 65
Hohenzollern, Wilhelm, 57
Holbach, Paul Henri Dietrich d', 321
Holbein, Hans, 328
Holszański, Ivan, 26
Holszański family, 23
Hołsztyńska, Zofia, 10
Homer, 106

Honta (Gonta), Ivan, 272
Horace, 97, 321
Hozjusz (Hosius), Stanisław, 56–57, 219
Hube, Michał, 325
Hubertusburg, treaty of, 266
Humanism: introduction of, 36, 96–97; Italian and German influence, 97; native school of, 97–98; Modrzewski's writings, 98–100. *See also* Renaissance
Hunashevsky, Mykhailo, 228
Hungary: founds Polish dynasty, 5, 8, 88; foreign policy issues, 17, 22, 32, 33, 46, 47, 48; Jagiellonian and Habsburg rivalry, 22–23, 32–33, 46–47, 117; and Humanism, 36, 97; peasant uprising in, 70; trade, 75, 76, 80, 82, 83, 300; Batory plans to conquer, 122–23, 125–27; and Sobieski campaigns, 239–40; and August II campaign, 247; hosts anti-Poniatowski forces, 269, 272; Hasidism in, 333
Hunyadi, János (John), 22
Hussitism: Hussite Wars, 3, 19–20, 31, 38; in Poland, 22, 42, 95

Iaroslav (Jarosław), 124, 205
Incompatibilites, 34, 37. *See also* Execution of the Laws
Industry: textiles, 74, 75, 76, 78, 79, 80, 82, 113, 144, 192, 197, 202, 300, 302, 304, 307; mining, 80, 83, 300, 301; guilds, 82, 198, 201–2, 221, 296, 297, 303–4; industrial growth, 82–83; in Gdańsk, 198; eighteenth-century revival of, 295–96, 297, 300, 307–8. *See also* Burghers; Cities; Jews; Trade
Inowrocław, 295
Insurrection of 1794, 285–87, 297, 322
Isaac ben Aaron Prostitz, 108

INDEX 363

Isaac ben Abraham Troki, 231
Israel ben Eliezer (Besht, Ba'al Shem Tov), 332–33, 334
Isserles, Moses, 110
Istanbul, 32
Itsakowicz, Szmul (Samuel ben Isaac), 302
Ivan III, 33
Ivan IV the Terrible, 26, 57, 59, 126
Izmail, 146

Jabłonowski, Stanisław Jan, 250
Jacigny, Jean Dubois de, 326
Jacob Joseph of Polonnoe, 333
Jadwiga (daughter of Zygmunt I), 37
Jadwiga ("King" of Poland), 3, 4, 7, 8, 67, 95, 214
Jaenichen, Peter, 310
Jaffe, Mordechai, 110
Jagiełło (Jogaila): in Lithuania, 3–5, 10–11; in Poland, 5, 7–10; struggles with Teutonic Order, 15–19; Hussite policy, 17, 19–20; taxation, 88; supports artists, 114. *See also* Lithuania
Jagiellonian University (Cracow Academy): foundation of, 19, 94–95, 96, 97, 100, 101, 126, 136; Mazovian students, 44; adds subjects, 218–19; students attack Jews, 230; Kołłataj reforms, 278, 314, 315, 318, 326; Załuski reforms, 310–11, 312, 313
Jakub ben Abraham of Międzyrzecz, 230
Jakub of Paradyż, 95
James Stuart, 233
Jan III Sobieski (John): son of Jakub Sobieski, 135; and revenues, 187; builds Wilanów palace, 222; and reform, 234, 236, 237–38; election of, 236–37; relations with Jews, 237, 241, 301, 303, 330; and Lithuanian autonomy, 239;
military affairs of, 239–41, 300; last years of, 241
Jan Kazimierz (John Casimir): early years, 154, 159–60; and great Cossack revolt, 160–61; the royal couple, 162–64; and Cossack wars, 164–65; and Cossack-Russian alliance, 165–66; and Swedish invasion, 166–69; and Ducal Prussian, 169–70; and the partition of Ukrainian lands, 170–72; and Hetman state, 172–73; and Jewish settlement in Ukraine, 173–74; and the Lubomirski revolt, 174–76, 234; abdication and death of, 176, 233; and revenues, 187; cries, 213; and Mazepa, 255
Jan of the Lithuanian Princes, 37
Jan Olbracht (John Albert): domestic policies of, 23, 28, 30, 31; Moldavian failure, 32–33; dies, 35
Jan (John) of Wiślica, 98
Janicki, Klement, 98
Janosik, 267
Jansenism, 219
Janusz III, 43
Jarzębski, Adam, 224
Jasiński, Jakub, 287, 312, 321
Jaskiewicz, Jan (John), 326
Jasna Góra monastery, 114, 168, 272, 333
Jaworów, 237
Jedlnia privilege, 10
Jędrzejów, 134
Jerusalem Boulevard (*Aleje Jerozolimskie*), 298
Jesuits (Society of Jesus): introduced, 56; cultural activities of, 103, 104, 107, 126, 224–25, 251; political attitudes and growth of, 137; imitated by Basilians, 138; and Jan Kazimierz, 160; build churches, 200; schools, 213, 215, 219; favor August II, 248; abol-
ished, 274, 313; education reforms of, 312, 313, 315; cultural influence of, 270, 316, 317, 323, 324
Jews: accused of Judaizing, 42, 87–88; accused of ritual crimes, 57, 87, 205, 208–9, 230, 330–31; community formed, 83–85; economic activities of, 85–86, 200, 202–4; population, 86, 204; restrictions on, 86–87; printing and literature, 108–9, 230; and Renaissance education, 109–10; and mysticism, 110, 229; supported by Jakub Sobieski, 136; in Ukrainian lands, 146, 173–74; and liquor trade, 203, 290–291, 302, 304; self-government of, 204–7; and Jan Sobieski, 237, 241; and Zamoyski law code, 276; and Great Parliament, 280, 282, 283–84; Praga massacre, 287; in suburbs and private cities, 296–99, 302–5; Magnate-Jewish symbiosis, 301–2; Hasidism and Jewish Enlightenment, 305, 331–34, 335; and decline of communal government, 305–7; synagogue architecture, 327; Polish-Lithuanian heritage, 338. *See also* Cities; Karaites; Nobles
Jezierski, Franciszek Salezy, 318
Jezierski, Jacek (Jack), 300
Joachim Friedrich, 143
Jogaila. *See* Jagiełło
Johan, Duke of Finland and King of Sweden, 59, 118, 131–32
Johann Friedrich, 143
Johann Georg II, 246
Johann Georg III, 246
Johann Georg IV, 246
Johann Sigismund, 143
Jordaens, Jacob, 221
Jósefowicz, Abraham, 84

Jósefowicz, Michał, 84
Journalism. *See under* Enlightenment
Juliana (wife of Algirdas), 3
Junginen, Ulrich von, 16

Kabrun, Josef, 328
Kadłubek, Wincenty, 95
Kaffa (Feodosiya), 32
Kalahore, Matthew, 330
Kaliningrad. *See* Königsberg
Kalisz, battle of, 252
Kalkstein, Albrecht, 170
Kalkstein-Stoliński, Christian Ludwig, 170, 234
Kallimach. *See* Buonaccorsi, Philipo
Kamianets-Podilskyi, 235, 240, 249, 267
Kamień, 117
Kamieniec, 178
Kamieński, Maciej, 324, 325
Kaniv (Kaniew), 146, 276
Karaites, 231, 338
Karl (Charles), 133; takes Swedish throne, 139–40; death of, 142
Karl X Gustav (Charles Gustavus), 166–69, 237
Karl XII (Charles), 249–53, 255
Karl, Duke of Lorraine, 233, 234
Karl, Duke of Saxony, 266
Karlowitz, treaty of, 240, 249
Karmichel, 79
Karnkowski, Stanisław, 56, 59, 100, 123
Karol Ferdynand Vasa (Charles Ferdinand), 162, 223
Karpiński, Franciszek, 321–22
Katarzyna (Catherine) the Jagiellonian, 59, 131
Kaufman, Paweł, 79
Kausch, Johann Joseph, 302
Kazanowski, Adam, 224
Kazimierz III the Great (Casimir), 5, 7, 94, 116
Kazimierz IV the Jagiellonian (Casimir), 36, 44, 52, 79, 96; character of, 23; Lithuanian policies 23–24;

centralization policies, 26–28; alliance with lesser nobility 27–28; union with Prussia, 28–31; Turkish policy, 32; Jewish laws, 87; taxation, 88; protects Kallimach, 97; tomb by Stwosz, 114
Kazimierz (suburb of Cracow), 86, 198
Kazimierz Dolny, 113
Keckermann, Benedikt, 220
Kejdany Accord, 167
Kestutis (Kiejstut), 3, 4
Kettler, Gotthard, 58
Khazar kingdom, 83
Kherson, 297, 300
Khmelnytsky, Bohdan (Bogdan Chmielnicki), 160–61, 162, 164–74
Khmelnytsky, Tymish (Timothy), 165
Khmelnytsky, Yurii, 170, 171, 172
Khodkevich, Grigorii (Grzegorz Chodkiewicz), 108
Khotyn (Chocim), 135, 145, 146, 151, 153, 236, 238
Kielce, 83, 214
Kiev, 3, 4, 10, 139, 147, 156, 157, 162, 164–66, 170, 173, 196, 226, 255, 267, 273, 276, 292, 304, 310, 335. *See also* Ruthenian territories
Kievan Rus, 4, 157, 228
Kiliia, 32, 146
Kingship: Jagiellonian, 5–6, 9–10, 26–28, 37–40; and constitutional powers, 119–20; 177–78; royalism, 133–34, 174–75, 234, 249, 254; and May constitution, 280–81. *See also* Constitutional reform; Elective kingship; Parliament
Kirchholm, battle of, 140
Kiszka, Leon, 334
Kitowicz, Andrzej (Andrew), 261
Klabon, Krzysztof (Christopher),223

Klaipėda (Kłajpeda, Memel), 11, 235, 238, 329
Kleczewski, Stanisław, 315
Kleparz, 199
Kluk, Krzysztof (Christopher), 291, 326
Klushino, battle of, 141
Knapski, G., 218
Kniaziewicz, Karol, 312
Kniaźnin, Dionizy, 322
Knyszyn, 66, 117
Kochanowska, Urszula, 106
Kochanowski, Jan (John), 104, 105–6, 111, 125
Kochanowski, Piotr, 215
Kochowski, Wespazjan, 234
Kodak, 151, 156
Kołłątaj, Hugo: university rector, 278; proposes reforms, 279, 280, 284, 293, 317–18; rejected by Targowica, 285; in 1794 insurrection, 286; educational reforms of, 278, 314; Kołłątaj's Forge, 316, 317–18
Koloff, Wawrzyniec Mitzler de, 291, 311, 315
Komarzewski, Jan (John), 276
Konarski, Adam, 119
Konarski, Jan (John), 103
Konarski, Stanisław, 311–12
Koniecpolski, Aleksander, 158
Koniecpolski, Stanisław, 147, 151, 158, 195
Koniecpolski family, 146, 193
Königsberg, 18, 30, 31, 43, 105, 168, 170, 235. *See also* Ducal Prussia
Konrad, Duke of Mazovia, 14
Kopczyński, Onufry, 315
Kopystensky, Zakharia, 228
Korczyń, 70
Koretsky family, 146
Korsun, 161
Korybut, Zygmunt, 20
Kościelecki, Andrzej (Andrew), 37
Kościuszko, Tadeusz (Thaddeus), 284, 285–87, 293, 312, 322
Kosiński, Krzysztof (Christopher), 145

INDEX   365

Kosiv, Sylvester, 164
Kossakowski, Józef (Joseph), 321
Kossakowski, Szymon (Simon), 285, 287
Kossakowski family, 250
Kozak, Jan (John), 225
Kozłowski, Józef (Joseph), 324
Krasicki, Ignacy, 270, 315, 320–21
Krasiński, Jan Dobrogosta, 222
Kriavas (Krevo, Krewo). *See* Union of Kriavas
Kristina, Queen of Sweden, 154, 167, 233
Król, Marcin (Marcin z Żurawicy), 109
Kromer, Marcin (Martin), 38
Krzycki, Andrzej (Andrew), 98
Kujawy, 292, 306
Kumejki, battle of, 156
Kurpie region, 267, 292, 294
Kysil (Kisiel), Adam, 156–57, 162, 164

Łaski, Jan (the elder), 34–35, 38, 89, 102
Łaski, Jan (the younger), 103
Lassus, Orlando di, 224
Lateran Council, 102
Laterna, Marcin, 126
Latin language, 12, 14, 25, 46, 96–104, 137, 154, 217–19, 225, 228, 231, 268, 309, 311–12, 315, 322, 331, 355
Latvia, 4
Lauxmin, Zygmunt, 328
Lavoisier, Antoine-Laurent, 326
Łazieńki Palace, 296
Lehmann, Berend, 301
Leiden, 317
Leipzig, 247, 254, 266, 310
Lengnich, Gottfried, 310, 329–30
Leonardo da Vinci, 328
Leopold I, 209, 234
Leopolita, Marcin (Martin), 110–11
Leszczyńska, Maria, 260
Leszczyński, Andrzej (Andrew), 175, 178

Leszczyński, Rafał (Raphael), 36, 43, 54, 250
Leszczyński, Stanisław: election of, 250–51, 263; as king, 251–53; forces cross Poland-Lithuania, 253; and Mazepa, 256; and 1733 election, 260; peasant support for, 267; reforms of, 293, 311
Leszczyński family, 302
Leszno (Lissa), 251, 302–3, 306
Lettou, Jan (John), 102
Levin (Satanower), Mendel, 334
Levko (Leib), 85
Lewenhaupt, Adam Ludwik, 252
Liberum veto: established, 153, 175, 181–83, 185, 212, 234, 236, 254, 255, 261, 263, 264, 265, 336; suspended, 269, 275; modified, 271, 329; abolished, 280, 281, 317, 318; restored, 285. *See also* Constitutional reform; Parliament
Lilius (Gigli), Vencentius, 223
Linköping, battle of, 140
Lipsius, Justus, 153
Lisowczycy, 160
Literature. *See under* Baroque; Enlightenment; Renaissance
Lithuania: before 1386, 3–5; relations with Poland, 10–12; relations with Ruthenians, 11–14, 25–26; civil war, 22, 250; national consciousness, 23–25, 184, 225; and Thirteen Years War, 30; emergence of parliament, 33–34; under Zygmunt I, 44–45; agriculture of, 72; nobility of, 78; and election of Henri Valois, 118–19; Batory encourages, 125; economic development of, 195; and Protestantism, 216–17; and Sobieski, 238, 239;

and Ottoman war, 249; federal status challenged, 282–83; Grodno parliament, 285; in the 1794 insurrection, 287; impact of mid-seventeenth-century wars on, 290; language decline, 290; economic recovery, 291–92; educational district, 313; and Enlightenment cultural revival, 316, 328–29; and Polish-Lithuanian heritage, 337. *See also* Partitions of Poland
Little Poland (Małopolska), 6, 44, 96, 117, 134, 167, 193, 196, 216, 250, 300, 313
Liubartas, 3
Livonia, 191; Livonian Knights, 4, 15, 47, 238; Livonian War, 57–59, 66, 126, 127; Swedish-Polish rivalry for, 132, 137, 139, 142, 166, 169; August II aims to conquer, 249, 251
Lizard Union, 15
Lobzów, 149
Locci, Augustino, 222
Łojko, Feliks, 326
Lorraine, 261, 311
Louis XIV, 238, 245, 247, 248
Louis XV, 260, 261
Louis XVI, 321
Louis, duc de Condée, 233, 234
Louis the Great, 5
Louis of Hungary, 5, 8, 76, 88
Louis the Jagiellonian, 47, 48
Louise Marie Gonzaga: as wife of Władysław IV, 150, 155; as wife of Jan Kazimierz, 160, 162–63; cultural influence of, 163–64, 223
Louvain, 153
Łowicz, 117
Lübeck, 31, 74, 310
Lublin, 76, 81, 98, 108, 114, 117, 137, 192, 201, 205, 217, 230, 250, 325
Lubomirski, Jerzy (George): blocks parliament, 152; opposition to Jan

366 INDEX

Lubomirski, Jerzy (George) (*continued*)
  Kazimierz, 164–65; wins victories, 169, 172, 174, 237, 241; revolt, 174–76
Lubomirski, Sebastian, 193
Lubomirski, Stanisław, 193
Lubomirski, Stanisław (Czartoryski family), 275
Lubomirski family, 193, 299
Lubrański, Jan (John), 98, 109
Lucchesini, Girolomo, 277
Łuków, 300
Lunéville, 261, 311
Luria, Salomon, 110
Lusatia, 36, 265
Łuskina, Stefan, 316
Łuszkowska, Jadwiga, 150
Luther, Martin, 42
Lutsk (Łuck), 171, 334
Lützen, battle of, 154
Lviv (Lvov, Lwów), 85, 86, 97, 108, 111, 174, 202, 228, 236, 249, 267, 298, 303, 305, 323, 325, 334

Mably, Gabriel, 272
Machiavelli, Nicolo, 212
Maciej of Miechów, 23
Maciejowice, battle of, 287
Maciejowski, Samuel, 103
Madaliński, Antoni (Anthony), 286
Magna, Valeriano, 163
Magnates. *See* Nobles
Maimon, Salomon, 334
Małachowski, Jan (John), 311
Małachowski, Stanisław, 318
Malbork (Marienburg), 14, 17, 29, 168
Mantua, 155
Marcuse, Moses, 334
Maria Josefa Habsburg, 260
Maria Theresia, 260, 265
Marie Casimire d'Arquien (Marysieńka), 162, 236–37
Mariensztat, 296
Masons, 257–58
Massalski, Ignacy, 314
Massalski family, 250
Matejko, Jan (John), 49
Mateuš of Cracow, 95

Mątwy, battle of, 237
Maurice de Saxe, 247, 257
Maximilian (Austrian archduke), 132
Maximilian I, Holy Roman Emperor, 47, 52, 57, 110
Maximilian II, Holy Roman Emperor, 122
May 3, 1791 Constitution, 209, 260, 280–83, 285, 293, 322, 324
Mazepa, Ivan, 251–52, 255–56
Mazovia: legal status of, 7; ignores Thirteen Years War, 30; incorporated into Poland-Lithuania, 43–44, 89; staunchly Catholic, 55; trade with Teutonic Order, 74; election of Henri Valois, 117; towns of, 196; and Pasek, 213; agriculture, 292; education, 313; Jews, 331. *See also* Elective Kingship
Mažvydas, Martynas (Martin), 107
Medicine. *See* Science and medicine
Medzhybizh (Międzybóż), 169, 299, 302, 332
Meissen, 245, 257
Melanchthon, Philip, 99
Memling, Hans, 114
Mendelssohn, Moses, 334
Metropolitanate of Kiev, 13, 46, 335
Meyer, Józef (Joseph), 316
Mickiewicz, Adam, 63, 337
Mielczewski, Marcin, 223–24
Mielnik, privilege of, 34
Mieszko, Duke of Poland, 5
Mikołaj of Radom, 110
Miłosz, Czes{l}aw, 337
Miłwid, Antoni (Anthony), 323
Mindaugas, 3
Ministers, 177–78. *See also* Kingship
Minsk, 4
Mniszech, Jerzy (George), 140
Mniszech, Marina, 140
Modrzewski, Andrzej Frycz, 40, 92, 98–100, 101

Mohács, battle of, 48
Mohyla, Petro (Peter), 156, 157, 228. *See also* Education
Mokronowski, Andrzej (Andrew), 312
Moldavia, 5, 8, 16, 32, 50, 66, 145, 152, 158, 238, 239, 240, 249, 252, 253, 271, 273, 277
Molière (Jean-Baptiste Poquelin), 319
Mollwitz, battle of, 265
Monastic orders, 214, 215, 305, 311. *See also* Jesuits; Piarist order
Mongols, 3, 4
Montelupi, Sebastian, 79
Monti, Antoine Felix de, 260
Montluc, Jean, 118
Morando, Bernardo, 113, 199
Moravia, 83, 117, 300
Morocco, 158
Morsztyn family, 79
Moscow (Muscovy). *See* Russia
Moszkowicz, Jezue, 301
Moussorgsky, Modest, 324
Mstislavl family, 13
Müller, Burchard, 168
Murad IV, 152
Music. *See under* Baroque; Enlightenment; Renaissance
Myszkowski, Piotr, 111, 117

Nalyvaiko, Severyn, 145
Napierski, Aleksander Kostka, 165
Naples, 318
Narew River, 44
Naronowicz-Naroński, Józef (Joseph), 328
Naruszewicz, Adam, 315, 321, 326
Narva, 57, 58, 59, 139, 249, 251
National Education Commission, 274–75, 284, 310, 311, 313, 314–15, 318, 325, 326, 336. *See also* Education

Nemours, Samuel Dupont de, 313
Nemyrych, Yurii (Jerzy Niemirycz), 171
Netherlands, 278
Nevsky, Alexander, 57
Nicholas V, 29
Nicholas of Leiden, 113
Niegoszewski, Stanisław, 104
Niemcewicz, Julian Ursyn, 313, 322, 325
Niemen River, 300
Niemiriv, 174
Nieszawa, Privilege of, 28
Nihil novi, 34–35
Nizhni-Novgorod, 76
Nobles: legal privileges of, 10, 77, 101; transformed into agriculturalists, 77–78; social divisions among, 78, 291, 294–95; in Lithuania, 78; magnate elite, 193–95, 224, 323; in private cities, 199–200; attitudes towards cities, 200–1, 327–28; lead Ruthenian revival, 226–27; taxed, 278, 308; Magnate-Jewish symbiosis, 301–2; and industries, 307. *See also* Cities; Constitutional Reform; Jews; Peasants
Norblin, Jean Pierre, 328
Novgorod, 3, 25–26, 126
Noyers, Pierre des, 164
Nüremberg, 79
Nystad, treaty of, 255

Ochakiv (Ochakov), 158
Ogiński, Andrzej (Andrew), 324
Ogiński, Michał Kleofas (Michael), 324
Ogiński family 250
Old Market (Altmark, Stary Targ), truce of, 143
Olelkevych, Mykhailo, 26
Oleśnicki, Zbigniew: at Grunwald, 16; policies under Władysław III, 21–23, 96, 97; biography of, 97
Oliwa, 248
Oliwa, treaty of, 169

Olkienniki, battle of, 250
Olszowski, Andrzej (Andrew), 233, 235
Ondraszek, 267
Opaliński, Krzysztof (Christopher), 167, 201
Opaliński, Łukasz (Lucas), 152–53, 175
Opaliński, Piotr (Peter), 152–53
Opatów (Apt), 299
Opawa, Duchy of 36
Opole-Raciborz, Duchy of, 155
Oppenheimer, Samuel, 301
Oraczewski, Feliks, 314
Orsha, battle of, 47
Orthodox Church: in Lithuania, 5, 13, 19, 46; and Union of Brest, 137–39; revival of, 147–48, 226–29; legality restored, 156; attitude towards Cossack revolt, 164, 173; and dissident issue under Poniatowski, 270–71
Orzechowski, Stanisław, 100–1, 106
Ossian, 322
Ossoliński, Jerzy (George): appointed chancellor, 152; blocks war, 158; policy toward Cossack revolt, 162, 164; as art patron, 221
Ostrianin, Yakiv (Jacob), 157
Ostrih, 203, 215, 226
Ostroróg, Jakub (Jacob), 43
Ostroróg, Jan (John), 27–28
Ostrowo. *See* Astravas Agreement
Ostrożska, Anna Alojza (Ostrozky), 215–16
Ostrozsky family, 146, 193, 262
Ostrozky, Konstiantyn (Constantine) the older, 38, 46, 47
Ostrozky, Konstiantyn (Constantine) the younger: opposes Union of Brest, 138–39; promotes Orthodox revival, 147–48, 226; employs Jews, 203; Ostrozky entail, 262
Oświęcim (Auschwitz), 64, 106, 295
Ottoman Empire: expansion of 32, 135; relations with Zygmunt I, 49–50; war with Zygmunt III, 144–45; relations with Władysław IV, 152, 158, 160; cultural influence of, 213, 323; war with Poland-Lithuania, 235–36, 238–40, 248–49; war with Russia, 272–74, 276–77
Ozylia, 59

Pac, Krzysztof (Christopher), 176
Pac, Krzysztof Zygmunt (Christopher Sigmund), 239, 250
Pac, Michał (Michael), 239, 250
Pacelli, Asprilli, 223
Pacta conventa, 119, 182, 248. *See also* Kingship
Padua, 98, 105, 123, 219
Palanga (Połąga), 11, 300
Paleologus, Sophia, 33
Paleologus family, 155
Palestine, 332
Palestrina, 224
Palij, Simon, 251, 255
Panin, Nikita, 269, 270
Paris, 119, 312. *See also* France
Párkány, battle of, 240
Parliament: origins of, 5; takes form, 28, 33–34; under Zygmunt I, 38, 40–41; inquisitional parliament, 133; organization and powers of, 178–83; *liberum veto*, 181–83; confederated parliaments, 184, 269–70, 273–82; role of cities, 185–86; silent parliament, 254, 330; partition parliament, 274–75, 313; great parliament, 276–82. *See also* Constitutional Reform

Partitions of Poland, 7, 338; first, 273–74, 300, 320, 330; second, 284–85, 297; third, 287–88, 328
Pascal, Blaise, 163
Pasek, Jan Chrysostom, 213–14, 234
Patkul, Johann Reinhold von, 249
Paul II, 97
Paweł of Krosno (Paul), 98
Peasants: obligations of, 69–70; social structure of, 70–72; revolts of, 165, 267, 292, 294; Zamoyski proposals concerning, 270, 276; in May 3 constitution, 282, 282; in 1794 insurrection, 286, 287; in eighteenth century, 290–94; and reform, 293–94, 317, 318; and parish schools, 314. *See also* Agriculture
Pękiel, Bartłomiej (Bartholemew), 224
Pereiaslav, agreement of, 165, 170, 171, 172. *See also* Cossacks
Perekop, 146
Permanent Council, 274, 275, 277
Persia (Iran), 158
Peter I, 249–52, 254, 260
Peter III, 263, 266, 269
Petryca, Sebastian, 218
Philip II, 54
Philip Wilhelm, Duke of Neuburg, 176
Physiocratism, 326–27
Piarist order: music, 225; education, 311–12, 313, 314, 315
Piast, 7, 96, 233, 259
Piątek, battle of, 167
Piattoli, Scippione, 279, 283
Piccolomini, Aeneas Sylvia (Pius II), 97
Piła, 317
Pińsk, 331
Piotrków, 34, 53, 330
Piramowicz, Grzegorz (Gregory), 313

Pius III, 102
Plato, 97, 110
Plauen, Heinrich von, 17
Pletenetsky, Elisei 227
Płock, 44, 86, 105, 117, 162, 222, 223, 274
Plutarch, 326
Poczobutt, Marcin (Martin), 314, 325
Podhajce, battle of, 249
Podhale, 267
Podhorce, 195
Podlasie, 45
Podlecki, Tadeusz (Thaddeus), 316
Podolia, 11, 124, 145, 171, 172, 173, 176, 235, 236, 239, 249, 267, 271, 273, 292, 299, 302, 331, 333
Podoski, Gabriel, 271
Pokuti (Pokucia), 47
Poland. *See* Great Poland; Little Poland; Partitions of Poland
Połaniec Decree, 286, 294
Polianovka (Polanów), agreement of, 152
Pollak, Jacob, 109
Polonius, 106
Polonus, Jan (John), 102
Polonus, Stanislaus, 102
Polotsk, 4, 47, 126, 335
Poltava, 173
Poltava, battle of, 252, 256
Pomerania, 7, 48, 96, 169, 246, 317, 326
Pomerelia, 17
Poniatowska, Konstancja (Constance) née Czartoryska, 268
Poniatowski, Andrzej (Andrew), 268, 328
Poniatowski, Józef (Joseph), 276, 280, 284, 285, 286
Poniatowski, Kazimierz (Casimir), 263, 264, 268, 328
Poniatowski, Michał, 268, 274, 276, 313, 314, 318
Poniatowski, Stanisław (father) 261, 262, 310, 311
Poniatowski, Stanisław (nephew), 276

Poniatowski, Stanisław. *See* Stanisław II August Poniatowski
Pope, Alexander, 321
Population, 12, 44, 67–68, 86, 190, 204, 231, 253, 273, 290, 291, 295, 296–97, 298
Potemkin, Grigorii, 275, 276
Potii, Ipatii, Lutsk, 138
Potocka, Zofia, 321
Potocki, Antoni (Anthony), 264
Potocki, Felix, 249
Potocki, Franciszek Salezy (Francis), 264
Potocki, Ignacy: opposes Stanisław August, 275, 276, 278; proposes reforms, 279, 280; emigrates, 285; in 1794 insurrection, 286; educational interests of, 313
Potocki, Józef (Joseph), 252, 264, 303
Potocki, Mikołaj (Nicholas), 156
Potocki, Prot, 308
Potocki, Stanisław (Hetman), 168
Potocki, Stanisław (Count), 275, 328
Potocki, Szczęsny, 279, 284, 285, 321
Potocki, Teodor, 264
Potocki, Wacław, 163
Potocki family: 146, 193, 294, 303; opposes Czartoryskis, 257, 264–65
Powązki, 328
Poznań, 6, 37, 86, 87, 98, 109, 113, 119, 137, 152, 196, 201, 251, 295, 323, 325, 330
Praga (Warsaw), 287, 296, 297, 321
Prague, 233, 312, 327
Prażmowski, Mikołaj Jan (Nicholas John), 175, 234
Prešov, 272
Printing. *See under* Renaissance; Baroque
Proćpak, 267
Protestantism: Reformation,

40–41; and Zygmunt I, 41–43; Anabaptism, 42, 43, 156; Calvinism, 43, 55, 56, 216; Czech Brethren, 43, 250; and Zygmunt II, 55–57; and unification, 56; and humanist influence, 100; and early printing, 107; weakened by Counter Reformation, 136–37; religions in Gdańsk, 197; decline of, 216; in Lithuania, 216–17; Arians, 217; and August II, 247, 257; and Poniatowski, 270–71. *See also* Toleration, religious
Prussia: before 1386, 14; in Teutonic Order State, 14–15; Prussian Estates 18–19, 65; union with Poland, 28–31; becomes sovereign, 249; war of the Austrian succession, 265–68; participation in first partition, 273–74; stimulates the Great Parliament, 277; renounces Polish alliance, 285; dominates Vistula trade, 300, 308; and Polish-Lithuanian heritage, 338. *See also* Ducal Prussia; Royal Prussia
Prut, treaty of, 256
Prut River, 32, 144
Przemyśl, 83, 100, 334
Przybyła brothers' residence, 113
Przyłuski, Jakub, 39
Pskov, 25–26, 126
Pułaski, Kazimierz (Casimir), 272
Puławy, 299, 321–22
Pyliavtsi, battle of, 161

Quadro, Giovanni Battista, 113

Racławice, battle of, 286
Radom, 11, 105, 110
Radvilas. *See* Radziwiłł
Radwan, Jan (John), 225
Radziejowski, Michał, 248, 249, 250
Radziwiłł, Barbara, 52, 53
Radziwiłł, "Black" Mikołaj (Nicholas), 52, 53, 111
Radziwiłł, Bogusław, 167–68, 169, 183
Radziwiłł, Hieronim Florian, 302
Radziwiłł, Jan II, 53
Radziwiłł, Janusz, 167, 173
Radziwiłł, Jerzy (George), 53
Radziwiłł, Karol (Charles), 264, 271, 323
Radziwiłł, Krzysztof (Christopher), 142, 152, 153
Radziwiłł, Michał (Michael), 264
Radziwiłł, Mikołaj II (Nicholas), 52
Radziwiłł, "Red" Mikołaj (Nicholas), 52, 53
Radziwiłł family, 45, 250, 329; rise of, 52–53; wealth of, 193, 294, 307; political role of, 262
Rákoczy, György II (George), 164, 169, 171
Raphael, 221
Rashi, 230
Rava Ruska, 249
Rawa, 43
Regalian rights, 5, 88, 246
Rej, Mikołaj (Nicholas), 92, 104–5, 106
Rejtan, Tadeusz, 209
Rembrandt, Harmenszoon van Rijn, 221, 328
Renaissance: political thought, 27–28, 98–99; humanism, 96–102; and printing, 102–3, 107–9; religious texts, 103–4, 227; literature, 104–7; education, 109–10; music, 110–11; architecture and urban design, 111–13; fine arts, 113–15. *See also* Science and medicine
Reni, Guido, 149, 221, 328
Repnin, Nikolai, 270–71
Republican faction. *See* Potocki family
Reytan, Tadeusz, 209, 273

Riga, 15, 57, 58, 127, 140, 249, 251
Romanov, Mikhail (Michael), 141
Rome, 55, 97, 112, 318, 322
Rorantist Choir, 111
Roth, Hieronymous (Jerome), 170
Rottenstein, Konrad Zollner von, 16
Rotunda, Augustinas, 63
Rousseau, Jean-Jacques, 272, 317, 319
Royal Prussia: 44, reorganized, 49, 64–65; settlement and ethnicity in, 72–73; trade with Poland, 73–75; Copernicus in, 101; negotiates with Batory, 123; and Jesuit schooling, 137; attacked by Gustav Adolf, 142–43; attacked by Karl X, 167; cities of, 199; Sarmatian variant, 212, 330; as cultural center, 218; and market agriculture, 292; and Enlightenment trends, 309–10; and separatist trends, 329–30. *See also* Ducal Prussia; Gdańsk; Prussia
Różycki, Jacek (Jack), 248, 322
Rubens, Peter Paul, 149, 221, 328
Rubinowicz, Yisrael, 301
Ruhig (Ruigys), Filip, 329
Rumelia, 144
Rurik, 4
Rurikovichi, 13
Russia (Muscovy), 4, 160; relations with Zygmunt I, 47; war with Batory, 126–27; Time of Troubles, 140–42, 145; war with Władysław IV, 152; proposed Polish-Russian alliance, 157, 158; alliance with Cossacks, 165–66; "eternal peace," 240; in Great Northern War, 249–53; supports August III, 261, 265; Poniatowski era, 268–88; trade, 303, 304. *See also* Trade

Russian Assembly (*Zemsky Sobor*), 141, 165
Russo-Polish War, 284–85, 324
Russo-Turkish War, 276–77, 287
Ruthenian territories: before 1386, 4–5; languages, 4; Ruthenian identity in the 1400s, 11–14; decline under Kazimierz IV, 25–26; under Zygmunt I, 45–46; under Zygmunt II, 64; economy of, 76, 193, 195, 292, 303; and early printing, 107–8; and Union of Brest, 137–39; and emergence of Cossacks, 145–47; under Władysław IV, 156–58; and great Cossack revolt, 160–61, 164–66, 170–73; and national consciousness, 225–29, 328; and term "Ukraine," 229; and Great Northern War, 251–53, 255–56; reorganization of, 265, 292; educational districts of, 313; and Polish-Lithuanian heritage, 337. *See also* Cossacks; Greek Catholic Church; Orthodox Church; Partitions of Poland
Rutsky, Yosyf (Joseph), 229
Rybiński, Jan (John), 220
Rymsza, Andrzej (Andrew), 225
Rzewuski, Seweryn, 275, 279, 284, 285
Rzewuski, Wacław, 271, 323

Safed, 110
St. Germain des Près, 176
St. Petersburg, 284, 288, 299, 310
St. Stanisław, 96
St. Stanisław Kostka, 214
Saltykov-Shchedrin Library, 311
Samogitia (Żmudź/Żemaitia), 3, 11, 17, 23, 64, 232
Samoilovich, Ivan, 228, 255
Samuel ben Moses, 306

Sandomierz, 103, 250
Sandomierz, confederation of, 251, 252
Sandomierz, Union of, 56
Sanguszko, Janusz, 262, 323
Sanguszko family, 299
Sanok, 96, 97, 110, 289
Santa Gucci, 112
Sapieha, Jan (John), 250
Sapieha, Kazimierz Nestor (Casimir Nestor), 283
Sapieha, Leon, 148
Sapieha family, 193, 250, 294, 329
Saratoga, battle of, 286
Sarmatianism: ideology of, 211–12, 309, 319, 338; Prussian variant, 212; behavior, 212–13, 320, 322; and anti-Semitism, 330
Satanower, Isaac, 334
Satonwer, Mendel Levin, 334
Saxony: 245–46, 248, 253–54, 260, 264, 269, 279, 302, 308, 310. *See also* August II, August III
Schlesinger, Marx, 301
Schlüter, Andreas, 222
Schultz, Daniel, 221
Schwetz (Świecie), 17
Science and medicine, 90, 94–95, 96, 101–2, 109, 150, 210, 217, 218–19, 220, 291, 310, 311–12, 313, 314, 325–26, 330, 334. *See also* Gregorian calendar
Sebastian of Felsztyn, 110
Sejm. *See* Parliament
Sejmik. *See* Dietines
Seklucjan, Jan (John), 103
Senate, 179–80. *See also* Parliament
Seneca, 97
Serfdom. *See* Agriculture; Peasants
Seven Years War, 266
Seville, 102
Sforza, Bona, 37, 48, 52, 53, 98; policies of, 39–40; leaves Poland, 54–55
Shabbateanism, 305
Shabbetai Zvi, 331–32

Shakespeare, William, 106
Shein, Mikhail (Michael), 152
Shklov (Szkłów), 299
Shuiskii, Vasilii (Basil), 140
Siaulias (Szawle), 292
Siciński, Władysław, 183
Siemowit III, Duke of Mazovia, 7
Siemowit IV, Duke of Mazovia, 7, 44
Sieniawa, 79
Sieniawska, Elżbieta (Elizabeth) née Lubomirska, 299, 301–2
Sieniawski, Adam, 252
Sienieński, Jakub, 217
Sierkowski, Wacław, 323
Sigismund of Luxemburg, 11, 16, 17, 20
Silesia, 5, 7, 36, 40, 68, 83, 96, 117, 155, 167, 168, 195, 201, 248, 265, 273, 299, 300, 302
Simon ben Zarach, 306
Sirvydas, Constantine, 225
Sixtus V, 127
Skania, 169, 249
Skarga, Piotr (Peter), 92, 103, 126, 137, 181, 215, 230
Skirgaila, 10
Skrzetuski, Kajetan, 326
Skrzetuski, Wincenty, 326
Śleszkowski, Sebastian, 220
Słonim, 334
Slovakia, 80, 112, 27
Smolensk, 4, 13, 23, 47, 75, 141, 152, 160, 172, 251
Smotrych River, 235
Smotrytsky, Herasym, 227
Smotrytsky, Meletii, 226, 227–28
Śniadecki, Jan (John), 325
Sobieski, Jakub (Jacob), father of Jan III Sobieski, 135–36, 153
Sobieski, Jakub (Jacob), son of Jan III Sobieski, 241, 250
Sobieski, Jan (John). *See* Jan III Sobieski
Sobieski, Marek, 135
Sochaczew, 43
Social customs, 209, 212–14

INDEX 371

Socinus, Faustus, 217
Solomon ben Aaron Troki, 231
Sołtyk, Kajetan, 271, 276
Sonia, wife of Władysław II, 97
Spiš (Szepesség, Spisz, Zips), 273, 326
Spytek of Melsztyn, 22
Środa, 152
Stackelberg, Otto Magnus, Russian ambassador, 274, 275, 277
Stadnicki, Stanisław, 54
Stalbovo, peace of, 141
Stanislavian Age. *See* Enlightenment
Stanisław, Duke of Mazovia, 43
Stanisław II August Poniatowski: and revenues, 187, 308; election of, 268–69; Russians and conservatives, 270–71; and war of the Bar Confederation, 271–72; and Haidamak rebellion of 1768, 272–73; and first partition 273–74; and reform, 274–76; and Great Parliament, 276–80; and May 3 constitution, 280–82; new regime, 282; and Lithuanian identity, 282–83; relations with Jews, 283–84, 306; Russo-Polish war and second partition, 284–85; and 1794 insurrection, 285–87; and third partition, 287–88; economic relations, 296, 297, 301, 304; educational interests of, 312–13; Stanislavian culture, 315–29
Stanisławów, 296
Starzechowski, Jan (John), 124
Staszic, Stanisław, 317–18
Statorius, Peter, 102, 103
Stefani, Jan (John), 324, 325
Stepan (Stephen) the Great, 32, 33
Stoutman, Pieter, 221
Stradom, 199
Straub, Kaspar, 102

Stroynowski, Hieronim (Gerald), 326–27
Stryjkowski, Mateusz (Matthew), 107, 225
Stwosz, Wit (Veit Stoss), 80, 113–14
Styria, 300
Subotiv, 160
Suburbs. *See* Cities
Suceava, 33
Sucharzewski, Jan (John), 209
Sukiennice, 112–13
Sulkes, Isaac, 108
Sułkowski, Aleksander Józef (Alexander Joseph), 262
Sułkowski, August, 296
Sułkowski, Franciszek (Francis), 323
Sułkowski family, 302
Sulyma, Ivan, 156
Suvorov, Alexander, 287
Suwałki (Suvalkai), 64
Švitrigaila (Świdrygiełło), 11, 22, 23
Sweden, 59, 74, 160, 272; and Zygmunt III, 131, 136, 139–40; Gustav Adolf attacks Poland-Lithuania, 142–43; invasion by Karl X, 163, 166–69; massacres of Jews, 174; economic impact of invasion, 195; plans with Sobieski, 238, 239; military tactics of, 240; and Great Northern War, 249–53
Świtkowski, Piotr (Peter), 316, 331
Syreniusz, Szymon (Simon), 218
Szadek, Tomasz (Thomas), 111
Szarzyński, Mikołaj Sęp (Nicholas Sęp), 215
Szarzyński, Stanisław, 323
Szczecin, 74
Szczekociny, battle of, 286
Szczucki, Stanisław, 153
Szczurowski, Jacek (Jack), 33
Szepielewicze, battle of, 166
Sztumska Wieś (Stumsdorf), peace of, 154
Szulc, Jan (John), 329

Szydłowiecki, Krzysztof (Christopher), 36
Szymonowic, Szymon (Simon), 219

Tacitus, 321
Tallinn (Reval), 57, 59, 132
Targowica confederation, 282, 283, 284, 285, 286, 314, 316, 321, 324, 325
Tarło, Adam, 264, 268
Tarnogród, 79
Tarnogród Confederation, 254
Tarnów, 113
Tarnowski, Jan (John), 38, 55, 100, 101
Tasso, 215
Taszycki, Mikołaj (Nicholas), 38
Tatars, 3, 13, 32, 49–50, 152, 253, 332, 338; Crimean Tatar state, 144; proposed war with, 158; participation in great Cossack revolt, 161, 165–66; Tatar community, 231–32; and Jan III Sobieski, 236, 237, 240
Taxation, 58, 88–89, 186–87, 204, 238, 241, 245, 253, 255, 269, 278, 283, 293, 294, 298, 303, 308
Tchaikovsky, Peter Ilich, 324
Tęczyńska, Izabela, 154
Tęczynski, Jan (John), 105, 121
Telemann, Georg Philipp, 324
Telnetz, Catherine von, 37
Tencalli, Constantine, 222
Teofan, Patriarch of Jerusalem, 148
Tepper, Piotr (Peter), 297, 307
Tepper, Piotr Fergusson, 297, 307
Teutonic Knights, 5, 7, 8, 10, 95, 310; Teutonic Order State, 14–15; relations with Poland-Lithuania, 15–17, 19; decline of, 17–19; lose Royal Prussia, 28–30, 330; continuing tensions, 30–31; 65; trading practices of, 74–75. *See also* Prussia

Teutonic Order. *See* Teutonic Knights
Theater, 149, 163, 220, 230, 312, 319, 321
Thirteen Years War, 29–30
Thirty Years War, 142, 151
Tiapkin (Russian envoy), 239
Tiavzin (Teusina), treaty of, 139
Tilsit, 238, 329
Titian, 221
Toleration, religious: Reformation and Catholic resurgence, 40–43; principle established, 120; Sarmatian attitudes, 212; lessens, 255; non-Catholics excluded from royal election, 259; dissident issue under Poniatowski, 270–71. *See also* Jews; Orthodox Church; Protestantism
Tomicki, Piotr (Peter), 98
Toruń (Thorn): in Teutonic order state, 14, 17, 18, 29; First Peace of, 17; Second Peace of, 30, 47, 96; in seventeenth century, 169, 196, 200; and education, 219, 220; in partition era, 273, 278, 285, 309, 310, 330. *See also* Cities; Royal Prussia
Trade: with England, 18, 73, 74, 80, 82, 197, 198, 303; with Russia, 57–58, 75, 76, 139, 251, 290, 299, 300, 303, 304; livestock, 68, 69, 71, 76, 192, 195, 198, 307; timber, 73, 74, 192, 300; grain, 73–75, 193, 195, 197, 290, 297, 299, 300, 304; staple right, 75–76, 136; with Germanies 76, 80, 195, 203, 299, 302, 304; and Great Northern War, 194–95, 299; by nobles, 200–1; and first partition, 273–74, 300; in eighteenth century, 297, 299–300. *See also* Cities; Jews; Industry
Trakai (Troki), 10, 46, 52, 53

Transylvania, 122
Treasury: under Jagiellonians, 6, 40, 64, 65, 88–89; and Teutonic order, 15; and Henri III, 120; under the Vasas, 134, 141, 153, 175, 186, 188; and Hetman State, 166, 171; in eighteenth century, 187, 274, 276, 280, 283, 306, 308; and Sobieski, 238, 241. *See also* Taxation
Trebizond, 146
Trembecki, Stanisław, 321
Trepka, Walerian Nekanda, 194–95
Turks. *See* Ottoman Empire
Turzo, Jan (John), 80
Țuțora (Cecora), battle of, 144, 146
Tver, 3
Twardowski, Samuel, 215
Tykocin, 107
Tyszowce, confederation of, 168
Tyzenhauz, Antoni (Anthony), 274, 291–92, 323
Tyzenhauz family, 329

Uchański, Jakub, 117
Ujazdów, 200, 224, 327
Ujście, capitulation of, 167
Ukraine. *See* Cossacks; Greek Catholic Church; Orthodox Church; Ruthenian territories
Uman, 272–73
Uniate. *See* Greek Catholic Church
Union of Brest, 25, 137–39, 161, 228
Union of Horodło, 11, 13
Union of Kriavas 8, 10, 13
Union of Lublin, 53, 58, 61–64, 145, 147, 148, 173, 179, 192, 221, 225, 283, 330
Union of Warsaw, 120

Vaclav IV, 17
Valois. *See* Henri III Valois
Varna, 146
Varna, battle of, 22

Vasilii (Basil) III, 26, 47
Vatican, 157, 158, 248, 257, 315, 317, 331
Veliki Luki, 126, 127
Venice, 97, 158, 240, 322
Versailles, 327
Vienna, 97, 132, 160, 233, 312, 327
Vienna, battle of, 239–40
Vienna, treaty of, 47, 53
Vilnius, 8, 11, 23, 35, 37, 46, 52, 79, 106, 107, 137, 196, 219, 287, 290, 291, 325, 329, 330, 333, 334, 337
Vilnius, treaty of, 169
Virgil, 96
Vishnevetsky. *See* Wiśniowiecki
Vistula River (Wisła), 16, 30, 44, 117, 200, 287, 300, 301, 308
Vitebsk, 47, 60
Vladimir, 13
Vladimir, Prince of Kievan Rus, 226
Volhynia, 4, 11, 13, 46, 139, 157, 171, 172, 193, 195, 203, 261, 267, 273, 292, 318
Voltaire (François-Marie Arouet), 320
Vorskla, battle of, 10
Vyhovsky, Ivan, 170–72, 173, 228
Vyshensky, Ivan, 147
Vytautas (Witold), 4, 8, 10, 20, 33, 52, 231. *See also* Lithuania

Wackerbarth, August Christopher von, 247
Wacław of Szamotuł, 111
Waiglowa (Weigel), Katarzyna Malcherowa, 42
Walachia, 178, 273
Wallenrode, Friedrich von, 16
Wallenrode, Jan (John), 19
Warmia, 30, 64, 98, 101, 320
War of the Austrian Succession, 265, 268
War of the Bar Confederation, 271–72

War of the Polish Succession, 261, 267
Warsaw, 113, 197, 233, 235, 249, 255, 308; and urban development, 43–44, 80–81, 163, 196, 199, 200, 202, 220–23, 295–98, 307, 327–28; and royal elections, 117, 121, 247, 250–52, 253, 260, 261, 269; wars and political events, 161, 167–69, 183, 235, 272, 283, 286, 288; cultural life, 224, 257, 262, 311, 318, 322, 323, 325
Warsaw, battles of, 168, 237, 251
Warsaw, treaties of, 251, 254
Warszewicki, Krzysztof (Christopher), 137
Warszycki, Stanisław, 234
Warta parliament, 10,
Watteau, Antoine, 328
Watzenrode, Lucas, 30
Wawel Castle, 35, 112, 121, 176, 220–21, 323
Wawrzyniec of Raciborz, 95
Węgierski, Kajetan, 321
Wehlau (Welawa), treaty of, 169, 308
West Point, 285
Wettin dynasty. *See* August II and August III
Wielhorski, Michał, 272
Wieliczka, 83, 257, 300
Wieluń, 294
Wietor, Hieronim, 108
Wilanów, 222, 248
Williams, Charles Hanbury, 269
Wiśniowiecki, Dmitri, 146
Wiśniowiecki, Jeremi (Jerome): leads army, 158; fights great Cossack revolt, 161, 164; wealth, 193; son, Michał, 233
Wiśniowiecki, Michał Korybut (Michael), 233–236
Wiśniowiecki family, 13
Witchcraft, 208
Witold. *See* Vytautas
Wittenberg, 42

Wittenberg, Arvid, 167
Władysław, King of Bohemia and Hungary, 32, 36, 47
Władysław I Łokietek, 5
Władysław II Jagiełło. *See* Jagiełło
Władysław III, 21, 22, 97
Władysław IV, 133, 135, 140; Russian tsar, 141–42; personality and election of, 149–50; military reform and war with Russia, 151–52; and parliamentary reform, 152–54; failed Baltic policy of, 154–55; alliance with France, 155; religious policy of, 156; and Ruthenian question, 156–57; planned war with Turkey, 158; death of, 158, 237; patron of the arts, 224
Włocławek, 97
Włodkowic, Paweł (Paulus Vladimiri), 19, 95
Wojciech z Brudzewa, 109
Wola, 122, 149, 247, 260, 296
Wołborz (Great Poland), 98
Wolff, Christian, 311
Woloczko (Wolf), 85
Women: and families, 90–93, 202; crimes of, 207–8; Jewish, 108, 205, 304; as victims of war, 144, 161, 273; fashions of, 163, 197; Tatar marriages of, 232; immigration to Warsaw, 297
Wrocław (Breslau), 102, 265
Wschowa, 252, 298
Wujek, Jakub (Jacob), 104, 215
Wybicki, Józef (Joseph), 317, 319
Wyrwicz, Karol (Charles), 326

Zabłocki, Franciszek (Francis), 319
Zabłudów, 108
Zalizniak, Maksym, 272
Załuski, Andrzej (Andrew), 263, 310, 311
Załuski, Józef Andrzej (Joseph Andrew), 310, 311

INDEX 373

Zamość: founding and design, 79, 113, 124, 199–200; pays ransom, 161; Wiśniowiecki born, 233; synod, 334
Zamoyska, Gryzelda, 233
Zamoyski, Andrzej (Andrew): 1764 reforms, 269–70; prepares law code, 275, 276, 282, 293–94, 317; educational interests, 313, 317
Zamoyski, Jan (John): supports the arts, 106, 111; founds Zamość, 113, 199; election of Henri Valois, 118; negotiates with Gdańsk, 123; rise to power, 123–5; as general, 126; and Zygmunt III, 132–34; election proposals of, 153; estates of, 193, 194; grandfather of Michał Wiśniowiecki, 233; and Staszic book, 317
Zamoyski, Jan (John) the younger, 162, 237
Zamoyski family, 146
Zaslavsky family, 13, 193
Zator, 64
Zawadzki, Teodor (Theodore), 218
Zbaraski, Krzysztof (Christopher), 153
Zbarazh, siege of, 164
Zbarazhsky family, 13, 146
Zbarski, Jerzy (George), 148
Zboriv, agreement of, 164
Zborowski, Krzysztof (Christopher), 125
Zborowski, Samuel, 125
Zborowski family, 125
Zbytkower, Shmuel (Samuel), 297–98, 301, 304
Zebrzydowski, Mikołaj (Nicholas), 134
Zebrzydowski Revolt, 134–35, 182
Żemaitia. *See* Samogitia
Zhovti Vody (Żółte Wody, Yellow Waters), battle of, 161
Zieliński, Konstantin, 251

374 INDEX

Zieliński, Mikołaj (Nicholas), 223
Żmudź. *See* Samogitia
Żoliborz, 296
Żółkiew (Zholkva), 136, 303, 305
Żółkiewski, Stefan (Stephen): defeats Zebrzydkowski, 134; funeral, 135; conquers Moscow, 141; loses at Ţutora, 144; supresses Cossack revolt, 145
Zwinger palace, 247, 254
Żygimantas (Zygmunt Kiejstutowicz), 11, 22, 23
Zygmunt Kazimierz (Sigmund Casimir), 150, 158
Zygmunt I (Sigmund): early years, 23, 26, 30, 32, 35, 36–37, 103; marriages of, 37, 39; strengthens royal authority, 37–39; conflict over "execution of the laws," 40–41; attitude toward Protestant Reformation, 41–43; foreign policy, 46–48; 53, 57; relies on Jan Boner, 79–80; and revenues, 89, 187; architectural interests of, 112. *See also* Sforza, Bona
Zygmunt II August (Sigmund Augustus): administrative skills of, 38, 126, 187; early election of, 39, 40, 51; as Supreme Duke in Lithuania, 52–53; and religious moderation, 52, 55, 100; political conflicts of, 53–55; and union with Lithuania, 59–64; and status of Prussia, 59, 64–65, 123, 197; death of, 66, 117; as patron of the arts, 111–12, 115. *See also* Execution of the Laws
Zygmunt III (Sigmund): elected king, 131–32; relations with parliament, 132–43, 183; and Zebrzydowski revolt, 134–35; and senatorial reform, 135–36; Counter Reformation policies of, 136–37, 219; and Union of Brest 137–39; loses Swedish throne, 139–40; intervenes in Russian Time of Troubles, 140–42; and renewed conflict with Sweden, 142–43; fails to keep Ducal Prussia, 143–144; and war with Turks and Tatars, 144–45; and emergence of Zaprozhian Cossacks, 145–47; and revival of Orthodox Church, 147–48, 227; and continued Lithuanian separatism, 148; and taxes, 186; and carnival celebration, 209; as art patron, 220; makes Warsaw his capital, 221–23; as music patron, 223
Żywiec, 267
Zápolya, Barbara, 37
Zápolya, János (John), 48, 65